Applying Macroeconomics to the Real World

Symbols Used in This Book

A	productivity		W	nominal wage
B	government debt		Y	total income or output
$BASE$	monetary base		$\overline{Y}$	full-employment output
C	consumption			
CA	current account balance			
CU	currency held by nonbank public		a	individual wealth or assets
DEP	bank deposits		c	individual consumption; consumption per worker
E	worker effort			
G	government purchases		cu	currency–deposit ratio
I	investment		d	depreciation rate
INT	net interest payments		e	real exchange rate
K	capital stock		e_{nom}	nominal exchange rate
KFA	capital and financial account balance		$\overline{e}_{\text{nom}}$	official value of nominal exchange rate
M	money supply		i	nominal interest rate
MC	marginal cost		i^m	nominal interest rate on money
MPK	marginal product of capital		k	capital–labor ratio
MPN	marginal product of labor		n	growth rate of labor force
$MRPN$	marginal revenue product of labor		p_K	price of capital goods
N	employment, labor		r	expected real interest rate
$\overline{N}$	full-employment level of employment		r^w	world real interest rate
			$r_{\text{a-t}}$	expected after-tax real interest rate
NFP	net factor payments		res	reserve–deposit ratio
NM	nonmonetary assets		s	individual saving; saving rate
NX	net exports		t	income tax rate
P	price level		u	unemployment rate
P^e	expected price level		$\overline{u}$	natural unemployment rate
P_{sr}	short-run price level		uc	user cost of capital
R	real seignorage revenue		w	real wage
RES	bank reserves		y	individual labor income; output per worker
S	national saving			
S_{pvt}	private saving		π	inflation rate
S_{govt}	government saving		π^e	expected inflation rate
T	taxes		η_Y	income elasticity of money demand
TR	transfers		τ	tax rate on firm revenues
V	velocity			

MACROECONOMICS

SEVENTH EDITION

Andrew B. Abel
The Wharton School of the
University of Pennsylvania

Ben S. Bernanke

Dean Croushore
Robins School of Business
University of Richmond

Addison-Wesley

Boston Columbus Indianapolis New York San Francisco Upper Saddle River
Amsterdam Cape Town Dubai London Madrid Milan Munich Paris Montréal Toronto
Delhi Mexico City São Paulo Sydney Hong Kong Seoul Singapore Taipei Tokyo

The Pearson Series in Economics

Abel/Bernanke/Croushore
*Macroeconomics**

Bade/Parkin
*Foundations of Economics**

Bierman/Fernandez
Game Theory with Economic Applications

Blanchard
Macroeconomics

Blau/Ferber/Winkler
The Economics of Women, Men, and Work

Boardman/Greenberg/Vining/Weimer
Cost-Benefit Analysis

Boyer
Principles of Transportation Economics

Branson
Macroeconomic Theory and Policy

Brock/Adams
The Structure of American Industry

Bruce
Public Finance and the American Economy

Carlton/Perloff
Modern Industrial Organization

Case/Fair/Oster
*Principles of Economics**

Caves/Frankel/Jones
World Trade and Payments: An Introduction

Chapman
Environmental Economics: Theory, Application, and Policy

Cooter/Ulen
Law & Economics

Downs
An Economic Theory of Democracy

Ehrenberg/Smith
Modern Labor Economics

Ekelund/Ressler/Tollison
*Economics**

Farnham
Economics for Managers

Folland/Goodman/Stano
The Economics of Health and Health Care

Fort
Sports Economics

Froyen
Macroeconomics

Fusfeld
The Age of the Economist

Gerber
International Economics

Gordon
Macroeconomics

Greene
Econometric Analysis

Gregory
Essentials of Economics

Gregory/Stuart
Russian and Soviet Economic Performance and Structure

Hartwick/Olewiler
The Economics of Natural Resource Use

Heilbroner/ Milberg
The Making of the Economic Society

Heyne/Boettke/Prychitko
The Economic Way of Thinking

Hoffman/Averett
Women and the Economy: Family, Work, and Pay

Holt
Markets, Games, and Strategic Behavior

Hubbard
Money, the Financial System, and the Economy

Hubbard/O'Brien
*Economics**

Hughes/Cain
American Economic History

Husted/Melvin
International Economics

Jehle/Reny
Advanced Microeconomic Theory

Johnson-Lans
A Health Economics Primer

Keat/Young
Managerial Economics

Klein
Mathematical Methods for Economics

Krugman/Obstfeld
*International Economics: Theory & Policy**

Laidler
The Demand for Money

Leeds/von Allmen
The Economics of Sports

Leeds/von Allmen/Schiming
Economics*

Lipsey/Ragan/Storer
Economics*

Lynn
Economic Development: Theory and Practice for a Divided World

Melvin
International Money and Finance

Miller
Economics Today*

Understanding Modern Economics

Miller/Benjamin
The Economics of Macro Issues

Miller/Benjamin/North
The Economics of Public Issues

Mills/Hamilton
Urban Economics

Mishkin
The Economics of Money, Banking, and Financial Markets*

The Economics of Money, Banking, and Financial Markets, Business School Edition*

Murray
Econometrics: A Modern Introduction

Nafziger
The Economics of Developing Countries

O'Sullivan/Sheffrin/Perez
Economics: Principles, Applications and Tools*

Parkin
Economics*

Perloff
Microeconomics*

Microeconomics: Theory and Applications with Calculus

Perman/Common/McGilvray/Ma
Natural Resources and Environmental Economics

Phelps
Health Economics

Pindyck/Rubinfeld
Microeconomics*

Riddell/Shackelford/Stamos/Schneider
Economics: A Tool for Critically Understanding Society

Ritter/Silber/Udell
Principles of Money, Banking & Financial Markets*

Roberts
The Choice: A Fable of Free Trade and Protection

Rohlf
Introduction to Economic Reasoning

Ruffin/Gregory
Principles of Economics

Sargent
Rational Expectations and Inflation

Sawyer/Sprinkle
International Economics

Scherer
Industry Structure, Strategy, and Public Policy

Schiller
The Economics of Poverty and Discrimination

Sherman
Market Regulation

Silberberg
Principles of Microeconomics

Stock/Watson
Introduction to Econometrics

Introduction to Econometrics, Brief Edition

Studenmund
Using Econometrics: A Practical Guide

Tietenberg/Lewis
Environmental and Natural Resource Economics

Environmental Economics and Policy

Todaro/Smith
Economic Development

Waldman
Microeconomics

Waldman/Jensen
Industrial Organization: Theory and Practice

Weil
Economic Growth

Williamson
Macroeconomics

 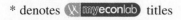

Editorial Director:	Sally Yagen
Editor in Chief:	Donna Battista
AVP/Executive Editor, Print:	David Alexander
Senior Marketing Manager:	Elizabeth A. Averbeck
Marketing Assistant:	Ian Gold
Managing Editor:	Nancy H. Fenton
Senior Production Project Manager:	Kathryn Dinovo
Senior Manufacturing Buyer:	Carol Melville
Senior Media Buyer:	Ginny Michaud
Text Designer:	Elm Street Publishing Services
Cover Designer:	Elena Sidorova
Cover Art:	Bryan P. Rippeon
Text Permissions Project Supervisor:	Michael Joyce
Director of Media:	Susan Schoenberg
Content Leads, MyEconLab:	Douglas A. Ruby and Noel Lotz
Senior Media Producer:	Melissa Honig
Media Project Manager:	Lisa Rinaldi
Supplements Production Coordinator:	Alison Eusden
Full-Service Project Management/Composition:	Elm Street Publishing Services/Integra Software Services Pvt. Ltd.
Printer/Binder:	Courier, Kendallville
Cover Printer:	Lehigh Phoenix
Text Font:	Palatino

Credits and acknowledgments borrowed from other sources and reproduced, with permission, in this textbook appear on appropriate page within text.

Microsoft® and Windows® are registered trademarks of the Microsoft Corporation in the U.S.A. and other countries. Screen shots and icons reprinted with permission from the Microsoft Corporation. This book is not sponsored or endorsed by or affiliated with the Microsoft Corporation.

Many of the designations by manufacturers and sellers to distinguish their products are claimed as trademarks. Where those designations appear in this book, and the publisher was aware of a trademark claim, the designations have been printed in initial caps or all caps.

Library of Congress Cataloging-in-Publication Data

Abel, Andrew B., 1952–
    Macroeconomics / Andrew B. Abel, Ben S. Bernanke, Dean Croushore.—7th ed.
        p.   cm. — (The Pearson series in economics)
    Includes bibliographical references and index.
    ISBN 978-0-13-611452-9 (alk. paper)
    1. Macroeconomics.   2. United States—Economic conditions.   I. Bernanke, Ben, 1953–
II. Croushore, Dean Darrell, 1956–   III. Title.

HB172.5.A24   2011
339—dc22   2009046996

10 9 8 7 6 5 4 3 2 1

Addison-Wesley
is an imprint of

www.pearsonhighered.com

ISBN 13: 978-0-13-611452-9
ISBN 10:   0-13-611452-0

About the Authors

Andrew B. Abel

The Wharton School of the University of Pennsylvania

Ronald A. Rosenfeld Professor of Finance at The Wharton School and professor of economics at the University of Pennsylvania, Andrew Abel received his A.B. *summa cum laude* from Princeton University and his Ph.D. from the Massachusetts Institute of Technology.

He began his teaching career at the University of Chicago and Harvard University and has held visiting appointments at both Tel Aviv University and The Hebrew University of Jerusalem.

A prolific researcher, Abel has published extensively on fiscal policy, capital formation, monetary policy, asset pricing, and Social Security—as well as serving on the editorial boards of numerous journals. He has been honored as an Alfred P. Sloan Fellow, a Fellow of the Econometric Society, and a recipient of the John Kenneth Galbraith Award for teaching excellence. Abel has served as a visiting scholar at the Federal Reserve Bank of Philadelphia, as a member of the Panel of Economic Advisers at the Congressional Budget Office, and as a member of the Technical Advisory Panel on Assumptions and Methods for the Social Security Advisory Board. He is also a Research Associate of the National Bureau of Economic Research and a member of the Advisory Board of the Carnegie-Rochester Conference Series.

Ben S. Bernanke

Previously the Howard Harrison and Gabrielle Snyder Beck Professor of Economics and Public Affairs at Princeton University, Ben Bernanke received his B.A. in economics from Harvard University *summa cum laude*—capturing both the Allyn Young Prize for best Harvard undergraduate economics thesis and the John H. Williams prize for outstanding senior in the Economics Department. Like coauthor Abel, he holds a Ph.D. from the Massachusetts Institute of Technology.

Bernanke began his career at the Stanford Graduate School of Business in 1979. In 1985 he moved to Princeton University, where he served as chair of the Economics Department from 1995 to 2002. He has twice been visiting professor at M.I.T. and once at New York University, and has taught in undergraduate, M.B.A., M.P.A., and Ph.D. programs. He has authored more than 60 publications in macroeconomics, macroeconomic history, and finance.

Bernanke has served as a visiting scholar and advisor to the Federal Reserve System. He is a Guggenheim Fellow and a Fellow of the Econometric Society. He has also been variously honored as an Alfred P. Sloan Research Fellow, a Hoover Institution National Fellow, a National Science Foundation Graduate Fellow, and a Research Associate of the National Bureau of Economic Research. He has served as editor of the *American Economic Review*. In 2005 he became Chairman of the President's Council of Economic Advisers. He is currently Chairman and a member of the Board of Governors of the Federal Reserve System.

Dean Croushore

Robins School of Business, University of Richmond

Dean Croushore is professor of economics and Rigsby Fellow at the University of Richmond and chair of the Economics Department. He received his A.B. from Ohio University and his Ph.D. from Ohio State University.

Croushore began his career at Pennsylvania State University in 1984. After teaching for five years, he moved to the Federal Reserve Bank of Philadelphia, where he was vice president and economist. His duties during his fourteen years at the Philadelphia Fed included heading the macroeconomics section, briefing the bank's president and board of directors on the state of the economy and advising them about formulating monetary policy, writing articles about the economy, administering two national surveys of forecasters, and researching current issues in monetary policy. In his role at the Fed, he created the Survey of Professional Forecasters (taking over the defunct ASA/NBER survey and revitalizing it) and developed the Real-Time Data Set for Macroeconomists.

Croushore returned to academia at the University of Richmond in 2003. The focus of his research in recent years has been on forecasting and how data revisions affect monetary policy, forecasting, and macroeconomic research. Croushore's publications include articles in many leading economics journals and a textbook on money and banking. He is associate editor of several journals and visiting scholar at the Federal Reserve Bank of Philadelphia.

Brief Contents

Detailed Contents

xiv Detailed Contents

Preface

Since February 2006, Ben Bernanke has been chairman of the Board of Governors of the Federal Reserve System. Federal ethics rules prohibited him from making substantive contributions to the sixth and seventh editions.

In preparing the seventh edition, we viewed our main objective to be keeping the book fresh and up-to-date, especially in light of the recent crises in housing and financial markets and their impact on the macroeonomy. Thus, we have also added new applications, boxes, and problems throughout and made many revisions of the text to reflect recent events and developments in the field. In addition, the empirical problems at the end of most chapters direct students to appropriate data in the FRED database on the Web site of the Federal Reserve Bank of St. Louis. Because this database is frequently updated and is available free of charge, students will develop familiarity and facility with a current data source that they can continue to use after completing the course.

A summary of our revisions follows.

New and Updated Coverage

What is taught in intermediate macroeconomics courses—and how it is taught—has changed substantially in recent years. Previous editions of *Macroeconomics* played a major role in these developments. The seventh edition provides lively coverage of a broad spectrum of macroeconomic issues and ideas, including a variety of new and updated topics:

- *Monetary policy.* In response to the financial crisis in 2008, the Federal Reserve introduced new tools to prop up the financial system and to influence economic activity, so we have added a substantial amount of material to discuss many different aspects of these policy changes. In addition, because most central banks now rely primarily on targeting interest rates, we derive a new (horizontal) curve (the *LR* curve) in place of the *LM* curve and show how to use this modified *IS–LM* model to analyze monetary policy in the context of interest-rate targeting. These two major changes have led us to rewrite Chapter 14 on monetary policy substantially. *New or substantially revised coverage*: In Chapter 14 we now discuss the money multiplier during severe financial crises, comparing the money supply during the Great Depression to that from 2007–2009, illustrate the changes in the Federal Reserve's balance sheet during the recent financial crisis, describe the Federal Reserve's payment of interest on reserves, and expand our analysis of both the Taylor rule and inflation targeting.

- *Long-term economic growth.* Because the rate of economic growth plays a central role in determining living standards, we devote much of Part 2 to growth and related issues. We first discuss factors contributing to growth, such as productivity (Chapter 3) and rates of saving and investment (Chapter 4); then in Chapter 6 we turn to a full-fledged analysis of the growth process, using tools such as growth accounting and the Solow model. Growth-related topics covered include the post-1973 productivity slowdown, the factors that determine long-run living standards, and the productivity "miracle" of the 1990s. *Revised coverage*: Updated data and a discussion of the recent growth of China's economy.

■ *International macroeconomic issues.* We address the increasing integration of the world economy in two ways. First, we frequently use cross-country comparisons and applications that draw on the experiences of nations other than the United States. For example, in Chapter 3, we compare U.S. and European labor markets; in Chapter 6 we compare the long-term economic growth rates of several countries; in Chapter 7 we compare inflation experiences among European countries in transition; in Chapter 8 we compare the growth in industrial production in several countries; in Chapter 12 we compare sacrifice ratios among various countries; and in Chapter 14 we discuss strategies used for making monetary policy around the world. Second, we devote two chapters, 5 and 13, specifically to international issues. In Chapter 5 we show how the trade balance is related to a nation's rates of saving and investment, and then apply this framework to discuss issues such as the U.S. trade deficit and the relationship between government budget deficits and trade deficits. In Chapter 13 we use a simple supply–demand framework to examine the determination of exchange rates. The chapter features innovative material on fixed exchange rates and currency unions, including an explanation of why a currency may face a speculative run. *Revised coverage*: The text includes updated data comparing U.S. and European labor markets (Chapter 3) and a discussion of the impact of globalization on the U.S. economy (Chapter 5).

■ *Business cycles.* Our analysis of business cycles begins with facts rather than theories. In Chapter 8 we give a history of U.S. business cycles and then describe the observed cyclical behavior of a variety of important economic variables (the "business cycle facts"). In Chapters 9–11 we evaluate alternative classical and Keynesian theories of the cycle by how well they explain the facts. *New to this edition*: The text now includes a description of the Fed's preferred inflation measures (Chapter 2), contains a discussion of the housing crisis that began in 2007 (Chapter 7), shows how the rate of job loss and job finding vary across the business cycle (Chapter 8), and presents new coincident indexes (Chapter 8).

■ *Fiscal policy.* The effects of macroeconomic policies are considered in nearly every chapter, in both theory and applications. We present classical (Chapter 10), Keynesian (Chapter 11), and monetarist (Chapter 14) views on the appropriate use of policy. *New or substantially revised coverage*: The text now discusses evidence on how consumers respond to tax rebates (Chapter 2) and a description of the fiscal stimulus package of 2009 and its impact on the debt–GDP ratio (Chapter 15).

■ *Labor market issues.* We pay close attention to issues relating to employment, unemployment, and real wages. We introduce the basic supply–demand model of the labor market, as well as unemployment, early, in Chapter 3. We discuss unemployment more extensively in Chapter 12, which covers the inflation–unemployment trade-off, the costs of unemployment, and government policies for reducing unemployment. Other labor market topics include household production and how it affects the business cycle (Chapter 10), efficiency wages (Chapter 11), and the effects of marginal and average tax rate changes on labor supply (Chapter 15). *New or substantially revised coverage*: The text now discusses in greater detail the degree to which jobs are lost and gained over the course of the business cycle, showing data based on recent research.

A Solid Foundation

The seventh edition builds on the strengths that underlie the book's lasting appeal to instructors and students, including:

- *Real-world applications.* A perennial challenge for instructors is to help students make active use of the economic ideas developed in the text. The rich variety of applications in this book shows by example how economic concepts can be put to work in explaining real-world issues such as the housing crisis that began in 2007 and the financial crisis of 2008, the contrasting behavior of unemployment in the United States and Europe, the slowdown and revival in productivity growth, the challenges facing the Social Security system and the Federal budget, the impact of globalization on the U.S. economy, and new approaches to making monetary policy that were used in response to the financial crisis in 2008. The seventh edition offers new applications as well as updates of the best applications and analyses of previous editions.

- *Broad modern coverage.* From its conception, *Macroeconomics* has responded to students' desires to investigate and understand a wider range of macroeconomic issues than is permitted by the course's traditional emphasis on short-run fluctuations and stabilization policy. This book provides a modern treatment of these traditional topics but also gives in-depth coverage of other important macroeconomic issues such as the determinants of long-run economic growth, the trade balance and financial flows, labor markets, and the institutional framework of policymaking. This comprehensive coverage also makes the book a useful tool for instructors with differing views about course coverage and topic sequence.

- *Reliance on a set of core economic ideas.* Although we cover a wide range of topics, we avoid developing a new model or theory for each issue. Instead we emphasize the broad applicability of a set of core economic ideas (such as the production function, the trade-off between consuming today and saving for tomorrow, and supply–demand analysis). Using these core ideas, we build a theoretical framework that encompasses all the macroeconomic analyses presented in the book: long-run and short-run, open-economy and closed-economy, and classical and Keynesian.

- *A balanced presentation.* Macroeconomics is full of controversies, many of which arise from the split between classicals and Keynesians (of the old, new, and neo-varieties). Sometimes the controversies overshadow the broad common ground shared by the two schools. We emphasize that common ground. First, we pay greater attention to long-run issues (on which classicals and Keynesians have less disagreement). Second, we develop the classical and Keynesian analyses of short-run fluctuations within a single overall framework, in which we show that the two approaches differ principally in their assumptions about how quickly wages and prices adjust. Where differences in viewpoint remain— for example, in the search versus efficiency-wage interpretations of unemployment—we present and critique both perspectives. This balanced approach exposes students to all the best ideas in modern macroeconomics. At the same time, an instructor of either classical or Keynesian inclination can easily base a course on this book.

■ *Innovative pedagogy.* The seventh edition, like its predecessors, provides a variety of useful tools to help students study, understand, and retain the material. Described in more detail later in the preface, these tools include summary tables, key diagrams, key terms, and key equations to aid students in organizing their study, and four types of questions and problems for practice and developing understanding, including problems that encourage students to do their own empirical work, using data readily available on the Internet. Several appendices illustrate how to solve numerical exercises that are based on the algebraic descriptions of the *IS-LM/AS-AD* model.

A Flexible Organization

The seventh edition maintains the flexible structure of earlier editions. In Part 1 (Chapters 1–2), we introduce the field of macroeconomics and discuss issues of economic measurement. In Part 2 (Chapters 3–7), we focus on long-run issues, including productivity, saving, investment, the trade balance, growth, and inflation. We devote Part 3 (Chapters 8–11) to the study of short-run economic fluctuations and stabilization policy. Finally, in Part 4 (Chapters 12–15), we take a closer look at issues and institutions of policymaking. Appendix A at the end of the book reviews useful algebraic and graphical tools.

Instructors of intermediate macroeconomics have different preferences as to course content, and their choices are often constrained by their students' backgrounds and the length of the term. The structure of *Macroeconomics* accommodates various needs. In planning how to use the book, instructors might find it useful to consider the following points:

■ *Core chapters.* We recommend that every course include these six chapters:
Chapter 1   Introduction to Macroeconomics
Chapter 2   The Measurement and Structure of the National Economy
Chapter 3   Productivity, Output, and Employment
Chapter 4   Consumption, Saving, and Investment
Chapter 7   The Asset Market, Money, and Prices
Chapter 9   The *IS–LM/AD–AS* Model: A General Framework for Macroeconomic Analysis

Chapters 1 and 2 provide an introduction to macroeconomics, including national income accounting. The next four chapters in the list make up the analytical core of the book: Chapter 3 examines the labor market, Chapters 3 and 4 together develop the goods market, Chapter 7 discusses the asset market, and Chapter 9 combines the three markets into a general equilibrium model usable for short-run analysis (in either a classical or Keynesian mode).

■ *Suggested additions.* To a syllabus containing these six chapters, instructors can add various combinations of the other chapters, depending on the course focus. The following are some possible choices:

Short-run focus. Instructors who prefer to emphasize short-run issues (business cycle fluctuations and stabilization policy) may omit Chapters 5 and 6 without loss of continuity. They could also go directly from Chapters 1 and 2 to Chapters 8 and 9, which introduce business cycles and the *IS–LM/AD–AS* framework. Although the presentation in Chapters 8 and 9 is self-contained, it will be helpful for instructors who skip Chapters 3–7 to provide some background and motivation for the various behavioral relationships and equilibrium conditions.

Classical emphasis. For instructors who want to teach the course with a modern classical emphasis, we recommend assigning all the chapters in Part 2. In Part 3, Chapters 8–10 provide a self-contained presentation of classical business cycle theory. Other material of interest includes the Friedman–Phelps interpretation of the Phillips curve (Chapter 12), the role of credibility in monetary policy (Chapter 14), and Ricardian equivalence with multiple generations (Chapter 15).

Keynesian emphasis. Instructors who prefer a Keynesian emphasis may choose to omit Chapter 10 (classical business cycle analysis). As noted, if a short-run focus is preferred, Chapter 5 (full-employment analysis of the open economy) and Chapter 6 (long-run economic growth) may also be omitted without loss of continuity.

International focus. Chapter 5 discusses saving, investment, and the trade balance in an open economy with full employment. Chapter 13 considers exchange rate determination and macroeconomic policy in an open-economy model in which short-run deviations from full employment are possible. (Chapter 5 is a useful but not essential prerequisite for Chapter 13.) Both chapters may be omitted for a course focusing on the domestic economy.

Applying Macroeconomics to the Real World

Economists sometimes get caught up in the elegance of formal models and forget that the ultimate test of a model or theory is its practical relevance. In the previous editions of *Macroeconomics,* we dedicated a significant portion of each chapter to showing how the theory could be applied to real events and issues. Our efforts were well received by instructors and students. The seventh edition continues to help students learn how to "think like an economist" by including the following features:

- *Applications.* Applications in each chapter show students how they can use theory to understand an important episode or issue. Examples of topics covered in Applications include the macroeconomic consequences of the boom and bust in stock prices (Chapter 4), how people respond to tax rebates (Chapter 4), the United States as international debtor (Chapter 5), the recent surge in U.S. productivity growth (Chapter 6), calibrating the business cycle (Chapter 10), how the introduction of euro currency affected exchange rates (Chapter 13), inflation targeting (Chapter 14), and labor supply and tax reform (Chapter 15).
- *In Touch with Data and Research.* These boxes give the reader further insight into new developments in economic research as well as a guide to keeping abreast of new developments in the economy. Research topics in these boxes include discussions of biases in inflation measurement (Chapter 2), the link between capital investment and the stock market (Chapter 4), flows of U.S. dollars abroad (Chapter 7), DSGE models and the classical–Keynesian debate (Chapter 10), the Lucas critique (Chapter 12), and the fiscal stimulus package passed in 2009 (Chapter 15). Keeping abreast of the economy requires an understanding of what data are

available, as well as their strengths and shortcomings. We provide a series of boxes to show where to find key macroeconomic data—such as labor market data (Chapter 3), balance of payments data (Chapter 5), and exchange rates (Chapter 13)—and how to interpret them. Online data sources are featured along with more traditional media.

Learning Features

The following features of this book aim to help students understand, apply, and retain important concepts:

- *Detailed, full-color graphs.* The book is liberally illustrated with data graphs, which emphasize the empirical relevance of the theory, and analytical graphs, which guide students through the development of model and theory in a step-by-step manner. For both types of graphs, descriptive captions summarize the details of the events shown.

- The use of color in an analytical graph is demonstrated by the figure on the next page, which shows the effects of a shifting curve on a set of endogenous variables. Note that the original curve is in black, whereas its new position is marked in red, with the direction of the shift indicated by arrows. A peach-colored "shock box" points out the reason for the shift, and a blue "result box" lists the main effects of the shock on endogenous variables. These and similar conventions make it easy for students to gain a clear understanding of the analysis.

- *Key diagrams.* Key diagrams, a unique study feature at the end of selected chapters, are self-contained descriptions of the most important analytical graphs in the book (see the end of the Detailed Contents for a list). For each key diagram, we present the graph (for example, the production function, p. 95, or the *AD–AS* diagram, p. 346) and define and describe its elements in words and, where appropriate, equations. We then analyze what the graph reveals and discuss the factors that shift the curves in the graph.

- *Summary tables.* Throughout the book, summary tables bring together the main results of an analysis and reduce the time that students must spend writing and memorizing results, allowing a greater concentration on understanding and applying these results.

- *End-of-chapter review materials.* To facilitate review, at the end of each chapter students will find a chapter summary, covering the chapter's main points; a list of key terms with page references; and an annotated list of key equations.

- *End-of-chapter questions and problems.* An extensive set of questions and problems includes review questions, for student self-testing and study; numerical problems, which have numerical solutions and are especially useful for checking students' understanding of basic relationships and concepts; analytical problems, which ask students to use or extend a theory qualitatively; and empirical problems that direct students to use data from the FRED database of the Federal Reserve Bank of St. Louis and allow them to see for themselves how well theory explains real-world data. Answers to these problems (except the empirical problems, the answers to which change over time) appear in the *Instructor's Manual*. All end-of-chapter Review Questions, Numerical Problems, and most Analytical Problems can be assigned in and automatically graded by MyEconLab.

Figure 9.14

Monetary neutrality in the *AD–AS* framework
If we start from general equilibrium at point *E*, a 10% increase in the nominal money supply shifts the *AD* curve up and to the right from AD^1 to AD^2. The points on the new *AD* curve are those for which the price level is 10% higher at each level of output demanded, because a 10% increase in the price level is needed to keep the real money supply, and thus the aggregate quantity of output demanded, unchanged. In the new short-run equilibrium at point *F*, the price level is unchanged, and output is higher than its full-employment level. In the new long-run equilibrium at point *H*, output is unchanged at $\overline{Y}$, and the price level P_2 is 10% higher than the initial price level P_1. Thus money is neutral in the long run.

- *Worked numerical problems at the end of selected chapters.* The *IS-LM/AD-AS* model is the analytic centerpiece of Parts 3 and 4 of the book. In addition to providing algebraic descriptions of this model in appendixes at the end of selected chapters in Parts 3 and 4, separate appendixes illustrate worked-out numerical problems using this model.

- *Review of useful analytical tools.* Although we use no mathematics beyond high school algebra, some students will find it handy to have a review of the book's main analytical tools. Appendix A (at the end of the text) succinctly discusses functions of one variable and multiple variables, graphs, slopes, exponents, and formulas for finding the growth rates of products and ratios.

- *Glossary.* The glossary at the end of the book defines all key terms (boldface within the chapter and also listed at the end of each chapter) and refers students to the page on which the term is fully defined and discussed.

The seventh edition includes end-of-chapter problems that can be assigned in and automatically graded by **MyEconLab**. **MyEconLab** delivers rich online content and innovative learning tools to your classroom. Instructors who use **MyEconLab** gain access to powerful communication and assessment tools, and their students receive access to the additional learning resources described below.

Students and MyEconLab.   This online homework and tutorial system puts students in control of their own learning through a suite of study and practice tools correlated with the online, interactive version of the textbook and other media tools. Within **MyEconLab**'s structured environment, students practice what they learn, test their understanding, and then pursue a study plan that **MyEconLab** generates for them based on their performance on practice tests.

Instructors and MyEconLab.   **MyEconLab** provides flexible tools that allow instructors to easily and effectively customize online course materials to suit their needs. Instructors can create and assign tests, quizzes, or homework assignments. **MyEconLab** saves time by automatically grading all questions and tracking results in an online gradebook. **MyEconLab** can even grade assignments that require students to draw a graph.

After registering for **MyEconLab** instructors have access to downloadable supplements such as an instructor's manual, PowerPoint lecture notes, and a test bank. The test bank can also be used within **MyEconLab,** giving instructors ample material from which they can create assignments.

For advanced communication and customization, **MyEconLab** is delivered in CourseCompass. Instructors can upload course documents and assignments, and use advanced course management features. For more information about **MyEconLab** or to request an instructor access code, visit *www.myeconlab.com*.

Additional **MyEconLab** resources include:

- *Animated figures.* Key figures from the textbook are presented in step-by-step animations with audio explanations of the action.
- *Research Navigator* (CourseCompass version only). Extensive help on the research process and four exclusive databases of accredited and reliable source material including *The New York Times, The Financial Times,* and peer-reviewed journals.

Additional Supplementary Resources

A full range of additional supplementary materials to support teaching and learning accompanies this book. All of these items are available to qualified domestic adopters but in some cases may not be available to international adopters.

- The *Study Guide* provides a review of each chapter, as well as multiple-choice and short-answer problems (and answers).
- The *Instructor's Manual* offers guidance for instructors on using the text, solutions to all end-of-chapter problems in the book (except the empirical questions), and suggested topics for class discussion.
- The *Test Item File* contains a generous selection of multiple-choice questions and problems, all with answers. All questions and problems are also available in TestGen.
- *PowerPoint Lectures* provide slides for all the basic text material, including all tables and figures from the textbook.

Acknowledgments

A textbook isn't the lonely venture of its author or coauthors but rather is the joint project of dozens of skilled and dedicated people. We extend special thanks to Denise Clinton, David Alexander, executive editor; and project managers Gavin Broady and Rachel Mattison, for their superb work on the seventh edition. For their efforts, care, and craft, we also thank Kathryn Dinovo, the senior production project manager; Debbie Meyer, the project editor from Elm Street Publishing Services; Melissa Honig, the senior media producer; Doug Ruby and Noel Lotz, the MyEconLab content leads; and Elizabeth Averbeck, the senior marketing manager.

We also appreciate the contributions of the reviewers and colleagues who have offered valuable comments on succeeding drafts of the book in all seven editions thus far:

Ugur Aker, *Hiram College*

Krishna Akkina, *Kansas State University*

Terence J. Alexander, *Iowa State University*

Edward Allen, *University of Houston*

Richard G. Anderson, *Federal Reserve Bank of St. Louis*

David Aschauer, *Bates College*

Martin A. Asher, *The Wharton School, University of Pennsylvania*

David Backus, *New York University*

Daniel Barbezat, *Amherst College*

Parantap Basu, *Fordham University*

Valerie R. Bencivenga, *University of Texas*

Haskel Benishag, *Kellogg Graduate School of Management, Northwestern University*

Charles A. Bennett, *Gannon University*

Joydeep Bhattacharya, *Iowa State University*

Robert A. Blewett, *Saint Lawrence University*

Scott Bloom, *North Dakota State University*

Bruce R. Bolnick, *Northeastern University*

David Brasfield, *Murray State University*

Viacheslav Breusov, *University of Pennsylvania*

Audie Brewton, *Northeastern Illinois University*

Stacey Brook, *University of Sioux Falls*

Nancy Burnett, *University of Wisconsin, Oshkosh*

Maureen Burton, *California Polytechnic University, Pomona*

John Campbell, *Harvard University*

Kevin Carey, *American University*

J. Lon Carlson, *Illinois State University*

Wayne Carroll, *University of Wisconsin, Eau Claire*

Arthur Schiller Casimir, *Western New England College*

Stephen Cecchetti, *Brandeis University*

Anthony Chan, *Woodbury University*

Leo Chan, *University of Kansas*

S. Chandrasekhar, *Pennsylvania State University*

Henry Chappell, *University of South Carolina*

Jen–Chi Cheng, *Wichita State University*

Menzie Chinn, *University of California, Santa Cruz*

K. A. Chopra, *State University of New York, Oneonta*

Nan-Ting Chou, *University of Louisville*

Jens Christiansen, *Mount Holyoke College*

Reid Click, *Brandeis University*

John P. Cochran, *Metropolitan State College of Denver*

Juan Carlos Cordoba, *Rice University*

Steven R. Cunningham, *University of Connecticut*

Bruce R. Dalgaard, *St. Olaf College*

Joe Daniels, *Marquette University*

Edward Day, *University of Central Florida*

Robert Dekle, *University of Southern California*

Greg Delemeester, *Marietta College*

Wouter J. Den Haan, *University of Amsterdam*

Johan Deprez, *Texas Tech University*

James Devine, *Loyola Marymount University*

Wael William Diab, *Cisco Systems*

Aimee Dimmerman, *George Washington University*

Peter Dohlman, *International Monetary Fund*

Patrick Dolenc, *Keene State College*

Allan Drazen, *University of Maryland*

Robert Driskill, *Vanderbilt University*

Bill Dupor, *Ohio State University*

Donald H. Dutkowsky, *Syracuse University*

James E. Eaton, *Bridgewater College*

Janice C. Eberly, *Northwestern University*

Andrew Economopoulos, *Ursinus College*

Alejandra Cox Edwards, *California State University, Long Beach*

Martin Eichenbaum, *Northwestern University*

Carlos G. Elias, *Manhattan College*

Kirk Elwood, *James Madison University*

Sharon J. Erenburg, *Eastern Michigan University*

Christopher Erickson, *New Mexico State University*

James Fackler, *University of Kentucky*

Steven Fazzari, *Washington University*

J. Peter Ferderer, *Clark University*

Abdollah Ferdowsi, *Ferris State University*

David W. Findlay, *Colby College*

Thomas J. Finn, *Wayne State University*

Charles C. Fischer, *Pittsburg State University*

John A. Flanders, *Central Methodist College*

Juergen Fleck, *Hollins College*

Adrian Fleissig, *California State University, Fullerton*

R. N. Folsom, *San Jose State University*

Kevin Foster, *City University of New York*

J. E. Fredland, *U.S. Naval Academy*

James R. Gale, *Michigan Technological University*

Edward N. Gamber, *Lafayette College*

William T. Ganley, *Buffalo State College*

Charles B. Garrison, *University of Tennessee, Knoxville*

Kathie Gilbert, *Mississippi State University*

Carlos G. Glias, *Manhattan College*

Roger Goldberg, *Ohio Northern University*

Joao Gomes, *The Wharton School, University of Pennsylvania*

Fred C. Graham, *American University*

John W. Graham, *Rutgers University*

Stephen A. Greenlaw, *Mary Washington College*

Alan F. Gummerson, *Florida International University*

A. R. Gutowsky, *California State University, Sacramento*

David R. Hakes, *University of Northern Iowa*

Michael Haliassos, *University of Maryland*

George J. Hall, *Brandeis University*

John C. Haltiwanger, *University of Maryland*

James Hamilton, *University of California, San Diego*

David Hammes, *University of Hawaii*

Reza Hamzaee, *Missouri Western State College*

Robert Stanley Herren, *North Dakota University*

Charles Himmelberg, *Federal Reserve Bank of New York*

Barney F. Hope, *California State University, Chico*

Fenn Horton, *Naval Postgraduate School*

Christopher House, *University of Michigan*

E. Philip Howrey, *University of Michigan*

John Huizinga, *University of Chicago*

Nayyer Hussain, *Tougaloo College*

Steven Husted, *University of Pittsburgh*

Matthew Hyle, *Winona State University*

Matteo Iacoviello, *Boston College*

Selo Imrohoroglu, *University of Southern California*

Kenneth Inman, *Claremont McKenna College*

Liana Jacobi, *Washington University*

Philip N. Jefferson, *Swarthmore College*

Urban Jermann, *The Wharton School, University of Pennsylvania*

Charles W. Johnston, *University of Michigan, Flint*

Barry E. Jones, *Binghamton University*

Paul Junk, *University of Minnesota*

James Kahn, *Yeshiva University*

George Karras, *University of Illinois, Chicago*

Roger Kaufman, *Smith College*

Adrienne Kearney, *University of Maine*

James Keeler, *Kenyon College*

Patrick R. Kelso, *West Texas State University*

Kusum Ketkar, *Seton Hall University*

F. Khan, *University of Wisconsin, Parkside*

Robert King, *Boston University*

Milka S. Kirova, *Saint Louis University*

Nobuhiro Kiyotaki, *Princeton University*

Michael Klein, *Tufts University*

Peter Klenow, *Stanford University*

Kenneth Koelln, *University of North Texas*

Douglas Koritz, *Buffalo State College*

Eugene Kroch, *Villanova University*

Corinne Krupp, *University of North Carolina, Chapel Hill*

Kishore Kulkarni, *Metropolitan State College of Denver*

Krishna B. Kumar, *University of Southern California*

Maureen Lage, *Miami University*

John S. Lapp, *North Carolina State University*

G. Paul Larson, *University of North Dakota*

Sven R. Larson, *Skidmore College*

James Lee, *Fort Hays State University*

Junsoo Lee, *University of Alabama*

Keith J. Leggett, *Davis and Elkins College*

Carol Scotese Lehr, *Virginia Commonwealth University*

John Leyes, *Florida International University*

Ming Chien Lo, *University of Virginia*

Mary Lorely, *Syracuse University*

Cara Lown, *Federal Reserve Bank of New York*

Richard MacDonald, *St. Cloud State University*

Thampy Mammen, *St. Norbert College*

Linda M. Manning, *University of Missouri*

Michael Marlow, *California Polytechnic State University*

Kathryn G. Marshall, *Ohio State University*

Patrick Mason, *University of California, Riverside*

Ben Matta, *New Mexico State University*

Stephen McCafferty, *Ohio State University*

J. Harold McClure, Jr., *Villanova University*

Ken McCormick, *University of Northern Iowa*

John McDermott, *University of South Carolina*

Michael B. McElroy, *North Carolina State University*

Randolph McGee, *University of Kentucky*

Michael McPherson, *University of North Texas*

Tim Miller, *Denison University*

Bruce Mizrach, *Rutgers University*

Tommaso Monacelli, *Boston College*

B. Moore, *Wesleyan University*

W. Douglas Morgan, *University of California, Santa Barbara*

Jon Nadenichek, *California State University, Northridge*

K. R. Nair, *West Virginia Wesleyan College*

Emi Nakamura, *Columbia University*

John Neri, *University of Maryland*

Jeffrey Nugent, *University of Southern California*

Maurice Obstfeld, *University of California, Berkeley*

Stephen A. O'Connell, *Swarthmore College*

William P. O'Dea, *State University of New York, Oneonta*

Heather O'Neill, *Ursinus College*

Athanasios Orphanides, *Federal Reserve Board*

Spencer Pack, *Connecticut College*

Walter Park, *American University*

Randall Parker, *East Carolina University*

Allen Parkman, *University of New Mexico*

David Parsley, *Vanderbilt University*

James E. Payne, *Eastern Kentucky University*

Rowena Pecchenino, *Michigan State University*

Peter Pedroni, *Williams College*

Mark Pernecky, *St. Olaf College*

Christopher Phelan, *University of Minnesota*

Kerk Phillips, *Brigham Young University*

Paul Pieper, *University of Illinois, Chicago*

Andrew J. Policano, *State University of New York, Stony Brook*

Richard Pollock, *University of Hawaii, Manoa*

Jay B. Prag, *Claremont McKenna College*

Kojo Quartey, *Talladega College*

Vaman Rao, *Western Illinois University*

Neil Raymon, *University of Missouri, Columbia*

Colin Read, *University of Alaska, Fairbanks*

Michael Redfearn, *University of North Texas*

Robert R. Reed, *University of Alabama*

Charles Revier, *Colorado State University*

Patricia Reynolds, *International Monetary Fund*

Jack Rezelman, *State University of New York, Potsdam*

Robert Rich, *Federal Reserve Bank of New York*

Libby Rittenberg, *Colorado College*

Helen Roberts, *University of Illinois, Chicago*

Kenneth Rogoff, *Harvard University*

Rosemary Rossiter, *Ohio University*

Benjamin Russo, *University of North Carolina*

Heajin Heidi Ryoo, *La Trobe University*

Plutarchos Sakellaris, *University of Maryland*

Christine Sauer, *University of New Mexico*

Edward Schmidt, *Randolph–Macon College*

Stacey Schreft, *Federal Reserve Bank of Kansas City*

William Seyfried, *Rose-Hulman Institute of Technology*

Tayyeb Shabbir, *University of Pennsylvania*

Andrei Shevchenko, *Michigan State University*

Virginia Shingleton, *Valparaiso University*

Dorothy Siden, *Salem State College*

Scott Simkins, *University of North Carolina, Greensboro*

Tara Sinclair, *George Washington University*

Abdol Soofi, *University of Wisconsin*

Nicholas Souleles, *The Wharton School, University of Pennsylvania*

David E. Spencer, *Brigham Young University*

Don Stabile, *St. Mary's College*

Richard Startz, *University of Washington*

Gabriel Talmain, *State University of New York, Albany*

Bryan Taylor, *California State University, Los Angeles*

Susan Washburn Taylor, *Millsaps College*

M. Dekalb Terrell, *Kansas State University*

Henry S. Terrell, *University of Maryland*

Willem Thorbecke, *George Mason University*

Stephen J. Turnovsky, *University of Washington*

Michael Twomey, *University of Michigan, Dearborn*

Michael Ulan, *U.S. Department of State*

Vic Valcarcel, *University of Kansas*

Victor Valcarcel, *Texas Tech University*

Dietrich Vollrath, *University of Houston*

Ronald Warren, *University of Georgia*

Chong K. Yip, *Chinese University of Hong Kong*

We thank John Haltiwanger of the University of Maryland for supplying data on job creation and destruction used in Chapter 10 and Shigeru Fujita of the Federal Reserve Bank of Philadelphia for data on the rates of job loss and job finding used in Chapter 8. We would also like to thank Robert H. Rasche, research director at the Federal Reserve Bank of St. Louis, for assisting us in our use of the FRED database cited at the end of each chapter in the "Working with Macroeconomic Data" exercises.

The authors and the editor also wish to thank Bryan P. Rippeon for his contribution of the art used on the cover of this text. Bryan is a current art student at the University of Maryland, graduating in May 2010.

Finally, we thank Mark Gertler, Rick Mishkin, and Steve Zeldes for valuable assistance with the first edition. Also, we are grateful to several cohorts of students at the University of Pennsylvania and Princeton University who—not entirely of their own free will but nonetheless very graciously—assisted us in the development of this textbook. Last and most important, we thank our families for their patience and support. We dedicate this book to them.

A. B. A.
Wynnewood, PA
B. S. B.
Washington, DC
D. C.
Richmond, VA

CHAPTER 1

Introduction to Macroeconomics

1.1 What Macroeconomics Is About

Macroeconomics is the study of the structure and performance of national economies and of the policies that governments use to try to affect economic performance. The issues that macroeconomists address include the following:

- *What determines a nation's long-run economic growth?* In 1870, income per capita was smaller in Norway than in Argentina. But today, income per capita is about three times as high in Norway as in Argentina. Why do some nations' economies grow quickly, providing their citizens with rapidly improving living standards, while other nations' economies are relatively stagnant?

- *What causes a nation's economic activity to fluctuate?* The 1990s exhibited the longest period of uninterrupted economic growth in U.S. economic history, but economic performance in the 2000s was much weaker. A mild recession in 2001 was followed by a weak recovery that lasted only until December 2007. The recession that began at the end of 2007 was worsened by the financial crisis in 2008, which contributed to a sharp decline in output at the end of 2008 and in early 2009. Why do economies sometimes experience sharp short-run fluctuations, lurching between periods of prosperity and periods of hard times?

- *What causes unemployment?* During the 1930s, one-quarter of the work force in the United States was unemployed. A decade later, during World War II, less than 2% of the work force was unemployed. Why does unemployment sometimes reach very high levels? Why, even during times of relative prosperity, is a significant fraction of the work force unemployed?

- *What causes prices to rise?* The rate of inflation in the United States crept steadily upward during the 1970s, and exceeded 10% per year in the early 1980s, before dropping to less than 4% per year in the mid 1980s and dropping even further to less than 2% per year in the late 1990s. Germany's inflation experience has been much more extreme: Although Germany has earned a reputation for low inflation in recent decades, following its defeat in World War I Germany experienced an eighteen-month period (July 1922–December 1923) during which prices rose by a factor of several billion! What causes inflation and what can be done about it?

■ *How does being part of a global economic system affect nations' economies?* In the late 1990s, the U.S. economy was the engine of worldwide economic growth. The wealth gained by Americans in the stock market led them to increase their spending on consumer goods, including products made abroad, spurring greater economic activity in many countries. How do economic links among nations, such as international trade and borrowing, affect the performance of individual economies and the world economy as a whole?

■ *Can government policies be used to improve a nation's economic performance?* In the 1980s and 1990s, the U.S. economy's output, unemployment rate, and inflation rate fluctuated much less than they did in the 1960s and 1970s. Some economists credit good government policy for the improvement in economic performance. In the financial crisis of 2008, the Federal Reserve and the federal government used extraordinary measures to keep banks and other financial institutions from failing. But some economists criticized these measures for going too far in trying to stabilize the economy, at the expense of creating incentives for increased risk taking by financial firms. How should economic policy be conducted so as to keep the economy as prosperous and stable as possible?

Macroeconomics seeks to offer answers to such questions, which are of great practical importance and are constantly debated by politicians, the press, and the public. In the rest of this section, we consider these key macroeconomic issues in more detail.

Long-Run Economic Growth

If you have ever traveled in a developing country, you could not help but observe the difference in living standards relative to those of countries such as the United States. The problems of inadequate food, shelter, and health care experienced by the poorest citizens of rich nations often represent the average situation for the people of a developing country. From a macroeconomic perspective, the difference between rich nations and developing nations may be summarized by saying that rich nations have at some point in their history experienced extended periods of rapid economic growth but that the poorer nations either have never experienced sustained growth or have had periods of growth offset by periods of economic decline.

Figure 1.1 summarizes the growth in output of the U.S. economy since 1869.[1] The record is an impressive one: Over the past century and a third, the annual output of U.S. goods and services has increased by more than 100 times. The performance of the U.S. economy is not unique, however; other industrial nations have had similar, and in some cases higher, rates of growth over the same period of time. This massive increase in the output of industrial economies is one of the central facts of modern history and has had enormous political, military, social, and even cultural implications.

In part, the long-term growth of the U.S. economy is the result of a rising population, which has meant a steady increase in the number of available workers. But another significant factor is the increase in the amount of output that can be produced with a given amount of labor. The amount of output produced per unit

---

[1]Output is measured in Fig. 1.1 by two very similar concepts, real gross national product (real GNP) until 1929 and real gross domestic product (real GDP) since 1929, both of which measure the physical volume of production in each year. We discuss the measurement of output in detail in Chapter 2.

Figure 1.1

Output of the U.S. economy, 1869–2008
In this graph the output of the U.S. economy is measured by real gross domestic product (real GDP) for the period 1929–2008 and by real gross national product (real GNP) for the period prior to 1929, with goods and services valued at their 2005 prices in both cases (see Chapter 2). Note the strong upward trend in output over time, as well as sharp fluctuations during the Great Depression (1929–1940), World War II (1941–1945), and the recessions of 1973–1975, 1981–1982, 1990–1991, 2001 and 2007.

Sources: Real GNP 1869–1928 from Christina D. Romer, "The Prewar Business Cycle Reconsidered: New Estimates of Gross National Product, 1869–1908," *Journal of Political Economy,* 97, 1 (February 1989), pp. 22–23; real GDP 1929 onward from FRED database, Federal Reserve Bank of St. Louis, *research.stlouisfed.org/fred2/series/GDPCA.* Data from Romer were rescaled to 2005 prices.

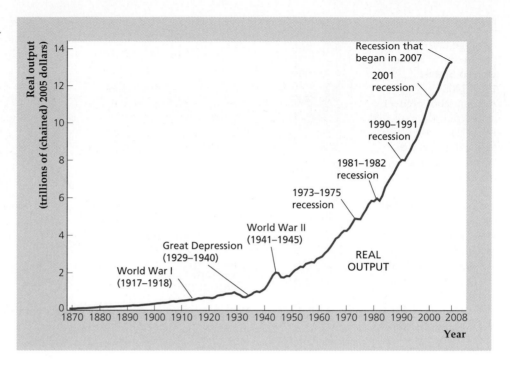

of labor input—for example, per worker or per hour of work—is called **average labor productivity.** Figure 1.2 shows how average labor productivity, defined in this case as output per employed worker, has changed since 1900. In 2008, the average U.S. worker produced more than six times as much output as the average worker at the beginning of the twentieth century, despite working fewer hours over the course of the year. Because today's typical worker is so much more productive, Americans enjoy a significantly higher standard of living than would have been possible a century ago.

Although the long-term record of productivity growth in the U.S. economy is excellent, productivity growth slowed from the early 1970s to the mid-1990s and only recently has picked up. Output per worker grew about 2.5% per year from 1949 to 1973, but only 1.1% per year from 1973 to 1995. More recently, from 1995 to 2008, output per worker has increased 1.7% per year, a pace that has improved the health of the U.S. economy significantly.

Because the rates of growth of output and, particularly, of output per worker ultimately determine whether a nation will be rich or poor, understanding what determines growth is one of the most important goals of macroeconomics. Unfortunately, explaining why economies grow is not easy. Why, for example, did resource-poor Japan and Korea experience growth rates that transformed them in a generation or two from war-torn nations into industrial powers, whereas several resource-rich nations of Latin America have had erratic or even negative growth in recent years? Although macroeconomists have nothing close to a complete answer to the question of what determines rates of economic growth, they do have some ideas to offer. For example, as we discuss in some detail in this book, most macroeconomists believe that rates of saving and investment are important for growth. Another key determinant of growth we discuss is the rate at which technological change and other factors help increase the productivity of machines and workers.

Figure 1.2

Average labor productivity in the United States, 1900–2008

Average labor productivity (output per employed worker) has risen over time, with a peak during World War II reflecting increased wartime production. Productivity growth was particularly strong in the 1950s and 1960s, slowed in the 1970s, and picked up again in the mid 1990s. For the calculation of productivity, output is measured as in Fig. 1.1.

Sources: Employment in thousands of workers 14 and older for 1900–1947 from *Historical Statistics of the United States, Colonial Times to 1970,* pp. 126–127; workers 16 and older for 1948 onward from FRED database, Federal Reserve Bank of St. Louis, *research.stlouisfed.org/fred2/ series/CE16OV.* Average labor productivity is output divided by employment, where output is from Fig. 1.1.

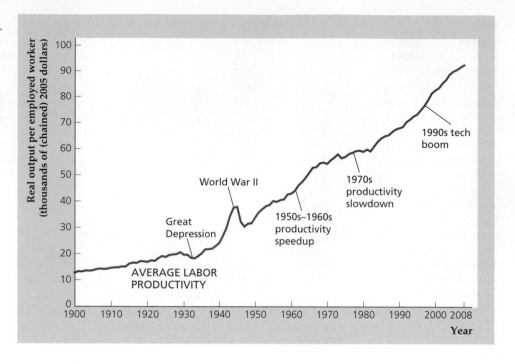

Business Cycles

If you look at the history of U.S. output in Fig. 1.1, you will notice that the growth of output isn't always smooth but has hills and valleys. Most striking is the period between 1929 and 1945, which spans the Great Depression and World War II. During the 1929–1933 economic collapse that marked the first major phase of the Great Depression, the output of the U.S. economy fell by nearly 30%. Over the period 1939–1944, as the United States entered World War II and expanded production of armaments, output nearly doubled. No fluctuations in U.S. output since 1945 have been as severe as those of the 1929–1945 period. However, during the postwar era there have been periods of unusually rapid economic growth, such as during the 1960s and 1990s, and times during which output actually declined from one year to the next, as in 1973–1975, 1981–1982, and 1990–1991.

Macroeconomists use the term *business cycle* to describe short-run, but sometimes sharp, contractions and expansions in economic activity.[2] The downward phase of a business cycle, during which national output may be falling or perhaps growing only very slowly, is called a recession. Even when they are relatively mild, recessions mean hard economic times for many people. Recessions are also a major political concern, because almost every politician wants to be reelected and the chances of reelection are better if the nation's economy is expanding rather than declining. Macroeconomists put a lot of effort into trying to figure out what causes business cycles and deciding what can or should be done about them. In this book we describe a variety of features of business cycles, compare alternative explanations for cyclical fluctuations, and evaluate the policy options that are available for affecting the course of the cycle.

---

[2]A more exact definition is given in Chapter 8. Business cycles do not include fluctuations lasting only a few months, such as the increase in activity that occurs around Christmas.

Figure 1.3

The U.S. unemployment rate, 1890–2008

The figure shows the percentage of the civilian labor force (excluding people in the military) that was unemployed in each year since 1890. Unemployment peaked during the depression of the 1890s and the Great Depression of the 1930s, and reached low points in 1920 and during World War II. Since World War II, the highest unemployment rates occurred during the 1973–1975 and 1981–1982 recessions.

Sources: Civilian unemployment rate (people aged 14 and older until 1947, aged 16 and older after 1947) for 1890–1947 from *Historical Statistics of the United States, Colonial Times to 1970*, p. 135; for 1948 onward from FRED database Federal Reserve Bank of St. Louis, *research.stlouisfed.org/fred2/ series/UNRATE*.

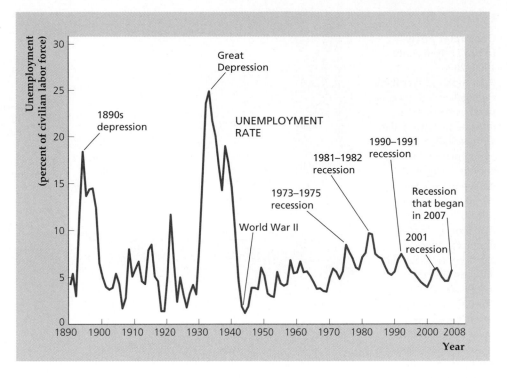

Unemployment

One important aspect of recessions is that they usually are accompanied by an increase in **unemployment,** or the number of people who are available for work and are actively seeking work but cannot find jobs. Along with growth and business cycles, the problem of unemployment is a third major issue in macroeconomics.

The best-known measure of unemployment is the unemployment rate, which is the number of unemployed divided by the total labor force (the number of people either working or seeking work). Figure 1.3 shows the unemployment rate in the United States over the past century. The highest and most prolonged period of unemployment occurred during the Great Depression of the 1930s. In 1933, the unemployment rate was 24.9%, indicating that about one of every four potential workers was unable to find a job. In contrast, the tremendous increase in economic activity that occurred during World War II significantly reduced unemployment. In 1944, at the peak of the wartime boom, the unemployment rate was 1.2%.

Recessions have led to significant increases in unemployment in the postwar period. For example, during the 1981–1982 recession the U.S. unemployment rate reached 10.8%.[3] Even during periods of economic expansion, however, the unemployment rate remains well above zero, as you can see from Fig. 1.3. In 2000, after nine years of economic growth with no recession, the unemployment rate was still about 4%. Why the unemployment rate can remain fairly high even when the economy as a whole is doing well is another important question in macroeconomics.

---

[3]The unemployment rate was 10.8% in November and December 1982. The unemployment rate plotted in Fig. 1.3 is not this high because the graph only shows annual data—the average unemployment rate over the 12 months of each year—which was 9.7% in 1982.

Figure 1.4

Consumer prices in the United States, 1800–2008

Prior to World War II, the average level of prices faced by consumers remained relatively flat, with periods of inflation (rising prices) offset by periods of deflation (falling prices). Since World War II, however, prices have risen more than tenfold. In the figure, the average level of prices is measured by the consumer price index, or CPI (see Chapter 2). The CPI measures the cost of a fixed set, or basket, of consumer goods and services relative to the cost of the same goods and services in a base period—in this case, 1982–1984. Thus a CPI of 215.20 in 2008 means that a basket of consumer goods and services that cost $100 in 1982–1984 would cost $215.20 in 2008.

Sources: Consumer price index, 1800–1946 (1967 = 100) from *Historical Statistics of the United States, Colonial Times to 1970,* pp. 210–211; 1947 onward (1982–1984 = 100) from FRED database, Federal Reserve Bank of St. Louis, *research. stlouisfed.org/fred2/series/ CPIAUCSL.* Data prior to 1971 were rescaled to a base with 1982–1984 = 100.

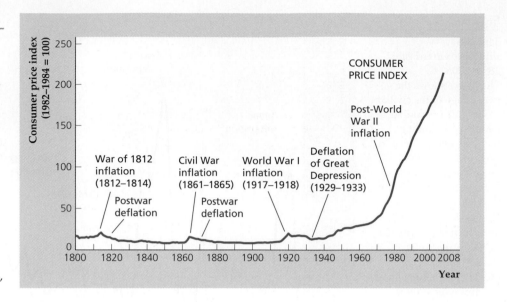

Inflation

When the prices of most goods and services are rising over time, the economy is said to be experiencing **inflation.** Figure 1.4 shows a measure of the average level of prices faced by consumers in the United States over the past two centuries.[4] Note that prior to World War II inflation usually occurred only during wartime, such as during the War of 1812, the Civil War, and World War I. These wartime periods of inflation were followed by periods of **deflation,** during which the prices of most goods and services fell. The result of these offsetting periods of inflation and deflation was that, over the long run, the level of prices was fairly constant. For example, prices at the end of World War I (1918) stood at about the same level as in 1800, more than a century earlier.

The last significant deflation in the United States occurred during 1929–1933, the initial phase of the Great Depression. Since then, inflation, without offsetting deflation, has become the normal state of affairs, although inflation was fairly low in the 1990s and 2000s. Figure 1.4 shows that consumer prices have risen significantly since World War II, with the measure of prices shown increasing tenfold.

The percentage increase in the average level of prices over a year is called the inflation rate. If the inflation rate in consumer prices is 10%, for example, then on average the prices of items that consumers buy are rising by 10% per year. Rates of inflation may vary dramatically both over time and by country, from 1 or 2 percent per year in low-inflation countries (such as Switzerland) to 1000% per year or more in countries (such as a number of the former Soviet republics in the early 1990s) that are experiencing hyperinflations, or extreme inflations. When the inflation rate reaches an extremely high level, with prices changing daily or hourly, the economy

---

[4]This measure is called the consumer price index, or CPI, which is discussed in Chapter 2. Conceptually, the CPI is intended to measure the cost of buying a certain fixed set, or "basket," of consumer goods and services. However, the construction of a consumer price index over a period as long as two centuries involves many compromises. For instance, the basket of goods and services priced by the CPI is not literally the same over the entire period shown in Fig. 1.4 but is periodically changed to reflect the different mix of consumer goods and services available at different times.

tends to function poorly. High inflation also means that the purchasing power of money erodes quickly. This situation forces people to scramble to spend their money almost as soon as they receive it.

The International Economy

Today every major economy is an **open economy,** or one that has extensive trading and financial relationships with other national economies. (In contrast, a **closed economy** doesn't interact economically with the rest of the world.) Macroeconomists study patterns of international trade and borrowing to understand better the links among national economies. For example, an important topic in macroeconomics is how international trade and borrowing relationships can help transmit business cycles from country to country.

Another issue for which international considerations are central is trade imbalances. Figure 1.5 shows the historical behavior of the imports and exports of goods and services by the United States. U.S. imports are goods and services produced

Figure 1.5

U.S. exports and imports, 1869–2008
The figure shows U.S. exports (black) and U.S. imports (red), each expressed as a percentage of total output. Exports and imports need not be equal in each year: U.S. exports exceeded imports (shaded gray) during much of the twentieth century. During the 1980s, 1990s, and early 2000s, however, U.S. exports were smaller than U.S. imports (shaded pink).

Sources: Imports and exports of goods and services: 1869–1959 from *Historical Statistics of the United States, Colonial Times to 1970,* pp. 864–865; 1960 onward from FRED database, Federal Reserve Bank of St. Louis, *research.stlouisfed.org/ fred2/series/BOPX* and *BOPM;* output is from Fig. 1.1.

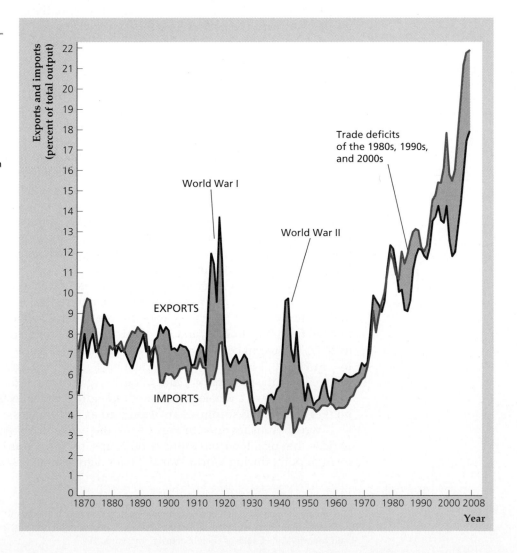

abroad and purchased by people in the United States; U.S. exports are goods and services produced in the United States and sold to people in other countries. To give you a sense of the relative importance of international trade, Fig. 1.5 expresses exports and imports as percentages of total U.S. output. Currently, both exports and imports are larger fractions of U.S. output than they were during the 1950s and 1960s, reflecting both the recovery of trade from the disruptions of the Great Depression and World War II and the trend toward greater economic interdependence among nations. Note, though, that a century ago exports and imports already were important relative to the size of the overall economy.

Figure 1.5 demonstrates that exports and imports need not be equal in each year. For example, following World War I and World War II, U.S. exports outstripped U.S. imports because the country was sending large quantities of supplies to countries whose economies had been damaged by war. When exports exceed imports, a **trade surplus** exists. In the 1980s, however, U.S. exports declined sharply relative to imports, a situation that has persisted through the 1990s and into the 2000s, as you can see from Fig. 1.5. This recent excess of imports over exports, or **trade deficit,** has received considerable attention from policymakers and the news media. What causes these trade imbalances? Are they bad for the U.S. economy or for the economies of this country's trading partners? These are among the questions that macroeconomists try to answer.

Macroeconomic Policy

A nation's economic performance depends on many factors, including its natural and human resources, its capital stock (buildings, machines, and software), its technology, and the economic choices made by its citizens, both individually and collectively. Another extremely important factor affecting economic performance is the set of macroeconomic policies pursued by the government.

Macroeconomic policies affect the performance of the economy as a whole. The two major types of macroeconomic policies are fiscal policy and monetary policy. **Fiscal policy,** which is determined at the national, state, and local levels, concerns government spending and taxation. **Monetary policy** determines the rate of growth of the nation's money supply and is under the control of a government institution known as the central bank. In the United States, the central bank is the Federal Reserve System, or the Fed.

One of the main macroeconomic policy issues of recent years in the United States has been in the realm of fiscal policy. Large Federal budget surpluses emerged in the late 1990s, but these gave way to large Federal budget deficits, averaging 2% of GDP from 2001 to 2008, and (as of this writing) projected to be over 11% of GDP in 2009. The recent behavior of the Federal budget is put into a long-term perspective in Figure. 1.6, which presents data on Federal government spending and tax revenues for the past century and a third.[5] Again, so that their importance relative to the economy as a whole is indicated, spending, tax collections, and government budget deficits and surpluses are expressed as percentages of total output.

Two obvious features of Fig. 1.6 are the peaks in government spending and deficits that resulted from military buildups in World War I and World War II. At its high point during World War II, Federal government spending exceeded 43%

---

[5]Government spending includes both government purchases of goods and services, such as purchases of military equipment and the salaries of government officials, and government benefits paid to individuals, such as Social Security payments.

Figure 1.6

U.S. Federal government spending and tax collections, 1869–2008

U.S. Federal government spending (red) and U.S. Federal government tax collections (black) are shown as a percentage of total output. Deficits (excesses of spending over tax collections) are shaded pink, and surpluses (excesses of taxes over spending) are shaded gray. The government sector's share of the economy has grown since World War II. Large deficits occurred during the two world wars, the Great Depression, and during the 1980s and much of the 1990s.

Sources: Federal spending and receipts: 1869–1929 from *Historical Statistics of the United States, Colonial Times to 1970,* p. 1104; 1930 onward from *Historical Tables, Budget of the U.S. Government,* Table 1.2; Output, 1869–1928 (GNP) from Christina D. Romer, "The Prewar Business Cycle Reconsidered: New Estimates of Gross National Product, 1869–1908," *Journal of Political Economy,* 97, 1 (February 1989), pp. 22–23; 1929 onward (GDP) from BEA Web site, www.bea.gov.

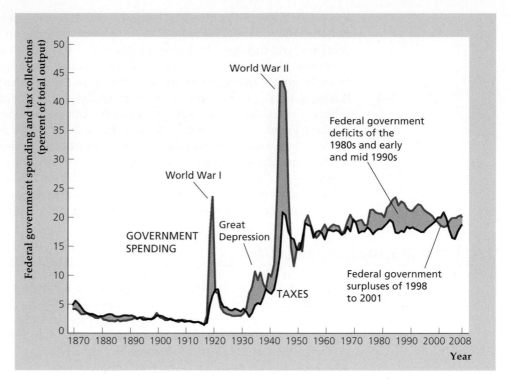

of total output. Significant deficits also occurred during the Great Depression of the 1930s because the government increased its spending on various programs designed to help the economy, such as government-financed jobs programs. Also shown clearly is the increase in the size of the government sector since World War II, an increase reflected in the major upward shift in government spending and in tax collections relative to national output that occurred in about 1940 as well as the mild upward trend in both variables that has occurred since then.

The large and persistent Federal budget deficits of the 1980s and early and mid 1990s were historically unusual in that they occurred during a period of peace and relative prosperity. The emergence of large Federal deficits in the 1980s coincided with the emergence of large trade deficits (see Fig. 1.5). Indeed, the Federal budget deficit and the trade deficit have been called the "twin deficits." Are these deficits related? If so, what can be done about them? These questions also fall within the purview of macroeconomics.

The possible link between the government's budget deficit and the trade imbalance illustrates an important aspect of macroeconomics: Macroeconomic issues and problems are frequently interconnected. For this reason, studying one macroeconomic question, such as the effects of the government budget deficit, in isolation generally is not sufficient. Instead, macroeconomists usually study the economy as a complete system, recognizing that changes in one sector or market may affect the behavior of the entire economy.

Aggregation

Macroeconomics is one of two broad areas within the field of economics, the other being microeconomics. Macroeconomics and microeconomics have many basic economic ideas and methods in common; the difference between them is the level at which the economy is studied. Microeconomists focus on individual consumers, workers, and firms, each of which is too small to have an impact on the national economy. Macroeconomists ignore the fine distinctions among the many different kinds of goods, firms, and markets that exist in the economy and instead focus on national totals. For example, in their analyses macroeconomists do not care whether consumers are buying Microsoft Xboxes or Sony PlayStations, beef or chicken, Pepsi or Coke. Instead, they add consumer expenditures on all goods and services to get an overall total called aggregate consumption. The process of summing individual economic variables to obtain economywide totals is called **aggregation.** The use of aggregation and the emphasis on aggregate quantities such as aggregate consumption, aggregate investment, and aggregate output are the primary factors that distinguish macroeconomics from microeconomics.

1.2 What Macroeconomists Do

How do macroeconomists use their skills, and what do they do with all the data they gather and the theories they develop? Besides teaching economics, macroeconomists engage in a wide variety of activities, including forecasting, macroeconomic analysis, basic research, and data development for government, nonprofit organizations, and private businesses.

Macroeconomic Forecasting

Many people believe that economists spend most of their time trying to forecast the performance of the economy. In fact, except for a relatively small number of forecasting specialists, forecasting is a minor part of what macroeconomists do. One reason macroeconomists don't emphasize forecasting is that on the whole they are not terribly good at it! Forecasting is difficult not only because our understanding of how the economy works is imperfect, but also because it is impossible to take into account *all* the factors—many of them not strictly economic—that might affect future economic trends. Here are some questions that a forecaster, in trying to project the course of the economy, might have to try to answer: How will events abroad affect congressional authorizations for military spending over the next few years? What oil price will the Organization of Petroleum Exporting Countries (OPEC) decide on at its next meeting? Will there be a severe drought in agricultural regions, with adverse effects on food quantities and prices? Will productivity rise as rapidly in the future as it did in the late 1990s and early 2000s as businesses increasingly adopted computer technology? Because answers to such questions are highly uncertain, macroeconomic forecasters rarely offer a single prediction. Instead, they usually combine a "most likely" forecast with "optimistic" and "pessimistic" alternative scenarios.

Does the fact that macroeconomics can't be used to make highly accurate forecasts of economic activity mean that it is a pointless field of study? Some people may think so, but that's really an unreasonable standard. Meteorology is an example of a field in which forecasting is difficult (will it *definitely* be sunny this weekend?) but in which there is also a lot of useful knowledge (meteorologists helped discover the depletion of the earth's ozone layer and pointed out its dangers). Similarly, cardiologists usually can't predict if or when a patient will have a heart attack—they can only talk about probabilities. Like meteorologists and doctors, economists deal with a system whose complexity makes gaining a thorough understanding difficult and forecasting the system's behavior even more difficult. Rather than predicting what will happen, most macroeconomists are engaged in analyzing and interpreting events as they happen (macroeconomic analysis) or in trying to understand the structure of the economy in general (macroeconomic research).

Macroeconomic Analysis

Macroeconomic analysts monitor the economy and think about the implications of current economic events. Many analysts are employed in the private sector, such as in banks or large corporations. Private-sector analysts try to determine how general economic trends will affect their employers' financial investments, their opportunities for expansion, the demand for their products, and so on. Some private firms specialize in macroeconomic analysis and assist clients on a fee-for-service basis.

The public sector, which includes national and regional governments and international agencies such as the World Bank and the International Monetary Fund, also employs many macroeconomic analysts. The main function of public-sector analysts is to assist in policymaking—for example, by writing reports that assess various macroeconomic problems and by identifying and evaluating possible policy options. Among U.S. policymakers, the officials who set monetary policy may call on the aid of several hundred Ph.D. economists employed within the Federal Reserve System, and the President has the advice of the Council of Economic Advisers and the professional staffs of numerous departments and agencies. For members of Congress, a frequent source of macroeconomic analysis is the Congressional Budget Office. Economic policymakers also often go outside the government to seek the advice of macroeconomists from business or academia.

If a country has many well-trained macroeconomic analysts, as is true in the United States, does that mean that its macroeconomic policies will always be intelligent and farsighted? The answer, unfortunately, is "no." Because of the complexity of the economy, macroeconomic policy analysis, like macroeconomic forecasting, often is difficult and uncertain. Perhaps even more important, *politicians, not economists, often make economic policy.* Politicians are typically less concerned with the abstract desirability of a policy than with the policy's immediate effects on their constituents. Thus in late 1990 international talks intended to reduce trade barriers failed because European governments found it politically inadvisable to reduce high subsidy payments to their farmers—despite the nearly universal opposition of economists to both trade barriers and farm price support payments. In 2002, the Bush administration gave in to pressure from the steel industry and imposed tariffs on certain types of imported steel—despite the nearly universal opposition of economists to trade barriers.

Although the technical advice provided by macroeconomic analysts is not the sole basis on which macroeconomic policy is made, such advice is probably necessary for making good policy decisions, especially if dramatic changes are being considered. Since the 1990s, for example, a number of countries in Eastern Europe, Latin America, and elsewhere have undertaken radical reforms of their economies. In most of these cases, the countries' leaders have sought the technical advice of domestic and foreign economists, and this advice has been influential in policymaking. In the former Soviet Union, economists have played an important role in the debate over restructuring and reform, both as technical specialists and as political advocates.

Macroeconomic Research

Macroeconomic research takes an amazing variety of forms, from abstract mathematical analysis to psychological experimentation to simulation projects in which computers are used to generate random numbers that represent the randomness of day-to-day economic activity. Nevertheless, the goal of all macroeconomic research is to make general statements about how the economy works. The general insights about the economy gained from successful research form the basis for the analyses of specific economic problems, policies, or situations.

To see why research is important, imagine that you are an economist with the International Monetary Fund whose task is to help a small African country control its high rate of inflation. On what basis can you offer advice? Basically, you should know what inflation-fighting policies other countries have used in the past, what the results have been, how the results have depended on the characteristics of the country employing the policy, and so on. Particularly if the situation you are analyzing is not identical to any of the previous cases, having some theoretical principles would also help you identify and understand the main factors contributing to that country's inflation. Analyzing the historical cases and working out the theoretical principles by yourself from scratch might involve many years' effort. The value of ongoing research activities is that many of the results and ideas that you need will already be available in books or professional journals or circulated in unpublished form. Because it forms the basis for activities such as economic analysis and forecasting, in a very real sense macroeconomic research is the engine that pulls the whole enterprise of macroeconomics behind it.

Macroeconomic research takes place primarily in colleges and universities, in nonprofit institutions (such as the National Bureau of Economic Research, the Brookings Institution, and the American Enterprise Institute), and in the public sector (the government and international agencies). Particularly in the public sector, the line between economic analysis and macroeconomic research is much fuzzier than we have drawn it here. The reason is that many economists move back and forth between analysis of specific problems (such as an African country's inflation problem) and more basic macroeconomic research (such as an analysis of inflation in general).

Economic Theory.   How is macroeconomic research carried out? As in many other fields, macroeconomic research proceeds primarily through the formulation and testing of theories. An **economic theory** is a set of ideas about the economy that has been organized in a logical framework. Most economic theories are developed in terms of an **economic model,** which is a simplified description of some aspect of the economy, usually expressed in mathematical form. Economists evaluate an economic model or theory by applying four criteria:

1. Are its assumptions reasonable and realistic?
2. Is it understandable and manageable enough to be used in studying real problems?
3. Does it have implications that can be tested by **empirical analysis?** That is, can its implications be evaluated by comparing them with data obtained in the real world?
4. When the implications and the data are compared, are the implications of the theory consistent with the data?

IN TOUCH WITH DATA AND RESEARCH

Developing and Testing an Economic Theory

To illustrate the process of developing and testing an economic theory, suppose that we want to develop a theory that explains the routes that people take when they commute from home to work and back. Such a theory would be useful, for example, to a traffic planner who is concerned about how a proposed housing development will affect traffic patterns. Here are the steps we would take.

Step 1. State the research question.

Example: What determines traffic flows in the city during rush hours?

Step 2. Make provisional assumptions that describe the economic setting and the behavior of the economic actors. These assumptions should be simple yet capture the most important aspects of the problem.

Example: The setting is described by the map of the city. The assumption about behavior is that commuters choose routes that minimize driving time.

Step 3. Work out the implications of the theory.

Example: Use the map of the city to plot a route that minimizes driving time between home and place of work.

Step 4. Conduct an *empirical analysis* to compare the implications of the theory with the data.

Example: Conduct a survey of commuters to identify (1) home locations; (2) work locations; and (3) routes taken to work. Then determine whether the routes predicted by the model are generally the same as those reported in the commuter survey.

Step 5. Evaluate the results of your comparisons.

If the theory fits the data well: Use the theory to predict what would happen if the economic setting or economic policies change.

Example: Use the minimum-driving-time assumption to evaluate the traffic effects of a new housing development by figuring out which routes the residents of the development are likely to take.

If the theory fits the data poorly: Start from scratch with a new model. Repeat Steps 2–5.

Example: Change the provisional behavioral assumption to the following: Commuters choose the route that minimizes the *distance* they must drive (not the time they spend driving).

If the theory fits the data moderately well: Either make do with a partially successful theory or modify the model with additional assumptions and then repeat Steps 3–5.

Example: A possible modification of the minimum-driving-time assumption is that commuters will choose more scenic over less scenic routes, if driving time is not increased by more than a certain number of minutes. To test the model with this modified assumption, you must determine which routes are more scenic (those that pass a lake) and which are less scenic (those that pass a dump).

For a theory or model—of any type, not just economic—to be useful, the answer to each of these questions must be "yes." Unfortunately, though, economists may not always agree in their evaluation of a particular model, with the result that controversies sometimes persist about the best way to model a given economic situation.

We present a summary of the main steps in developing and testing an economic theory or model in "In Touch with Data and Research: Developing and Testing an Economic Theory," p. 13.

Data Development

The collection of economic data is a vital part of macroeconomics, and many economists are involved in the data development process. In the United States as well as all other major countries, data on thousands of economic variables are collected and analyzed. We have already presented some important macroeconomic data series, such as measures of output and the price level, and will look at these and others in more detail in Chapter 2. Macroeconomists use economic data to assess the current state of the economy, make forecasts, analyze policy alternatives, and test macroeconomic theories.

Most economic data are collected and published by the Federal government—for example, by agencies such as the Bureau of the Census, the Bureau of Labor Statistics, and the Bureau of Economic Analysis in the United States, and by central banks such as the Federal Reserve. To an increasing degree, however, these activities also take place in the private sector. For example, marketing firms and private economic forecasting companies are important collectors, users, and sellers of economic data. In this book, many of the boxes called "In Touch with Data and Research" describe major macroeconomic data series and tell you how they are collected and where to find them; other "In Touch with Data and Research" boxes describe topics and issues in macroeconomic research.

Much of the data collection and preparation process is routine. However, because providers of data want their numbers to be as useful as possible while keeping costs down, the organization of major data collection projects is typically the joint effort of many skilled professionals. Providers of data must decide what types of data should be collected on the basis of who is expected to use the data and how. They must take care that measures of economic activity correspond to abstract concepts (such as "capital" and "labor") that are suggested by economic theory. In addition, data providers must guarantee the confidentiality of data that may reveal information about individual firms and people in the economy. In a large data-gathering organization such as the Bureau of the Census, each of these issues is exhaustively analyzed by economists and statisticians before data collection begins.[6]

1.3 Why Macroeconomists Disagree

Over the years, the efforts of thousands of analysts, data collectors, and researchers have greatly enhanced the understanding of macroeconomic phenomena. Yet no matter what the macroeconomic issue, the news media seemingly can find an economist to argue either side of it. Why do macroeconomists appear to disagree so much?[7]

---

[6]For a readable discussion of issues that face data collectors, see Janet L. Norwood, "Distinguished Lecture on Economics in Government: Data Quality and Public Policy," *Journal of Economic Perspectives*, Spring 1990, pp. 3–12.

[7]Not only do macroeconomists often seem to disagree with one another, but they also sometimes are accused of not being able to agree with themselves. President Harry Truman expressed the frustration of many policymakers when he said he wanted a one-handed economist—one who wouldn't always say, "On the one hand, . . . ; on the other hand. . . ."

To a certain extent, the amount of disagreement among macroeconomists is exaggerated by the tendency of the public and the media to focus on the most difficult and controversial issues. In addition, the very fact that economic policy and performance are of such broad interest and concern contributes to the intensity of debate: More than controversies in many other fields, debates in macroeconomics tend to take place in public, rather than in the seminar room or the laboratory. Although important disagreements among macroeconomists certainly exist, there also are many areas of substantial agreement in macroeconomics.

We can provide an insight into why macroeconomists disagree by drawing the important distinction between positive and normative analyses of economic policy. A **positive analysis** of an economic policy examines the economic consequences of a policy but doesn't address the question of whether those consequences are desirable.

A **normative analysis** of policy tries to determine whether a certain policy *should* be used. For example, if an economist is asked to evaluate the effects on the economy of a 5% reduction in the income tax, the response involves a positive analysis. But if asked whether the income tax *should* be reduced by 5%, the economist's response requires a normative analysis. This normative analysis will involve not only the economist's objective, scientific understanding of how the economy works but also personal value judgments—for example, about the appropriate size of the government sector or the amount of income redistribution that is desirable.

Economists may agree on the positive analysis of a question yet disagree on the normative part because of differences in values. Value differences also are common in other fields: Physicists may be in perfect agreement on what would happen *if* a nuclear bomb were detonated (a positive analysis). But physicist "hawks" and physicist "doves" may disagree strongly about whether nuclear weapons *should* be deployed (a normative question).

Disagreement may occur on positive issues, however, and these differences are important in economics. In macroeconomics there always have been many schools of thought, each with a somewhat different perspective on how the economy works. Examples include monetarism and supply-side economics, both of which we discuss in this book. However, the most important—and enduring—disagreements on positive issues in macroeconomics involve the two schools of thought called the classical approach and the Keynesian approach.

Classicals Versus Keynesians

The classical approach and the Keynesian approach are the two major intellectual traditions in macroeconomics. We discuss the differences between the two approaches briefly here and in much greater detail later in the book.

The Classical Approach.   The origins of the classical approach go back more than two centuries, at least to the famous Scottish economist Adam Smith. In 1776 Smith published his classic, *The Wealth of Nations,* in which he proposed the concept of the "invisible hand." The idea of the **invisible hand** is that, if there are free markets and individuals conduct their economic affairs in their own best interests, the overall economy will work well. As Smith put it, in a market economy, individuals pursuing their own self-interests seem to be led by an invisible hand to maximize the general welfare of everyone in the economy.

However, we must not overstate what Smith claimed: To say that an invisible hand is at work does *not* mean that no one in a market economy will be hungry or dissatisfied; free markets cannot insulate a nation from the effects of drought, war, or political instability. Nor does the invisible hand rule out the existence of great inequalities between the rich and the poor, because in Smith's analysis he took the initial distribution of wealth among people as given. Rather, the invisible-hand idea says that given a country's resources (natural, human, and technological) and its initial distribution of wealth, the use of free markets will make people as economically well off as possible.

Validity of the invisible-hand idea depends on a key assumption: The various markets in the economy, including financial markets, labor markets, and markets for goods and services, must function smoothly and without impediments such as minimum wages and interest rate ceilings. In particular, wages and prices must adjust rapidly enough to maintain **equilibrium**—a situation in which the quantities demanded and supplied are equal—in all markets. In markets where quantity demanded exceeds quantity supplied, prices must rise to bring the market into equilibrium. In markets where more of a good is available than people want to buy, prices must fall to bring the market into equilibrium.

Wage and price flexibility is crucial to the invisible-hand idea, because in a free-market system, changes in wages and prices are the signals that coordinate the actions of people in the economy. To illustrate, suppose that war abroad disrupts oil imports. This drop in supply will drive up the price of oil. A higher oil price will make it profitable for domestic oil suppliers to pump more oil and to drill more wells. The higher price will also induce domestic consumers to conserve oil and to switch to alternative sources of energy. Increased demand for alternative energy sources will raise their prices and stimulate *their* production, and so on. Thus, in the absence of impediments such as government price controls, the adjustment of prices helps the free-market economy respond in a constructive and coordinated way to the initial disruption of supplies.

The classical approach to macroeconomics builds on Smith's basic assumptions that people pursue their own economic self-interests and that prices adjust reasonably quickly to achieve equilibrium in all markets. With these two assumptions as a basis, followers of the classical approach attempt to construct models of the macroeconomy that are consistent with the data and that can be used to answer the questions raised at the beginning of this chapter.

The use of the classical approach carries with it some strong policy implications. Because the classical assumptions imply that the invisible hand works well, classical economists often argue (as a normative proposition) that the government should have, *at most*, a limited role in the economy. As a positive proposition, classical economists also often argue that government policies will be ineffective or counterproductive at achieving their stated goals. Thus, for example, most classicals believe that the government should not try actively to eliminate business cycles.

The Keynesian Approach. Compared with the classical approach, the Keynesian approach is relatively recent. The book that introduced it, *The General Theory of Employment, Interest, and Money,* by British economist John Maynard Keynes, appeared in 1936—160 years after Adam Smith's *The Wealth of Nations*. In 1936 the world was suffering through the Great Depression: Unprecedentedly high rates of unemployment had afflicted most of the world's economies for years, and the invisible hand of free markets seemed completely ineffective. From the viewpoint of 1936, the classical theory appeared to be seriously inconsistent with the data, creating a need for a new macroeconomic theory. Keynes provided this theory.

In his book, Keynes offered an explanation of persistently high unemployment.[8] He based this explanation on an assumption about wage and price adjustment that was fundamentally different from the classical assumption. Instead of assuming that wages and prices adjust rapidly to achieve equilibrium in each market, as in the classical tradition, Keynes assumed that wages and prices adjust slowly. Slow wage and price adjustment meant that markets could be out of equilibrium—with quantities demanded not equal to quantities supplied—for long periods of time. In the Keynesian theory, unemployment can persist because wages and prices don't adjust quickly enough to equalize the number of people that firms want to employ with the number of people who want to work.

Keynes's proposed solution to high unemployment was to have the government increase its purchases of goods and services, thus raising the demand for output. Keynes argued that this policy would reduce unemployment because, to meet the higher demands for their products, businesses would have to employ more workers. In addition, Keynes suggested, the newly hired workers would have more income to spend, creating another source of demand for output that would raise employment further. More generally, in contrast to classicals, Keynesians tend to be skeptical about the invisible hand and thus are more willing to advocate a role for government in improving macroeconomic performance.

The Evolution of the Classical–Keynesian Debate.   Because the Great Depression so strongly shook many economists' faith in the classical approach, the Keynesian approach dominated macroeconomic theory and policy from World War II until about 1970. At the height of Keynesian influence, economists widely believed that, through the skillful use of macroeconomic policies, the government could promote economic growth while avoiding inflation or recession. The main problems of macroeconomics apparently had been solved, with only some details to be filled in.

However, in the 1970s the United States suffered from both high unemployment and high inflation—called **stagflation,** or stagnation plus inflation. This experience weakened economists' and policymakers' confidence in the traditional Keynesian approach, much as the Great Depression had undermined the traditional classical approach. In addition, the Keynesian assumption that prices and wages adjust slowly, so that markets may be out of equilibrium, was criticized as being without sound theoretical foundations. While the Keynesian approach was coming under attack, developments in economic theory made classical macroeconomics look more interesting and attractive to many economists. Starting in the early 1970s, a modernized classical approach enjoyed a major resurgence among macroeconomic researchers, although classical macroeconomics did not achieve the dominance that Keynesianism had enjoyed in the early postwar years.

In the past three decades, advocates of both approaches have reworked them extensively to repair their weaknesses. Economists working in the classical tradition have improved their explanations of business cycles and unemployment.

---

[8]Actually, Keynes presented a number of explanations of unemployment in his book, and debate continues about "what Keynes really meant." Our interpretation of what Keynes meant is the one adopted by his major followers.

Keynesians have worked on the development of sound theoretical foundations for the slow adjustment of wages and prices, and Keynesian models can now accommodate stagflation. Currently, excellent research is being conducted with both approaches, and substantial communication and cross-fertilization are occurring between them.

A Unified Approach to Macroeconomics

In writing this book, we needed a strategy to deal with the fact that there are two major macroeconomic schools of thought. One strategy would have been to emphasize one of the two schools of thought and to treat the other only briefly. The problem with that strategy is that it would not expose you to the full range of ideas and insights that compose modern macroeconomics. Alternatively, we might have presented the two approaches separately and then compared and contrasted their conclusions—but you would have missed the opportunity to explore the large common ground shared by the two schools of thought.

Our choice was to take an approach to macroeconomics that is as balanced and unified as possible. In keeping with this unified approach, all our analyses in this book—whether of economic growth, business cycles, inflation, or policy, and whether classical or Keynesian in spirit—are based on a *single economic model*, or on components or extensions of the basic model. This economic model, which draws heavily from both the classical and Keynesian traditions, has the following characteristics.

1. *Individuals, firms, and the government interact in goods markets, asset markets, and labor markets.* We have already discussed the need for aggregation in macroeconomics. In the economic model of this book we follow standard macroeconomic practice and aggregate all the markets in the economy into three major markets: the market for goods and services, the asset market (in which assets such as money, stocks, bonds, and real estate are traded), and the labor market. We show how participants in the economy interact in each of these three markets and how these markets relate to one another and to the economy as a whole.

2. *The model's macroeconomic analysis is based on the analysis of individual behavior.* Macroeconomic behavior reflects the behaviors of many individuals and firms interacting in markets. To understand how individuals and firms behave, we take a "bottom-up" approach and focus our analysis at the level of individual decision making (as in "In Touch with Data and Research: Developing and Testing an Economic Theory," p. 13, where we discuss a model of individual choices about the route to take to work). The insights gained are then used for studying the economy as a whole.

The guiding principle in analyzing the behavior of individuals and firms is the assumption that they *try to maximize their own economic satisfaction, given their needs, desires, opportunities, and resources.* Although the founder of classical economics, Adam Smith, emphasized this assumption, it is generally accepted by Keynesians and classicals alike, and it is used in virtually all modern macroeconomic research.

3. Although Keynesians reject the classical assumption that wages and prices quickly adjust to achieve equilibrium in the short run, *Keynesians and classicals both agree that, in the long run, prices and wages fully adjust to achieve equilibrium in the markets for goods, assets, and labor.* Because complete flexibility of wages and prices in the long run is not controversial, we examine the long-term behavior of the economy (Chapters 3–7) before discussing short-run issues associated with business cycles (Chapters 8–13).

   4. *The basic model that we present may be used with either the classical assumption that wages and prices are flexible or the Keynesian assumption that wages and prices are slow to adjust.* This aspect of the model allows us to compare classical and Keynesian conclusions and policy recommendations within a common theoretical framework.

CHAPTER SUMMARY

1. Macroeconomics is the study of the structure and performance of national economies and the policies that governments use to try to affect economic performance. Important topics in macroeconomics include the determinants of long-run economic growth, business cycles, unemployment, inflation, international trade and lending, and macroeconomic policy.

2. Because macroeconomics covers the economy as a whole, macroeconomists ignore the fine distinctions among different kinds of goods, firms, or markets and focus on national totals such as aggregate consumption. The process of adding individual economic variables to obtain economywide totals is called aggregation.

3. The activities engaged in by macroeconomists include (in addition to teaching) forecasting, macroeconomic analysis, macroeconomic research, and data development.

4. The goal of macroeconomic research is to be able to make general statements about how the economy works. Macroeconomic research makes progress toward this goal by developing economic theories and testing them empirically—that is, by seeing whether they are consistent with data obtained from the real world. A useful economic theory is based on reasonable and realistic assumptions, is easy to use, has implications that can be tested in the real world,

and is consistent with the data and the observed behavior of the real-world economy.

5. A positive analysis of an economic policy examines the economic consequences of the policy but does not address the question of whether those consequences are desirable. A normative analysis of a policy tries to determine whether the policy *should* be used. Disagreements among macroeconomists may arise because of differences in normative conclusions, as the result of differences in personal values and beliefs, and because of differences in the positive analysis of a policy proposal.

6. The classical approach to macroeconomics is based on the assumptions that individuals and firms act in their own best interests and that wages and prices adjust quickly to achieve equilibrium in all markets. Under these assumptions the invisible hand of the free-market economy works well, with only a limited scope for government intervention in the economy.

7. The Keynesian approach to macroeconomics assumes that wages and prices do not adjust rapidly and thus the invisible hand may not work well. Keynesians argue that, because of slow wage and price adjustment, unemployment may remain high for a long time. Keynesians are usually more inclined than classicals to believe that government intervention in the economy may help improve economic performance.

KEY TERMS

REVIEW QUESTIONS

All review questions are available in at **www.myeconlab.com**.

1. How have total output and output per worker changed over time in the United States? How have these changes affected the lives of typical people?

2. What is a business cycle? How does the unemployment rate behave over the course of a business cycle? Does the unemployment rate ever reach zero?

3. Define *inflation* and *deflation*. Compare the behavior of consumer prices in the United States in the years before and after World War II.

4. Historically, when has the Federal government been most likely to run budget deficits? What has been the recent experience?

5. Define *trade deficit* and *trade surplus*. In recent years, has the U.S. economy had trade deficits or trade surpluses? What was the U.S. experience from 1900 to 1970?

6. List the principal professional activities of macroeconomists. What role does macroeconomic research play in each of these activities?

7. What steps are involved in developing and testing an economic theory or model? What are the criteria for a useful theory or model?

8. Might two economists agree about the effects of a particular economic policy but disagree about the desirability of implementing the policy? Explain your answer.

9. Compare the classical and Keynesian views on the speed of wage and price adjustment. What are the important consequences of the differences in their views?

10. What was stagflation, and when did it occur? How did it change economists' views about macroeconomics?

NUMERICAL PROBLEMS

All numerical problems are available in at **www.myeconlab.com**.

1. Here are some macroeconomic data for the country of Oz for the years 2008 and 2009.

	2008	2009
Output	12,000 tons of potatoes	14,300 tons of potatoes
Employment	1,000 workers	1,100 workers
Unemployed	100 workers	50 workers
Total labor force	1,100 workers	1,150 workers
Prices	2 shekels/ton of potatoes	2.5 shekels/ton of potatoes

As the data suggest, Oz produces only potatoes, and its monetary unit is the shekel. Calculate each of the following macroeconomic variables for Oz, being sure to give units.

a. Average labor productivity in 2008 and 2009.

b. The growth rate of average labor productivity between 2008 and 2009.

c. The unemployment rate in 2008 and 2009.

d. The inflation rate between 2008 and 2009.

2. In a recent issue of the *Survey of Current Business*, find the data section entitled "Selected NIPA Tables." In Table 1.1.5, "Gross Domestic Product," find data on gross domestic product (a measure of total output), exports, and imports. In Table 3.2, "Federal Government Current Receipts and Expenditures,"find data on the government's total receipts (taxes) and expenditures. These tables from the *Survey of Current Business* can be accessed from the home page of the Bureau of Economic Analysis at *www.bea.gov*.

a. Calculate the ratio of exports to GDP, the ratio of imports to GDP, and the ratio of the trade imbalance to GDP in the latest reported quarter. Compare the answers with the values reported for the previous two complete years.

b. Calculate the ratio of Federal government receipts to GDP, the ratio of Federal government expenditures to GDP, and the ratio of the budget deficit to GDP, for the most recent quarter and for the previous two complete years.

ANALYTICAL PROBLEMS

1. Can average labor productivity fall even though total output is rising? Can the unemployment rate rise even though total output is rising?

2. Prices were much higher in the United States in 2009 than in 1890. Does this fact mean that people were economically better off in 1890? Why or why not?

3. State a theory for why people vote Republican or Democratic that potentially could satisfy the criteria for a useful theory given in the text. How would you go about testing your theory?

4. Which of the following statements are positive in nature and which are normative?

   a. A tax cut will raise interest rates.

   b. A reduction in the payroll tax would primarily benefit poor and middle-class workers.

   c. Payroll taxes are too high.

   d. A cut in the payroll tax would improve the President's popularity ratings.

   e. Payroll taxes should not be cut unless capital gains taxes are cut also.

5. In 2002, President George W. Bush imposed tariffs on certain types of imported steel. He argued that foreign steel producers were dumping their steel on the U.S. market at low prices. The foreign steel producers were able to sell steel cheaply because they received subsidies from their governments. The Bush administration argued that the influx of steel was disrupting the U.S. economy, harming the domestic steel industry, and causing unemployment among U.S. steel workers. What might a classical economist say in response to these claims? Would a Keynesian economist be more or less sympathetic to the imposition of tariffs? Why?

WORKING WITH MACROECONOMIC DATA

For data to use in these exercises, go to the Federal Reserve Bank of St. Louis FRED database at research.stlouisfed.org/fred2.

1. a. Calculate the total percentage growth in average labor productivity in the U.S. economy for the 1950s, 1960s, 1970s, 1980s, and 1990s. Define average labor productivity for any year as real gross domestic product in the last quarter of the year divided by civilian employment in the last month of the year. In which decades did average labor productivity grow the most quickly overall? The most slowly? Express the growth rates for each decade in annualized terms by using the formula

$$(1 + g)^{10} = 1 + G$$

where g is the annual growth rate, expressed as a decimal (for example, 0.05 for 5%), and G is the growth rate for the decade (the change in productivity during the decade divided by the initial productivity level). For each of the five decades, use your calculated values for G and the formula above to solve for g.

   b. Calculate annual labor productivity growth rates for each year since 2000 for which data are available. How do the recent growth rates compare with those of the five previous decades?

2. Graph the behavior of the civilian unemployment rate from 1961 until the present using monthly data. Can you see the periods of recession that occurred in 1969–1970, 1973–1975, 1980, 1981–1982, 1990–1991, and 2001? In terms of the unemployment rate, how does the recession that began in 2007 compare in severity with those earlier downturns? How does the behavior of the unemployment rate over the 2000s compare to its behavior in the 1960s, 1970s, 1980s, and 1990s?

3. Using data on the consumer price index (CPI) for all urban consumers, calculate and graph the annual U.S. inflation rate (the percentage change in the price index, December to December) for each year since 1948. In which periods within the postwar era did the United States experience the most severe inflation problems? In which periods has inflation been the most stable (that is, roughly constant from one year to the next)?

CHAPTER 2

The Measurement and Structure of the National Economy

Measurement is a crucial part of scientific study. Accurate measurement is essential for making new discoveries, evaluating competing theories, and predicting future events or trends. During the first half of the twentieth century, painstaking research by economists such as Nobel Prize winner Simon Kuznets (the first person to obtain comprehensive measures of national output) and the team of Arthur Burns and Wesley Mitchell (who performed detailed measurements of the stages of the business cycle) showed that careful economic measurement is not only possible but also necessary for any serious understanding of the economy. Their work, and the efforts of many other researchers, transformed economics from a field in which scholars relied on informal observations and broad generalizations to one in which numbers and statistical analysis play an essential role.

In this chapter we present some of the conceptual and practical issues involved in measuring the macroeconomy. We focus on the national income accounts, a framework for measuring economic activity that is widely used by economic researchers and analysts. Learning about the national income accounts will familiarize you with some useful economic data. In addition, because the national income accounts are set up in a logical way that mirrors the structure of the economy, working through these accounts is an important first step toward understanding how the macroeconomy works. When you finish this chapter, you will have a clearer understanding of the relationships that exist among key macroeconomic variables and among the different sectors of the economy.

2.1 National Income Accounting: The Measurement of Production, Income, and Expenditure

The **national income accounts** are an accounting framework used in measuring current economic activity. Almost all countries have some form of official national income accounts. (For background information on the U.S. national income accounts, see "In Touch with Data and Research: The National Income and Product Accounts," p. 24.)

The national income accounts are based on the idea that the amount of economic activity that occurs during a period of time can be measured in terms of

1. the amount of output produced, excluding output used up in intermediate stages of production (the product approach);
2. the incomes received by the producers of output (the income approach); and
3. the amount of spending by the ultimate purchasers of output (the expenditure approach).

Each approach gives a different perspective on the economy. However, the fundamental principle underlying national income accounting is that, except for problems such as incomplete or misreported data, *all three approaches give identical measurements of the amount of current economic activity.*

We can illustrate why these three approaches are equivalent by an example. Imagine an economy with only two businesses, called OrangeInc and JuiceInc. OrangeInc owns and operates orange groves. It sells some of its oranges directly to the public. It sells the rest of its oranges to JuiceInc, which produces and sells orange juice. The following table shows the transactions of each business during a year.

OrangeInc Transactions	
Wages paid to OrangeInc employees	$15,000
Taxes paid to government	5,000
Revenue received from sale of oranges	35,000
Oranges sold to public	10,000
Oranges sold to JuiceInc	25,000
JuiceInc Transactions	
Wages paid to JuiceInc employees	$10,000
Taxes paid to government	2,000
Oranges purchased from OrangeInc	25,000
Revenue received from sale of orange juice	40,000

OrangeInc pays $15,000 per year in wages to workers to pick oranges, and it sells these oranges for $35,000 ($10,000 worth of oranges to households and $25,000 worth of oranges to JuiceInc). Thus OrangeInc's profit before taxes is $35,000 − $15,000 = $20,000. Because OrangeInc pays taxes of $5000, its after-tax profit is $15,000.

JuiceInc buys $25,000 of oranges from OrangeInc and pays wages of $10,000 to workers to process the oranges into orange juice. It sells the orange juice for $40,000, so its profit before taxes is $5000 ($40,000 − $25,000 − $10,000). After paying taxes of $2000, its after-tax profit is $3000.

What is the total value, measured in dollars, of the economic activity generated by these two businesses? The product approach, income approach, and expenditure approach are three different ways of arriving at the answer to this question; all yield the same answer.

1.   The **product approach** measures economic activity by adding the market values of goods and services produced, excluding any goods and services used up in intermediate stages of production. This approach makes use of the value-added concept. The **value added** of any producer is the value of its output minus the value of the inputs it purchases from other producers. The product approach computes economic activity by summing the value added by all producers.

IN TOUCH WITH DATA AND RESEARCH

The National Income and Product Accounts

In the United States, the national income accounts are officially called the National Income and Product Accounts, or NIPA. These accounts provide comprehensive measurements of production, income, and expenditure for the U.S. economy. Developed in the 1930s and 1940s by the Department of Commerce, the U.S. national income accounts were used for economic planning during World War II. Official accounts have been constructed as far back as 1929, and some official data are available from as early as 1909.

Currently, the accounts are constructed quarterly by government economists and statisticians in the Bureau of Economic Analysis (BEA), a part of the Department of Commerce. In constructing the accounts, the BEA relies heavily on data provided by other government agencies, such as the Census Bureau and the Bureau of Labor Statistics. The BEA also uses data from tax returns and from private sources, such as industry associations.

Initial estimates of quarterly economic activity are released about one month after the end of each quarter. The data are then revised about one month later, and revised a second time about one month after that.

Historical NIPA data may be obtained from numerous sources, including the *Survey of Current Business* (the BEA's monthly publication) and the *Economic Report of the President*, which is issued each February by the President's Council of Economic Advisers. Latest-quarter NIPA data appear in the business press, which gives extensive coverage to the BEA's monthly releases. The BEA's home page at *www.bea.gov* provides access to current and historical data. Data on many NIPA variables can be downloaded conveniently from the Federal Reserve Bank of St. Louis FRED database at *research.stlouisfed.org/fred2*. National income accounts data for other countries are available in *National Accounts*, a publication of the Organization for Economic Cooperation and Development (OECD), in *World Economic Outlook* (published by the International Monetary Fund), and in the United Nations' *National Accounts Statistics*.

In our example, OrangeInc produces output worth $35,000 and JuiceInc produces output worth $40,000. However, measuring overall economic activity by simply adding $35,000 and $40,000 would "double count" the $25,000 of oranges that JuiceInc purchased from OrangeInc and processed into juice. To avoid this double counting, we sum value added rather than output: Because JuiceInc processed oranges worth $25,000 into a product worth $40,000, JuiceInc's value added is $15,000 ($40,000 − $25,000). OrangeInc doesn't use any inputs purchased from other businesses, so its value added equals its revenue of $35,000. Thus total value added in the economy is $35,000 + $15,000 = $50,000.

2. The **income approach** measures economic activity by adding all income received by producers of output, including wages received by workers and profits received by owners of firms. As you have seen, the (before-tax) profits of OrangeInc equal its revenues of $35,000 minus its wage costs of $15,000, or $20,000. The profits of JuiceInc equal its revenues of $40,000 minus the $25,000 the company paid to buy oranges and the $10,000 in wages paid to its employees, or $5000. Adding the $20,000 profit of OrangeInc, the $5000 profit of JuiceInc, and the $25,000 in wage income received by the employees of the two companies, we get a total of $50,000, the same amount determined by the product approach.

In this calculation we added the before-tax incomes of workers and firm owners. Equivalently, we could have added the after-tax incomes of producers of output and the taxes received by the government. Recall that, when taxes are subtracted, OrangeInc's after-tax profits are $15,000 and JuiceInc's after-tax profits are $3000. Adding the two firms' after-tax profits of $18,000, total wage income of $25,000 (we assumed that workers pay no taxes), and the $7000 in taxes received by the government, we again obtain $50,000 as the measure of economic activity.

3.   Finally, the **expenditure approach** measures activity by adding the amount spent by all ultimate users of output. In this example, households are ultimate users of oranges. JuiceInc is not an ultimate user of oranges because it sells the oranges (in processed, liquid form) to households. Thus ultimate users purchase $10,000 of oranges from OrangeInc and $40,000 of orange juice from JuiceInc for a total of $50,000, the same amount computed in both the product and the expenditure approaches.[1]

Why the Three Approaches Are Equivalent

That the product, income, and expenditure approaches all give the same answer is no accident. The logic of these three approaches is such that they must *always* give the same answer.

To see why, first observe that the market value of goods and services produced in a given period is *by definition* equal to the amount that buyers must spend to purchase them. JuiceInc's orange juice has a market value of $40,000 only because that is what people are willing to spend to buy it. The market value of a good or service and the spending on that good or service are always the same, so the product approach (which measures market values) and the expenditure approach (which measures spending) must give the same measure of economic activity.[2]

Next, observe that what the seller receives must equal what the buyers spend. The seller's receipts in turn equal the total income generated by the economic activity, including the incomes paid to workers and suppliers, taxes paid to the government, and profits (whatever is left over). Thus total expenditure must equal total income generated, implying that the expenditure and income approaches must also produce the same answer. Finally, as both product value and income equal expenditure, they also must be equal.

Because of the equivalence of the three approaches, over any specified time period

$$\text{total production} = \text{total income} = \text{total expenditure}, \qquad \textbf{(2.1)}$$

---

[1] In the example, each business also purchases labor services from employees, but because these services are used in production, they aren't counted as services purchased by ultimate users.

[2] Our explanation implicitly assumes that everything produced is sold. What if a firm produces some goods that it can't sell? As we discuss shortly, the national income accounts treat unsold goods as though they were purchased by the firm from itself; that is, accumulation of unsold goods in inventory is treated as part of expenditure. Thus expenditure and production remain equal even if some goods remain unsold.

where production, income, and expenditure all are measured in the same units (for example, in dollars). Equation (2.1) is called the **fundamental identity of national income accounting** and forms the basis for national income accounting. (An identity is an equation that is true by definition.) In Section 2.2, we show how this fundamental identity is used in measuring current economic activity for the economy as a whole.

2.2 Gross Domestic Product

The broadest measure of aggregate economic activity, as well as the best-known and most often used, is the gross domestic product, or GDP. As in the example in Section 2.1, a country's GDP may be measured by the product approach, the expenditure approach, or the income approach. Although the three approaches arrive at the same value for GDP, each views GDP differently. Using all three approaches gives a more complete picture of an economy's structure than any single approach could.

The Product Approach to Measuring GDP

The product approach defines a nation's **gross domestic product** (GDP) as the market value of final goods and services newly produced within a nation during a fixed period of time. In working through the various parts of this definition, we discuss some practical issues that arise in measuring GDP.

Market Value. Goods and services are counted in GDP at their market values—that is, at the prices at which they are sold. The advantage of using market values is that it allows adding the production of different goods and services. Imagine, for example, that you want to measure the total output of an economy that produces 7 cars and 100 pairs of shoes. Adding the number of cars and the number of pairs of shoes to get a total output of 107 wouldn't make much sense because cars and shoes aren't of equal economic value. But suppose that each car sells for $20,000 and each pair of shoes sells for $60. Taking these market-determined prices as measures of relative economic values, you can calculate the value of cars produced as $140,000 ($7 \times \$20,000$) and the value of shoes produced as $6000 ($100 \times \$60$). The total market value of production, or GDP, is $140,000 + $6000 = $146,000. Using market values to measure production makes sense because it takes into account differences in the relative economic importance of different goods and services.

A problem with using market values to measure GDP is that some useful goods and services are not sold in formal markets. Ideally, GDP should be adjusted upward to reflect the existence of these goods and services. However, because of the difficulty of obtaining reliable measures, some nonmarket goods and services simply are ignored in the calculation of GDP. Homemaking and child-rearing services performed within the family without pay, for example, are not included in GDP, although homemaking and child care that are provided for pay (for example, by professional housecleaners or by private day-care centers) are included. Similarly, because the benefits of clean air and water aren't bought and sold in markets, actions to reduce pollution or otherwise improve environmental quality usually are not reflected in GDP (see "In Touch with Data and Research: Natural Resources, the Environment, and the National Income Accounts," p. 29).

Some nonmarket goods and services are partially incorporated in official GDP measures. An example is activities in the so-called underground economy.

The **underground economy** includes both legal activities hidden from government record keepers (to avoid payment of taxes or compliance with regulations, for example) and illegal activities such as drug dealing, prostitution, and (in some places) gambling. Some might argue that activities such as drug dealing are "bads" rather than "goods" and shouldn't be included in GDP anyway—although a consistent application of this argument might rule out many goods and services currently included in GDP. Clearly, though, the services of a housepainter who is paid in cash to avoid taxes should be included in GDP. Government statisticians are unable to reliably adjust GDP figures to include estimates of the underground economy's size, but they do make some adjustments for underreported income.[3]

A particularly important component of economic activity that does not pass through markets is the value of the services provided by government, such as defense, public education, and the building and maintenance of roads and bridges. The fact that most government services are not sold in markets implies a lack of market values to use when calculating the government's contribution to GDP. In this case, the solution that has been adopted is to value government services at their cost of production. Thus the contribution of national defense to GDP equals the government's cost of providing defense: the salaries of service and civilian personnel, the costs of building and maintaining weapons and bases, and so on. Similarly, the contribution of public education to GDP is measured by the cost of teachers' salaries, new schools and equipment, and so on.

Newly Produced Goods and Services. As a measure of current economic activity, GDP includes only goods or services that are newly produced within the current period. GDP excludes purchases or sales of goods that were produced in previous periods. Thus, although the market price paid for a newly constructed house would be included in GDP, the price paid in the sale of a used house is not counted in GDP. (The value of the used house would have been included in GDP for the year it was built.) However, the value of the services of the real estate agent involved in the sale of the used house is part of GDP, because those services are provided in the current period.

Final Goods and Services. Goods and services produced during a period of time may be classified as either intermediate goods and services or final goods and services. **Intermediate goods and services** are those used up in the production of other goods and services *in the same period that they themselves were produced*. For example, flour that is produced and then used to make bread in the same year is an intermediate good. The trucking company that delivers the flour to the bakery provides an intermediate service.

Final goods and services are those goods and services that are not intermediate. Final goods and services are the end products of a process. For example, bread produced by the bakery is a final good, and a shopper's bus ride home from the bakery is a final service. Because the purpose of economic activity is the production of final

---

[3]Discussion of NIPA adjustments for the underground economy is given in "Taking the Pulse of the Economy: Measuring GDP" by J. Steven Landefeld, Eugene P. Seskin, and Barbara M. Fraumeni, *Journal of Economic Perspectives* 22 (Spring 2008), pp. 193–216. On estimating the size of the underground economy, see Edgar Feige, "Measuring Underground (Unobserved, Non-observed, Unrecorded) Economies in Transition Countries: Can We Trust GDP?" *Journal of Comparative Economics* 36 (June 2008), pp. 287–306.

goods and services, with intermediate goods being but a step along the way, only final goods and services are counted in GDP.

Sometimes the distinction between intermediate goods and final goods is subtle. For example, is a new lathe sold to a furniture manufacturer an intermediate good or a final good? Although the lathe is used to produce other goods, it is not used up during the year. Hence it is not an intermediate good; it is a final good. In particular, the lathe is an example of a type of final good called a capital good. Other more general examples of capital goods include factories, office buildings, equipment, and software. A **capital good** is a good that is itself produced (which rules out natural resources such as land) and is used to produce other goods; however, unlike an intermediate good, a capital good is not used up in the same period that it is produced. The preparers of the national income accounts decided to classify capital goods as final goods and thus to include their production in GDP. Their reasoning was that the addition to productive capacity from new capital goods represents economic activity.

Another subtle distinction between intermediate and final goods arises in the treatment of inventory investment. **Inventories** are stocks of unsold finished goods, goods in process, and raw materials held by firms. Inventory investment is the amount by which inventories increase during the year.[4] For example, suppose that a baker began the year with $1000 worth of flour in her storeroom and that at the end of the year she is holding $1100 worth of flour. The difference between her beginning and ending stocks, or $100 worth of flour, equals the baker's inventory investment during the year. Even though the ultimate purpose of the baker's flour is for making bread, her increase in inventory represents production of flour that is not used up during the year.[5] As in the case of capital goods, inventory investment is treated as a final good and thus part of GDP because increased inventories on hand imply greater productive capacity in the future.

In the OrangeInc–JuiceInc example, we showed that total economic activity could be measured by summing the value added (value of output minus value of purchased inputs) for each producer. The advantage of the value-added technique is that it automatically includes final goods and excludes intermediate goods from the measure of total output. If you go back to that example, you will see that, by summing the value added of the two companies, we obtained a measure of economic activity that included the value of final sales of the two businesses to the public but excluded the intermediate goods (unprocessed oranges) sold to JuiceInc by OrangeInc.

GNP Versus GDP.   Until 1991, most economists working with U.S. data focused on a measure of economic activity known as gross national product (GNP) rather than on GDP. However, in 1991, primarily to conform with national income accounting practices in other major industrialized countries, the Department of Commerce began to use GDP as its basic measure of economic activity. The difference between GNP and GDP lies in the treatment of output produced by capital and labor working outside its home (domestic) country. Specifically, **gross national product** is the market value of final goods and services newly produced

---

[4]When inventories decline during the year, inventory investment is negative.

[5]Inventory investment is the change in the physical quantity of goods in inventory multiplied by their price. Changes in the valuation of inventories arising from price changes (capital gains or losses) are not considered inventory investment.

IN TOUCH WITH DATA AND RESEARCH

Natural Resources, the Environment, and the National Income Accounts

Much of any country's economic well-being flows from natural, rather than human-made, assets—land, rivers and oceans, natural resources (such as oil and timber), and indeed the air that everyone breathes. Ideally, for the purposes of economic and environmental planning, the use and misuse of natural resources and the environment should be appropriately measured in the national income accounts. Unfortunately, they are not. There are at least two important conceptual problems with the way the national income accounts currently handle the economic use of natural resources and the environment.

1. *Natural resource depletion.* When an oil driller pumps oil from an underground field, the value of the oil produced is counted as part of the nation's GDP; there is no offsetting deduction to account for the fact that nonrenewable resources are being depleted. In principle, the draining of the oil field can be thought of as a type of negative inventory investment because in a sense it reduces the inventory of oil. If it were included in the national income accounts, this negative inventory investment would reduce the computed value of GDP.

2. *The costs and benefits of pollution control.* Imagine that a company has the following choices: It can produce $100 million worth of output and in the process pollute the local river by dumping its wastes; alternatively, by using 10% of its workers to dispose properly of its wastes, it can avoid polluting but will get only $90 million of output. Under current national income accounting rules, if the firm chooses to pollute rather than not to pollute, its contribution to GDP will be larger ($100 million rather than $90 million) because the national income accounts attach no explicit value to a clean river. In an ideal accounting system, the economic costs of environmental degradation would be subtracted in the calculation of a firm's contribution to output, and activities that improve the environment—because they provide real economic benefits—would be added to output.

Discussing the national income accounting implications of resource depletion and pollution may seem to trivialize these important problems. Actually, because GDP and related statistics are used continually in policy analyses, abstract questions of measurement often may turn out to have significant real effects. For example, economic development experts have expressed concern that some poor countries, in attempting to raise measured GDP as quickly as possible, have done so in part by overexploiting their natural resources and harming the environment. Conceivably, explicitly incorporating "hidden" resource and environmental costs into official measures of economic growth might cause these policies to be modified. Similarly, in industrialized countries, political debates about the environment at times have emphasized the impact on conventionally measured GDP of proposed pollution control measures, rather than their impact on overall economic welfare. Better accounting for environmental quality might serve to refocus these debates to the more relevant question of whether, for any particular environmental proposal, the benefits (economic and noneconomic) exceed the costs.

by domestic factors of production during the current period, whereas GDP is production taking place within a country.

When U.S. capital and labor—also called factors of production—are used abroad, they produce output and earn income. This output and income are included in U.S. GNP but not in U.S. GDP because they don't represent production taking place within the United States. So, for example, the value of roads built by a U.S. construction company in Saudi Arabia, as measured by the fees that the construction company receives from the Saudi government, is counted in U.S. GNP but not in U.S. GDP. Similarly, when foreign capital or labor is used in the United States, the output produced and the income earned are part of U.S. GDP (because the production occurs within the United States) but not of U.S. GNP (they are counted in the foreign country's GNP instead). For example, the portion of the value of Japanese cars built in the United States that is attributable to Japanese capital and management counts in Japanese GNP and U.S. GDP, but not in U.S. GNP.

We define **net factor payments from abroad** (*NFP*) to be income paid to domestic factors of production by the rest of the world minus income paid to foreign factors of production by the domestic economy. Using this concept, we express the relationship between GDP and GNP as

$$\text{GDP} = \text{GNP} - \text{NFP}. \tag{2.2}$$

For the United States, GDP and GNP give similar measures of economic activity. For example, in 2008 the U.S. GDP was $14,441 billion and the U.S. GNP was $14,583 billion, a difference of about 1%. The distinction between GNP and GDP is more important for countries such as Egypt and Turkey that have many citizens working abroad. The reason is that income earned by workers abroad is part of a country's GNP but not its GDP.

The Expenditure Approach to Measuring GDP

A different perspective on the components of GDP is obtained by looking at the expenditure side of the national income accounts. The expenditure approach measures GDP as total spending on final goods and services produced within a nation during a specified period of time. Four major categories of spending are added to get GDP: consumption, investment, government purchases of goods and services, and net exports of goods and services. In symbols,

$$
\begin{aligned}
Y = \text{GDP} &= \text{total production (or output)} \\
&= \text{total income} \\
&= \text{total expenditure;}
\end{aligned}
$$

$$
\begin{aligned}
C &= \text{consumption;} \\
I &= \text{investment;} \\
G &= \text{government purchases of goods and services;} \\
NX &= \text{net exports of goods and srevices.}
\end{aligned}
$$

With these symbols, we express the expenditure approach to measuring GDP as

$$Y = C + I + G + NX. \tag{2.3}$$

Equation (2.3), like Eq. (2.1), is one of the basic relationships in macroeconomics. Equation (2.3) is called the **income–expenditure identity** because it states that income, Y, equals total expenditure, $C + I + G + NX$. Recent U.S. data for the four

Table 2.1

Expenditure Approach to Measuring GDP in the United States, 2008

	Billions of dollars	Percent of GDP
Personal consumption expenditures (C)	10130	70.1
Consumer durables	1095	7.6
Nondurable goods	2308	16.0
Services	6727	46.6
Gross private domestic investment (I)	2136	14.8
Business fixed investment	1694	11.7
Nonresidential structures	610	4.2
Equipment and software	1084	7.5
Residential investment	477	3.3
Inventory investment	−35	−0.2
Government purchases of goods and services (G)	2883	20.0
Federal	1083	7.5
National defense	738	5.1
Nondefense	345	2.4
State and local	1801	12.5
Net exports (NX)	−708	−4.9
Exports	1831	12.7
Imports	2539	17.6
Total (equals GDP) (Y)	14441	100.0

Note: Numbers may not add to totals shown owing to rounding.
Source: Bureau of Economic Analysis Web site, *www.bea.gov*, Table 1.1.5, July 31, 2009

categories of spending, along with some major subcategories, are given in Table 2.1. As you read the rest of this section, you should look at Table 2.1 to get a feel for the relative sizes of different components of spending in the U.S. economy.

Consumption.   **Consumption** is spending by domestic households on final goods and services, including those produced abroad.[6] It is the largest component of expenditure, usually accounting for about two-thirds of GDP in the United States. Consumption expenditures are grouped into three categories:

1. *consumer durables*, which are long-lived consumer items, such as cars, televisions, furniture, and major appliances (but not houses, which are classified under investment);
2. *nondurable goods*, which are shorter-lived items, such as food, clothing, and fuel; and
3. *services*, such as education, health care, financial services, and transportation.

Investment.   **Investment** includes both spending for new capital goods, called *fixed investment*, and increases in firms' inventory holdings, called *inventory investment*. Fixed investment in turn has two major components:

1. *business fixed investment*, which is spending by businesses on structures (factories, warehouses, and office buildings, for example) and equipment (such as machines, vehicles, computers, and furniture) and software; and

---

[6]Later, we subtract imports from total expenditures and add exports to calculate total spending on the goods and services produced by the domestic economy.

2. *residential investment*, which is spending on the construction of new houses and apartment buildings. Houses and apartment buildings are treated as capital goods because they provide a service (shelter) over a long period of time.

Like consumption, investment includes spending on foreign-produced goods. Overall, fixed investment in the United States usually is about one-sixth of GDP.

As we have mentioned, increases in inventories are included in investment spending, regardless of why inventories rose. In particular, if a firm produces goods that it can't sell, the resulting rise in inventories counts as investment by the firm. For the purposes of national income accounting, the firm has, in effect, purchased the unsold goods from itself. This accounting rule is useful because it guarantees that production and expenditure will always be equal in the national income accounts. Anything that is produced must, by definition, either be bought by a customer or "purchased" by the firm itself.

Government Purchases of Goods and Services.   **Government purchases** of goods and services, which include any expenditure by the government for a currently produced good or service, foreign or domestic, is the third major component of spending. Government purchases in the United States recently have been about one-fifth of GDP. Note in Table 2.1 that in the United States the majority of government purchases are made by state and local governments, not the Federal government.

Not all the checks written by the government are for purchases of current goods and services. **Transfers**, a category that includes government payments for Social Security and Medicare benefits,[7] unemployment insurance, welfare payments, and so on, are payments (primarily to individuals) by the government that are not made in exchange for current goods or services. As a result, they are excluded from the government purchases category and are not counted in GDP as calculated by the expenditure approach. Similarly, interest payments on the national debt are not counted as part of government purchases.

Much like the distinction between private-sector consumption and investment, some part of government purchases goes toward current needs (such as employee salaries) and some is devoted to acquiring capital goods (such as office buildings). In the U.S. national income and product accounts, government spending on capital goods (buildings, equipment, and software) has been broken out from other government purchases. Investment by the government is fairly sizable—more than $400 billion annually in recent years, or about one-fifth of the amount invested annually by the private sector. When we speak of "investment" in the national income accounts, however, we are generally referring to investment by the private sector, I; for simplicity, we include government investment with other government purchases of goods and services, G.

Net Exports.   **Net exports** are exports minus imports. As discussed in Chapter 1, exports are the goods and services produced within a country that are purchased

---

[7]Although it might seem that Medicare benefits are a current expenditure by the government and not a transfer, in the NIPAs the medical expenditure is considered consumption spending by households, and the government payment to cover the medical expenditure is a transfer payment from the government to the household.

by foreigners; imports are the goods and services produced abroad that are purchased by a country's residents. Net exports are positive if exports are greater than imports and negative if imports exceed exports.

Exports are added to total spending because they represent spending (by foreigners) on final goods and services produced in a country. Imports are subtracted from total spending because consumption, investment, and government purchases are defined to include imported goods and services. Subtracting imports ensures that total spending, $C + I + G + NX$, reflects spending only on output produced in the country. For example, an increase in imports may mean that Americans are buying Japanese cars instead of American cars. For fixed total spending by domestic residents, therefore, an increase in imports lowers spending on domestic production.

The Income Approach to Measuring GDP

The third and final way to measure GDP is the income approach. It calculates GDP by adding the incomes received by producers, including profits, and taxes paid to the government. A key part of the income approach is a concept known as national income. **National income** is the sum of eight types of income (see Table 2.2 for recent U.S. data).

1. *Compensation of employees.* Compensation of employees is the income of workers (excluding the self-employed) and includes wages, salaries, employee benefits (including contributions by employers to pension plans), and employer contributions to Social Security. As you can see from Table 2.2, compensation of employees is the largest component of national income, accounting for 55.7% of GDP in 2008.

2. *Proprietors' income.* Proprietors' income is the income of the nonincorporated self-employed. Because many self-employed people own some capital (examples are a farmer's tractor or a dentist's X-ray machine), proprietors' income includes both labor income and capital income. Proprietors' income was 7.7% of GDP in 2008.

3. *Rental income of persons.* Rental income of persons, a small item, is the income earned by individuals who own land or structures that they rent to others. Some miscellaneous types of income, such as royalty income paid to authors, recording artists, and others, also are included in this category. Rental income of persons was about 1.5% of GDP in 2008.[8]

4. *Corporate profits.* Corporate profits are the profits earned by corporations and represent the remainder of corporate revenue after wages, interest, rents, and other costs have been paid. Corporate profits are used to pay taxes levied on corporations, such as the corporate income tax, and to pay dividends to shareholders. The rest of corporate profits after taxes and dividends, called retained earnings, are kept by the corporations. Corporate profits generally are a modest fraction of GDP (9.4% of GDP in 2008), but the amount of profits earned by corporations may change dramatically from year to year or even from quarter to quarter.

---

[8]Rental income of persons is a tiny fraction of GDP because it represents net rental income, or rents received minus the cost of replacing worn-out or depreciated structures. Also, rental income of persons does not include all rents paid in the economy because it excludes rents received by corporations.

Table 2.2

Income Approach to Measuring GDP in the United States, 2008

	Billions of dollars	Percent of GDP
Compensation of employees	8037	55.7
Proprietors' income	1106	7.7
Rental income of persons	210	1.5
Corporate profits	1360	9.4
Net interest	815	5.6
Taxes on production and imports	994	6.9
Business current transfer payments	119	0.8
Current surplus of government enterprises	−7	0.0
Total (equals **National Income**)	12635	87.5
Plus Statistical discrepancy	101	0.7
Equals **Net National Product** (NNP)	12736	88.2
Plus Consumption of fixed capital	1847	12.8
Equals **Gross National Product** (GNP)	14583	101.0
Less Factor income received from rest of world	809	5.6
Plus Payments of factor income to rest of world	667	4.6
Equals **Gross Domestic Product** (GDP)	14441	100.0

Note: Numbers may not add to totals shown owing to rounding.
Source: Bureau of Economic Analysis Web site, *www.bea.gov*, Tables 1.7.5 and 1.12, July 31, 2009

   5.   *Net interest.* Net interest is interest earned by individuals from businesses and foreign sources minus interest paid by individuals. Net interest has varied from 4% to 8% of GDP each year over the past 25 years.
   6.   *Taxes on production and imports.* Taxes on production and imports include indirect business taxes, such as sales and excise taxes, that are paid by businesses to Federal, state, and local governments, as well as customs duties and taxes on residential real estate and motor vehicle licenses paid by households. These taxes have averaged about 7% of GDP for the past 25 years.
   7.   *Business current transfer payments (net).* Business current transfer payments are payments made by businesses to individuals or governments or foreigners, but not for wages or taxes or as payment for services. Instead, such transactions as charitable donations, insurance payments, FDIC insurance premiums paid by banks, and legal settlements are covered by this category of income. Business current transfer payments have been between 0.5% and 0.9% of GDP each year for the past 25 years.
   8.   *Current surplus of government enterprises.* Current surplus of government enterprises is essentially the profit of businesses that are owned by governments, such as water, electric, and sewer companies, trash companies, mass transit firms, and housing firms. Current surplus of government enterprises is often negative when the firms suffer losses, as has occurred in 7 of the past 25 years, though the losses have never been more than 0.11% of GDP.

   In addition to the eight components of national income just described, three other items need to be accounted for to obtain GDP:

- statistical discrepancy;
- depreciation; and
- net factor payments.

Statistical discrepancy arises because data on income are compiled from different sources than data on production; the production measure minus the income measure equals the statistical discrepancy. Thus, a positive statistical discrepancy means that the income measure adds up to less than the production measure. National income plus the statistical discrepancy equals **net national product** (NNP), as indicated in Table 2.2.

Depreciation (also known as consumption of fixed capital) is the value of the capital that wears out during the period over which economic activity is being measured.[9] In the calculation of the components of national income (specifically, proprietors' income, corporate profits, and rental income), depreciation is subtracted from total, or gross, income. Thus, to compute the total or gross amount of income, we must add back in depreciation. The sum of net national product and depreciation is gross national product (GNP). Gross national product and gross domestic product are called gross because they measure the nation's total production or output of goods and services without subtracting depreciation.

As we discussed earlier, to go from GNP to GDP we have to subtract net factor payments from abroad, *NFP* (see Eq. 2.2). As we have already mentioned and as you can see from Table 2.2, for the United States net factor payments are relatively small and so GDP and GNP are very close.

Private Sector and Government Sector Income. In this section we have measured economic activity as the sum of all the incomes received in an economy. Sometimes, however, economists need to know how much of total income was received by the private sector (households and businesses) and how much accrues to the government sector, which in the United States consists of Federal, state, and local governments. For example, in trying to predict the demand for consumer goods, focusing on the income available to the private sector might be more useful than focusing on the income of the economy as a whole.

The income of the private sector, known as **private disposable income**, measures the amount of income the private sector has available to spend. In general, as for an individual family, the disposable income of the private sector as a whole equals income received from private-sector activities, plus payments received by the private sector from the government, minus taxes paid to the government. The precise definition is

$$\text{private disposable income} = Y + NFP + TR + INT - T, \qquad (2.4)$$

where

$$Y = \text{gross domestic product (GDP)};$$
$$NFP = \text{net factor payments from abroad};$$
$$TR = \text{transfers received from the government};$$
$$INT = \text{interest payments on the government's debt};$$
$$T = \text{taxes}.$$

---

[9]Depreciation (consumption of fixed capital) includes both capital that physically wears out and capital that is scrapped because it is no longer economically useful. For instance, still-functioning computers that are scrapped because they have been made obsolete by newer models would be included in depreciation.

As you can see from Eq. (2.4), private disposable income equals private sector income earned at home (GDP) and abroad (net factor payments from abroad, *NFP*);[10] plus payments to the private sector from the government sector (transfers, *TR*, and interest on the government debt, *INT*); minus taxes paid to the government, *T*.

The part of GDP that is not at the disposal of the private sector is the net income of the government sector. **Net government income** equals taxes paid by the private sector, *T*, minus payments from the government to the private sector (transfers, *TR*, and interest payments on the government debt, *INT*):

$$\text{net government income} = T - TR - INT. \tag{2.5}$$

Adding Eqs. (2.4) and (2.5) yields the sum of private disposable income and net government income, $Y + NFP$, which is gross national product.

2.3 Saving and Wealth

If you wanted to assess the economic situation of a household, the current income of the household would be an important piece of information. However, someone with a high current income isn't necessarily better off economically than someone with a low current income. For example, a retired tycoon who has no current earnings but owns real estate worth $10 million probably is economically better off than a newly graduated doctor with a high salary but heavy debts left over from medical school. To determine how well off a household is, in addition to knowing current income, you also need to know what the household owns (its assets) and owes (its liabilities). The value of assets minus the value of liabilities is called **wealth**.

As for a household, the economic well-being of a country depends not only on its income but also on its wealth. The wealth of an entire nation is called **national wealth**.

An important determinant of wealth is the rate of saving: A family that puts aside a quarter of its income each month will accumulate wealth much more quickly than a family with the same income that saves only 2% of its income. Similarly, the rate at which national wealth increases depends on the rate at which individuals, businesses, and governments in the economy save. Thus rates of saving and wealth accumulation are closely related.

In this section we present some concepts of aggregate saving and wealth and examine the relationships among them. Our main interest here is measurement. Questions such as what determines the rate of saving in a country are covered in later chapters.

Measures of Aggregate Saving

In general, the **saving** of any economic unit is the unit's current income minus its spending on current needs. The saving *rate* of an economic unit is its saving divided by its income. From a macroeconomic perspective, three important measures of saving are private saving, government saving, and national saving. Summary table 1 outlines the definitions of each measure.

---

[10]Note that the sum of incomes earned at home and abroad, GDP + *NFP*, equals GNP.

SUMMARY 1

Measures of Aggregate Saving

Saving measure	Definition and formula
Private saving	Private disposable income less consumption
	$$S_{pvt} = (Y + NFP - T + TR + INT) - C$$
Government saving	Government receipts less government outlays
	$$S_{govt} = (T - TR - INT) - G$$
National saving	Private saving plus government saving; also GNP ($Y + NFP$) less consumption and government purchases
	$$\begin{aligned} S &= S_{pvt} + S_{govt} \\ &= Y + NFP - C - G \end{aligned}$$

Private Saving. The saving of the private sector, known as **private saving**, equals private disposable income minus consumption. Using the definition of private disposable income from Eq. (2.4), we have

$$S_{pvt} = \text{private disposable income} - \text{consumption} \tag{2.6}$$
$$= (Y + NFP - T + TR + INT) - C,$$

where S_{pvt} is private saving. Consumption is subtracted from private disposable income to obtain private saving because consumption represents the private sector's spending to meet current needs. Investment, although part of private sector spending, is not subtracted from private disposable income because capital goods are purchased to enhance future productive capacity rather than to satisfy current needs. The private saving *rate* is private saving divided by private disposable income.

Government Saving. **Government saving** is defined as net government income, Eq. (2.5), less government purchases of goods and services. Using S_{govt} for government saving, we write this definition of government saving as

$$S_{govt} = \text{net government income} - \text{government purchases} \tag{2.7}$$
$$= (T - TR - INT) - G.$$

Equation (2.7) treats total government purchases, G, as the government's spending to meet current needs. Thus the definition of government saving fits the general definition of saving as income less spending on current needs.

However, as we discussed earlier, not all government purchases are in fact devoted to satisfying current needs; some part of G is devoted to the acquisition of long-lived capital, such as schools, highways, and dams. The national income and product accounts break total government purchases into the portion devoted to current needs (referred to as *government consumption*[11]) and the portion spent on long-lived capital goods (referred to as *government investment*). Under

---

[11]The measure of government consumption includes depreciation of the government's capital goods.

this breakdown, government saving could be defined as net government income less government consumption only, rather than net government income less all government purchases. This alternative approach would increase the amount of measured saving and investment in the U.S. economy by the amount of government investment, an amount exceeding $400 billion per year.[12]

Although the new definition of government saving is conceptually more correct, for most analyses in this book, keeping track of government consumption and government investment separately is an unnecessary complication. To keep things simple, we usually ignore government investment, assuming that government purchases are made up entirely of government consumption. With this assumption, we can use the traditional definition of government saving, Eq. (2.7). When considering issues such as the government budget deficit, however, keep in mind that, in fact, some government spending is devoted to building or acquiring long-lived capital goods.

Another, probably more familiar, name for government saving is the government budget surplus. The government **budget surplus** equals government receipts minus government outlays. **Government receipts** equal tax revenue, T. **Government outlays** are the sum of government purchases of goods and services, G, transfers, TR, and interest payments on government debt, INT. Thus the government budget surplus equals $T - (G + TR + INT)$, which, as you can see from Eq. (2.7), is the same as government saving.

When government receipts are less than government outlays, the difference between outlays and receipts is known as the government **budget deficit**. Thus, when the government runs a budget deficit, with its outlays greater than its receipts, government saving is negative.

National Saving.   **National saving**, or the saving of the economy as a whole, equals private saving plus government saving. Using the definitions of private and government saving, Eqs. (2.6) and (2.7), we obtain national saving, S:

$$\begin{aligned} S &= S_{\text{pvt}} + S_{\text{govt}} \\ &= (Y + NFP - T + TR + INT - C) + (T - TR - INT - G) \\ &= Y + NFP - C - G. \end{aligned} \tag{2.8}$$

Equation (2.8) shows that national saving equals the total income of the economy, $Y + NFP$ (which equals GNP), minus spending to satisfy current needs (consumption, C, and government purchases, G).

The Uses of Private Saving

How is private saving in an economy put to use? Private saving is used to fund new capital investment, provide the resources the government needs to finance its budget deficits, and acquire assets from or lend to foreigners.

To derive an important identity that illustrates the uses of private saving, we first use the income–expenditure identity (Eq. 2.3) and substitute $C + I + G + NX$ for Y in the expression for national saving (Eq. 2.8):

$$S = (C + I + G + NX) + NFP - C - G.$$

---

[12]Note that, by similar reasoning, household spending on cars and other long-lived consumer durables should not be subtracted from private disposable income in the calculation of private saving; however, in practice they are subtracted.

Simplifying this expression, we obtain

$$S = I + (NX + NFP). \tag{2.9}$$

The expression for national saving in Eq. (2.9) contains the term $NX + NFP$, which is the sum of net exports and net factor payments, and is called the current account balance, CA.[13] The **current account balance** equals payments received from abroad in exchange for currently produced goods and services (including factor services), minus the analogous payments made to foreigners by the domestic economy. Substituting CA for $NX + NFP$ in Eq. (2.9), we obtain

$$S = I + CA. \tag{2.10}$$

We now have an expression for national saving, S; our goal is an expression for private saving, S_{pvt}. Equation (2.8) shows that private saving, S_{pvt}, equals national saving, S, minus government saving, S_{govt}. Then, subtracting S_{govt} from both sides of Eq. (2.10), we get

$$S_{pvt} = I + (-S_{govt}) + CA, \tag{2.11}$$

where $-S_{govt}$ is the government budget deficit.

Equation (2.11) is another important macroeconomic identity, called the **uses-of-saving identity**. It states that an economy's private saving is used in three ways.

1. *Investment (I).* Firms borrow from private savers to finance the construction and purchase of new capital (including residential capital) and inventory investment.

2. *The government budget deficit* $(-S_{govt})$. When the government runs a budget deficit (so that S_{govt} is negative and $-S_{govt}$ is positive), it must borrow from private savers to cover the difference between outlays and receipts.

3. *The current account balance (CA).* When the U.S. current account balance is positive, foreigners' receipts of payments from the United States are not sufficient to cover the payments they make to the United States. To make up the difference, foreigners must either borrow from U.S. private savers or sell to U.S. savers some of their assets, such as land, factories, stocks, and bonds. Thus financing the current account balance is a use of a country's private saving.

In contrast, when the U.S. current account balance is negative, as it was during most of the 1980s, 1990s, and 2000s, U.S. receipts of payments from foreigners are not sufficient to cover U.S. payments to foreigners. To offset this excess of payments over receipts, the United States must borrow from foreigners or sell to foreigners some U.S. assets. In this case, foreigners use their saving to lend to the United States or to acquire U.S. assets.[14]

Relating Saving and Wealth

Saving is a key economic variable because it is closely related to the rate of wealth accumulation. In the rest of this section we discuss the relationship of saving and wealth. To do so, however, we must first introduce the concept of stocks versus flows.

---

[13]Actually, the current account balance also includes the term *net unilateral transfers,* which measures transfers between countries such as private gifts or official foreign aid (see Chapter 5). In our analysis we generally ignore this term.

[14]The current account and its relationship to international borrowing and lending are discussed in greater detail in Chapter 5.

Stocks and Flows.   The economic variables we have discussed so far in this chapter—such as GDP and the various types of expenditure, income, and saving—are measured per unit of time (for example, per quarter or per year). For instance, annual GDP figures measure the economy's production per year. Variables that are measured per unit of time are called **flow variables**.

In contrast, some economic variables, called **stock variables**, are defined at a point in time. Examples of stock variables include the amount of money in your bank account on September 15 of this year and the total value of all houses in the United States on January 1, 2010.

In many applications, a flow variable is the rate of change in a stock variable. A classic example is a bathtub with water flowing in from a faucet. The amount of water in the tub at any moment is a stock variable. The units of a stock variable (gallons, in this case) don't have a time dimension. The rate at which water enters the tub is a flow variable; its units (gallons per minute) have a time dimension. In this case the flow equals the rate of change of the stock.

Wealth and Saving as Stock and Flow.   Saving and wealth are related to each other in much the same way that the flow and stock of water in a bathtub are related. The wealth of any economic unit (a household, firm, or government), also called net worth, is its assets (the things that it owns, including IOUs from other economic units) minus its liabilities (what it owes to other units). Wealth is measured in dollars at a point in time and is a stock variable. Saving is measured in dollars per unit time and is a flow variable. Because saving takes the form of an accumulation of assets or a reduction in liabilities (for example, if saving is used to pay off debts), it adds to wealth just as water flowing into a bathtub adds to the stock of water.

National Wealth.   National wealth is the total wealth of the residents of a country. National wealth consists of two parts: (1) the country's domestic physical assets, such as its stock of capital goods and land;[15] and (2) its net foreign assets. The **net foreign assets** of a country equal the country's foreign assets (foreign stocks, bonds, and factories owned by domestic residents) minus its foreign liabilities (domestic physical and financial assets owned by foreigners). Net foreign assets are part of national wealth because they represent claims on foreigners that are not offset by foreigners' claims on the domestic economy.

Domestic financial assets held by domestic residents are not part of national wealth because the value of any domestic financial asset is offset by a domestic financial liability. For example, a checking account of a U.S. resident in a U.S. bank is an asset for the depositor but a liability for the bank; it thus does not represent wealth for the economy as a whole. In contrast, a U.S. resident's checking account in a foreign bank has no corresponding domestic liability (it is a liability of a foreigner) and so is part of U.S. national wealth.

National wealth can change in two ways over time. First, the value of the existing assets or liabilities that make up national wealth may change. For example, the dramatic increase in the stock market during the 1990s increased U.S. national wealth.

[15]In principle, national wealth should also include the value of the skills and training of the country's residents—what economists call human capital. In practice, because of measurement problems, human capital is not usually included in measures of national wealth.

The wearing out or depreciation of physical assets, which corresponds to a drop in the value of those assets, reduces national wealth.

The second way that national wealth can change is through national saving. Over any particular period of time, with the value of existing assets and liabilities held constant, each extra dollar of national saving adds a dollar to national wealth. That is,

$$S = I + CA,$$

which you will recognize as Eq. (2.10). This equation shows that national saving has two uses: (1) to increase the stock of domestic physical capital through investment, I, and (2) to increase the nation's stock of net foreign assets by lending to foreigners or acquiring foreign assets in an amount equal to the current account balance, CA. But each dollar by which domestic physical assets or net foreign assets increase is a dollar by which national wealth increases. Thus, as we claimed, increases in national saving increase national wealth dollar for dollar. As in the example of water flowing into a bathtub, the more rapid the flow of national saving, the more quickly the stock of national wealth will rise.

How do national saving and investment in the United States compare to that in other countries? The United States is a relatively low-saving country, compared with other industrialized nations. Investment is also relatively low in the United States, according to the official statistics.[16] However, investment rates in the United States are generally higher than saving rates. Using the relationship $S = I + CA$, we see that, if investment, I, is greater than national saving, S, then the current account balance, CA, must be negative. As we mentioned earlier, the U.S. current account has indeed been in deficit nearly every year since 1980. In contrast, high-saving countries such as China have typically had investment rates lower than their saving rates, resulting in consistently positive current account balances for those countries.

2.4 Real GDP, Price Indexes, and Inflation

All of the key macroeconomic variables that we have discussed so far in this chapter—GDP, the components of expenditure and income, national wealth, and saving—are measured in terms of current market values. Such variables are called **nominal variables**. The advantage of using market values to measure economic activity is that it allows summing of different types of goods and services.

However, a problem with measuring economic activity in nominal terms arises if you want to compare the values of an economic variable—GDP, for example—at two different points in time. If the current market value of the goods and services included in GDP changes over time, you can't tell whether this change reflects changes in the quantities of goods and services produced, changes in the prices of goods and services, or a combination of these factors. For example, a large increase in the current market value of GDP might mean that a country has greatly expanded its production of goods and services, or it might mean that the country has experienced inflation, which raised the prices of goods and services.

---

[16]Some economists have suggested that the low U.S. saving and investment rates reflect various measurement problems as much as fundamental differences in behavior. See, for example, William Dewald and Michael Ulan, "Appreciating U.S. Saving and Investment," *Business Economics*, January 1992, pp. 42–46.

Real GDP

Economists have devised methods for breaking down changes in nominal variables into the part owing to changes in physical quantities and the part owing to changes in prices. Consider the numerical example in Table 2.3, which gives production and price data for an economy that produces two types of goods: computers and bicycles. The data are presented for two different years. In year 1, the value of GDP is $46,000 (5 computers worth $1200 each and 200 bicycles worth $200 each). In year 2, the value of GDP is $66,000 (10 computers worth $600 each and 250 bicycles worth $240 each), which is 43.5% higher than the value of GDP in year 1. This 43.5% increase in nominal GDP does not reflect either a 43.5% increase in physical output or a 43.5% increase in prices. Instead, it reflects changes in both output and prices.

How much of the 43.5% increase in nominal output is attributable to an increase in physical output? A simple way to remove the effects of price changes, and thus to focus on changes in quantities of output, is to measure the value of production in each year by using the prices from some base year. For this example, let's choose year 1 as the base year. Using the prices from year 1 ($1200 per computer and $200 per bicycle) to value the production in year 2 (10 computers and 250 bicycles) yields a value of $62,000, as shown in Table 2.4. We say that $62,000 is the value of *real* GDP in year 2, measured using the prices of year 1.

In general, an economic variable that is measured by the prices of a base year is called a **real variable**. Real economic variables measure the physical quantity of economic activity. Specifically, **real GDP**, also called *constant-dollar GDP*, measures the physical volume of an economy's final production using the prices of a base year. **Nominal GDP**, also called *current-dollar GDP*, is the dollar value of an economy's final output measured at current market prices. Thus nominal GDP in year 2 for our example is $66,000, which we computed earlier using current (that is, year 2) prices to value output.

What is the value of real GDP in year 1? Continuing to treat year 1 as the base year, use the prices of year 1 ($1200 per computer and $200 per bicycle) to value production. The production of 5 computers and 200 bicycles has a value of $46,000. Thus the value of real GDP in year 1 is the same as the value of nominal GDP in year 1. This result is a general one: Because current prices and base-year prices are the same in the base year, real and nominal values are always the same in the base year. Specifically, real GDP and nominal GDP are equal in the base year.

Table 2.3

Production and Price Data

	Year 1	Year 2	Percent change from year 1 to year 2
Product (quantity)			
Computers	5	10	+100%
Bicycles	200	250	+25%
Price			
Computers	$1,200/computer	$600/computer	−50%
Bicycles	$200/bicycle	$240/bicycle	+20%
Value			
Computers	$6,000	$6,000	0
Bicycles	$40,000	$60,000	+50%
Total	$46,000	$66,000	+43.5%

Table 2.4

Calculation of Real Output with Alternative Base Years

Calculation of real output with base year = Year 1

	Current quantities		Base-year prices		
Year 1					
Computers	5	×	$1,200	=	$6,000
Bicycles	200	×	$200	=	$40,000
				Total =	**$46,000**
Year 2					
Computers	10	×	$1,200	=	$12,000
Bicycles	250	×	$200	=	$50,000
				Total =	**$62,000**

Percentage growth of real GDP = ($62,000 − $46,000)/$46,000 = **34.8%**

Calculation of real output with base year = Year 2

	Current quantities		Base-year prices		
Year 1					
Computers	5	×	$600	=	$3,000
Bicycles	200	×	$240	=	$48,000
				Total =	**$51,000**
Year 2					
Computers	10	×	$600	=	$6,000
Bicycles	250	×	$240	=	$60,000
				Total =	**$66,000**

Percentage growth of real GDP = ($66,000 − $51,000)/$51,000 = **29.4%**

Now we are prepared to calculate the increase in the physical production from year 1 to year 2. Real GDP is designed to measure the physical quantity of production. Because real GDP in year 2 is $62,000, and real GDP in year 1 is $46,000, output, as measured by real GDP, is 34.8% higher in year 2 than in year 1.

Price Indexes

We have seen how to calculate the portion of the change in nominal GDP owing to a change in physical quantities. Now we turn our attention to the change in prices by using price indexes. A **price index** is a measure of the average level of prices for some specified set of goods and services, relative to the prices in a specified base year. For example, the **GDP deflator** is a price index that measures the overall level of prices of goods and services included in GDP, and is defined by the formula

$$\text{real GDP} = \text{nominal GDP}/(\text{GDP deflator}/100).$$

The GDP deflator (divided by 100) is the amount by which nominal GDP must be divided, or "deflated," to obtain real GDP. In our example, we have already computed nominal GDP and real GDP, so we can now calculate the GDP deflator by rewriting the preceding formula as

$$\text{GDP deflator} = 100 \times \text{nominal GDP}/\text{real GDP}.$$

In year 1 (the base year in our example), nominal GDP and real GDP are equal, so the GDP deflator equals 100. This result is an example of the general principle that the GDP deflator always equals 100 in the base year. In year 2, nominal GDP is $66,000 (see Table 2.3) and real GDP is $62,000 (see Table 2.4), so the GDP deflator in year 2 is $100 \times \$66,000/\$62,000 = 106.5$, which is 6.5% higher than the value of the GDP deflator in year 1. Thus the overall level of prices, as measured by the GDP deflator, is 6.5% higher in year 2 than in year 1.

The measurement of real GDP and the GDP deflator depends on the choice of a base year. "In Touch with Data and Research: The Computer Revolution and Chain-Weighted GDP" demonstrates that the choice of a base year can have important effects on the calculated growth of real output, which in turn affects the calculated change in the price level.

IN TOUCH WITH DATA AND RESEARCH

The Computer Revolution and Chain-Weighted GDP

The widespread use of computers has revolutionized business, education, and leisure throughout much of the developed world. The fraction of the real spending in the United States devoted to computers quintupled between the mid-1980s and the mid-1990s,* while computer prices fell by more than 10% per year on average.[†] The sharp increase in the real quantity of computers and the sharp decline in computer prices highlight the problem of choosing a base year in calculating the growth of real GDP.

We can use the example in Tables 2.3 and 2.4, which includes a large increase in the quantity of computers coupled with a sharp decrease in computer prices, to illustrate the problem. We have shown that, when we treat year 1 as the base year, real output increases by 34.8% from year 1 to year 2. However, as we will see in this box using Table 2.4, we get a substantially different measure of real output growth if we treat year 2 as the base year. Treating year 2 as the base year means that we use the prices of year 2 to value output. Specifically, each computer is valued at $600 and each bicycle is valued at $240. Thus the real value of the 5 computers and 200 bicycles produced in year 1 is $51,000. If we continue to treat year 2 as the base year, the real value of output in year 2 is the same as the nominal value of output, which we have already calculated to be $66,000. Thus, by treating year 2 as the base year, we see real output grow from $51,000 in year 1 to $66,000 in year 2, an increase of 29.4%.

Let's summarize our calculations so far. Using year 1 as the base year, the calculated growth of output is 34.8%, but using year 2 as the base year, the calculated growth of output is only 29.4%. Why does this difference arise? In this example, the quantity of computers grows by 100% (from 5 to 10) and the quantity of bicycles grows by 25% (from 200 to 250) from year 1 to year 2. The computed growth of overall output—34.8% using year 1 as the base year or 29.4% using year 2 as the base year—is between the growth rates of the two individual goods. The overall growth rate is a sort of weighted average of the growth rates of the individual goods. When year 1 is the base year, we use year 1 prices to value output, and in year 1 computers are much more expensive than

*See Joseph Haimowitz, "Has the Surge in Computer Spending Fundamentally Changed the Economy?" *Federal Reserve Bank of Kansas City Economic Review*, Second Quarter 1998, pp. 27–42.

[†]These prices are for computer and peripheral equipment in Table 1 of Stephen D. Oliner and Daniel E. Sichel, "Computers and Output Growth Revisited: How Big Is the Puzzle?" *Brookings Papers on Economic Activity*, 2: 1994, pp. 273–317.

bicycles. Thus the growth of overall output is closer to the very high growth rate of computers than when the growth rate is computed using year 2 as the base year.

Which base year is the "right" one to use? There is no clear reason to prefer one over the other. To deal with this problem, in 1996 the Bureau of Economic Analysis introduced chain-weighted indexes to measure real GDP. Chain-weighted real GDP represents a mathematical compromise between using year 1 and using year 2 as the base year. The growth rate of real GDP computed using chain-weighted real GDP is a sort of average of the growth rate computed using year 1 as the base year and the growth rate computed using year 2 as the base year. (In this example, the growth rate of real GDP using chain-weighting is 32.1%, but we will not go through the details of that calculation here.)‡

Before the Bureau of Economic Analysis adopted chain-weighting, it used 1987 as the base year to compute real GDP. As time passed, it became necessary to update the base year so that the prices used to compute real GDP would reflect the true values of various goods being produced. Every time the base year was changed, the Bureau of Economic Analysis had to calculate new historical data for real GDP. Chain-weighting effectively updates the base year automatically. The annual growth rate for a given year is computed using that year and the preceding year as base years. As time goes on, there is no need to recompute historical growth rates of real GDP using new base years. Nevertheless, chain-weighted real GDP has a peculiar feature. Although the income–expenditure identity, $Y = C + I + G + NX$, always holds exactly in nominal terms, for technical reasons, this relationship need not hold exactly when GDP and its components are measured in real terms when chain-weighting is used. Because the discrepancy is usually small, we assume in this book that the income–expenditure identity holds in both real and nominal terms.

Chain-weighting was introduced to resolve the problem of choosing a given year as a base year in calculating real GDP. How large a difference does chain-weighting make in the face of the rapidly increasing production of computers and plummeting computer prices? Using 1987 as the base year, real GDP in the fourth quarter of 1994 was computed to be growing at a 5.1% annual rate. Using chain-weighting, real GDP growth during this quarter was a less impressive 4.0%. The Bureau of Economic Analysis estimates that computers account for about three-fifths of the difference between these two growth rates.**

---

‡For discussions of chain-weighting, see Charles Steindel, "Chain-Weighting: The New Approach to Measuring GDP," *Current Issues in Economics and Finance*, New York: Federal Reserve Bank of New York, December 1995, and "A Guide to the NIPAs," on the Web site of the Bureau of Economic Analysis, *www.bea.gov/national/pdf/nipaguid.pdf*.

**These figures are from p. 36 of J. Steven Landefeld and Robert P. Parker, "Preview of the Comprehensive Revision of the National Income and Product Accounts: BEA's New Featured Measures of Output and Prices," *Survey of Current Business*, July 1995, pp. 31–38.

The Consumer Price Index.   The GDP deflator measures the average level of prices of goods and services included in GDP. The **consumer price index**, or CPI, measures the prices of consumer goods. Unlike the GDP deflator, which is calculated quarterly, the CPI is available monthly. The Bureau of Labor Statistics constructs the CPI by sending people out each month to find the current prices of a fixed list, or "basket," of consumer goods and services, including many specific items of food, clothing, housing, and fuel. The CPI for that month is then calculated as 100 times the current cost of the basket of consumer items divided by the cost of the same basket of items in the reference base period.

The calculation of the consumer price index requires the use of a reference base period, for comparing prices over time, and an expenditure base period, for determining the basket of goods used in the index. Currently the reference base period is 1982–1984, which means that the consumer price index is constructed so it averages 100 for the three-year period from January 1982 to December 1984. So, if the CPI averages 215 in 2008, that means the average level of consumer prices is 115% higher than it was in the 1982–1984 period.

The expenditure base period for the CPI is the period on which the Bureau of Labor Statistics bases the basket of goods, which is currently 2005–2006. A survey of consumers' expenditure patterns over the years 2005–2006 is used to weight the goods and services for constructing the CPI. Currently the reference base period differs from the expenditure base period. The government updates the expenditure base period every few years and does not want to recalculate the past values of the index by changing the reference base period. Even though the government updates the expenditure base period every few years, there is reason to think that the CPI inflation rate is biased upward, as discussed in "In Touch with Data and Research: Does CPI Inflation Overstate Increases in the Cost of Living?"

IN TOUCH WITH DATA AND RESEARCH

Does CPI Inflation Overstate Increases in the Cost of Living?

In 1995–1996 a government commission, headed by Michael Boskin of Stanford University, prepared a report on the accuracy of official inflation measures. The commission concluded that inflation as measured by the CPI may overstate true increases in the cost of living by as much as 1–2 percentage points per year. In other words, if the official inflation rate is 3% per year, the "true" inflation rate may well be only 1%–2% per year.

Why might increases in the CPI overstate the actual rate at which the cost of living rises? One reason is the difficulty that government statisticians face in trying to measure changes in the quality of goods. For example, if the design of an air conditioner is improved so that it can put out 10% more cold air without an increased use of electricity, then a 10% increase in the price of the air conditioner should not be considered inflation; although paying 10% more, the consumer is also receiving 10% more cooling capacity. However, if government statisticians fail to account for the improved quality of the air conditioner and simply note its 10% increase in price, the price change will be incorrectly interpreted as inflation.

Although measuring the output of an air conditioner isn't difficult, for some products (especially services) quality change is hard to measure. For example, by what percentage does the availability of 24-hour cash machines improve the quality of banking services? To the extent that the CPI fails to account for quality improvements in the goods and services people use, inflation will be overstated. This overstatement is called the *quality adjustment bias*.

Another problem with CPI inflation as a measure of cost of living increases can be illustrated by the following example. Suppose that consumers like chicken and turkey about equally well and in the base year consume equal amounts of each. But then for some reason the price of chicken rises sharply, leading consumers to switch to eating turkey almost exclusively. Because consumers are about equally satisfied with chicken and turkey, this switch doesn't make them significantly worse off; their true cost of living has not been affected much by the rise in the price of chicken. However, the official CPI, which measures the cost of buying the base-year basket of goods and services, will register a significant increase when the price of chicken skyrockets. Thus the rise in the CPI exaggerates the true increase in the cost of living. The problem is that the CPI is based on the assumption that consumers purchase a basket of goods and services that is fixed over time, ignoring the fact that consumers can (and do) substitute cheaper goods or services for more expensive ones. This source of overstatement of the true increase in the cost of living is called the *substitution bias*.

If official inflation measures do, in fact, overstate true inflation, there are important implications. First, if cost of living increases are overstated, then increases in important quantities such as real family income (the purchasing power of a typical family's income) are correspondingly understated. As a result, the bias in the CPI may lead to too gloomy a view of how well the U.S. economy has done over the past few decades. Second, many government payments and taxes are tied, or indexed, to the CPI. Social Security benefits, for example, automatically increase each year by the same percentage as the CPI. If CPI inflation overstates true inflation, then Social Security recipients have been receiving greater benefit increases than necessary to compensate them for increases in the cost of living. If Social Security and other transfer program payments were set to increase at the rate of "true" inflation, rather than at the CPI inflation rate, the Federal government would save billions of dollars each year.

In response to the Boskin commission's report, the Bureau of Labor Statistics (BLS) made several technical changes in the way it constructs the CPI to reduce substitution bias. These changes have reduced the overstatement of the "true" inflation rate by 0.2 to 0.4 percentage points per year. However, the substitution bias was originally larger than the Boskin Commission's estimate, so the bias in the inflation rate is still 1% per year, or perhaps even higher.

Note: For a detailed discussion of biases in the CPI, see David Lebow and Jeremy Rudd, "Measurement Error in the Consumer Price Index: Where Do We Stand?" *Journal of Economic Literature*, March 2003, pp. 159–201; and Robert J. Gordon, "The Boskin Commission Report: A Retrospective One Decade Later," NBER Working Paper No. 12311, June 2006.

Inflation.   An important variable that is measured with price indexes is the inflation rate. The inflation rate equals the percentage rate of increase in the price index per period. Thus, if the GDP deflator rises from 100 in one year to 105 the next, the inflation rate between the two years is $(105 - 100)/100 = 5/100 = 0.05 = 5\%$ per year. If in the third year the GDP deflator is 112, the inflation rate between the second and third years is $(112 - 105)/105 = 7/105 = 0.0667 = 6.67\%$ per year. More generally, if P_t is the price level in period t and P_{t+1} is the price level in period $t + 1$, the inflation rate between t and $t + 1$, or π_{t+1}, is

$$\pi_{t+1} = \frac{P_{t+1} - P_t}{P_t} = \frac{\Delta P_{t+1}}{P_t},$$

Figure 2.1

The inflation rate in the United States, 1960–2008

Here, inflation is measured as the annual percentage change in the GDP deflator. Inflation rose during the 1960s and 1970s, fell sharply in the early 1980s, and fell more in the 1990s, but had an upward trend in the first half of the 2000s before declining later in the decade.

Source: Implicit price deflator for GDP, from FRED database, Federal Reserve Bank of St. Louis, *research.stlouisfed.org/fred2/series/GDPCTPI.*

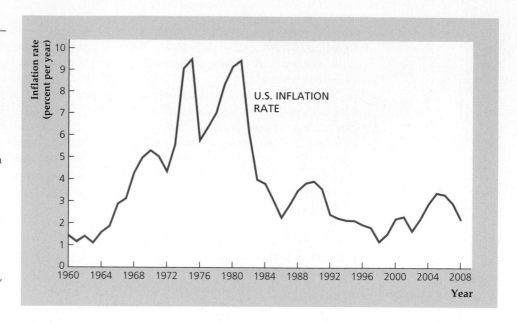

where ΔP_{t+1}, or $P_{t+1} - P_t$, represents the change in the price level from date t to date $t + 1$.

Figure 2.1 shows the U.S. inflation rate for 1960–2008, based on the GDP deflator as the measure of the price level. Inflation rose during the 1960s and 1970s, fell sharply in the early 1980s, fell more in the 1990s, trended upward from 1998 to 2005, and declined from 2005 to 2008.

APPLICATION

The Federal Reserve's Preferred Inflation Measures

Our discussion of price indexes describes the GDP deflator and the consumer price index (CPI). But the Federal Reserve (the Fed, for short), in reporting its forecasts of the economy, focuses on a different measure of prices: the personal consumption expenditures (PCE) price index, which is the measure of consumer prices in the national income and product accounts. The Fed announced in November 2007 that it would forecast inflation and other variables four times each year (instead of twice each year as it had done before). It also said that it would forecast both the overall inflation rate in the PCE price index and the core inflation rate of the same index, which excludes food and energy prices.

In the 1990s, the Fed provided forecasts of the inflation rate based on the CPI. But the Boskin Commission's finding (see "In Touch with Data and Research: Does CPI Inflation Overstate Increases in the Cost of Living?" p. 46) that the CPI measure of inflation substantially overstates increases in the cost of living caused the Fed to move away from focusing on the CPI and to pay more attention to the PCE price index.[17] Because the PCE price index is based on actual household expenditures on

---

[17]See the Federal Reserve Board of Governors, *Monetary Policy Report to the Congress*, February 2000, p. 4.

various goods and services, it avoids the substitution bias inherent in the CPI.[18] In addition, the Fed suggested that the PCE measure of consumption spending is broader than the CPI, and the PCE measure has the advantage of being revised when better data are available, whereas the CPI is not revised.

Other differences between the CPI and PCE price index include differences in the formulas used to calculate the index, the coverage of different items, and the weights given to different items.[19] The CPI is an index with a given base year while the PCE price index is a chain-weighted index, as discussed in "In Touch with Data and Research: The Computer Revolution and Chain-Weighted GDP," p. 44. The PCE price index covers more types of goods and services, as the CPI is based on the average spending habits of people who live in urban areas, whereas the PCE price index covers all spending on consumer goods in the economy. The weights on different spending categories differ as well; for example, homeowner-ship costs are about 20% of the CPI but only about 11% of the PCE price index.

The Fed used the rate of change of the PCE price index as its main measure of infla-tion beginning in 2000, but became somewhat dissatisfied with it because short-term shocks to food or energy prices frequently caused sharp fluctuations in the inflation rate. So, in 2004, the Fed switched its main inflation variable to the PCE price index excluding food and energy prices. We call the inflation rate using this index the *core* PCE inflation rate and we call the inflation rate that includes food and energy prices the *overall* PCE inflation rate. In announcing the switch in 2004, the Fed argued that the core PCE inflation rate was a better measure of "underlying inflation trends."[20]

In November 2007, however, the Fed decided that it should provide forecasts to the public for both the overall PCE inflation rate and the core PCE inflation rate. The rationale was laid out in a speech by Federal Reserve governor Frederic Mishkin, who noted that although monetary policymakers should focus on core inflation for determining monetary policy, there was good reason also to keep an eye on overall inflation.[21] After all, that measure more closely matches the goods and services actually bought by households, and if unwatched, it may deviate from core inflation in ways that are detrimental to households.

Figure 2.2 shows how overall PCE inflation differs from core PCE inflation. The figure shows the inflation rates from January 1960 to June 2009.[22] You can see in the figure that overall PCE inflation and core PCE inflation differed from each other

---

[18]The PCE price measure may still suffer from some of the other problems, such as quality adjustment bias, that plague the CPI.

[19]For more details, see the article by Todd E. Clark, "A Comparison of the CPI and the PCE Price Index," Federal Reserve Bank of Kansas City *Economic Review* (Third Quarter 1999), pp. 15–29.

[20]See the Federal Reserve Board of Governors, *Monetary Policy Report to the Congress,* July 2004, p. 3.

[21]"Headline versus Core Inflation in the Conduct of Monetary Policy," speech at the conference on Busi-ness Cycles, International Transmission, and Macroeconomic Policies, HEC Montreal, October 20, 2007.

[22]The data plotted in Figure 2.2 are the inflation rates between one month and the same month one year earlier. The inflation rate is calculated by dividing the price index for a particular month by the value twelve months earlier, then subtracting 1 and multiplying by 100 to put the result in percentage points. That is, the inflation rate is $\pi_t = \left[\left(\frac{P_t}{P_{t-12}}\right) - 1\right] \times 100$ where P_t is the price index in month t.

(continued)

Figure 2.2

Overall PCE inflation rate and core PCE inflation rate, 1960–2009
The overall PCE inflation rate usually differs from the core PCE inflation rate. However, the overall PCE inflation rate tends to revert to the core PCE inflation rate.

Source: Federal Reserve Bank of St. Louis FRED database at *research.stlouisfed.org/fred2/ series/PCEPI and PCEPILFE.*

substantially in many years. Large increases in the price of oil in the mid 1970s and again in the late 1970s caused the overall PCE inflation rate to be above the core PCE inflation rate during these episodes. However, as the relative price of oil declined in the 1980s, the overall PCE inflation rate was less than the core PCE inflation rate from 1982 to 1987. After that, the core PCE inflation rate has not varied as much as the overall PCE inflation rate. Generally, the overall PCE inflation rate tends to revert to the core PCE inflation rate after several years of being above it or below it.

2.5 Interest Rates

Interest rates are another important—and familiar—type of economic variable. An **interest rate** is a rate of return promised by a borrower to a lender. If, for example, the interest rate on a $100, one-year loan is 8%, the borrower has promised to repay the lender $108 one year from now, or $8 interest plus repayment of the $100 borrowed.

As we discuss in more detail in Chapter 4, there are many different interest rates in the economy. Interest rates vary according to who is doing the borrowing, how long the funds are borrowed for, and other factors (see "In Touch with Data and Research: Interest Rates," p. 114). There are also many assets in the economy, such as shares of corporate stock, that do not pay a specified interest rate but do pay their holders a return; for shares of stock, the return comes in the form of dividends and capital gains (increases in the stock's market price). The existence of so many different assets, each with its own rate of return, has the potential to complicate greatly the study of macroeconomics. Fortunately, however, most interest rates and other rates of return tend to move up and down together. For purposes of macroeconomic analysis we usually speak of "the" interest rate, as if there were only one. If we say that a certain policy causes "the" interest rate to rise, for example, we mean that interest rates and rates of return in general are likely to rise.

Real Versus Nominal Interest Rates.   Interest rates and other rates of return share a measurement problem with nominal GDP: An interest rate indicates how quickly the nominal, or dollar, value of an interest-bearing asset increases over time, but it does not reveal how quickly the value of the asset changes in real, or purchasing-power, terms. Consider, for example, a savings account with an interest rate of 4% per year that has $300 in it at the beginning of the year. At the end of the year the savings account is worth $312, which is a relatively good deal for the depositor if inflation is zero; with no inflation the price level is unchanged over the year, and $312 buys 4% more goods and services in real terms than the initial $300 did one year earlier. If inflation is 4%, however, what cost $300 one year earlier now costs $312, and in real terms the savings account is worth no more today than it was a year ago.

To distinguish changes in the real value of assets from changes in nominal value, economists frequently use the concept of the real interest rate. The **real interest rate** (or real rate of return) on an asset is the rate at which the real value or purchasing power of the asset increases over time. We refer to conventionally measured interest rates, such as those reported in the media, as nominal interest rates, to distinguish them from real interest rates. The **nominal interest rate** (or nominal rate of return) is the rate at which the nominal value of an asset increases over time. The symbol for the nominal interest rate is i.

The real interest rate is related to the nominal interest rate and the inflation rate as follows:

$$\text{real interest rate} = \text{nominal interest rate} - \text{inflation rate} \qquad \textbf{(2.12)}$$
$$= i - \pi.$$

We derive and discuss Eq. (2.12) further at the end of the book in Appendix A, Section A.7.[23] For now, consider again the savings account paying 4% interest. If the inflation rate is zero, the real interest rate on that savings account is the 4% nominal interest rate minus the 0% inflation rate, which equals 4%. A 4% real interest rate on the account means that the depositor will be able to buy 4% more goods and services at the end of the year than at the beginning. But if inflation is 4%, the real interest rate on the savings account is the 4% nominal interest rate minus the 4% inflation rate, which equals 0%. In this case, the purchasing power of the account is no greater at the end of the year than at the beginning.

Nominal and real interest rates for the United States for 1960–2008 are shown in Fig. 2.3. The real interest rate was unusually low in the mid 1970s; indeed, it was negative, which means that the real values of interest-bearing assets actually were declining over time. Both nominal and real interest rates rose to record highs in the early 1980s before returning to a more normal level in the 1990s. But the real interest rate turned negative in the early 2000s and was close to zero in 2008.

The Expected Real Interest Rate.   When you borrow, lend, or make a bank deposit, the nominal interest rate is specified in advance. But what about the real interest rate? For any nominal interest rate, Eq. (2.12) states that the real interest rate depends on the rate of inflation over the period of the loan or deposit—say, one year. However, the rate of inflation during the year generally can't be determined until the year is over. Thus, at the time that a loan or deposit is made, the real interest rate that will be received is uncertain.

---

[23]Equation (2.12) is an approximation rather than an exact relationship. This approximation holds most closely when interest rates and inflation rates are not too high.

Figure 2.3

Nominal and real interest rates in the United States, 1960–2008

The nominal interest rate shown is the interest rate on three-year Treasury securities. The real interest rate is measured as the nominal interest rate minus the average inflation rate (using the GDP deflator) over the current and subsequent two years. The real interest rate was unusually low (actually negative) in the mid 1970s. In the early 1980s, both the nominal and real interest rates were very high. Nominal and real interest rates returned to more normal levels in the 1990s, then fell sharply in the early 2000s.

Source: The implicit price deflator for GDP is the same as for Fig. 2.1. Inflation rates for 2009 and 2010 are assumed to be 2%. The nominal interest rate on three-year Treasury securities is from the Board of Governors of the Federal Reserve System, Statistical Release H15, *www.federalreserve.gov/releases.*

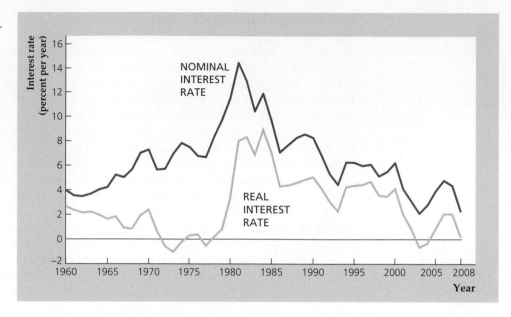

Because borrowers, lenders, and depositors don't know what the actual real interest rate will be, they must make their decisions about how much to borrow, lend, or deposit on the basis of the real interest rate they expect to prevail. They know the nominal interest rate in advance, so the real interest rate they expect depends on what they think inflation will be. The **expected real interest rate** is the nominal interest rate minus the expected rate of inflation, or

$$r = i - \pi^e, \tag{2.13}$$

where r is the expected real interest rate and π^e is the expected rate of inflation.

Comparing Eqs. (2.13) and (2.12), you can see that if people are correct in their expectations—so that expected inflation and actual inflation turn out to be the same—the expected real interest rate and the real interest rate actually received will be the same.

The expected real interest rate is the correct interest rate to use for studying most types of economic decisions, such as people's decisions about how much to borrow or lend. However, a problem in measuring the expected real interest rate is that economists generally don't know exactly what the public's expected rate of inflation is. Economists use various means to measure expected inflation. One approach is to survey the public and simply ask what rate of inflation people expect. A second method is to assume that the public's expectations of inflation are the same as publicly announced government or private forecasts. A third possibility is to assume that people's inflation expectations are an extrapolation of recently observed rates of inflation. Unfortunately, none of these methods is perfect, so the measurement of the expected real interest rate always contains some error.

CHAPTER SUMMARY

1. The national income accounts are an accounting framework used in measuring current economic activity. The national income accounts measure activity in three ways: the product approach, the expenditure approach, and the income approach. Although each gives the same value for current economic activ-

ity, all three approaches are used because each gives a different perspective on the economy.

2. Gross domestic product (GDP) is the broadest measure of aggregate economic activity occurring during a specified period of time. The product approach measures GDP by adding the market values of final

goods and services newly produced in an economy; this approach sums the value added by all producers. The expenditure approach measures GDP by adding the four categories of spending: consumption, investment, government purchases, and net exports. The income approach measures GDP by adding all the incomes, including taxes and profits, generated by economic activity.

3. The income of the private sector (domestic households and businesses) is called private disposable income. Private disposable income equals income received from private-sector activities (GDP plus net factor payments from abroad, or GNP) plus payments received from the government (transfers and interest on government debt) minus taxes paid to the government. The net income of the government sector equals taxes collected minus transfer payments and interest paid on government debt. Private disposable income and net government income sum to GNP.

4. Saving is the portion of an economic unit's current income that it doesn't spend to meet current needs. Saving by the private sector, called private saving, equals private disposable income minus consumption. Government saving, which is the same as the government budget surplus, equals the government's net income minus its purchases of goods and services (assuming that government purchases are devoted solely to government consumption rather than partially to government investment). Equivalently, government saving equals government receipts minus government outlays. National saving is the sum of private saving and government saving; it equals GDP plus net factor payments from abroad minus consumption and government purchases.

5. The uses-of-saving identity states that private saving equals the sum of investment, the government budget deficit, and the current account balance. Equivalently, national saving equals the sum of investment and the current account balance.

6. The national wealth of a country equals its physical assets, such as capital, plus its net foreign assets. National wealth increases in two ways: through changes in the value of existing assets and through national saving. National saving adds to national wealth because national saving is used either for investment, thus adding to physical capital, or for lending to foreigners an amount that equals the current account balance, which increases the country's net foreign assets.

7. Nominal GDP is the value of an economy's final output measured at current market prices. Real GDP is a measure of the economy's final output valued in terms of prices in a base year. Real GDP equals nominal GDP divided by the GDP deflator/100.

8. A price index is a measure of the current price level relative to a base year. The GDP deflator measures the overall price level of goods and services included in GDP. The consumer price index (CPI) measures the price level of a basket of consumer goods. The rate of inflation is the percentage rate of change of the price level, as measured by percentage rate of change of a price index such as the GDP deflator or the CPI.

9. An interest rate is a rate of return promised by a borrower to a lender. The nominal interest rate is the rate at which the nominal value of an interest-bearing asset increases over time. The real interest rate, or the nominal interest rate minus the rate of inflation, is the rate at which the value of an asset grows in real, or purchasing-power, terms. Borrowing and lending decisions are based on the expected real interest rate, which is the nominal interest rate less the expected rate of inflation.

KEY TERMS

budget deficit, p. 38
budget surplus, p. 38
capital good, p. 28
consumer price index, p. 45
consumption, p. 31
current account balance, p. 39
depreciation, p. 35
expected real interest rate, p. 52
expenditure approach, p. 25
final goods and services, p. 27
flow variables, p. 40

fundamental identity of national income accounting, p. 26
GDP deflator, p. 43
government outlays, p. 38
government purchases, p. 32
government receipts, p. 38
government saving, p. 37
gross domestic product, p. 26
gross national product, p. 28
income approach, p. 24
income–expenditure identity, p. 30

interest rate, p. 50
intermediate goods and services, p. 27
inventories, p. 28
investment, p. 31
national income, p. 33
national income accounts, p. 22
national saving, p. 38
national wealth, p. 36
net exports, p. 32

net factor payments from
   abroad, p. 30

net foreign assets, p. 40

net government income, p. 36

net national product, p. 35

nominal GDP, p. 42

nominal interest rate, p. 51

nominal variables, p. 41

price index, p. 43

private disposable income, p. 35

private saving, p. 37

product approach, p. 23

real GDP, p. 42

real interest rate, p. 51

real variable, p. 42

saving, p. 36

statistical discrepancy, p. 35

stock variables, p. 40

transfers, p. 32

underground economy, p. 27

uses-of-saving identity, p. 39

value added, p. 23

wealth, p. 36

KEY EQUATIONS

$$\frac{\text{total}}{\text{production}} = \frac{\text{total}}{\text{income}} = \frac{\text{total}}{\text{expenditure}} \qquad (2.1)$$

The *fundamental identity of national income accounting* states that the same value of total economic activity is obtained whether activity is measured by the production of final goods and services, the amount of income generated by the economic activity, or the expenditure on final goods and services.

$$Y = C + I + G + NX \qquad (2.3)$$

According to the *income-expenditure identity*, total income or product or output, Y, equals the sum of the four types of expenditure: consumption, C, investment, I, government purchases, G, and net exports, NX.

$$S_{\text{pvt}} = (Y + NFP - T + TR + INT) - C \qquad (2.6)$$

Private saving equals private disposable income less consumption, C. Private sector disposable income equals gross domestic product, Y, plus net factor payments from abroad, NFP, plus transfers, TR, and interest, INT, received from the government, less taxes paid, T.

$$S_{\text{govt}} = (T - TR - INT) - G \qquad (2.7)$$

Government saving equals government receipts from taxes, T, less outlays for transfers, TR, interest on the national debt, INT, and government purchases, G.

Government saving is the same as the government budget surplus and is the negative of the government budget deficit.

$$S = S_{\text{pvt}} + S_{\text{govt}} = Y + NFP - C - G \qquad (2.8)$$

National saving, S, is the sum of private saving and government saving. Equivalently, national saving equals gross domestic product, Y, plus net factor payments from abroad, NFP, less consumption, C, and government purchases, G.

$$S = I + CA \qquad (2.10)$$

National saving, S, has two uses: to finance investment, I, and to lend to foreigners (or to acquire foreign assets) an amount that equals the current account balance, CA. The current account balance equals the increase in net foreign assets.

$$S_{\text{pvt}} = I + (-S_{\text{govt}}) + CA \qquad (2.11)$$

According to the *uses-of-saving identity*, private saving is used to finance investment spending, I, to provide the government with the funds it needs to cover its budget deficit, $-S_{\text{govt}}$, and to lend to foreigners (or to acquire foreign assets) an amount that equals the current account balance, CA.

$$r = i - \pi^e \qquad (2.13)$$

The expected real interest rate, r, equals the nominal interest rate, i, minus expected inflation π^e.

REVIEW QUESTIONS

All review questions are available in (X) myeconlab at www.myeconlab.com.

1. What are the three approaches to measuring economic activity? Why do they give the same answer?

2. Why are goods and services counted in GDP at market value? Are there any disadvantages or problems in using market values to measure production?

3. What is the difference between intermediate and final goods and services? In which of these categories do

capital goods, such as factories and machines, fall? Why is the distinction between intermediate and final goods important for measuring GDP?

4. How does GDP differ from GNP? If a country employs many foreign workers, which is likely to be higher: GDP or GNP?

5. List the four components of total spending. Why are imports subtracted when GDP is calculated in the expenditure approach?

6. Define private saving. How is private saving used in the economy? What is the relationship between private saving and national saving?

7. What is national wealth, and why is it important? How is national wealth linked to national saving?

8. For the purposes of assessing an economy's growth performance, which is the more important statistic: real GDP or nominal GDP? Why?

9. Describe how the CPI and CPI inflation are calculated. What are some reasons that CPI inflation may overstate the true increase in the cost of living?

10. Explain the differences among the nominal interest rate, the real interest rate, and the expected real interest rate. Which interest rate concept is the most important for the decisions made by borrowers and lenders? Why?

NUMERICAL PROBLEMS

All numerical problems are available in ![myeconlab] at **www.myeconlab.com.**

1. After a boat rescues everyone else from Gilligan's Island, the Professor and Gilligan remain behind, afraid of getting shipwrecked again with the same bunch of people. The Professor grows coconuts and catches fish. Last year he harvested 1000 coconuts and caught 500 fish. He values one fish as worth two coconuts. The Professor gave 200 coconuts to Gilligan in exchange for help in the harvest, and he gave Gilligan 100 fish in exchange for collecting worms for use in fishing. The Professor stored 100 of his coconuts in his hut for consumption at some future time. Gilligan consumed all his coconuts and fish.

In terms of fish, what is the GDP of Gilligan's Island? What are consumption and investment? What are the incomes of the Professor and Gilligan?

2. National income and product data are generally revised. What effects would the following revisions have on consumption, investment, government purchases, net exports, and GDP?

  a. It is discovered that consumers bought $6 billion more furniture than previously thought. This furniture was manufactured in North Carolina.

  b. It is discovered that consumers bought $6 billion more furniture than previously thought. This furniture was manufactured in Sweden.

  c. It is discovered that businesses bought $6 billion more furniture than previously thought. This furniture was manufactured in North Carolina.

  d. It is discovered that businesses bought $6 billion more furniture than previously thought. This furniture was manufactured in Sweden.

3. ABC Computer Company has a $20,000,000 factory in Silicon Valley. During the current year ABC builds $2,000,000 worth of computer components. ABC's costs are labor, $1,000,000; interest on debt, $100,000; and taxes, $200,000.

ABC sells all its output to XYZ Supercomputer. Using ABC's components, XYZ builds four supercom-

puters at a cost of $800,000 each ($500,000 worth of components, $200,000 in labor costs, and $100,000 in taxes per computer). XYZ has a $30,000,000 factory.

XYZ sells three of the supercomputers for $1,000,000 each. At year's end, it had not sold the fourth. The unsold computer is carried on XYZ's books as an $800,000 increase in inventory.

  a. Calculate the contributions to GDP of these transactions, showing that all three approaches give the same answer.

  b. Repeat part (*a*), but now assume that, in addition to its other costs, ABC paid $500,000 for imported computer chips.

4. For each of the following transactions, determine the contribution to the current year's GDP. Explain the effects on the product, income, and expenditure accounts.

  a. On January 1, you purchase 10 gallons of gasoline at $2.80 per gallon. The gas station purchased the gasoline the previous week at a wholesale price (transportation included) of $2.60 per gallon.

  b. Colonel Hogwash purchases a Civil War–era mansion for $1,000,000. The broker's fee is 6%.

  c. A homemaker enters the work force, taking a job that will pay $40,000 over the year. The homemaker must pay $16,000 over the year for professional child care services.

  d. A Japanese company builds an auto plant in Tennessee for $100,000,000, using only local labor and materials. (*Hint*: The auto plant is a capital good produced by Americans and purchased by the Japanese.)

  e. You are informed that you have won $3,000,000 in the New Jersey State Lottery, to be paid to you, in total, immediately.

  f. The New Jersey state government pays you an additional $5000 fee to appear in a TV commercial publicizing the state lottery.

  g. Hertz Rent-a-Car replaces its rental fleet by buying $100,000,000 worth of new cars from General

Motors. It sells its old fleet to a consortium of used-car dealers for $40,000,000. The consortium resells the used cars to the public for a total of $60,000,000.

5. You are given the following information about an economy:

Gross private domestic investment = 40
Government purchases of goods and services = 30
Gross national product (GNP) = 200
Current account balance = −20
Taxes = 60
Government transfer payments to the domestic private sector = 25
Interest payments from the government to the domestic private sector = 15 (Assume all interest payments by the government go to domestic households.)
Factor income received from rest of world = 7
Factor payments made to rest of world = 9

Find the following, assuming that government investment is zero:

a. Consumption
b. Net exports
c. GDP
d. Net factor payments from abroad
e. Private saving
f. Government saving
g. National saving

6. Consider an economy that produces only three types of fruit: apples, oranges, and bananas. In the base year (a few years ago), the production and price data were as follows:

Fruit	Quantity	Price
Apples	3,000 bags	$2 per bag
Bananas	6,000 bunches	$3 per bunch
Oranges	8,000 bags	$4 per bag

In the current year the production and price data are as follows:

Fruit	Quantity	Price
Apples	4,000 bags	$3 per bag
Bananas	14,000 bunches	$2 per bunch
Oranges	32,000 bags	$5 per bag

a. Find nominal GDP in the current year and in the base year. What is the percentage increase since the base year?
b. Find real GDP in the current year and in the base year. By what percentage does real GDP increase from the base year to the current year?
c. Find the GDP deflator for the current year and the base year. By what percentage does the price level change from the base year to the current year?
d. Would you say that the percentage increase in nominal GDP in this economy since the base year is due more to increases in prices or increases in the physical volume of output?

7. For the consumer price index values shown, calculate the rate of inflation in each year from 1930 to 1933. What is unusual about this period, relative to recent experience?

Year	1929	1930	1931	1932	1933
CPI	51.3	50.0	45.6	40.9	38.8

8. Hy Marks buys a one-year government bond on January 1, 2009, for $500. He receives principal plus interest totaling $545 on January 1, 2010. Suppose that the CPI is 200 on January 1, 2009, and 214 on January 1, 2010. This increase in prices is more than Hy had anticipated; his guess was that the CPI would be at 210 by the beginning of 2010. Find the nominal interest rate, the inflation rate, the real interest rate, Hy's expected inflation rate, and Hy's expected real interest rate.

9. The GDP deflator in Econoland is 200 on January 1, 2008. The deflator rises to 242 by January 1, 2010, and to 266.2 by January 1, 2011.

a. What is the annual rate of inflation over the two-year period between January 1, 2008, and January 1, 2010? In other words, what constant yearly rate of inflation would lead to the price rise observed over those two years?
b. What is the annual rate of inflation over the three-year period from January 1, 2008, to January 1, 2011?
c. In general, if P_0 is the price level at the beginning of an n-year period, and P_n is the price level at the end of that period, show that the annual rate of inflation π over that period satisfies the equation

$$(1 + \pi)^n = P_n/P_0.$$

ANALYTICAL PROBLEMS

1. A reputable study shows that a particular new workplace safety regulation will reduce the growth of real GDP. Is this an argument against implementing the regulation? Explain.

2. Consider a closed economy with a single telephone company, Calls-R-Us. The residents of the country make 2 million phone calls per year and pay $3 per phone call. One day a new phone company, CheapCall, enters

the market and charges only $2 per phone call. All of the residents immediately stop using Calls-R-Us and switch to CheapCall. They still make 2 million phone calls per year. The executives of CheapCall are proud of their market share. Moreover, they post billboards stating, "Our country has increased its national saving by $2 million per year by switching to CheapCall." Comment on the accuracy of the statement on the billboards.

3. Economists have tried to measure the GDPs of virtually all the world's nations. This problem asks you to think about some practical issues that arise in that effort.

   a. Before the fall of communism, the economies of the Soviet Union and Eastern Europe were centrally planned. One aspect of central planning is that most prices are set by the government. A government-set price may be too low, in that people want to buy more of the good at the fixed price than there are supplies available; or the price may be too high, so that large stocks of the good sit unsold on store shelves.

      What problem does government control of prices create for economists attempting to measure a country's GDP? Suggest a strategy for dealing with this problem.

   b. In very poor, agricultural countries, many people grow their own food, make their own clothes, and provide services for one another within a family or village group. Official GDP estimates for these countries are often extremely low, perhaps just a few

hundred dollars per person. Some economists have argued that the official GDP figures underestimate these nations' actual GDPs. Why might this be so? Again, can you suggest a strategy for dealing with this measurement problem?

4. Government saving is defined as $T - (G + TR + INT)$, where G is government purchases. But suppose that we split government purchases into two parts: government consumption expenditures (GCE) and government investment (GI) and that we define a new version of government saving, which is $T - (GCE + TR + INT)$. With this new definition of government saving, which treats government investment similarly to private investment, how would the uses-of-savings identity be modified?

   To investigate how much difference this redefinition would make, look at the NIPA section of a recent issue of the *Survey of Current Business* or online at www. bea.gov, and find Table 5.1, "Gross Saving and Investment." The table refers to private saving as gross private saving, to investment as gross private domestic investment, to the current account balance as net foreign investment, to government investment as gross government investment, and to the new version of government saving as gross government saving. Verify that both the old and new definitions of the uses-of-savings identity are valid, except for statistical discrepancies.

WORKING WITH MACROECONOMIC DATA

For data to use in these exercises, go to the Federal Reserve Bank of St. Louis FRED database at research.stlouisfed.org/fred2.

1. Graph the four main expenditure components of GDP, in real terms, since the first quarter of 1947. Also graph the expenditure components as a share of total real GDP. Do you see any significant trends?

2. On the same figure, graph national saving and investment as fractions of real GDP, using quarterly U.S. data since 1947. (Note that national saving is called gross saving in the FRED database.) How does the behavior of these variables in the past ten years compare to their behavior in earlier periods? How is it possible for investment to exceed national saving, as it does in some periods?

3. Graph the annual (December to December) CPI inflation rate and the annual (fourth quarter to fourth quarter) GDP deflator inflation rate since 1960 on the same figure. What are the conceptual differences between these two measures of inflation? Judging from your

graph, would you say that the two measures give similar or different estimates of the rate of inflation in the economy?

4. If the real interest rate were approximately constant, then in periods in which inflation is high, the nominal interest rate should be relatively high (because the nominal interest rate equals the real interest rate plus the inflation rate). Using annual data since 1948, graph the three-month Treasury bill interest rate ("Discount rate on new ninety-one-day Treasury bills") and the CPI inflation rate for the U.S. economy. (Take annual averages of monthly interest rates and measure annual inflation rates as the change in the CPI from December to December.) Is it generally true that nominal interest rates rise with inflation? Does the relationship appear to be one-for-one (so that each additional percentage point of inflation raises the nominal interest rate by one percentage point), as would be the case if the real interest rate were constant? Calculate the real interest rate and graph its behavior since 1948.

CHAPTER 3

Productivity, Output, and Employment

In Chapter 2 we discussed the measurement of several economic variables used to gauge the economy's health. The measurement of economic performance is a prelude to the main objective of macroeconomics: *to understand how the economy works.* Understanding how the economy works requires a shift from economic *measurement* to economic *analysis.*

In Part 2 of this book, which begins with this chapter, we have two main goals. The first is to analyze the factors that affect the longer-term performance of the economy, including the rate of economic growth, productivity and living standards, the long-run levels of employment and unemployment, saving and capital formation, and the rate of inflation, among others.

The second goal is to develop a theoretical model of the macroeconomy that you can use to analyze the economic issues covered in this book and others that you may encounter in the future. As outlined in Chapter 1, our model is based on the assumption that individuals, firms, and the government interact in three aggregate markets: the labor market (covered in this chapter), the goods market (Chapter 4), and the asset market (Chapter 7). In developing and using this model in Part 2, we generally assume that the economy is at full employment, with quantities supplied and demanded being equal in the three major markets. As we are focusing on the long-term behavior of the economy, this assumption is a reasonable one. In Part 3, in which we explore business cycles, we allow for the possibility that quantities supplied and demanded may not be equal in the short run.

In this chapter, we begin the discussion of how the economy works with what is perhaps the most fundamental determinant of economic well-being in a society: the economy's productive capacity. Everything else being equal, the greater the quantity of goods and services an economy can produce, the more people will be able to consume in the present and the more they will be able to save and invest for the future.

In the first section of the chapter we show that the amount of output an economy produces depends on two factors: (1) the quantities of inputs (such as labor, capital, and raw materials) utilized in the production process; and (2) the **productivity** of the inputs—that is, the effectiveness with which they are used. As discussed in Chapter 1, an economy's productivity is basic to determining living standards. In this chapter we show how productivity affects people's incomes by helping to determine how many workers are employed and how much they receive in wages.

Of the various inputs to production, the most important (as measured by share of total cost) is labor. For this reason, we spend most of the chapter analyzing the labor market, using the tools of supply and demand. We first consider the factors that affect the quantity of labor demanded by employers and supplied by workers and then look at the forces that bring the labor market into equilibrium. Equilibrium in the labor market determines wages and employment; in turn, the level of employment, together with the quantities of other inputs (such as capital) and the level of productivity, determines how much output an economy produces.

Our basic model of the labor market rests on the assumption that the quantities of labor supplied and demanded are equal so that all labor resources are fully utilized. In reality, however, there are always some unemployed workers. In the latter part of the chapter, we introduce unemployment and look at the relationship between the unemployment rate and the amount of output produced in the economy.

3.1 How Much Does the Economy Produce? The Production Function

Every day the business news reports many economic variables that influence the economy's performance—the rate of consumer spending, the value of the dollar, the gyrations of the stock market, the growth rate of the money supply, and so on. All of these variables are important. However, no determinant of economic performance and living standards is more basic than the economy's physical capacity to produce goods and services. If an economy's factories, farms, and other businesses all shut down for some reason, other economic factors wouldn't mean much.

What determines the quantity of goods and services that an economy can produce? A key factor is the quantity of inputs—such as capital goods, labor, raw materials, land, and energy—that producers in the economy use. Economists refer to inputs to the production process as **factors of production**. All else being equal, the greater the quantities of factors of production used, the more goods and services are produced.

Of the various factors of production, the two most important are capital (factories and machines, for example) and labor (workers). Hence we focus on these two factors in discussing an economy's capacity to produce goods and services. In modern economies, however, output often responds strongly to changes in the supply of other factors, such as energy or raw materials. Later in this chapter, the Application "Output, Employment, and the Real Wage During Oil Price Shocks," p. 85, discusses the effects of a disruption in oil supplies on the economy.

The quantities of capital and labor (and other inputs) used in production don't completely determine the amount of output produced. Equally important is how effectively these factors are used. For the same stocks of capital and labor, an economy with superior technologies and management practices, for example, will produce a greater amount of output than an economy without those strengths.

The effectiveness with which capital and labor are used may be summarized by a relationship called the production function. The **production function** is a mathematical expression relating the amount of output produced to quantities of capital and labor utilized. A convenient way to write the production function is

$$Y = AF(K, N), \tag{3.1}$$

where

$$Y = \text{real output produced in a given period of time;}$$
$$A = \text{a number measuring overall productivity;}$$
$$K = \text{the capital stock, or quantity of capital used in the period;}$$
$$N = \text{the number of workers employed in the period;}$$
$$F = \text{a function relating output } Y \text{ to capital } K \text{ and labor } N.$$

The production function in Eq. (3.1) applies both to an economy as a whole (where Y, K, and N refer to the economy's output, capital stock, and number of workers, respectively) and to an individual firm, in which case Y, K, and N refer to the firm's output, capital, and number of workers, respectively.

According to Eq. (3.1), the amount of output Y that an economy (or firm) can produce during any period of time depends on the size of the capital stock K and the number of workers N. The symbol A in Eq. (3.1), which multiplies the function $F(K, N)$, is a measure of the overall effectiveness with which capital and labor are used. We refer to A as **total factor productivity,** or simply productivity. Note that, for any values of capital and labor, an increase in productivity of, say, 10% implies a 10% increase in the amount of output that can be produced. Thus increases in productivity, A, correspond to improvements in production technology or to any other change in the economy that allows capital and labor to be utilized more effectively.

APPLICATION

The Production Function of the U.S. Economy and U.S. Productivity Growth

Empirical studies show that the relationship between output and inputs in the U.S. economy is described reasonably well by the following production function:[1]

$$Y = AK^{0.3}N^{0.7}. \tag{3.2}$$

The production function in Eq. (3.2) is a specific example of the general production function in Eq. (3.1), in which we set the general function $F(K, N)$ equal to $K^{0.3}N^{0.7}$. (Note that this production function contains exponents; if you need to review the properties of exponents, see Appendix A, Section A.6.)

Equation (3.2) shows how output, Y, relates to the use of factors of production, capital, K, and labor, N, and to productivity, A, in the United States. Table 3.1 presents data on these variables for the U.S. economy for 29 years beginning in 1979. Columns (1), (2), and (3) show output (real GDP), capital stock, and labor for each year. Real GDP and the capital stock are measured in billions of 2000 dollars, and labor is measured in millions of employed workers. Column (4) shows the U.S. economy's productivity for each year.

Output, capital, and labor in Table 3.1 are measured directly, but there is no way to measure productivity directly. Instead, the productivity index, A, shown in column

---

[1]This type of production function is called a Cobb-Douglas production function. Cobb-Douglas production functions take the form $Y = AK^aN^{1-a}$, where $0 < a < 1$. Under certain conditions, the parameter a in the Cobb-Douglas production function corresponds to the share of income received by owners of capital, whereas labor receives a share of income equal to $1-a$. Thus observing the actual shares of income received by capital and labor provides a way of estimating the parameter a.

Table 3.1

The Production Function of the United States, 1979–2007

Year	(1) Real GDP, Y (billions of 2000 dollars)	(2) Capital stock, K (billions of 2000 dollars)	(3) Labor, N (millions of workers)	(4) A^a	(5) Growth in A (% change in A)
1979	5173	5615	98.8	15.58	
1980	5162	5831	99.3	15.32	−1.7
1981	5292	6060	100.4	15.40	0.6
1982	5189	6236	99.5	15.07	−2.2
1983	5424	6383	100.8	15.50	2.8
1984	5814	6614	105.0	15.98	3.1
1985	6054	6863	107.2	16.22	1.5
1986	6264	7060	109.6	16.38	1.0
1987	6475	7239	112.4	16.51	0.8
1988	6743	7429	115.0	16.79	1.7
1989	6981	7623	117.3	17.01	1.3
1990	7113	7809	118.8	17.06	0.3
1991	7101	7932	117.7	17.06	0.0
1992	7337	8045	118.5	17.47	2.4
1993	7533	8208	120.3	17.64	1.0
1994	7836	8396	123.1	17.94	1.7
1995	8032	8638	124.9	18.04	0.6
1996	8329	8917	126.7	18.35	1.7
1997	8704	9242	129.6	18.67	1.8
1998	9067	9605	131.5	19.03	1.9
1999	9470	9986	133.5	19.44	2.1
2000	9817	10,392	136.9	19.57	0.6
2001	9891	10,669	136.9	19.55	−0.1
2002	10,049	10,841	136.5	19.82	1.3
2003	10,301	10,986	137.7	20.10	1.5
2004	10,676	11,147	139.3	20.59	2.4
2005	10,990	11,333	141.7	20.83	1.2
2006	11,295	11,584	144.4	20.99	0.8
2007	11,524	11,849	146.0	21.10	0.6

^{a}Total factor productivity is calculated by the formula $A = Y/(K^{0.3}N^{0.7})$. The calculation of A in this table is based on more precise values for Y, N, and K, so the reported numbers for A here may differ very slightly from what you would calculate by using the numbers in this table for Y, N, and K.

Sources: Y is real GDP in billions of 2000 chained dollars from the St. Louis FRED database, *research.stlouisfed.org/ fred2/ series/*GDPCA; K is real net stock of fixed private nonresidential capital in billions of 2000 dollars from Bureau of Economic Analysis, *www.bea.gov/bea/dn/faweb/AllFATables.asp*; N is civilian employment in millions of workers from Bureau of Labor Statistics, *ftp://ftp.bls.gov/pub/special.requests/lf/aat1.txt.*

(4) is measured indirectly by assigning to A the value necessary to satisfy Eq. (3.2). Specifically, for each year A is determined by the formula $A = Y/(K^{0.3}N^{0.7})$, which is just another way of writing Eq. (3.2). In 2007, for example, $Y = 11,523.9$, $K = 11,848.7$, and $N = 146.05$; therefore the value of A for 2007 is $11,523.9/[(11,848.7)^{0.3}(146.05)^{0.7}]$ or $A = 21.103$. Calculating productivity in this way ensures that the production function relationship, Eq. (3.2), is satisfied exactly for each year.

The levels of the productivity index, A, reported in Table 3.1 depend on the units in which output, capital, and labor are measured—for example, the values of A would change if workers were measured in thousands rather than millions—and thus are

(continued)

difficult to interpret. In contrast, the year-to-year growth rates of the productivity measure shown in column (5) are units-free and are therefore easier to work with. A close look at the productivity growth rates shown in Table 3.1 emphasizes two points.

First, productivity growth can vary sharply from year to year. Most strikingly, productivity in the United States fell 2.2% in 1982, a deep recession year, then rose 2.8% in 1983 and 3.1% in 1984, a period of economic recovery. Productivity also fell slightly during the 2001 recession. Productivity normally falls in recessions and rises in recoveries, but explanations for its behavior over the business cycle are controversial. We return to this issue in Part 3 of this book.

Second, from 1980 to 1995, productivity in the United States had been growing relatively slowly, averaging about 0.9% per year. This result is better than the performance in the 1970s, when productivity growth was only 0.4% per year, but notably less than in the 1950s and 1960s, when productivity growth averaged about 2.1% per year. But since 1995, productivity growth has increased, averaging 1.3% per year. This recent increase in productivity growth is good news if it is sustained, because the rate of productivity growth is closely related to the rate of improvement of living standards. In Chapter 6 we discuss the relationship between productivity and living standards in greater detail.

The Shape of the Production Function

The production function in Eq. (3.1) can be shown graphically. The easiest way to graph it is to hold one of the two factors of production, either capital or labor, constant and then graph the relationship between output and the other factor.[2] Suppose that we use the U.S. production function for the year 2007 and hold labor N at its actual 2007 value of 146.05 million workers (see Table 3.1). We also use the actual 2007 value of 21.103 for A. The production function (Eq. 3.2) becomes

$$Y = AK^{0.3}N^{0.7} = (21.103)(K^{0.3})(146.05^{0.7}) = 691.03K^{0.3}.$$

This relationship is graphed in Fig. 3.1, with capital stock K on the horizontal axis and output Y on the vertical axis. With labor and productivity held at their 2007 values, the graph shows the amount of output that could have been produced in that year for any value of the capital stock. Point A on the graph shows the situation that actually occurred in 2007: The value of the capital stock ($11,849 billion) appears on the horizontal axis, and the value of real GDP ($11,524 billion) appears on the vertical axis.

The U.S. production function graphed in Fig. 3.1 shares two properties with most production functions:

1. *The production function slopes upward from left to right.* The slope of the production function reveals that, as the capital stock increases, more output can be produced.
2. *The slope of the production function becomes flatter from left to right.* This property implies that although more capital always leads to more output, it does so at a decreasing rate.

Before discussing the economics behind the second property of the production function, we can illustrate it numerically, using Fig. 3.1. Suppose that we are

---

[2]To show the relationship among output and both factors of production simultaneously would require a three-dimensional graph.

Figure 3.1

The production function relating output and capital

This production function shows how much output the U.S. economy could produce for each level of U.S. capital stock, holding U.S. labor and productivity at 2007 levels. Point *A* corresponds to the actual 2007 output and capital stock. The production function has diminishing marginal productivity of capital: Raising the capital stock by $1000 billion to move from point *B* to point *C* raises output by $874 billion, but adding another $1000 billion in capital to go from point *C* to point *D* increases output by only $688 billion.

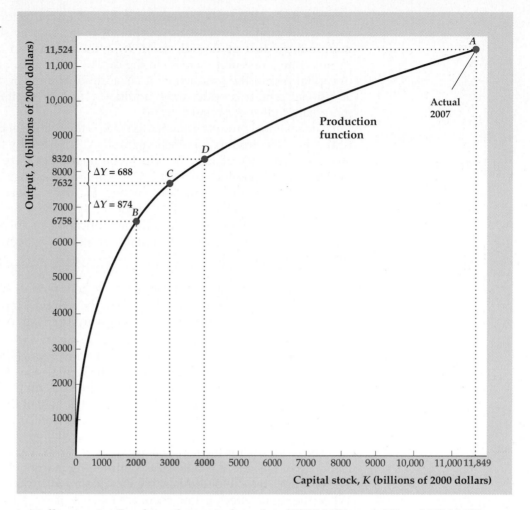

initially at point *B*, where the capital stock is $2000 billion. Adding $1000 billion in capital moves us to point *C*, where the capital stock is $3000 billion. How much extra output has this expansion in capital provided? The difference in output between points *B* and *C* is $874 billion ($7632 billion output at *C* minus $6758 billion output at *B*). This extra $874 billion in output is the benefit from raising the capital stock from $2000 billion to $3000 billion, with productivity and employment held constant.

Now suppose that, starting at *C*, we add another $1000 billion of capital. This new addition of capital takes us to *D*, where the capital stock is $4000 billion. The difference in output between *C* and *D* is only $688 billion ($8320 billion output at *D* minus $7632 billion output at *C*), which is less than the $874 billion increase in output between *B* and *C*. Thus, although the second $1000 billion of extra capital raises total output, it does so by less than did the first $1000 billion of extra capital. This result illustrates that the production function rises less steeply between points *C* and *D* than between points *B* and *C*.

The Marginal Product of Capital. The two properties of the production function are closely related to a concept known as the marginal product of capital. To understand this concept, we can start from some given capital stock, *K*, and increase the capital stock by some amount, ΔK (other factors held constant). This increase in capital would cause output, Y, to increase by some amount, ΔY. The **marginal product of capital,** or *MPK,* is the increase in output produced that results from a one-unit increase in the capital stock. Because ΔK additional units of capital permit the production of ΔY additional units of output, the amount of additional output produced per additional unit of capital is $\Delta Y/\Delta K$. Thus the marginal product of capital is $\Delta Y/\Delta K$.

The marginal product of capital, $\Delta Y/\Delta K$, is the change in the variable on the vertical axis of the production function graph, ΔY, divided by the change in the variable on the horizontal axis, ΔK, which you might recognize as a slope.[3] For small increases in the capital stock, the *MPK* can be measured by the slope of a line drawn tangent to the production function. Figure 3.2 illustrates this way of measuring the *MPK.* When the capital stock is 2000, for example, the *MPK* equals the slope of the line tangent to the production function at point B.[4] We can use the concept of the marginal product of capital to restate the two properties of production functions listed earlier.

1. *The marginal product of capital is positive.* Whenever the capital stock is increased, more output can be produced. Because the marginal product of capital is positive, the production function slopes upward from left to right.
2. *The marginal product of capital declines as the capital stock is increased.* Because the marginal product of capital is the slope of the production function, the slope of the production function decreases as the capital stock is increased. As Fig. 3.2 shows, the slope of the production function at point D, where the capital stock is 4000, is smaller than the slope at point B, where the capital stock is 2000. Thus the production function becomes flatter from left to right.

The tendency for the marginal product of capital to decline as the amount of capital in use increases is called the **diminishing marginal productivity** of capital. The economic reason for diminishing marginal productivity of capital is as follows: When the capital stock is low, there are many workers for each machine, and the benefits of increasing capital further are great; but when the capital stock is high, workers already have plenty of capital to work with, and little benefit is to be gained from expanding capital further. For example, in a business firm's call center in which there are many more staff members than workstations (phones and computer terminals), each workstation is constantly being utilized, and the staff must waste time waiting for a free workstation. In this situation, the benefit in terms of increased output of adding extra workstations is high. However, if there are already as many workstations as staff members, so that workstations are often idle and there is no waiting for a workstation to become available, little additional output can be obtained by adding yet another workstation.

The Marginal Product of Labor.   In Figs. 3.1 and 3.2 we graphed the relationship between output and capital implied by the 2007 U.S. production function, holding constant the amount of labor. Similarly, we can look at the relationship between

---

[3]For definitions and a discussion of slopes of lines and curves, see Appendix A, Section A.2.

[4]We often refer to the slope of the line tangent to the production function at a given point as simply the slope of the production function at that point, for short.

Figure 3.2

The marginal product of capital

The marginal product of capital (*MPK*) at any point can be measured as the slope of the line tangent to the production function at that point. Because the slope of the line tangent to the production function at point *B* is greater than the slope of the line tangent to the production function at point *D*, we know that the *MPK* is greater at *B* than at *D*. At higher levels of capital stock, the *MPK* is lower, reflecting diminishing marginal productivity of capital.

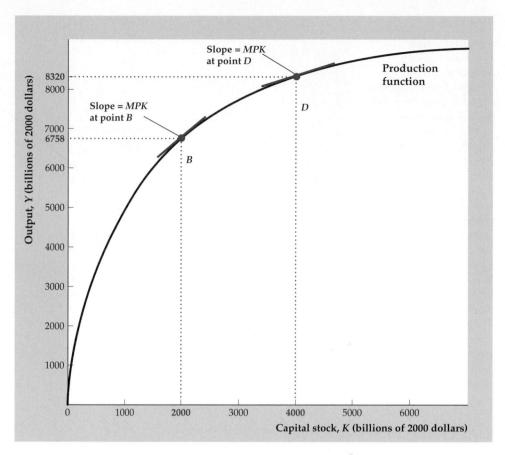

output and labor, holding constant the quantity of capital. Suppose that we fix capital, *K*, at its actual 2007 value of $11,848.7 billion and hold productivity, *A*, at its actual 2007 value of 21.103 (see Table 3.1). The production function (Eq. 3.2) becomes

$$Y = AK^{0.3}N^{0.7} = (21.103)(11,848.7^{0.3})(N^{0.7}) = 351.92N^{0.7}.$$

This relationship is shown graphically in Fig. 3.3. Point *A*, where *N* = 146.0 million workers and *Y* = $11,524 billion, corresponds to the actual 2007 values.

The production function relating output and labor looks generally the same as the production function relating output and capital.[5] As in the case of capital, increases in the number of workers raise output but do so at a diminishing rate. Thus the principle of diminishing marginal productivity also applies to labor, and for similar reasons: the greater the number of workers already using a fixed amount of capital and other inputs, the smaller the benefit (in terms of increased output) of adding even more workers.

The **marginal product of labor,** or *MPN,* is the additional output produced by each additional unit of labor, $\Delta Y/\Delta N$. As with the marginal product of capital, for small increases in employment, the *MPN* can be measured by the slope of the line tangent to a production function that relates output and labor. In Fig. 3.3, when

---

[5]Because *N* is raised to the power of 0.7 but *K* is raised to the power of 0.3, the production function relating output and labor is not as sharply bowed as the production function relating output and capital. The closer the power is to 1, the closer the production function will be to a straight line.

Figure 3.3

The production function relating output and labor
This production function shows how much output the U.S. economy could produce at each level of employment (labor input), holding productivity and the capital stock constant at 2007 levels. Point A corresponds to actual 2007 output and employment. The marginal product of labor (*MPN*) at any point is measured as the slope of the line tangent to the production function at that point. The *MPN* is lower at higher levels of employment, reflecting diminishing marginal productivity of labor.

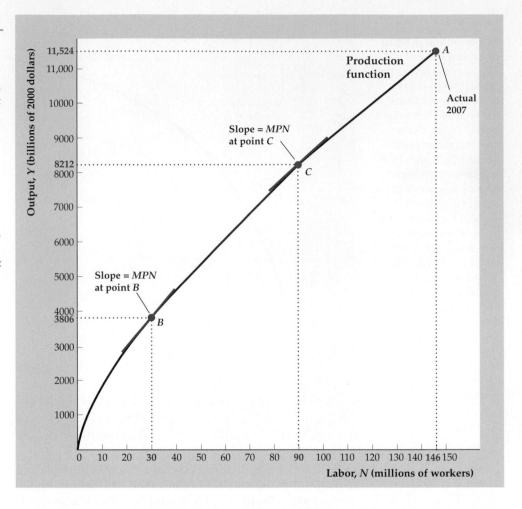

employment equals 30 million workers, the *MPN* equals the slope of the line tangent to the production function at point *B*; when employment is 90 million workers, the *MPN* is the slope of the line that touches the production function at point *C*. Because of the diminishing marginal productivity of labor, the slope of the production function relating output to labor is greater at *B* than at *C*, and the production function flattens from left to right.

Supply Shocks

The production function of an economy doesn't usually remain fixed over time. Economists use the term **supply shock**—or, sometimes, productivity shock—to refer to a change in an economy's production function.[6] A positive, or beneficial, supply shock raises the amount of output that can be produced for given quantities of capital and labor. A negative, or adverse, supply shock lowers the amount of output that can be produced for each capital-labor combination.

Real-world examples of supply shocks include changes in the weather, such as a drought or an unusually cold winter; inventions or innovations in management

---

[6]The term *shock* is a slight misnomer. Not all changes in the production function are sharp or unpredictable, although many are.

Figure 3.4

An adverse supply shock that lowers the *MPN*

An adverse supply shock is a downward shift of the production function. For any level of labor, the amount of output that can be produced is now less than before. The adverse shock reduces the slope of the production function at every level of employment.

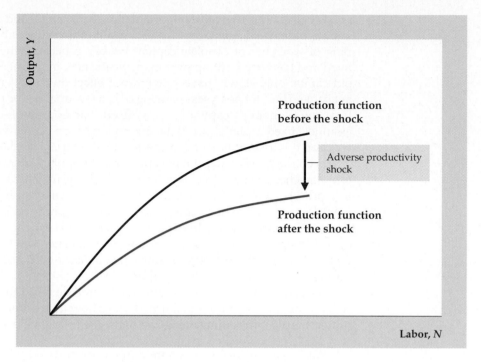

techniques that improve efficiency, such as computerized inventory control or statistical analysis in quality control; and changes in government regulations, such as antipollution laws, that affect the technologies or production methods used. Also included in the category of supply shocks are changes in the supplies of factors of production *other than capital and labor* that affect the amount that can be produced.

Figure 3.4 shows the effects of an adverse supply shock on the production function relating output and labor. The negative supply shock shifts the production function downward so that less output can be produced for specific quantities of labor and capital. In addition, the supply shock shown reduces the slope of the production function so that the output gains from adding a worker (the marginal product of labor) are lower at every level of employment.[7] Conversely, a beneficial supply shock makes possible the production of more output with given quantities of capital and labor and thus shifts the production function upward.[8]

3.2 The Demand for Labor

We have shown that the amount of output produced by a country, or by a firm, depends both on productivity and the quantities of inputs used in the production process. In Section 3.1 our focus was on productivity—its measurement and factors such as supply shocks that cause it to change. In this section, we examine what determines the quantities of inputs that producers use.

---

[7]Logically, an adverse supply shock need not always reduce the marginal products of labor and capital; for example, the production function could make a parallel downward shift. However, thinking of an adverse supply shock reducing marginal products as being the normal case seems reasonable. A shift of the production function like that shown in Fig. 3.4 would occur if there were a decline in total factor productivity, *A*, for example.

[8]The effects of supply shocks on the production function relating output and capital would be similar.

Recall that the two most important inputs are capital and labor. The capital stock in an economy changes over time as a result of investment by firms and the scrapping of worn-out or obsolete capital. However, because the capital stock is long-lived and has been built up over many years, new investment and the scrapping of old capital only slowly have a significant effect on the overall quantity of capital available. Thus, for analyses spanning only a few quarters or years, economists often treat the economy's capital stock as fixed. For now we follow this practice and assume a fixed capital stock. In taking up long-term economic growth in Chapter 6, we drop this assumption and examine how the capital stock evolves over time.

In contrast to the amount of capital, the amount of labor employed in the economy can change fairly quickly. For example, firms may lay off workers or ask them to work overtime without much notice. Workers may quit or decide to enter the work force quickly. Thus year-to-year changes in production often can be traced to changes in employment. To explain why employment changes, for the remainder of this chapter we focus on how the labor market works, using a supply and demand approach. In this section we look at labor demand, and in Section 3.3 we discuss factors affecting labor supply.

As a step toward understanding the overall demand for labor in the economy, we consider how an individual firm decides how many workers to employ. To keep things simple for the time being, we make the following assumptions:

1. *Workers are all alike.* We ignore differences in workers' aptitudes, skills, ambitions, and so on.
2. *Firms view the wages of the workers they hire as being determined in a competitive labor market and not set by the firms themselves.* For example, a competitive firm in Cleveland that wants to hire machinists knows that it must pay the going local wage for machinists if it wants to attract qualified workers. The firm then decides how many machinists to employ.
3. *In making the decision about how many workers to employ, a firm's goal is to earn the highest possible level of profit* (the value of its output minus its costs of production, including taxes). The firm will demand the amount of labor that maximizes its profit.

To figure out the profit-maximizing amount of labor, the firm must compare the costs and benefits of hiring each additional worker. The cost of an extra worker is the worker's wage, and the benefit of an extra worker is the value of the additional goods or services the worker produces. As long as the benefits of additional labor exceed the costs, hiring more labor will increase the firm's profits. The firm will continue to hire additional labor until the benefit of an extra worker (the value of extra goods or services produced) equals the cost (the wage).

The Marginal Product of Labor and Labor Demand: An Example

Let's make the discussion of labor demand more concrete by looking at The Clip Joint, a small business that grooms dogs. The Clip Joint uses both capital, such as clippers, tubs, and brushes, and labor to produce its output of groomed dogs.

The production function that applies to The Clip Joint appears in Table 3.2. For given levels of productivity and the capital stock, it shows how The Clip Joint's daily output of groomed dogs, column (2), depends on the number of workers employed, column (1). The more workers The Clip Joint has, the greater its daily output is.

Table 3.2

The Clip Joint's Production Function

(1) Number of workers, N	(2) Number of dogs groomed, Y	(3) Marginal product of labor, MPN	(4) Marginal revenue product of labor, $MRPN = MPN \times P$ (when $P = \$30$ per grooming)
0	0		
		11	$330
1	11		
		9	$270
2	20		
		7	$210
3	27		
		5	$150
4	32		
		3	$90
5	35		
		1	$30
6	36		

The MPN of each worker at The Clip Joint is shown in column (3). Employing the first worker raises The Clip Joint's output from 0 to 11, so the MPN of the first worker is 11. Employing the second worker raises The Clip Joint's output from 11 to 20, an increase of 9, so the MPN of the second worker is 9; and so on. Column (3) also shows that, as the number of workers at The Clip Joint increases, the MPN falls so that labor at The Clip Joint has diminishing marginal productivity. The more workers there are on the job, the more they must share the fixed amount of capital (tubs, clippers, brushes), and the less benefit there is to adding yet another worker.

The marginal product of labor measures the benefit of employing an additional worker in terms of the extra *output* produced. A related concept, the **marginal revenue product of labor**, or $MRPN$, measures the benefit of employing an additional worker in terms of the extra *revenue* produced. To calculate the $MRPN$, we need to know the price of the firm's output. If The Clip Joint receives $30 for each dog it grooms, the $MRPN$ of the first worker is $330 per day (11 additional dogs groomed per day at $30 per grooming). More generally, the marginal revenue product of an additional worker equals the price of the firm's output, P, times the extra output gained by adding the worker, MPN:

$$MRPN = P \times MPN. \tag{3.3}$$

At The Clip Joint the price of output, P, is $30 per grooming, so the $MRPN$ of each worker, column (4), equals the MPN of the worker, column (3), multiplied by $30.

Now suppose that the wage, W, that The Clip Joint must pay to attract qualified workers is $240 per day. (We refer to the wage, W, when measured in the conventional way in terms of today's dollars, as the *nominal wage*.) How many workers should The Clip Joint employ to maximize its profits? To answer this question, The Clip Joint compares the benefits and costs of employing each additional worker. The benefit of employing an additional worker, in dollars per day, is the worker's marginal revenue product, $MRPN$. The cost of an additional worker, in dollars per day, is the nominal daily wage, W.

Table 3.2 shows that the *MRPN* of the first worker is $330 per day, which exceeds the daily wage of $240, so employing the first worker is profitable for The Clip Joint. Adding a second worker increases The Clip Joint's profit as well because the *MRPN* of the second worker ($270 per day) also exceeds the daily wage. However, employing a third worker reduces The Clip Joint's profit because the third worker's *MRPN* of $210 per day is less than the $240 daily wage. Therefore, The Clip Joint's profit-maximizing level of employment at $240/day—equivalently, the quantity of labor demanded by The Clip Joint—is two workers.

In finding the quantity of labor demanded by The Clip Joint, we measured the benefits and costs of an extra worker in nominal, or dollar, terms. If we measure the benefits and costs of an extra worker in real terms, the results would be the same. In real terms the benefit to The Clip Joint of an extra worker is the number of extra groomings that the extra worker provides, which is the marginal product of labor, *MPN*. The real cost of adding another worker is the **real wage**, which is the wage measured in terms of units of output. Algebraically, the real wage, w, equals the nominal wage, W, divided by the price of output, P.

In this example the nominal wage, W, is $240 per day and the price of output, P, is $30 per grooming, so the real wage, w, equals ($240 per day)/($30 per grooming), or 8 groomings per day. To find the profit-maximizing level of employment, The Clip Joint compares this real cost of an additional worker with the real benefit of an additional worker, the *MPN*. The *MPN* of the first worker is 11 groomings per day, which exceeds the real wage of 8 groomings per day, so employing this worker is profitable. The second worker also should be hired, as the second worker's *MPN* of 9 groomings per day also exceeds the real wage of 8 groomings per day. However, a third worker should not be hired, as the third worker's *MPN* of 7 groomings per day is less than the real wage. The quantity of labor demanded by The Clip Joint is therefore two workers, which is the same result we got when we compared costs and benefits in nominal terms.

This example shows that, when the benefit of an additional worker exceeds the cost of an additional worker, the firm should increase employment so as to maximize profits. Similarly, if at the firm's current employment level the benefit of the last worker employed is less than the cost of the worker, the firm should reduce employment. For example, if The Clip Joint currently employed three workers, the *MRPN* of the third worker is $210, which is less than the nominal wage of $240, so the firm should fire one worker. Summary table 2 compares benefits and costs of additional labor in both real and nominal terms. In the choice of the profit-maximizing level of employment, a comparison of benefits and costs in either real or nominal terms is equally valid.

A Change in the Wage

The Clip Joint's decision to employ two workers was based on a nominal wage of $240 per day. Now suppose that for some reason the nominal wage needed to attract qualified workers drops to $180 per day. How will the reduction in the nominal wage affect the number of workers that The Clip Joint wants to employ?

To find the answer, we can compare costs and benefits in either nominal or real terms. Let's make the comparison in real terms. If the nominal wage drops to $180 per day while the price of groomings remains at $30, the real wage falls to ($180 per day)/($30 per grooming), or 6 groomings per day. Column (3) of

Table 3.2 shows that the *MPN* of the third worker is 7 groomings per day, which is now greater than the real wage. Thus, at the lower wage, expanding the quantity of labor demanded from two to three workers is profitable for The Clip Joint. However, the firm will not hire a fourth worker because the *MPN* of the fourth worker (5 groomings per day) is less than the new real wage (6 groomings per day).

This example illustrates a general point about the effect of the real wage on labor demand: All else being equal, *a decrease in the real wage raises the amount of labor demanded.* Similarly, *an increase in the real wage decreases the amount of labor demanded.*

The Marginal Product of Labor and the Labor Demand Curve

Using The Clip Joint as an example, we showed the negative relationship between the real wage and the quantity of labor that a firm demands. Figure 3.5 shows in more general terms how the link between the real wage and the quantity of labor demanded is determined. The amount of labor, *N*, is on the horizontal axis. The *MPN* and the real wage, both of which are measured in goods per unit of labor, are on the vertical axis. The downward-sloping curve is the *MPN* curve; it relates the marginal product of labor, *MPN*, to the amount of labor employed by the firm, *N*. The *MPN* curve slopes downward because of the diminishing marginal productivity of labor. The horizontal line represents the real wage firms face in the labor market, which the firms take as given. Here, the real wage is w^*.

For any real wage, w^*, the amount of labor that yields the highest profit (and therefore the amount of labor demanded) is determined at point *A*, the intersection of the real-wage line and the *MPN* curve. At *A* the quantity of labor demanded is N^*. Why is N^* a firm's profit-maximizing level of labor input? At employment levels less than N^*, the marginal product of labor exceeds the real wage (the *MPN* curve lies above the real-wage line); thus, if the firm's employment is initially less than N^*, it can increase its profit by expanding the amount of labor it uses. Similarly, if the firm's employment is initially greater

SUMMARY 2

Comparing the Benefits and Costs of Changing the Amount of Labor

To maximize profits, the firm should:	Increase employment if, for an additional worker	Decrease employment if, for the last worker employed
Real terms	$MPN > w$ $(MPN > W/P)$	$MPN < w$ $(MPN < W/P)$
Nominal terms	$P \times MPN > W$ $(MRPN > W)$	$P \times MPN < W$ $(MRPN < W)$

MPN = marginal product of labor
P = price of output
$MRPN$ = marginal revenue product of labor = $P \times MPN$
W = nominal wage
w = real wage = W/P

Figure 3.5

The determination of labor demand
The amount of labor demanded is determined by locating the point on the *MPN* curve at which the *MPN* equals the real wage rate; the amount of labor corresponding to that point is the amount of labor demanded. For example, when the real wage is w^*, the *MPN* equals the real wage at point A and the quantity of labor demanded is N^*. The labor demand curve, *ND*, shows the amount of labor demanded at each level of the real wage. The labor demand curve is identical to the *MPN* curve.

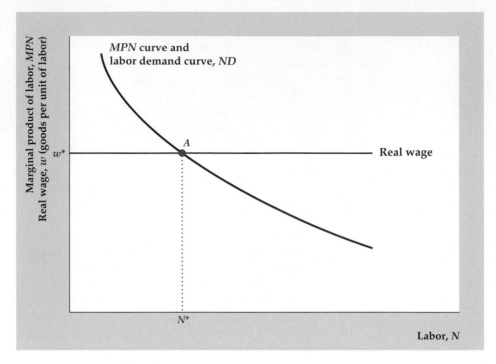

than N^*, the marginal product of labor is less than the real wage ($MPN < w^*$) and the firm can raise profits by reducing employment. Only when employment equals N^* will the firm be satisfied with the number of workers it has. More generally, for any real wage, the profit-maximizing amount of labor input—labor demanded—corresponds to the point at which the *MPN* curve and the real-wage line intersect.

The graph of the relationship between the amount of labor demanded by a firm and the real wage that the firm faces is called the *labor demand curve*. Because the *MPN* curve also shows the amount of labor demanded at any real wage, *the labor demand curve is the same as the MPN curve,* except that the vertical axis measures the real wage for the labor demand curve and measures the marginal product of labor for the *MPN* curve.[9] Like the *MPN* curve, the labor demand curve slopes downward, indicating that the quantity of labor demanded falls as the real wage rises.

This labor demand curve is more general than that in the example of The Clip Joint in a couple of ways that are worth mentioning. First, we referred to the demand for labor and not specifically to the demand for workers, as in The Clip Joint example. In general, labor, N, can be measured in various ways—for example, as total hours worked, total weeks worked, or the number of employees—depending on the application. Second, although we assumed in the example that The Clip Joint had to hire a whole number of workers, the labor demand curve shown in Fig. 3.5 allows labor, N, to have any positive value, whole or fractional. Allowing N to take any value is sensible because people may work fractions of an hour.

---

[9]Recall that the real wage and the *MPN* are measured in the same units, goods per unit of labor.

Factors That Shift the Labor Demand Curve

Because the labor demand curve shows the relation between the real wage and the amount of labor that firms want to employ, changes in the real wage are represented as movements *along* the labor demand curve. Changes in the real wage do not cause the labor demand curve to shift. The labor demand curve shifts in response to factors that change the amount of labor that firms want to employ *at any given level of the real wage.* For example, we showed earlier in this chapter that beneficial, or positive, supply shocks are likely to increase the *MPN* at all levels of labor input and that adverse, or negative, supply shocks are likely to reduce the *MPN* at all levels of labor input. Thus a beneficial supply shock shifts the *MPN* curve upward and to the right and raises the quantity of labor demanded at any given real wage; an adverse supply shock does the reverse.

The effect of a supply shock on The Clip Joint's demand for labor can be illustrated by imagining that the proprietor of The Clip Joint discovers that playing New Age music soothes the dogs. It makes them more cooperative and doubles the number of groomings per day that the same number of workers can produce. This technological improvement gives The Clip Joint a new production function, as described in Table 3.3. Note that doubling total output doubles the *MPN* at each employment level.

The Clip Joint demanded two workers when faced with the original production function (Table 3.2) and a real wage of 8 groomings per day. Table 3.3 shows that the productivity improvement increases The Clip Joint's labor demand at the given real wage to four workers, because the *MPN* of the fourth worker (10 groomings per day) now exceeds the real wage. The Clip Joint will not hire a fifth worker, however, because this worker's *MPN* (6 groomings per day) is less than the real wage.

The effect of a beneficial supply shock on the labor demand curve is shown in Fig. 3.6. The shock causes the *MPN* to increase at any level of labor input, so the *MPN* curve shifts upward and to the right. Because the *MPN* and labor demand

Table 3.3

The Clip Joint's Production Function After a Beneficial Productivity Shock

(1) Number of workers, N	(2) Number of dogs groomed, Y	(3) Marginal product of labor, MPN	(4) Marginal revenue product of labor, $MRPN = MPN \times P$ (when $P = \$30$ per grooming)
0	0		
		22	$660
1	22		
		18	$540
2	40		
		14	$420
3	54		
		10	$300
4	64		
		6	$180
5	70		
		2	$60
6	72		

Figure 3.6

The effect of a beneficial supply shock on labor demand
A beneficial supply shock that raises the *MPN* at every level of labor shifts the *MPN* curve upward and to the right. Because the labor demand curve is identical to the *MPN* curve, the labor demand curve shifts upward and to the right from ND^1 to ND^2. For any real wage, firms demand more labor after a beneficial supply shock.

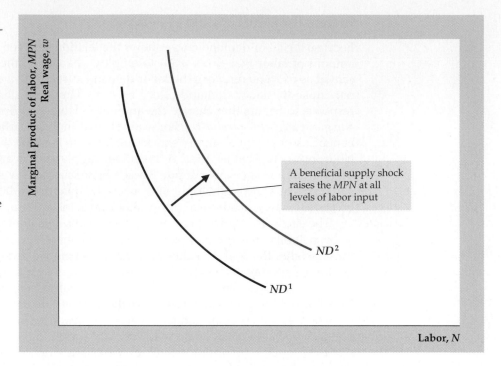

A beneficial supply shock raises the *MPN* at all levels of labor input

curves are identical, the labor demand curve also shifts upward and to the right, from ND^1 to ND^2 in Fig. 3.6. When the labor demand curve is ND^2, the firm hires more workers at any real wage level than when the labor demand curve is ND^1. Thus worker productivity and the amount of labor demanded are closely linked.

Another factor that may affect labor demand is the size of the capital stock. Generally, an increase in the capital stock, K—by giving each worker more machines or equipment to work with—raises workers' productivity and increases the *MPN* at any level of labor. Hence an increase in the capital stock will cause the labor demand curve to shift upward and to the right, raising the amount of labor that a firm demands at any particular real wage.[10]

SUMMARY 3

Factors That Shift the Aggregate Labor Demand Curve

An increase in	Causes the labor demand curve to shift	Reason
Productivity	Right	Beneficial supply shock increases MPN and shifts MPN curve up and to the right.
Capital stock	Right	Higher capital stock increases MPN and shifts MPN curve up and to the right.

[10]An increase in the capital stock may reduce the demand for labor if the new capital substitutes for the use of labor. For example, the installation of automatic tollbooths has reduced the marginal product of toll takers and thus the demand for these workers.

Aggregate Labor Demand

So far we have focused on the demand for labor by an individual firm, such as The Clip Joint. For macroeconomic analysis, however, we usually work with the concept of the **aggregate demand for labor,** or the sum of the labor demands of all the firms in an economy.

Because the aggregate demand for labor is the sum of firms' labor demands, the factors that determine the aggregate demand for labor are the same as those for an individual firm. Thus the aggregate labor demand curve looks the same as the labor demand curve for an individual firm (Fig. 3.5). Like the firm's labor demand curve, the aggregate labor demand curve slopes downward, showing that an increase in the economywide real wage reduces the total amount of labor that firms want to use. Similarly, a beneficial supply shock or an increase in the aggregate capital stock shifts the aggregate labor demand curve upward and to the right; an adverse supply shock or a drop in the aggregate capital stock shifts it downward and to the left. The factors affecting aggregate labor demand are listed for convenience in Summary table 3.

3.3 The Supply of Labor

The demand for labor is determined by firms, but the supply of labor is determined by individuals or members of a family making a joint decision. Each person of working age must decide how much (if at all) to work in the wage-paying sector of the economy versus non-wage-paying alternatives, such as taking care of the home and children, going to school, or being retired. The **aggregate supply of labor** is the sum of the labor supplied by everyone in the economy.

Recall that, in determining how much labor to demand, firms compare the costs and benefits of hiring additional workers. Similarly, in deciding how much to work, an individual should weigh the benefits against the costs of working. Beyond any psychological satisfaction gained from having a job, the principal benefit of working is the income earned, which can be used to buy necessities and luxuries. The principal cost of working is that it involves time and effort that are no longer available for other activities. Economists use the term **leisure**[11] for all off-the-job activities, including eating, sleeping, working around the house, spending time with family and friends, and so on. To make themselves as well off as possible, individuals should choose to supply labor up to the point at which the income obtained from working an extra hour just makes up for the extra hour of leisure they have to forgo.

The Income–Leisure Trade-Off

To illustrate how the trade-off between income and leisure affects the labor supply decision, let's look at an example. Consider a tennis instructor named Ace who offers tennis lessons. After paying taxes and job-related expenses, Ace can earn $60 per hour, which we will call his (after-tax) nominal wage rate. Ace enjoys

---

[11]The term *leisure* does not imply that all off-the-job activities (housework or schoolwork, for example) are "leisurely"!

a reputation as an outstanding tennis instructor and could work as many hours per year as he chooses. He is reluctant to work too much, however, because every day he spends teaching tennis means one less day available to devote to his real passion, skydiving. The decision Ace faces is how many hours to work this year—or, in other words, how much labor to supply.

Ace approaches this question by asking himself: Economically speaking, what really makes me happy? After a little reflection, Ace concludes that his level of happiness, or *utility,* depends on the amount of goods and services he consumes and on the amount of leisure time he has available to jump out of airplanes. His question can therefore be recast as follows: How much should I work this year so as to obtain the highest possible level of utility?

To find the level of labor supply that maximizes his utility, Ace must compare the costs and benefits of working an extra hour. The cost of an extra hour of work is the loss of an hour of leisure; this cost can be measured as the loss in utility that Ace experiences when he must work for an hour instead of skydive. The benefit of working an extra hour is an increase of $60 in income, which allows Ace to enjoy more consumption.

If the benefit of working an extra hour (the utility gained from extra income) exceeds the cost (the utility lost by reducing leisure), Ace should work the extra hour. In fact, he should continue to increase his time at work until the utility he receives from the additional income of $60 just equals the loss of utility associated with missing an hour of leisure. Ace's labor supply at that point is the one that maximizes his utility.[12] Using the idea that the labor supply decision results from a trade-off of leisure against income, we can discuss factors that influence the amount of labor supplied by Ace.

Real Wages and Labor Supply

The real wage is the amount of real income that a worker receives in exchange for giving up a unit of leisure (an hour, a day, or a week, for example) for work. It is an important determinant of the quantity of labor that is supplied.

Generally, an increase in the real wage affects the labor supply decision in two ways. First, an increase in the real wage raises the benefit (in terms of additional real income) of working an additional hour and thus tends to make the worker want to supply more labor. The tendency of workers to supply more labor in response to a higher reward for working is called the **substitution effect of a higher real wage** on the quantity of labor supplied.

Second, an increase in the real wage makes workers effectively wealthier because for the same amount of work they now earn a higher real income. Someone who is wealthier will be better able to afford additional leisure and, as a result, will supply less labor. The tendency of workers to supply less labor in response to becoming wealthier is called the **income effect of a higher real wage** on the quantity of labor supplied. Note that the substitution and income effects of a higher real wage operate in opposite directions, with the substitution effect tending to raise the quantity of labor supplied and the income effect tending to reduce it.

---

[12]Not everyone can choose his or her labor supply as flexibly as Ace; for example, some jobs are available for forty hours a week or not at all. Nevertheless, by choosing to work overtime, part-time, or at a second job, or by varying the number of family members who are working, households do have a significant amount of latitude over how much labor to supply.

A Pure Substitution Effect: A One-Day Rise in the Real Wage.   We can illustrate the substitution effect by supposing that, after some consideration, Ace decides to work forty-eight hours per week, by working eight hours per day for six days each week. He leaves every Wednesday free to go skydiving. Although Ace could work and earn $60 per hour each Wednesday, his highest utility is obtained by taking leisure on that day instead.

Now imagine that one Tuesday, an eccentric tennis player calls Ace and requests a lesson on Wednesday to help him prepare for a weekend amateur tournament. He offers Ace his regular wage of $60 per hour, but Ace declines, explaining that he plans to go skydiving on Wednesday. Not willing to take "no" for an answer, the tennis player then offers to pay Ace $600 per hour for an all-day lesson on Wednesday. When Ace hears this offer to work for ten times his usual wage rate, he thinks: "I don't get offers like this one every day. I'll go skydiving some other day, but this Wednesday I'm going to work."

Ace's decision to work rather than skydive (that is, to substitute labor for leisure) on this particular Wednesday represents a response to a very high reward, in terms of additional income, that each additional hour of work on that day will bring. His decision to work the extra day results from the substitution effect. Because receiving a very high wage for only one day doesn't make Ace substantially wealthier, the income effect of the one-day wage increase is negligible. Thus the effect of a one-day increase in the real wage on the quantity of labor supplied by Ace is an almost pure example of the substitution effect.

A Pure Income Effect: Winning the Lottery.   In addition to skydiving, Ace enjoys playing the state lottery. As luck would have it, a week after spending the Wednesday teaching the eccentric tennis player, Ace wins $300,000 in the state lottery. Ace's response is to reduce his workweek from six to five days, because the additional $300,000 of wealth enables him to afford to take more time off from work—and so he does. Because the lottery prize has made him wealthier, he reduces his labor supply. As the lottery prize does not affect the current reward for giving up an hour of leisure to work—Ace's wage is still $60 per hour—there is no substitution effect. Thus, winning the lottery is an example of a pure income effect.

Another example of a pure income effect is an increase in the expected future real wage. Suppose that the aging tennis pro at the posh country club in Ace's community announces that he will retire the following year, and the country club agrees to hire Ace beginning one year from now. Ace will earn $100 per hour (after taxes) for as many hours as he wants to teach tennis.[13] Ace recognizes that this increase in his future wage has effectively made him wealthier by increasing the future income he will receive for any given amount of labor supplied in the future. Looking at his lifetime income, Ace realizes that he is better able to afford leisure today. That is, the increase in the future real wage has an income effect that leads Ace to reduce his current labor supply. Because this increase in the future wage does not change Ace's current wage, and thus does not affect the current reward for giving up an hour of leisure to work an additional hour, there is no substitution effect on Ace's current labor supply. Thus the increase in the future real wage has a pure income effect on Ace's labor supply.

---

[13]We assume that zero inflation is expected over the next year, so the $100 per hour wage rate in the following year is an increase in Ace's real wage rate as well as an increase in his nominal wage rate.

The Substitution Effect and the Income Effect Together: A Long-Term Increase in the Real Wage.   The aging tennis pro at the country club quits suddenly, and the country club asks Ace to start work immediately. Ace accepts the offer and earns $100 per hour (after taxes) for as many hours as he wants to teach tennis.

On his new job, will Ace work more hours or fewer hours than he did before? In this case, the two effects work in opposite directions. On the one hand, because the reward for working is greater, Ace will be tempted to work more than he did previously. This tendency to increase labor supply in response to a higher real wage is the substitution effect. On the other hand, at his new, higher wage, Ace can pay for food, rent, and skydiving expenses by working only three or four days each week, so he is tempted to work less and spend more time skydiving. This tendency to reduce labor supply because he is wealthier is the income effect.

Which effect wins? One factor that will influence Ace's decision is the length of time he expects his new, higher wage to last. The longer the higher wage is expected to last, the larger its impact on Ace's lifetime resources is, and the stronger the income effect is. Thus, if Ace expects to hold the new job until he retires, the income effect is strong (he is much wealthier) and he is more likely to reduce the amount of time that he works. In contrast, if Ace believes that the job may not last very long, the income effect is weak (the increase in his lifetime resources is small) and he may choose to work more so as to take advantage of the higher wage while he can. In general, the longer an increase in the real wage is expected to last, the larger the income effect is and the more likely it is that the quantity of labor supplied will be reduced.

Empirical Evidence on Real Wages and Labor Supply.   Because of conflicting income and substitution effects, some ambiguity exists regarding how a change in the real wage will affect labor supply. What is the empirical evidence?

Research on labor supply generally shows that the aggregate amount of labor supplied rises in response to a temporary increase in the real wage but falls in response to a permanent increase in the real wage.[14] The finding that a temporary increase in the real wage raises the amount of labor supplied confirms the substitution effect: If the reward for working rises for a short period, people will take advantage of the opportunity to work more. The result that a permanent increase in the real wage lowers the aggregate amount of labor supplied indicates that for long-lived increases in the real wage, the income effect outweighs the substitution effect: If permanently higher wages make workers much better off, they will choose to work less. The size of these effects depends on a person's family situation (married or not and whether the family has children) and the tax rate (which determines how much income can be kept after taxes are paid).

The Labor Supply Curve

We have discussed how the amount of labor supplied by an individual depends on the current and expected future real wage rates. The *labor supply curve* of an individual relates the amount of labor supplied to the current real wage rate, holding

---

[14]For a detailed review of research on labor supply, see the article by Richard Blundell and Thomas MaCurdy, "Labor Supply: A Review of Alternative Approaches," in O. Ashenfelter and D. Card, eds., *Handbook of Labor Economics*, volume 3 (Amsterdam: North-Holland, 1999), pp. 1559–1695.

Figure 3.7

The labor supply curve of an individual worker
The horizontal axis shows the amount of labor that a worker will supply for any given current real wage on the vertical axis. The labor supply curve slopes upward, indicating that—with other factors, including the expected future real wage, held constant—an increase in the current real wage raises the amount of labor supplied.

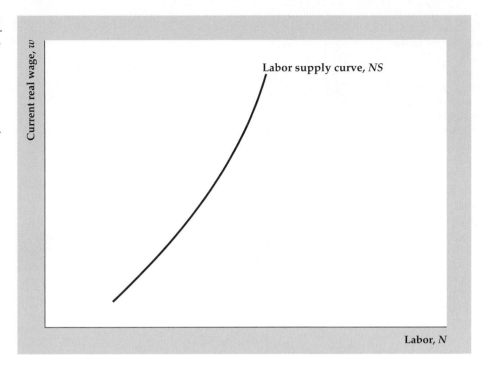

constant all other factors (including the expected future real wage rate) that affect the amount of labor supplied. Figure 3.7 presents a graph of a typical labor supply curve. The current real wage is measured on the vertical axis, and the amount of labor supplied is measured on the horizontal axis. The labor supply curve slopes upward because an increase in the current real wage (holding constant the expected future real wage) leads to an increase in the amount of labor supplied.

Factors That Shift the Labor Supply Curve.   Any factor that changes the amount of labor supplied at a given level of the current real wage shifts the labor supply curve. Specifically, any factor that increases the amount of labor supplied at a given level of the real wage shifts the labor supply curve to the right, and any factor that decreases the amount of labor supplied at a given real wage shifts the labor supply curve to the left. We have already discussed how an increase in wealth (say, from winning the lottery) has a pure income effect that reduces the amount of labor supplied at a given real wage. Thus, as shown in Fig. 3.8, an increase in wealth shifts the labor supply curve to the left. We have also discussed how an increase in the expected future real wage has a pure income effect that reduces the amount of labor supplied at a given real wage. Figure 3.8 also depicts the response of the labor supply curve to an increase in the expected future real wage.

Aggregate Labor Supply

As we mentioned earlier, the aggregate supply of labor is the total amount of labor supplied by everyone in the economy. Just as the quantity of labor supplied by an individual rises when the person's current real wage rises, the aggregate quantity of labor supplied increases when the economywide real wage rises. An increase in

Figure 3.8

The effect on labor supply of an increase in wealth

An increase in wealth reduces the amount of labor supplied at any real wage. Therefore an increase in wealth causes the labor supply curve to shift to the left. Similarly, an increase in the expected future real wage, which has the effect of making the worker wealthier, reduces the amount of labor supplied at any given current real wage and shifts the labor supply curve to the left.

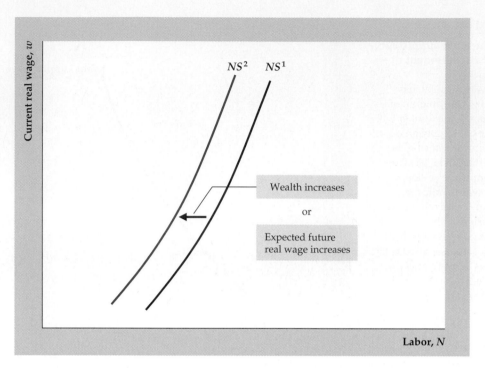

the current economywide real wage raises the aggregate quantity of labor supplied for two reasons. First, when the real wage rises, people who are already working may supply even more hours—by offering to work overtime, by changing from part-time to full-time work, or by taking a second job. Second, a higher real wage may entice some people who are not currently in the labor force to decide to look for work. Because higher current real wages induce people to want to work more, the aggregate labor supply curve—which shows the relation between the aggregate amount of labor supplied and the current real wage—slopes upward.

Factors other than the current real wage that change the amount of labor that people want to supply cause the aggregate labor supply curve to shift. Summary

SUMMARY 4

Factors That Shift the Aggregate Labor Supply Curve

An increase in	Causes the labor supply curve to shift	Reason
Wealth	Left	Increase in wealth increases amount of leisure workers can afford.
Expected future real wage	Left	Increase in expected future real wage increases amount of leisure workers can afford.
Working-age population	Right	Increased number of potential workers increases amount of labor supplied.
Participation rate	Right	Increased number of people wanting to work increases amount of labor supplied.

APPLICATION

Comparing U.S. and European Labor Markets

Most of our discussion in this chapter relates to the labor market in the United States, but the same theory and analysis apply to other countries. Although the theory is the same, there are many differences in labor market institutions and government policy between the United States and other countries. In this application, we compare U.S. and European labor markets.

Economists have studied Europe's labor markets with particular interest in the past decade because unemployment rates in the United States and Europe were similar in the 1970s and early 1980s but have diverged since then. In the 1990s, the unemployment rate fell to a low level in the United States but rose to high levels in several European countries, as Fig. 3.9 illustrates. Even in 2008, during a recession, the U.S. unemployment rate of 5.8% was well below the rates of most countries in Europe. Why has the U.S. labor market performed so well while most European labor markets have stagnated?

Research has suggested several possible reasons for high unemployment in Europe. These include generous unemployment insurance systems, high income tax rates, and government policies that interfere with labor markets. We consider these possible factors in turn.

European countries generally have more generous unemployment insurance systems than the United States. For one thing, the replacement rate—the fraction of lost wages a worker receives as unemployment payments—is higher in Europe than in the United States. Also, unemployed European workers can receive unemployment payments for a longer period than can unemployed U.S. workers. As a result, unemployed workers have a strong incentive to remain unemployed longer in Europe, and so the unemployment rate is higher.

Some economists have challenged the view that Europe's generous unemployment benefits have caused the high unemployment. They point out that Europe has

Figure 3.9

Unemployment rates in the United States and Europe, 1982–2008 Unemployment rates in Germany, Italy, and France rose in the 1990s, while the U.S. rate declined. Spain's unemployment rate has historically been higher than rates in the other countries shown. The question is, why are unemployment rates in Europe so high relative to the United States?

Source: OECD Factbook 2009, Harmonised Unemployment Rates.

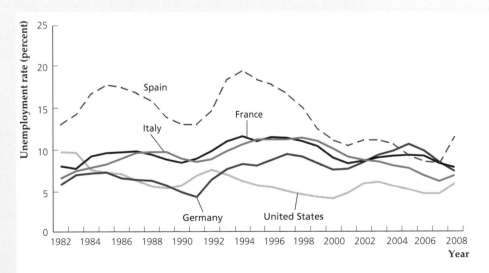

(continued)

had generous unemployment benefits for many decades, but that the high unemployment rates (relative to U.S. rates) began only in the mid-1980s for most countries. However, according to Lars Ljungqvist and Thomas Sargent, European unemployment was lower in earlier decades because the economy was tranquil in the 1950s to 1970s, before becoming much more turbulent in the 1980s and 1990s.[15] Although there had been no need to do so in earlier decades, workers took advantage of the system of unemployment benefits as the chances of losing a job increased.

A country that reforms its unemployment benefits system can bring its unemployment rate down substantially. Two cases in point are Ireland and the Netherlands. Both countries engaged in major reforms in the 1990s, substantially reducing the generosity of unemployment benefits.[16] Ireland's unemployment rate declined from 15.6% in 1993 to 4.3% in 2005, while the Netherlands' unemployment rate fell from 7.7% in 1982 to 2.2% in 2001.

In Ireland and the Netherlands, however, reform of the unemployment benefits system was not the only change. Ireland reduced income tax rates, and the Netherlands reduced government restrictions on part-time work.

Recall now that some economists think that it is the high income tax rates in most European countries that largely explain Europe's weak labor markets. Notable in this group is Nobel laureate Edward Prescott. High income tax rates, Prescott points out, give people little incentive to work.[17] Prescott suggests that differences in tax rates are the main reason why Americans work so much relative to Europeans: Americans get to keep more of what they earn and give less to the government.

Also recall that other researchers have emphasized government meddling in labor markets as a factor in Europe's high unemployment. Governments in Europe generally do interfere more in labor markets than is the case in the United States. For example, some European countries restrict firms' ability to fire workers. This restriction causes labor supply to shift to the right and labor demand to shift to the left. As we will consider in Chapter 11, when this happens and when wages cannot decline to clear the labor market, unemployment increases. European governments have interfered in the labor market in other ways as well. The Netherlands' government, for example, restricted part-time work. When the government loosened those restrictions beginning in 1982, many more women immediately entered the labor force than before, and the unemployment rate of women fell dramatically because labor demand increased even more than labor supply.

Thus, there is significant evidence that unemployment rates are high in Europe relative to the United States because of generous unemployment benefits, high tax rates, and laws that restrict part-time work. Countries that have removed these impediments to the labor market have experienced lower unemployment rates. For example, in 2008, the unemployment rate in the Netherlands was significantly lower than the unemployment rate in the United States, whereas the opposite was true for most other European countries.

---

[15]"A Supply-Side Explanation of European Unemployment," Federal Reserve Bank of Chicago, *Economic Perspectives* (September 1996), pp. 2–15.

[16]See the article by Cédric Tille and Kei-Mu Yi, "Curbing Unemployment in Europe: Are There Lessons from Ireland and the Netherlands?" Federal Reserve Bank of New York, *Current Issues in Economics and Finance* (May 2001).

[17]See Edward C. Prescott, "Why Do Americans Work So Much More Than Europeans?" Federal Reserve Bank of Minneapolis, *Quarterly Review* (July 2004), pp. 2–13.

table 4 lists the factors that shift aggregate labor supply. We have discussed the first two factors in the table, wealth and the expected future real wage. Aggregate labor supply will also increase if the country's working-age population increases (for example, because of an increased birth rate or immigration), or if changes in the social or legal environment cause a greater proportion of the working-age population to enter the labor force (increased labor force participation). For example, evolving attitudes about the role of women in society contributed to a large increase in the number of women in the U.S. labor market from the late 1960s to the mid-1990s; and the elimination of mandatory retirement in many fields may increase the participation rates of older workers.

3.4 Labor Market Equilibrium

Equilibrium in the labor market requires that the aggregate quantity of labor demanded equal the aggregate quantity of labor supplied. The basic supply–demand model of the labor market introduced here (called the *classical model of the labor market*) is based on the assumption that the real wage adjusts reasonably quickly to equate labor supply and labor demand. Thus, if labor supply is less than labor demand, firms competing for scarce workers bid up the real wage, whereas if many workers are competing for relatively few jobs, the real wage will tend to fall.

Labor market equilibrium is represented graphically by the intersection of the aggregate labor demand curve and the aggregate labor supply curve at point E in Fig. 3.10. The equilibrium level of employment, achieved after the complete adjustment of wages and prices, is known as the **full-employment level of employment**, $\bar{N}$. The corresponding market-clearing real wage is $\bar{w}$.

Figure 3.10

Labor market equilibrium
The quantity of labor demanded equals the quantity of labor supplied at point E. The equilibrium real wage is w, and the corresponding equilibrium level of employment is $\bar{N}$, the full-employment level of employment.

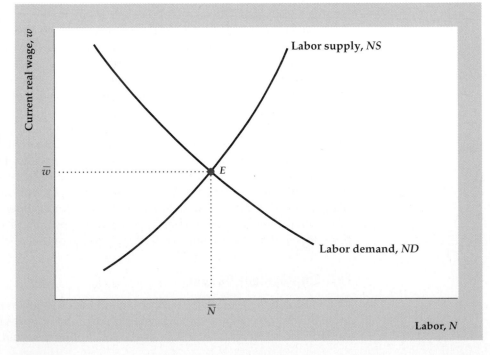

Figure 3.11

Effects of a temporary adverse supply shock on the labor market
An adverse supply shock that lowers the marginal product of labor (see Fig. 3.4) reduces the quantity of labor demanded at any real wage level. Thus the labor demand curve shifts left, from ND^1 to ND^2, and the labor market equilibrium moves from point A to point B. The adverse supply shock causes the real wage to fall from $\overline{w}_1$ to $\overline{w}_2$ and reduces the full-employment level of employment from $\overline{N}_1$ to $\overline{N}_2$.

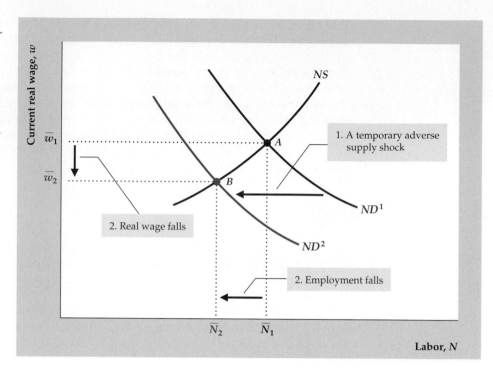

Factors that shift either the aggregate labor demand curve or the aggregate labor supply curve affect both the equilibrium real wage and the full-employment level of employment. An example of such a factor is a temporary adverse supply shock. A temporary adverse supply shock—because of, say, a spell of unusually bad weather—decreases the marginal product of labor at every level of employment. As Fig. 3.11 shows, this decrease causes the labor demand curve to shift to the left, from ND^1 to ND^2. Because the supply shock is temporary, however, it is not expected to affect future marginal products or the future real wage, so the labor supply curve doesn't shift. Equilibrium in the labor market moves from point A to point B. Thus the model predicts that a temporary supply shock will lower both the current real wage (from $\overline{w}_1$ to $\overline{w}_2$) and the full-employment level of employment (from $\overline{N}_1$ to $\overline{N}_2$).

The classical supply–demand model of the labor market has the virtue of simplicity and is quite useful for studying how economic disturbances or changes in economic policy affect employment and the real wage. However, a significant drawback of this basic model is that it cannot be used to study unemployment. Because it assumes that any worker who wants to work at the equilibrium real wage can find a job, the model implies zero unemployment, which never occurs. We discuss unemployment later in this chapter, but in the meantime we will continue to use the classical supply–demand model of the labor market.

Full-Employment Output

By combining labor market equilibrium and the production function, we can determine the amount of output that firms want to supply. **Full-employment output**, $\overline{Y}$, sometimes called *potential output*, is the level of output that firms in the economy supply when wages and prices have fully adjusted. Equivalently, full-employment output is the level of output supplied when aggregate employment equals its full-employment level, $\overline{N}$. Algebraically, we define full-employment output, $\overline{Y}$, by using the production function (Eq. 3.1):

$$\overline{Y} = AF(K, \overline{N}). \tag{3.4}$$

Equation (3.4) shows that, for constant capital stock, K, full-employment output is determined by two general factors: the full-employment level of employment, $\overline{N}$, and the production function relating output to employment.

Anything that changes either the full-employment level of employment, $\overline{N}$, or the production function will change full-employment output, $\overline{Y}$. For example, an adverse supply shock that reduces the MPN (Fig. 3.11) works in two distinct ways to lower full-employment output:

1. The adverse supply shock lowers output directly, by reducing the quantity of output that can be produced with any fixed amounts of capital and labor. This direct effect can be thought of as a reduction in the productivity measure A in Eq. (3.4).

2. The adverse supply shock reduces the demand for labor and thus lowers the full-employment level of employment $\overline{N}$, as Fig. 3.11 shows. A reduction in $\overline{N}$ also reduces full-employment output, $\overline{Y}$, as Eq. (3.4) confirms.

APPLICATION

Output, Employment, and the Real Wage During Oil Price Shocks

Among the most severe supply shocks hitting the U.S. and world economies since World War II were sharp increases in the prices of oil and other energy products. Figure 3.12 shows how the price of energy paid by firms, measured relative to the GDP deflator (the general price level of all output), varied during the period 1960–2008. Three adverse oil price shocks stand out: one in 1973–1974, when the Organization of Petroleum Exporting Countries (OPEC) first imposed an oil embargo and then greatly increased crude oil prices; a second in 1979–1980, after the Iranian revolution disrupted oil supplies; and a third in 2003–2008, when surging demand for oil by large rapidly developing countries such as China and India, combined with weak supply (because of insufficient production capacity, hurricanes that damaged Gulf of Mexico production, and geopolitical concerns in the Middle East, Russia, Venezuela, and Nigeria) caused the price of oil to rise sharply. The 1979–1980 oil price shock turned out to be temporary, as energy prices subsequently fell. The increase in oil prices following Iraq's invasion of Kuwait in August 1990 had less of an impact on overall energy prices than the three oil price shocks mentioned above and thus doesn't appear as much more than a blip in Fig. 3.12.

When a reduction or disruption in the supply of oil causes energy prices to rise, firms cut back on energy use, implying that less output is produced at any particular levels of capital and labor, which is an adverse supply shock. How large is the effect on GDP from an oil price shock? It is difficult to disentangle everything else going on in the economy when such a shock occurs, and the outcome depends on the government's policy response. But empirical research suggests that an increase

Figure 3.12

Relative price of energy, 1960–2008

The figure shows the producer price index of fuels and related products and power (an index of energy prices paid by producers) relative to the GDP deflator. Note the impact of the 1973–1974, 1979–1980, and 2003–2008 oil shocks and the decline in energy prices in the first half of the 1980s.

Sources: Producer price index for fuels and related products and power from *research.stlouisfed.org/fred2/series/PPIENG*; GDP deflator from *research.stlouisfed.org/fred2/GDPDEF*. Data were scaled so that the relative price of energy equals 100 in year 2000.

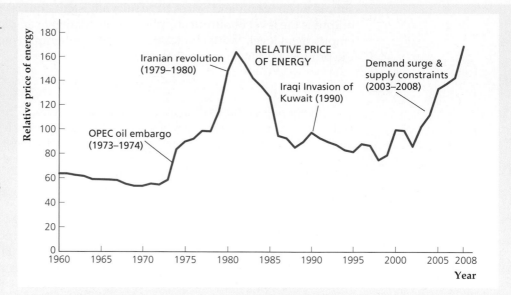

of 10% in the price of oil reduces GDP by about 0.4 percentage points.[18] Thus the 96% increase in oil prices from 2002 to 2008 leads GDP to be about 3.8% lower than it would have been in the absence of the increase in oil prices.

Our analysis predicts that an adverse supply shock will lower labor demand, reducing employment and the real wage, as well as reducing the supply of output. In fact, the economy went into recession, with negative GDP growth, following the increases in oil prices resulting from restrictions in the supply of oil in 1973-1974, 1979–1980, and 1990. In each case, employment and the real wage fell. Care must be taken in interpreting these results because macroeconomic policies and other factors were changing at the same time; however, our model appears to account for the response of the economy to these major oil price increases.

---

[18]See Charles T. Carlstrom and Timothy S. Fuerst, "Oil Prices, Monetary Policy, and the Macroeconomy," Federal Reserve Bank of Cleveland, *Economic Commentary* (July 2005), and John Fernald and Bharat Trehan, "Why Hasn't the Jump in Oil Prices Led to a Recession?" Federal Reserve Bank of San Francisco, *Economic Letter*, Number 2005-31, November 18, 2005.

3.5 Unemployment

Our classical model of the labor market, which relies on supply–demand analysis, is useful for studying the wage rate and the level of employment in an economy and for showing how these variables are linked to output and productivity. However, this model of the labor market is based on the strong assumption that, when the labor market is in equilibrium, all workers who are willing to work at the prevailing wage are able to find jobs. In reality, of course, not everyone who would like to work has a job; there is always some unemployment. The existence of unemployment implies that, at any time, not all of society's labor resources are actively involved in producing goods and services.

We discuss the problem of unemployment several times in this book, notably in Chapter 12. Here we introduce the topic by presenting some basic facts about unemployment and then turning to a preliminary economic analysis of it.

Measuring Unemployment

To estimate the unemployment rate in the United States, each month the Bureau of Labor Statistics (BLS) surveys about 60,000 households. Each person over age 16 in the surveyed households is assigned to one of three categories:

1. *employed*, if the person worked full-time or part-time during the past week (or was on sick leave or vacation from a job);
2. *unemployed*, if the person didn't work during the past week but looked for work during the past four weeks; or
3. *not in the labor force*, if the person didn't work during the past week and didn't look for work during the past four weeks (examples are full-time students, homemakers, and retirees).

Table 3.4 shows the number of people in each category in June 2009. (Good sources for these and other data about the labor market are described in "In Touch with Data and Research: Labor Market Data," p. 88.) In that month there were 140.2 million employed and 14.7 million unemployed workers. The **labor force** consists of all employed and unemployed workers, so in June 2009 it totaled 154.9 million workers (140.2 million employed plus 14.7 million unemployed). The adult (over age 16) population in June 2009 was 235.7 million, which leaves 80.8 million adults not in the labor force (total population of 235.7 million less 154.9 million in the labor force).

Some useful measures of the labor market are the unemployment rate, the participation rate, and the employment ratio. The **unemployment rate** is the fraction of the labor force that is unemployed. In June 2009, the unemployment

Table 3.4

Employment Status of the U.S. Adult Population, June 2009

Category	Number (millions)	Share of labor force (percent)	Share of adult population (percent)
Employed workers	140.2	90.5	59.5 (employment ratio)
Unemployed workers	14.7	9.5 (unemployment rate)	6.2
Labor force (employed + unemployed workers)	154.9	100.0	65.7 (participation rate)
Not in labor force	80.8		34.3
Adult population (labor force + not in labor force)	235.7		100.0

Note: Figures may not add up because of rounding.
Source: The Employment Situation, June 2009, Table A-1.

IN TOUCH WITH DATA AND RESEARCH

Labor Market Data

Government agencies collect and distribute a remarkable variety of data pertaining to the labor market. A useful summary of labor market data can be found in *The Employment Situation*, a monthly report issued by the Bureau of Labor Statistics (available online at *www.bls.gov/news.release/pdf/empsit.pdf*). This report, which is usually released on the first Friday of the month, includes data for the previous month on employment, unemployment, average hours worked each week, and average weekly and hourly earnings. The data are presented for the aggregate U.S. economy and for various categories of workers based on age, gender, race, occupation, and industry. Many of these data are later reprinted in a variety of sources, including *Employment and Earnings*, the *Economic Report of the President*, and electronic databases such as the FRED database at *research.stlouisfed.org/fred2*.

The data in *The Employment Situation* are obtained from two different surveys, a household survey and an establishment survey. The household survey is the monthly survey described in this chapter and is used to calculate employment and the unemployment rate. The establishment survey (also known as the payroll survey) is based on the responses of almost 400,000 business establishments about their employment, hours worked, and employee earnings.

Both the household survey and the establishment survey provide information on employment, but they sometimes give conflicting signals about what happened to employment in the previous month. An important difference between the two surveys is that the establishment survey counts *jobs* whereas the household survey counts *people*. Thus a worker with two jobs could be counted twice in the establishment survey but only once in the household survey. The employment data from the establishment survey are more comprehensive and are more closely related to output than are the employment data from the household survey.* However, the household survey provides information about unemployment and the establishment survey doesn't.

---

*See Robert Ingenito and Bharat Trehan, "Using Monthly Data to Predict Quarterly Output," Federal Reserve Bank of San Francisco, *Economic Review*, 1996, no. 3: pp. 3–11.

rate was 9.5% (14. 7 million unemployed divided by 154.9 million in the labor force). Figure 1.3 shows the U.S. unemployment rate for the period since 1890.

The fraction of the adult population in the labor force is the **participation rate.** Of the 235.7 million adults in the United States in June 2009, 154.9 million were in the labor force, so the participation rate was 65.7% (because 154.9/235.7 = 0.657 = 65.7%).

The **employment ratio** is the employed fraction of the adult population. In June 2009 the employment ratio was 59.5% (140.2 million employed divided by the adult population of 235.7 million). With an employment ratio of 59.5%, 40.5% of the adult population was not employed in June 2009. Of this 40.5%, 6.2% reflected unemployment and the remaining 34.3% reflected people not in the labor force. Thus a large majority of adults who are not employed at any given time are not in the labor force rather than unemployed.

Figure 3.13

Changes in employment status in a typical month (June 2007)
The arrows between two boxes represent changes from one employment status to another; the labels on the arrows show the fraction of the people in one status who switch to the other status in a typical month. For example, the arrow from the unemployed box to the employed box indicates that 28% of unemployed workers become employed the following month; the arrow from the employed box to the unemployed box indicates that 1% of employed workers become unemployed the following month.

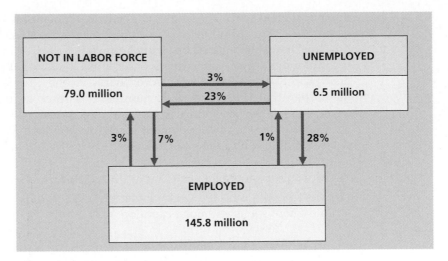

Changes in Employment Status

The labor market is in a constant state of flux. Even when the unemployment rate remains unchanged from one month to the next, during the month hundreds of thousands of U.S. workers become unemployed and hundreds of thousands become employed.

Figure 3.13 shows how workers change their employment status (that is, whether they are employed, unemployed, or not in the labor force) in a typical month (the numbers are from June 2007). The arrows between each pair of boxes represent changes from one employment status to another, and the number on each arrow shows the fraction of the people in one status that switch to the other status in a typical month.[19] For example, the arrow from the employed box to the unemployed box has the label 1%, indicating that 1% of employed workers will become unemployed by the following month.

What are the employment prospects of an unemployed worker? Figure 3.13 shows that 28% of the unemployed people in a typical month will be employed the following month and that 23% of the unemployed people will be out of the labor force the next month. The remaining 49% of the unemployed people will still be unemployed the following month. Of the 23% of the unemployed who leave the labor force each month, some are **discouraged workers**, or people who have become so discouraged by lack of success at finding a job that they stop searching. Other unemployed workers leave the labor force to engage in some activity outside the labor market, such as homemaking or going to school.

How Long Are People Unemployed?

Of the 49% of those unemployed in a typical month who remain unemployed the following month, some may remain unemployed for a considerable period of time. The period of time that an individual is continuously unemployed is called an

---

[19]Figure 3.13 makes use of data on transition rates between employment, unemployment, and not-in-the-labor-force status. The rates are from the Bureau of Labor Statistics research series on labor force status flows from the Current Population Survey, *www.bls.gov/cps/cps_flows.htm*.

unemployment spell. The length of time that an unemployment spell lasts is called its **duration**. The duration of an unemployment spell determines in large part the degree of hardship suffered by an unemployed worker. At one extreme, a one-week unemployment spell will cost a worker a week's pay but probably will not seriously affect the worker's standard of living. At the other extreme, an unemployment spell that lasts for several months may force an unemployed worker to exhaust his or her life savings or to sell a car or house.

The duration of unemployment spells in the United States is characterized by two seemingly contradictory statements:

1. Most unemployment spells are of short duration, about two months or less.
2. Most people who are unemployed on a given date are experiencing unemployment spells with long duration.

To understand how both of these statements can be true, consider an economy with 100 people in the labor force. Suppose that at the beginning of every month, two workers become unemployed and remain unemployed for one month before finding new jobs. In addition, at the beginning of every year four workers become unemployed and remain unemployed for the entire year.

In this example, there are twenty-eight spells of unemployment during a year: twenty-four spells that last one month, and four spells that last one year. Thus twenty-four of twenty-eight, or 86%, of the spells last only one month, which is consistent with the first statement: Most spells are short.

How many people are unemployed on a given day—say, on May 15? There are six unemployed workers on May 15: two unemployed workers who began one-month spells of unemployment on May 1, and four unemployed workers who began one-year spells of unemployment on January 1. Thus, four of six, or 67%, of the workers unemployed on May 15 are experiencing one-year spells of unemployment, which is consistent with the second statement: Most people who are unemployed on a given date are experiencing long spells of unemployment.

Why There Always Are Unemployed People

Even when the economy is growing vigorously and many new jobs are being created, some people remain unemployed. Why is unemployment apparently a permanent feature of the economy? Here we discuss frictional unemployment and structural unemployment, two types of unemployment that always exist in the labor market and thus prevent the unemployment rate from ever reaching zero.

Frictional Unemployment. The labor market is characterized by a great deal of searching by both workers and firms. Unemployed workers search for suitable jobs, and firms with vacancies search for suitable workers. If all workers were identical and all jobs were identical, these searches would be short and easy: Unemployed workers would simply have to find firms that had vacancies and they would immediately be hired. The problem, of course, is that neither jobs nor workers are identical. Workers vary in their talents, skills, experience, goals, geographic location (and willingness to move), and amount of time and energy they are willing to commit to their job. Similarly, jobs vary in the skills and experience required, working conditions, location, hours, and pay. Because of these differences, an unemployed worker may search for several weeks or more before finding a suitable job; similarly, a firm may search for a considerable time before it is able to hire a suitable worker.

The unemployment that arises as workers search for suitable jobs and firms search for suitable workers is called **frictional unemployment**. Because the economy is dynamic, with jobs continually being created and destroyed and workers continually entering and exiting the labor force, there is always some frictional unemployment as workers are matched with appropriate jobs.

Structural Unemployment. In addition to those suffering long spells of unemployment, many people are chronically unemployed. Although their unemployment spells may be broken by brief periods of employment or being out of the labor force, workers who are **chronically unemployed** are unemployed a large part of the time. Long spells of unemployment and chronic unemployment can't be attributed primarily to the matching process. People in these situations don't seem to search for work very intensively and don't generally find stable employment. The long-term and chronic unemployment that exists even when the economy is not in a recession is called **structural unemployment**.

Structural unemployment occurs for two primary reasons. First, unskilled or low-skilled workers often are unable to obtain desirable, long-term jobs. The jobs available to them typically offer relatively low wages and little chance for training or advancement. Most directly related to the issue of structural unemployment is the fact that jobs held by low-skilled workers often don't last long. After a few months the job may end, or the worker may quit or be fired, thus entering another spell of unemployment. Some workers with low skill levels eventually get enough training or experience to obtain more secure, long-term jobs. Because of factors such as inadequate education, discrimination, and language barriers, however, some unskilled workers never make the transition to long-term employment and remain chronically unemployed.

The second source of structural unemployment is the reallocation of labor from industries that are shrinking, or regions that are depressed, to areas that are growing. When industries find that their products are no longer in demand (for example, buggy whip manufacturers) or that they are no longer competitive (for example, U.S. producers of color television sets that lost much of the market to producers in Asia), workers in these industries lose their jobs. At the same time, some industries will be growing (for example, health care providers and computer software developers). To prevent unemployment from rising requires that workers who lose jobs in declining industries be matched somehow with jobs in growing industries. This matching may involve a long period of unemployment, especially if workers need to relocate or be trained for a new job.

The Natural Rate of Unemployment. Because of the combination of frictional and structural unemployment, an economy's unemployment rate is never zero, even when the economy is at its full-employment level. The rate of unemployment that prevails when output and employment are at the full-employment level is called the **natural rate of unemployment**, $\bar{u}$. The natural rate of unemployment reflects unemployment owing to frictional and structural causes. Although there is no single official measure of the natural rate of unemployment, many economists believe that the natural rate was about 4% or 5% during the 1950s and increased gradually to about 6% in the 1980s. Many economists think that the natural rate fell toward 5.5% or lower during the 1990s and 2000s. In Chapter 12 we discuss the reasons for the variations in the natural rate.

As output fluctuates around its full-employment level, the unemployment rate fluctuates around the natural rate. The difference between the actual unemployment rate and the natural rate of unemployment is called **cyclical unemployment.** Specifically, cyclical unemployment $= u - \bar{u}$, where u is the actual unemployment rate and $\bar{u}$ is the natural rate. Cyclical unemployment is positive whenever the economy's output and employment are below full-employment levels; it is negative when output and employment exceed full-employment levels.

3.6 Relating Output and Unemployment: Okun's Law

Earlier in this chapter we said that many short-run output fluctuations result from changes in employment. When employment falls and unemployment rises, the reduction in the number of people working leads to a decline in the quantity of goods and services produced. We can use the concept of cyclical unemployment to provide a more precise link between the state of the labor market and aggregate output.

The quantitative impact on aggregate output of a change in the unemployment rate is described by Okun's law, a rule of thumb (rather than a "law") first stated by Arthur Okun, chairman of the Council of Economic Advisers in the 1960s during the Johnson administration. According to **Okun's law**, the gap between an economy's full-employment output and its actual level of output increases by 2 percentage points for each percentage point the unemployment rate increases.[20,21] We express Okun's law algebraically as

$$\frac{\overline{Y} - Y}{\overline{Y}} = 2(u - \bar{u}). \tag{3.5}$$

The left side of Eq. (3.5) equals the amount by which actual output, Y, falls short of full-employment output, $\overline{Y}$, expressed as a percentage of $\overline{Y}$. Thus Eq. (3.5) says that the percentage gap between potential and actual output equals 2 times the cyclical unemployment rate.

Let's apply Okun's law by supposing that the natural rate of unemployment is 6% and that the full-employment level of output is $15,000 billion. If the actual unemployment rate is 7%, or 1 percentage point above the natural rate, cyclical unemployment, $u - \bar{u}$, equals 1%. If cyclical unemployment is 1%, Okun's law predicts that actual output, Y, will be 2% (2 times 1%) lower than full-employment output, $\overline{Y}$. Because $\overline{Y}$ equals $15,000 billion, Okun's law says that actual output will be $300 billion below the full-employment level (2% times $15,000 billion).

You may wonder why a 1 percentage point increase in the unemployment rate, which reduces employment by about 1%, leads (according to Okun's law) to

---

[20]When the unemployment rate increases, for example, from 6% to 9%, we say that it increases by 3 percentage points (9%–6%), or that it increases by 50 percent (3% is 50 percent of 6%).

[21]In Okun's original work ("Potential GNP: Its Measurement and Significance," reprinted in Arthur Okun, *The Political Economy of Prosperity,* Washington, D.C.: Brookings Institution, 1970, pp. 132–145), the "Okun's law coefficient" was about 3 rather than 2, so each percentage point of cyclical unemployment was associated with a difference between actual output and full-employment output of 3 percentage points. Current estimates put the Okun's law coefficient closer to 2.

Figure 3.14

Okun's law in the United States: 1951–2008

This figure shows the relation between the growth rate of real GDP (vertical axis) and the change in the unemployment rate (horizontal axis). Line OL is a graph of Okun's law (Eq. 3.6). The slope of this line is −2, indicating that a 1 percentage point change in the unemployment rate changes the growth rate of output by 2 percentage points in the opposite direction. The horizontal line at 3% shows the approximate average growth rate of full-employment output, equaling the rate at which actual output would grow if there were no change in the unemployment rate (Δu = 0).

Sources: Real GDP growth rate from Table 1.1.1 from Bureau of Economic Analysis Web site, *www.bea.gov/bea/dn/nipaweb.* Civilian unemployment rate for all civilian workers from Bureau of Labor Statistics Web site, *data.bls.gov.*

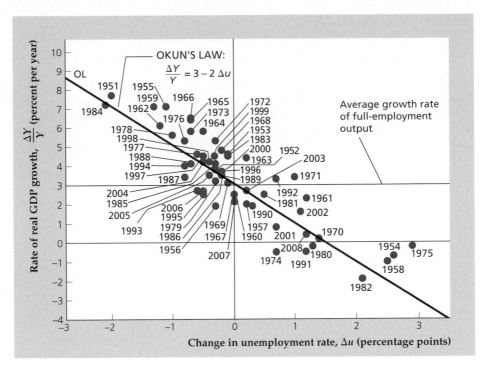

a drop in output that is about twice as large in percentage terms. The reason is that when cyclical unemployment increases, other factors that determine output—the number of people in the labor force, the number of hours each worker works per week, the average productivity of labor—also fall, which magnifies the effect of the increase in unemployment. Numerical Problem 10 at the end of this chapter illustrates this point.

Sometimes we express Okun's law in a slightly different form:

$$\frac{\Delta Y}{Y} = 3 - 2\Delta u \tag{3.6}$$

where $\Delta Y/Y$ is the percentage growth rate of output and Δu is the change in the actual unemployment rate from one year to the next. Equation (3.6) says that when unemployment is rising ($\Delta u > 0$), actual output, Y, is growing more slowly than 3% per year, which is the average growth rate of full-employment output in the United States. Equation (3.6), which requires the assumption that the natural rate of unemployment is constant, is called the growth rate form of Okun's law. See Appendix 3.A at the end of this chapter for a derivation of Eq. (3.6).

Figure 3.14 illustrates the growth rate form of Okun's law. The figure shows the relation between the annual change in the unemployment rate (measured on the horizontal axis) and the annual growth rate of U.S. output (measured on the vertical axis) for the period 1951–2008. Line OL in this figure represents Okun's law. Its slope is −2, indicating that a 1 percentage point increase in the unemployment rate is associated with a 2% drop in output. The vertical line rising from 0 on the horizontal axis intersects OL at 3%. This intercept indicates that, when no change occurs in the unemployment rate, the growth rate of actual output is 3%, or the approximate average growth rate of full-employment output in the United States.

CHAPTER SUMMARY

1. The production function tells us the amount of output that can be produced with any given quantities of capital and labor. It can be graphed as a relationship between output and capital, holding labor fixed, or as a relationship between output and labor, holding capital fixed. In either case, the production function slopes upward, implying that greater use of capital or labor leads to more output. A shift in the production function, which indicates a change in the amount of output that can be produced with given amounts of capital and labor, is called a supply shock.

2. The extra output that can be produced when the capital stock is increased by one unit, with labor held constant, is called the marginal product of capital (MPK). In a graph of the production function relating output to capital, the MPK can be measured as the slope of the production function. The MPK falls as the capital stock increases, reflecting the diminishing marginal productivity of capital. Similarly, the marginal product of labor (MPN) is the extra output that can be produced when labor increases by one unit, with capital held constant. The MPN—which can be measured as the slope of the production function relating output to labor—falls as employment rises, indicating that labor also has diminishing marginal productivity.

3. To maximize profits, firms demand labor to the point that the marginal revenue product of labor ($MRPN$) equals the nominal wage, W; or, equivalently, to the point that the MPN equals the real wage, w.

4. The labor demand curve is identical to the MPN curve. Because an increase in the real wage causes firms to demand less labor, the labor demand curve slopes downward. Factors that increase the amount of labor demanded at any real wage, such as a beneficial supply shock or an increase in the capital stock, shift the labor demand curve to the right. Aggregate labor demand is the sum of the labor demands of firms in the economy.

5. An individual's decision about how much labor to supply reflects a comparison of the benefit and cost of working an additional hour. The benefit of working an additional hour is the additional real income earned, which can be used to increase consumption. The cost of working an extra hour is the loss of an hour's leisure. An individual's happiness, or utility, is maximized by supplying labor to the point where the cost of working an extra hour (the utility lost because of reduced leisure) equals the benefit (the utility gained because of increased income).

6. An increase in the real wage has competing substitution and income effects on the amount of labor supplied. The substitution effect of a higher real wage increases the amount of labor supplied, as the worker responds to the increased reward for working. The income effect reduces the amount of labor supplied, as the higher real wage makes the worker wealthier and thus able to afford a greater amount of leisure. The longer an increase in the real wage is expected to last, the stronger the income effect is. Thus a temporary increase in the real wage will increase the amount of labor supplied. A permanent increase in the real wage will increase the amount of labor supplied by a smaller amount than a temporary increase in the real wage of the same size, however, and may even lead to a decrease in the amount of labor supplied.

7. The labor supply curve relates the amount of labor supplied to the current real wage. The labor supply curve slopes upward, indicating that an increase in the current real wage—with other factors, including the expected future real wage, held fixed—raises the amount of labor supplied. Factors that decrease the quantity of labor supplied at the current real wage, and thus shift the labor supply curve to the left, include an increase in wealth and an increase in the expected future real wage. Aggregate labor supply, which is the sum of labor supplies of the individuals in the economy, is also influenced by changes in the adult population and social or legal factors that affect the number of people participating in the labor market.

8. The classical supply–demand model of the labor market is based on the assumption that the real wage adjusts relatively quickly to equalize the quantities of labor demanded and supplied. The equilibrium level of employment, which arises when wages and prices in the economy have fully adjusted, is called the full-employment level of employment. Fluctuations in employment and the real wage result from factors that shift the labor supply curve and/or the labor demand curve.

9. Full-employment output, or potential output, is the amount of output produced when employment is at its full-employment level. Increases in the full-employment level of employment or beneficial supply shocks increase the full-employment level of output.

10. Adults without jobs are classified as unemployed if they looked for work during the preceding four weeks; they are classified as not in the labor force if they haven't been looking for work. The labor force consists of all employed workers plus all unemployed workers. The unemployment rate is the fraction of the labor force that is unemployed.

11. Frictional unemployment reflects the time required for potential workers to find suitable jobs and for firms with vacancies to find suitable workers. Structural unemployment—long-term and chronic unemployment that exists even when the economy isn't in recession—occurs because some workers don't have the skills needed to obtain long-term employment, or because of delays as workers relocate from economically depressed areas to those that are growing.

Frictional and structural unemployment together account for the natural rate of unemployment, which is the unemployment rate that exists when employment is at its full-employment level. Cyclical unemployment is the excess of the actual unemployment rate over the natural rate of unemployment.

12. According to Okun's law, a 1 percentage point increase in the rate of cyclical unemployment reduces output by 2 percent.

KEY DIAGRAM 1

The production function

The production function indicates how much output an economy or a firm can produce with any given quantities of capital and labor.

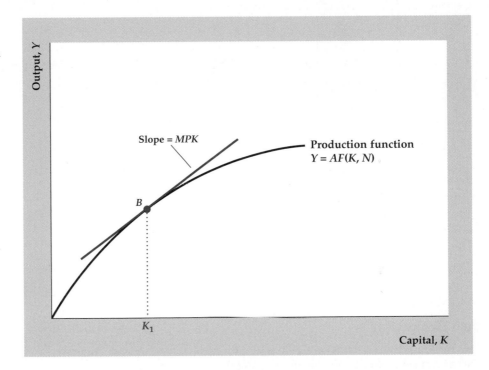

Diagram Elements

■ The production function graphed here has the amount of output produced, Y, on the vertical axis and the quantity of capital used, K, on the horizontal axis, with labor, N, held constant. It can also be drawn as a relationship between output and labor, with capital held constant. The production function relating output to labor looks like the graph shown here.

■ The equation for the production function is $Y = AF(K, N)$, where A (total factor productivity, or simply productivity) measures how effectively the economy uses capital and labor.

Analysis

■ The production function slopes upward, reflecting the fact that an increase in the quantity of capital will allow more output to be produced.

■ The production function becomes flatter from left to right, implying that the larger the capital stock already is, the less extra output is gained by adding another unit of capital. The fact that extra capital becomes less productive as the capital stock grows is called diminishing marginal productivity of capital.

■ With labor held constant, if an increase in capital of ΔK leads to an increase in output of ΔY, then $\Delta Y / \Delta K$ is called the marginal product of capital, or MPK. The MPK is measured graphically by the slope of the line tangent to the production function. For example, in the diagram the MPK when the capital stock is K_1 equals the slope of the line tangent to the production function at point B.

Factors That Shift the Curve

■ Any change that allows more output to be produced for given quantities of capital and labor—a beneficial supply shock—shifts the production function upward. Examples of beneficial supply shocks include new inventions and improved management techniques.

■ Any change that reduces the amount of output that can be produced for given quantities of capital and labor—an adverse supply shock—shifts the production function downward. Examples of adverse supply shocks include bad weather and the depletion of natural resources.

KEY DIAGRAM 2

The labor market
An economy's level of employment and the real wage are determined in the labor market.

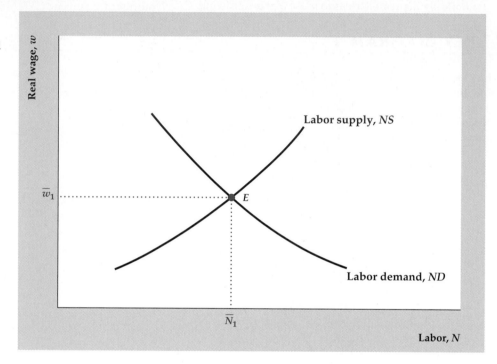

Diagram Elements

■ The current real wage, w, is on the vertical axis, and the level of employment, N, is on the horizontal axis. The variable N may also represent alternative measures of labor, such as total hours worked.

■ The labor demand curve, ND, shows the amount of labor that firms want to employ at each current real wage. The labor demand curve slopes downward because firms find hiring more labor profitable when the real wage falls. The labor demand curve for an individual firm is the same as the MPN curve, which shows the marginal product of labor at each level of employment.

■ The labor supply curve, NS, shows the amount of labor offered by workers at each current real wage. The labor supply curve slopes upward because an increase in the current real wage, with other factors held constant, increases the amount of labor supplied.

Analysis

■ Equilibrium in the labor market occurs when the quantity of labor demanded equals the quantity

of labor supplied. In the figure, equilibrium employment is $\overline{N}_1$ and the equilibrium real wage is $\overline{w}_1$. The equilibrium level of employment, which occurs after wages and prices have fully adjusted, is called the full-employment level of employment.

Factors That Shift the Curves

■ Any factor that increases the amount of labor demanded at a given current real wage shifts the labor demand curve to the right. Such factors include an increase in productivity that increases the marginal product of labor and an increase in the capital stock. See Summary table 3 on page 74.

■ Any factor that increases the amount of labor supplied at a given current real wage shifts the labor supply curve to the right. Such factors include a decline in wealth, a drop in the expected future real wage, an increase in the adult population, and an increase in labor force participation. See Summary table 4 on page 80.

KEY TERMS

aggregate demand for labor, p. 75

aggregate supply of labor, p. 75

chronically unemployed, p. 91

cyclical unemployment, p. 92

diminishing marginal
productivity, p. 64

discouraged workers, p. 89

duration, p. 90

employment ratio, p. 88

factors of production, p. 59

frictional unemployment, p. 91

full-employment level of
employment, p. 83

full-employment output, p. 84

income effect of a higher
real wage, p. 76

labor force, p. 87

leisure, p. 75

marginal product of capital
(*MPK*), p. 64

marginal product of labor
(*MPN*), p. 65

marginal revenue product of labor
(*MRPN*), p. 69

natural rate of
unemployment, p. 91

Okun's law, p. 92

participation rate, p. 88

production function, p. 59

productivity, p. 58

real wage, p. 70

structural unemployment, p. 91

substitution effect of a higher
real wage, p. 76

supply shock, p. 66

total factor productivity, p. 60

unemployment rate, p. 87

unemployment spell, p. 90

KEY EQUATIONS

$$Y = AF(K, N) \qquad (3.1)$$

The *production function* indicates how much output, Y, can be produced for given quantities of capital, K, and labor, N, and for a given level of total factor productivity, A.

$$\overline{Y} = AF(K, \overline{N}) \qquad (3.4)$$

Full-employment output, $\overline{Y}$, is the quantity of output supplied by firms when wages and prices have fully adjusted, and employment equals its equilibrium value, $\overline{N}$.

$$\frac{\overline{Y} - Y}{\overline{Y}} = 2(u - \bar{u}) \qquad (3.5)$$

Okun's law states that a 1 percentage point increase in the unemployment rate, u, reduces output, Y, by 2% of the

full-employment level of output, $\overline{Y}$. When the unemployment rate equals the natural rate of unemployment, $\bar{u}$, output equals its full-employment level.

$$\frac{\Delta Y}{Y} = 3 - 2\Delta u \qquad (3.6)$$

The growth rate form of Okun's law relates the growth rate of output, $\Delta Y/Y$, to the average growth rate of full-employment output in the United States, 3%, and the change in the unemployment rate, Δu. According to Eq. (3.6), output grows more slowly than full-employment output when unemployment is rising and more quickly than full-employment output when unemployment is falling. This version of Okun's law is based on the assumption that the natural rate of unemployment is constant.

REVIEW QUESTIONS

All review questions are available in (X) myeconlab at **www.myeconlab.com.**

1. What is a production function? What are some factors that can cause a nation's production function to shift over time? What do you have to know besides an economy's production function to know how much output the economy can produce?

2. The production function slopes upward, but its slope declines from left to right. Give an economic interpretation of each of these properties of the production function.

3. Define *marginal product of capital*, or *MPK*. How can the *MPK* be shown graphically?

4. Explain why the profit-maximizing level of employment for a firm occurs when the marginal revenue product of labor equals the nominal wage. How can this profit-maximizing condition be expressed in real terms?

5. What is the *MPN* curve? How is the *MPN* curve related to the production function? How is it related to labor demand?

6. Use the concepts of income effect and substitution effect to explain why a temporary increase in the real wage increases the amount of labor supplied, but a permanent increase in the real wage may decrease the quantity of labor supplied.

7. What two variables are related by the aggregate labor supply curve? What are some factors that cause the aggregate labor supply curve to shift?

8. Define *full-employment output*. How is full-employment output affected by an increase in labor supply? By a beneficial supply shock?

9. Why is the classical model of the labor market discussed in this chapter not very useful for studying unemployment?

10. Define the following: *labor force, unemployment rate, participation rate,* and *employment ratio*.

11. Define *unemployment spell* and *duration*. What are the two seemingly contradictory facts about unemployment spells? Why are the two facts not actually contradictory?

12. What is frictional unemployment? Why is a certain amount of frictional unemployment probably necessary in a well-functioning economy?

13. What is structural unemployment? What are the two principal sources of structural unemployment?

14. Define the *natural rate of unemployment* and *cyclical unemployment*. What does negative cyclical unemployment mean?

15. What is Okun's law? If the unemployment rate increases by 2 percentage points between this year and next year, by how much will output change during the same period? Assume that the natural unemployment rate and full-employment output are constant. Use the form of Okun's Law in Eq. (3.5).

NUMERICAL PROBLEMS

All numerical problems are available in myeconlab at www.myeconlab.com.

1. The following data give real GDP, Y, capital, K, and labor, N, for the U.S. economy in various years.

Year	Y	K	N
1960	2502	2695	65.8
1970	3772	4044	78.7
1980	5162	5831	99.3
1990	7113	7809	118.8
2000	9817	10,392	136.9
2007	11,524	11,849	146.0

Units and sources are the same as in Table 3.1. Assume that the production function is $Y = AK^{0.3}N^{0.7}$.

a. By what percentage did U.S. total factor productivity grow between 1960 and 1970? Between 1970 and 1980? Between 1980 and 1990? Between 1990 and 2000? Between 2000 and 2007?

b. What happened to the marginal product of labor between 1960 and 2007? Calculate the marginal product numerically as the extra output gained by adding 1 million workers in each of the two years. (The data for employment, N, are measured in millions of workers, so an increase of 1 million workers is an increase of 1.0.)

2. An economy has the production function
$$Y = 0.2(K + \sqrt{N}).$$
In the current period, $K = 100$ and $N = 100$.

a. Graph the relationship between output and capital, holding labor constant at its current value. What is the MPK? Does the marginal productivity of capital diminish?

b. Graph the relationship between output and labor, holding capital constant at its current value. Find the MPN for an increase of labor from 100 to 110. Compare this result with the MPN for an increase in labor from 110 to 120. Does the marginal productivity of labor diminish?

3. Acme Widget, Inc., has the following production function.

Number of Workers	Number of Widgets Produced
0	0
1	8
2	15
3	21
4	26
5	30
6	33

a. Find the MPN for each level of employment.

b. Acme can get $5 for each widget it produces. How many workers will it hire if the nominal wage is $38? If it is $27? If it is $22?

c. Graph the relationship between Acme's labor demand and the nominal wage. How does this graph differ from a labor demand curve? Graph Acme's labor demand curve.

d. With the nominal wage fixed at $38, the price of widgets doubles from $5 each to $10 each. What happens to Acme's labor demand and production?

e. With the nominal wage fixed at $38 and the price of widgets fixed at $5, the introduction of a new automatic widget maker doubles the number of widgets that the same number of workers can produce. What happens to labor demand and production?

f. What is the relationship between your answers to part (d) and part (e)? Explain.

4. The marginal product of labor (measured in units of output) for a certain firm is

$$MPN = A(100 - N),$$

where A measures productivity and N is the number of labor hours used in production. The price of output is $2.00 per unit.

a. If $A = 1.0$, what will be the demand for labor if the nominal wage is $10? If it is $20? Graph the demand curve for labor. What is the equilibrium real wage if the supply of labor is fixed at 95?

b. Repeat part (a) for $A = 2.0$.

5. Consider an economy in which the marginal product of labor MPN is $MPN = 309 - 2N$, where N is the amount of labor used. The amount of labor supplied, NS, is given by $NS = 22 + 12w + 2T$, where w is the real wage and T is a lump-sum tax levied on individuals.

a. Use the concepts of income effect and substitution effect to explain why an increase in lump-sum taxes will increase the amount of labor supplied.

b. Suppose that $T = 35$. What are the equilibrium values of employment and the real wage?

c. With T remaining equal to 35, the government passes minimum-wage legislation that requires firms to pay a real wage greater than or equal to 7. What are the resulting values of employment and the real wage?

6. Suppose that the production function is $Y = 9K^{0.5}N^{0.5}$. With this production function, the marginal product of labor is $MPN = 4.5K^{0.5}N^{-0.5}$. The capital stock is $K = 25$. The labor supply curve is $NS = 100[(1 - t)w]^2$, where w is the real wage rate, t is the tax rate on labor income, and hence $(1 - t)w$ is the after-tax real wage rate.

a. Assume that the tax rate on labor income, t, equals zero. Find the equation of the labor demand curve. Calculate the equilibrium levels of the real wage and employment, the level of full-employment output, and the total after-tax wage income of workers.

b. Repeat part (a) under the assumption that the tax rate on labor income, t, equals 0.6.

c. Suppose that a minimum wage of $w = 2$ is imposed. If the tax rate on labor income, t, equals zero, what are the resulting values of employment and the real wage? Does the introduction of the minimum wage increase the total income of workers, taken as a group?

7. Consider an economy with 500 people in the labor force. At the beginning of every month, 5 people lose their jobs

and remain unemployed for exactly one month; one month later, they find new jobs and become employed. In addition, on January 1 of each year, 20 people lose their jobs and remain unemployed for six months before finding new jobs. Finally, on July 1 of each year, 20 people lose their jobs and remain unemployed for six months before finding new jobs.

a. What is the unemployment rate in this economy in a typical month?

b. What fraction of unemployment spells lasts for one month? What fraction lasts for six months?

c. What is the average duration of an unemployment spell?

d. On any particular date, what fraction of the unemployed are suffering a long spell (six months) of unemployment?

8. Use the data in Fig. 3.13 to calculate how many people become unemployed during a typical month. How many become employed? How many leave the labor force?

9. You are given the following data on the unemployment rate and output.

Year	1	2	3	4
Unemployment rate	8%	6%	7%	5%
Output	950	1030	1033.5	1127.5

a. Assume that the natural rate of unemployment is 6% and that $(\bar{Y} - Y)/\bar{Y} = 2(u - \bar{u})$. Find the full-employment level of output in each year.

b. Calculate the growth rate of full-employment output in years 2, 3, and 4 two different ways. First, calculate the growth rates by using the values for full-employment output that you found in part (a). Then calculate the growth rate of full-employment output by using only the change in the unemployment rate, the growth rate of output, and the growth rate version of Okun's law, $\Delta Y/Y = \Delta \bar{Y}/\bar{Y} - 2\Delta u$, which is similar to Eq. (3.6), except that in Eq. (3.6), $\Delta \bar{Y}/\bar{Y} = 3$ for the United States, where for this economy, $\Delta \bar{Y}/\bar{Y}$ could differ from 3. Compare your answers from the two sets of calculations.

10. Consider an economy that initially has a labor force of 2000 workers. Of these workers, 1900 are employed and each works 40 hours per week. Ten units of output are produced by each hour of labor.

a. What is the total number of hours worked per week in the economy? What is the total output per week in the economy? What is the unemployment rate?

b. The economy enters a recession. Employment falls by 4%, and the number of hours per week worked by each employed worker falls by 2.5%. In addition,

0.2% of the labor force becomes discouraged at the prospect of finding a job and leaves the labor force. Finally, suppose that whenever total hours fall by 1%, total output falls by 1.4%.

After the recession begins, what is the size of the labor force? How many workers are unemployed and what is the unemployment rate? What is the total output per week in the economy?

By what percentage has total output fallen relative to the initial situation? What is the value of the Okun's law coefficient relating the loss of output to the increase in the unemployment rate?

ANALYTICAL PROBLEMS

1. *a.* A technological breakthrough raises a country's total factor productivity *A* by 10%. Show how this change affects the graphs of both the production function relating output to capital and the production function relating output to labor.

   b. Show that a 10% increase in *A* also increases the *MPK* and the *MPN* by 10% at any level of capital and labor. (*Hint:* What happens to Δ*Y* for any increase in capital, Δ*K*, or for any increase in labor, Δ*N*?)

   c. Can a beneficial supply shock leave the *MPK* and *MPN* unaffected? Show your answer graphically.

2. How would each of the following affect the current level of full-employment output? Explain.

   a. A large number of immigrants enter the country.

   b. Energy supplies become depleted.

   c. New teaching techniques improve the educational performance of high school seniors.

   d. A new law mandates the shutdown of some unsafe forms of capital.

3. During the 1980s and 1990s the average rate of unemployment in Europe was high. Some economists claimed that this rate was in part the result of "real-wage rigidity," a situation in which unions kept real wages above their market-clearing levels.

   a. Accepting for the sake of argument that real wages were too high in Europe in the 1980s and 1990s, show how this situation would lead to unemployment (a situation where people who would like to work at the going wage cannot find jobs).

   b. What is the effect of real-wage rigidity on the output actually supplied by firms, relative to the output they would supply if there were no real-wage rigidity?

4. How would each of the following affect Helena Handbasket's supply of labor?

   a. The value of Helena's home triples in an unexpectedly hot real estate market.

   b. Originally an unskilled worker, Helena acquires skills that give her access to a higher-paying job. Assume that her preferences about leisure are not affected by the change in jobs.

   c. A temporary income tax surcharge raises the percentage of her income that she must pay in taxes, for the current year only. (Taxes are proportional to income in Helena's country.)

5. Suppose that under a new law all businesses must pay a tax equal to 6% of their sales revenue. Assume that this tax is not passed on to consumers. Instead, consumers pay the same prices after the tax is imposed as they did before. What is the effect of this tax on labor demand? If the labor supply curve is unchanged, what will be the effect of the tax on employment and the real wage?

6. Can the unemployment rate and the employment ratio rise during the same month? Can the participation rate fall at the same time that the employment ratio rises? Explain.

7. Self-employed workers in the United States must pay Social Security taxes equal to 12.4% of any income up to $106,800 in 2009. This income level of $106,800 is known as the "cap." Income in excess of the cap is not subject to Social Security tax, so self-employed workers with incomes exceeding $106,800 pay $106,800 × 0.124 = $13,243. Now consider two proposals designed to increase Social Security tax revenue. Proposal A increases the cap to $129,194, so that Social Security taxes equal 12.4% of income up to $129,194. Proposal B increases the Social Security tax rate to 15%, but leaves the cap unchanged at $106,800. For people with income that always exceeds the cap, the amount of Social Security tax is the same under Proposal A ($129,194 × 0.124 = $16,020) as under Proposal B ($106,800 × 0.15 = $16,020). There are no planned changes in future Social Security benefits anticipated by current workers.

   a. Sally is self-employed and earns $150,000 per year. What are the effects of Proposal A and Proposal B on Sally's labor supply? Under which proposal would she supply a greater amount of labor? Explain your answers using the concepts of income effect and substitution effect.

   b. Fred is self-employed and earns $50,000 per year. What are the effects of Proposal A and Proposal B on Fred's labor supply? Under which proposal would he supply a greater amount of labor? Explain your answers using the concepts of income effect and substitution effect.

WORKING WITH MACROECONOMIC DATA

For data to use in these exercises, go to the Federal Reserve Bank of St. Louis FRED database at research.stlouisfed.org/fred2.

1. Using the production function in Equation (3.2) and annual data for real GDP, the capital stock, and civilian employment from the sources in Table 3.1, calculate and graph U.S. total factor productivity for the period since 1948.

   Calculate and graph the growth rate of total factor productivity. In what period was total factor productivity growth highest? Lowest? Compare your graph to a graph of the civilian unemployment rate. How does productivity behave in periods around recessions? How was productivity affected by the oil shocks of 1973–1975, 1979–1980, 1990, and 2003–2008?

2. Using monthly data from 1948 to the present, calculate and graph the total working-age population (called the civilian noninstitutional population), the number of employed workers, the number of unemployed workers, and the number of workers in the labor force.

   At the Web site of the Bureau of Labor Statistics, *www.bls.gov/cps/cpsatabs.htm*, find data and graph the labor force participation rate for the overall working-age population, and graph the labor force participation rates for males aged 20 and older and for females aged 20 and older. What are the major changes in these variables that have occurred over the postwar period?

3. Plot a graph of quarterly data for real GDP and full-employment GDP from 1970 to the present. (In the FRED database, full-employment GDP is called Real Potential GDP.) Which variable is "smoother"? Can you pick out the dates of recessions (1953–1954, 1957–1958, 1960–1961, 1969–1970, 1973–1975, 1980, 1981–1982, 1990–1991, and 2001) on the graph?

The Growth Rate Form of Okun's Law

To derive the growth rate form of Okun's law, Eq. (3.6), we start with the basic form of Okun's law, Eq. (3.5):

$$\frac{\overline{Y} - Y}{\overline{Y}} = 2(u - \bar{u}). \qquad (3.5)$$

After multiplying by −1, we rewrite Eq. (3.5) as

$$-1 + \frac{Y}{\overline{Y}} = -2u + 2\bar{u}.$$

We now calculate the change from the previous year to the current year for each side of this equation. Setting the change on the left side equal to the change on the right side, and assuming that $\bar{u}$ is constant (so that $\Delta\bar{u} = 0$), we get

$$\Delta(Y/\overline{Y}) = -2\Delta u$$

The left side of this equation, which is the change in $Y/\overline{Y}$, is very close to the growth rate of $Y/\overline{Y}$, which is $\Delta(Y/\overline{Y})/(Y/\overline{Y})$. (To go from the change to the growth rate, we divide by $Y/\overline{Y}$, which is a number close to 1.) Approximating the change in $Y/\overline{Y}$ by its growth rate, and using the formula that states that the growth rate of a ratio is the growth rate of the numerator minus the growth rate of the denominator (Appendix A, Section A.7), we rewrite the equation once more as

$$\frac{\Delta Y}{Y} - \frac{\Delta \overline{Y}}{\overline{Y}} = -2\Delta u.$$

In the United States, the average growth rate of full-employment output is 3% per year. Substituting 3% into this equation and rearranging gives the growth rate form of Okun's law, Eq. (3.6).

CHAPTER 4

Consumption, Saving, and Investment

In Chapter 3 we focused on some of the factors determining the amount of output produced, or *supplied*, in the economy. In this chapter we consider the factors that underlie the economywide *demand* for goods and services. In other words, we move from examining how much is produced to examining how that production is used.

Recall from Chapter 2 that aggregate demand (spending) in the economy has four components: the demand for consumer goods and services by households (consumption), the demand for new capital goods by firms and new homes by households (investment), government purchases of goods and services, and the net demand for domestic goods by foreigners (net exports). Because the level of government purchases is determined primarily by the political process, macroeconomic analysis usually treats that component of spending as given. For this chapter we also assume that the economy is closed so that net exports are zero (we drop the closed-economy assumption in Chapter 5). That leaves two major components of spending—consumption and investment—to be discussed in this chapter. In Section 4.1 we present the factors that determine how much households choose to consume, and in Section 4.2 we look at the decision by firms about how much to invest.

We have said that this chapter is about the aggregate demand for goods and services. However, we could just as easily say that it is about a seemingly very different (but equally important) topic: the determination of saving and capital formation. Studying the aggregate demand for goods and services is the same as studying the factors that determine saving and capital formation for the following reasons. First, saving is simply what is left after an economic unit (say, a household) decides how much of its income to consume. Thus the decision about how much to consume is the same as the decision about how much to save. Second, investment spending is part of the aggregate demand for goods and services, but it also represents the acquisition of new capital goods by firms. In studying investment spending, we therefore are also looking at the factors that lead an economy to acquire new factories, machines, and housing. In effect, we do two things at once in this chapter:

- We explore the determinants of the aggregate demand for goods, which prepares you for future discussions of topics such as the role of spending fluctuations in business cycles.
- While exploring aggregate demand we also examine the factors affecting saving and capital formation, which prepares you for future discussions of the sources of economic growth and other issues.

In making many economic decisions, including those we consider in this chapter, people must trade off the present against the future. In deciding how much to consume and save, for example, a household must weigh the benefits of enjoying more consumption today against the benefits of putting aside some of its income as saving for the future. Similarly, in deciding how much to invest, a firm's manager must determine how much to spend today so as to increase the firm's productive capacity one, five, or even twenty years from now. In making these trade-offs, households and firms must take into account their expectations about the future of the economy, including expectations about government policy.

In Chapter 3 we asked, What forces act to bring the labor market into equilibrium? We close this chapter by asking the same question for the goods market. The goods market is in equilibrium when the quantity of goods and services that producers want to supply (discussed in Chapter 3) equals the quantity of goods and services demanded by households, firms, and the government (discussed in this chapter). Equivalently, the goods market is in equilibrium when desired saving in the economy equals desired investment. We show that the real interest rate plays a key role in bringing the goods market into equilibrium.

4.1 Consumption and Saving

We begin consideration of the demand for goods and services by discussing the factors that affect consumer spending. Because consumption spending by households is by far the largest component of the demand for goods and services—accounting for more than two-thirds of total spending in the United States—changes in consumers' willingness to spend have major implications for the behavior of the economy.

Besides the sheer size of consumption spending, another reason to study consumption is that the individual's or household's decision about how much to consume is closely linked to another important economic decision, the decision about how much to save. Indeed, for given levels of disposable income, the decision about how much to consume and the decision about how much to save are really the same decision. For example, a college student with a part-time job that pays $4000 per year after taxes might decide to spend $3700 per year on clothes, food, entertainment, and other consumption. If she does consume this amount, her saving will automatically be $300 ($4000 minus $3700) per year. Equivalently, she might decide to save $300 per year. If she succeeds in saving $300, her consumption automatically is $3700 ($4000 minus $300) per year. Because the decision about how much to consume and the decision about how much to save actually are two sides of the same coin, we analyze them together.

From a macroeconomic perspective, we are interested in the aggregate, or national, levels of consumption and saving. We define the national level of *desired consumption*, C^d, as the aggregate quantity of goods and services that households want to consume, given income and other factors that determine households' economic opportunities. We will analyze desired consumption and its response to various factors, such as income and interest rates, by examining the consumption decisions of individual households. The aggregate level of desired consumption, C^d, is obtained by adding up the desired consumption of all households. Thus any factor that increases the desired consumption of individual households will increase C^d, and any factor that decreases the desired consumption of individual households will decrease C^d.

Just as a household's consumption decision and saving decision are closely linked, a country's desired consumption is closely linked to its desired national saving. Specifically, *desired national saving, S^d,* is the level of national saving that occurs when aggregate consumption is at its desired level. Recall from Chapter 2 (Eq. 2.8) that if net factor payments from abroad *(NFP)* equal zero (as must be true in a closed economy), national saving, S, equals $Y - C - G$, where Y is output, C is consumption, and G is government purchases. Because desired national saving, S^d, is the level of national saving that occurs when consumption equals its desired level, we obtain an expression for desired national saving by substituting desired consumption, C^d, for consumption, C, in the definition of national saving. This substitution yields

$$S^d = Y - C^d - G. \tag{4.1}$$

We can gain insight into the factors that affect consumption and saving at the national level by considering how consumption and saving decisions are made at the individual level. Appendix 4.A provides a more formal analysis of this decision-making process.

The Consumption and Saving Decision of an Individual

Let's consider the case of Prudence, a bookkeeper for the Spectacular Eyeglasses Company. Prudence earns $60,000 per year after taxes. Hence she could, if she chose, consume $60,000 worth of goods and services every year. Prudence, however, has two other options.

First, she can save by consuming less than $60,000 per year. Why should Prudence consume less than her income allows? The reason is that she is thinking about the future. By consuming less than her current income, she will accumulate savings that will allow her, at some time in the future, to consume more than her income. For example, Prudence may expect her income to be very low when she retires; by saving during her working life, she will be able to consume more than her income during retirement. Indeed, the desire to provide for retirement is an important motivation for saving in the real world.

Alternatively, Prudence could consume more than her current income by borrowing or by drawing down previously accumulated savings. If she borrows $5000 from a bank, for example, she could consume as much as $65,000 worth of goods and services this year even though her income is only $60,000. Consuming more than her income is enjoyable for Prudence, but the cost to her is that at some future time, when she must repay the loan, she will have to consume less than her income.

If Prudence consumes less today, she will be able to consume more in the future, and vice versa. In other words, she faces a *trade-off* between current consumption and future consumption. The rate at which Prudence trades off current and future consumption depends on the real interest rate prevailing in the economy. Suppose that Prudence can earn a real interest rate of r per year on her saving and, for simplicity, suppose that if she borrows, she must pay the same real interest rate r on the loan. These assumptions imply that Prudence can trade one unit of current (this year's) consumption for $1 + r$ units of future (next year's) consumption. For example, suppose Prudence reduces her consumption today by one dollar, thereby increasing her saving by one dollar. Because she earns a real interest rate of r on her saving, the dollar she saves today will be worth $1 + r$ dollars one year from now.[1] Under the assumption that Prudence uses the extra $1 + r$ dollars to increase her next year's consumption, she has effectively traded one dollar's worth of consumption today for $1 + r$ dollars of consumption a year from now.

Similarly, Prudence can trade $1 + r$ real dollars of future consumption for one extra dollar of consumption today. She does so by borrowing and spending an extra dollar today. In a year she will have to repay the loan with interest, a total of $1 + r$ dollars. Because she has to repay $1 + r$ dollars next year, her consumption next year will be $1 + r$ dollars less than it would be otherwise. So the "price" to Prudence of one dollar's worth of extra consumption today is $1 + r$ dollars' worth of consumption in the future.

The real interest rate r determines the relative price of current consumption and future consumption. Given this relative price, how should Prudence choose between consuming today and consuming in the future? One extreme possibility would be for her to borrow heavily and consume much more than her income today. The problem with this strategy is that, after repaying her loan, Prudence would be able to consume almost nothing in the future. The opposite, but equally extreme, approach would be for Prudence to save nearly all of her current income. This strategy would allow her to consume a great deal in the future, but at the cost of near-starvation today.

Realistically, most people would choose neither of those extreme strategies but would instead try to avoid sharp fluctuations in consumption. The desire to have a relatively even pattern of consumption over time—avoiding periods of very high or very low consumption—is known as the **consumption-smoothing motive.** Because of her consumption-smoothing motive, Prudence will try to spread her consumption spending more or less evenly over time, rather than bingeing in one period and starving in another.

Next, we will see how the consumption-smoothing motive guides Prudence's behavior when changes occur in some important determinants of her economic well-being, including her current income, her expected future income, and her wealth. As we consider each of these changes, we will hold constant the real interest rate r and, hence, the relative price of current consumption and future consumption. Later, we will discuss what happens if the real interest rate changes.

Effect of Changes in Current Income

Current income is an important factor affecting consumption and saving decisions. To illustrate, suppose that Prudence receives a one-time bonus of $6000 at work, which increases her current year's income by $6000. (We ignore income taxes; equivalently, we can assume that the bonus is actually larger than $6000 but that, after paying her taxes, Prudence finds that her current income has increased by $6000.) What will she do with this extra income? Prudence could splurge and spend the entire bonus on a trip to Hawaii. If she spends the entire bonus, her current consumption will increase by $6000 but, because she has not increased her saving, her future consumption will be unchanged. Alternatively, she could save the entire bonus, leaving her current consumption unchanged but using the bonus

---

[1]We are assuming that there is zero inflation over the coming year, so that $1 purchases the same amount of real goods in each period. Alternatively, we could say that since the real interest rate is r, each *real* dollar Prudence saves today will be worth $1 + r$ *real* dollars one year from now.

plus the interest it earns to increase her consumption in the future. Because of the consumption-smoothing motive, however, Prudence is unlikely to follow either of these extreme strategies. Instead, she will spend part of the bonus (increasing current consumption) and save the rest (enabling her to increase future consumption as well).

The portion of her bonus that Prudence spends will depend on factors such as her willingness to defer gratification and her assessment of her current and future needs. We define Prudence's **marginal propensity to consume,** or *MPC,* as the fraction of additional current income that she consumes in the current period. Because Prudence consumes some but not all of her extra income, her *MPC* will be between zero and one. Suppose, for example that Prudence has an *MPC* equal to 0.4, so that she consumes 0.4, or 40%, of an increase in current income. Then, when she receives a $6000 bonus, Prudence will increase her current consumption by $0.4 \times \$6000 = \$2400$. Because the part of income that is not consumed is saved, her saving also increases by the amount of $\$6000 - \$2400 = \$3600$.

The marginal propensity to consume also applies to *declines* in current income. For example, if Prudence were temporarily laid off from her bookkeeping job so that her current year's income decreased by $8000, she would reduce both her consumption and her saving. If we assume that her marginal propensity to consume remains 0.4, she would reduce her consumption by $0.4 \times \$8000 = \$3200$, and her saving would therefore have to diminish by $\$8000 - \$3200 = \$4800$.

Aggregate income and consumption reflect the decisions of millions of individuals and households, so that the lessons we learned from thinking about the case of Prudence also apply at the macroeconomic level. Just as an increase in Prudence's income caused her to consume more, we would expect an increase in aggregate output (income) Y to lead to an increase in aggregate desired consumption, C^d, as well. Because marginal propensities to consume are less than 1, however, the increase in C^d will be less than the increase in Y. As not all of the increase in Y is spent, desired national saving S^d will also rise when Y rises.

Effect of Changes in Expected Future Income

Today's consumption decisions may depend not only on current income, but also on the income that one expects to earn in the future. For example, an individual who is currently not employed but who has a contract to begin a high-paying job in three months will probably consume more today than another unemployed individual with no job prospects.

To illustrate the effect of changes in expected future income, suppose that instead of receiving the $6000 bonus during the current year, Prudence learns that she will receive a $6000 bonus (after taxes) next year. The promise of the bonus is legally binding, and Prudence has no doubt that she will receive the extra income next year. How will this information affect Prudence's consumption and saving in the current year?

Because her current income is unaffected, Prudence could leave her current consumption and saving unchanged, waiting until she actually receives the bonus to increase her consumption. If her decisions are guided by a consumption-smoothing motive, however, she will prefer to use the bonus to increase her current consumption as well as her future consumption. She can increase her current consumption, despite the fact that her current income remains unchanged, by reducing her current saving (she could even "dissave," or have negative current saving, with current consumption exceeding current income, by using her accumulated assets or by borrowing). Suppose, for example, that Prudence decides to consume $1000 more this year. Because her current income is unchanged, Prudence's $1000 increase in current consumption is equivalent to a $1000 reduction in current saving.

The $1000 reduction in current saving will reduce Prudence's available resources in the next year, relative to the situation in which her saving is unchanged, by $1000 × (1 + r). For example, if the real interest rate is 0.05, cutting current saving by $1000 reduces Prudence's available resources next year by $1000 × 1.05 = $1050. Overall, her available resources next year will increase by $6000 because of the bonus but will decrease by $1050 because of reduced current saving, giving a net increase in resources of $6000 − $1050 = $4950, which can be used to increase consumption next year or in the following years. Effectively, Prudence can use the increase in her expected future income to increase consumption both in the present and in the future.

To summarize, an increase in an individual's expected future income is likely to lead that person to increase current consumption and decrease current saving. The same result applies at the macroeconomic level: If people expect that aggregate output and income, Y, will be higher in the future, current desired consumption, C^d, should increase and current desired national saving, S^d, should decrease.

Economists can't measure expected future income directly, so how do they take this variable into account when predicting consumption and saving behavior? One approach is to survey consumers and ask them about their expectations. Their answers can be useful for assessing developments in the macroeconomy, as the Application "Consumer Sentiment and Forecasts of Consumer Spending" shows.

APPLICATION

Consumer Sentiment and Forecasts of Consumer Spending

Indexes that focus on consumer sentiment are widely reported in the press. The University of Michigan, The Conference Board, and ABC News/Washington Post each conduct their own survey, in which they ask consumers about their perceptions of current and future economic conditions. Consumer sentiment is closely associated with consumer spending. News about the stock market, wars, and elections causes consumer sentiment to change and affects consumer spending.

Economists on Wall Street and at the Federal Reserve pay attention to the indexes, thinking that they provide useful information about future spending by consumers. But do they? The question is: Even if consumer sentiment today is closely associated with consumer spending today, can consumer sentiment help economists forecast *future* consumer spending? Recent research suggests that these measures of consumer sentiment may not be helpful in doing so.

To see whether indexes of consumer sentiment facilitate accurate forecasting, we begin by examining the data. Figure 4.1 shows the monthly values of the University of Michigan (U of M) index, plotted over time from January 1978 to May 2009, with shaded bars indicating when the economy was in a recession.[2]

---

[2]The Conference Board survey and the ABC News/Washington Post survey show similar results. As their data are not as readily available as the University of Michigan survey data, we focus here on the U of M survey data.

Figure 4.1

University of Michigan Index of Consumer Sentiment, January 1978–May 2009

The U of M index of consumer sentiment is based on what consumers tell interviewers about their current economic situation and their expectations for the future of the economy. The index turned down before some recessions, but not all of them.

Source: Index of Consumer Sentiment (© University of Michigan) from FRED database, series UMCSENT.

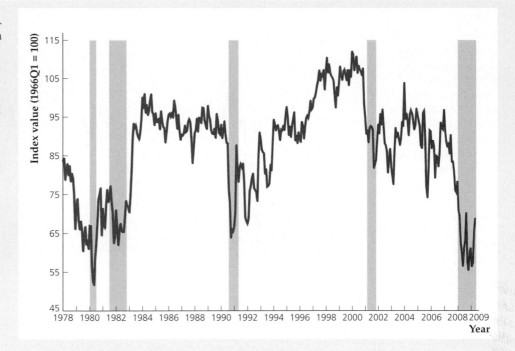

The University of Michigan consumer sentiment index turns down sharply during recessions. But it does not always give any warning before a recession begins, and it often turns down sharply but no recession occurs. Thus, the consumer sentiment index may not be useful for forecasting recessions.

If consumer sentiment indexes help economists on Wall Street and at the Federal Reserve forecast any economic variables, the likeliest such variable is consumer spending. We know that people base their spending decisions on their incomes and other variables, and it is a reasonable conjecture that their views of the current and future state of the economy would influence their consumption decisions.

To see whether consumer sentiment indexes are correlated with people's spending decisions, we look at the data in Fig. 4.2. The figure shows values from 1978 to 2009 of the U of M index of consumer sentiment (the scale on the left vertical axis) compared with consumer spending (the scale on the right vertical axis), as measured by the percentage change in consumer spending from the same month one year earlier (so the value reported for May 2009 is the percentage change in the amount of consumer spending in May 2009 from its value in May 2008).

The general movements of the two series correspond fairly closely (the correlation between them is 0.71). They declined together from 1978 to 1980, rose sharply together after the recession ended in 1982, and drifted slowly downward together in the 1980s. In the 1990s, the University of Michigan index rose earlier than the growth rate of consumption spending, but both were very high in the late 1990s and fell together in the early 2000s. Both series moved down sharply in 2007 and 2008.

Sometimes, however, the consumer sentiment index moves differently than consumer spending. For example, consumer sentiment fell sharply in 1978, but consumer spending grew briskly throughout the year and did not exhibit substantially slower growth until the spring of 1979. We find another example in late 1998, when

Figure 4.2

University of Michigan Index of Consumer Sentiment and Consumption Spending, January 1978–May 2009

The index of consumer sentiment and growth in consumption spending appear to move together reasonably well, suggesting that consumer sentiment might be useful for explaining consumption spending.

Source: Index of Consumer Sentiment (© University of Michigan) from *research.stlouisfed.org/fred2/ series/UMCSENT*; consumption spending from *research. stlouisfed.org/fred2/ series/PCEC96.*

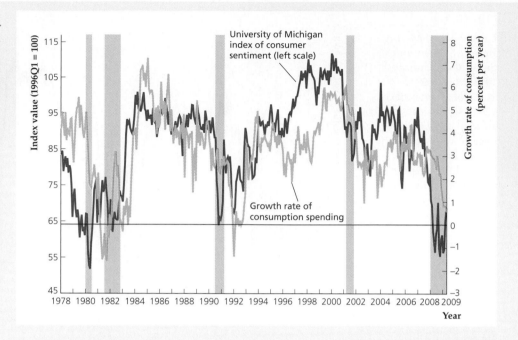

the Russian government defaulted on its debt and a large hedge fund failed, leading to chaotic financial conditions around the world. Consumer sentiment declined sharply, but consumer spending was unaffected.

So there are reasons to think that consumer sentiment might be useful in forecasting consumer spending, as well as reasons to think it may not be helpful. The only way to tell is to use formal statistical methods to test whether consumer sentiment improves the forecasting performance of a model.

Jason Bram of the Federal Reserve Bank of New York and Sydney Ludvigson of New York University examined the use of consumer sentiment indexes in forecasting consumer spending.[3] They asked the question: If a forecaster used a model to forecast the amount of consumer spending in the next three months, would those forecasts be improved if the forecaster included data on consumer sentiment in the model? Bram and Ludvigson found that for forecasting changes in consumer spending, a model including past consumer spending, personal income, stock prices, and interest rates is good, and the model's forecasts would not be improved by adding either the University of Michigan index or The Conference Board index.

Consumer sentiment indexes usefully inform us about consumers' perceptions of the current and future state of the economy and help to explain past changes in consumer spending. But they do not appear to be useful in forecasting consumer spending. Consumers may be worried about the current economic situation, but it appears that their future spending is governed mainly by their incomes and financial variables, not by current consumer sentiment.

---

[3]See Jason Bram and Sydney Ludvigson, "Does Consumer Confidence Forecast Household Expenditure? A Sentiment Index Horse Race." Federal Reserve Bank of New York, *Economic Policy Review* (June 1998), pp. 59–78.

Effect of Changes in Wealth

Another factor that affects consumption and saving is wealth. Recall from Chapter 2 that the wealth of any entity, such as a household or an entire nation, equals its assets minus its liabilities.

To see how consumption and saving respond to an increase in wealth, suppose that while cleaning out her attic Prudence finds a stock certificate for 50 shares of stock in a pharmaceutical company. Prudence's grandmother bought this stock for Prudence when she was born, and Prudence did not know about it. She immediately calls her broker and learns that the stock is now worth $6000. This unexpected $6000 increase in Prudence's wealth has the same effect on her available resources as the $6000 increase in current income that we examined earlier. As in the case involving an increase in her current income, Prudence will use her increase in wealth to increase her current consumption by an amount smaller than $6000 so that she can use some of the additional $6000 to increase her future consumption. Because Prudence's current income is not affected by finding the stock certificate, the increase in her current consumption is matched by a decrease in current saving of the same size. In this way, an increase in wealth increases current consumption and reduces current saving. The same line of reasoning leads to the conclusion that a decrease in wealth reduces current consumption and increases saving.

The ups and downs in the stock market are an important source of changes in wealth, and the effects on consumption of changes in the stock market are explored in the Application, "Macroeconomic Consequences of the Boom and Bust in Stock Prices," p. 138.

Effect of Changes in the Real Interest Rate

We have seen that the real interest rate is the price of current consumption in terms of future consumption. We held the real interest rate fixed when we examined the effects of changes in current income, expected future income, and wealth. Now we let the real interest rate vary, examining the effect on current consumption and saving of changes in the real interest rate.

How would Prudence's consumption and saving change in response to an increase in the real interest rate? Her response to such an increase reflects two opposing tendencies. On the one hand, because each real dollar of saving in the current year grows to $1 + r$ real dollars next year, an increase in the real interest rate means that each dollar of current saving will have a higher payoff in terms of increased future consumption. This increased reward for current saving tends to increase saving.

On the other hand, a higher real interest rate means that Prudence can achieve any future savings target with a smaller amount of current saving. For example, suppose that she is trying to accumulate $1400 to buy a new laptop computer next year. An increase in the real interest rate means that any current saving will grow to a larger amount by next year, so the amount that she needs to save this year to reach her goal of $1400 is lower. Because she needs to save less to reach her goal, she can increase her current consumption and thus reduce her saving.

The two opposing effects described above are known as the substitution effect and the income effect of an increase in the real interest rate. The **substitution effect of the real interest rate on saving** reflects the tendency to reduce current consumption and increase future consumption as the price of current consumption,

$1 + r$, increases. In response to an increase in the price of current consumption, consumers *substitute* away from current consumption, which has become relatively more expensive, toward future consumption, which has become relatively less expensive. The reduction in current consumption implies that current saving increases. Thus the substitution effect implies that current saving increases in response to an increase in the real interest rate.

The **income effect of the real interest rate on saving** reflects the change in current consumption that results when a higher real interest rate makes a consumer richer or poorer. For example, if Prudence has a savings account and has not borrowed any funds, she is a recipient of interest payments. She therefore benefits from an increase in the real interest rate because her interest income increases. With a higher interest rate, she can afford to have the same levels of current and future consumption as before the interest rate change, and she would have some additional resources to spend. These extra resources are effectively the same as an increase in her wealth, so she will increase both her current and her future consumption. Thus, for a saver, who is a recipient of interest payments, the income effect of an increase in the real interest rate is to increase current consumption and reduce current saving. Therefore, for a saver, the income and substitution effects of an increase in the real interest rate work in opposite directions, with the income effect reducing saving and the substitution effect increasing saving.

The income effect of an increase in the real interest rate is different for a payer of interest, such as a borrower. An increase in the real interest rate increases the amount of interest payments that a borrower must make, thereby making the borrower unable to afford the same levels of current and future consumption as before the increase in the real interest rate. The borrower has effectively suffered a loss of wealth as a result of the increase in the real interest rate, and responds to this decline in wealth by reducing both current consumption and future consumption. The reduction in current consumption means that current saving increases (that is, borrowing decreases). Hence, for a borrower, the income effect of an increase in the real interest rate is to increase saving. Thus both the substitution effect and the income effect of an increase in the real interest rate increase the saving of a borrower.

Let's summarize the effect of an increase in the real interest rate. For a saver, who is a recipient of interest, an increase in the real interest rate tends to increase saving through the substitution effect but to reduce saving through the income effect. Without additional information, we cannot say which of these two opposing effects is larger. For a borrower, who is a payer of interest, both the substitution effect and the income effect operate to increase saving. Consequently, the saving of a borrower unambiguously increases.

What is the effect of an increase in the real interest rate on national saving? Because the national economy is composed of both borrowers and savers, and because, in principle, savers could either increase or decrease their saving in response to an increase in the real interest rate, economic theory cannot answer this question. As economic theory does not indicate whether national saving increases or decreases in response to an increase in the real interest rate, we must rely on empirical studies that examine this relationship using actual data. Unfortunately, interpretation of the empirical evidence from the many studies done continues to inspire debate. The most widely accepted conclusion seems to be that an increase in the real interest rate reduces current consumption and increases saving, but this effect isn't very strong.

Taxes and the Real Return to Saving. In discussing the real return that savers earn, we have not yet mentioned an important practical consideration: Interest earnings (and other returns on savings) are taxed. Because part of interest earnings must be paid as taxes, the real return earned by savers is actually less than the difference between the nominal interest rate and expected inflation.

A useful measure of the returns received by savers that recognizes the effects of taxes is the *expected after-tax real interest rate*. To define this concept, we let i represent the nominal interest rate and t the rate at which interest income is taxed. In the United States, for example, most interest earnings are taxed as ordinary income, so t is the income tax rate. Savers retain a fraction $(1 - t)$ of total interest earned so that the after-tax nominal interest rate, received by savers after payment of taxes, is $(1 - t)i$. The **expected after-tax real interest rate**, r_{a-t}, is the after-tax nominal interest rate minus the expected inflation rate, π^e, or

$$r_{a-t} = (1 - t)i - \pi^e. \tag{4.2}$$

The expected after-tax real interest rate is the appropriate interest rate for consumers to use in making consumption and saving decisions because it measures the increase in the purchasing power of their saving after payment of taxes.

Table 4.1 shows how to calculate the after-tax nominal interest rate and the expected after-tax real interest rate. Note that, given the nominal interest rate and expected inflation, a reduction in the tax rate on interest income increases the nominal and real after-tax rates of return that a saver receives. Thus, by reducing the rate at which it taxes interest, the government can increase the real rate of return earned by savers and (possibly) increase the rate of saving in the economy.

The stimulation of saving is the motivation for tax provisions such as individual retirement accounts (IRAs), which allow savers to shelter part of their interest earnings from taxes and thus earn higher after-tax rates of return. Unfortunately, because economists disagree about the effect of higher real interest rates on saving, the effectiveness of IRAs and similar tax breaks for saving also is in dispute.

Fiscal Policy

We've just demonstrated how government tax policies can affect the real return earned by savers and thus, perhaps, the saving rate. However, even when government fiscal policies—decisions about spending and taxes—aren't intentionally

Table 4.1

Calculating After-Tax Interest Rates

i = nominal interest rate = 5% per year
π^e = expected inflation rate = 2% per year

Example 1
t = tax rate on interest income = 30%
After-tax nominal interest rate = $(1 - t)i = (1 - 0.30)5\% = 3.5\%$
Expected after-tax real interest rate = $(1 - t)i - \pi^e = (1 - 0.30)5\% - 2\% = 1.5\%$

Example 2
t = tax rate on interest income = 20%
After-tax nominal interest rate = $(1 - t)i = (1 - 0.20)5\% = 4\%$
Expected after-tax real interest rate = $(1 - t)i - \pi^e = (1 - 0.20)5\% - 2\% = 2\%$

directed at affecting the saving rate, these policies have important implications for the amount of consumption and saving that takes place in the economy. Although understanding the links between fiscal policy and consumer behavior requires some difficult economic reasoning, these links are so important that we introduce them here. Later we discuss several of these issues further, particularly in Chapter 15.

To make the discussion of fiscal policy effects as straightforward as possible, we take the economy's aggregate output, Y, as a given. That is, we ignore the possibility that the changes in fiscal policy that we consider could affect the aggregate supply of goods and services. This assumption is valid if the economy is at full employment (as we are assuming throughout Part 2 of this book) and if the fiscal policy changes don't significantly affect the capital stock or employment. Later we relax the fixed-output assumption and discuss both the classical and Keynesian views about how fiscal policy changes can affect output.

In general, fiscal policy affects *desired consumption*, C^d, primarily by affecting households' current and expected future incomes. More specifically, fiscal changes that increase the tax burden on the private sector, either by raising current taxes or by leading people to expect that taxes will be higher in the future, will cause people to consume less.

For a given level of output, Y, government fiscal policies affect *desired national saving*, S^d, or $Y - C^d - G$, in two basic ways. First, as we just noted, fiscal policy can influence desired consumption: For any levels of output, Y, and government purchases, G, a fiscal policy change that reduces desired consumption, C^d, by one dollar will at the same time raise desired national saving, S^d, by one dollar. Second, for any levels of output and desired consumption, increases in government purchases directly lower desired national saving, as is apparent from the definition of desired national saving, $S^d = Y - C^d - G$.

IN TOUCH WITH DATA AND RESEARCH

Interest Rates

Although in our theoretical discussions we refer to "the" interest rate, as if there were only one, actually there are many different interest rates, each of which depends on the identity of the borrower and the terms of the loan. Shown here are some interest rates that appeared in Federal Reserve statistical release H.15 on July 20, 2009.

The prime rate is the basic rate that banks charge on loans to their best customers. The Federal funds rate is the rate at which banks make overnight loans to one another. Treasury bills, notes, and bonds are debts of the U.S. government, and

	July 2009	July 2008
Prime rate	3.25%	5.00%
Federal funds	0.15	1.98
3-month Treasury bills	0.19	1.48
6-month Treasury bills	0.28	1.93
10-year Treasury notes	3.61	4.09
30-year Treasury bonds	4.47	4.64
Municipal bonds	4.69	4.77

municipal bonds are obligations of state and local governments. With the exception of the prime rate, these interest rates vary continuously as financial market conditions change. The prime rate is an average of lending rates set by major banks and changes less frequently.

The interest rates charged on these different types of loans need not be the same. One reason for this variation is differences in the risk of nonrepayment, or default. Federal government debt is believed to be free from default risk, but there is always a chance that a business, bank, or municipality may not be able to repay what it borrowed. Lenders charge risky borrowers extra interest to compensate themselves for the risk of default. Thus the prime rate, the Federal funds rate, and the municipal bond rate are higher than they would be if there were no default risk.

A second factor affecting interest rates is the length of time for which the funds are borrowed. The relationship between the life of a bond (its *maturity*) and the interest rate it pays is called the *yield curve*. The accompanying figure shows the yield curve in July 2009 and the yield curve one year earlier. Because longer maturity bonds typically pay higher interest rates than shorter maturity bonds, the yield curve generally slopes upward. We will discuss how interest rates relate to the maturity of a bond in the section "Time to Maturity" in Chapter 7, pp. 245–246.

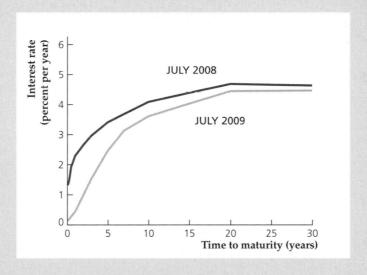

A final factor affecting interest rates is tax status. Because interest on municipal bonds is not taxable, lenders are willing to accept a lower interest rate on these loans than if the interest were taxable.

Although the levels of the various interest rates are quite different, interest rates go up and down together most of the time. All of the interest rates discussed here, including those on Treasury bills, notes, and bonds of various maturities and on municipal bonds, decreased between July 2008 and July 2009. As a general rule, interest rates tend to move together, so in our economic analyses we usually refer to "the" interest rate, as if there were only one.

To illustrate these general points, we consider how desired consumption and desired national saving would be affected by two specific fiscal policy changes: an increase in government purchases and a tax cut.

Government Purchases.   Suppose that current government purchases, G, increase by $10 billion, perhaps because the government increases military spending. Assume that this increase in G is temporary so that plans for future government purchases are unchanged. (Analytical Problem 5 at the end of this chapter looks at the case of a permanent increase in government purchases.) For any fixed level of output, Y, how will this change in fiscal policy affect desired consumption and desired national saving in the economy?

Let's start by finding the effect of the increased government purchases on consumption. As already mentioned, changes in government purchases affect consumption because they affect private-sector tax burdens. Suppose for example that the government pays for the extra $10 billion in military spending by raising current taxes by $10 billion. For a given total (before-tax) output, Y, this tax increase implies a $10 billion decline in consumers' current (after-tax) incomes. We know that consumers respond to a decline in their current incomes by reducing consumption, although by less than the decline in current income.[4] So, in response to the $10 billion tax increase, consumers might, for example, reduce their current consumption by $6 billion.

What happens to consumption if the government doesn't raise current taxes when it increases its purchases? The analysis in this case is more subtle. If the government doesn't raise current taxes, it will have to borrow the $10 billion to pay for the extra spending. The government will have to repay the $10 billion it borrows, plus interest, sometime in the future, implying that future taxes will have to rise. If taxpayers are clever enough to understand that increased government purchases today mean higher taxes in the future, households' expected future (after-tax) incomes will fall, and again they will reduce desired consumption. For the sake of illustration, we can imagine that they again reduce their current consumption by $6 billion, although the reduction in consumption might be less if some consumers don't understand that their future taxes are likely to rise.

What about the effects on desired national saving? The increase in government purchases affects desired national saving, $Y - C^d - G$, directly by increasing G and indirectly by reducing desired consumption, C^d. In our example, the increase in government purchases reduces desired consumption by $6 billion, which by itself would raise national saving by $6 billion. However, this effect is outweighed by the increase in G of $10 billion so that overall desired national saving, $Y - C^d - G$, falls by $4 billion, with output, Y, held constant.[5] More generally, because the decline in desired consumption can be expected to be less than the initial increase in government purchases, a temporary increase in government purchases will lower desired national saving.

To summarize, for a given current level of output, Y, we conclude that a temporary increase in government purchases reduces both desired consumption and desired national saving.

---

[4]Recall that the marginal propensity to consume out of current income is positive but less than 1.

[5]Note that national saving would fall by even more than $4 billion if consumers ignored the prospect of future tax increases and thus didn't reduce their current consumption.

Taxes.   Now suppose that government purchases, G, remain constant but that the government reduces current taxes, T, by $10 billion. To keep things as simple as possible, we suppose that the tax cut is a *lump sum*, giving each taxpayer the same amount (think of the country's 100 million taxpayers receiving $100 each). With government purchases, G, and output, Y, held constant, desired national saving, $Y - C^d - G$, will change only if desired consumption, C^d, changes. So the question is, How will desired consumption respond to the cut in current taxes?

Again the key issue is, How does the tax cut affect people's current and expected future incomes? The $10 billion current tax cut directly increases current (after-tax) incomes by $10 billion, so the tax cut should increase desired consumption (by somewhat less than $10 billion). However, the $10 billion current tax cut also should lead people to expect *lower* after-tax incomes in the future. The reason is that, because the government hasn't changed its spending, to cut taxes by $10 billion today the government must also increase its current borrowing by $10 billion. Because the extra $10 billion of government debt will have to be repaid with interest in the future, future taxes will have to be higher, which in turn implies lower future disposable incomes for households. All else being equal, the decline in expected future incomes will cause people to consume less today, offsetting the positive effect of increased current income on desired consumption. Thus, in principle, a current tax cut—which raises current incomes but lowers expected future incomes—could either raise or lower current desired consumption.

Interestingly, some economists argue that the positive effect of increased current income and the negative effect of decreased future income on desired consumption should exactly cancel so that the overall effect of a current tax cut on consumption is zero! The idea that tax cuts do not affect desired consumption and (therefore) also do not affect desired national saving,[6] is called the **Ricardian equivalence proposition.**[7]

The Ricardian equivalence idea can be briefly explained as follows (see Chapter 15 for a more detailed discussion). In the long run, all government purchases must be paid for by taxes. Thus, if the government's current and planned purchases do not change, a cut in current taxes can affect the *timing* of tax collections but (advocates of Ricardian equivalence emphasize) not the ultimate tax burden borne by consumers. A current tax cut with no change in government purchases doesn't really make consumers any better off (any reduction in taxes today is balanced by tax increases in the future), so they have no reason to respond to the tax cut by changing their desired consumption.

Although the logic of the Ricardian equivalence proposition is sound, many economists question whether it makes sense in practice. Most of these skeptics argue that, even though the proposition predicts that consumers will not increase consumption when taxes are cut, in reality lower current taxes likely will lead to increased desired consumption and thus reduced desired national saving. One

---

[6]In this example, private disposable income rises by $10 billion, so if desired consumption doesn't change, desired private saving rises by $10 billion. However, the government deficit also rises by $10 billion because of the tax cut, so government saving falls by $10 billion. Therefore desired national saving—private saving plus government saving—doesn't change.

[7]The argument was first advanced by the nineteenth-century economist David Ricardo, although he expressed some reservations about its applicability to real-world situations. The word "equivalence" refers to the idea that, if Ricardian equivalence is true, taxes and government borrowing have equivalent effects on the economy.

SUMMARY 5

Determinants of Desired National Saving

An increase in	Causes desired national saving to	Reason
Current output, Y	Rise	Part of the extra income is saved to provide for future consumption.
Expected future output	Fall	Anticipation of future income raises current desired consumption, lowering current desired saving.
Wealth	Fall	Some of the extra wealth is consumed, which reduces saving for given income.
Expected real interest rate, r	Probably rise	An increased return makes saving more attractive, probably outweighing the fact that less must be saved to reach a specific savings target.
Government purchases, G	Fall	Higher government purchases directly lower desired national saving.
Taxes, T	Remain unchanged or rise	Saving doesn't change if consumers take into account an offsetting future tax cut; saving rises if consumers don't take into account a future tax cut and thus reduce current consumption.

reason that consumption may rise after a tax cut is that many—perhaps most—consumers do not understand that increased government borrowing today is likely to lead to higher taxes in the future. Thus consumers may simply respond to the current tax cut, as they would to any other increase in current income, by increasing their desired consumption.

The effects of a tax cut on consumption and saving may be summarized as follows: According to the Ricardian equivalence proposition, with no change in current or planned government purchases, a tax cut doesn't change desired consumption and desired national saving. However, the Ricardian equivalence proposition may not apply if consumers fail to take account of possible future tax increases in their planning; in that case, a tax cut will increase desired consumption and reduce desired national saving.

The factors that affect consumption and saving are listed in Summary table 5.

APPLICATION

How Consumers Respond to Tax Rebates

In 2008, during the recession that began in December 2007, the government gave consumers a tax rebate, hoping to stimulate the economy. But if Ricardian equivalence holds, such a tax rebate is not likely to be effective at stimulating consumer spending or the economy.

Some evidence suggesting that consumer spending would not rise much in response to a tax rebate was provided by Matthew D. Shapiro and Joel Slemrod of the University of Michigan in a study of the tax rebate given to consumers in the

2001 recession.[8] They found that fewer than one-quarter of households said they mostly spent the tax rebates they received in 2001. This finding indicates that the tax rebates did not stimulate the economy as much as the government had hoped when it passed the tax cuts into law.

New evidence on the impact of the tax rebates in 2001 has been developed recently by Sumit Agarwal of the Federal Reserve Bank of Chicago, Chunlin Liu of the University of Nevada, and Nicholas Souleles of the University of Pennsylvania.[9] They found evidence consistent with the results in the study by Shapiro and Slemrod, which is that most consumers saved most of the rebate they received, at least initially. But, using a novel data set of credit-card purchases and balances by about 75,000 households from a large credit-card issuer, they found that in the months after the rebate was received, a typical household gradually increased its purchases and increased its credit-card debt.

Agarwal, Liu, and Souleles first examined the pattern of how credit-card payments changed after the rebate is received by a household. Then they looked to see if credit-card purchases subsequently rose. Finally, they were able to examine the change in the amount of credit-card debt the household had. Since the rebate checks were mailed out over a three-month period depending on the social security numbers of taxpayers, Agarwal, Liu, and Souleles were able to calculate exactly when each household received its rebate check. This information enabled them to determine the response of payments, purchases, and credit-card debt.

One clear impact of the tax rebates in 2001 was to spur people to increase payments to their credit-card issuers. Though many people at first made additional payments on their credit cards, they also changed their purchasing behavior in response to the tax rebate. At first, households did not increase their credit-card purchases. But after a few months, they began to increase their purchases and after nine months had spent an additional $60 on average on their credit cards because of the tax rebate.

Because initially purchases did not change but payments increased, the average amount of credit-card debt declined at first. As households began to purchase more over time, the amount of credit-card debt began to rise. Nine months after receiving its tax rebate, the average household ended up with a little over $25 of additional credit-card debt, which is a small increase relative to average debt levels of about $2000 and is not statistically significant.

Because the main results take the average across many different households, it may be worthwhile to look at different segments of the population to see how they responded to the tax rebates. In particular, in Appendix 4.A we discuss how binding borrowing constraints (which prevent people from borrowing as much as they would like) can affect consumption behavior. In particular, someone who is unable to borrow any more because of a binding borrowing constraint (perhaps resulting from a credit-card limit imposed by its bank) is likely to spend more of the tax rebate than someone who is not constrained. Most likely, younger people (whose future income tends to be higher than current income) and those with low limits on their credit cards are likely to face binding borrowing constraints.

[8]"Did the 2001 Tax Rebate Stimulate Spending? Evidence from Taxpayer Surveys," in James Poterba, ed., *Tax Policy and the Economy* 17 (Cambridge, MA: MIT Press, 2003), pp. 83–109.
[9]"The Reaction of Consumer Spending and Debt to Tax Rebates – Evidence from Consumer Credit Data," *Journal of Political Economy,* December 2007, pp. 986–1019.

To see if young people responded more to the tax rebates than others, Agarwal, Liu, and Souleles split their data into three age groups: young people (less than 35 years old), middle-aged people, and old people (over 60 years old). They found that nine months after receiving the tax rebate, young people had increased their purchases by about $200, which was substantially more than the other groups. Also, debt increased by about $130 for young households but by much less for older households.

Agarwal, Liu, and Souleles performed a similar split based on the credit-card limits faced by the household. People in the low-credit-limit group have limits of less than $7,500, while people in the high-limit group have limits exceeding $10,500. The results indicate that people with high credit limits paid off more of their balances, spent less, and reduced their credit-card debt more than the other groups. Thus, it appears that people with high credit limits, who may be less likely to face binding borrowing constraints, mainly responded to the tax rebates closer to the manner suggested by the Ricardian equivalence theory, while those facing binding borrowing constraints did not. We might expect a similar response to the 2008 tax rebates, but will have wait until new data become available to know.

4.2 Investment

Let's now turn to a second major component of spending: investment spending by firms. Like consumption and saving decisions, the decision about how much to invest depends largely on expectations about the economy's future. Investment also shares in common with saving and consumption the idea of a trade-off between the present and the future. In making a capital investment, a firm commits its current resources (which could otherwise be used, for example, to pay increased dividends to shareholders) to increasing its capacity to produce and earn profits in the future.

Recall from Chapter 2 that investment refers to the purchase or construction of capital goods, including residential and nonresidential buildings, equipment and software used in production, and additions to inventory stocks. From a macroeconomic perspective, there are two main reasons to study investment behavior. First, more so than the other components of aggregate spending, investment spending fluctuates sharply over the business cycle, falling in recessions and rising in booms. Even though investment is only about one-sixth of GDP, in the typical recession half or more of the total decline in spending is reduced investment spending. Hence explaining the behavior of investment is important for understanding the business cycle, which we explore further in Part 3.

The second reason for studying investment behavior is that investment plays a crucial role in determining the long-run productive capacity of the economy. Because investment creates new capital goods, a high rate of investment means that the capital stock is growing quickly. As discussed in Chapter 3, capital is one of the two most important factors of production (the other is labor). All else being equal, output will be higher in an economy that has invested rapidly and thus built up a large capital stock than in an economy that hasn't acquired much capital.

The Desired Capital Stock

To understand what determines the amount of investment, we must consider how firms decide how much capital they want. If firms attempt to maximize profit, as we assume, a firm's **desired capital stock** is the amount of capital that allows the firm to earn the largest expected profit. Managers can determine the profit-maximizing level of the capital stock by comparing the costs and benefits of using additional capital—a new machine, for example. If the benefits outweigh the costs, expanding the capital stock will raise profits. But if the costs outweigh the benefits, the firm shouldn't increase its planned capital stock and may even want to reduce it. As you might infer from this brief description, the economic logic underlying a firm's decision about how much capital to use is similar to the logic of its decision about how many workers to employ, discussed in Chapter 3.

In real terms, the benefit to a firm of having an additional unit of capital is the marginal product of capital, MPK. Recall from Chapter 3 that the MPK is the increase in output that a firm can obtain by adding a unit of capital, holding constant the firm's work force and other factors of production. Because lags occur in obtaining and installing new capital, the expected *future* marginal product of capital, MPK^f, is the benefit from increasing investment today by one unit of capital. This expected future benefit must be compared to the expected cost of using that extra unit of capital, or the user cost of capital.

The User Cost of Capital. To make the discussion of the user cost of capital more concrete, let's consider the case of Kyle's Bakery, Inc., a company that produces specialty cookies. Kyle, the bakery's owner-manager, is considering investing in a new solar-powered oven that will allow him to produce more cookies in the future. If he decides to buy such an oven, he must also determine its size. In making this decision, Kyle has the following information:

1. A new oven can be purchased in any size at a price of $100 per cubic foot, measured in real (base-year) dollars.
2. Because the oven is solar powered, using it does not involve energy costs. The oven also does not require maintenance expenditures.[10] However, the oven becomes less efficient as it ages: With each year that passes, the oven produces 10% fewer cookies. Because of this depreciation, the real value of an oven falls 10% per year. For example, after one year of use, the real value of the oven is $90 per cubic foot.
3. Kyle can borrow (from a bank) or lend (to the government, by buying a one-year government bond) at the prevailing expected real interest rate of 8% per year.

In calculating the user cost of capital, we use the following symbols (the numerical values are from the example of Kyle's Bakery):

$$p_K = \text{real price of capital goods (\$100 per cubic foot)};$$
$$d = \text{rate at which capital depreciates (10\% per year)};$$
$$r = \text{expected real interest rate (8\% per year)}.$$

[10]These assumptions simplify the example. If there were operating costs, such as fuel and maintenance costs, we would subtract them from the expected future marginal product of capital when calculating the benefit of using the oven.

The **user cost of capital** is the expected real cost of using a unit of capital for a specified period of time. For Kyle's Bakery, we consider the expected costs of purchasing a new oven, using it for a year, and then selling it. The cost of using the oven has two components: depreciation and interest.

In general, the depreciation cost of using capital is the value lost as the capital wears out. Because of depreciation, after one year the oven for which Kyle pays $100 per cubic foot when new will be worth only $90 per cubic foot. The $10-per-cubic-foot loss that Kyle suffers over the year is the depreciation cost of using the oven. Even if Kyle doesn't sell the oven at the end of a year, he suffers this loss because at the end of the year the asset's (the oven's) economic value will be 10% less.

The interest cost of using capital equals the expected real interest rate times the price of the capital. As the expected real interest rate is 8%, Kyle's interest cost of using the oven for a year is 8% of $100 per cubic foot, or $8 per cubic foot. To see why the interest cost is a cost of using capital, imagine first that Kyle must borrow the funds necessary to buy the oven; in this case, the interest cost of $8 per cubic foot is the interest he pays on the loan, which is obviously part of the total cost of using the oven. Alternatively, if Kyle uses profits from the business to buy the oven, he gives up the opportunity to use those funds to buy an interest-bearing asset, such as a government bond. For every $100 that Kyle puts into the oven, he is sacrificing $8 in interest that he would have earned by purchasing a $100 government bond. This forgone interest is a cost to Kyle of using the oven. Thus the interest cost is part of the true economic cost of using capital, whether the capital's purchase is financed with borrowed funds or with the firm's own retained profits.

The user cost of capital is the sum of the depreciation cost and the interest cost. The interest cost is rp_K, the depreciation cost is dp_K, and the user cost of capital, uc, is

$$uc = rp_K + dp_K = (r + d)p_K \qquad (4.3)$$

In the case of Kyle's Bakery,

$$\begin{aligned} uc &= (0.08 \text{ per year} \times \$100 \text{ per cubic foot}) \\ &\quad + (0.10 \text{ per year} \times \$100 \text{ per cubic foot}) \\ &= \$18 \text{ per cubic foot per year.} \end{aligned}$$

Thus Kyle's user cost of capital is $18 per cubic foot per year.

Determining the Desired Capital Stock.   Now we can find a firm's profit-maximizing capital stock, or desired capital stock. A firm's desired capital stock is the capital stock at which the expected future marginal product of capital equals the user cost of capital.

Figure 4.3 shows the determination of the desired capital stock for Kyle's Bakery. The capital stock, K, expressed as cubic feet of oven capacity, is measured along the horizontal axis. Both the MPK^f and the user cost of capital are measured along the vertical axis.

The downward-sloping curve shows the value of the MPK^f for different sizes of the capital stock, K; at each level of K, the MPK^f equals the expected real value of the extra cookies that could be produced per year if oven capacity were expanded an additional cubic foot. The MPK^f curve slopes downward because the marginal product of capital falls as the capital stock is increased (we discussed reasons for the

Figure 4.3

Determination of the desired capital stock
The desired capital stock (5000 cubic feet of oven capacity in this example) is the capital stock that maximizes profits. When the capital stock is 5000 cubic feet, the expected future marginal product of capital, MPK^f, is equal to the user cost of capital, uc. If the MPK^f is larger than uc, as it is when the capital stock is 4000 cubic feet, the benefit of extra capital exceeds the cost, and the firm should increase its capital stock. If the MPK^f is smaller than uc, as it is at 6000 cubic feet, the cost of extra capital exceeds the benefit, and the firm should reduce its capital stock.

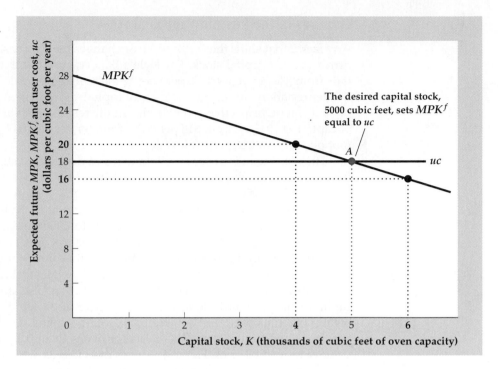

diminishing marginal productivity of capital in Chapter 3). The user cost (equal to $18 per cubic foot per year in the example) doesn't depend on the amount of capital and is represented by a horizontal line.

The amount of capital that maximizes the expected profit of Kyle's Bakery is 5000 cubic feet, represented by point A in Fig. 4.3. At A, the expected benefit of an additional unit of capital, MPK^f, equals the user cost, uc. For any amount of oven capacity less than 5000 cubic feet, Kyle's Bakery could increase its expected profit by increasing oven capacity. For example, Fig. 4.3 shows that at a planned capacity of 4000 cubic feet the MPK^f of an additional cubic foot is $20 worth of cookies per year, which exceeds the $18 per year expected cost of using the additional cubic foot of capacity. Starting from a planned capacity of 4000 cubic feet, if Kyle adds an extra cubic foot of capacity, he will gain an additional $20 worth of future output per year while incurring only $18 per year in expected future costs. Thus expanding beyond 4000 cubic feet is profitable for Kyle. Similarly, Fig. 4.3 shows that at an oven capacity of more than 5000 cubic feet the expected future marginal product of capital, MPK^f, is less than the user cost, uc; in this case Kyle's Bakery could increase expected profit by reducing its capital stock. Only when $MPK^f = uc$ will the capital stock be at the level that maximizes expected profit.

As mentioned earlier, the determination of the desired capital stock is similar to the determination of the firm's labor demand, described in Chapter 3. Recall that the firm's profit-maximizing level of employment is the level at which the marginal product of labor equals the wage. Analogously, the firm's profit-maximizing level of capital is the level at which the expected future marginal product of capital equals the user cost, which can be thought of as the "wage" of capital (the cost of using capital for one period).

Changes in the Desired Capital Stock

Any factor that shifts the MPK^f curve or changes the user cost of capital changes the firm's desired capital stock. For Kyle's Bakery, suppose that the real interest rate falls from 8% per year to 6% per year. If the real interest rate, r, is 0.06 per year and the depreciation rate, d, and the price of capital, p_K, remain at 0.10 per year and $100 per cubic foot, respectively, the decline in the real interest rate reduces the user cost of capital, $(r + d)p_K$, from $18 per cubic foot per year to $(0.06 + 0.10)$100 per cubic foot per year, or $16 per cubic foot per year.

This decline in the user cost is shown as a downward shift of the user cost line, from uc^1 to uc^2 in Fig. 4.4. After that shift, the MPK^f at the original desired capital stock of 5000 cubic feet (point A), or $18 per cubic foot per year, exceeds the user cost of capital, now $16 per cubic foot per year (point B). Kyle's Bakery can increase its profit by raising planned oven capacity to 6000 cubic feet, where the MPK^f equals the user cost of $16 per cubic foot per year (point C). This example illustrates that a decrease in the expected real interest rate—or any other change that lowers the user cost of capital—increases the desired capital stock.

Technological changes that affect the MPK^f curve also affect the desired stock of capital. Suppose that Kyle invents a new type of cookie dough that requires less baking time, allowing 12.5% more cookies to be baked daily. Such a technological advance would cause the MPK^f curve for ovens to shift upward by 12.5% at each value of the capital stock. Figure 4.5 shows this effect as a shift of the MPK^f curve from MPK^f_1 to MPK^f_2. If the user cost remains at $18 per cubic foot per year, the technological advance causes Kyle's desired capital stock to rise from 5000 to 6000 cubic feet. At 6000 cubic feet (point D) the MPK^f again equals the user cost of capital. In general, with the user cost of capital held constant, an increase in the expected future marginal product of capital at any level of capital raises the desired capital stock.

Figure 4.4

A decline in the real interest rate raises the desired capital stock
For the Kyle's Bakery example, a decline in the real interest rate from 8% to 6% reduces the user cost, uc, of oven capacity from $18 to $16 per cubic foot per year and shifts the user-cost line down from uc^1 to uc^2. The desired capital stock rises from 5000 (point A) to 6000 (point C) cubic feet of oven capacity. At 6000 cubic feet the MPK^f and the user cost of capital again are equal, at $16 per cubic foot per year.

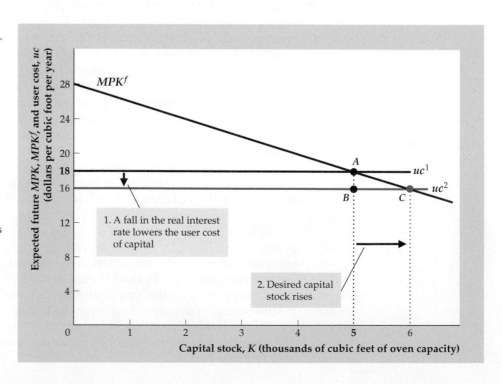

Figure 4.5

An increase in the expected future *MPK* raises the desired capital stock

A technological advance raises the expected future marginal product of capital, *MPK^f*, shifting the *MPK^f* curve upward from MPK_1^f to MPK_2^f. The desired capital stock increases from 5000 (point *A*) to 6000 (point *D*) cubic feet of oven capacity. At 6000 cubic feet the *MPK^f* equals the user cost of capital *uc* at $18 per cubic foot per year.

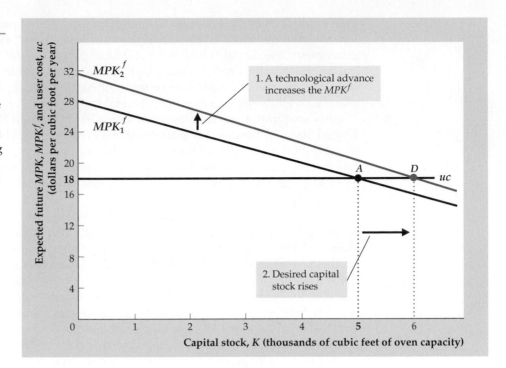

Taxes and the Desired Capital Stock.   So far we have ignored the role of taxes in the investment decision. But Kyle is interested in maximizing the profit his firm gets to keep after paying taxes. Thus he must take into account taxes in evaluating the desirability of an additional unit of capital.

Suppose that Kyle's Bakery pays 20% of its revenues in taxes. In this case, extra oven capacity that increases the firm's future revenues by, say, $20 will raise Kyle's after-tax revenue by only $16, with $4 going to the government. To decide whether to add this extra capacity, Kyle should compare the after-tax *MPK^f* of $16 per cubic foot per year—not the before-tax *MPK^f* of $20 per cubic foot per year— with the user cost. In general, if τ is the tax rate on firm revenues, the after-tax future marginal product of capital is $(1 - \tau)MPK^f$. The desired capital stock is the one for which the after-tax future marginal product equals the user cost, or

$$(1 - \tau)MPK^f = uc.$$

Dividing both sides of this equation by $1 - \tau$, we obtain

$$MPK^f = \frac{uc}{1 - \tau} = \frac{(r + d)p_K}{1 - \tau}. \tag{4.4}$$

In Eq. (4.4), the term $uc/(1 - \tau)$ is called the tax-adjusted user cost of capital. The **tax-adjusted user cost of capital** shows how large the before-tax future marginal product of capital must be for a firm to willingly add another unit of capital. An increase in the tax rate τ raises the tax-adjusted user cost and thus reduces the desired stock of capital.

To derive the tax-adjusted user cost, we assumed that taxes are levied as a proportion of firms' revenues. However, actual corporate taxes in the United States and other countries are much more complicated. Firms generally pay taxes on their profits rather than on their revenues, and the part of profit that is considered taxable may depend on how much the firm invests. For example, when a firm purchases some capital, it is allowed to deduct part of the purchase price of the capital from its taxable profit in both the year of purchase and in subsequent years. By reducing the amount of profit to be taxed, these deductions, known as *depreciation allowances*, allow the firm to reduce its total tax payment.

Another important tax provision, which has been used at various times in the United States, is the *investment tax credit*. An investment tax credit permits the firm to subtract a percentage of the purchase price of new capital directly from its tax bill. So, for example, if the investment tax credit is 10%, a firm that purchases a $15,000 piece of equipment can reduce its taxes by $1500 (10% of $15,000) in the year the equipment is purchased.

Economists summarize the many provisions of the tax code affecting investment by a single measure of the tax burden on capital called the **effective tax rate.** Essentially, the idea is to ask: What tax rate τ on a firm's revenue would have the same effect on the desired capital stock as do the actual provisions of the tax code? The hypothetical tax rate that answers this question is the effective tax rate. Changes in the tax law that, for example, raise the effective tax rate are equivalent to an increased tax on firm revenue and a rise in the tax-adjusted user cost of capital. Thus, all else being equal, an increase in the effective tax rate lowers the desired capital stock.

Table 4.2 shows effective tax rates on capital for countries in the Organization for Economic Cooperation and Development (OECD) in 2007. The effective tax rate on capital ranges from −3.4% in Belgium to 37.1% in Korea. Also shown are the ratios of gross investment to GDP in each of these countries. Because an increase in the effective tax rate on capital increases the tax-adjusted user cost of capital, we would expect countries with high effective tax rates on capital to have low rates of

Table 4.2

Effective Tax Rate on Capital, 2007

	ETR	I/GDP		ETR	I/GDP
Australia	29.3	27.7	Korea (Rep. of)	37.1	28.8
Austria	26.4	22.2	Luxembourg	19.1	19.6
Belgium	−3.4	21.7	Mexico	15.4	20.8
Canada	31.9	22.6	Netherlands	16.6	20.0
Czech Republic	17.0	24.3	New Zealand	20.1	22.9
Denmark	18.6	22.2	Norway	24.5	21.3
Finland	20.1	20.3	Poland	14.0	21.7
France	35.9	21.5	Portugal	19.0	21.8
Germany	35.1	18.7	Slovak Republic	12.6	26.1
Greece	11.9	22.5	Spain	28.7	31.0
Hungary	13.5	21.0	Sweden	21.1	19.0
Iceland	12.8	27.5	Switzerland	17.2	22.0
Ireland	13.2	26.3	Turkey	9.2	21.5
Italy	33.4	21.1	United Kingdom	30.3	17.8
Japan	35.0	23.2	United States	36.0	18.4

Note: ETR is effective tax rate on capital in 2007, in percent. *I/GDP* is the ratio of gross capital formation to GDP, in percent, for 2007.
Sources: ETR from Duanjie Chen and Jack Mintz, *Still a Wallflower: The 2008 Report on Canada's International Tax Competitiveness* (Toronto: C. D. Howe Institute, 2008): Table 1, p. 3. *I/GDP* from Organization for Economic Cooperation and Development, OECD Factbook 2009, *www.oecd.org*.

APPLICATION

Measuring the Effects of Taxes on Investment

Does the effective tax rate significantly affect investment patterns? Determining the empirical relationship between tax rates and investment isn't easy. One problem is that the factors other than taxes that affect the desired capital stock—such as the expected future marginal product of capital and real interest rates—are always changing, making it difficult to isolate the "pure" effects of tax changes. Another problem is that changes in the tax code don't happen randomly but reflect the government's assessment of economic conditions. For example, Congress is likely to reduce taxes on investment when investment spending is expected to be unusually low so as to boost spending. But if Congress does so, low taxes on capital will tend to be associated with periods of low investment, and an econometrician might mistakenly conclude that tax cuts reduce rather than increase investment spending. For example, Congress passed an economic stimulus plan in early 2002 designed to increase investment by allowing firms to depreciate capital for tax purposes faster than the true depreciation on the capital, effectively reducing the tax rate on the capital. But gross private domestic investment had already declined from 18% of GDP in 2000 to 16% in 2001, and it fell to 15% in 2002 despite the tax cut. More recently, the stimulus package passed by Congress in early 2009 provided an $8000 tax credit for qualified first-time homebuyers, which reduces the tax-adjusted user cost of housing for recipients of the credit, and was intended to stimulate residential investment. But by the first quarter of 2009 residential investment had fallen to 2.7% of GDP from 5.0% of GDP in the first quarter of 2007, and 3.7% of GDP in the first quarter of 2008, and, as of this writing, residential investment for 2009 was forecast to remain low.

An interesting study that attempted to solve both of these problems was carried out by Jason Cummins and R. Glenn Hubbard of Columbia University and Kevin Hassett of the Board of Governors of the Federal Reserve System.[11] To get around the problem that factors other than taxes are always changing, Cummins, Hubbard, and Hassett focused on the periods around thirteen major tax reforms, beginning with the investment tax credit initiated by President Kennedy in 1962 and ending with the major tax reform of 1986, passed under President Reagan. The authors' idea was that, by looking at occasions when the tax code changed significantly in a short period of time, they could reasonably assume that most of the ensuing change in investment was the result of the tax change rather than other factors. To get around the second problem, that tax cuts tend to take place when aggregate investment is low, Cummins, Hubbard, and Hassett didn't look at the behavior of aggregate investment; instead, they compared the investment responses of a large number of individual corporations to each tax reform. Because the tax laws treat different types of capital differently (for example, a machine and a factory are taxed differently) and because companies use capital in different combinations, the authors argued that observing how different companies changed their

---

[11]"A Reconsideration of Investment Behavior Using Tax Reforms as Natural Experiments," *Brookings Papers on Economic Activity*, 1994:2, pp. 1–59. For a survey of work on taxation and investment, see Kevin Hassett and R. Glenn Hubbard, "Tax Policy and Investment," in A. J. Auerbach, ed., *Fiscal Policy: Lessons from Economic Research*, Cambridge: MIT Press, 1997.

investment after each tax reform would provide information on the effects of the tax changes. For example, if a tax reform cuts taxes on machines relative to taxes on factories and taxes are an important determinant of investment, companies whose investment is concentrated in machinery should respond relatively more strongly to the tax change than companies who invest primarily in factories.

Cummins, Hubbard, and Hassett found considerably stronger effects of tax changes on investment than reported in previous studies, possibly because the earlier studies didn't deal effectively with the two problems that we identified. These authors found an empirical elasticity of about −0.66. That is, according to their estimates, a tax change that lowers the user cost of capital by 10% would raise aggregate investment by about 6.6%, a significant amount. Most previous studies had found this elasticity to be about −0.25. Thus, more recent research shows that the effective tax rate significantly affects investment.

investment, all else being equal. However, all else is not equal in the various countries in Table 4.2, and, in fact, there is little statistical relationship between the effective tax rate and investment in this group of countries. In the following application, we describe a successful approach to measuring the impact of taxes on investment.

From the Desired Capital Stock to Investment

Now let's look at the link between a firm's desired capital stock and the amount it invests. In general, the capital stock (of a firm or of a country) changes over time through two opposing channels. First, the purchase or construction of new capital goods increases the capital stock. We've been calling the total purchase or construction of new capital goods that takes place each year "investment," but its precise name is **gross investment.** Second, the capital stock depreciates or wears out, which reduces the capital stock.

Whether the capital stock increases or decreases over the course of a year depends on whether gross investment is greater or less than depreciation during the year; when gross investment exceeds depreciation, the capital stock grows. The change in the capital stock over the year—or, equivalently, the difference between gross investment and depreciation—is **net investment.**

We express these concepts symbolically as

$$I_t = \text{gross investment during year } t,$$
$$K_t = \text{capital stock at the beginning of year } t, \text{ and}$$
$$K_{t+1} = \text{capital stock at the beginning of year } t + 1$$
$$\text{(equivalently, at the end of year } t\text{).}$$

Net investment, the change in the capital stock during period t, equals $K_{t+1} - K_t$. The amount of depreciation during year t is dK_t, where d is the fraction of capital that depreciates each year. The relationship between net and gross investment is

$$\text{net investment} = \text{gross investment} - \text{depreciation};\qquad(4.5)$$
$$K_{t+1} - K_t = I_t - dK_t.$$

In most but not all years, gross investment is larger than depreciation so that net investment is positive and the capital stock increases. Figure 4.6 shows the

Figure 4.6

Gross and net investment, 1929–2008
Gross and net investment in the United States since 1929 are shown as percentages of GDP. During some years of the Great Depression and World War II net investment was negative, implying that the capital stock was shrinking.

Sources: GDP, gross private domestic investment, and net private domestic investment from BEA Web site, Tables 1.1.5, 5.1, and 5.2.5.

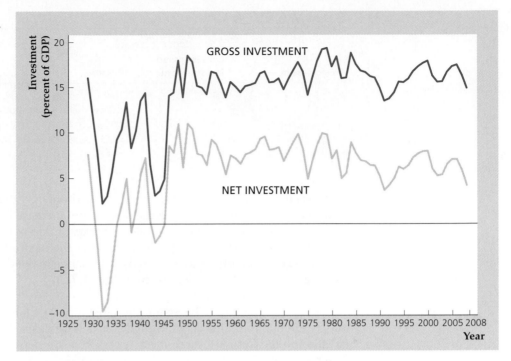

behavior since 1929 of gross and net investment in the United States, expressed as percentages of GDP; the difference between gross and net investment is depreciation. Note the occasional large swings in both gross and net investment and the negative rates of net investment that occurred in some years during the Great Depression of the 1930s and World War II (1941–1945).

We use Eq. (4.5) to illustrate the relationship between the desired capital stock and investment. First, rewriting Eq. (4.5) gives

$$I_t = K_{t+1} - K_t + dK_t,$$

which states that gross investment equals net investment plus depreciation.[12]

Now suppose that firms use information available at the beginning of year t about the expected future marginal product of capital and the user cost of capital and determine the desired capital stock, K^*, they want by the end of year t (the beginning of year $t + 1$). For the moment, suppose also that capital is easily obtainable so that firms can match the actual capital stock at the end of year t, K_{t+1}, with the desired capital stock, K^*. Substituting K^* for K_{t+1} in the preceding equation yields

$$I_t = K^* - K_t + dK_t. \tag{4.6}$$

Equation (4.6) shows that firms' gross investment, I_t, during a year has two parts: (1) the desired net increase in the capital stock over the year, $K^* - K_t$; and (2) the investment needed to replace worn-out or depreciated capital, dK_t. The amount

---

[12]In this equation, we are implicitly assuming that the relative price of capital is constant and equal to 1. More generally, the price of capital could be different from 1, in which case the equation would be:

$$I_t = p_K(K_{t+1} - K_t + dK_t).$$

SUMMARY 6

Determinants of Desired Investment

An increase in	Causes desired investment to	Reason
Real interest rate, r	Fall	The user cost increases, which reduces desired capital stock.
Effective tax rate, τ	Fall	The tax-adjusted user cost increases, which reduces desired capital stock.
Expected future MPK	Rise	The desired capital stock increases.

of depreciation that occurs during a year is determined by the depreciation rate and the initial capital stock. However, the desired net increase in the capital stock over the year depends on the factors—such as taxes, interest rates, and the expected future marginal product of capital—that affect the desired capital stock. Indeed, Eq. (4.6) shows that any factor that leads to a change in the desired capital stock, K^*, results in an equal change in gross investment, I_t.

Lags and Investment. The assumption just made—that firms can obtain capital quickly enough to match actual capital stocks with desired levels each year—isn't realistic in all cases. Although most types of equipment are readily available, a skyscraper or a nuclear power plant may take years to construct. Thus, in practice, a $1 million increase in a firm's desired capital stock may not translate into a $1 million increase in gross investment within the year; instead, the extra investment may be spread over several years as planning and construction proceed. Despite this qualification, factors that increase firms' desired capital stocks also tend to increase the current rate of investment. Summary table 6 brings together the factors that affect investment. In "In Touch with Data and Research: Investment and the Stock Market," p. 131, we discuss an alternative approach to investment, which relates investment to stock prices.

Investment in Inventories and Housing

Our discussion so far has emphasized what is called business fixed investment, or investment by firms in structures (such as factories and office buildings), equipment (such as drill presses and jetliners), and software. However, there are two other components of investment spending: inventory investment and residential investment. As discussed in Chapter 2, inventory investment equals the increase in firms' inventories of unsold goods, unfinished goods, or raw materials. Residential investment is the construction of housing, such as single-family homes, condominiums, or apartment buildings.

Fortunately, the concepts of future marginal product and the user cost of capital, which we used to examine business fixed investment, apply equally well to inventory investment and residential investment. Consider, for example, a new-car dealer trying to decide whether to increase the number of cars she normally keeps on her lot from 100 to 150—that is, whether to make an inventory investment of 50 cars. The benefit of having more cars to show is that potential car buyers will have a greater variety of models from which to select and may not have to wait for delivery, enabling the car dealer to sell more cars. The increase in sales commissions the car dealer expects to make, measured in real terms and with the same sales

IN TOUCH WITH DATA AND RESEARCH

Investment and the Stock Market

Fluctuations in the stock market can have important macroeconomic effects. Changes in stock prices may cause households to change how much they consume and save (see the Application, "Macroeconomic Consequences of the Boom and Bust in Stock Prices," p. 138). Similarly, economic theory suggests that rises and falls in the stock market should lead firms to change their rates of capital investment in the same direction. The relationship between stock prices and firms' investment in physical capital is captured by the "q theory of investment," developed by James Tobin, who was a Nobel laureate at Yale University.

Tobin argued that the rate of investment in any particular type of capital can be predicted by looking at the ratio of the capital's market value to its replacement cost. When this ratio, often called "Tobin's q," is greater than 1, it is profitable to acquire additional capital because the value of capital exceeds the cost of acquiring it. Similarly, when Tobin's q is smaller than 1, the value of capital is less than the cost of acquiring it, so it is not profitable to invest in additional capital.

Because much of the value of firms comes from the capital they own, we can use the stock market value of a firm as a measure of the market value of the firm's capital stock. If we let V be the stock market value of a firm, K be the amount of capital the firm owns, and p_K be the price of new capital goods, then for an individual firm

$$\text{Tobin's } q = \frac{V}{p_K K}$$

where $p_K K$ is the replacement cost of the firm's capital stock. If the replacement cost of capital isn't changing much, a boom in the stock market (an increase in V) will cause Tobin's q to rise for most firms, leading to increased rates of investment. Essentially, when the stock market is high, firms find it profitable to expand.

Figure 4.7 shows quarterly data on Tobin's q and real private nonresidential investment. Consistent with the theory, the two are closely related; Tobin's q and investment rose together throughout the 1990s and then both fell sharply in 2000 and 2008. However, in specific episodes, such as the 1987 stock market crash and the mid 2000s, Tobin's q and investment are less closely related. In the graph, Tobin's q declined significantly after the decline in stock prices in 1987 and did not recover for a long time, but investment spending continued to grow at a fairly rapid pace for several years.

Although it may seem different, the q theory of investment is very similar to the theory of investment discussed in this chapter. In the theory developed in this chapter we identified three main factors affecting the desired capital stock: the expected future marginal product of capital, MPK^f; the real interest rate, r; and the purchase price of new capital, p_K. Each of these factors also affects Tobin's q: (1) An increase in the expected marginal product of capital tends to increase the expected future earnings of the firm, which raises the stock market value of the firm and thus increases q; (2) a reduction in the real interest rate also

Figure 4.7

Investment and Tobin's q, 1987–2009
The graph shows the amount of real private nonresidential fixed investment, labeled investment, whose values are shown on the left axis, and the value of Tobin's q, whose values are shown on the right axis from 1987 to the first quarter of 2009. Note that investment and Tobin's q usually move together, rising or falling at about the same time.

Source: Investment from St. Louis Fed Web site at *research.stlouisfed.org/fred2/series/ PNFIC1*; Tobin's q from Federal Reserve Flow of Funds Accounts, Table B.102, for nonfarm nonfinancial corporate business, market value plus liabilities divided by assets.

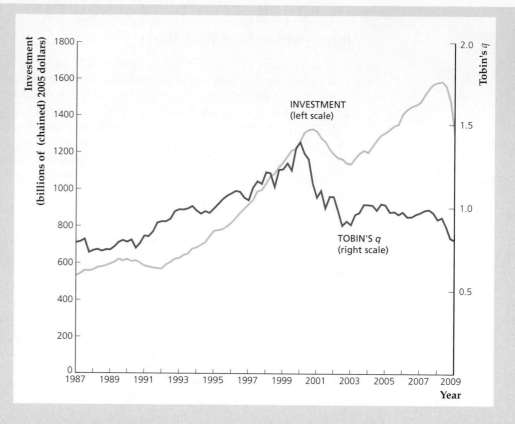

tends to raise stock prices (and hence q), as financial investors substitute away from low-yielding bonds and bank deposits and buy stocks instead; and (3) a decrease in the purchase price of capital reduces the denominator of the q ratio and thus increases q. Because all three types of change increase Tobin's q, they also increase the desired capital stock and investment, as predicted by our analysis in this chapter.

force, is the expected future marginal product of the increased inventory. The cost of holding more cars reflects (1) depreciation of the cars sitting on the lot and (2) the interest the car dealer must pay on the loan obtained to finance the higher inventory. The car dealer will make the inventory investment if the expected benefits of increasing her inventory, in terms of increased sales commissions, are at least as great as the interest and depreciation costs of adding 50 cars. This principle is the same one that applies to business fixed investment.

We can also use this same approach to analyze residential investment. The expected future marginal product of an apartment building, for example, is the real value of rents that can be collected from the tenants, minus taxes and operating costs. The user cost of capital for an apartment building during a year is its depreciation, or loss of value from wear and tear, plus the interest cost (reflected in mortgage payments, for example). As for other types of capital, constructing an apartment building is profitable only if its expected future marginal product is at least as great as its user cost.

4.3 Goods Market Equilibrium

In Chapter 3, we showed that the quantity of goods and services supplied in an economy depends on the level of productivity—as determined, for example, by the technology used—and on the quantity of inputs, such as the capital and labor used. In this chapter we have discussed the factors that affect the demand for goods and services, particularly the demand for consumption goods by households and the demand for investment goods by firms. But how do we know that the amount of goods and services that consumers and investors want to buy will be the same as the amount that producers are willing to provide? Putting the question another way, What economic forces bring the goods market into equilibrium, with quantities demanded equal to quantities supplied? In this section, we show that the real interest rate is the key economic variable whose adjustments help bring the quantities of goods supplied and demanded into balance; thus a benefit of our analysis is an explanation of what determines interest rates. Another benefit is that, by adding the analysis of goods market equilibrium to the analysis of labor market equilibrium in Chapter 3, we take another large step toward constructing a complete model of the macroeconomy.

The goods market is in equilibrium when the aggregate quantity of goods supplied equals the aggregate quantity of goods demanded. (For brevity, we refer only to "goods" rather than to "goods and services," but services always are included.) Algebraically, this condition is

$$Y = C^d + I^d + G. \tag{4.7}$$

The left side of Eq. (4.7) is the quantity of goods, Y, supplied by firms, which is determined by the factors discussed in Chapter 3. The right side of Eq. (4.7) is the aggregate demand for goods. If we continue to assume no foreign sector, so that net exports are zero, the quantity of goods demanded is the sum of desired consumption by households, C^d, desired investment by firms, I^d, and government purchases, G.[13] Equation (4.7) is called the *goods market equilibrium condition*.

The goods market equilibrium condition is different in an important way from the income–expenditure identity for a closed economy, $Y = C + I + G$ (this identity is Eq. 2.3, with $NX = 0$). The income–expenditure identity is a relationship between actual income (output) and actual spending, which, by definition, is always satisfied. In contrast, the goods market equilibrium condition does not always have to be satisfied. For example, firms may produce output faster than consumers want to buy it so that undesired inventories pile up in firms' warehouses. In this situation, the income–expenditure identity is still satisfied (because the undesired additions to firms' inventories are counted as part of total spending—see Chapter 2), but the goods market wouldn't be in equilibrium because production exceeds *desired* spending (which does *not* include the undesired increases in inventories). Although in principle the goods market equilibrium condition need not always hold, strong forces act to bring the goods market into equilibrium fairly quickly.

A different, but equivalent, way to write the goods market equilibrium condition emphasizes the relationship between desired saving and desired investment.

---

[13]We assume that G always equals the level desired by the government and so we don't distinguish between desired and actual G.

To obtain this alternative form of the goods market equilibrium condition, we first subtract $C^d + G$ from both sides of Eq. (4.7):

$$Y - C^d - G = I^d.$$

The left side of this equation, $Y - C^d - G$, is desired national saving, S^d (see Eq. 4.1). Thus the goods market equilibrium condition becomes

$$S^d = I^d. \tag{4.8}$$

This alternative way of writing the goods market equilibrium condition says that the goods market is in equilibrium when desired national saving equals desired investment.

Because saving and investment are central to many issues we present in this book and because the desired-saving-equals-desired-investment form of the goods market equilibrium condition often is easier to work with, we utilize Eq. (4.8) in most of our analyses. However, we emphasize once again that Eq. (4.8) is equivalent to the condition that the supply of goods equals the demand for goods, Eq. (4.7).

The Saving–Investment Diagram

For the goods market to be in equilibrium, then, the aggregate supply of goods must equal the aggregate demand for goods, or equivalently, desired national saving must equal desired investment. We demonstrate in this section that adjustments of the real interest rate allow the goods market to attain equilibrium.[14]

The determination of goods market equilibrium can be shown graphically with a saving–investment diagram (Fig. 4.8). The real interest rate is measured along the

Figure 4.8

Goods market equilibrium
Goods market equilibrium occurs when desired national saving equals desired investment. In the figure, equilibrium occurs when the real interest rate is 6% and both desired national saving and desired investment equal 1000. If the real interest rate were, say, 3%, desired investment (1500) would not equal desired national saving (850), and the goods market would not be in equilibrium. Competition among borrowers for funds would then cause the real interest rate to rise until it reaches 6%.

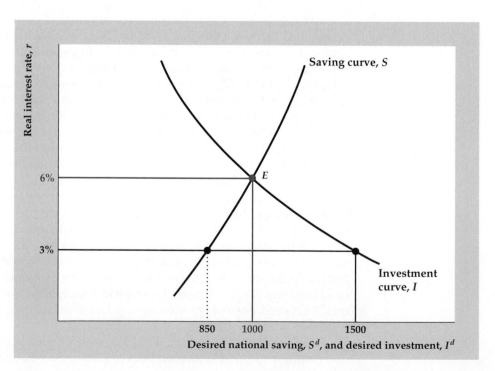

---

[14]Strictly speaking, we should refer to the expected real interest rate rather than simply the real interest rate. The two are the same if expected inflation and actual inflation are equal.

vertical axis, and national saving and investment are measured along the horizontal axis. The saving curve, S, shows the relationship between desired national saving and the real interest rate. The upward slope of the saving curve reflects the empirical finding (Section 4.1) that a higher real interest rate raises desired national saving. The investment curve, I, shows the relationship between desired investment and the real interest rate. The investment curve slopes downward because a higher real interest rate increases the user cost of capital and thus reduces desired investment.

Goods market equilibrium is represented by point E, at which desired national saving equals desired investment, as required by Eq. (4.8). The real interest rate corresponding to E (6% in this example) is the only real interest rate that clears the goods market. When the real interest rate is 6%, both desired national saving and desired investment equal 1000.

How does the goods market come to equilibrium at E, where the real interest rate is 6%? Suppose instead that the real interest rate is 3%. As Fig. 4.8 shows, when the real interest rate is 3%, the amount of investment that firms want to undertake (1500) exceeds desired national saving (850). With investors wanting to borrow more than savers want to lend, the "price" of saving—the real interest rate that lenders receive—will be bid up. The return to savers will rise until it reaches 6%, and desired national saving and desired investment are equal. Similarly, if the real interest rate exceeds 6%, the amount that savers want to lend will exceed what investors want to borrow, and the real return paid to savers will be bid down. Thus adjustments of the real interest rate, in response to an excess supply or excess demand for saving, bring the goods market into equilibrium.

Although Fig. 4.8 shows goods market equilibrium in terms of equal saving and investment, keep in mind that an equivalent way to express goods market equilibrium is that the supply of goods, Y, equals the demand for goods, $C^d + I^d + G$ (Eq. 4.7). Table 4.3 illustrates this point with a numerical example consistent with the values shown in Fig. 4.8. Here the assumption is that output, Y, and government purchases, G, are fixed at values of 4500 and 1500, respectively. Desired consumption, C^d, and desired investment, I^d, depend on the real interest rate. Desired consumption depends on the real interest rate because a higher real interest rate raises desired saving, which necessarily reduces desired consumption. Desired investment depends on the real interest rate because an increase in the real interest rate raises the user cost of capital, which lowers desired investment.

In the example in Table 4.3, when the real interest rate is 6%, desired consumption $C^d = 2000$. Therefore desired national saving $S^d = Y - C^d - G = 4500 - 2000 - 1500 = 1000$. Also, when the real interest rate is 6%, desired investment $I^d = 1000$. As desired national saving equals desired investment when $r = 6\%$, the equilibrium real interest rate is 6%, as in Fig. 4.8.

Table 4.3

Components of Aggregate Demand for Goods (An Example)

Real Interest Rate, r	Output, Y	Desired Consumption, C^d	Desired Investment, I^d	Government Purchases, G	Desired National Saving, $S^d = Y - C^d - G$	Aggregate Demand for Goods, $C^d + I^d + G$
3%	4500	2150	1500	1500	850	5150
6%	4500	2000	1000	1500	1000	4500

Note, moreover, that when the real interest rate is at the equilibrium value of 6%, the aggregate supply of goods, Y, which is 4500, equals the aggregate demand for goods, $C^d + I^d + G = 2000 + 1000 + 1500 = 4500$. Thus, both forms of the goods market equilibrium condition, Eqs. (4.7) and (4.8), are satisfied when the real interest rate equals 6%.

Table 4.3 also illustrates how adjustments of the real interest rate bring about equilibrium in the goods market. Suppose that the real interest rate initially is 3%. Both components of private-sector demand for goods (C^d and I^d) are higher when the real interest rate is 3% than when it is 6%. The reason is that consumers save less and firms invest more when real interest rates are relatively low. Thus, at a real interest of 3%, the demand for goods ($C^d + I^d + G = 2150 + 1500 + 1500 = 5150$) is greater than the supply of goods ($Y = 4500$). Equivalently, at a real interest rate of 3%, Table 4.3 shows that desired investment ($I^d = 1500$) exceeds desired saving ($S^d = 850$). As Fig. 4.8 shows, an increase in the real interest rate to 6% eliminates the disequilibrium in the goods market by reducing desired investment and increasing desired national saving. An alternative explanation is that the increase in the real interest rate eliminates the excess of the demand for goods over the supply of goods by reducing both consumption demand and investment demand.

Shifts of the Saving Curve.   For any real interest rate, a change in the economy that raises desired national saving shifts the saving curve to the right, and a change that reduces desired national saving shifts the saving curve to the left. (Summary table 5 on p. 118 lists the factors affecting desired national saving.)

A shift of the saving curve leads to a new goods market equilibrium with a different real interest rate and different amounts of saving and investment. Figure 4.9

Figure 4.9

A decline in desired saving

A change that reduces desired national saving, such as a temporary increase in current government purchases, shifts the saving curve to the left, from S^1 to S^2. The goods market equilibrium points moves from E to F. The decline in desired saving raises the real interest rate, from 6% to 7%, and lowers saving and investment, from 100 to 850.

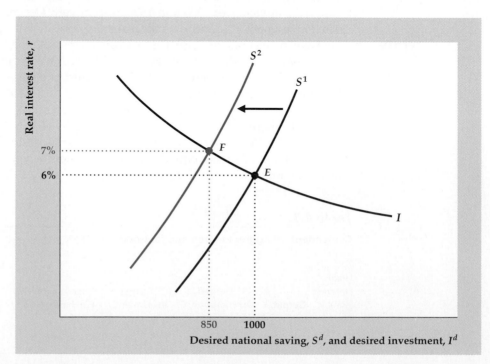

illustrates the effects of a decrease in desired national saving—resulting, for example, from a temporary increase in current government purchases. The initial equilibrium point is at E, where (as in Fig. 4.8) the real interest rate is 6% and desired national saving and desired investment both equal 1000. When current government purchases increase, the resulting decrease in desired national saving causes the saving curve to shift to the left, from S^1 to S^2. At the new goods market equilibrium point, F, the real interest rate is 7%, reflecting the fact that at the initial real interest rate of 6% the demand for funds by investors now exceeds the supply of saving.

Figure 4.9 also shows that, in response to the increase in government purchases, national saving and investment both fall, from 1000 to 850. Saving falls because of the initial decrease in desired saving, which is only partially offset by the increase in the real interest rate. Investment falls because the higher real interest rate raises the user cost of capital that firms face. When increased government purchases cause investment to decline, economists say that investment has been *crowded out*. The crowding out of investment by increased government purchases occurs, in effect, because the government is using more real resources, some of which would otherwise have gone into investment.

Shifts of the Investment Curve. Like the saving curve, the investment curve can shift. For any real interest rate, a change in the economy that raises desired investment shifts the investment curve to the right, and a change that lowers desired investment shifts the investment curve to the left. (See Summary table 6 on p. 130 for the factors affecting desired investment.)

The effects on goods market equilibrium of an increase in desired investment—as from an invention that raises the expected future marginal product of capital—are shown in Fig. 4.10. The increase in desired investment shifts the investment curve to

Figure 4.10

An increase in desired investment
A change in the economy that increases desired investment, such as an invention that raises the expected future MPK, shifts the investment curve to the right, from I^1 to I^2. The goods market equilibrium point moves from E to G. The real interest rate rises from 6% to 8%, and saving and investment also rise, from 1000 to 1100.

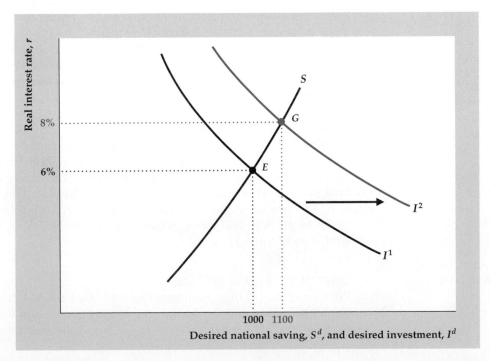

Desired national saving, S^d, and desired investment, I^d

the right, from I^1 to I^2, changing the goods market equilibrium point from E to G. The real interest rate rises from 6% to 8% because the increased demand for investment funds causes the real interest rate to be bid up. Saving and investment also increase, from 1000 to 1100, with the higher saving reflecting the willingness of savers to save more when the real interest rate rises.

In these last two chapters, we have presented supply–demand analyses of the labor and goods markets and developed tools needed to understand the behavior of various macroeconomic variables, including employment, the real wage, output, saving, investment, and the real interest rate. These concepts—and a few more developed in the study of asset markets in Chapter 7—form the basis for the economic analysis presented in the rest of this book. In Chapter 5, we use the concepts developed so far to examine the determinants of trade flows and international borrowing and lending. In Chapter 6, we use them to tackle the fundamental question of why some countries' economies grow more quickly than others.

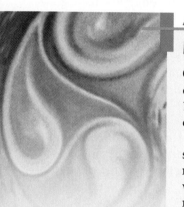

APPLICATION

Macroeconomic Consequences of the Boom and Bust in Stock Prices

On October 19, 1987, stock prices took their biggest-ever one-day plunge. The Standard and Poor's index of 500 stocks dropped 20% that day, after having fallen by 16% from the market's peak in August of the same year. About $1 trillion of financial wealth was eliminated by the decline in stock prices on that single day.

Stock prices in the United States soared during the 1990s, especially during the second half of the decade, but then tumbled sharply early in the first year of the new century. Stock prices continued to fall for several years, and stockholders lost wealth of about $5 trillion, an amount equal to about half of a year's GDP. After rising from 2003 to 2007, stock prices plunged during the financial crisis of 2008, with stocks losing 48% of their value in real terms. By the first quarter of 2009, real stock prices were at their lowest level since 1995.

What are the macroeconomic effects of such booms and busts in stock prices? We have emphasized two major macroeconomic channels for stock prices: a wealth effect on consumption and an effect on capital investment through Tobin's q. Let's see how each of those effects worked after the stock market crash of 1987, the increase in stock values in the 1990s, the decline in stock market wealth in the early 2000s, and the financial crisis of 2008.

The *wealth effect* on consumption arises because stocks are a component of households' financial assets. Because a stock market boom makes households better off financially, they should respond by consuming more; and likewise, a bust in the stock market reduces household wealth and should reduce consumption. To show how consumption and stock prices are related, Fig. 4.11 plots the value of the S&P 500 index, adjusted for inflation, along with the ratio of consumption spending to GDP.

Consumption and the 1987 Crash

We would expect that following the 1987 stock market crash, consumers would reduce spending, but the decline in consumption should have been much smaller than the $1 trillion decline in wealth, because consumers would spread the effects

Figure 4.11

Real U.S. stock prices and the ratio of consumption to GDP, 1987–2009

The graph shows the values of the real (inflation-adjusted) S&P 500, which covers a broad cross-section of U.S. corporations, and the ratio of consumption spending to GDP from 1987 to the first quarter of 2009. The variables move together in some episodes and in opposite directions in other episodes.

Source: S&P 500 from Yahoo finance Web site, *finance.yahoo. com*; real S&P 500 calculated as S&P 500 divided by GDP deflator; GDP deflator, consumption spending, and GDP from St. Louis Fed Web site at *research.stlouisfed.org/fred2*.

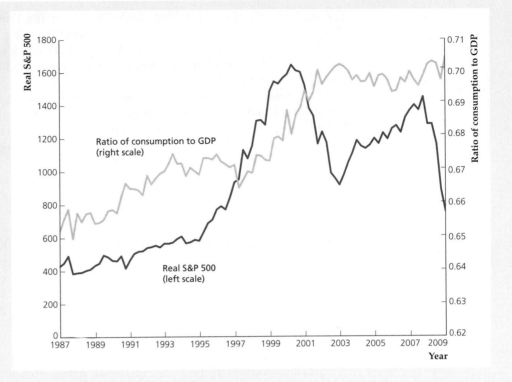

of their losses over a long period of time by reducing planned future consumption as well as current consumption. If consumers spread changes in their wealth over 25 years, then we might guess that current consumption spending would decline by about $40 billion (assuming the real interest rate is near zero). However, consumers might also worry that the stock market crash would lead to a recession, so they might cut consumption further; such a scenario suggests that consumption should decline by more than $40 billion. However, economists who estimated the actual decline in consumption suggest that it fell less than $40 billion.[15] Why did consumption decline less than economic theory suggests? Perhaps the reason is that the rise in stock prices had been very recent—stock prices had risen 39% in the 8 months preceding the crash. Because the increase in stock prices occurred so rapidly, it is possible that by August 1987, stockholders had not yet fully adjusted their consumption to reflect the higher level of wealth. Thus, when the market fell, consumption did not have to decline by very much to fall back into line with wealth.[16]

---

[15]See C. Alan Garner, "Has the Stock Market Crash Reduced Consumer Spending?" *Economic Review*, Federal Reserve Bank of Kansas City, April 1988, pp. 3–6, and David Runkle, "Why No Crunch from the Crash?" *Quarterly Review*, Federal Reserve Bank of Minneapolis, Winter 1988, pp. 2–7.

[16]In "Consumption, Aggregate Wealth, and Expected Stock Returns," *Journal of Finance*, June 2001, pp. 815–849, Martin Lettau and Sydney Ludvigson noted that, prior to the crash, aggregate consumption was unusually low relative to stock market wealth. Their analysis indicates that this behavior reflected consumers' expectations of a decline in the stock market.

Consumption and the Rise in Stock Market Wealth in the 1990s

The U.S. stock market enjoyed tremendous growth during the 1990s. The S&P 500 index more than tripled in real terms by the end of the decade. Our theory predicts that such gains in stock market wealth should be associated with increased consumption spending.

However, contrary to our theory that an increase in wealth should increase consumption, consumption does not appear to have been closely correlated with stock prices in the 1990s. Research by Jonathan Parker of Northwestern University shows that there has been a long-run increase in the ratio of consumption to GDP that began in 1979.[17] He concludes that no more than one-fifth of the increase in the ratio of consumption to GDP in the 1980s and 1990s resulted from increased wealth associated with the stock market boom. And in Fig. 4.11, we can see that stock prices increased significantly from 1995 to 1998, yet consumption declined relative to GDP in that period.

Consumption and the Decline in Stock Prices in the Early 2000s

Following the peak of the stock market in early 2000, stock prices declined for three years, erasing about $5 trillion in wealth. Our theory suggests that consumers should respond by reducing their consumption spending. Yet Fig. 4.11 shows that, in fact, consumption spending increased significantly relative to GDP during that period, rising from 67% of GDP in 1999 to 70% in 2002. Several reasons may explain why consumption did not decline after stock prices fell: (1) the reduction in people's wealth is spread throughout their lifetimes, so there is not a large immediate impact on consumption; (2) at the same time stock prices declined, home prices rose, so many people who lost wealth in the stock market gained it back in real estate; and (3) people may have just viewed their gains in the late 1990s as "paper profits" that were lost in the early 2000s, so neither the gains nor the losses affected consumption.

Investment and the Declines in the Stock Market in the 2000s

As we have seen in Fig. 4.11, the stock market fell precipitously in 2000 and 2008. The large declines in the stock market led to large declines in Tobin's q, the ratio of the market value of firms to the replacement cost of their capital, as you can see in Figure 4.7 in "In Touch with Data and Research: Investment and the Stock Market," p. 132. This figure also shows very sharp declines in real investment beginning shortly after the stock market and Tobin's q began to fall in 2000 and again in 2008. The slight delay in the fall in investment, relative to the fall in the stock market, reflects the lags in the process of making investment decisions, planning capital formation, and implementing the plans. But despite these lags, the declines in investment following large declines in the stock market are quite evident.

The Financial Crisis of 2008

During the financial crisis of 2008, stock prices plunged rapidly. In the six months from August 2008 to February 2009, U.S. stock prices declined in nominal terms by 43%, one of the fastest declines in stock prices on record. Investors feared that a depression was possible because of a meltdown in the financial sector, which had taken excessive risks, especially in real-estate markets. The recession that had

[17]"Spendthrift in America? On Two Decades of Decline in the U.S. Saving Rate," in B. Bernanke and J. Rotemberg, eds., *NBER Macroeconomics Annual, 1999*, Cambridge: MIT Press, 1999.

begun in December 2007 became much worse, and the unemployment rate increased dramatically. In this case, unlike the episode in the early 2000s, home prices also declined, and the simultaneous decline in housing prices and stock values translated into a nearly 20% decline in household net wealth, which fell from $62.6 trillion at the end of 2007 to $50.4 trillion by the end of March 2009. Yet the ratio of consumption to GDP only declined about 1 percentage point in 2008, as Fig. 4.11 shows, and then it rebounded in early 2009.

CHAPTER SUMMARY

1. Because saving equals income minus consumption, a household's decisions about how much to consume and how much to save are really the same decision. Individuals and households save because they value both future consumption and current consumption; for the same amount of income, an increase in current saving reduces current consumption but increases the amount that the individual or household will be able to consume in the future.

2. For an individual or household, an increase in current income raises both desired consumption and desired saving. Analogously, at the national level, an increase in current output raises both desired consumption and desired national saving. At both the household and national levels, an increase in expected future income or in wealth raises desired consumption; however, because these changes raise desired consumption without affecting current income or output, they cause desired saving to fall.

3. An increase in the real interest rate has two potentially offsetting effects on saving. First, a higher real interest rate increases the price of current consumption relative to future consumption (each unit of current consumption costs $1 + r$ units of forgone future consumption). In response to the increased relative price of current consumption, people substitute future consumption for current consumption by saving more today. This tendency to increase saving in response to an increase in the relative price of current consumption is called the substitution effect of the real interest rate on saving. Second, a higher real interest rate increases the wealth of savers by increasing the interest payments they receive, while reducing the wealth of borrowers by increasing the amount of interest they must pay. By making savers wealthier, an increase in the real interest rate leads savers to consume more and reduce their saving; however, because it makes borrowers poorer, an increase in the real interest rate causes borrowers to reduce their consumption and increase their saving. The change in current consumption that results

because a consumer is made richer or poorer by an increase in the real interest rate is called the income effect of the real interest rate on saving.

For a saver, the substitution effect of an increase in the real interest rate (which tends to boost saving) and the income effect (which tends to reduce saving) work in opposite directions, so that the overall effect is ambiguous. For a borrower, both the substitution effect and the income effect of a higher real interest rate act to increase saving. Overall, empirical studies suggest that an increase in the real interest rate increases desired national saving and reduces desired consumption, but not by very much.

The real interest rate that is relevant to saving decisions is the expected after-tax real interest rate, which is the real return that savers expect to earn after paying a portion of the interest they receive in taxes.

4. With total output held constant, a temporary increase in government purchases reduces desired consumption. The reason is that higher government purchases imply increases in present or future taxes, which makes consumers feel poorer. However, the decrease in desired consumption is smaller than the increase in government purchases, so that desired national saving, $Y - C^d - G$, falls as a result of a temporary increase in government purchases.

5. According to the Ricardian equivalence proposition, a current lump-sum tax cut should have no effect on desired consumption or desired national saving. The reason is that, if no change occurs in current or planned government purchases, a tax cut that increases current income must be offset by future tax increases that lower expected future income. If consumers do not take into account expected future tax changes, however, the Ricardian equivalence proposition will not hold and a tax cut is likely to raise desired consumption and lower desired national saving.

6. The desired capital stock is the level of capital that maximizes expected profits. At the desired capital stock, the expected future marginal product of capital

equals the user cost of capital. The user cost of capital is the expected real cost of using a unit of capital for a period of time; it is the sum of the depreciation cost (the loss in value because the capital wears out) and the interest cost (the interest rate times the price of the capital good).

7. Any change that reduces the user cost of capital or increases the expected future marginal product of capital increases the desired capital stock. A reduction in the taxation of capital, as measured by the effective tax rate, also increases the desired capital stock.

8. Gross investment is spending on new capital goods. Gross investment minus depreciation (worn-out or scrapped capital) equals net investment, or the change in the capital stock. Firms invest so as to achieve their desired level of capital stock; when the desired capital stock increases, firms invest more.

9. The goods market is in equilibrium when the aggregate quantity of goods supplied equals the aggregate quantity of goods demanded, which (in a closed economy) is the sum of desired consumption, desired investment, and government purchases of goods and services. Equivalently, the goods market is in equilibrium when desired national saving equals desired investment. For any given level of output, the goods market is brought into equilibrium by changes in the real interest rate.

10. The determination of goods market equilibrium, for any fixed supply of output, Y, is represented graphically by the saving–investment diagram. The saving curve slopes upward because empirical evidence suggests that a higher real interest rate raises desired saving. The investment curve slopes downward because a higher real interest rate raises the user cost of capital, which lowers firms' desired capital stocks and thus the amount of investment they do. Changes in variables that affect desired saving or investment shift the saving or investment curves and change the real interest rate that clears the goods market.

KEY DIAGRAM 3

The saving–investment diagram
In an economy with no foreign trade, the goods market is in equilibrium when desired national saving equals desired investment. Equivalently, the goods market is in equilibrium when the aggregate quantity of goods supplied equals the aggregate quantity of goods demanded.

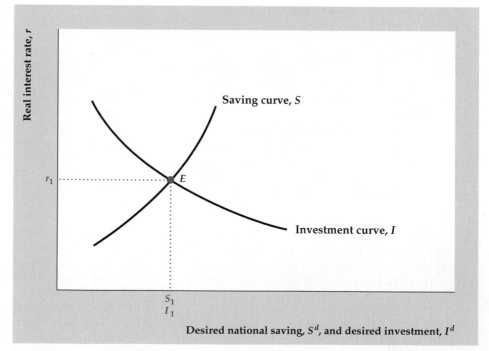

Diagram Elements

■ The real interest rate, r, is on the vertical axis; desired national saving, S^d, and desired investment, I^d, are on the horizontal axis.

■ The saving curve, S, shows the level of desired national saving at each real interest rate. The saving curve slopes upward because a higher real interest rate increases the reward for saving and causes households to save more. (Empirically, this effect outweighs the tendency of a higher real interest rate to lower saving by reducing the amount of saving necessary to reach any specified target.) Desired national saving is defined as $S^d = Y - C^d - G$, where is output, is desired consumption, and is government purchases.

■ The investment curve, I, shows the amount that firms want to invest in new capital goods at each real interest rate. The investment curve slopes downward because a higher real interest rate raises the user cost of capital and thus lowers the amount of capital that firms want to use.

Analysis

■ Goods market equilibrium requires that desired national saving equal desired investment, or $S^d = I^d$.

■ Goods market equilibrium occurs in the diagram at point E, where the saving curve and investment curve intersect. At E, desired national saving equals S_1, desired investment equals I_1, and $S_1 = I_1$. The real interest rate at E, r_1, is the real interest rate that clears the goods market.

■ An alternative way to express the goods market equilibrium condition is as follows: The quantity of goods supplied, Y, equals the quantity of goods demanded by households, C^d, firms, I^d, and the government, G, or $Y = C^d + I^d + G$. As $S^d = Y - C^d - G$, this condition is equivalent to $S^d = I^d$.

Factors That Shift the Curves

■ Any factor that raises desired national saving at a given real interest rate shifts the saving curve to the right; similarly, any factor that lowers desired national saving shifts the saving curve to the left. Factors that affect desired national saving are listed in Summary table 5, page 118. Similarly, factors that change desired investment for a given real interest rate shift the investment curve; see Summary table 6, page 130, for factors that affect desired investment. Shifts of either curve change the goods market equilibrium point and thus change national saving, investment, and the real interest rate.

KEY TERMS

consumption-smoothing motive, p. 106

desired capital stock, p. 121

effective tax rate, p. 126

expected after-tax real interest rate, p. 113

gross investment, p. 128

income effect of the real interest rate on saving, p. 112

marginal propensity to consume, p. 107

net investment, p. 128

Ricardian equivalence proposition, p. 117

substitution effect of the real interest rate on saving, p. 111

tax-adjusted user cost of capital, p. 125

user cost of capital, p. 122

KEY EQUATIONS

$$S^d = Y - C^d - G \qquad (4.1)$$

Desired national saving, S^d, is the level of national saving that occurs when consumption is at its desired level. Equation (4.1) is obtained by substituting desired consumption, C^d, for actual consumption, C, in the definition of national saving.

$$r_{a-t} = (1 - t)i - \pi^e \qquad (4.2)$$

The expected after-tax real interest rate, r_{a-t}, is the after-tax nominal interest rate, $(1 - t)i$, minus the expected rate of inflation, π^e. The expected after-tax real interest rate is the real return earned by a saver when a portion, t, of interest income must be paid as taxes.

$$uc = rp_K + dp_K = (r + d)p_K \qquad (4.3)$$

The user cost of capital, uc, is the sum of the interest cost, rp_K, and the depreciation cost, dp_K, where d is the depreciation rate and p_K is the price of a new capital good.

$$MPK^f = \frac{uc}{1 - \tau} = \frac{(r + d)p_K}{1 - \tau} \qquad (4.4)$$

The desired capital stock, or the capital stock that maximizes the firm's expected profits, is the capital stock for which the expected future marginal product of capital, MPK^f, equals the tax-adjusted user cost of capital, $uc/(1 - \tau)$, where τ is the tax rate on the firm's revenues (equivalently, the effective tax rate).

$$Y = C^d + I^d + G \qquad (4.7)$$

The *goods market equilibrium condition* in a closed economy says that the goods market is in equilibrium when the aggregate quantity of goods supplied, Y, equals the aggregate quantity of goods demanded, $C^d + I^d + G$.

$$S^d = I^d \qquad (4.8)$$

Another way of stating the goods market equilibrium condition is that desired national saving, S^d, must equal desired investment, I^d. This equation is equivalent to Eq. (4.7).

REVIEW QUESTIONS

All review questions are available in [X myeconlab] at www.myeconlab.com.

1. Given income, how are consumption and saving linked? What is the basic motivation for saving?

2. How are desired consumption and desired saving affected by increases in current income, expected future income, and wealth?

3. Use the concepts of income effect and substitution effect to explain why the effect on desired saving of an increase in the expected real interest rate is potentially ambiguous.

4. Define the expected after-tax real interest rate. If the tax rate on interest income declines, what happens to the expected after-tax real interest rate?

5. What effect does a temporary increase in government purchases—for example, to fight a war—have on desired consumption and desired national saving, for a constant level of output? What is the effect on desired national saving of a lump-sum tax increase? Why is the effect of a lump-sum tax increase controversial?

6. What are the two components of the user cost of capital? Explain why each is a cost of using a capital good.

7. What is the desired capital stock? How does it depend on the expected future marginal product of capital, the user cost of capital, and the effective tax rate?

8. What is the difference between gross investment and net investment? Can gross investment be positive when net investment is negative?

9. Give two equivalent ways of describing equilibrium in the goods market. Use a diagram to show how goods market equilibrium is attained.

10. Explain why the saving curve slopes upward and the investment curve slopes downward in the saving–investment diagram. Give two examples of changes that would shift the saving curve to the right, and two examples of changes that would shift the investment curve to the right.

NUMERICAL PROBLEMS

All numerical problems are available in [X myeconlab] at www.myeconlab.com.

1. A consumer is making saving plans for this year and next. She knows that her real income after taxes will be $50,000 in both years. Any part of her income saved this year will earn a real interest rate of 10% between this year and next year. Currently, the consumer has no wealth (no money in the bank or other financial assets, and no debts). There is no uncertainty about the future.

   The consumer wants to save an amount this year that will allow her to (1) make college tuition payments next year equal to $12,600 in real terms; (2) enjoy exactly the same amount of consumption this year and next year, not counting tuition payments as part of next year's consumption; and (3) have neither assets nor debts at the end of next year.

   a. How much should the consumer save this year? How much should she consume?

   How are the amounts that the consumer should save and consume affected by each of the following changes (taken one at a time, with other variables held at their original values)?

   b. Her current income rises from $50,000 to $54,200.

   c. The income she expects to receive next year rises from $50,000 to $54,200.

   d. During the current year she receives an inheritance of $1050 (an increase in wealth, not income).

   e. The expected tuition payment for next year rises from $12,600 to $14,700 in real terms.

   f. The real interest rate rises from 10% to 25%.

2. Hula hoop fabricators cost $100 each. The Hi-Ho Hula Hoop Company is trying to decide how many of these machines to buy. HHHHC expects to produce the following number of hoops each year for each level of capital stock shown.

Number of Fabricators	Number of Hoops Produced per Year
0	0
1	100
2	150
3	180
4	195
5	205
6	210

Hula hoops have a real value of $1 each. HHHHC has no other costs besides the cost of fabricators.

a. Find the expected future marginal product of capital (in terms of dollars) for each level of capital. The MPK^f for the third fabricator, for example, is the real value of the extra output obtained when the third fabricator is added.

b. If the real interest rate is 12% per year and the depreciation rate of capital is 20% per year, find the user cost of capital (in dollars per fabricator per year). How many fabricators should HHHHC buy?

c. Repeat Part (b) for a real interest rate of 8% per year.

d. Repeat Part (b) for a 40% tax on HHHHC's sales revenues.

e. A technical innovation doubles the number of hoops a fabricator can produce. How many fabricators should HHHHC buy when the real interest rate is 12% per year? 8% per year? Assume that there are no taxes and that the depreciation rate is still 20% per year.

3. You have just taken a job that requires you to move to a new city. In relocating, you face the decision of whether to buy or rent a house. A suitable house costs $300,000 and you have saved enough for the down payment. The (nominal) mortgage interest rate is 10% per year, and you can also earn 10% per year on savings. Mortgage interest payments are tax deductible, interest earnings on savings are taxable, and you are in a 30% tax bracket. Interest is paid or received, and taxes are paid, on the last day of the year. The expected inflation rate is 5% per year.

The cost of maintaining the house (replacing worn-out roofing, painting, and so on) is 6% of the value of the house. Assume that these expenses also are paid entirely on the last day of the year. If the maintenance is done, the house retains its full real value. There are no other relevant costs or expenses.

a. What is the expected after-tax real interest rate on the home mortgage?

b. What is the user cost of the house?

c. If all you care about is minimizing your living expenses, at what (annual) rent level would you be just indifferent between buying a house and renting

a house of comparable quality? Rent is also paid on the last day of the year.

4. The Missing Link Chain-Link Fence Company is trying to determine how many chain-link fabricating machines to buy for its factory. If we define a chain-link fence of some specified length to be equal to one unit of output, the price of a new fabricating machine is 60 units of output, and the price of a one-year-old machine is 51 units of output. These relative prices are expected to be the same in the future. The expected future marginal product of fabricating machines, measured in units of output, is $165 - 2K$, where K is the number of machines in use. There are no taxes of any sort. The real interest rate is 10% per year.

a. What is the user cost of capital? Specify the units in which your answer is measured.

b. Determine the number of machines that will allow Missing Link to maximize its profit.

c. Suppose that Missing Link must pay a tax equal to 40% of its gross revenue. What is the optimal number of machines for the company?

d. Suppose that in addition to the 40% tax on revenue described in Part (c), the firm can take advantage of a 20% investment tax credit, which allows it to reduce its taxes paid by 20% of the cost of any new machines purchased. What is Missing Link's desired capital stock now? (*Hint:* An investment tax credit effectively reduces the price of capital to the firm.)

5. An economy has full-employment output of 9000, and government purchases are 2000. Desired consumption and desired investment are as follows:

Real Interest Rate (%)	Desired Consumption	Desired Investment
2	6100	1500
3	6000	1400
4	5900	1300
5	5800	1200
6	5700	1100

a. Why do desired consumption and desired investment fall as the real interest rate rises?

b. Find desired national saving for each value of the real interest rate.

c. If the goods market is in equilibrium, what are the values of the real interest rate, desired national saving, and desired investment? Show that both forms of the goods market equilibrium condition, Eqs. (4.7) and (4.8), are satisfied at the equilibrium. Assume that output is fixed at its full-employment level.

d. Repeat Part (c) for the case in which government purchases fall to 1600. Assume that the amount people desire to consume at each real interest rate is unchanged.

6. An economy has full-employment output of 6000. Government purchases, G, are 1200. Desired consumption and desired investment are

$$C^d = 3600 - 2000r + 0.10Y, \text{ and}$$
$$I^d = 1200 - 4000r,$$

where Y is output and r is the real interest rate.

a. Find an equation relating desired national saving, S^d, to r and Y.

b. Using both versions of the goods market equilibrium condition, Eqs. (4.7) and (4.8), find the real interest rate that clears the goods market. Assume that output equals full-employment output.

c. Government purchases rise to 1440. How does this increase change the equation describing desired national saving? Show the change graphically. What happens to the market-clearing real interest rate?

7. Suppose that the economywide expected future marginal product of capital is $MPK^f = 20 - 0.02K$, where K is the future capital stock. The depreciation rate of capital, d, is 20% per period. The current capital stock is 900 units of capital. The price of a unit of capital is 1 unit of output. Firms pay taxes equal to 15% of their output. The consumption function in the economy is $C = 100 + 0.5Y - 200r$, where C is consumption, Y is output, and r is the real interest rate. Government purchases equal 200, and full-employment output is 1000.

a. Suppose that the real interest rate is 10% per period. What are the values of the tax-adjusted user cost of capital, the desired future capital stock, and the desired level of investment?

b. Now consider the real interest rate determined by goods market equilibrium. This part of the problem will guide you to this interest rate.

   i. Write the tax-adjusted user cost of capital as a function of the real interest rate r. Also write the desired future capital stock and desired investment as functions of r.

   ii. Use the investment function derived in Part (i) along with the consumption function and

government purchases, to calculate the real interest rate that clears the goods market. What are the goods market-clearing values of consumption, saving, and investment? What are the tax-adjusted user cost of capital and the desired capital stock in this equilibrium?

8. (Appendix 4.A) A consumer has initial real wealth of 20, current real income of 90, and future real income of 110. The real interest rate is 10% per period.

a. Find the consumer's $PVLR$.

b. Write the equation for the consumer's budget constraint (using the given numerical values) and graph the budget line.

Suppose that the consumer's goal is to smooth consumption completely. That is, he wants to have the same level of consumption in both the current and the future period.

c. How much will he save and consume in the current period?

d. How will his current saving and consumption be affected by an increase of 11 in current income?

e. How will his current saving and consumption be affected by an increase of 11 in future income?

f. How will his current saving and consumption be affected by an increase of 11 in his initial wealth?

9. (Appendix 4.A) A consumer lives three periods, called the learning period, the working period, and the retirement period. Her income is 200 during the learning period, 800 during the working period, and 200 again during the retirement period. The consumer's initial assets are 300. The real interest rate is zero. The consumer desires perfectly smooth consumption over her lifetime.

a. What are consumption and saving in each period, assuming no borrowing constraints? What happens if the consumer faces a borrowing constraint that prevents her from borrowing?

b. Assume that the consumer's initial wealth is zero instead of 300. Repeat Part (a). Does being borrowing-constrained mean that consumption is lower in all three periods of the consumer's life than it would be if no borrowing constraints applied?

ANALYTICAL PROBLEMS

1. Use the saving–investment diagram to analyze the effects of the following on national saving, investment, and the real interest rate. Explain your reasoning.

a. Consumers become more future-oriented and thus decide to save more.

b. The government announces a large, one-time bonus payment to veterans returning from a war. The bonus will be financed by additional taxes levied on the general population over the next five years.

c. The government introduces an investment tax credit (offset by other types of taxes, so total tax collections remain unchanged).

d. A large number of accessible oil deposits are discovered, which increases the expected future marginal product of oil rigs and pipelines. It also causes an increase in expected future income.

2. A country loses much of its capital stock to a war.

a. What effects should this event have on the country's current employment, output, and real wage?

b. What effect will the loss of capital have on desired investment?

c. The effects on desired national saving of the wartime losses are ambiguous. Give one reason for desired saving to rise and one reason for it to fall.

d. Assume that desired saving doesn't change. What effect does the loss of capital have on the country's real interest rate and the quantity of investment?

3. a. Analyze the effects of a temporary increase in the price of oil (a temporary adverse supply shock) on current output, employment, the real wage, national saving, investment, and the real interest rate. Because the supply shock is temporary, you should assume that the expected future *MPK* and households' expected future incomes are unchanged. Assume throughout that output and employment remain at full-employment levels (which may change).

b. Analyze the effects of a permanent increase in the price of oil (a permanent adverse supply shock) on current output, employment, the real wage, national saving, investment, and the real interest rate. Show that in this case, unlike the case of a temporary supply shock, the real interest rate need not change. (*Hint:* A permanent adverse supply shock lowers the current productivity of capital and labor, just as a temporary supply shock does. In addition, a permanent supply shock lowers both the expected future *MPK* and households' expected future incomes.)

4. Economists often argue that a temporary increase in government purchases—say, for military purposes—will crowd out private investment. Use the saving–investment diagram to illustrate this point, explaining why the curve(s) shift. Does it matter whether the

temporary increase in military spending is funded by taxes or by borrowing?

Alternatively, suppose that the temporary increase in government purchases is for infrastructure (roads, sewers, bridges) rather than for military purposes. The government spending on infrastructure makes private investment more productive, increasing the expected future *MPK* at each level of the capital stock. Use the saving–investment diagram to analyze the effects of government infrastructure spending on current consumption, national saving, investment, and the real interest rate. Does investment by private firms get crowded out by this kind of government investment? If not, what kind of spending, if any, does get crowded out? Assume that there is no change in current productivity or current output and assume also (for simplicity) that households do not expect a change in their future incomes.

5. "A permanent increase in government purchases has a larger effect than a temporary increase of the same amount." Use the saving–investment diagram to evaluate this statement, focusing on effects on consumption, investment, and the real interest rate for a fixed level of output. (*Hint:* The permanent increase in government purchases implies larger increases in current and future taxes.)

6. (Appendix 4.A) Draw a budget line and indifference curves for a consumer who initially is a borrower. Be sure to indicate the no-borrowing, no-lending point and the optimal consumption point. Then show the effect on the budget line and the consumer's optimal consumption of an increase in the real interest rate. Using an intermediate budget line, show the income effect and the substitution effect. Do they work in the same direction or in opposite directions? Explain your answer.

7. (Appendix 4.A) Consumers typically pay a higher real interest rate to borrow than they receive when they lend (by making bank deposits, for example). Draw a consumer's budget line under the assumption that the real interest rate earned on funds lent, r_l, is lower than the real interest rate paid to borrow, r_b. Show how the budget line is affected by an increase in r_b, an increase in r_b, or an increase in the consumer's initial wealth.

Show that changes in r_l and r_b may leave current and future consumption unchanged. (*Hint:* Draw the consumer's indifference curves so that the consumer initially chooses the no-borrowing, no-lending point.)

WORKING WITH MACROECONOMIC DATA

For data to use in these exercises, go to the Federal Reserve Bank of St. Louis FRED database at research.stlouisfed.org/fred2.

1. Graph the index of consumer sentiment, using data since 1965. Can you pick out the recessions of 1969–1970,

1973–1975, 1980, 1981–1982, 1990–1991, and 2001 and the recession that began in December 2007?

Construct scatter plots relating the consumer sentiment index to the growth rates of real consumption expenditures and real consumption expenditures on durables, using quarterly data since 1965. Generally speaking, does consumption grow more quickly when consumers are more optimistic? Compare the growth rates of real consumption and of real consumption expenditures on durables during recessions.

2. The S&P 500 stock market index measures the total dollar value of a large set of stocks traded on the stock market. The real value of the S&P index, which measures the real value of the wealth represented by that set of stocks, is obtained by dividing the index by a measure of the price level, such as the CPI. (To obtain monthly data on the S&P 500, go to the Web site *finance.yahoo.com* and get data for ticker symbol: ^GSPC.)

Using monthly data for the period since 1961, graph the real value of the S&P 500 stock market index. What striking difference do you see in comparing the values in the 1970s with the values in the rest of the period? According to the theory, what effect should the behavior of stock market wealth during the 1970s have had on the national saving rate during that period, relative to the 1960s and 1980s? Look at a graph of the national saving rate for 1961 to the present from NIPA Table 5.1 at *www.bea.gov*. Would you say that the prediction is borne out? Discuss.

3. This problem asks you to calculate the actual (as opposed to the expected) after-tax real interest rate using annual data from 1961 to the present. The formula for the actual after-tax real interest rate is $(1 - t)i - \pi$, where i is the nominal interest rate, t is the tax rate, and π is the inflation rate.

Use the average for each year of the three-month Treasury bill interest rate for the nominal interest rate i and measure annual inflation π by the CPI inflation rate from December to December. Take the tax rate t to be the ratio of total (Federal plus state and local) government receipts to nominal GDP in the fourth quarter of each year. In what periods did financial conditions favor savers? Borrowers?

4. Using quarterly data from 1947 to the present, graph residential fixed investment relative to GDP.

a. Compare the graph of residential investment relative to GDP to a graph of the civilian unemployment rate. What happens to residential investment during recessions? In this respect, is residential investment similar to or different from other types of investment?

b. During the two decades after World War II, there was an upsurge in population growth and household formation known as the "baby boom." The baby boom was followed by a "baby bust" during which population growth slowed. How are these demographic trends connected to the behavior of residential investment relative to GDP shown in your graph?

5. The chapter claims that interest rates tend to move together. Using monthly data since 1975, graph the interest rate on three-month Treasury bills, the yield on high-grade corporate bonds, the interest rate on FHA mortgages, the prime rate charged by banks, and the yield on ten-year Treasury bonds. Which interest rates tend to be highest? Lowest? Explain. Which interest rates tend to move together? Explain.

6. Graph real equipment and software investment and real structures investment since 1948. How has the relative emphasis on the two types of investment changed in the past three decades or so? Can you think of an explanation? (*Hint:* What is the most important new technology to be introduced in the past three decades?)

APPENDIX 4.A

A Formal Model of Consumption and Saving

This appendix analyzes more formally the decision about how much to consume and how much to save. We focus on the decisions of a consumer named Prudence, who was introduced in Chapter 4. To help keep the analysis manageable, we make three simplifying assumptions:

1. The time horizon over which Prudence makes plans consists of only two periods: the present, or current, period and the future period. The current period might represent Prudence's working years and the future period might represent her retirement years, for example.
2. Prudence takes her current income, future income, and wealth as given.
3. Prudence faces a given real interest rate and can choose how much to borrow or save at that rate.

How Much Can the Consumer Afford? The Budget Constraint

To analyze Prudence's decision about how much to consume and save, we first examine the choices available to her. To have some specific numbers to analyze, let's suppose that Prudence receives a fixed after-tax income, measured in real terms,[1] of 42,000 in the current period and expects to receive a real income of 33,000 in the future period. In addition, she begins the current period with real wealth of 18,000 in a savings account, and she can borrow or lend at a real interest rate of 10% per period.

Next, we list the symbols used to represent Prudence's situation:

y = Prudence's current real income (42,000);
y^f = Prudence's future real income (33,000);[2]
a = Prudence's real wealth (assets) at the beginning of the current period (18,000);
r = real interest rate (10%);
c = Prudence's current real consumption (not yet determined);
c^f = Prudence's future real consumption (not yet determined).

In general, any amount of current consumption, c, that Prudence chooses will determine the amount of future consumption, c^f, that she will be able to afford. To work out this relationship, note that the funds that Prudence has on hand in the current period are her current income, y, and her initial wealth, a. If her current consumption is c, then at the end of the current period she has $y + a - c$ left.

---

[1]The units in which Prudence's income is measured are base-year dollars.

[2]We do not include in future income y^f, the interest that Prudence earns on her saving. Future income, y^f, includes only labor income or transfers received, such as Social Security payments.

Prudence can put these leftover current resources, $y + a - c$, in the bank to earn interest. If the real interest rate that she can earn on her deposit is r, the real value of her bank account (principal plus interest) in the future period will be $(y + a - c)(1 + r)$. In addition to the real value of her bank account in the future period, Prudence receives income of y^f, so her total resources in the future period equal $(y + a - c)(1 + r) + y^f$. Because the future period is the last period of Prudence's life, she spends all of her remaining resources on consumption.[3] Thus Prudence's future consumption, c^f, is

$$c^f = (y + a - c)(1 + r) + y^f. \tag{4.A.1}$$

Equation (4.A.1) is called the *budget constraint*. It shows for any level of current consumption, c, how much future consumption, c^f, Prudence can afford, based on her current and future income and initial wealth.[4] The budget constraint in Eq. (4.A.1) is represented graphically by the *budget line*, which shows the combinations of current and future consumption that Prudence can afford, based on her current and future income, her initial level of wealth, and the real interest rate. Figure 4.A.1 depicts Prudence's budget line, with current consumption, c, on the horizontal axis and future consumption, c^f, on the vertical axis.

The budget line slopes downward, reflecting the trade-off between current and future consumption. If Prudence increases her current consumption by one unit, her saving falls by one unit. Because saving earns interest at rate r, a one-unit

Figure 4.A.1

The budget line
The budget line shows the combinations of current and future consumption, c and c^f, available to Prudence. The slope of the budget line is $-(1 + r) = -1.10$. The horizontal intercept is at $c = 90,000$, which equals *PVLR* as defined in Eq. (4.A.2); the vertical intercept is at $c^f = 99,000$. You can verify that the combinations of current and future consumption at each of the lettered points (as well as any point on the budget line) satisfies the equation $c + c^f/(1 + r) = 90,000$, which equals *PVLR* as defined in Eq. (4.A.2).

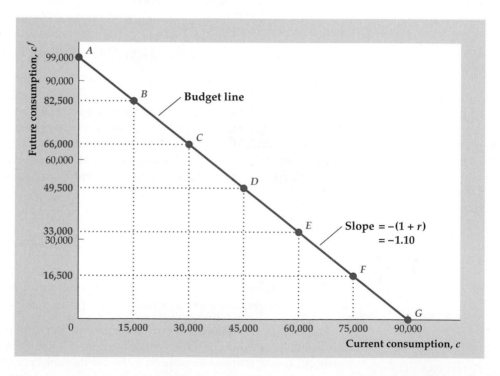

---

[3]Here we assume that Prudence does not want to leave a bequest to anyone. Later we will briefly examine the effect of bequests on saving decisions.

[4]In our derivation of Eq. (4.A.1), we assumed that Prudence's current consumption was less than her total current resources so that she had some resources left to deposit in the bank. However, the budget constraint, Eq. (4.A.1), still works if Prudence's current consumption exceeds her total current resources so that she must borrow from the bank. Note that this works as long as y^f exceeds $[c - (y + a)] \times (1 + r)$, so that $c^f > 0$.

decline in saving today implies that Prudence's future resources—and thus her future consumption—will be lower by $1 + r$ units. Because a one-unit increase in current consumption lowers future consumption by $1 + r$ units, the slope of the budget line is $-(1 + r)$. In our numerical example, the real interest rate is 10%, so the slope of the budget line in Fig. 4.A.1 is –1.10.

Present Values

We can conveniently represent Prudence's budget constraint by using the concept of *present value*. The present value measures the value of payments to be made in the future in terms of today's dollars or goods. To illustrate this concept, suppose that you must make a payment of $13,200 one year from now. How much money would you have to put aside today so that you could make that future payment? The answer to this question is called the present value.

The present value of a future payment depends on the interest rate. If the current nominal interest rate, i, is 10% per year, the present value of $13,200 to be paid one year from now is $12,000. The reason is that $12,000 deposited in the bank today at a 10% interest rate will earn $1200 (10% of $12,000) of interest in one year, which, when added to the initial $12,000, gives the $13,200. Therefore, at an interest rate of 10%, having $13,200 one year from now is economically equivalent to having $12,000 today. Thus, we say that the present value of $13,200 in one year equals $12,000.

More generally, if the nominal interest rate is i per year, each dollar in the bank today is worth $1 + i$ dollars one year from now. To have $13,200 one year from now requires $13,200/(1 + i)$ in the bank today; thus the present value of $13,200 to be paid one year from now is $13,200/(1 + i)$. As we have already shown, if $i = 10\%$ per year, the present value of $13,200 one year from now is $13,200/1.10 = \$12,000$. If $i = 20\%$ per year, the present value of $13,200 one year in the future is $13,200/1.20 = \$11,000$. Hence an increase in the interest rate reduces the present value of a future payment. Similarly, a decline in the interest rate increases the present value of a future payment.

If future payments are measured in nominal terms, as in the preceding example, the appropriate interest rate for calculating present values is the nominal interest rate, i. If future payments are measured in real terms, present values are calculated in exactly the same way, except that we use the real interest rate, r, rather than the nominal interest rate, i. In analyzing Prudence's consumption–saving decision, we're measuring everything in real terms, so we use the real interest rate, r, to calculate the present values of Prudence's future income and consumption.

Present Value and the Budget Constraint

We define the *present value of lifetime resources* (PVLR) as the present value of the income that a consumer expects to receive in current and future periods plus initial wealth. In the two-period case, the present value of lifetime resources is

$$PVLR = a + y + y^f/(1 + r) \qquad \text{(4.A.2)}$$

which is the sum of current income, y,[5] the present value of future income, $y^f/(1 + r)$, and current wealth, a. In our example, Prudence has $PVLR = 42,000 + (33,000/1.10) + 18,000 = 90,000$.

---

[5]Note that the present value of current income is just current income.

Next, we divide both sides of Eq. (4.A.1) by $(1 + r)$ and then add c to both sides to get

$$c + c^f/(1 + r) = a + y + y^f/(1 + r) \qquad \text{(4.A.3)}$$
$$PVLC = PVLR.$$

The left side of Eq. (4.A.3) is the present value of lifetime consumption, $c + c^f/(1 + r)$, which we denote $PVLC$. The budget constraint in Eq. (4.A.3) states that the *present value of lifetime consumption (PVLC)* equals the present value of lifetime resources $PVLR$.

In terms of Fig. 4.A.1, and indeed for any graph of the budget line, $PVLR$ equals the value of current consumption, c, at the horizontal intercept of the budget line because the horizontal intercept is the point on the budget line at which future consumption, c^f, equals zero. Setting future consumption, c^f, to zero in Eq. (4.A.3) yields current consumption, c, on the left side of the equation, which must equal $PVLR$ on the right side. Thus $c = PVLR$ at the horizontal intercept of the budget line.

What Does the Consumer Want? Consumer Preferences

The budget constraint, represented graphically as the budget line, shows the combinations of current and future consumption *available* to Prudence. To determine which of the many possible consumption combinations Prudence will choose, we need to know something about Prudence's preferences for current versus future consumption.

Economists use the term *utility* to describe the satisfaction or well-being of an individual. Preferences about current versus future consumption are summarized by how much utility a consumer obtains from each combination of current and future consumption. We can graphically represent Prudence's preferences for current versus future consumption through *indifference curves*, which represent all combinations of current and future consumption that yield the same level of utility. Because Prudence is equally happy with all consumption combinations on an indifference curve, she doesn't care (that is, she is indifferent to) which combination she actually gets. Figure 4.A.2 shows two of Prudence's indifference curves. Because the consumption combinations corresponding to points X, Y, and Z all are on the same indifference curve, IC^1, Prudence would obtain the same level of utility at X, Y, and Z.

Indifference curves have three important properties, each of which has an economic interpretation and each of which appears in Fig. 4.A.2:

1. *Indifference curves slope downward from left to right.* To understand why, let's suppose that Prudence has selected the consumption combination at point Y, where $c = 45,000$ and $c^f = 45,000$.[6] Now suppose that Prudence must reduce her current consumption to $c = 39,000$. Clearly, if she reduces current consumption while maintaining future consumption at 45,000, she will suffer a reduction in utility. However, Prudence can be compensated for this reduction in current consumption by additional future consumption. Suppose that, if she increases her future consumption to $c^f = 63,000$ when her current consumption falls to

---

[6]Point Y lies below Prudence's budget line, shown in Fig. 4.A.1, which means that not only could Prudence afford this consumption combination, but she would have resources left over at the end of the future period. Unless she wants to leave a bequest, she would not actually choose such a combination for the resources shown in Fig. 4.A.1.

Figure 4.A.2

Indifference curves
All points on an indifference curve represent consumption combinations that yield the same level of utility. Indifference curves slope downward because a consumer can be compensated for a reduction in current consumption by an appropriate increase in future consumption. All points on IC^2 represent consumption combinations that are preferred to all consumption combinations represented by points on IC^1. Indifference curves are bowed toward the origin to reflect the consumption-smoothing motive. Prudence prefers the consumption combination at point W, which is an average of the combinations at points X and Z because W represents a smoother pattern of consumption. Thus the indifference curve containing $W(IC^2)$ lies above and to the right of the indifference curve containing X, Y, and Z (IC^1).

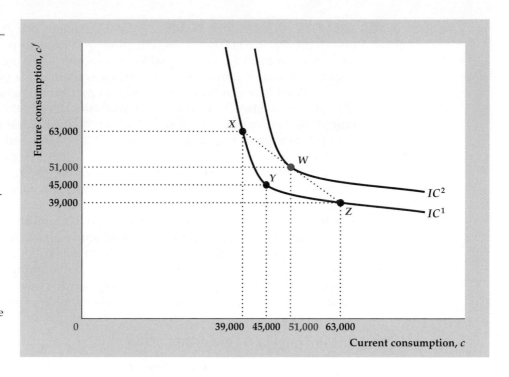

$c = 39,000$, so that she moves to point X, her level of utility remains unchanged. In such a case, she is indifferent between the consumption combinations at X and Y, and points X and Y must lie on the same indifference curve. In general, any change in the level of current consumption must be accompanied by a change in the *opposite* direction in the level of future consumption so as to keep Prudence's level of utility unchanged. Thus indifference curves, which represent consumption combinations with equal levels of utility, must slope downward from left to right.

2. *Indifference curves that are farther up and to the right represent higher levels of utility.* Consider for example point W, which lies above and to the right of point Y in Fig. 4.A.2. Both current consumption and future consumption are higher at W than at Y. Because Prudence obtains utility from both current and future consumption, W offers a higher level of utility than does Y; that is, Prudence prefers W to Y. In fact, as all points on the indifference curve IC^1 yield the same level of utility as Y, Prudence prefers W to all points on the indifference curve IC^1. Furthermore, as all points on indifference curve IC^2 yield the same level of utility as W, Prudence prefers all points on IC^2 to all points on IC^1. In general, for any two indifference curves, consumers prefer consumption combinations on an indifference curve that is above and to the right of the other indifference curve.

3. *Indifference curves are bowed toward the origin.* This characteristic shape of indifference curves captures the consumption-smoothing motive, discussed in Chapter 4. Under the consumption-smoothing motive, consumers prefer a relatively smooth pattern of consumption over time to having large amounts of consumption in one period and small amounts in another period. We can illustrate the link between the shape of indifference curves and the consumption-smoothing motive by considering the following three consumption combinations in

Fig. 4.A.2: point X ($c = 39{,}000$; $c^f = 63{,}000$), point W ($c = 51{,}000$; $c^f = 51{,}000$), and point Z ($c = 63{,}000$; $c^f = 39{,}000$). Note that W corresponds to complete consumption smoothing, with equal consumption occurring in both periods. In contrast, X and Z represent consumption combinations with large changes in consumption between the first period and the second period. In addition, note that W represents a consumption combination that is the average of the consumption combinations at X and Z: Current consumption at W, 51,000, is the average of current consumption at X and Z, 39,000 and 63,000, respectively; similarly, future consumption at W, also 51,000, is the average of future consumption at X and Z, 63,000 and 39,000, respectively.

Even though point W essentially is an average of points X and Z, and Prudence is indifferent between X and Z, she prefers W to X and Z because W represents much "smoother" (more even) consumption. Graphically, her preference for W over X and Z is indicated by W's position above and to the right of indifference curve IC^1 (which runs through X and Z). Note that W lies on a straight line drawn between X and Z. The only way that W can lie above and to the right of IC^1 is if IC^1 bows toward the origin, as depicted in Fig. 4.A.2. Thus the bowed shape of the indifference curve reflects the consumption-smoothing motive.

The Optimal Level of Consumption

Combining Prudence's budget line (which describes her available consumption combinations) and her indifference curves (which describe her preferences for current versus future consumption), we can find the levels of current consumption and saving that make her happiest. This best available, or *optimal*, level of current consumption and saving is re presented graphically by the point at which Prudence's budget line is tangent to an indifference curve, shown as point D in Fig. 4.A.3.

Figure 4.A.3

The optimal consumption combination
The optimal (highest utility) combination of current and future consumption is represented by the point of tangency between the budget line and an indifference curve (point D). All other points on the budget line, such as B and E, lie on indifference curves below and to the left of indifference curve IC^* and thus yield lower utility than the consumption combination at D, which lies on IC^*. Prudence would prefer the consumption combination at point T to the one at D, but as T lies above the budget line she can't afford the consumption combination that T represents.

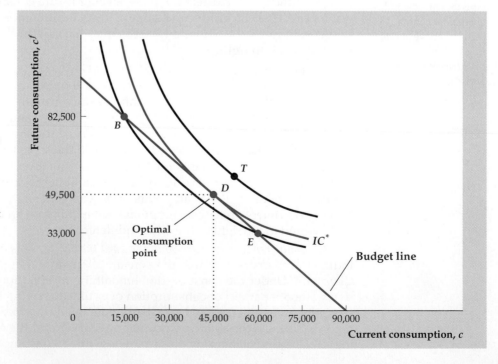

To see why Prudence achieves her highest possible level of satisfaction, or utility, at point D, first note that D lies on indifference curve IC^*, which means that all consumption combinations on IC^* yield the same level of utility as D. All points on Prudence's budget line other than point D—points such as B and E, for example—lie on indifference curves that are below and to the left of IC^*. Thus the consumption combinations represented by all of these other points yield a lower level of utility than the consumption combination at D. Prudence would prefer the consumption combination represented by a point such as T in Fig. 4.A.3 to the consumption combination represented by D, because T lies on an indifference curve above and to the right of IC^*; because T also lies above the budget line, however, Prudence can't afford the consumption combination represented by that point. With her budget constraint, Prudence can't do any better than D.

We conclude that Prudence's utility-maximizing consumption and saving choice is represented by point D, where her budget line is tangent to an indifference curve. Here, her optimal level of current consumption is 45,000, and her optimal level of future consumption is 49,500. Prudence's choice of current consumption automatically determines her current saving, s, which equals her current income minus her optimal current consumption:

$$s = y - c = 42,000 - 45,000 = -3000.$$

Thus Prudence chooses to dissave (decrease her initial assets) by 3000.

The Effects of Changes in Income and Wealth on Consumption and Saving

The formal model developed in this appendix provides a helpful insight: *The effect on consumption of a change in current income, expected future income, or wealth depends only on how that change affects the consumer's present value of lifetime resources, or PVLR.*

An Increase in Current Income

Suppose that Prudence receives a bonus at work of 12,000, which raises her current real income from 42,000 to 54,000. Her initial assets (18,000), future income (33,000), and the real interest rate (10%) remain unchanged; hence the increase of 12,000 in current income implies an equal increase in Prudence's present value of lifetime resources, or $PVLR$. If she hasn't yet committed herself to her original consumption–saving plan, how might Prudence revise that plan in light of her increased current income?

We use the graph in Fig. 4.A.4 to answer this question. In Fig. 4.A.4, BL^1 is Prudence's original budget line, and point D, where $c = 45,000$ and $c^f = 49,500$, represents Prudence's original, pre-bonus consumption plan. Prudence's bonus will allow her to consume more, both now and in the future, so the increase in her income causes her budget line to shift. To see exactly how it shifts, note that the increase of 12,000 in Prudence's current income implies that her $PVLR$ also increases by 12,000. Because the horizontal intercept of the budget line occurs at $c = PVLR$, the bonus shifts the horizontal intercept to the right by 12,000. The slope of the budget line, $-(1 + r) = -1.10$, remains unchanged because the real interest rate r is unchanged. Thus the increase in current income of 12,000 causes a parallel shift of the budget line to the right by 12,000, from BL^1 to BL^2.

Figure 4.A.4

An increase in income or wealth
An increase in current income, future income, and/or initial wealth that raises Prudence's *PVLR* by 12,000 causes the budget line to make a parallel shift to the right by 12,000, from BL^1 to BL^2. If Prudence's original consumption plan was to consume at point *D*, she could move to point *H* by spending all the increase on future consumption and none on current consumption; or she could move to point *K* by spending all the increase on current consumption and none on future consumption. However, if Prudence has a consumption-smoothing motive she will move to point *J*, which has both higher current consumption and higher future consumption than *D*. Point *J* is optimal because it lies where the new budget line BL^2 is tangent to an indifference curve, *IC***.

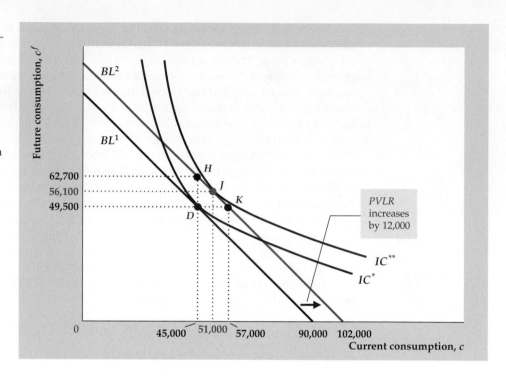

That shift demonstrates graphically that, after receiving her bonus, Prudence can enjoy greater current and future consumption. One strategy for Prudence, represented by point *K* on the new budget line BL^2, is to use the entire bonus to increase her current consumption by 12,000 while leaving her future consumption unchanged. Another strategy, represented by point *H* on BL^2, is to save all of her bonus while keeping her current consumption unchanged, and then use both the bonus and the interest of 1,200 earned on the bonus to increase her future consumption by 13,200.

If Prudence operates under a consumption-smoothing motive, she will use her bonus to increase *both* her current consumption and (by saving part of her bonus) her future consumption, thereby choosing a point on BL^2 between point *K* (consume the entire bonus) and point *H* (save the entire bonus). If her indifference curves are as shown in Fig. 4.A.4, she will move to *J*, where her new budget line, BL^2, is tangent to the indifference curve *IC***. At *J*, current consumption, *c*, is 51,000, future consumption, c^f, is 56,100, and saving, *s*, is 54,000 − 51,000 = 3000. Both current and future consumption are higher at *J* than at *D* (where *c* = 45,000 and c^f = 49,500). Prudence's current saving of 3000 at *J* is higher than her saving was at *D* (where she dissaved by 3000) because the increase in her current consumption of 6000 is less than the increase in her current income of 12,000. This example illustrates that an increase in current income raises both current consumption and current saving.

An Increase in Future Income
Suppose that Prudence doesn't receive her bonus of 12,000 in the current period, so that her current income, *y*, remains at its initial level of 42,000. Instead, because of an improved company pension plan, she learns that her future income will increase by 13,200, so y^f rises from 33,000 to 46,200. How will this good news affect Prudence's current consumption and saving?

At a real interest rate of 10%, the improvement in the pension plan increases the present value of Prudence's future income by 13,200/1.10, or 12,000. So, as in the case of the current-period bonus just discussed, the improved pension plan raises Prudence's *PVLR* by 12,000 and causes a parallel shift of the budget line to the right by that amount. The effects on current and future consumption are therefore exactly the same as they were for the increase of 12,000 in current income (and Fig. 4.A.4 applies equally well here).

Although increases in current income and expected future income that are equal in present value will have the same effects on current and planned future consumption, the effects of these changes on current saving are different. Previously, we showed that an increase in current income raises current saving. In contrast, because the increase in future income raises current consumption (by 6000 in this example) but doesn't affect current income, it causes saving to fall (by 6000, from –3000 to –9000). Prudence knows that she will be receiving more income in the future, so she has less need to save today.

An Increase in Wealth

Changes in wealth also affect consumption and saving. As in the cases of current and future income, the effect of a change in wealth on consumption depends only on how much the *PVLR* changes. For example, if Prudence finds a passbook savings account in her attic worth 12,000, her *PVLR* increases by 12,000. To illustrate this situation, we use Fig. 4.A.4 again. Prudence's increase in wealth raises her *PVLR* by 12,000 and thus shifts the budget line to the right by 12,000, from BL^1 to BL^2. As before, her optimal consumption choice goes from point D (before she finds the passbook) to point J (after her increase in wealth). Because the increase in wealth raises current consumption (from 45,000 at D to 51,000 at J) but leaves current income (42,000) unchanged, it results in a decline in current saving (from –3000 at D to –9000 at J). Being wealthier, Prudence does not have to save as much of her current income (actually, she is increasing her dissaving) to provide for the future.

The preceding analyses show that changes in current income, future income, and initial wealth all lead to parallel shifts of the budget line by the amount that they change the *PVLR*. Economists use the term *income effect* to describe the impact of any change that causes a parallel shift of the budget line.

The Permanent Income Theory

In terms of our model, a temporary increase in income represents a rise in current income, y, with future income, y^f, held constant. A permanent increase in income raises *both* current income, y, *and* future income, y^f. Therefore a permanent one-unit increase in income leads to a larger increase in *PVLR* than does a temporary one-unit increase in income. Because income changes affect consumption only to the extent that they lead to changes in *PVLR*, our theory predicts that a permanent one-unit increase in income will raise current and future consumption more than a temporary one-unit increase in income will.

This distinction between the effects of permanent and temporary income changes is emphasized in the *permanent income theory* of consumption and saving, developed in the 1950s by Nobel laureate Milton Friedman. He pointed out that income should affect consumption only through the *PVLR* in a many-period version of the model we present here. Thus permanent changes in income, because they last for many periods, may have much larger effects on consumption than temporary changes in income. As a result, temporary income increases would be mostly saved, and permanent income increases would be mostly consumed.[7]

Consumption and Saving over Many Periods: The Life-Cycle Model

The two-period model suggests that a significant part of saving is intended to pay for retirement. However, it doesn't reflect other important aspects of a consumer's lifetime income and consumption patterns. For example, income typically rises over most of a person's working life, and people save for reasons other than retirement. The *life-cycle model* of consumption and saving, originated in the 1950s by Nobel laureate Franco Modigliani and his associates, extends the model from two periods to many periods and focuses on the patterns of income, consumption, and saving throughout an individual's life.

The essence of the life-cycle model is shown in Fig. 4.A.5. In Fig. 4.A.5(a), the typical consumer's patterns of income and consumption are plotted against the consumer's age, from age twenty (the approximate age of economic independence) to age eighty (the approximate age of death). Two aspects of Fig. 4.A.5(a) are significant.

First, the average worker experiences steadily rising real income, with peak earnings typically occurring between the ages of fifty and sixty. After retirement, income (excluding interest earned from previous saving) drops sharply.

Second, the lifetime pattern of consumption is much smoother than the pattern of income over time, which is consistent with the consumption-smoothing motive discussed earlier. Although shown as perfectly flat in Fig. 4.A.5(a), consumption, in reality, varies somewhat by age; for example, it will be higher during years of high child-rearing expenses. An advantage of using the life-cycle model to study consumption and saving is that it may be easily modified to allow for various patterns of lifetime income and consumption.

The lifetime pattern of saving, shown in Fig. 4.A.5(b), is the difference between the income and consumption curves in Fig. 4.A.5(a). This overall hump-shaped pattern has been confirmed empirically. Saving is minimal or even negative during the early working years, when income is low. Maximum saving occurs when the worker is between ages fifty and sixty, when income is highest. Finally, dissaving occurs during retirement as the consumer draws down accumulated wealth to meet living expenses.

An important implication of the hump-shaped pattern of saving is that national saving rates depend on the age distribution of a country's population. Countries with unusually young or unusually old populations have low saving rates, and countries with relatively more people in their middle years have higher saving rates.

Bequests and Saving

We have assumed that the consumer plans to spend all of his or her wealth and income during his or her lifetime, leaving nothing to heirs. In reality, many people leave bequests, or inheritances, to children, charities, and others. To the extent that consumers desire to leave bequests, they will consume less and save more than when they simply consume all their resources during their lifetimes.

---

[7]Friedman also provided some of the first empirical evidence for this theory. For example, he found that the consumption of farm families, on average, responded less to changes in income than did the consumption of nonfarm families. Friedman's explanation was that, because farm incomes depend heavily on weather and crop prices, both of which are volatile, changes in farm incomes are much more likely to be temporary than are changes in nonfarm incomes. Current changes in farm incomes have a smaller effect on the *PVLR* and therefore have a smaller effect on current consumption.

Figure 4.A.5

Life-cycle consumption, income, and saving
(a) Income and consumption are plotted against age. Income typically rises gradually throughout most of a person's working life and peaks shortly before retirement. The desire for a smooth pattern of consumption means that consumption varies less than income over the life cycle. Consumption here is constant.
(b) Saving is the difference between income and consumption; the saving pattern is hump-shaped. Early in a person's working life consumption is larger than income, so saving is negative. In the middle years saving is positive; the excess of income over consumption is used to repay debts incurred earlier in life and to provide for retirement. During retirement people dissave.

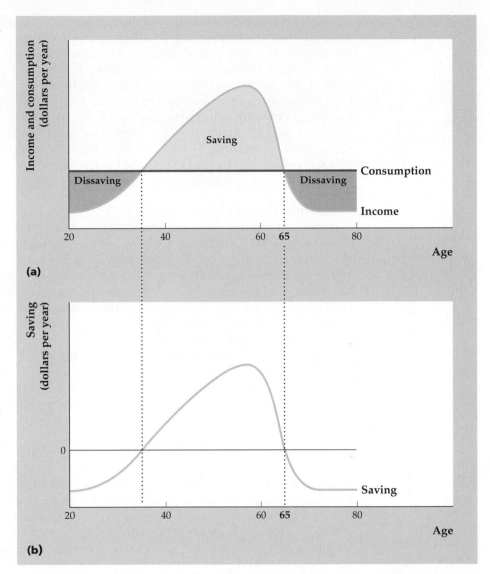

Ricardian Equivalence

One of the most significant results of analyzing our model is that changes in income or wealth affect desired consumption only to the extent that they affect the consumer's *PVLR*. The point made by advocates of Ricardian equivalence, discussed in Chapter 4, is that, holding current and future government purchases constant, *a change in current taxes does not affect the consumer's* PVLR *and thus should not affect desired consumption,* C^d, *or desired national saving,* $Y - C^d - G$.

To illustrate this idea, suppose that the government cuts Prudence's current taxes by 300. This tax reduction increases Prudence's current income by 300, which (all else being equal) would cause her to consume more. Because the government's revenue has been reduced by 300 and its expenditures have not changed, however, the government must increase its current borrowing from the public by 300 (per taxpayer). Furthermore, the government must pay interest on its borrowings. For example, if the real interest rate that the government must pay on its debt is 10%, in the future period the government's outstanding debt will be 330 greater than it would have been without the tax cut.

As a taxpayer, Prudence is ultimately responsible for the government's debts. Suppose that the government decides to repay its borrowings and accumulated interest in the future period (Chapter 15 discusses what happens if the government's debt is left for Prudence's descendants to repay). To repay its debt plus interest, the government must raise taxes in the future period by 330, so Prudence's expected future income falls by 330. Overall, then, the government's tax program has raised Prudence's current income by 300 but reduced her future income by 330. At a real interest rate of 10%, the present value of the future income change is –300, which cancels out the increase in current income of 300. Thus Prudence's *PVLR* is unchanged by the tax cut, and (as the Ricardian equivalence proposition implies) she should not change her current consumption.

Excess Sensitivity and Borrowing Constraints

A variety of studies have confirmed that consumption is affected by current income, expected future income, and wealth, and that permanent income changes have larger effects on consumption than do temporary income changes—all of which are outcomes implied by the model. Nevertheless, some studies show that the response of consumption to a change in current income is greater than would be expected on the basis of the effect of the current income change on *PVLR*. This tendency of consumption to respond to current income more strongly than the model predicts is called the *excess sensitivity* of consumption to current income.

One explanation for excess sensitivity is that people are more short-sighted than assumed in our model and thus consume a larger portion of an increase in current income than predicted by it. Another explanation, which is more in the spirit of the model, is that the amount that people can borrow is limited. A restriction imposed by lenders on the amount that someone can borrow against future income is called a *borrowing constraint*.

The effect of a borrowing constraint on the consumption–saving decision depends on whether the consumer would want to borrow in the absence of a borrowing constraint. If the consumer wouldn't want to borrow even if borrowing were possible, the borrowing constraint is said to be *nonbinding*. When a consumer wants to borrow but is prevented from doing so, the borrowing constraint is said to be *binding*. A consumer who faces a binding borrowing constraint will spend all available current income and wealth on current consumption so as to come as close as possible to the consumption combination desired in the absence of borrowing constraints. Such a consumer would consume the entire amount of an increase in current income. Thus the effect of an increase in current income on current consumption is greater for a consumer who faces a binding borrowing constraint than is predicted by our simple model without borrowing constraints. In macroeconomic terms, this result implies that—if a significant number of consumers face binding borrowing constraints—the response of aggregate consumption to an increase in aggregate income will be greater than implied by the basic theory in the absence of borrowing constraints. In other words, if borrowing constraints exist, consumption may be excessively sensitive to current income.[8]

---

[8]Although we have no direct way of counting how many consumers are constrained from borrowing, several studies estimate that, to account for the observed relationship between consumption and current income, during any year some 20% to 50% of U.S. consumers face binding borrowing constraints. See, for example, John Y. Campbell and N. Gregory Mankiw, "Consumption, Income, and Interest Rates: Reinterpreting the Time Series Evidence," in O. Blanchard and S. Fischer, eds., *NBER Macroeconomics Annual*, Cambridge, Mass.: MIT Press, 1989; and Robert E. Hall and Frederic S. Mishkin, "The Sensitivity of Consumption to Transitory Income: Estimates from Panel Data on Households," *Econometrica*, March 1982, pp. 461–481.

Figure 4.A.6

The effect of an increase in the real interest rate on the budget line
The figure shows the effect on Prudence's budget line of an increase in the real interest rate, r, from 10% to 76%. Because the slope of a budget line is $-(1 + r)$ and the initial real interest rate is 10%, the slope of Prudence's initial budget line, BL^1, is -1.10. The initial budget line, BL^1, also passes through the no-borrowing, no-lending point, E, which represents the consumption combination that Prudence obtains by spending all her current income and wealth on current consumption. Because E can still be obtained when the real interest rate rises, it also lies on the new budget line, BL^2. However, the slope of BL^2 is -1.76, reflecting the rise in the real interest rate to 76%. Thus the higher real interest rate causes the budget line to pivot clockwise around the no-borrowing, no-lending point.

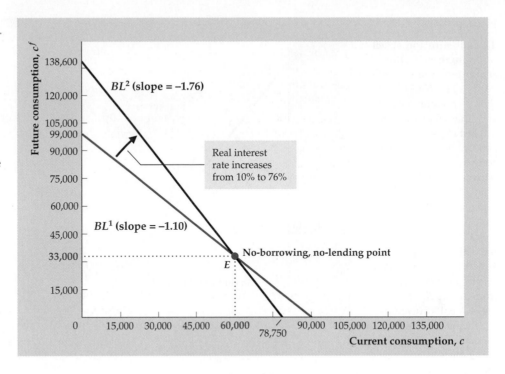

The Real Interest Rate and the Consumption–Saving Decision

To explore the effects of a change in the real interest rate on consumption and saving, let's return to the two-period model and Prudence's situation. Recall that Prudence initially has current real income, y, of 42,000, future income, y^f, of 33,000, initial wealth, a, of 18,000, and that she faces a real interest rate, r, of 10%. Her budget line, which is the same as in Fig. 4.A.1, is shown in Fig. 4.A.6 as BL^1. Now let's see what happens when for some reason the real interest rate jumps from 10% to 76%.[9]

The Real Interest Rate and the Budget Line

To see how Prudence's budget line is affected when the real interest rate rises, let's first consider point E on the budget line BL^1. Point E is special in that it is the only point on the budget line at which current consumption equals current income plus initial wealth ($c = y + a = 60,000$) and future consumption equals future income ($c^f = y^f = 33,000$). If Prudence chooses this consumption combination, she doesn't need to borrow (her current income and initial wealth are just sufficient to pay for her current consumption), nor does she have any current resources left to deposit in (lend to) the bank. Thus E is the *no-borrowing, no-lending point*. Because E involves neither borrowing nor lending, the consumption combination it represents is available to Prudence regardless of the real interest rate. Thus the no-borrowing, no-lending point remains on the budget line when the real interest rate changes.

Next, recall that the budget line's slope is $-(1 + r)$. When the real interest rate, r, jumps from 10% to 76%, the slope of the budget line changes from -1.10 to -1.76; that is, the new budget line becomes steeper. Because the budget line becomes steeper but still passes through the no-borrowing, no-lending point, E, it pivots clockwise around point E.

---

[9]A 76% real interest rate isn't realistic, but assuming this large a change makes its effects more obvious.

Figure 4.A.7

The substitution effect of an increase in the real interest rate
We assume that Prudence's preferences are such that when the real interest rate is 10% she chooses the consumption combination at the no-borrowing, no-lending point, E, on the initial budget line BL^1. Point E lies on the indifference curve IC^1. An increase in the real interest rate to 76% causes the budget line to pivot clockwise from BL^1 to BL^2, as in Fig. 4.A.6. By substituting future consumption for current consumption along the new budget line, BL^2, Prudence can reach points that lie above and to the right of IC^1; these points represent consumption combinations that yield higher utility than the consumption combination at E. Her highest utility is achieved by moving to point V, where the new budget line, BL^2, is tangent to indifference curve IC^2. The drop in current consumption (by 9000) and the resulting equal rise in saving that occur in moving from E to V reflect the substitution effect of the increase in the real interest rate.

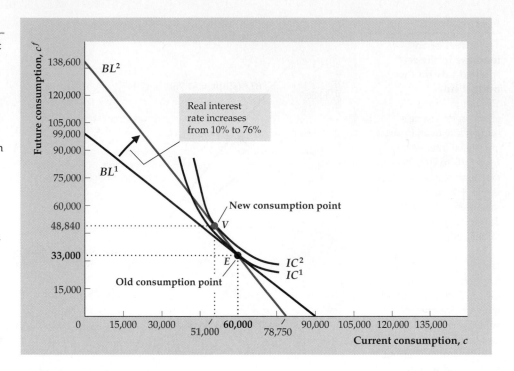

The Substitution Effect

As we discussed in Chapter 4, the price of current consumption in terms of future consumption is $1 + r$, because if Prudence increases her consumption by one unit today, thereby reducing her saving by one unit, she will have to reduce her future consumption by $1 + r$ units. When the real interest rate increases, current consumption becomes more expensive relative to future consumption. In response to this increase in the relative price of current consumption, Prudence substitutes away from current consumption toward future consumption by increasing her saving. This increase in saving reflects *the substitution effect of the real interest rate on saving*, introduced in Chapter 4.

The substitution effect is illustrated graphically in Fig. 4.A.7. Initially, the real interest rate is 10% and the budget line is BL^1. Suppose for now that Prudence's preferences are such that BL^1 is tangent to an indifference curve, IC^1, at the no-borrowing, no-lending point, E.[10] At a real interest rate of 10%, Prudence chooses the consumption combination at E.

When the real interest rate rises from 10% to 76%, the budget line pivots clockwise to BL^2. Because Prudence's original consumption point—the no-borrowing, no-lending point, E—also lies on the new budget line, BL^2, she has the option of remaining at E and enjoying the same combination of current and future consumption after the real interest rate rises. Points along BL^2 immediately above and to the left of E lie above and to the right of IC^1, however. These points represent consumption combinations that are available to Prudence and yield a higher level of utility than the consumption combination at E. Prudence can attain the highest level of utility along BL^2 at point V, where indifference curve IC^2 is tangent to BL^2. In response to the increase in the relative price of current consumption, Prudence reduces her current consumption, from 60,000 to 51,000, and moves from E to V on BL^2. Her reduction of 9000 in current consumption between E and V is equivalent

[10]Note that Prudence's indifference curves in Fig. 4.A.7 are different from those in Fig. 4.A.4.

to an increase of 9000 in saving. The increase in saving between E and V reflects the substitution effect on saving of a higher real interest rate.

The Income Effect
If Prudence's current consumption initially equals her current resources (current income plus initial wealth) so that she is neither a lender nor a borrower, a change in the real interest rate has only a substitution effect on her saving, as shown in Fig. 4.A.7. If her current consumption initially is not equal to her current resources, however, then an increase in the real interest rate also has an income effect. As we discussed in Chapter 4, if Prudence is initially a saver (equivalently, a lender), with current consumption less than her current resources (current income plus initial wealth), an increase in the real interest rate makes her financially better off by increasing the future interest payments that she will receive. In response to this increase in future interest income, she increases her current consumption and reduces her current saving. On the other hand, if Prudence is initially a borrower, with current consumption exceeding her current resources, an increase in the real interest rate increases the interest she will have to pay in the future. Having to make higher interest payments in the future makes Prudence financially worse off overall, leading her to reduce her current consumption. Thus, for a borrower, the income effect of an increase in the real interest rate leads to reduced current consumption and increased saving.

The Substitution Effect and the Income Effect Together
Figure 4.A.8 illustrates the full impact of an increase in the real interest rate on Prudence's saving, including the substitution and income effects—assuming that Prudence initially is a lender. As before, Prudence's original budget line is BL^1 when the real interest rate is 10%. We now assume that Prudence's preferences are such that BL^1 is tangent to an indifference curve, IC^1, at point D. Thus, at a 10% real interest rate, Prudence plans current consumption of 45,000 and future consumption of 49,500. Her current resources equal 60,000 (current income of 42,000 plus initial assets of 18,000), so if she enjoys current consumption of 45,000 she will have resources of 15,000 to lend. Her chosen point, D, is located to the left of the no-borrowing, no-lending point, E (current consumption is lower at D than at E), showing that Prudence is a lender.

The increase in the real interest rate from 10% to 76% causes Prudence's budget line to pivot clockwise through the no-borrowing, no-lending point, E, ending at BL^2 as before. To separate the substitution and income effects of the increase in the real interest rate, think of the movement of the budget line from BL^1 to BL^2 as taking place in two steps.

First, imagine that the original budget line, BL^1, pivots clockwise around Prudence's original consumption combination, point D, until it is parallel to the new budget line, BL^2 (that is, its slope is -1.76). The resulting intermediate budget line is the dotted line, BL^{int}. Second, imagine that BL^{int} makes a parallel shift to the right to BL^2.

The response of Prudence's saving and current consumption to the increase in the real interest rate can also be broken into two steps. First, consider her response to the pivot of the budget line through point D, from BL^1 to BL^{int}. If this change were the only one in Prudence's budget line, she would move from D to P ($c = 36,600$ and $c^f = 64,284$) on BL^{int}. At P, she would save more and enjoy less current consumption than at D. The increase in saving between D and P, similar to Prudence's shift from E to V in Fig. 4.A.7, measures the substitution effect on Prudence's saving of the increase in the real interest rate.

Second, consider the effect of the parallel shift from BL^{int} to BL^2. The new budget line, BL^2, is tangent to an indifference curve, IC^3, at point Q, so Prudence

An increase in the real interest rate with both an income effect and a substitution effect
We assume that Prudence initially consumes at point D on the original budget line, BL^1. An increase in the real interest rate from 10% to 76% causes the budget line to pivot clockwise, from BL^1 to the new budget line, BL^2. We break the overall shift of the budget line into two parts: (1) a pivot around the original consumption point, D, to yield an intermediate budget line, BL^{int}, and (2) a parallel shift from BL^{int} to the final budget line, BL^2. The substitution effect is measured by the movement from the original consumption point, D, to point P on BL^{int}, and the income effect is measured by the movement from P to Q on BL^2. As drawn, the substitution effect is larger than the income effect so that the overall effect is for current consumption to fall and saving to rise.

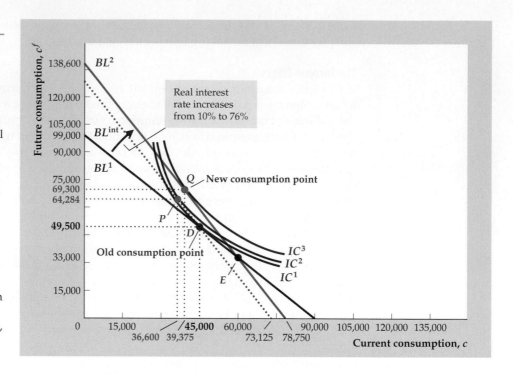

will choose the consumption combination at Q. Current and future consumption are higher, and saving is lower, at Q than at P. The increase in current consumption and the decrease in saving between P and Q reflect the income effect of the increase in the real interest rate. Thus, as discussed earlier, income effects occur when a change in some variable causes a parallel shift of the budget line.

The total change in Prudence's consumption and saving resulting from the rise in the real interest rate is depicted in Fig. 4.A.8 as the change in saving between point D and point Q. This change is the sum of the substitution effect, measured by the increase in saving in moving from D to P, and the income effect, measured by the decline in saving in moving from P to Q. In Fig. 4.A.8, current consumption is lower and saving is higher at the final point, Q, than at the original point, D. However, we could just as easily draw the curves so that saving is less at the final point, Q, than at the initial point, D. Thus the theory fails to predict whether Prudence's saving will rise or fall in response to an increase in the real interest rate, because the income and substitution effects work in opposite directions for a lender.

As we discussed in Chapter 4, for a borrower the income and substitution effects work in the same direction (Analytical Problem 6 at the end of Chapter 4 asks you to explain this result). A higher real interest rate increases a borrower's reward for saving (equivalently, it increases the relative price of current consumption), so he or she tends to save more (the substitution effect); because a borrower pays rather than receives interest, a higher real interest rate also makes him or her poorer, leading to less consumption and more saving.

To summarize, the two-period model implies that an increase in the real interest rate increases saving by borrowers. Nevertheless, because of conflicting income and substitution effects, economic theory isn't decisive about the effect of the real interest rate on the saving of lenders. As we discussed in Chapter 4, empirical studies have shown that an increase in the real interest rate tends to increase desired national saving, though this effect is not very strong.

CHAPTER **5**

Saving and Investment in the Open Economy

With virtually no exceptions, modern economies are open economies, which means that they engage in international trade of goods and services and in international borrowing and lending. Economic openness is of tremendous benefit to the average person. Because the United States is an open economy, U.S. consumers can enjoy products from around the world (Japanese MP3 players, Italian shoes, Irish woolens) and U.S. businesses can find new markets abroad for their products (computers, beef, financial services). Similarly, the internationalization of financial markets means that U.S. savers have the opportunity to purchase German government bonds or shares in Taiwanese companies as well as domestic assets, and U.S. firms that want to finance investment projects can borrow in London or Tokyo as well as in New York.

Beyond the economic diversity and opportunity it creates, economic openness carries another important implication: In an open economy, *a country's spending need not equal its production in every period,* as would be required in a closed economy with no foreign trade and no international borrowing and lending. In particular, by importing more than they export and borrowing from abroad to pay for the difference, the residents of an open economy can temporarily spend more than they produce.

The ability of an open economy to spend more than it produces is both an opportunity and a potential problem. For example, by borrowing abroad (and by selling off U.S.-owned assets to foreign investors), the United States was able to finance a large excess of imports over exports during the 1980s, 1990s, and 2000s. As a result, U.S. citizens enjoyed higher levels of consumption, investment, and government purchases than they could have otherwise. At the same time, however, they incurred foreign debts that may be a future burden to the U.S. economy.

Why do countries sometimes borrow abroad to pay for an excess of imports over exports but at other times export more than they import and lend the difference to other countries? Why doesn't each country just balance its books and import as much as it exports each year? As we explain in this chapter, the fundamental determinants of a country's trade position are the country's saving and investment decisions. Thus although the issues of trade balances and international lending introduced here may seem at first to be unrelated to the topics covered in Chapter 4, the two sets of questions actually are closely related.

To explore how desired national saving and desired investment help determine patterns of international trade and lending, we extend the idea of goods market

165

equilibrium, described by the saving–investment diagram, to include a foreign sector. We show that, unlike the situation in a closed economy, in an open economy desired national saving and desired investment don't have to be equal. Instead, we show that, when a country's desired national saving exceeds its desired investment, the country will be a lender in the international capital market and will have a current account surplus. Similarly, when a country's desired national saving is less than its desired investment, the country will be an international borrower and will have a current account deficit.

By emphasizing saving and investment, we develop an important theme of this part of the book. However, to focus on the role of saving and investment, we ignore some other factors that also influence international trade and lending. The most important of these factors is the exchange rate, or the rate at which domestic currency can be exchanged for foreign currency. We fully discuss exchange rates and their role in the open economy in Chapter 13.

5.1 Balance of Payments Accounting

Examining the factors that affect international trade and lending first requires an understanding of the basics of balance of payments accounting. The **balance of payments accounts,** which are part of the national income accounts discussed in Chapter 2, are the record of a country's international transactions. ("In Touch with Data and Research: The Balance of Payments Accounts," p. 168, contains information about how the balance of payments accounts are constructed and where to find these data.) As you read this section, you should refer to Table 5.1, which presents U.S. balance of payments data for 2008; note that some of the numbers are positive and that others are negative. To sort out which international transactions are entered with a plus sign and which are entered with a minus sign, keep the following principle in mind: Any transaction that involves a flow of funds *into* the United States is a *credit* item and is entered with a plus sign; any transaction that involves a flow of funds *out of* the United States is a *debit* item and is entered with a minus sign. We illustrate this principle as we discuss the various components of the balance of payments accounts.

The Current Account

The **current account** measures a country's trade in currently produced goods and services, along with unilateral transfers between countries. For convenience we divide the current account into three separate components: (1) net exports of goods and services, (2) net income from abroad, and (3) net unilateral transfers.

Net Exports of Goods and Services.   We discussed the concept of net exports, *NX*, or exports minus imports, as part of the expenditure approach to measuring GDP in Chapter 2. Here we point out that net exports often are broken into two categories: goods and services.

Examples of internationally traded goods include U.S. soybeans, French perfume, Brazilian coffee, and Japanese cars. When a U.S. consumer buys a Japanese car, for example, the transaction is recorded as an import of goods for the United States (a debit item for the United States, because funds flow out of the United States to pay for the car) and an export of goods for Japan (a credit item for Japan because funds flow into Japan to pay for the car).

Table 5.1

Balance of Payments Accounts of the United States, 2008 (Billions of Dollars)

Current Account			
Net exports of goods and services (NX)			−681.1
Exports of goods and services		1835.8	
Goods	1291.4		
Services	544.4		
Imports of goods and services		−2516.9	
Goods	−2112.2		
Services	−404.7		
Net income from abroad (NFP)			127.6
Income receipts from abroad		755.5	
Income payments to residents of other countries		−627.9	
Net unilateral transfers			−119.7
Current Account Balance (CA)			−673.3

Capital and Financial Account			
Capital Account			
Net capital account transactions			−2.6
Financial Account			
Net financial flows			546.6
Increase in U.S.-owned assets abroad (financial outflow)		−52.5	
U.S. official reserve assets	−4.8		
Other U.S.-owned assets abroad	−47.6		
Increase in foreign-owned assets in U.S. (financial inflow)		599.0	
Foreign official assets	421.4		
Other foreign-owned assets	177.6		
Capital and Financial Account Balance (KFA)			544.0
Statistical Discrepancy			129.3
Memoranda:			
Balance on goods and services (trade balance)			−681.1
Balance on goods, services, and income			−553.5
Official settlements balance =			
Balance of payments =			
Increase in U.S. official reserve assets minus increase in foreign official assets = 4.8–421.4			−416.6

Note: Numbers may not add to totals shown owing to rounding.
Source: "U.S. International Transactions: Fourth Quarter of 2008 and Year 2008," Table A, p. 12 and Tables F and G, p. 26, *Survey of Current Business*, April 2009.

Internationally traded services include tourism, insurance, education, and financial services. The Application "The Impact of Globalization on the U.S. Economy," p. 185, discusses trade in business services. When a U.S. family spends a week's vacation in Mexico, for example, the family's expenditures for accommodations, food, sight-seeing tours, and so on, are in the U.S. current account as an import of tourism services (a debit item for the United States because funds are flowing out of the country). The family's expenditures are an export of tourism services for Mexico (a credit item in the Mexican current account). Similarly, when a foreign student attends college in the United States, her tuition payments are an export of services for the United States and an import of services for her home country.

IN TOUCH WITH DATA AND RESEARCH

The Balance of Payments Accounts

The data on U.S. international transactions that make up the balance of payments accounts are produced quarterly by the Bureau of Economic Analysis (BEA) in the U.S. Department of Commerce. The BEA releases data to the public about two and one-half months after the end of the quarter to which those data refer, and detailed figures appear in the January, April, July, and October issues of *Survey of Current Business.* Balance of payments data for recent years are revised each June to reflect more complete information, and these revisions are published in the July issue of *Survey of Current Business.* Summary data, much like those that appear in Table 5.1, appear in various publications including the FRED database of the Federal Reserve Bank of St. Louis and the *Economic Report of the President,* which is published each February. Balance of payments data can also be obtained by going to the BEA's Web site at *www.bea.gov* and clicking on "Balance of Payments" under the heading "International."

Although full information about the balance of payments accounts is available only quarterly, some components of the accounts are released monthly. The best-known example is the trade balance, which equals exports of goods and services minus imports of goods and services. These data are initially tabulated by the U.S. Bureau of the Census (which then passes them on to the BEA) and are based primarily on information provided by the U.S. Customs Service, the government agency responsible for monitoring flows of goods and services in and out of the country. In recent years, the Census Bureau has also negotiated with the data collection agencies of major U.S. trading partners to swap information about trade flows. The benefit of exchanging trade information is that it allows the Census Bureau to find out, for example, whether Canadian estimates of the imports they receive from the United States are similar to U.S. estimates of exports shipped to Canada. In principle, of course, the two numbers should be the same.

For more information, see Bureau of Economic Analysis, *The Balance of Payments of the United States: Concepts, Data Sources, and Estimating Procedures,* Washington, D.C.: U.S. Government Printing Office, 1990, available at *www.bea.gov/scb/pdf/internat/bpa/meth/bopmp.pdf.*

Net Income from Abroad.   Net income from abroad equals income receipts from abroad minus income payments to residents of other countries. It is almost equal to net factor payments from abroad, *NFP*, discussed in Chapter 2.[1] We will ignore the difference between *NFP* and net income from abroad and treat the two as equivalent concepts.

The income receipts flowing into a country, which are credit items in the current account, consist of compensation received from residents working abroad

---

[1] Net factor payments from abroad are presented in the national income and product accounts (NIPA), and net income from abroad is presented in the balance of payments accounts (BPA). The Bureau of Economic Analysis publishes a "reconciliation table" (in the Appendix section of BEA Current and Historical Data in *Survey of Current Business*) to account for the relatively minor differences between the NIPA and BPA accounts.

plus investment income from assets abroad. Investment income from assets abroad includes interest payments, dividends, royalties, and other returns that residents of a country receive from assets (such as bonds, stocks, and patents) that they own in other countries. For example, the interest that a U.S. saver receives from a French government bond she owns, or the profits that a U.S. company receives from a foreign subsidiary, qualify as income receipts from abroad.

The income payments flowing out of a country, which are debit items in the current account, consist of compensation paid to foreign residents working in the country plus payments to foreign owners of assets in the country. For example, the wages paid by a U.S. company to a Swedish engineer who is temporarily residing in the United States, or the dividends paid by a U.S. automobile company to a Mexican owner of stock in the company, are both income payments to residents of other countries.

Net Unilateral Transfers.   **Unilateral transfers** are payments from one country to another that do not correspond to the purchase of any good, service, or asset. Examples are official foreign aid (a payment from one government to another) or a gift of money from a resident of one country to family members living in another country. When the United States makes a transfer to another country, the amount of the transfer is a debit item because funds flow out of the United States. A country's net unilateral transfers equal unilateral transfers received by the country minus unilateral transfers flowing out of the country. The negative value of net unilateral transfers in Table 5.1 shows that the United States is a net donor to other countries.

Current Account Balance.   Adding all the credit items and subtracting all the debit items in the current account yields a number called the **current account balance.** If the current account balance is positive—with the value of credit items exceeding the value of debit items—the country has a current account surplus. If the current account balance is negative—with the value of debit items exceeding the value of credit items—the country has a current account deficit. As Table 5.1 shows, in 2008 the United States had a $673.3 billion current account deficit, equal to the sum of net exports of goods and services ($NX = -\$681.1$ billion), net income from abroad ($NFP = \$127.6$ billion), and net unilateral transfers ($-\$119.7$ billion).

The Capital and Financial Account

International transactions involving assets, either real or financial, are recorded in the **capital and financial account,** which consists of a capital account and a financial account. The **capital account** encompasses unilateral transfers of assets between countries, such as debt forgiveness or migrants' transfers (the assets that migrants take with them when they move into or out of a country). The **capital account balance** measures the net flow of assets unilaterally transferred into the country. As you can see in Table 5.1, the dollar value of the capital account balance in the United States was $-\$2.6$ billion in 2008.

Most transactions involving the flow of assets into or out of a country are recorded in the **financial account.** (Before July 1999, this account was called the *capital account,* so beware: If you use data from a source published before 1999, the term "capital account" refers to a measure currently known as the financial account. Even many current discussions still use the term "capital account" to refer to the "capital and financial account.") When the home country sells an asset to another country, the transaction is recorded as a **financial inflow** for the home country and as a credit item in the financial account of the home country. For example, if a U.S. hotel is sold to Italian investors, the transaction is counted as a financial inflow to the United States and therefore as a credit item in the U.S. financial account because funds flow *into* the United States to pay for the hotel. Similarly, when the home country buys an asset from abroad—say a U.S. resident opens a Swiss bank account—the transaction involves a **financial outflow** from the home country (the United States in this example) and is recorded as a debit item in the home country's financial account because funds are flowing *out* of the home country.

The **financial account balance** equals the value of financial inflows (credit items) minus the value of financial outflows (debit items). When residents of a country sell more assets to foreigners than they buy from foreigners, the financial account balance is positive, creating a financial account surplus. When residents of the home country purchase more assets from foreigners than they sell, the financial account balance is negative, creating a financial account deficit. Table 5.1 shows that in 2008 U.S. residents increased their holdings of foreign assets (ignoring unilaterally transferred assets) by $52.5 billion while foreigners increased their holdings of U.S. assets by $599.0 billion. Thus the United States had a financial account surplus of $546.6 billion in 2008 ($599.0 billion minus $52.5 billion with a small difference because of rounding). The **capital and financial account balance** is the sum of the capital account balance and the financial account balance. Because the capital account balance of the United States is so small, the capital and financial account balance is almost equal to the financial account balance.

The Official Settlements Balance.   In Table 5.1 one set of financial account transactions—transactions in official reserve assets—has been broken out separately. These transactions differ from other financial account transactions in that they are conducted by central banks (such as the Federal Reserve in the United States), which are the official institutions that determine national money supplies. Held by central banks, **official reserve assets** are assets, other than domestic money or securities, that can be used in making international payments. Historically, gold was the primary official reserve asset, but now the official reserves of central banks also include government securities of major industrialized economies, foreign bank deposits, and special assets created by the International Monetary Fund.

Central banks can change the quantity of official reserve assets they hold by buying or selling reserve assets on open markets. For example, the Federal Reserve could increase its reserve assets by using dollars to buy gold. According to Table 5.1 (see the line "U.S. official reserve assets"), in 2008 the U.S. central bank bought $4.8 billion of official reserve assets.[2] In the same year foreign central banks increased their holdings of dollar-denominated reserve assets by $421.4 billion (see the line "Foreign official assets"). The **official settlements balance**—also called the

---

[2]Remember that a negative number in the financial account indicates a financial outflow, or purchase of assets.

balance of payments—is the net increase (domestic less foreign) in a country's official reserve assets. A country that increases its net holdings of reserve assets during a year has a balance of payments surplus, and a country that reduces its net holdings of reserve assets has a balance of payments deficit. For the United States in 2008 the official settlements balance was −$416.6 billion (equal to the $4.8 billion increase in U.S. reserve assets minus the $421.4 billion increase in foreign dollar-denominated reserve assets). Thus the United States had a balance of payments deficit of $416.6 billion in 2008.

For the issues we discuss in this chapter, the balances on current account and on capital and financial account play a much larger role than the balance of payments. We explain the macroeconomic significance of the balance of payments in Chapter 13 when we discuss the determination of exchange rates.

The Relationship Between the Current Account and the Capital and Financial Account

The logic of balance of payments accounting implies a close relationship between the current account and the capital and financial account. Except for errors arising from problems of measurement, *in each period the current account balance and the capital and financial account balance must sum to zero.* That is, if

$$CA = \text{current account balance and}$$
$$KFA = \text{capital and financial account balance,}$$

then

$$CA + KFA = 0. \tag{5.1}$$

The reason that Eq. (5.1) holds is that every international transaction involves a swap of goods, services, or assets between countries. The two sides of the swap always have offsetting effects on the sum of the current account and the capital and financial account balances, $CA + KFA$. Thus the sum of the current account and the capital and financial account balances must equal zero.

Table 5.2 helps clarify this point. Suppose that a U.S. consumer buys an imported British sweater, paying $75 for it. This transaction is an import of goods to the United States and thus reduces the U.S. current account balance by $75. However, the British exporter who sold the sweater now holds $75. What will he do with it? There are several possibilities, any of which will offset the effect of the purchase of the sweater on the sum of the current account and the capital and financial account balances.

The Briton may use the $75 to buy a U.S. product—say, a computer game. This purchase is a $75 export for the United States. This U.S. export together with the original import of the sweater into the United States results in no net change in the U.S. current account balance CA. The U.S. capital and financial account balance KFA hasn't changed, as no assets have been traded. Thus the sum of CA and KFA remains the same.

A second possibility is that the Briton will use the $75 to buy a U.S. asset—say, a bond issued by a U.S. corporation. The purchase of this bond is a financial inflow to the United States. This $75 increase in the U.S. capital and financial account offsets the $75 reduction in the U.S. current account caused by the original import of the sweater. Again, the sum of the current account and the capital and financial account balances, $CA + KFA$, is unaffected by the combination of transactions.

Table 5.2

Why the Current Account Balance and the Capital and Financial Account Balance Sum to Zero: An Example (Balance of Payments Data Refer to the United States)

Case I: United States Imports $75 Sweater from Britain;
Britain Imports $75 Computer Game from United States

Current Account	
Exports	+$75
Imports	−$75
Current account balance, *CA*	0
Capital and Financial Account	
No transaction	
Capital and financial account balance, *KFA*	0
Sum of current and capital and financial account balances, *CA* + *KFA*	0

Case II: United States Imports $75 Sweater from Britain;
Britain Buys $75 Bond from United States

Current Account	
Imports	−$75
Current account balance, *CA*	−$75
Capital and Financial Account	
Financial inflow	+$75
Capital and financial account balance, *KFA*	+$75
Sum of current and capital and financial account balances, *CA* + *KFA*	0

Case III: United States Imports $75 Sweater from Britain;
Federal Reserve Sells $75 of British Pounds to British Bank

Current Account	
Imports	−$75
Current account balance, *CA*	−$75
Capital and Financial Account	
Financial inflow (reduction in U.S. official reserve assets)	+$75
Capital and financial account balance, *KFA*	+$75
Sum of current and capital and financial account balances, *CA* + *KFA*	0

Finally, the Briton may decide to go to his bank and trade his dollars for British pounds. If the bank sells these dollars to another Briton for the purpose of buying U.S. exports or assets, or if it buys U.S. assets itself, one of the previous two cases is repeated. Alternatively, the bank may sell the dollars to the Federal Reserve in exchange for pounds. But in giving up $75 worth of British pounds, the Federal Reserve reduces its holdings of official reserve assets by $75, which counts as a financial inflow. As in the previous case, the capital and financial account balance rises by $75, offsetting the decline in the current account balance caused by the import of the sweater.[3]

This example shows why, conceptually, the current account balance and the capital and financial account balance must always sum to zero. In practice, problems in measuring international transactions prevent this relationship from holding exactly. The amount that would have to be added to the sum of the current

---

[3]In this case the balance of payments falls by $75, reflecting the Fed's loss of official reserves. We didn't consider the possibility that the Briton would just hold $75 in U.S. currency. As dollars are an obligation of the United States (in particular, of the Federal Reserve), the Briton's acquisition of dollars would be a credit item in the U.S. capital and financial account, which would offset the effect of the sweater import on the U.S. current account.

IN TOUCH WITH DATA AND RESEARCH

Does Mars Have a Current Account Surplus?

The exports and imports of any individual country need not be equal in value. However, as every export is somebody else's import, for the world as a whole exports must equal imports and the current account surplus must be zero.

Or must it? When official current account figures for all nations are added up, the result is a current account deficit for the world. For example, International Monetary Fund (IMF) projections for 2009 show that advanced economies had a collective $371.3 billion current account deficit, and emerging market and developing countries had a $262.4 billion surplus, which adds up to a current account deficit for the world as a whole of $108.9 billion. Is planet Earth a net importer, and does Mars have a current account surplus?

As extraterrestrial trade seems unlikely, the explanation of the Earth's current account deficit must lie in statistical and measurement problems. A study by the IMF concluded that the main problem is the misreporting of income from assets held abroad. For example, interest earned by a U.S. investor on a foreign bank account should in principle be counted as a credit item in the U.S. current account and a debit item in the current account of the foreign country. However, if the U.S. investor fails to report this interest income to the U.S. government, it may show up only as a debit to the foreign current account, leading to a measured Earthwide current account deficit. The fact that the world's current account deficit is generally larger during periods of high interest rates provides some support for this explanation.

Sources: International Monetary Fund, *Report on the World Current Account Discrepancy,* September 1987; and IMF, *World Economic Outlook,* April 2009, Statistical Appendix Table A10, p. 208, available at *www.imf.org.*

account and the capital and financial account balances for this sum to reach its theoretical value of zero is called the **statistical discrepancy.** As Table 5.1 shows, in 2008 the statistical discrepancy was $129.3 billion. "In Touch with Data and Research: Does Mars Have a Current Account Surplus?" describes a puzzle that arises because of statistical discrepancies in the balance of payments accounts.

Net Foreign Assets and the Balance of Payments Accounts

In Chapter 2, we defined the net foreign assets of a country as the foreign assets held by the country's residents (including, for example, foreign stocks, bonds, or real estate) minus the country's foreign liabilities (domestic physical and financial assets owned by foreigners). Net foreign assets are part of a country's national wealth, along with the country's domestic physical assets, such as land and the capital stock. The total value of a country's net foreign assets can change in two ways: (1) the value of existing foreign assets and foreign liabilities can change, as when stock held by a U.S. citizen in a foreign corporation increases in value or the value of U.S. farmland owned by a foreigner declines; and (2) the country can acquire new foreign assets or incur new foreign liabilities.

What determines the quantity of new foreign assets that a country can acquire? In any period *the net amount of new foreign assets that a country acquires equals its current account surplus.* For example, suppose a country exports $10 billion more in goods and services than it imports and thus runs a $10 billion current account surplus (assuming that net factor payments from abroad, *NFP*, and net unilateral transfers both are zero). The country must then use this $10 billion to acquire foreign assets or reduce foreign liabilities. In this case we say that the country has undertaken net foreign lending of $10 billion.

Similarly, if a country has a $10 billion current account deficit, it must cover this deficit either by selling assets to foreigners or by borrowing from foreigners. Either action reduces the country's net foreign assets by $10 billion. We describe this situation by saying that the country has engaged in net foreign borrowing of $10 billion.

One important way in which a country borrows from foreigners occurs when a foreign business firm buys or builds capital goods; this is known as **foreign direct investment.** For example, when the Honda Motor Company from Japan builds a new auto production facility in Ohio, it engages in foreign direct investment. Because the facility is built in the United States but is financed by Japanese funds, foreign-owned assets in the United States increase, so the capital and financial account balance increases. Foreign direct investment is different from portfolio investment, in which a foreigner acquires securities sold by a U.S. firm or investor. An example of portfolio investment occurs when a French investor buys shares of stock in General Motors Corporation. This transaction also increases the capital and financial account balance, as it represents an increase in foreign-owned assets in the United States.

Equation (5.1) emphasizes the link between the current account and the acquisition of foreign assets. Because $CA + KFA = 0$, if a country has a current account surplus, it must have an equal capital and financial account deficit. In turn, a capital and financial account deficit implies that the country is increasing its net holdings of foreign assets. Similarly, a current account deficit implies a capital and financial account surplus and a decline in the country's net holdings of foreign assets. Summary table 7 presents some equivalent ways of describing a country's current account position and its acquisition of foreign assets.

SUMMARY 7

Equivalent Measures of a Country's International Trade and Lending
Each Item Describes the Same Situation
A current account surplus of $10 billion
A capital and financial account deficit of $10 billion
Net acquisition of foreign assets of $10 billion
Net foreign lending of $10 billion
Net exports of $10 billion (if net factor payments, *NFP*, and net unilateral transfers equal zero)

APPLICATION

The United States as International Debtor

From about World War I until the 1980s, the United States was a net creditor internationally; that is, it had more foreign assets than liabilities. Since the early 1980s, however, the United States has consistently run large annual current account deficits. These current account deficits have had to be financed by net foreign borrowing (which we define broadly to include the sale of U.S.-owned assets to foreigners as well as the incurring of new foreign debts).

The accumulation of foreign debts and the sale of U.S. assets to foreigners have, over time, changed the United States from a net creditor internationally to a net debtor. Figure 5.1 shows the U.S. ownership of foreign assets and foreign ownership of U.S. assets, both measured as a percent of U.S. GDP, since 1982. As you can see, foreign ownership of U.S. assets overtook the U.S. ownership of foreign assets in the mid 1980s and the gap between the two has grown substantially since then. According to estimates by the Bureau of Economic Analysis, at the end of 2008 the United States had net foreign assets of −$3469 billion, measured at current market prices. Equivalently, we could say that the United States had net foreign debt of $3469 billion.[4] This international obligation of more than $3 trillion is larger than that of any other country, making the United States the world's largest international debtor. This figure represented an increase of indebtedness of $1331 billion from yearend 2007. The U.S. current account deficit in 2008 was $673 billion. But the net debt of the United States rose nearly twice that much in part because of decreases in the value of U.S.-owned assets abroad relative to the value of foreign-owned assets in the United States.

Although the international debt of the United States is large and growing, the numbers need to be put in perspective. First, the economic burden created by any debt depends not on the absolute size of the debt but on its size relative to the debtor's economic resources. Even at $3469 billion, the U.S. international debt is only about 24% of one year's GDP (U.S. GDP in 2008 was $14,441 billion). By contrast, some countries, especially certain developing countries, have ratios of net foreign debt to annual GDP that exceed 100%. Second, the large negative net foreign asset position of the United States doesn't imply that it is being "bought up" or "controlled" by foreigners. If we focus on foreign direct investment, in which a resident of one country has ownership in a business in another country and has influence over the management of that business, it appears that the United States has a stronger presence in other countries then they do in the United states. At the end of 2008, the market value of U.S. direct investment in foreign countries was $3699 billion, and the market value of foreign direct investment in the United States was $2647 billion.[5]

---

[4]These and other data in this application are from Elena L. Nguyen, "The International Investment Position of the United States at Yearend 2008," *Survey of Current Business*, July 2009, pp. 10–19.

[5]See Nguyen, pp. 14–16. Incidentally, the largest direct investor in the United States isn't Japan, as is commonly believed, but the United Kingdom. The United Kingdom also is the country that receives the most direct investment from the United States. For data on the distribution of U.S. direct investment abroad and foreign direct investment in the United States, see Marilyn Ibarra and Jennifer Koncz, "Direct Investment Positions for 2008: Country and Industry Detail," *Survey of Current Business*, July 2009, pp. 20–34.

(continued)

Figure 5.1

International ownership of assets relative to U.S. GDP, 1982–2008

The chart shows annual values for ownership of foreign assets by U.S. residents and ownership of U.S. assets by foreigners, each as a percentage of U.S. GDP for the period 1982 to 2008.

Sources: International ownership of assets: Bureau of Economic Analysis, International Economic Accounts, International Investment Position, Table 2, available at *www.bea. gov/international/xls/intinv08_t2. xls.* GDP: Bureau of Economic Analysis, National Income and Product Accounts, available at *research.stlouisfed.org/fred2/ series/GDPCA.*

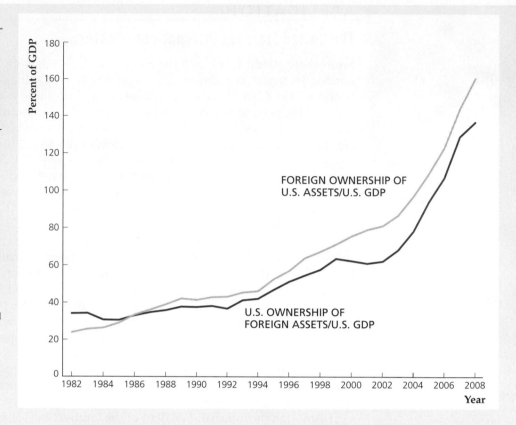

In evaluating the economic significance of a country's foreign debt, you should also keep in mind that net foreign assets are only part of a country's wealth; the much greater part of wealth is a country's physical capital stock and (though it isn't included in the official national income accounts) its "human capital"—the economically valuable skills of its population. Thus, if a country borrows abroad but uses the proceeds of that borrowing to increase its physical and human capital, the foreign borrowing is of less concern than when a country borrows purely to finance current consumption spending. Unfortunately, the deterioration of the U.S. net foreign asset position doesn't appear to have been accompanied by any significant increase in the rates of physical investment or human capital formation in the United States. In that respect, the continued high rate of U.S. borrowing abroad is worrisome but unlikely to create an immediate crisis.

5.2 Goods Market Equilibrium in an Open Economy

We are now ready to investigate the economic forces that determine international trade and borrowing. In the remainder of this chapter we demonstrate that a country's current account balance and foreign lending are closely linked to its domestic spending and production decisions. Understanding these links first requires developing the open-economy version of the goods market equilibrium condition.

In Chapter 4 we derived the goods market equilibrium condition for a closed economy. We showed that this condition can be expressed either as desired national saving equals desired investment or, equivalently, as the aggregate supply of goods equals the aggregate demand for goods. With some modification, we can use these same two conditions to describe goods market equilibrium in an open economy.

Let's begin with the open-economy version of the condition that desired national saving equals desired investment. In Chapter 2 we derived the national income accounting identity (Eq. 2.9):

$$S = I + CA = I + (NX + NFP). \tag{5.2}$$

Equation (5.2) is a version of the uses-of-saving identity. It states that national saving, S, has two uses: (1) to increase the nation's stock of capital by funding investment, I, and (2) to increase the nation's stock of net foreign assets by lending to foreigners (recall that the current account balance, CA, equals the amount of funds that the country has available for net foreign lending). Equation (5.2) also reminds us that (assuming no net unilateral transfers) the current account, CA, is the sum of net exports, NX, and net factor payments from abroad, NFP.

Because Eq. (5.2) is an identity, it must always hold (by definition). For the economy to be in goods market equilibrium, actual national saving and investment must also equal their desired levels. If actual and desired levels are equal, Eq. (5.2) becomes

$$S^d = I^d + CA = I^d + (NX + NFP), \tag{5.3}$$

where S^d and I^d represent desired national saving and desired investment, respectively. Equation (5.3) is the goods market equilibrium condition for an open economy, in which the current account balance, CA, equals net lending to foreigners, or financial outflows.[6] Hence Eq. (5.3) states that *in goods market equilibrium in an open economy, the desired amount of national saving, S^d, must equal the desired amount of domestic investment, I^d, plus the amount lent abroad, CA.* Note that the closed-economy equilibrium condition is a special case of Eq. (5.3), with $CA = 0$.

In general, the majority of net factor payments, NFP, are determined by past investments and aren't much affected by current macroeconomic developments. If for simplicity we assume that net factor payments, NFP, are zero, the current account equals net exports and the goods market equilibrium condition, Eq. (5.3), becomes

$$S^d = I^d + NX. \tag{5.4}$$

Equation (5.4) is the form of the goods market equilibrium condition that we will work with. Under the assumption that net factor payments are zero, we can refer to the term NX interchangeably as net exports or as the current account balance.

As for the closed economy, we can also write the goods market equilibrium condition for the open economy in terms of the aggregate supply and aggregate demand for goods. In an open economy, where net exports, NX, are part of the aggregate demand for goods, this alternative condition for goods market equilibrium is

$$Y = C^d + I^d + G + NX, \tag{5.5}$$

---

[6]Throughout this section and for the remainder of this book, we ignore unilateral transfers of capital, so the capital account balance equals zero. The financial account balance therefore has the same size but the opposite sign as the current account balance.

where Y is output, C^d is desired consumption spending, and G is government purchases. This way of writing the goods market equilibrium condition is equivalent to the condition in Eq. (5.4).[7]

We can rewrite Eq. (5.5) as

$$NX = Y - (C^d + I^d + G). \tag{5.6}$$

Equation (5.6) states that in goods market equilibrium the amount of net exports a country sends abroad equals the country's total output (gross domestic product), Y, less total desired spending by domestic residents, $C^d + I^d + G$. Total spending by domestic residents is called **absorption.** Thus Eq. (5.6) states that an economy in which output exceeds absorption will send goods abroad ($NX > 0$) and have a current account surplus and that an economy that absorbs more than it produces will be a net importer ($NX < 0$), with a current account deficit.

5.3 Saving and Investment in a Small Open Economy

To show how saving and investment are related to international trade and lending, we first present the case of a small open economy. A **small open economy** is an economy that is too small to affect the world real interest rate. The **world real interest rate** is the real interest rate that prevails in the international capital market—that is, the market in which individuals, businesses, and governments borrow and lend across national borders. Because changes in saving and investment in the small open economy aren't large enough to affect the world real interest rate, this interest rate is fixed in our analysis, which is a convenient simplification. Later in this chapter we consider the case of an open economy, such as the U.S. economy, that is large enough to affect the world real interest rate.

As with the closed economy, we can describe the goods market equilibrium in a small open economy by using the saving–investment diagram. The important new assumption that we make is that residents of the economy can borrow or lend in the international capital market at the (expected) world real interest rate, r^w, which for now we assume is fixed. If the world real interest rate is r^w, the domestic real interest rate must be r^w as well, as no domestic borrower with access to the international capital market would pay more than r^w to borrow, and no domestic saver with access to the international capital market would accept less than r^w to lend.[8]

Figure 5.2 shows the saving and investment curves for a small open economy. In a closed economy, goods market equilibrium would be represented by point E, the intersection of the curves. The equilibrium real interest rate in the closed economy would be 4% (per year), and national saving and investment would be $3 billion (per year). In an open economy, however, desired national saving need not

---

[7]To see that Eq. (5.5) is equivalent to Eq. (5.4), subtract $C^d + G$ from both sides of Eq. (5.5) to obtain $Y - C^d - G = I^d + NX$. The left side of this equation equals desired national saving, S^d, so it is the same as Eq. (5.4).

[8]For simplicity, we ignore factors such as differences in risk or taxes that might cause the domestic real interest rate to differ from the world rate. We also assume that there are no legal barriers to international borrowing and lending (when they exist, such barriers are referred to as capital controls).

Figure 5.2

A small open economy that lends abroad

The graph shows the saving–investment diagram for a small open economy. The country faces a fixed world real interest rate of 6%. At this real interest rate, national saving is $5 billion (point *B*) and investment is $1 billion (point *A*). The part of national saving not used for investment is lent abroad, so foreign lending is $4 billion (distance *AB*).

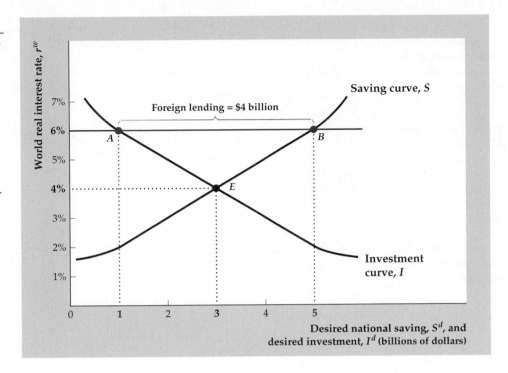

equal desired investment. If the small open economy faces a fixed world real interest rate, r^w, higher than 4%, desired national saving will be greater than desired investment. For example, if r^w is 6%, desired national saving is $5 billion and desired investment is $1 billion, so desired national saving exceeds desired investment by $4 billion.

Can the economy be in equilibrium when desired national saving exceeds desired investment by $4 billion? In a closed economy it couldn't. The excess saving would have no place to go, and the real interest rate would have to fall to bring desired saving and desired investment into balance. However, in the open economy the excess $4 billion of saving can be used to buy foreign assets. This financial outflow uses up the excess national saving so that there is no disequilibrium. Instead, the goods market is in equilibrium with desired national saving of $5 billion, desired investment of $1 billion, and net foreign lending of $4 billion (see Eq. 5.4 and recall that net exports, *NX*, and net foreign lending are the same).

Alternatively, suppose that the world real interest rate, r^w, is 2% instead of 6%. As Fig. 5.3 shows, in this case desired national saving is $1 billion and desired investment is $5 billion so that desired investment exceeds desired saving by $4 billion. Now firms desiring to invest will have to borrow $4 billion in the international capital market. Is this also a goods market equilibrium? Yes it is, because desired national saving ($1 billion) again equals desired investment ($5 billion) plus net foreign lending (minus $4 billion). Indeed, a small open economy can achieve goods market equilibrium for any value of the world real interest rate. All that is required is that net foreign lending equal the difference between the country's desired national saving and its desired investment.

A more detailed version of the example illustrated in Figs. 5.2 and 5.3 is presented in Table 5.3. As shown in the top panel, we assume that in this small country gross domestic product, *Y*, is fixed at its full-employment value of $20 billion

Figure 5.3

A small open economy that borrows abroad
The same small open economy shown in Fig. 5.2 now faces a fixed world real interest rate of 2%. At this real interest rate, national saving is $1 billion (point C) and investment is $5 billion (point D). Foreign borrowing of $4 billion (distance CD) makes up the difference between what investors want to borrow and what domestic savers want to lend.

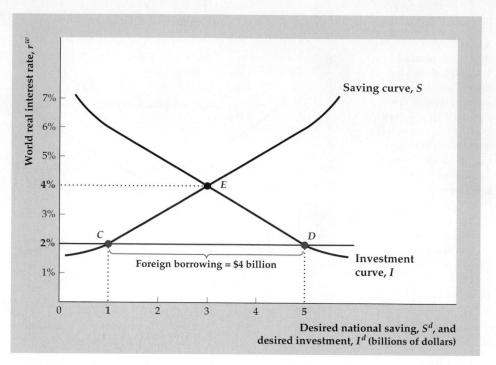

and government purchases, G, are fixed at $4 billion. The middle panel shows three possible values for the world real interest rate, r^w, and the assumed levels of desired consumption and desired investment at each of these values of the real interest rate. Note that higher values of the world real interest rate imply lower levels of desired consumption (because people choose to save more) and lower desired investment. The bottom panel shows the values of various economic quantities implied by the assumed values in the top two panels.

The equilibrium in this example depends on the value of the world real interest rate, r^w. Suppose that $r^w = 6\%$, as shown in Fig. 5.2. Column (3) of Table 5.3

Table 5.3

Goods Market Equilibrium in a Small Open Economy: An Example (Billions of Dollars)

Given			
Gross domestic product, Y	20		
Government purchases, G	4		
Effect of real interest rate on desired consumption and investment			
	(1)	(2)	(3)
(1) World real interest rate, r^w (%)	2	4	6
(2) Desired consumption, C^d	15	13	11
(3) Desired investment, I^d	5	3	1
Results			
(4) Desired absorption, $C^d + I^d + G$	24	20	16
(5) Desired national saving, $S^d = Y - C^d - G$	1	3	5
(6) Net exports, $NX = Y -$ desired absorption	−4	0	4
(7) Desired foreign lending, $S^d - I^d$	−4	0	4

Note: We assume that net factor payments, *NFP*, and net unilateral transfers equal zero.

shows that, if $r^w = 6\%$, desired consumption, C^d, is \$11 billion (row 2) and that desired investment, I^d, is \$1 billion (row 3). With C^d at \$11 billion, desired national saving, $Y - C^d - G$, is \$5 billion (row 5). Desired net foreign lending, $S^d - I^d$, is \$4 billion (row 7)—the same result illustrated in Fig. 5.2.

If $r^w = 2\%$, as in Fig. 5.3, column (1) of Table 5.3 shows that desired national saving is \$1 billion (row 5) and that desired investment is \$5 billion (row 3). Thus desired foreign lending, $S^d - I^d$, equals $-\$4$ billion (row 7)—that is, foreign borrowing totals \$4 billion. Again, the result is the same as illustrated in Fig. 5.3.

An advantage of working through the numerical example in Table 5.3 is that we can also use it to demonstrate how the goods market equilibrium, which we've been interpreting in terms of desired saving and investment, can be interpreted in terms of output and absorption. Suppose again that $r^w = 6\%$, giving a desired consumption, C^d, of \$11 billion and a desired investment, I^d, of \$1 billion. Government purchases, G, are fixed at \$4 billion. Thus when r^w is 6%, desired absorption (the desired spending by domestic residents), $C^d + I^d + G$, totals \$16 billion (row 4, column 3).

In goods market equilibrium a country's net exports—the net quantity of goods and services that it sends abroad—equal gross domestic product, Y, minus desired absorption (Eq. 5.6). When r^w is 6%, Y is \$20 billion and desired absorption is \$16 billion so that net exports, NX, are \$4 billion. Net exports of \$4 billion imply that the country is lending \$4 billion abroad, as shown in Fig. 5.2. If the world real interest rate drops to 2%, desired absorption rises (because people want to consume more and invest more) from \$16 billion to \$24 billion (row 4, column 1). Because in this case absorption (\$24 billion) exceeds domestic production (\$20 billion), the country has to import goods and services from abroad ($NX = -\$4$ billion). Note that desired net imports of \$4 billion imply net foreign borrowing of \$4 billion, as shown in Fig. 5.3.

The Effects of Economic Shocks in a Small Open Economy

The saving–investment diagram can be used to determine the effects of various types of economic disturbances in a small open economy. Briefly, any change that increases desired national saving relative to desired investment at a given world real interest rate will increase net foreign lending, the current account balance, and net exports, which are all equivalent under our assumption that net factor payments from abroad and net unilateral transfers are zero. A decline in desired national saving relative to desired investment reduces those quantities. Let's look at two examples that arise frequently in various countries.

Example 1: A Temporary Adverse Supply Shock. Suppose that a small open economy is hit with a severe drought—an adverse supply shock—that temporarily lowers output. The effects of the drought on the nation's saving, investment, and current account are shown in Fig. 5.4. The initial saving and investment curves are S^1 and I^1, respectively. For the world real interest rate, r^w, initial net foreign lending (equivalently, net exports or the current account balance) is distance AB.

The drought brings with it a temporary decline in income. A drop in current income causes people to reduce their saving at any prevailing real interest rate, so the saving curve shifts left, from S^1 to S^2. If the supply shock is temporary, as we have assumed, the expected future marginal product of capital is unchanged. As a result, desired investment at any real interest rate is unchanged, and the investment curve does not shift. The world real interest rate is given and does not change.

Figure 5.4

A temporary adverse supply shock in a small open economy Curve S^1 is the initial saving curve, and curve I^1 is the initial investment curve of a small open economy. With a fixed world real interest rate of r^w, national saving equals the distance OB and investment equals distance OA. The current account surplus (equivalently, net foreign lending) is the difference between national saving and investment, shown as distance AB. A temporary adverse supply shock lowers current output and causes consumers to save less at any real interest rate, which shifts the saving curve left, from S^1 to S^2. National saving decreases to distance OD, and the current account surplus decreases to distance AD.

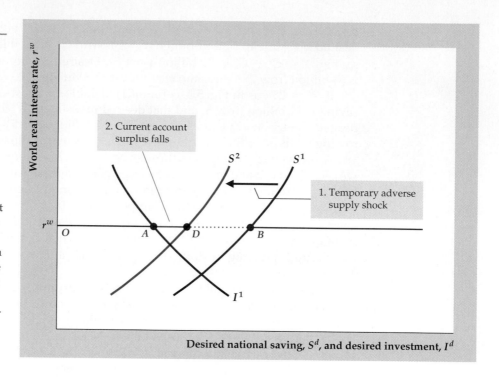

In the new equilibrium, net foreign lending and the current account have shrunk to distance AD. The current account shrinks because the country saves less and thus is not able to lend abroad as much as before.

In this example, we assumed that the country started with a current account surplus, which is reduced by the drought. If, instead, the country had begun with a current account deficit, the drought would have made the deficit larger. In either case the drought reduces (in the algebraic sense) net foreign lending and the current account balance.

Example 2: An Increase in the Expected Future Marginal Product of Capital. Suppose that technological innovations increase the expected future marginal product, MPK^f, of current capital investment. The effects on a small open economy are shown in Fig. 5.5. Again, the initial national saving and investment curves are S^1 and I^1, respectively, so that the initial current account surplus equals distance AB.

An increase in the MPK^f raises the capital stock that domestic firms desire to hold so that desired investment rises at every real interest rate. Thus the investment curve shifts to the right, from I^1 to I^2. The current account and net foreign lending shrink to length FB. Why does the current account fall? Because building capital has become more profitable in the home country, more of the country's output is absorbed by domestic investment, leaving less to send abroad.[9]

---

[9]A possibility that we have neglected so far is that technological innovations also cause savers to expect a higher future income, which would reduce current saving at every level of the world real interest rate. A leftward shift of the saving curve would further reduce the current account balance. This effect would only reinforce the effect on the country's current account of the rightward shift of the investment curve, so for simplicity we continue to ignore this potential change in desired saving.

Figure 5.5

An increase in the expected future *MPK* in a small open economy
As in Fig. 5.4, the small open economy's initial national saving and investment curves are S^1 and I^1, respectively. At the fixed world real interest rate of r^w, there is an initial current account surplus equal to the distance AB. An increase in the expected future marginal product of capital (MPK^f) shifts the investment curve right, from I^1 to I^2, causing investment to increase from distance OA to distance OF. The current account surplus, which is national saving minus investment, decreases from distance AB to distance FB.

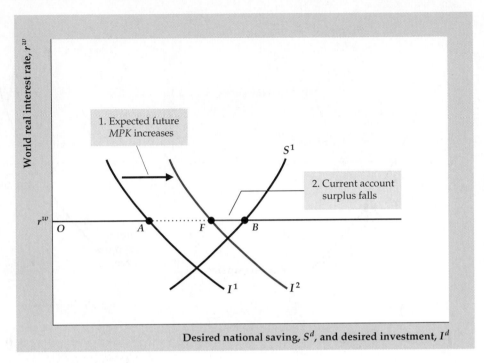

1. Expected future *MPK* increases

2. Current account surplus falls

Desired national saving, S^d, and desired investment, I^d

5.4 Saving and Investment in Large Open Economies

Although the model of a small open economy facing a fixed real interest rate is appropriate for studying many of the countries in the world, it isn't the right model to use for analyzing the world's major developed economies. The problem is that significant changes in the saving and investment patterns of a major economy can and do affect the world real interest rate, which violates the assumption made for the small open economy that the world real interest rate is fixed. Fortunately, we can readily adapt the analysis of the small open economy to the case of a **large open economy,** that is, an economy large enough to affect the world real interest rate.

To begin, let's think of the world as comprising only two large economies: (1) the home, or domestic economy, and (2) the foreign economy (representing the economies of the rest of the world combined). Figure 5.6 shows the saving–investment diagram that applies to this case. Figure 5.6(a) shows the saving curve, S, and the investment curve, I, of the home economy. Figure 5.6(b) displays the saving curve, S_{For}, and the investment curve, I_{For}, of the foreign economy. These saving and investment curves are just like those for the small open economy.

Instead of taking the world real interest rate as given, as we did in the model of a small open economy, we determine the world real interest rate within the model for a large open economy. What determines the value of the world real interest rate? Remember that for the closed economy the real interest rate was set by the condition that the amount that savers want to lend must equal the amount that investors want to borrow. Analogously, in the case of two large open economies, *the world real interest rate will be such that desired international lending by one country equals desired international borrowing by the other country.*

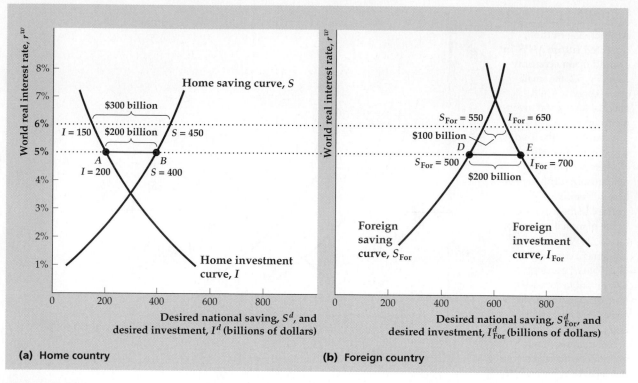

Figure 5.6

The determination of the world real interest rate with two large open economies
The equilibrium world real interest rate is the real interest rate at which desired international lending by one country equals desired international borrowing by the other country. In the figure, when the world real interest rate is 5%, desired international lending by the home country is $200 billion ($400 billion desired national saving less $200 billion desired investment, or distance AB), which equals the foreign country's desired international borrowing of $200 billion ($700 billion desired investment less $500 billion desired national saving, or distance DE). Thus 5% is the equilibrium world real interest rate. Equivalently, when the interest rate is 5%, the current account surplus of the home country equals the current account deficit of the foreign country (both are $200 billion).

To illustrate the determination of the equilibrium world real interest rate, we return to Fig. 5.6. Suppose, arbitrarily, that the world real interest rate, r^w, is 6%. Does this rate result in a goods market equilibrium? Figure 5.6(a) shows that, at a 6% real interest rate, in the home country desired national saving is $450 billion and desired investment is $150 billion. Because desired national saving exceeds desired investment by $300 billion, the amount that the home country would like to lend abroad is $300 billion.

To find how much the foreign country wants to borrow, we turn to Fig. 5.6(b). When the real interest rate is 6%, desired national saving is $550 billion and desired investment is $650 billion in the foreign country. Thus at a 6% real interest rate the foreign country wants to borrow $100 billion ($650 billion less $550 billion) in the international capital market. Because this amount is less than the $300 billion the home country wants to lend, 6% is *not* the real interest rate that is consistent with equilibrium in the international capital market.

At a real interest rate of 6%, desired international lending exceeds desired international borrowing, so the equilibrium world real interest rate must be less than 6%. Let's try a real interest rate of 5%. Figure 5.6(a) shows that at that interest rate desired national saving is $400 billion and desired investment is $200 billion in the home country, so the home country wants to lend $200 billion abroad. In Fig. 5.6(b), when the real interest rate is 5%, desired national saving in the foreign country is $500 billion and desired investment is $700 billion, so the foreign country's desired international borrowing is $200 billion. At a 5% real interest rate, desired international borrowing and desired international lending are equal (both are $200 billion), so the equilibrium world real interest rate is 5% in this example.

Graphically, the home country's desired lending when r^w equals 5% is distance AB in Fig. 5.6(a), and the foreign country's desired borrowing is distance DE in Fig. 5.6(b). Because distance AB equals distance DE, desired international lending and borrowing are equal when the world real interest rate is 5%.

We defined international equilibrium in terms of desired international lending and borrowing. Equivalently, we can define equilibrium in terms of international flows of goods and services. The amount the lending country desires to lend (distance AB in Fig. 5.6a) is the same as its current account surplus. The amount the borrowing country wants to borrow (distance DE in Fig. 5.6b) equals its current account deficit. Thus saying that desired international lending must equal desired international borrowing is the same as saying that the desired net outflow of goods and services from the lending country (its current account surplus) must equal the desired net inflow of goods and services to the borrowing country (its current account deficit).

In summary, for a large open economy the equilibrium world real interest rate is the rate at which the desired international lending by one country equals the desired international borrowing of the other country. Equivalently, it is the real interest rate at which the lending country's current account surplus equals the borrowing country's current account deficit.

Unlike the situation in a small open economy, for large open economies the world real interest rate is not fixed but will change when desired national saving or desired investment changes in either country. Generally, any factor that increases desired international lending relative to desired international borrowing at the initial world real interest rate causes the world real interest rate to fall. Similarly, a change that reduces desired international lending relative to desired international borrowing at the initial world real interest rate will cause the world real interest rate to rise.

APPLICATION

The Impact of Globalization on the U.S. Economy

Section 5.1, "Balance of Payments Accounting," showed how the international balance of payments accounts keep track of international trade and investment. These accounts reveal that the world's economies have become increasingly interdependent, as the volume of trade in goods and services has increased and as people in one country have increased their investment in other countries. This globalization is not without its consequences, and some people have argued that the United States needs to rein in the degree of globalization, restricting trade or international investment. To evaluate such proposals, we need to examine the facts about globalization, including how it has affected U.S. trade with other countries, how trade in services has changed, and how international investment has been altered.

(continued)

Figure 5.7

Exports and imports of goods and services as a percent of GDP, 1929–2008
The chart shows annual values for exports of goods and services from the United States and imports into the United States for the period 1929 to 2008.

Sources: Exports and imports: Bureau of Economic Analysis, Trade in Goods and Services, available at *research.stlouisfed. org/fred2/series/EXPGSCA* and *IMPGSCA.* GDP: Bureau of Economic Analysis, National Income and Product Accounts, available at *research.stlouisfed. org/fred2/series/GDPCA.*

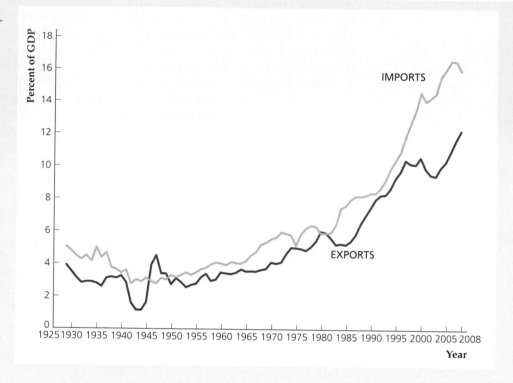

To begin, let's look at how U.S. trade with other countries has changed over time. If we examine exports of goods and services as a percentage of our GDP, we can see the relative importance of exports in the economy; similarly for imports. Figure 5.7 shows both statistics from 1929 to 2008. After World War II, both exports and imports rose gradually relative to GDP until the mid 1980s, when both began growing more rapidly. From the mid 1980s to 2006, imports have generally outpaced exports, thereby leading to a trade deficit that peaked at about 5.5% of GDP. The recession that began in 2007 led to a reduction in imports relative to GDP, reducing the trade deficit to just over 3%.

In addition to increased trade in goods and services, investors have also increased their investments in foreign countries over the past 30 years. As we saw in Figure 5.1 in the Application "The United States as International Debtor," p. 175, ownership of foreign assets by U.S. investors has increased rapidly, and that ownership of U.S. assets by foreign investors has increased even more rapidly, so that the United States has gone from being a net international creditor 30 years ago (with U.S. ownership of foreign assets exceeding foreign ownership of U.S. assets) to a net international debtor (with U.S. ownership of foreign assets being less than foreign ownership of U.S. assets) today.

As the U.S. economy has become more interdependent with other economies, there have been some costs and complaints. Increased openness means that jobs in some sectors of the U.S. economy may be eliminated, as a particular good is produced by workers in another country. Often workers complain that they have lost their jobs to foreign workers. And there have been instances, widely reported in the U.S. business press, in which a company shuts down a facility in the United States and opens one to do the same work in a foreign country. There are costs in foreign countries as well. In the fourth quarter of 2008, U.S. GDP declined about 6% because of the financial crisis and recession. But countries in Asia that produced many goods that they export to the United States suffered declines of 12% and more in their GDPs, as U.S. demand for their products declined dramatically.

Some people conclude that international trade destroys jobs. But international trade also creates jobs. Federal Reserve Chairman Ben Bernanke has noted, "Directly, trade creates jobs in the United States by expanding the potential market for U.S. goods and services. . . . Trade also creates jobs indirectly, in a variety of ways" including allowing firms to obtain cheaper or higher quality inputs to production and giving consumers greater variety of goods and services at lower prices.[10] Bernanke also recognized why people sometimes are fearful of increased trade: ". . . those who lose jobs for trade-related reasons are not necessarily the same people who get the new jobs created by trade. Trade, like other factors resulting in structural change, can have noticeable effects on the mix of jobs across industries, skill levels, and locations." But Bernanke also noted that the loss of jobs because of trade is very small relative to the loss of jobs every year for other reasons, so that trade is not a major factor in job loss.

In recent years, U.S. business firms have hired foreign workers in the business services industry. For example, call centers for customer service related to computers have been established in countries such as India, in part because those countries have educated workers who are fluent in English and because technological improvements have reduced the costs of international phone calls, thus allowing customers in the United States to call technicians in another country. This type of trade in services has become widespread, and some critics have objected to U.S. firms "moving jobs abroad."

However, the U.S. economy is the world leader in providing business services to other countries, not the other way around. Some U.S. politicians have proposed prohibiting U.S. companies from establishing call centers abroad, but this suggestion seems to ignore that the United States is the world leader in providing such services to other countries. U.S. exports of business services far exceed our imports of business services. So, if the United States ended all imports of business services, and other countries did the same, U.S. net exports would fall and the U.S. economy would be harmed, not helped, in terms of the short-term loss of jobs.

---

[10]Ben S. Bernanke, "Trade and Jobs." Remarks at the Distinguished Speaker Series, Fuqua School of Business, Duke University, March 30, 2004. These remarks were made by Bernanke when he was a Federal Reserve governor, before becoming chairman.

APPLICATION

Recent Trends in the U.S. Current Account Deficit

The United States has a very large current account deficit, as discussed in section 5.1, "Balance of Payments Accounting." But the current account deficit began to shrink in 2007 and 2008, thanks to the U.S. recession, which reduced demand for imported goods.

Figure 5.8 shows how the current account balance has changed since 1960. The figure shows that the current account balance was generally positive in the 1960s, bounced up and down around zero in the 1970s, and then fell sharply to about −3.5% of GDP by the mid 1980s. In the second half of the 1980s, the current account balance improved, becoming positive again in 1991. From 1991 to 2005, it deteriorated markedly, falling to −6.6% of GDP by the end of 2005. The housing downturn of 2006 and the recession that began in 2007 helped the current account balance improve to about −5% of GDP by mid 2008, as U.S. consumers bought fewer imported goods and services than before. When the financial crisis hit in late 2008, U.S. imports fell sharply and the current account balance improved to about −3% of GDP by the first quarter of 2009.

Economists have tried to explain why the current account balance declined steadily from 1991 to 2005. They developed four explanations: (1) a decline in demand by foreigners; (2) improved opportunities for international investment; (3) the rise in oil prices; (4) increased saving by developing countries.[11]

Figure 5.8

Current account balance as a percent of GDP, 1960–2009

The chart shows quarterly values for the current account balance as a percent of GDP for the period from the first quarter of 1960 to the first quarter of 2009.

Sources: Balance on current account: Bureau of Economic Analysis, available on-line at *research.stlouisfed.org/fred2/series/ BOPBCA*. GDP: Bureau of Economic Analysis, available at *research.stlouisfed.org/fred2/ series/GDP*.

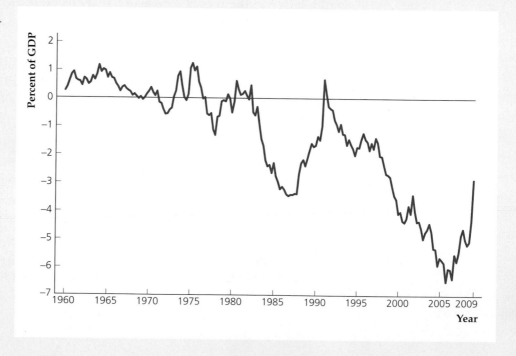

---

[11]For a useful summary of research on these reasons for the current account deficit, see Roger W. Ferguson, Jr. "U.S. Current Account Deficit: Causes and Consequences." Remarks to the Economics Club of the University of North Carolina at Chapel Hill, April 20, 2005; available at *www.federalreserve. gov/boarddocs/speeches/2005*.

The first explanation for the increased current account deficit was a slowdown in demand by foreigners, especially those in Japan and Europe. Economic growth in those areas was slow, and they ran current account surpluses. Both Japan and Germany increased their saving rates as the ratio of older workers to younger workers rose. As a result, they spent less (and thus imported fewer U.S. goods) and saved more, and the increased saving was often invested in the United States.

A second explanation for the increased U.S. current account deficit from 1991 to 2005 has to do with increased opportunities for international investment. U.S. investors sought to diversify their portfolios internationally, and foreign investors increasingly sought to invest in the United States. As foreigners perceived a rise in the return to U.S. investments in the second half of the 1990s, they invested more in the United States. The result was a U.S. capital and financial account surplus and a current account deficit. The increased return on U.S. equity increased the wealth of U.S. households and led to a lower personal saving rate and higher consumption spending. As Fig. 5.9 shows, the United States now finds itself with a net international investment position of about −24% of one year's GDP. (For more on this subject, see the Application "The United States as International Debtor," p. 175.)

A third reason for the widening current account deficit in recent years is the rise in oil prices. The average price of a barrel of crude oil increased twelve-fold from 1998 to 2008, and the United States imports far more oil than it exports. As a result, the value of U.S. net exports of oil decreased sharply, thereby increasing the U.S. current account deficit by 1% of GDP in the early 2000s, and by as much as 2.5% of GDP in 2008, as Fig. 5.10 shows.

Figure 5.9

Net international ownership of assets relative to U.S. GDP, 1982–2008

The chart shows annual values for the net international ownership of assets as a percent of U.S. GDP for the period 1982 to 2008.

Sources: Net international investment position: Bureau of Economic Analysis, International Investment Position of the United States at Yearend, available online at *www.bea.gov/international/xls/intinv08_t2.xls;* GDP: Bureau of Economic Analysis, available at *research.stlouisfed.org/fred2/series/GDP.*

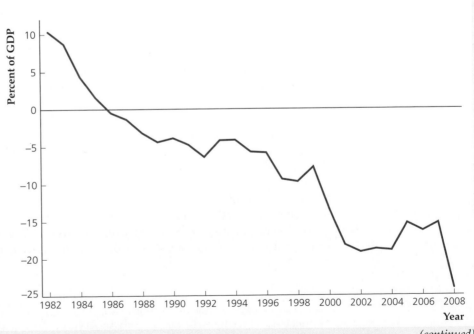

(continued)

Figure 5.10

Petroleum net exports as a percent of U.S. GDP, 1978–2008

The chart shows annual values for the net exports of petroleum and related products as a percent of U.S. GDP for the period 1978 to 2008.

Sources: Petroleum net exports: Bureau of Economic Analysis, U.S. International Transactions Accounts, Table 2b, Net Trade in Goods, available at *www.bea.gov.* GDP: Bureau of Economic Analysis, available at *research.stlouisfed.org/fred2/series/GDP.*

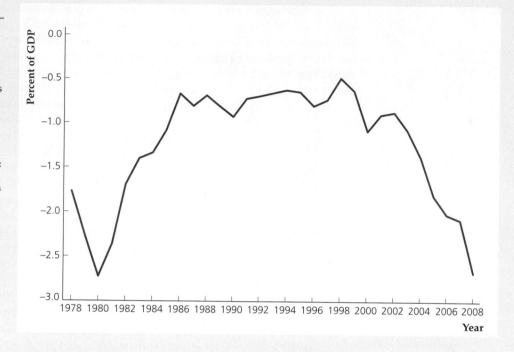

The final reason for the increase in the current account deficit from 1998 to 2005 was a change in the saving behavior of developing countries.[12] Developing nations that had borrowed from abroad in past decades began lending abroad, especially to the United States. In part, this change in behavior occurred as a result of past financial crises, such as Mexico experienced in 1994 and the countries of East Asia experienced in 1997–1998. Those crises were exacerbated by the fact that those countries had borrowed substantially from foreign countries. To prevent such crises from happening again, the countries increased their saving, built up foreign exchange reserves, and became net lenders to foreign countries instead of net borrowers.

A factor that may or may not be responsible for the increase in the current account deficit is the increase in the U.S. government budget deficit. As discussed in the Application "The Twin Deficits" on p. 193, both the current account deficit and government budget deficits grew sharply in early 2000s; however, they moved in opposite directions in late 1990s. In addition, countries such as Germany and Japan have had government budget deficits that are much larger (as a share of GDP) than that in the United States, but those countries ran large current account surpluses. Therefore, the large U.S. government budget deficit may be a cause of the large current account deficit, but the evidence on this issue is mixed.

---

[12]For an analysis of this view, see Ben S. Bernanke, "The Global Saving Glut and the U.S. Current Account Deficit." Sandridge Lecture, Virginia Association of Economists, Richmond, Virginia, March 10, 2005. Available at *www.federalreserve.gov/boarddocs/speeches/2005.*

5.5 Fiscal Policy and the Current Account

During the 1980s and 1990s the United States often had both large government budget deficits and large current account deficits. Are these two phenomena related? Many economists and other commentators argue that they are, suggesting that in fact the budget deficit is the primary cause of the current account deficit. Those supporting this view often use the phrase "twin deficits" to convey the idea that the government budget deficit and the current account deficit are closely linked. Not all economists agree with this interpretation, however; some argue that the two deficits are largely unrelated. In this section we briefly discuss what the theory has to say about this issue and then turn to the evidence.

The Critical Factor: The Response of National Saving

In theory, the issue of whether there is a link between the government budget deficit and the current account deficit revolves around the following proposition: *An increase in the government budget deficit will raise the current account deficit only if the increase in the budget deficit reduces desired national saving.*

Let's first look at why the link to national saving is crucial. Figure 5.11 shows the case of the small open economy. The world real interest rate is fixed at r^w. We draw the initial saving and investment curves, S^1 and I, so that, at the world real interest rate, r^w, the country is running a current account surplus, represented by distance AB. Now suppose that the government budget deficit rises. For simplicity, we assume throughout this section that the change in fiscal policy doesn't affect the tax treatment of investment so that the investment curve doesn't shift. Hence as Fig. 5.11 shows, the government deficit increase will change the current account balance only if it affects desired national saving.

The usual claim made by supporters of the twin-deficits idea is that an increase in the government budget deficit reduces desired national saving. If it does, the increase in the government deficit shifts the desired national saving curve to the left, from S^1 to S^2. The country still has a current account surplus, now equal to distance AC, but it is less than the original surplus, AB.

We conclude that in a small open economy an increase in the government budget deficit reduces the current account balance by the same amount that it reduces desired national saving. By reducing saving, the increased budget deficit reduces the amount that domestic residents want to lend abroad at the world real interest rate, thus lowering financial outflows. Equivalently, reduced national saving means that a greater part of domestic output is absorbed at home; with less output to send abroad, the country's current account balance falls. Similar results hold for the large open economy (you are asked to work out this case in Analytical Problem 4 at the end of the chapter).

The Government Budget Deficit and National Saving

Let's now turn to the link between the budget deficit and saving and consider two cases: a budget deficit arising from an increase in government purchases and a deficit rising from a cut in taxes.

A Deficit Caused by Increased Government Purchases. Suppose that the source of the government budget deficit is a temporary increase in government purchases,

Figure 5.11

The government budget deficit and the current account in a small open economy
An increase in the government budget deficit affects the current account only if the increased budget deficit reduces national saving. Initially, the saving curve is S^1 and the current account surplus is distance AB. If an increase in the government deficit reduces national saving, the saving curve shifts to the left, from S^1 to S^2. With no change in the effective tax rate on capital, the investment curve, I, doesn't move. Thus the increase in the budget deficit causes the current account surplus to decrease from distance AB to distance AC. In contrast, if the increase in the budget deficit has no effect on national saving, the current account also is unaffected and remains equal to distance AB.

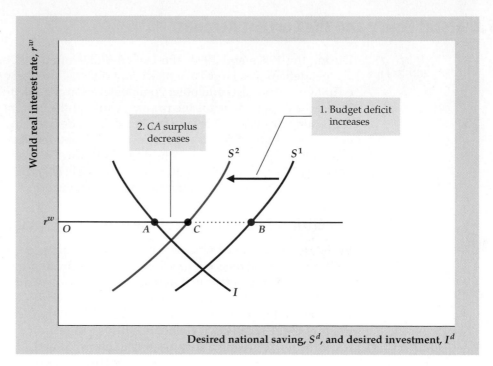

perhaps owing to a military buildup. In this case there is no controversy: Recall (Chapter 4) that, with output, Y, held constant at its full-employment level, an increase in government purchases, G, directly reduces desired national saving, $S^d = Y - C^d - G$.[13,14] Because economists agree that a deficit owing to increased government purchases reduces desired national saving, they also agree that a deficit resulting from increased government purchases reduces the nation's current account balance.

A Deficit Resulting from a Tax Cut.
Suppose instead that the government budget deficit is the result of a cut in current taxes, with current and planned future government purchases unchanged. With government purchases, G, unchanged and with output, Y, held constant at its full-employment level, the tax cut will cause desired national saving, $S^d = Y - C^d - G$, to fall only if it causes desired consumption, C^d, to rise.

Will a tax cut cause people to consume more? As we discussed in Chapter 4, believers in the Ricardian equivalence proposition argue that a lump-sum tax change (with current and future government purchases held constant) won't affect desired consumption or desired national saving. These economists point out that a cut in taxes today forces the government to borrow more to pay for its current

---

[13]Because the increase in government purchases also means that taxes may be raised in the future, lowering consumers' expected future income, desired consumption, C^d, may fall. However, because the increase in G is temporary so that the future tax increase need not be too large, this drop in C^d should not completely offset the effect of increased G on desired national saving.

[14]In general, in an open economy $S^d = Y + NFP - C^d - G$, but we are assuming that $NFP = 0$ so that $S^d = Y - C^d - G$.

purchases; when this extra borrowing plus interest is repaid in the future, future taxes will have to rise. Thus, although a tax cut raises consumers' current after-tax incomes, the tax cut creates the need for higher future taxes and lowers the after-tax incomes that consumers can expect to receive in the future. Overall, according to this argument, a tax cut doesn't benefit consumers and thus won't increase their desired consumption.

If the Ricardian equivalence proposition is true, a budget deficit resulting from a tax cut will have no effect on the current account because it doesn't affect desired national saving. However, as we noted in Chapter 4, many economists argue that—despite the logic of Ricardian equivalence—in practice many consumers do respond to a current tax cut by consuming more. For example, consumers simply may not understand that a higher deficit today makes higher taxes tomorrow more likely. If for any reason consumers do respond to a tax cut by consuming more, the deficit resulting from a tax cut will reduce national saving and thus also will reduce the current account balance.

APPLICATION

The Twin Deficits

The relationship between the U.S. government budget and the U.S. current account for the period 1960–2008 is illustrated in Fig. 5.12. This figure shows government purchases and net government income (taxes less transfers and interest) for the Federal government alone as well as for the combined Federal, state, and local governments, all measured as a percentage of GDP. Our discussion of the current account balance as the excess of national saving over investment leads us to focus on the broadest level of government, which includes state and local government in addition to the Federal government. We also present data on the purchases and net income of the Federal government alone because Federal budget deficits and surpluses are often the focus of public attention. In addition, as shown in Fig. 5.12, much of the movement in purchases and net income of the combined Federal, state, and local government reflects movement in the corresponding components of the Federal budget.

The excess of government purchases over net income is the government budget deficit, shown in pink.[15] Negative values of the current account balance indicate a current account deficit, also shown in pink. During the 1960s, the combined government sector in the United States ran a surplus, even though the Federal government ran modest budget deficits in the late 1960s. At the same time, the current account showed a modest surplus. The largest deficits—both government and current account—occurred during the 1980s and 1990s. Between 1979 and 1983, the budget deficit of the combined government sector increased from less than 0.1% of GDP to almost 5% of GDP, corresponding to an increase in the Federal budget deficit from about 0.5% of GDP to approximately 5% of GDP over the same period

---

[15]Government purchases are current expenditures minus transfer payments and interest. Thus government investment is not included in government purchases. The budget deficit is the current deficit; see Chapter 15 for a further discussion of this concept.

(continued)

Figure 5.12

The government budget deficit and the current account in the United States, 1960–2008

Shown are government purchases, net government income (taxes less transfers and interest), and the current account balance for the United States for 1960–2008. All data series are measured as a percentage of GDP. The government deficit (pink) is the excess of government purchases over net government income. The simultaneous appearance of the government budget deficit and the current account deficit in the 1980s and early 1990s is the twin-deficits phenomenon.

Sources: Total government and Federal government receipts, current expenditures, interest, and transfers: BEA Web site, *www.bea.gov,* NIPA Tables 3.1 and 3.2. GDP: BEA Web site, NIPA Table 1.1.5. Current account balance: BEA Web site, International transactions accounts Table 1.

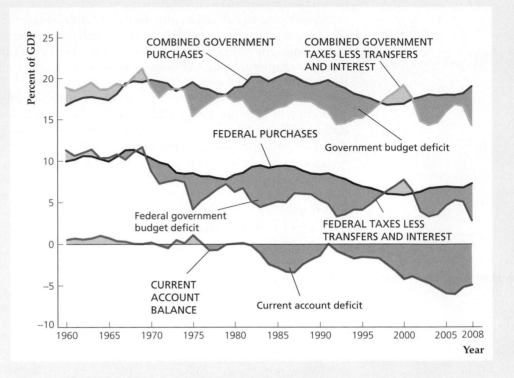

of time. This growth in the government budget deficit reflected a decline in net government income (particularly important in this respect were the tax cuts phased in following the Economic Recovery Tax Act of 1981), but military spending also increased. The current account, which was in surplus in 1981, fell to a deficit of 2.5% of GDP in 1984. Both the government budget deficit and the current account deficit remained large throughout the 1980s and the first half of the 1990s.[16]

The apparently close relationship between the U.S. government budget deficit and the current account deficit in the 1980s and the first half of the 1990s represents evidence in favor of the twin-deficits idea that budget deficits cause current account deficits. Because the rise in budget deficits primarily reflected tax cuts (or increases in transfers and interest payments, which reduced net government income) rather than increased government purchases, this behavior of the two deficits also seems to contradict the Ricardian equivalence proposition, which says that tax cuts should have no effect on saving or the current account.

Even though the U.S. experience during the 1980s and first half of the 1990s seems to confirm the link between government budget and the current account, evidence from other episodes is less supportive of the twin-deficits idea. For example, the United States simultaneously ran large government budget deficits and large current account surpluses in the periods around World War I and II (compare Figs. 1.5 and 1.6). Another situation in which the twin-deficits idea failed to hold

---

[16]During 1991 the current account deficit was less than 0.1% of GDP. This improvement was largely the result of one-time unilateral transfers to the United States from allies to help defray the costs of the Persian Gulf War.

occurred in 1975. A one-time Federal tax rebate contributed to a large (4.0% of GDP for the combined government; 4.2% of GDP for the Federal government) government budget deficit, yet the U.S. current account balance rose noticeably in 1975, as Fig. 5.12 shows. In the late 1990s, the Federal government budget and the combined government budget were both in surplus, yet the U.S. current account balance remained deeply in deficit because private saving fell and investment rose as a share of GDP at the same time. And at the end of 2008 and early 2009, the government budget deficit grew substantially as the government increased spending to stimulate the economy, but the current account deficit fell considerably as consumers cut back on their purchases of imported goods and services.

The evidence from other countries on the relationship between government budget and current account deficits is also mixed. For example, Germany's budget deficit and current account deficit both increased in the early 1990s following the reunification of Germany. This behavior is consistent with the twin-deficits idea. During the mid 1980s, however, Canada and Italy both ran government budget deficits that were considerably larger than those in the United States (as a percentage of GDP), without experiencing severe current account problems. Because of the lack of clear evidence, a good deal of disagreement persists among economists about the relationship between government budget deficits and the current account.[17] We can say for sure (because it is implied by the uses-of-saving identity, Eq. 2.11) that if an increase in the government budget deficit is not offset by an equal increase in private saving, the result must be a decline in domestic investment, a rise in the current account deficit, or both.

---

[17]For a review of recent research on twin deficits, see Michele Cavallo, "Understanding the Twin Deficits: New Approaches, New Results," Federal Reserve Bank of San Francisco, *Economic Letter*, No. 2005–16, July 22, 2005.

CHAPTER SUMMARY

1. The balance of payments accounts consist of the current account and the capital and financial account. The current account records trade in currently produced goods and services, income from abroad, and transfers between countries. The capital and financial account, which consists of the capital account and the financial account, records trade in existing assets, both real and financial. In the United States the capital account, which records unilateral transfers of assets, is very small.

2. In the current account, exports of goods and services, receipts of income from abroad, and unilateral transfers received from abroad count as credit (plus) items. Imports of goods and services, payments of income to foreigners holding assets or working in the home country, and unilateral transfers sent abroad are debit (minus) items in the current account. The current account balance, CA, equals the value of credit items less debit items in the current account. Ignoring net factor payments and net unilateral transfers, the current account

balance is the same as net exports, NX. The capital and financial account balance, KFA, is the value of assets sold to foreigners (financial inflows) minus the value of assets purchased from foreigners (financial outflows) plus net unilateral transfers of assets.

3. In each period, except for measurement errors, the current account balance, CA, and the capital and financial account balance, KFA, must sum to zero. The reason is that any international transaction amounts to a swap of goods, services, or assets between countries; the two sides of the swap always have offsetting effects on the sum of the current account and capital and financial account balances.

4. In an open economy, goods market equilibrium requires that the desired amount of national saving equal the desired amount of domestic investment plus the amount the country lends abroad. Equivalently, net exports must equal the country's output

(gross domestic product) less desired total spending by domestic residents (absorption).

5. A small open economy faces a fixed real interest rate in the international capital market. In goods market equilibrium in a small open economy, national saving and investment equal their desired levels at the prevailing world real interest rate; foreign lending, net exports, and the current account all equal the excess of national saving over investment. Any factor that increases desired national saving or reduces desired investment at the world real interest rate will increase the small open economy's foreign lending (equivalently, its current account balance).

6. The levels of saving and investment of a large open economy affect the world real interest rate. In a model of two large open economies, the equilibrium real interest rate in the international capital market is the rate at which desired international lending by one country equals desired international borrowing by the other country. Equivalently, it is the rate at which the lending country's current account surplus

equals the borrowing country's current account deficit. Any factor that increases desired national saving or reduces desired investment at the initial interest rate for either large country will increase the supply of international loans relative to the demand and cause the world real interest rate to fall.

7. According to the twin-deficits hypothesis, the large U.S. government budget deficits of the 1980s and the first half of the 1990s helped cause the sharply increased U.S. current account deficits of that period. Whether budget deficits cause current account deficits is the subject of disagreement. In theory, and if we assume no change in the tax treatment of investment, an increase in the government budget deficit will raise the current account deficit only if it reduces national saving. Economists generally agree that an increase in the budget deficit caused by a temporary increase in government purchases will reduce national saving, but whether an increase in the budget deficit caused by a tax cut reduces national saving remains controversial.

KEY DIAGRAM 4

National saving and investment in a small open economy

This open-economy version of the saving–investment diagram shows the determination of national saving, investment, and the current account balance in a small open economy that takes the world real interest rate as given.

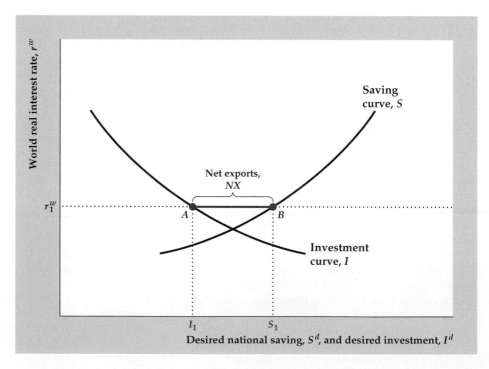

Diagram Elements

- The world real interest rate is measured on the vertical axis, and the small open economy's desired national saving, S^d, and desired investment, I^d, are measured on the horizontal axis.

- The world real interest rate, r^w, is fixed, as indicated by the horizontal line.

- The saving curve, S, and the investment curve, I, are the same as in the closed-economy saving–investment diagram, Key Diagram 3 (p. 142).

Analysis

- Goods market equilibrium in a small open economy requires that desired national saving equal desired investment plus net exports (Eq. 5.4). In the diagram when the world real interest rate is r_1^w, desired national saving is S_1 and desired investment is I_1. The country's net exports, NX, and current account balance, CA, or $S_1 - I_1$, is distance AB. Equivalently, distance AB, the excess of desired national saving over desired investment, is the amount that the small open economy is lending abroad, or its capital and financial account deficit, $-KFA$.

Factors That Shift the Curves

- Anything that increases desired national saving in the small open economy, for a fixed value of the world real interest rate, shifts the saving curve to the right. Factors that shift the saving curve to the right (see Summary table 5, p. 118) include

  an increase in current output, Y,

  a decrease in expected future output,

  a decrease in wealth,

  a decrease in current government purchases, G, and

an increase in current taxes, T, if Ricardian equivalence doesn't hold and taxes affect saving.

- Anything that increases desired investment at the prevailing real interest rate shifts the investment curve to the right. Factors that shift the investment curve to the right (see Summary table 6, p. 130) include an increase in the expected future marginal product of capital, MPK^f, and a decrease in the effective tax rate on capital.

- An increase in desired national saving shifts the saving curve to the right and raises net exports and the current account balance, CA. Equivalently, an increase in desired national saving raises the country's net foreign lending, which equals its capital and financial account deficit, $-KFA$. Similarly, an increase in desired investment shifts the investment curve to the right and lowers net exports, the current account balance, net foreign lending, and the capital and financial account deficit.

- An increase in the world real interest rate, r^w, raises the horizontal line in the diagram. Because an increase in the world real interest rate increases national saving and reduces investment, it raises net foreign lending, net exports, the current account surplus, and the capital and financial account deficit.

KEY DIAGRAM 5

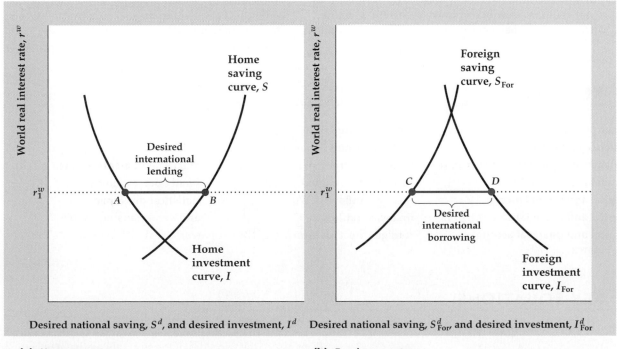

(a) Home country

(b) Foreign country

National saving and investment in large open economies

This diagram shows the determination of national saving, investment, and the current account balance in large open economies—that is, economies large enough to affect the world real interest rate.

Diagram Elements

■ The figure consists of two saving–investment diagrams, one for the home country and one for the foreign country (representing the rest of the world).

■ The world real interest rate, r^w, measured on the vertical axis, is the real interest rate faced by both countries in the international capital market.

■ The saving and investment curves in the home country (S and I) and in the foreign country (S_{For} and I_{For}) are the same as the saving and investment curves presented before (Key Diagram 3, p. 142, and Key Diagram 4).

Analysis

■ This case differs from the case of the small open economy (Key Diagram 4) in that the world real interest rate, r^w, is determined within the model, not given.

■ Goods market equilibrium for large open economies requires that the desired international lending of one country equal the desired international borrowing of the other. Equivalently, because a country's international lending equals its current account balance, goods market equilibrium requires that one country's current account surplus equal the other country's current account deficit.

■ The world real interest rate adjusts to achieve goods market equilibrium. In the diagram r_1^w is the equilibrium world real interest rate, because at that interest rate the home country's desired international lending (its desired national saving less desired investment, or distance AB) equals the foreign country's desired international borrowing (its desired investment less desired national saving, or distance CD).

Factors That Shift the Curves

■ The saving and investment curves in the two countries are shifted by the same factors as in Key Diagram 3, p. 142, and Key Diagram 4.

■ The world real interest rate changes when desired national saving or desired investment changes in either country. Any change that increases desired international lending relative to desired international borrowing at the initial world real interest rate will cause the world real interest rate to fall to restore equilibrium in the international capital market. Changes that increase desired international lending relative to desired international borrowing include an increase in desired national saving or a decrease in desired investment in either country. Similarly, a decrease in desired national saving or an increase in desired investment in either country reduces desired international lending relative to desired international borrowing and raises the world real interest rate.

KEY TERMS

KEY EQUATIONS

$$CA + KFA = 0 \qquad (5.1)$$

Except for problems of measurement, the current account balance, CA, and the capital and financial account balance, KFA, always sum to zero. The reason is that every inter-national transaction involves a swap of goods, services, or assets; the two sides of the swap always have offsetting effects on $CA + KFA$.

$$S^d = I^d + NX \qquad (5.4)$$

The goods market equilibrium condition in an open economy holds that desired national saving, S^d, must equal desired investment, I^d, plus the amount lent abroad. The amount lent abroad equals the current account balance, which (if we assume that net factor payments and unilateral transfers are zero) also equals net exports, NX.

$$NX = Y - (C^d + I^d + G) \qquad (5.6)$$

An alternative way of writing the goods market equilibrium condition, this equation states that net exports must equal the country's output, Y, less its desired absorption, $C^d + I^d + G$.

REVIEW QUESTIONS

All review questions are available in at **www.myeconlab.com.**

1. List the categories of credit items and debit items that appear in a country's current account. What is the current account balance? What is the relationship between the current account balance and net exports?

2. What is the key difference that determines whether an international transaction appears in the current account or the capital and financial account?

3. A U.S. publisher sells $200 worth of books to a resident of Brazil. By itself, this item is a credit item in the U.S. current account. Describe some offsetting transactions that could ensure that the U.S. current account and the capital and financial account balances would continue to sum to zero.

4. How do a country's current account and capital and financial account balances affect its net foreign assets? If country A has greater net foreign assets per citizen than does country B, is country A necessarily better off than country B?

5. Explain why, in a small open economy, (a) national saving does not have to equal investment, and (b) output does not have to equal absorption.

6. Generally, what types of changes in desired saving and desired investment lead to large current account deficits in a small open economy? What factors lead to these changes in desired saving and desired investment?

7. In a world with two large open economies, what determines the world real interest rate? What relationship between the current accounts of the two countries is satisfied when the world real interest rate is at its equilibrium value?

8. How does an increase in desired national saving in a large open economy affect the world real interest rate? How does an increase in desired investment affect it? Why do changes in desired saving or investment in large open economies affect the world real interest rate but changes in desired saving or investment in small open economies do not?

9. Under what circumstances will an increase in the government budget deficit affect the current account balance in a small open economy? In the cases in which the current account balance changes, by how much does it change?

10. What are the twin deficits? What is the connection between them?

NUMERICAL PROBLEMS

All numerical problems are available in 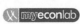 at **www.myeconlab.com.**

1. Here are some balance of payments data (without pluses and minuses):

Exports of goods, 100
Imports of goods, 125
Service exports, 90
Service imports, 80

Income receipts from abroad, 110
Income payments to foreigners, 150
Increase in home country's ownership of assets abroad, 160
Increase in foreign ownership of assets in home country, 200
Increase in home reserve assets, 30
Increase in foreign reserve assets, 35

Assuming that unilateral transfers equal zero, find net exports, the current account balance, the capital and financial account balance, the official settlements balance, and the statistical discrepancy. (*Note:* The increase in home reserve assets of 30 is included in the increase in the home country's ownership of assets abroad of 160, and the increase in foreign reserve assets of 35 is included in the increase in foreign ownership of assets in the home country of 200.)

2. In a small open economy, output (gross domestic product) is \$25 billion, government purchases are \$6 billion, and net factor payments from abroad are zero. Desired consumption and desired investment are related to the world real interest rate in the following manner:

World Real Interest Rate	Desired Consumption	Desired Investment
5%	\$12 billion	\$3 billion
4%	\$13 billion	\$4 billion
3%	\$14 billion	\$5 billion
2%	\$15 billion	\$6 billion

For each value of the world real interest rate, find national saving, foreign lending, and absorption. Calculate net exports as the difference between output and absorption. What is the relationship between net exports and foreign lending?

3. In a small open economy,
desired national saving, S^d = \$10 billion + (\$100 billion)r^w;
desired investment, I^d = \$15 billion − (\$100 billion)r^w;
output, Y = \$50 billion;
government purchases, G = \$10 billion;
world real interest rate, r^w = 0.03.

a. Find the economy's national saving, investment, current account surplus, net exports, desired consumption, and absorption.

b. Owing to a technological innovation that increases future productivity, the country's desired investment rises by \$2 billion at each level of the world real interest rate. Repeat Part (a) with this new information.

4. Consider two large open economies, the home economy and the foreign economy. In the home country the following relationships hold:
desired consumption, C^d = 320 + 0.4(Y − T) − 200r^w;
desired investment, I^d = 150 − 200r^w;

output, Y = 1000;
taxes, T = 200;
goverment purchases, G = 275.

In the foreign country the following relationships hold:
desired consumption, C^d_{For} = 480 + 0.4(Y_{For} − T_{For}) − 300r^w;
desired investment, I^d_{For} = 225 − 300r^w;
output, Y_{For} = 1500;
taxes, T_{For} = 300;
government purchases, G_{For} = 300.

a. What is the equilibrium interest rate in the international capital market? What are the equilibrium values of consumption, national saving, investment, and the current account balance in each country?

b. Suppose that in the home country government purchases increase by 50 to 325. Taxes also increase by 50 to keep the deficit from growing. What is the new equilibrium interest rate in the international capital market? What are the new equilibrium values of consumption, national saving, investment, and the current account balance in each country?

5. Consider a world with only two countries, which are designated the home country (H) and the foreign country (F). Output equals its full-employment level in each country. You are given the following information about each country:

Home Country
Consumption: C_H = 100 + 0.5Y_H − 500r^w
Investment: I_H = 300 − 500r^w
Government Purchases: G_H = 155
Full-employment Output: $\bar{Y}_H$ = 1000

Foreign Country
Consumption: C_F = 225 + 0.7Y_F − 600r^w
Investment: I_F = 250 − 200r^w
Government Purchases: G_F = 190
Full-employment Output: $\bar{Y}_F$ = 1200

a. Write national saving in the home country and in the foreign country as functions of the world real interest rate r^w.

b. What is the equilibrium value of the world real interest rate?

c. What are the equilibrium values of consumption, national saving, investment, the current account balance, and absorption in each country?

6. A small island nation is endowed with indestructible coconut trees. These trees live forever and no new trees can be planted. Every year \$1 million worth of coconuts fall off the trees and can be eaten locally or exported to other countries. In past years the island

nation ran current account surpluses and capital and financial account deficits, acquiring foreign bonds. It now owns $500,000 of foreign bonds. The interest rate on these bonds is 5% per year. The residents of the island nation consume $1,025,000 per year. What are the values of investment, national saving, the current account balance, the capital and financial account balance, net exports, GDP, and GNP in this country?

ANALYTICAL PROBLEMS

1. Explain how each of the following transactions would enter the U.S. balance of payments accounts. Discuss only the transactions described. Do not be concerned with possible offsetting transactions.

   a. The U.S. government sells F–16 fighter planes to a foreign government.

   b. A London bank sells yen to, and buys dollars from, a Swiss bank.

   c. The Federal Reserve sells yen to, and buys dollars from, a Swiss bank.

   d. A New York bank receives the interest on its loans to Brazil.

   e. A U.S. collector buys some ancient artifacts from a collection in Egypt.

   f. A U.S. oil company buys insurance from a Canadian insurance company to insure its oil rigs in the Gulf of Mexico.

   g. A U.S. company borrows from a British bank.

2. For each transaction described in Analytical Problem 1 that by itself changes the sum of the U.S. current account balance, *CA*, and the U.S. capital and financial account balance, *KFA*, give an example of an offsetting transaction that would leave *CA* + *KFA* unchanged.

3. A large country imposes capital controls that prohibit foreign borrowing and lending by domestic residents. Analyze the effects on the country's current account balance, national saving, and investment, and on domestic and world real interest rates. Assume that, before the capital controls were imposed, the large country was running a capital and financial account surplus.

4. The text showed, for a small open economy, that an increase in the government budget deficit raises the current account deficit only if it affects desired national saving in the home country. Show that this result is also true for a large open economy. Then assume that an increase in the government budget deficit does affect desired national saving in the home country. What effects will the increased budget deficit have on the foreign country's current account, investment in both countries, and the world real interest rate?

5. How would each of the following affect national saving, investment, the current account balance, and the real interest rate in a large open economy?

   a. An increase in the domestic willingness to save (which raises desired national saving at any given real interest rate).

   b. An increase in the willingness of foreigners to save.

   c. A temporary increase in foreign government purchases.

   d. An increase in foreign taxes (consider both the case in which Ricardian equivalence holds and the case in which it doesn't hold).

6. Analyze the effects on a large open economy of a temporary adverse supply shock that hits only the foreign economy. Discuss the impact on the home country's national saving, investment, and current account balance—and on the world real interest rate. How does your answer differ if the adverse supply shock is worldwide?

7. The chief economic advisor of a small open economy makes the following announcement: "We have good news and bad news: The good news is that we have just had a temporary beneficial productivity shock that will increase output; the bad news is that the increase in output and income will lead domestic consumers to buy more imported goods, and our current account balance will fall." Analyze this statement, taking as given that a beneficial productivity shock has indeed occurred.

8. The world is made up of only two large countries: Eastland and Westland. Westland is running a large current account deficit and often appeals to Eastland for help in reducing this current account deficit. Currently the government of Eastland purchases $10 billion of goods and services, and all of these goods and services are produced in Eastland. The finance minister of Eastland proposes that the government purchase half of its goods from Westland. Specifically, the government of Eastland will continue to purchase $10 billion of goods, but $5 billion will be from Eastland and $5 billion will be from Westland. The finance minister gives the following rationale: "Both countries produce identical goods so it does not really matter to us which country produced the goods we purchase. Moreover, this change in purchasing policy will help reduce Westland's large current account deficit." What are the effects of this change in purchasing policy on the current account balance in each country and on the world real interest rate? (*Hint:* What happens to net exports by the private sector in each country after the government of Eastland changes its purchasing policy?)

WORKING WITH MACROECONOMIC DATA

For data to use in these exercises, go to the Federal Reserve Bank of St. Louis FRED database at research.stlouisfed.org/fred2.

1. A popular measure of a country's "openness" to international trade is an index computed as the sum of the country's exports and imports divided by its GDP. Calculate and graph the openness index for the United States using quarterly data since 1947. What has been the postwar trend? Can you think of any factors that might help explain this trend? (*Hint:* Be careful with the data, as some databases record imports with a negative sign and then add them to exports to get net exports. If that is the case with your data, take the absolute value of imports before adding it to exports, because we are interested in the total volume of trade, not the balance of trade.)

2. Using quarterly data since 1961, graph output and absorption (both in real terms) in the same figure. In another figure, graph real investment, national saving, and the current account balance for the same period. (Use real GNP, which includes net factor payments, as the measure of output and/or income.) What is the relationship between the two figures?

3. Using quarterly data since 1960, graph the following four series, expressing each as a percent of GDP: exports of goods (sometimes called merchandise), exports of services, imports of goods (sometimes called merchandise), and imports of services. What trends do you notice in U.S. exports and imports of goods and services? When computing the percentage of GDP, you should note that quarterly data on exports and imports often are not expressed at annual rates, but the data on GDP are expressed at annual rates; if this is the case with your data, multiply your data on imports and exports by 4 to get the appropriate ratio relative to GDP.

CHAPTER 6

Long-Run Economic Growth

A nation's ability to provide improving standards of living for its people depends crucially on its long-run rate of economic growth. Over a long period of time, even an apparently small difference in the rate of economic growth can translate into a large difference in the income of the average person.

Compare, for example, the historical experiences of Australia and Japan. In 1870 real GDP per person was more than four times as large in Australia as in Japan, as the data on national growth performances in Table 6.1 show. Australia's economy didn't stand still after 1870. Over the next 136 years, Australian real GDP per person grew by 1.5% per year so that by 2006 the real income of the average Australian was more than seven times as great as it had been in 1870. However, during the same period Japanese real GDP per person grew at a rate of 2.5% per year, reaching a level in 2006 that was more than thirty times as large as it had been in 1870.

The Japanese growth rate of 2.5% per year may not seem dramatically greater than the Australian growth rate of 1.5% per year. Yet by 1990 Japan, which had been far poorer than Australia a century earlier, had surpassed its Pacific neighbor in per capita GDP by a margin of 10%. However, in the 1990s, sluggish growth in Japan allowed Australia to retake the lead by 1998. Other, similar comparisons can be drawn from Table 6.1; compare, for example, the long-term growth performance of the United Kingdom against that of Canada or Sweden. Note, however, that even those countries that grew relatively slowly have dramatically increased their output per person during the past century and a quarter.

Although the comparisons highlighted by Table 6.1 span a long period of time, a change in the rate of economic growth can have important effects over even a decade or two. For example, since about 1973 the United States and other industrialized countries have experienced a sustained slowdown in their rates of growth. Between 1947 and 1973, total (not per capita) real GDP in the United States grew by 4.0% per year, but between 1973 and 2008 U.S. real GDP grew by only 2.9% per year. To appreciate the significance of this slowdown, imagine that the 1947–1973 growth trend had continued—that is, suppose that real GDP in the United States had continued to grow at 4.0% per year instead of at the 2.9% per year rate actually achieved. Then in 2008 the U.S. real GDP would have been more than 45% higher than its actual value—a bonus of about $6.6 trillion, or $21,700 per person (in 2008 dollars).

Table 6.1

Economic Growth in Eight Major Countries, 1870–2006

	Levels of real GDP per capita				Annual growth rate
Country	1870	1913	1950	2006	1870–2006
Australia	3,273	5,157	7,412	24,343	1.5%
Canada	1,695	4,447	7,291	24,951	2.0
France	1,876	3,485	5,186	21,809	1.8
Germany	1,839	3,648	3,881	19,993	1.8
Japan	737	1,387	1,921	22,462	2.5
Sweden	1,662	3,096	6,739	24,204	2.0
United Kingdom	3,190	4,921	6,939	23,013	1.5
United States	2,445	5,301	9,561	31,049	1.9

Note: Figures are in U.S. dollars at 1990 prices, adjusted for differences in the purchasing power of the various national currencies.
Source: Data from Angus Maddison, *Statistics on World Population, GDP, and Per Capita GDP, 1–2006 AD* (March 2009, vertical file, copyright Angus Maddison), available at *www.ggdc.net/maddison*.

No one understands completely why economies grow, and no one has a magic formula for inducing rapid growth. Indeed, if such a formula existed, there would be no poor nations. Nevertheless, economists have gained useful insights about the growth process. In this chapter we identify the forces that determine the growth rate of an economy over long periods of time and examine various policies that governments may use to try to influence the rate of growth. Once again, saving and investment decisions play a central role in the analysis. Along with changes in productivity, the rates at which a nation saves and invests—and thus the rate at which it accumulates capital goods—are important factors in determining the standard of living that the nation's people can attain.

6.1 The Sources of Economic Growth

An economy's output of goods and services depends on the quantities of available inputs, such as capital and labor, and on the productivity of those inputs. The relationship between output and inputs is described by the production function, introduced in Chapter 3:

$$Y = AF(K,N). \tag{6.1}$$

Equation (6.1) relates total output, Y, to the economy's use of capital, K, and labor, N, and to productivity, A.

If inputs and productivity are constant, the production function states that output also will be constant—there will be no economic growth. For the quantity of output to grow, either the quantity of inputs must grow or productivity must improve, or both. The relationship between the rate of output growth and the rates of input growth and productivity growth is

$$\frac{\Delta Y}{Y} = \frac{\Delta A}{A} + a_K \frac{\Delta K}{K} + a_N \frac{\Delta N}{N} \tag{6.2}$$

where

$$\frac{\Delta Y}{Y} = \text{rate of output growth;}$$

$$\frac{\Delta A}{A} = \text{rate of productivity growth;}$$

$$\frac{\Delta K}{K} = \text{rate of capital growth;}$$

$$\frac{\Delta N}{N} = \text{rate of labor growth;}$$

$$a_K = \text{elasticity of output with respect to capital;}$$

$$a_N = \text{elasticity of output with respect to labor.}$$

In Eq. (6.2) the elasticity of output with respect to capital, a_K, is the percentage increase in output resulting from a 1% increase in the capital stock, and the elasticity of output with respect to labor, a_N, is the percentage increase in output resulting from a 1% increase in the amount of labor used. The elasticities a_K and a_N both are numbers between 0 and 1 that must be estimated from historical data.[1]

Equation (6.2), called the **growth accounting equation,** is the production function (Eq. 6.1) written in growth rate form. Some examples will be helpful for understanding the growth accounting equation.

Suppose that a new invention allows firms to produce 10% more output for the same amount of capital and labor. In terms of the production function, Eq. (6.1), for constant capital and labor inputs, a 10% increase in productivity, A, raises output, Y, by 10%. Similarly, from the growth accounting equation, Eq. (6.2), if productivity growth, $\Delta A/A$, equals 10% and capital and labor growth are zero, output growth, $\Delta Y/Y$, will be 10%. Thus the production function and the growth accounting equation give the same result, as they should.

Now suppose that firms' investments cause the economy's capital stock to rise by 10% ($\Delta K/K = 10\%$) while labor input and productivity remain unchanged. What will happen to output? The production function shows that, if the capital stock grows, output will increase. However, because of the diminishing marginal productivity of capital (see Chapter 3), the extra capital will be less productive than that used previously, so the increase in output will be less than 10%. Diminishing marginal productivity of capital is the reason that the growth rate of capital, $\Delta K/K$, is multiplied by a factor less than 1 in the growth accounting equation. For the United States this factor, a_K, the elasticity of output with respect to capital, is about 0.3. Thus the growth accounting equation, Eq. (6.2), indicates that a 10% increase in the capital stock, with labor and productivity held constant, will increase U.S. output by about 3%, or $0.3 \times 10\%$.

Similarly, the elasticity of output with respect to labor, a_N, is about 0.7 in the United States. Thus, according to Eq. (6.2), a 10% increase in the amount of labor used ($\Delta N/N = 10\%$), with no change in capital or productivity, will raise U.S. output by about 7%, or $0.7 \times 10\%$.[2]

---

[1]Elasticities and growth rate formulas such as Eq. (6.2) are discussed further in Appendix A, Sections A.3 and A.7.

[2]In Chapter 3 we examined the production function for the U.S. economy, $Y = AK^{0.3}N^{0.7}$. In that production function, called a Cobb-Douglas production function, the exponent on the capital stock, K, 0.3, equals the elasticity of output with respect to capital, and the exponent on the quantity of labor input, N, 0.7, equals the elasticity of output with respect to labor. See Appendix A, Section A.7.

Growth Accounting

According to Eq. (6.2), output growth, $\Delta Y/Y$, can be broken into three parts:

1. that resulting from productivity growth, $\Delta A/A$,
2. that resulting from increased capital inputs, $a_K \Delta K/K$, and
3. that resulting from increased labor inputs, $a_N \Delta N/N$.

Growth accounting measures empirically the relative importance of these three sources of output growth. A typical growth accounting analysis involves the following four steps (see Table 6.2 for a summary and numerical example):

■ *Step 1.* Obtain measures of the growth rates of output, $\Delta Y/Y$, capital, $\Delta K/K$, and labor, $\Delta N/N$, for the economy over any period of time. In the calculation of growth rates for capital and labor, more sophisticated analyses make adjustments for changing quality as well as quantity of inputs. For example, to obtain a quality-adjusted measure of N, an hour of work by a skilled worker is counted as more labor than an hour of work by an unskilled worker. Similarly, to obtain a quality-adjusted measure of K, a machine that can turn fifty bolts per minute is treated as being more capital than a machine that can turn only thirty bolts per minute.

■ *Step 2.* Estimate values for the elasticities a_K and a_N from historical data. Keep in mind the estimates for the United States of 0.3 for a_K and 0.7 for a_N.

Table 6.2

The Steps of Growth Accounting: A Numerical Example

Step 1. Obtain measures of output growth, capital growth, and labor growth over the period to be studied.

Example:

$$\text{output growth} = \frac{\Delta Y}{Y} = 40\%;$$

$$\text{capital growth} = \frac{\Delta K}{K} = 20\%;$$

$$\text{labor growth} = \frac{\Delta N}{N} = 30\%.$$

Step 2. Using historical data, obtain estimates of the elasticities of output with respect to capital and labor, a_K and a_N.

Example: $\quad a_K = 0.3 \quad \text{and} \quad a_N = 0.7.$

Step 3. Find the contributions to growth of capital and labor.

Example: $\quad$ contribution to output growth of growth in capital $= a_K \dfrac{\Delta K}{K} = 0.3 \times 20\% = 6\%;$

$\quad$ contribution to output growth of growth in labor $= a_N \dfrac{\Delta N}{N} = 0.7 \times 30\% = 21\%.$

Step 4. Find productivity growth as the residual (the part of output growth not explained by capital or labor).

Example: $\quad$ productivity growth $= \dfrac{\Delta A}{A} = \dfrac{\Delta Y}{Y} - a_K \dfrac{\Delta K}{K} - a_N \dfrac{\Delta N}{N}$

$$= 40\% - 6\% - 21\% = 13\%.$$

- *Step 3.* Calculate the contribution of capital to economic growth as $a_K \, \Delta K/K$ and the contribution of labor to economic growth as $a_N \, \Delta N/N$.
- *Step 4.* The part of economic growth assignable to neither capital growth nor labor growth is attributed to improvements in total factor productivity, A. The rate of productivity change, $\Delta A/A$, is calculated from the formula

$$\frac{\Delta A}{A} = \frac{\Delta Y}{Y} - a_K \frac{\Delta K}{K} - a_N \frac{\Delta N}{N},$$

which is the growth accounting equation, Eq. (6.2), rewritten with $\Delta A/A$ on the left side. Thus the growth accounting technique treats productivity change as a residual—that is, the portion of growth not otherwise explained.[3]

Growth Accounting and the Productivity Slowdown. What does growth accounting say about the sources of U.S. economic growth? Among the best-known research using the growth accounting framework was done at the Brookings Institution by Edward Denison. Table 6.3 summarizes Denison's findings for the period 1929–1982 and provides more recent data from the Bureau of Labor Statistics covering the period 1982–2008.

The last entry in column (4) shows that, over the 1929–1982 period, output grew at an average rate of 2.92% per year. According to Denison's measurements (column 4), the growth of labor accounted for output growth of 1.34% per year. The growth of labor in turn resulted primarily from an increase in population, an increase in the percentage of the population in the labor force, and higher educational levels, which raised workers' skills. (Offsetting these trends to a degree was a decline in the number of hours worked per person.) According to Denison, the growth of the capital stock accounted for output growth of 0.56% per year. So, taken together, labor and capital growth contributed 1.90% to the annual growth rate of output.

Table 6.3

Sources of Economic Growth in the United States (Percent per Year)

	(1) 1929–1948	(2) 1948–1973	(3) 1973–1982	(4) 1929–1982	(5) 1982–2008
Source of Growth					
Labor growth	1.42	1.40	1.13	1.34	0.89
Capital growth	0.11	0.77	0.69	0.56	0.84
Total input growth	1.53	2.17	1.82	1.90	1.73
Productivity growth	1.01	1.53	−0.27	1.02	1.01
Total output growth	**2.54**	**3.70**	**1.55**	**2.92**	**2.76**

Sources: Columns (1)–(4) from Edward F. Denison, *Trends in American Economic Growth, 1929–1982*, Washington, D.C.: The Brookings Institution, 1985, Table 8.1, p. 111. Column (5) from Bureau of Labor Statistics Web site, Multifactor Productivity Trends news release, Table 1, accessed through *www.bls.gov/news.release/prod3.t01.htm.*

[3]The growth accounting method for calculating productivity growth is similar to the method we used to find productivity growth in Section 3.1, where we also determined productivity growth as the part of output growth not explained by increases in capital and labor. The differences are that growth accounting uses the growth accounting equation, which is the production function in growth rate form, instead of using the production function directly, as we did in Chapter 3; and growth accounting analyses usually adjust measures of capital and labor for changes in quality, which we did not do in Chapter 3.

The difference between total growth (2.92%) and the amount of growth attributed to capital and labor growth (1.90%) is 1.02%. By the growth accounting method, this remaining 1.02% per year of growth is attributed to increases in productivity. Thus, according to Denison, increased quantities of factors of production and improvements in the effectiveness with which those factors were used both played an important role in U.S. growth after 1929.

Data for three shorter periods are given in columns (1)–(3) of Table 6.3. This breakdown highlights a striking conclusion: Productivity growth during 1973–1982 was negative (fourth entry in column 3). In other words, Denison estimated that any combination of capital and labor would have produced less output in 1982 than it could have in 1973! (See the Application "The Post–1973 Slowdown in Productivity Growth," for various hypotheses to explain this drop in productivity.) Comparing columns (2) and (3) reveals that the decline in U.S. productivity growth between the 1948–1973 and 1973–1982 periods of 1.80 percentage points (1.53 minus –0.27) accounts for the bulk of the overall slowdown in output growth between those periods of 2.15 percentage points (3.70 minus 1.55).

The slowdown in productivity growth after 1973 reported by Denison was confirmed by other studies, both for the United States and for other industrialized countries. This slowdown generated widespread concern, because a sustained reduction in the rate of productivity growth would have an adverse effect on future real wages and living standards. In addition, to the extent that future Social Security benefits will be paid by taxing the wage income of future workers, a long-term productivity slowdown would threaten the future of the Social Security system. But will the productivity slowdown continue? To shed light on this question, the final column of Table 6.3 extends Denison's calculations by adding 26 years of more recent data. During the period 1982–2008, productivity grew at an average annual rate of 1.01%. Although the return to a positive rate of productivity growth was a welcome development, the 1.01% growth rate was only about two-thirds of the productivity growth rate seen during the 25-year period preceding the 1973 slowdown. But beginning in the second half of the 1990s, productivity growth increased. From 1995 to 2008, it has averaged 1.38% per year, which is only 0.15 percentage points lower than it was from 1948 to 1973. For more details, see the Application "The Recent Surge in U.S. Productivity Growth," p. 211.

APPLICATION

The Post–1973 Slowdown in Productivity Growth

We have seen in Table 6.3 that productivity in the United States grew much more slowly after 1973 than in the quarter-century preceding 1973. Indeed, productivity growth was negative during the period 1973–1982. What caused productivity performance to deteriorate so sharply? In this application we discuss some alternative explanations, including possible measurement problems, deterioration in the legal and human environment, the effects of high oil prices, and the information technology revolution.

Measurement

Interestingly, several economists have suggested that the productivity slowdown really isn't a genuine economic problem. Instead, they argue, the slowdown is an illusion, the result of measurement problems that have overstated the extent of the decline.

The key issue in productivity measurement is whether the official output statistics adequately capture changes in quality. Consider the case of a firm producing personal computers that, using unchanged quantities of capital and labor, makes the same number of computers this year as last year. However, this year's computers are of much higher quality than last year's because they are faster and have more memory. The firm's output this year has a greater real economic value than last year's output, so the true productivity of the firm's capital and labor has risen over the year, even though the firm produces the same number of computers as before. However, if statisticians measuring the firm's output counted only the number of computers produced and failed to adjust for quality change, they would miss this improvement in productivity. Similar issues arise in the construction of price indexes; see "In Touch with Data and Research: Does CPI Inflation Overstate Increases in the Cost of Living?", p. 46.

In fact, official output measures do try to account for quality improvements— for example, by counting a faster computer as contributing more to output than a slower model. However, measuring quality change is difficult, and to the extent that improvements are not fully accounted for in the data, productivity growth will be underestimated. One study suggested that measurement problems could explain at most one-third of the reported post–1973 slowdown.[4] Thus, the productivity slowdown is not, for the most part, simply a measurement problem.

The Legal and Human Environment

In his growth accounting study, Edward Denison didn't stop at reporting the decline in productivity growth but went on to offer some explanations for the decline. One explanation given by Denison for the negative productivity growth during 1973–1982 is the change in what he called *the legal and human environment*, which includes several diverse factors. For example, since 1973 a cleaner environment and worker safety and health have been emphasized. To the extent that capital and labor are devoted to these goals, measured output and productivity will decline.[5]

The Oil Price Explanation

A popular explanation for the productivity slowdown is the large increase in energy prices that followed the OPEC oil embargo in 1973. The idea is that, as companies responded to high energy prices by using less energy, the amount of output they could produce with the same amount of capital and labor declined, reducing productivity. What makes this explanation plausible is not only that the timing is right— the productivity decline appears to have begun in earnest in about 1973—but that, unlike several of the other explanations, the oil price story explains why all major industrial countries, not just the United States, experienced a slowdown. However,

---

[4]Martin N. Baily and Robert J. Gordon, "The Productivity Slowdown, Measurement Issues, and the Explosion of Computer Power," *Brookings Papers on Economic Activity*, 1988:2, pp. 347–420.

[5]Of course, the reduction in measured productivity caused by reducing pollution or increasing worker safety is not in any way an argument against pursuing these goals. The proper criterion for evaluating proposed environmental regulations, for example, is whether the benefits to society of the regulations, in terms of cleaner air or water, exceed the costs they will impose. For a discussion of the problems of accounting for environmental quality when measuring output, see "In Touch with Data and Research: Natural Resources, the Environment, and the National Income Accounts," p.29.

(continued)

proponents of the oil price explanation face the problem of explaining why productivity growth did not resurge when oil prices fell in real terms in the 1980s.

The Beginning of a New Industrial Revolution?

In an article titled simply "1974," Jeremy Greenwood of the University of Pennsylvania and Mehmet Yorukoglu of the Central Bank of Turkey[6] argue that the slowdown in productivity after 1973 may have resulted from the onset of the information technology (IT) revolution. The development and commercial implementation of new information technologies required a substantial period of learning by both the developers of the new technology and the skilled workers who would work with the technology. During the learning process, productivity was temporarily depressed as developers and workers groped toward developing more powerful technologies and operating those technologies more efficiently. To support their view that productivity was depressed following the introduction of a new range of technologies, Greenwood and Yorukoglu present data showing that productivity in Great Britain fell in the late eighteenth century during the early part of the Industrial Revolution in that country. In the United States, productivity fell in the 1830s as the young country was beginning its industrialization.

This view of the post–1973 productivity slowdown offers an optimistic prospect for the future. In the previous industrial revolutions examined by Greenwood and Yorukoglu, the revolutionary ideas eventually paid off in terms of very large increases in productivity after a few decades of learning. If the productivity slowdown in the 1970s did, in fact, result from the IT revolution, then we should see increases in productivity growth in the not-too-distant future. In fact, proponents of this view suggest that the improved productivity growth in the 1990s reflects the IT revolution. Additional support for this hypothesis is provided by Bart Hobijn of the Federal Reserve Bank of New York and Boyan Jovanovic of New York University,[7] who argue that the stock market fell during the 1970s because the IT revolution would eventually benefit new firms that had not yet been formed, at the expense of existing firms then traded on the stock market. As these new firms were born, flourished, and became traded on the stock market in the 1980s and 1990s, the stock market boomed.

Of course, only time will tell whether predicted gains in productivity will materialize and whether the rise in the stock market in the 1990s will continue in the twenty-first century.

Conclusion

The problem involved in explaining the post–1973 slowdown in productivity growth may not be a lack of reasonable explanations but too many. We should not dismiss the possibility that there was no single cause of the slowdown but that many factors contributed to it. Unfortunately, if there are multiple explanations for the slowdown, no single policy action by itself is likely to rev up the productivity engine. Fortunately, however, since the mid-1990s, productivity growth has increased substantially, as we discuss in the Application "The Recent Surge in U.S. Productivity Growth."

---

[6]Jeremy Greenwood and Mehmet Yorukoglu, "1974," *Carnegie-Rochester Conference Series on Public Policy,* June 1997, pp. 49–95.

[7]Bart Hobijn and Boyan Jovanovic, "The Information Technology Revolution and the Stock Market: Preliminary Evidence," *American Economic Review,* December 2001, pp. 1203–1220.

APPLICATION

The Recent Surge in U.S. Productivity Growth

Our discussion of productivity growth in Table 6.3 showed that productivity growth slowed in the period from 1973 to 1982 but returned to a faster pace after 1982. In the late 1990s, labor productivity grew far more rapidly than it had for the preceding 20 years. In the past few years, labor productivity (output per hour in the nonfarm business sector) and total factor productivity (*A* in Equation 6.1) have continued to grow, and economists have developed new explanations for that growth.

If we examine the levels of productivity shown in Fig. 6.1, we see that both labor productivity and total factor productivity have grown fairly steadily in the past 26 years, since bottoming out in 1982. Labor productivity has grown somewhat faster than total factor productivity. (Note that both of the variables are indexed to have a value of 100 in year 2000. So, the levels of the indexes themselves have no inherent meaning.)

Figure 6.2 shows the growth rates of the productivity measures and illustrates a widening gap between labor productivity growth and total factor productivity growth since 1995. To understand the relationship between the growth rates of total factor productivity and average labor productivity, recall Equation (6.2), which is

$$\frac{\Delta Y}{Y} = \frac{\Delta A}{A} + a_K \frac{\Delta K}{K} + a_N \frac{\Delta N}{N}.$$

Figure 6.1

Productivity levels, 1948–2008

The chart shows annual values for labor productivity (output per hour in the nonfarm business sector) and total factor productivity (variable *A* in Equation 6.1) for the period 1948–2008.

Sources: Labor productivity: Bureau of Labor Statistics, Nonfarm Business Sector: Output Per Hour of All Persons, available at *research.stlouisfed.org/fred2/series/OPHNFB*. Total factor productivity: Bureau of Labor Statistics, Multifactor Productivity Trends, Table XG, available at *ftp://ftp.bls.gov/pub/special.requests/opt/mp/prod3.mfptablehis.zip*

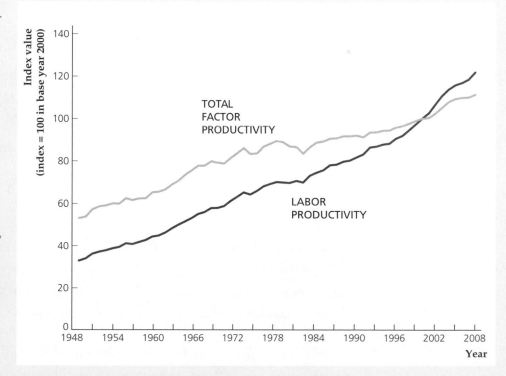

(continued)

Figure 6.2

Productivity growth, 1949–2008
The chart shows annual values of labor productivity growth and total factor productivity growth for the period 1949–2008.

Sources: Labor productivity: Bureau of Labor Statistics, Nonfarm Business Sector: Output Per Hour of All Persons, available at *research. stlouisfed.org/fred2/series/ OPHNFB*. Total factor productivity: Bureau of Labor Statistics, Multifactor Productivity Trends, Table XG, available at *ftp://ftp.bls.gov/pub/special. requests/opt/mp/prod3. mfptablehis.zip*

Empirically, the elasticity of output with respect to capital, a_K, plus the elasticity of output with respect to labor, a_N, equals one, so that $a_N = 1 - a_K$. Substituting $1 - a_K$ for a_N in Eq. (6.2) yields

$$\frac{\Delta Y}{Y} = \frac{\Delta A}{A} + a_K \frac{\Delta K}{K} + (1 - a_K) \frac{\Delta N}{N}.$$

Finally, subtracting the growth rate of labor, $\Delta N/N$, from both sides of this equation yields

$$\frac{\Delta Y}{Y} - \frac{\Delta N}{N} = \frac{\Delta A}{A} + a_K \left(\frac{\Delta K}{K} - \frac{\Delta N}{N} \right). \tag{6.3}$$

Notice that the left-hand side of Eq. (6.3), $\frac{\Delta Y}{Y} - \frac{\Delta N}{N}$, is the growth rate of Y/N, that is, it is the growth rate of average labor productivity. The amount of capital per unit of labor, K/N, grows at the rate $\frac{\Delta K}{K} - \frac{\Delta N}{N}$. Thus, Eq. (6.3) states that the growth rate of average labor productivity equals the growth rate of total factor productivity, $\Delta A/A$, plus a_K times the growth rate of capital per unit of labor. As shown in Fig. 6.2, because capital per unit of labor generally grows, so that $\frac{\Delta K}{K} - \frac{\Delta N}{N} > 0$, the growth rate of average labor productivity is generally higher than the growth rate of total factor productivity. Figure 6.2 also shows that excess of average labor productivity growth over total factor productivity growth has been unusually large since 1995, which is consistent with a higher growth rate of capital per unit of labor during this time.

The rise in labor productivity growth in the second half of the 1990s has mostly been attributed to the revolution in information and communications technologies (ICT). Recently, research by economists has challenged the view that the growth in U.S. labor productivity was largely the result of increased ICT growth. One reason that economists have looked more carefully at this issue is that many other countries also invested heavily in ICT but did not reap the same labor productivity rewards as in the United States.

Why did the United States see an appreciable gain in labor productivity from ICT, but Europe did not? Researchers have discovered a number of reasons.[8] European firms are subject to substantially more government regulations than U.S. firms, and consequently are slower to adopt new technologies. Government-owned firms in Europe often stifle innovation because of a lack of competitive pressure. Government regulations have also prevented the existence in Europe of "big box" retail outlets that efficiently provide goods to consumers, as in the United States. Shortages of workers in Europe who have the skills needed to use the new technologies have also slowed their adoption. In the United States, adaptable capital markets and research universities that foster innovation have contributed to the adoption of new technologies.

Another puzzle that has occupied researchers studying productivity is that, although economists attribute productivity gains to ICT investment, the timing is strange: There appears to be a long lag between investment in ICT and a rise in productivity. U.S. firms invested heavily in computers in the 1980s, but productivity growth did not rise very much—not nearly as much as it has since 1995. In addition, ICT investment fell sharply in 2000, but productivity growth has remained strong. As we discussed in the Application "The Post–1973 Slowdown in Productivity Growth," p. 208, this weak link in timing between ICT investment and productivity improvements may arise because the use of ICT requires more than just buying computers—it takes research and development expenditures, reorganization of the firm, and training of workers. These activities, which economists call investment in intangible capital, take time and may temporarily cause a firm's output to decline rather than to rise. Thus, investment in intangible capital can help explain the lag between increases in ICT investment and productivity growth.

Is the recent increase in productivity unique in U.S. history? Not at all. In fact, researchers have identified three similar periods in our past: 1873 to 1890, following the Civil War; 1917 to 1927, following World War I; and 1948 to 1973, following World War II.[9] In each of these episodes, productivity improvements led to a substantial increase in the U.S. standard of living. New technologies included steam power, railroad transportation, and communication by telegraph in the late 1800s; electrification in factories after World War I; and the transistor after World War II. Each of these periods was characterized not only by new technology but also by changes in how business firms were organized and by investments in workers (education and training).

The lesson from history is that it is not just the development of new technology that has improved productivity since 1995, but also the ability of U.S. firms to adapt and use that technology, with investments in intangible capital and reorganization to take advantage of what the new technologies offer.

---

[8]For a readable summary of this research with references to original sources, see Ben S. Bernanke, "Productivity." Remarks at the Peter C. McColough Roundtable Series on International Economics at the University of Arkansas at Little Rock, February 24, 2005. Available at *www.federalreserve.gov/boarddocs/speeches/2005.*

[9]For details, see Roger W. Ferguson, Jr., and William L. Wascher, "Lessons from Past Productivity Booms," *Journal of Economic Perspectives* 18 (Spring 2004), pp. 3–28.

6.2 Growth Dynamics: The Solow Model

Although growth accounting provides useful information about the sources of economic growth, it doesn't completely explain a country's growth performance. Because growth accounting takes the economy's rates of input growth as given, it can't explain why capital and labor grow at the rates that they do. The growth of the capital stock in particular is the result of the myriad saving and investment decisions of households and firms. By taking the growth of the capital stock as given, the growth accounting method leaves out an important part of the story.

In this section we take a closer look at the dynamics of economic growth, or how the growth process evolves over time. In doing so, we drop the assumption made in Chapter 3 that the capital stock is fixed and study the factors that cause the economy's stock of capital to grow. Our analysis is based on a famous model of economic growth developed in the late 1950s by Nobel laureate Robert Solow[10] of MIT, a model that has become the basic framework for most subsequent research on growth. Besides clarifying how capital accumulation and economic growth are interrelated, the Solow model is useful for examining two basic questions about growth:

1. What is the relationship between a nation's long-run standard of living and fundamental factors such as its saving rate, its population growth rate, and its rate of technical progress?
2. How does a nation's rate of economic growth evolve over time? Will economic growth stabilize, accelerate, or stop?

Setup of the Solow Model

The Solow model examines an economy as it evolves over time. To analyze the effects of labor force growth as well as changes in capital, we assume that the population is growing and that at any particular time a fixed share of the population is of working age. For any year, t,

$$N_t = \text{the number of workers available.}$$

We assume that the population and work force both grow at fixed rate n. So, if $n = 0.05$, the number of workers in any year is 5% greater than in the previous year.

At the beginning of each year, t, the economy has available a capital stock, K_t. (We demonstrate shortly how this capital stock is determined.) During each year, t, capital, K_t, and labor, N_t, are used to produce the economy's total output, Y_t. Part of the output produced each year is invested in new capital or in replacing worn-out capital. We further assume that the economy is closed and that there are no government purchases,[11] so the uninvested part of output is consumed by the population. If

$$Y_t = \text{output produced in year } t,$$
$$I_t = \text{gross (total) investment in year } t, \text{ and}$$
$$C_t = \text{consumption in year } t,$$

---

[10]The original article is Robert M. Solow, "A Contribution to the Theory of Economic Growth," *Quarterly Journal of Economics*, February 1956, pp. 65–94.

[11]Analytical Problem 3 at the end of this chapter adds government purchases to the model.

the relationship among consumption, output, and investment in each year is

$$C_t = Y_t - I_t. \tag{6.4}$$

Equation (6.4) states that the uninvested part of the economy's output is consumed.

Because the population and the labor force are growing in this economy, focusing on output, consumption, and the capital stock *per worker* is convenient. Hence we use the following notation:

$$y_t = \frac{Y_t}{N_t} = \text{output per worker in year } t;$$

$$c_t = \frac{C_t}{N_t} = \text{consumption per worker in year } t;$$

$$k_t = \frac{K_t}{N_t} = \text{capital stock per worker in year } t.$$

The capital stock per worker, k_t, is also called the **capital–labor ratio.** An important goal of the model is to understand how output per worker, consumption per worker, and the capital–labor ratio change over time.[12]

The Per-Worker Production Function. In general, the amount of output that can be produced by specific quantities of inputs is determined by the production function. Until now we have written the production function as a relationship between total output, Y, and the total quantities of capital and labor inputs, K and N. However, we can also write the production function in per-worker terms as

$$y_t = f(k_t). \tag{6.5}$$

Equation (6.5) indicates that, in each year t, output per worker, y_t, depends on the amount of available capital per worker, k_t.[13] Here we use a lower case f instead of an upper case F for the production function to emphasize that the measurement of output and capital is in *per-worker* terms. For the time being we focus on the role of the capital stock in the growth process by assuming no productivity growth and thus leaving the productivity term out of the production function, Eq. (6.5).[14] We bring productivity growth back into the model later.

The per-worker production function is graphed in Fig. 6.3. The capital–labor ratio (the amount of capital per worker), k_t, is measured on the horizontal axis, and output per worker, y_t, is measured on the vertical axis. The production function slopes upward from left to right because an increase in the amount of capital per worker allows each worker to produce more output. As with the standard production function, the bowed shape of the per-worker production function reflects

---

[12]For purposes of analysis, discussing output and consumption per worker is more convenient than discussing output and consumption per member of the population as a whole. Under the assumption that the labor force is a fixed fraction of the population and is fully employed, anything we say about the growth rate of output or consumption per worker also will be true of the growth rate of output or consumption per member of the population.

[13]To write the production function in the form of Eq. (6.5) requires the assumption of constant returns to scale, which means that an equal percentage increase in both capital and labor inputs results in the same percentage increase in total output. So, for example, with constant returns to scale, a 10% increase in both capital and labor raises output by 10%. In terms of the growth accounting equation, Eq. (6.2), constant returns to scale requires that $a_K + a_N = 1$. See Analytical Problem 6 at the end of this chapter.

[14]More precisely, we set the total factor productivity term A equal to 1.

Figure 6.3

The per-worker production function
The per-worker production function, $y_t = f(k_t)$, relates the amount of output produced per worker, y_t, to the capital–labor ratio, k_t. For example, when the capital–labor ratio is k_1, output per worker is y_1. The per-worker production function slopes upward from left to right because an increase in the capital–labor ratio raises the amount of output produced per worker. The bowed shape of the production function reflects the diminishing marginal productivity of capital.

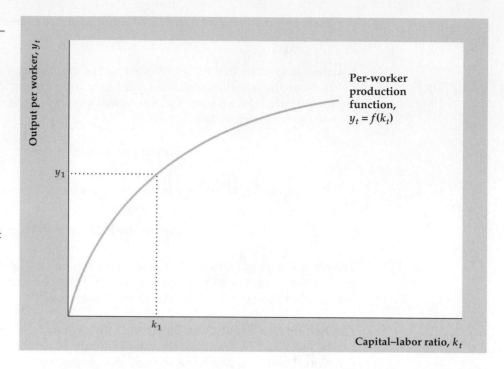

the diminishing marginal productivity of capital. Thus when the capital–labor ratio is already high, an increase in the capital–labor ratio has a relatively small effect on output per worker.

Steady States.   One of the most striking conclusions obtained from the Solow model is that in the absence of productivity growth the economy reaches a steady state in the long run. A **steady state** is a situation in which the economy's output per worker, consumption per worker, and capital stock per worker are constant—that is, in the steady state, y_t, c_t, and k_t don't change over time.[15] To explain how the Solow model works, we first examine the characteristics of a steady state and then discuss how the economy might attain it.

Let's begin by looking at investment in a steady state. In general, gross (total) investment in year t, I_t, is devoted to two purposes: (1) replacing worn-out or depreciated capital, and (2) expanding the size of the capital stock. If d is the capital depreciation rate, or the fraction of capital that wears out each year, the total amount of depreciation in year t is dK_t. The amount by which the capital stock is increased is net investment. What is net investment in a steady state? Because capital per worker, K_t/N_t, is constant in a steady state, the total capital stock grows at the same rate as the labor force—that is, at rate n. Net investment is therefore nK_t in a steady state.[16] To obtain steady-state gross investment, we add steady-state net investment nK_t and depreciation dK_t:

$$I_t = (n + d)K_t \text{ (in a steady state).} \tag{6.6}$$

---

[15]Note that if output, consumption, and capital per worker are constant, then total output, consumption, and capital all are growing at rate n, the rate of growth of the work force.

[16]Algebraically, net investment in year t is $K_{t+1} - K_t$. If total capital grows at rate n, then $K_{t+1} = (1 + n)K_t$. Substituting for K_{t+1} in the definition of net investment, we find that net investment $= (1 + n)K_t - K_t = nK_t$ in a steady state.

To obtain steady-state consumption (output less investment), we substitute Eq. (6.6) into Eq. (6.4):

$$C_t = Y_t - (n + d)K_t \text{ (in a steady state).} \tag{6.7}$$

Equation (6.7) measures consumption, output, and capital as economywide totals rather than in per-worker terms. To put them in per-worker terms, we divide both sides of Eq. (6.7) by the number of workers, N_t, recalling that $c_t = C_t/N_t$, $y_t = Y_t/N_t$, and $k_t = K_t/N_t$. Then we use the per-worker production function, Eq. (6.5), to replace y_t with $f(k_t)$ and obtain

$$c = f(k) - (n + d)k \text{ (in a steady state).} \tag{6.8}$$

Equation (6.8) shows the relationship between consumption per worker, c, and the capital–labor ratio, k, in the steady state. Because consumption per worker and the capital–labor ratio are constant in the steady state, we dropped the time subscripts, t.

Equation (6.8) shows that an increase in the steady-state capital–labor ratio, k, has two opposing effects on steady-state consumption per worker, c. First, an increase in the steady-state capital–labor ratio raises the amount of output each worker can produce, $f(k)$. Second, an increase in the steady-state capital–labor ratio increases the amount of output per worker that must be devoted to investment, $(n + d)k$. More goods devoted to investment leaves fewer goods to consume.

Figure 6.4 shows the trade-off between these two effects. In Fig. 6.4(a) different possible values of the steady-state capital–labor ratio, k, are measured on the horizontal axis. The curve is the per-worker production function, $y = f(k)$, as in Fig. 6.3. The straight line shows steady-state investment per worker, $(n + d)k$. Equation (6.8) indicates that steady-state consumption per worker, c, equals the height of the curve, $f(k)$, minus the height of the straight line, $(n + d)k$. Thus consumption per worker is the height of the shaded area.

The relationship between consumption per worker and the capital–labor ratio in the steady state is shown more explicitly in Fig. 6.4(b). For each value of the steady-state capital–labor ratio, k, steady-state consumption, c, is the difference between the production function and investment in Fig. 6.4(a). Note that, starting from low and medium values of k (values less than k_G in Fig. 6.4(b)), increases in the steady-state capital–labor ratio lead to greater steady-state consumption per worker. The level of the capital–labor ratio that maximizes consumption per worker in the steady state, shown as k_G in Fig. 6.4, is known as the **Golden Rule capital–labor ratio,** so-called because it maximizes the economic welfare of future generations.[17]

However, for high values of k (values greater than the Golden Rule capital–labor ratio, k_G), increases in the steady-state capital–labor ratio actually result in lower steady-state consumption per worker because so much investment is needed to maintain the high level of capital per worker. In the extreme case, where $k = k_{max}$ in Fig. 6.4, all output has to be devoted to replacing and expanding the capital stock, with nothing left to consume!

Policymakers often try to improve long-run living standards with policies aimed at increasing the capital–labor ratio by stimulating saving and investment.

---

[17]Readers familiar with calculus might try to use Eq. (6.8) to show that, at the Golden Rule capital–labor ratio, the marginal product of capital equals $n + d$.

Figure 6.4

The relationship of consumption per worker to the capital–labor ratio in the steady state

(a) For each value of the capital–labor ratio, k, steady-state output per worker, y, is given by the per-worker production function, $f(k)$. Steady-state investment per worker, $(n + d)k$, is a straight line with slope $n + d$. Steady-state consumption per worker, c, is the difference between output per worker and investment per worker (the peach-shaded area). For example, if the capital–labor ratio is k_G, steady-state consumption per worker is c_G. **(b)** For each value of the steady-state capital–labor ratio, k, steady-state consumption per worker, c, is derived in **(a)** as the difference between output per worker and investment per worker. Thus the shaded area (peach) in **(b)** corresponds to the shaded area in **(a)**. Note that, starting from a low value of the capital–labor ratio, an increase in the capital–labor ratio raises steady-state consumption per worker. However, starting from a capital–labor ratio greater than the Golden Rule level, k_G, an increase in the capital–labor ratio actually lowers consumption per worker. When the capital–labor ratio equals k_{max}, all output is devoted to investment, and steady-state consumption per worker is zero.

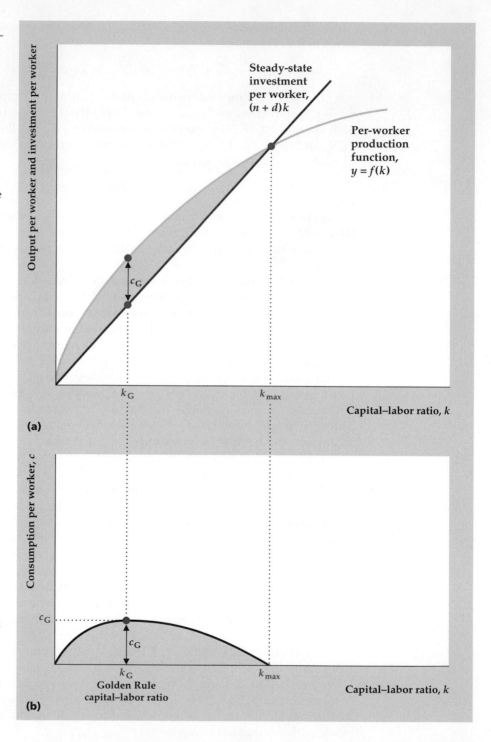

Figure 6.4 shows the limits to this strategy. A country with a low amount of capital per worker may hope to improve long-run (steady-state) living standards substantially by increasing its capital–labor ratio. However, a country that already has a high level of capital per worker may find that further increases in the capital–labor ratio fail to raise steady-state consumption much. The fundamental reason for this

outcome is the diminishing marginal productivity of capital—that is, the larger the capital stock already is, the smaller the benefit from expanding the capital stock further. Indeed, Fig. 6.4 shows that, theoretically, capital per worker can be so high that further increases will actually *lower* steady-state consumption per worker.

In any economy in the world today, could a higher capital stock lead to less consumption in the long run? An empirical study of seven advanced industrial countries concluded that the answer is "no." Even for high-saving Japan, further increases in capital per worker would lead to higher steady-state consumption per worker.[18] Thus in our analysis we will always assume that an increase in the steady-state capital–labor ratio raises steady-state consumption per worker.

Reaching the Steady State.   Our discussion of steady states leaves two loose ends. First, we need to say something about why an economy like the one we describe here eventually will reach a steady state, as we claimed earlier. Second, we have not yet shown *which* steady state the economy will reach; that is, we would like to know the steady-state level of consumption per worker and the steady-state capital–labor ratio that the economy will eventually attain.

To tie up these loose ends, we need one more piece of information: the rate at which people save. To keep things as simple as possible, suppose that saving in this economy is proportional to current income:

$$S_t = sY_t, \tag{6.9}$$

where S_t is national saving[19] in year t and s is the saving rate, which we assume to be constant. Because a \$1 increase in current income raises saving, but by less than \$1 (see Chapter 4), we take s to be a number between 0 and 1. Equation (6.9) ignores some other determinants of saving discussed in earlier chapters, such as the real interest rate. However, including these other factors wouldn't change our basic conclusions, so for simplicity we omit them.

In every year, national saving, S_t, equals investment, I_t. Therefore

$$sY_t = (n + d)K_t \text{ (in a steady state),} \tag{6.10}$$

where the left side of Eq. (6.10) is saving (see Eq. 6.9) and the right side of Eq. (6.10) is steady-state investment (see Eq. 6.6).

Equation (6.10) shows the relation between total output, Y_t, and the total capital stock, K_t, that holds in the steady state. To determine steady-state capital per worker, we divide both sides of Eq. (6.10) by N_t. We then use the production function, Eq. (6.5), to replace y_t with $f(k_t)$:

$$sf(k) = (n + d)k \text{ (in the steady state).} \tag{6.11}$$

Equation (6.11) indicates that saving per worker, $sf(k)$, equals steady-state investment per worker, $(n + d)k$. Because the capital–labor ratio, k, is constant in the steady state, we again drop the subscripts, t, from the equation.

With Eq. (6.11) we can now determine the steady-state capital–labor ratio that the economy will attain, as shown in Fig. 6.5. The capital–labor ratio is measured along the horizontal axis. Saving per worker and investment per worker are measured on the vertical axis.

---

[18]See Andrew B. Abel, N. Gregory Mankiw, Lawrence H. Summers, and Richard J. Zeckhauser, "Assessing Dynamic Efficiency: Theory and Evidence," *Review of Economic Studies*, January 1989, pp. 1–20.

[19]With no government in this model, national saving and private saving are the same.

Figure 6.5

Determining the capital–labor ratio in the steady state

The steady-state capital–labor ratio, k^*, is determined by the condition that saving per worker, $sf(k)$, equals steady-state investment per worker, $(n + d)k$. The steady-state capital–labor ratio, k^*, corresponds to point A, where the saving curve and the steady-state investment line cross. From any starting point, eventually the capital–labor ratio reaches k^*. If the capital–labor ratio happens to be below k^* (say, at k_1), saving per worker, $sf(k_1)$, exceeds the investment per worker, $(n + d)k_1$, needed to maintain the capital–labor ratio at k_1. As this extra saving is converted into capital, the capital–labor ratio will rise, as indicated by the arrows. Similarly, if the capital–labor ratio is greater than k^* (say, at k_2), saving is too low to maintain the capital–labor ratio, and the capital–labor ratio will fall over time.

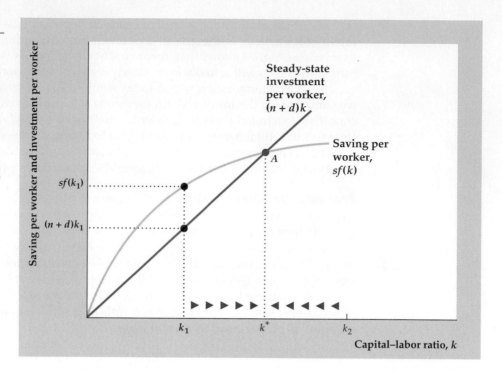

The bowed curve shows how the amount of saving per worker, $sf(k)$, is related to the capital–labor ratio. This curve slopes upward because an increase in the capital–labor ratio implies higher output per worker and thus more saving per worker. The saving-per-worker curve has the same general shape as the per-worker production function, because saving per worker equals the per-worker production function, $f(k)$, multiplied by the fixed saving rate, s.

The line in Fig. 6.5 represents steady-state investment per worker, $(n + d)k$. The steady-state investment line slopes upward because, as the capital–labor ratio rises, more investment per worker is required to replace depreciating capital and equip new workers with the same high level of capital.

According to Eq. (6.11), the steady-state capital–labor ratio must ensure that saving per worker and steady-state investment per worker are equal. The one level of the capital–labor ratio for which this condition is satisfied is shown in Fig. 6.5 as k^*, the value of k at which the saving curve and the steady-state investment line cross. For any other value of k, saving and steady-state investment won't be equal. Thus k^* is the only possible steady-state capital–labor ratio for this economy.[20]

With the unique steady-state capital–labor ratio, k^*, we can also find steady-state output and consumption per worker. From the per-worker production function, Eq. (6.5), if the steady-state capital–labor ratio is k^*, steady-state output per worker, y^*, is

$$y^* = f(k^*).$$

---

[20]Actually, there is also a steady state at the point $k = 0$, at which the capital stock, output, and consumption are zero forever. However, as long as the economy starts out with a positive amount of capital, it will never reach the zero-capital steady state.

From Eq. (6.8) steady-state consumption per worker, c^*, equals steady-state output per worker, $f(k^*)$, minus steady-state investment per worker, $(n + d)k^*$:

$$c^* = f(k^*) - (n + d)k^*.$$

Recall that, in the empirically realistic case, a higher value of the steady-state capital–labor ratio, k^*, implies greater steady-state consumption per worker, c^*.

Using the condition that in a steady state, national saving equals steady-state investment, we found the steady-state capital–labor ratio, k^*. When capital per worker is k^*, the amount that people choose to save will just equal the amount of investment necessary to keep capital per worker at k^*. Thus, when the economy's capital–labor ratio reaches k^*, it will remain there forever.

But is there any reason to believe that the capital–labor ratio will ever reach k^* if it starts at some other value? Yes, there is. Suppose that the capital–labor ratio happens to be less than k^*; for example, it equals k_1 in Fig. 6.5. When capital per worker is k_1, the amount of saving per worker, $sf(k_1)$, is greater than the amount of investment needed to keep the capital–labor ratio constant, $(n + d)k_1$. When this extra saving is invested to create new capital, the capital–labor ratio will rise. As indicated by the arrows on the horizontal axis, the capital–labor ratio will increase from k_1 toward k^*.

If capital per worker is initially greater than k^*—for example, if k equals k_2 in Fig. 6.5—the explanation of why the economy converges to a steady state is similar. If the capital–labor ratio exceeds k^*, the amount of saving that is done will be less than the amount of investment that is necessary to keep the capital–labor ratio constant. (In Fig. 6.5, when k equals k_2, the saving curve lies below the steady-state investment line.) Thus the capital–labor ratio will fall over time from k_2 toward k^*, as indicated by the arrows. Output per worker will also fall until it reaches its steady-state value.

To summarize, if we assume no productivity growth, the economy must eventually reach a steady state. In this steady state the capital–labor ratio, output per worker, and consumption per worker remain constant over time. (However, total capital, output, and consumption grow at rate n, the rate of growth of the labor force.) This conclusion might seem gloomy because it implies that living standards must eventually stop improving. However, that conclusion can be avoided if, in fact, productivity continually increases.

The Fundamental Determinants of Long-Run Living Standards

What determines how well off the average person in an economy will be in the long run? If we measure long-run well-being by the steady-state level of consumption per worker, we can use the Solow model to answer this question. Here, we discuss three factors that affect long-run living standards: the saving rate, population growth, and productivity growth (see Summary table 8).

The Saving Rate.   According to the Solow model, a higher saving rate implies higher living standards in the long run, as illustrated in Fig. 6.6. Suppose that the economy's initial saving rate is s_1 so that saving per worker is $s_1 f(k)$. The saving curve when the saving rate is s_1 is labeled "Initial saving per worker." The initial steady-state capital–labor ratio, k_1^*, is the capital–labor ratio at which the initial saving curve and the investment line cross (point A).

Suppose now that the government introduces policies that strengthen the incentives for saving, causing the country's saving rate to rise from s_1 to s_2. The

SUMMARY 8

The Fundamental Determinants of Long-Run Living Standards

An increase in	Causes long-run output, consumption, and capital per worker to	Reason
The saving rate, s	Rise	Higher saving allows for more investment and a larger capital stock.
The rate of population growth, n	Fall	With higher population growth more output must be used to equip new workers with capital, leaving less output available for consumption or to increase capital per worker.
Productivity	Rise	Higher productivity directly increases output; by raising incomes, it also raises saving and the capital stock.

increased saving rate raises saving at every level of the capital–labor ratio. Graphically, the saving curve shifts upward from $s_1 f(k)$ to $s_2 f(k)$. The new steady-state capital–labor ratio, k_2^*, corresponds to the intersection of the new saving curve and the investment line (point B). Because k_2^* is larger than k_1^*, the higher saving rate has increased the steady-state capital–labor ratio. Gradually, this economy will move to the higher steady-state capital–labor ratio, as indicated by the arrows on the horizontal axis. In the new steady state, output per worker and consumption per worker will be higher than in the original steady state.

Figure 6.6

The effect of an increased saving rate on the steady-state capital–labor ratio

An increase in the saving rate from s_1 to s_2 raises the saving curve from $s_1 f(k)$ to $s_2 f(k)$. The point where saving per worker equals steady-state investment per worker moves from point A to point B, and the corresponding capital–labor ratio rises from k_1^* to k_2^*. Thus a higher saving rate raises the steady-state capital–labor ratio.

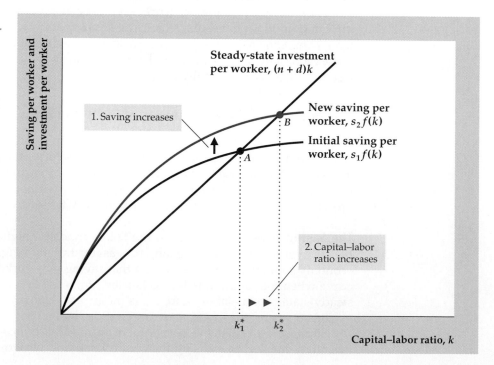

An increased saving rate leads to higher output, consumption, and capital per worker in the long run, so it might seem that a policy goal should be to make the country's saving rate as high as possible. However, this conclusion isn't necessarily correct: Although a higher saving rate raises consumption per worker in the long run, an increase in the saving rate initially causes consumption to fall. This decline occurs because, at the initial level of output, increases in saving and investment leave less available for current consumption. Thus higher future consumption has a cost in terms of lower present consumption. Society's choice of a saving rate should take into account this trade-off between current and future consumption. Beyond a certain point the cost of reduced consumption today will outweigh the long-run benefits of a higher saving rate.

Population Growth. In many developing countries a high rate of population growth is considered to be a major problem, and reducing it is a primary policy goal. What is the relationship between population growth and a country's level of development, as measured by output, consumption, and capital per worker?

The Solow model's answer to this question is shown in Fig. 6.7. An initial steady-state capital–labor ratio, k_1^*, corresponds to the intersection of the steady-state investment line and the saving curve at point A. Now suppose that the rate of population growth, which is the same as the rate of labor force growth, rises from an initial level of n_1 to n_2. What happens?

An increase in the population growth rate means that workers are entering the labor force more rapidly than before. These new workers must be equipped with capital. Thus, to maintain the same steady-state capital–labor ratio, the amount of investment per current member of the work force must rise. Algebraically, the rise in n increases steady-state investment per worker from $(n_1 + d)k$ to $(n_2 + d)k$. This increase in the population growth rate causes the steady-state investment line to pivot up and to the left, as its slope rises from $(n_1 + d)$ to $(n_2 + d)$.

After the pivot of the steady-state investment line, the new steady state is at point B. The new steady-state capital–labor ratio is k_2^*, which is lower than the original capital–labor ratio, k_1^*. Because the new steady-state capital–labor ratio is lower, the new steady-state output per worker and consumption per worker will be lower as well.

Thus the Solow model implies that increased population growth will lower living standards. The basic problem is that when the work force is growing rapidly, a large part of current output must be devoted just to providing capital for the new workers to use. This result suggests that policies to control population growth will indeed improve living standards.

There are some counterarguments to the conclusion that policy should aim to reduce population growth. First, although a reduction in the rate of population growth n raises consumption *per worker*, it also reduces the growth rate of *total* output and consumption, which grow at rate n in the steady state. Having fewer people means more for each person but also less total productive capacity. For some purposes (military, political) a country may care about its total output as well as output per person. Thus, for example, some countries of Western Europe are concerned about projections that their populations will actually shrink in the next century, possibly reducing their ability to defend themselves or influence world events.

Second, an assumption in the Solow model is that the proportion of the total population that is of working age is fixed. When the population growth rate changes dramatically, this assumption may not hold. For example, declining birth

Figure 6.7

The effect of a higher population growth rate on the steady-state capital–labor ratio

An increase in the population growth rate from n_1 to n_2 increases steady-state investment per worker from $(n_1 + d)k$ to $(n_2 + d)k$. The steady-state investment line pivots up and to the left as its slope rises from $n_1 + d$ to $n_2 + d$. The point where saving per worker equals steady-state investment per worker shifts from point A to point B, and the corresponding capital–labor ratio falls from k_1^* to k_2^*. A higher population growth rate therefore causes the steady-state capital–labor ratio to fall.

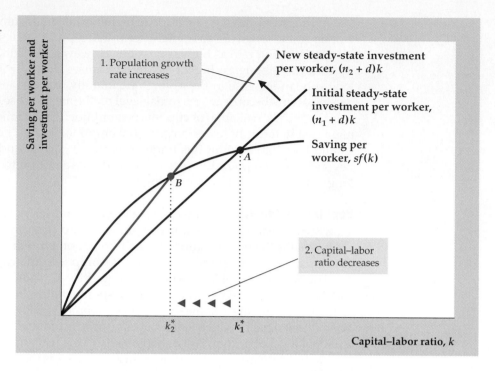

rates in the United States imply that the ratio of working-age people to retirees will become unusually low early in the twenty-first century, a development that may cause problems for Social Security funding and other areas such as health care.

Productivity Growth.   A significant aspect of the basic Solow model is that, ultimately, the economy reaches a steady state in which output per capita is constant. But in the introduction to this chapter we described how Japanese output per person has grown by a factor of more than 30 since 1870! How can the Solow model account for that sustained growth? The key is a factor that we haven't yet made part of the analysis: productivity growth.

The effects of a productivity improvement—the result of, say, a new technology—are shown in Figs. 6.8 and 6.9. An improvement in productivity corresponds to an upward shift in the per-worker production function because, at any prevailing capital–labor ratio, each worker can produce more output. Figure 6.8 shows a shift from the original production function, $y = f_1(k)$, to a "new, improved" production function, $y = f_2(k)$. The productivity improvement corresponds to a beneficial supply shock, as explained in Chapter 3.

Figure 6.9 shows the effects of this productivity improvement in the Solow model. As before, the initial steady state is determined by the intersection of the saving curve and the steady-state investment line at point A; the corresponding steady-state capital–labor ratio is k_1^*. The productivity improvement raises output per worker for any level of the capital–labor ratio. As saving per worker is a constant fraction, s, of output per worker, saving per worker also rises at any capital–labor ratio. Graphically, the saving curve shifts upward from $sf_1(k)$ to $sf_2(k)$, now intersecting the steady-state investment line at point B. The new steady-state capital–labor ratio is k_2^*, which is higher than the original steady-state capital–labor ratio, k_1^*.

Figure 6.8

An improvement in productivity
An improvement in productivity shifts the per-worker production function upward from the initial production function, $y = f_1(k)$, to the new production function, $y = f_2(k)$. After the productivity improvement, more output per worker, y, can be produced at any capital–labor ratio, k.

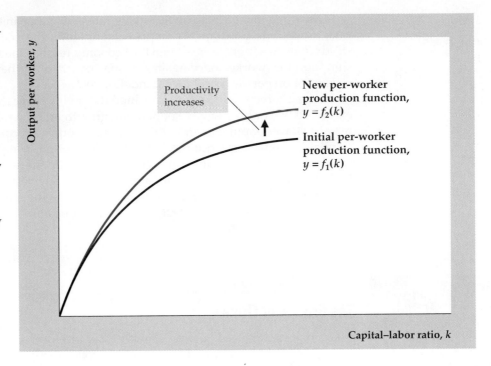

Figure 6.9

The effect of a productivity improvement on the steady-state capital–labor ratio
A productivity improvement shifts the production function upward from $f_1(k)$ to $f_2(k)$, raising output per worker for any capital–labor ratio. Because saving is proportional to output, saving per worker also rises, from $sf_1(k)$ to $sf_2(k)$. The point where saving per worker equals steady-state investment per worker shifts from point A to point B, and the corresponding steady-state capital–labor ratio rises from k_1^* to k_2^*. Thus a productivity improvement raises the steady-state capital–labor ratio.

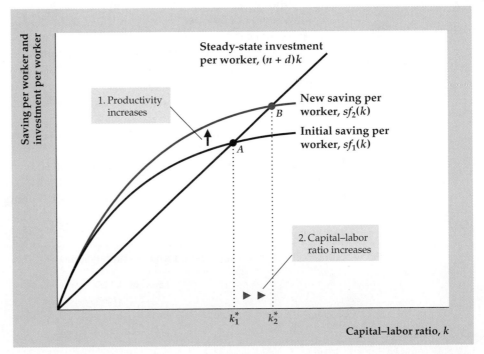

Overall, a productivity improvement raises steady-state output and consumption per worker in two ways. First, it directly increases the amount that can be produced at any capital–labor ratio. Second, as Fig. 6.9 shows, by raising the supply of saving, a productivity improvement causes the long-run capital–labor ratio to rise. Thus a productivity improvement has a doubly beneficial impact on the standard of living.

Like a one-time increase in the saving rate or decrease in the population growth rate, a one-time productivity improvement shifts the economy only from one steady state to a higher one. When the economy reaches the new steady state, consumption per worker once again becomes constant. Is there some way to keep consumption per worker growing indefinitely?

In reality, there are limits to how high the saving rate can rise (it certainly can't exceed 100%!) or how low the population growth rate can fall. Thus higher saving rates or slower population growth aren't likely sources of continually higher living standards. However, since the Industrial Revolution, if not before, people have shown remarkable ingenuity in becoming more and more productive. In the very long run, according to the Solow model, only these continuing increases in productivity hold the promise of perpetually better living standards. Thus we conclude that, *in the long run, the rate of productivity improvement is the dominant factor determining how quickly living standards rise.*

APPLICATION

The Growth of China

China has experienced soaring growth rates in recent years. Because of its size (population of 1.3 billion), China could become the next great world economic power. Although it has grown rapidly in the past few decades, China started from such a low level of GDP per capita that the country has a long way to go before its GDP per capita catches up to GDP per capita in advanced economies.

Table 6.4 shows that China's GDP per capita compares poorly with other countries. As recently as 1998, China's real GDP per capita was about 16% of Japan's, even though China and Japan were not very far apart in real GDP per capita in 1870. Real GDP per capita in China was actually lower in 1950 than it had been 80 years earlier in 1870.

In recent years, real GDP growth in China has been quite rapid. Figure 6.10 shows the growth rate of GDP in China compared with that in the United States. In the past eight years, China's GDP growth rate has averaged 10.2% per year, whereas the U.S. GDP growth rate averaged just 2.2% per year. Analysts have attributed the rapid growth rate in China to a tremendous increase in capital

Table 6.4

Economic Growth in China, Japan, and the United States

Country	Levels of real GDP per capita				Annual growth rate 1870–2006
	1870	1913	1950	2006	
China	530	552	448	6,048	1.8%
Japan	737	1,387	1,921	22,462	2.5
United States	2,445	5,301	9,561	31,049	1.9

Note: Figures are in U.S. dollars at 1990 prices, adjusted for differences in the purchasing power of the various national currencies.
Source: Data from Angus Maddison, *Statistics on World Population, GDP, and Per Capita GDP, 1–2006 AD* (March 2009, vertical file, copyright Angus Maddison), available at *www.ggdc.net/maddison*.

investment, fast productivity growth that has arisen in part from the transition from a centrally planned economy to a market economy, and increased trade with other countries.[21]

Because of its economic failures before 1979 when government central planners ran business firms, China has needed to rebuild its infrastructure, housing stock, and production facilities. As a result, investment in China is a much higher percentage of GDP than in most countries, including the United States. Consumption spending is low relative to consumption in other countries, so the saving rate in China is high. In fact, national saving in China is large enough to finance the large amount of investment spending and still enable China to run a current account surplus (see the goods market equilibrium condition in an open economy, Eq. 5.3).

Given that China has a population four times the size of the U.S. population, it may not be surprising that Chinese workers earn low wages and that China competes internationally in labor-intensive industries rather than capital-intensive industries. However, as China continues to grow and as its productivity keeps rising along with the growth of its capital stock, China should eventually experience higher wages and an increased standard of living. The main problems that China will face in the near future include a weak banking system, increasing income inequality, and high unemployment among rural workers.

Figure 6.10

Real GDP growth in China and the United States, 2001–2008
The chart shows annual values for real GDP growth for both China and the United States for the period 2001–2008.

Source: International Monetary Fund, World Economic Outlook, available at *www.imf.org/ external/pubs/ft/weo/2009/01/pdf/ tables.pdf.*

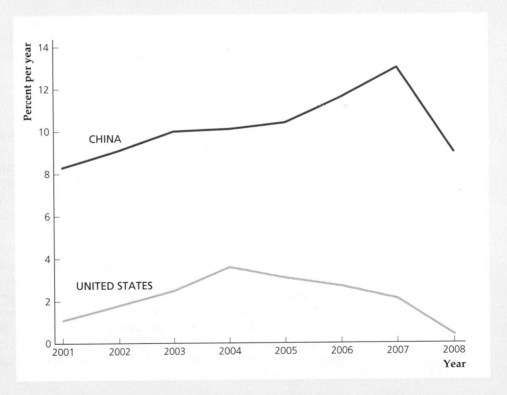

[21]For a readable and comprehensive review of China's economic growth, see Mathew Shane and Fred Gale, "China: A Study of Dynamic Growth," U.S. Department of Agriculture, Economic Research Service, WRS-04-08, October 2004; available at *www.ers.usda.gov.*

Endogenous Growth Theory

The traditional Solow model of economic growth has proved quite useful, but it nevertheless has at least one serious shortcoming as a model of economic growth. According to the Solow model, productivity growth is the only source of long-run growth of output per capita, so a full explanation of long-run economic growth requires an explanation of productivity growth. The model, however, simply takes the rate of productivity growth as given, rather than trying to explain how it is determined. That is, the Solow model *assumes,* rather than *explains,* the behavior of the crucial determinant of the long-run growth rate of output per capita.

In response to this shortcoming of the Solow model, a new branch of growth theory, **endogenous growth theory,** has been developed to try to explain productivity growth—and hence the growth rate of output—*endogenously,* or *within the model.*[22] As we will see, an important implication of endogenous growth theory is that a country's long-run growth rate depends on its rate of saving and investment, not only on exogenous productivity growth (as implied by the Solow model).

Here we present a simple endogenous growth model in which the number of workers remains constant, a condition implying that the growth rate of output per worker is simply equal to the growth rate of output. Our simple endogenous growth model is based on the aggregate production function

$$Y = AK \tag{6.12}$$

where Y is aggregate output and K is the aggregate capital stock. The parameter A in Eq. (6.12) is a positive constant. According to the production function in Eq. (6.12), each additional unit of capital increases output by A units, regardless of how many units of capital are used in production. Because the marginal product of capital, equal to A, does not depend on the size of the capital stock K, the production function in Eq. (6.12) does not imply diminishing marginal productivity of capital. The assumption that the marginal productivity is constant, rather than diminishing, is a key departure from the Solow growth model.

Endogenous growth theorists have provided a number of reasons to explain why, for the economy as a whole, the marginal productivity of capital may not be diminishing. One explanation emphasizes the role of **human capital,** the economists' term for the knowledge, skills, and training of individuals. As economies accumulate capital and become richer, they devote more resources to "investing in people," through improved nutrition, schooling, health care, and on-the-job training. This investment in people increases the country's human capital, which in turn raises productivity. If the physical capital stock increases while the stock of human capital remains fixed, there will be diminishing marginal productivity of physical capital, as each unit of physical capital effectively works with a smaller amount of human capital. Endogenous growth theory argues that, as an economy's physical capital stock increases, its human capital stock tends to increase in the same proportion. Thus, when the physical capital stock increases, each unit of physical capital effectively works with the same amount of human capital, so the marginal productivity of capital need not decrease.

---

[22]Two important early articles in endogenous growth theory are Paul Romer, "Increasing Returns and Long-Run Growth," *Journal of Political Economy,* October 1986, pp. 1002–1037, and Robert E. Lucas, Jr., "On the Mechanics of Economic Development," *Journal of Monetary Economics,* July 1988, pp. 3–42. A more accessible description of endogenous growth theory is in Paul Romer, "The Origins of Endogenous Growth," *Journal of Economic Perspectives,* Winter 1994, pp. 3–22.

A second rationalization of a constant marginal productivity of capital is based on the observation that, in a growing economy, firms have incentives to undertake research and development (R&D) activities. These activities increase the stock of commercially valuable knowledge, including new products and production techniques. According to this R&D-focused explanation, increases in capital and output tend to generate increases in technical know-how, and the resulting productivity gains offset any tendency for the marginal productivity of capital to decline.

Having examined why a production function like Eq. (6.12) might be a reasonable description of the economy as a whole, once factors such as increased human capital and research and development are taken into account, let's work out the implications of this equation. As in the Solow model, let's assume that national saving, S, is a constant fraction s of aggregate output, AK, so that $S = sAK$. In a closed economy, investment must equal saving. Recall that total investment equals net investment (the net increase in the capital stock) plus depreciation, or $I = \Delta K + dK$. Therefore, setting investment equal to saving, we have

$$\Delta K + dK = sAK. \tag{6.13}$$

Next, we divide both sides of Eq. (6.13) by K and then subtract d from both sides of the resulting equation to obtain the growth rate of the capital stock.

$$\frac{\Delta K}{K} = sA - d. \tag{6.14}$$

Because output is proportional to the capital stock, the growth rate of output $\frac{\Delta Y}{Y}$ equals the growth rate of the capital stock $\frac{\Delta K}{K}$. Therefore Eq. (6.14) implies

$$\frac{\Delta Y}{Y} = sA - d. \tag{6.15}$$

Equation (6.15) shows that, in the endogenous growth model, the growth rate of output depends on the saving rate s. As we are assuming that the number of workers remains constant over time, the growth rate of output per worker equals the growth rate of output given in Eq. (6.15), and thus depends on the saving rate s. The result that the saving rate affects the long-run growth rate of output stands in sharp contrast to the results of the Solow model, in which the saving rate does not affect the long-run growth rate. Saving affects long-run growth in the endogenous growth framework because, in that framework, higher rates of saving and capital formation stimulate greater investment in human capital and R&D. The resulting increases in productivity help to spur long-run growth. In summary, in comparison to the Solow model, the endogenous growth model places greater emphasis on saving, human capital formation, and R&D as sources of long-run growth.

Although endogenous growth theory remains in a developmental stage, the approach appears promising in at least two dimensions. First, this theory attempts to explain, rather than assumes, the economy's rate of productivity growth. Second, it shows how the long-run growth rate of output may depend on factors, such as the country's saving rate, that can be affected by government policies. Many economists working in this area are optimistic that endogenous growth theory will yield further insights into the creative processes underlying productivity growth, while providing lessons that might be applied to help the poorest nations of the world achieve substantially higher standards of living.

6.3 Government Policies to Raise Long-Run Living Standards

Increased growth and a higher standard of living in the long run often are cited by political leaders as primary policy goals. Let's take a closer look at government policies that may be useful in raising a country's long-run standard of living.

Policies to Affect the Saving Rate

The Solow model suggests that the rate of national saving is a principal determinant of long-run living standards. However, this conclusion doesn't necessarily mean that policymakers should try to force the saving rate upward, because more saving means less consumption in the short run. Indeed, if the "invisible hand" of free markets is working well, the saving rate freely chosen by individuals should be the one that optimally balances the benefit of saving more (higher future living standards) against the cost of saving more (less present consumption).

Despite the argument that saving decisions are best left to private individuals and the free market, some people claim that U.S. residents save too little and that U.S. policy should aim at raising the saving rate. One possible justification for this claim is that existing tax laws discriminate against saving by taxing away part of the returns to saving; a "pro-saving" policy thus is necessary to offset this bias. Another view is that people in the United States are just too shortsighted in their saving decisions and must be encouraged to save more.

What policies can be used to increase saving? If saving were highly responsive to the real interest rate, tax breaks that increase the real return that savers receive would be effective. For example, some economists advocate taxing households on how much they consume rather than on how much they earn, thereby exempting from taxation the income that is saved. But, as we noted in Chapter 4, although saving appears to increase when the expected real return available to savers rises, most studies find this response to be small.

An alternative and perhaps more direct way to increase the national saving rate is by increasing the amount that the government saves; in other words, the government should try to reduce its deficit or increase its surplus. Our analysis of the twin deficits debate (Chapter 5) indicated that reducing the deficit by reducing government purchases will lead to more national saving. Many economists also argue that raising taxes to reduce the deficit or increase the surplus will also increase national saving by leading people to consume less. However, believers in Ricardian equivalence contend that tax increases without changes in current or planned government purchases won't affect consumption or national saving.

Policies to Raise the Rate of Productivity Growth

Of the factors affecting long-run living standards, the rate of productivity growth may well be the most important in that—according to the Solow model—only ongoing productivity growth can lead to continuing improvement in output and consumption per worker. Government policy can attempt to increase productivity in several ways.[23]

---

[23]According to endogenous growth theory, an increase in the saving rate will increase the rate of productivity growth and hence increase the growth rates of output and consumption per worker. Thus, in addition to the policies discussed here, government may attempt to increase productivity growth by trying to increase the saving rate.

Improving Infrastructure.   Some research findings suggest a significant link between productivity and the quality of a nation's infrastructure—its highways, bridges, utilities, dams, airports, and other publicly owned capital.[24] The construction of the interstate highway system in the United States, for example, significantly reduced the cost of transporting goods and stimulated tourism and other industries. In the past quarter-century the rate of U.S. government investment in infrastructure has fallen, leading to a decline in the quality and quantity of public capital.[25] Reversing this trend, some economists argue, might help achieve higher productivity. However, not everyone agrees that more infrastructure investment is needed. For example, some critics have pointed out that the links between productivity growth and infrastructure aren't clear. If rich countries are more likely to build roads and hospitals, perhaps higher productivity growth leads to more infrastructure, rather than vice versa. Others worry that infrastructure investments by the government may involve political considerations (for example, favoring the districts of powerful members of Congress) more than promoting economic efficiency.

Building Human Capital.   Recent research findings point to a strong connection between productivity growth and human capital. The government affects human capital development through educational policies, worker training or relocation programs, health programs, and in other ways. Specific programs should be examined carefully to see whether benefits exceed costs, but a case may be made for greater commitment to human capital formation as a way to boost productivity growth.

One crucial form of human capital, which we haven't yet mentioned, is entrepreneurial skill. People with the ability to build a successful new business or to bring a new product to market play a key role in economic growth. Productivity growth may increase if the government were to remove unnecessary barriers to entrepreneurial activity (such as excessive red tape) and give people with entrepreneurial skills greater incentives to use those skills productively.[26]

Encouraging Research and Development.   The government also may be able to stimulate productivity growth by affecting rates of scientific and technical progress. The U.S. government directly supports much basic scientific research (through the National Science Foundation, for example). Most economists agree with this type of policy because the benefits of scientific progress, like those of human capital development, spread throughout the economy. Basic scientific research may thus be a good investment from society's point of view, even if no individual firm finds such research profitable. Some economists would go further and say that even more applied, commercially oriented research deserves government aid.

---

[24]See, for example, John G. Fernald, "Roads to Prosperity: Assessing the Link Between Public Capital and Productivity," *American Economic Review* 89 (June 1999), pp. 619–638.

[25]For data and discussion, see "Trends in Public Spending on Transportation and Water Infrastructure, 1956 to 2004," Congressional Budget Office, August 2007, available at *www.cbo.gov/ftpdocs/85xx/doc8517/08-08-Infrastructure.pdf.*

[26]For a discussion of entrepreneurial activity and how it affects productivity, see Douglas Holtz-Eakin and Chihwa Kao, "Entrepreneurship and Economic Growth: the Proof Is in the Productivity," Center for Policy Research working paper 50, Syracuse University, February 2003.

CHAPTER SUMMARY

1. Economic growth is the principal source of improving standards of living over time. Over long periods, even small differences in growth rates can have a large effect on nations' standards of living.

2. Growth accounting is a method for breaking total output growth into the portions resulting from growth in capital inputs, growth in labor inputs, and growth in productivity. All three factors have contributed to long-run economic growth in the United States. However, the slowdown in U.S. output growth after 1973 (and in other countries) primarily reflects a sharp decline in productivity growth. Part of this slowdown may be illusory, a product of measurement problems. Other explanations of the decline in productivity growth include the legal and human environment (for example, increased worker safety), increased oil prices, and the cost of adopting new information technologies.

3. The Solow model of economic growth examines the interaction of growth, saving, and capital accumulation over time. It predicts that in the absence of productivity growth the economy will reach a steady state in which output, consumption, and capital per worker are constant.

4. According to the Solow model, each of the following leads to higher output, consumption, and capital per worker in the long run: an increase in the saving rate, a decline in the population growth rate, and an increase in productivity.

5. Endogenous growth theory attempts to explain, rather than assumes, the economywide rate of productivity growth. One strand of this approach emphasizes the formation of human capital, including the acquisition of skills and training by workers. A second strand focuses on research and development activity by firms. Endogenous growth theorists argue that, because growth in capital and output engenders increased human capital and innovation, the marginal productivity of capital may not be diminishing for the economy as a whole. An implication of this theory is that the saving rate can affect the long-run rate of economic growth.

6. Government policies to raise long-run living standards include raising the rate of saving and increasing productivity. Possible ways of increasing productivity involve investing in public capital (infrastructure), encouraging the formation of human capital, and increasing research and development.

KEY TERMS

capital–labor ratio, p. 215
endogenous growth theory, p. 228
Golden Rule capital–labor
   ratio, p. 217

growth accounting, p. 206
growth accounting
   equation, p. 205

human capital, p. 228
steady state, p. 216

KEY EQUATIONS

$$\frac{\Delta Y}{Y} = \frac{\Delta A}{A} + a_K \frac{\Delta K}{K} + a_N \frac{\Delta N}{N} \qquad (6.2)$$

The growth accounting equation states that output growth, $\Delta Y/Y$, depends on the growth rate of productivity, $\Delta A/A$, the growth rate of capital, $\Delta K/K$, and the growth rate of labor, $\Delta N/N$. The elasticity of output with respect to capital, a_K, gives the percentage increase in output that results when capital increases by 1%. The elasticity of output with respect to labor, a_N, gives the percentage increase in output that results when labor increases by 1%.

$$y_t = f(k_t) \qquad (6.5)$$

For any year, t, the per-worker production function relates output per worker, y_t, to capital per worker (also called the capital–labor ratio), k_t.

$$c = f(k) - (n + d)k \qquad (6.8)$$

Steady-state consumption per worker, c, equals steady-state output per worker, $f(k)$, minus steady-state investment per worker, $(n + d)k$. Steady-state output per worker is determined by per-worker production, $f(k)$, where k is the steady-state capital–labor ratio. Steady-state investment per worker has two parts: equipping new workers with the per-worker capital stock, nk, and replacing worn-out or depreciated capital, dk.

$$sf(k) = (n + d)k \qquad (6.11)$$

The steady state is determined by the condition that saving per worker, $sf(k)$, equals steady-state investment per worker, $(n + d)k$. Saving per worker equals the saving rate s times output per worker, $f(k)$.

$$Y = AK \qquad (6.12)$$

Endogenous growth theory replaces the assumption of diminishing marginal productivity of capital with the assumption that the marginal productivity of capital is independent of the level of the capital stock. In the production function relating aggregate output Y to the aggregate capital stock K in Eq. (6.12), the marginal product of capital is constant and equal to the parameter A.

$$\frac{\Delta Y}{Y} = sA - d \qquad (6.15)$$

In an endogenous growth model, the growth rate of output, $\frac{\Delta Y}{Y}$, is determined endogenously by the saving rate, s. An increase in the saving rate increases the growth rate of output.

REVIEW QUESTIONS

All review questions are available in ⓧ **myeconlab** at **www.myeconlab.com**.

1. According to the growth accounting approach, what are the three sources of economic growth? From what basic economic relationship is the growth accounting approach derived?

2. Of the three sources of growth identified by growth accounting, which one is primarily responsible for the slowdown in U.S. economic growth after 1973? What explanations have been given for the decline in this source of growth?

3. How did technology increase U.S. economic growth in the 1990s?

4. Explain what is meant by a steady state. In the Solow model, which variables are constant in a steady state?

5. According to the Solow model of economic growth, if there is no productivity growth, what will happen to output per worker, consumption per worker, and capital per worker in the long run?

6. True or false? The higher the steady-state capital–labor ratio is, the more consumption each worker can enjoy in the long run. Explain your answer.

7. What effect should each of the following have on long-run living standards, according to the Solow model?
   a. An increase in the saving rate.
   b. An increase in the population growth rate.
   c. A one-time improvement in productivity.

8. What two explanations of productivity growth does endogenous growth theory offer? How does the production function in an endogenous growth model differ from the production function in the Solow model?

9. What types of policies are available to a government that wants to promote economic growth? For each type of policy you identify, explain briefly how the policy is supposed to work and list its costs or disadvantages. How does endogenous growth theory possibly change our thinking about the effectiveness of various pro-growth policies, such as increasing the saving rate?

NUMERICAL PROBLEMS

All numerical problems are available in ⓧ **myeconlab** at **www.myeconlab.com**.

1. Two economies, Hare and Tortoise, each start with a real GDP per person of $5000 in 1950. Real GDP per person grows 3% per year in Hare and 1% per year in Tortoise. In the year 2020, what will be real GDP per person in each economy? Make a guess first; then use a calculator to get the answer.

2. Over the past twenty years an economy's total output has grown from 1000 to 1300, its capital stock has risen from 2500 to 3250, and its labor force has increased from 500 to 575. All measurements are in real terms. Calculate the contributions to economic growth of growth in capital, labor, and productivity:

   a. assuming that $a_K = 0.3$ and $a_N = 0.7$.
   b. assuming that $a_K = 0.5$ and $a_N = 0.5$.

3. For a particular economy, the following capital input K and labor input N were reported in four different years:

Year	K	N
1	200	1000
2	250	1000
3	250	1250
4	300	1200

The production function in this economy is

$$Y = K^{0.3}N^{0.7},$$

where Y is total output.

a. Find total output, the capital–labor ratio, and output per worker in each year. Compare year 1 with year 3 and year 2 with year 4. Can this production function be written in per-worker form? If so, write algebraically the per-worker form of the production function.

b. Repeat Part (a) but assume now that the production function is $Y = K^{0.3}N^{0.8}$.

4. Use the data from Table 6.1 to calculate annual growth rates of GDP per capita for each country listed over the period 1950–2006. [*Note:* The annual growth rate z will satisfy the equation $(1 + z)^{56} = GDP_{2006}/GDP_{1950}$. To solve this equation for z using a calculator, take logs of both sides of the equation.] You will find that Germany and Japan, two countries that suffered extensive damage in World War II, had the two highest growth rates after 1950. Give a reason, based on the analysis of the Solow model, for these countries' particularly fast growth during this period.

5. An economy has the per-worker production function

$$y_t = 3k_t^{0.5}$$

where y_t is output per worker and k_t is the capital–labor ratio. The depreciation rate is 0.1, and the population growth rate is 0.05. Saving is

$$S_t = 0.3Y_t,$$

where S_t is total national saving and Y_t is total output.

a. What are the steady-state values of the capital–labor ratio, output per worker, and consumption per worker?

The rest of the problem shows the effects of changes in the three fundamental determinants of long-run living standards.

b. Repeat Part (a) for a saving rate of 0.4 instead of 0.3.

c. Repeat Part (a) for a population growth rate of 0.08 (with a saving rate of 0.3).

d. Repeat Part (a) for a production function of

$$y_t = 4k_t^{0.5}.$$

Assume that the saving rate and population growth rate are at their original values.

6. Consider a closed economy in which the population grows at the rate of 1% per year. The per-worker production function is $y = 6\sqrt{k}$, where y is output per worker and k is capital per worker. The depreciation rate of capital is 14% per year.

a. Households consume 90% of income and save the remaining 10% of income. There is no government. What are the steady-state values of capital per worker, output per worker, consumption per worker, and investment per worker?

b. Suppose that the country wants to increase its steady-state value of output per worker. What steady-state value of the capital–labor ratio is needed to double the steady-state value of output per capita? What fraction of income would households have to save to achieve a steady-state level of output per worker that is twice as high as in Part (a)?

7. Both population and the work force grow at the rate of $n = 1\%$ per year in a closed economy. Consumption is $C = 0.5(1 - t)Y$, where t is the tax rate on income and Y is total output. The per-worker production function is $y = 8\sqrt{k}$, where y is output per worker and k is the capital–labor ratio. The depreciation rate of capital is $d = 9\%$ per year. Suppose for now that there are no government purchases and the tax rate on income is $t = 0$.

a. Find expressions for national saving per worker and the steady-state level of investment per worker as functions of the capital–labor ratio, k. In the steady state, what are the values of the capital–labor ratio, output per worker, consumption per worker, and investment per worker?

b. Suppose that the government purchases goods each year and pays for these purchases using taxes on income. The government runs a balanced budget in each period and the tax rate on income is $t = 0.5$. Repeat Part (a) and compare your results.

ANALYTICAL PROBLEMS

1. According to the Solow model, how would each of the following affect consumption per worker in the long run (that is, in the steady state)? Explain.

a. The destruction of a portion of the nation's capital stock in a war.

b. A permanent increase in the rate of immigration (which raises the overall population growth rate).

c. A permanent increase in energy prices.

d. A temporary rise in the saving rate.

e. A permanent increase in the fraction of the population in the labor force (the population growth rate is unchanged).

2. An economy is in a steady state with no productivity change. Because of an increase in acid rain, the rate of capital depreciation rises permanently.

   a. According to the Solow model, what are the effects on steady-state capital per worker, output per worker, consumption per worker, and the long-run growth rate of the total capital stock?

   b. In an endogenous growth model, what are the effects on the growth rates of output, capital, and consumption of an increase in the depreciation rate of capital?

3. This problem adds the government to the Solow model. Suppose that a government purchases goods in the amount of g per worker every year; with N_t workers in year t, total government purchases are gN_t. The government has a balanced budget so that its tax revenue in year t, T_t, equals total government purchases. Total national saving, S_t, is

$$S_t = s(Y_t - T_t),$$

   where Y_t is total output and s is the saving rate.

   a. Graphically show the steady state for the initial level of government purchases per worker.

   b. Suppose that the government permanently increases its purchases per worker. What are the effects on the steady-state levels of capital per worker, output per worker, and consumption per worker? Does your result imply that the optimal level of government purchases is zero?

4. In a Solow-type economy, total national saving, S_t, is

$$S_t = sY_t - hK_t.$$

   The extra term, $-hK_t$, reflects the idea that when wealth (as measured by the capital stock) is higher, saving is lower. (Wealthier people have less need to save for the future.)

Find the steady-state values of per-worker capital, output, and consumption. What is the effect on the steady state of an increase in h?

5. Two countries are identical in every way except that one has a much higher capital–labor ratio than the other. According to the Solow model, which country's total output will grow more quickly? Does your answer depend on whether one country or the other is in a steady state? In general terms, how will your answer be affected if the two countries are allowed to trade with each other?

6. Suppose that total capital and labor both increase by the same percentage amount, so that the amount of capital per worker, k, doesn't change. Writing the production function in per-worker terms, $y = f(k)$, requires that this increase in capital and labor must not change the amount of output produced per worker, y. Use the growth accounting equation to show that equal percentage increases in capital and labor will leave output per worker unaffected only if $a_K + a_N = 1$.

7. An economy has a per-capita production function $y = Ak^a h^{1-a}$, where A and a are fixed parameters, y is per-worker output, k is the capital–labor ratio, and h is human capital per worker, a measure of the skills and training of the average worker. The production function implies that, for a given capital–labor ratio, increases in average human capital raise output per worker.

   The economy's saving rate is s, and all saving is used to create physical capital, which depreciates at rate d. Workers acquire skills on the job by working with capital; the more capital with which they have to work, the more skills they acquire. We capture this idea by assuming that human capital per worker is always proportional to the amount of physical capital per worker, or $h = Bk$, where B is a fixed parameter.

   Find the long-run growth rates of physical capital, human capital, and output in this economy.

WORKING WITH MACROECONOMIC DATA

For data to use in these exercises, go to the Federal Reserve Bank of St. Louis FRED database at research.stlouisfed.org/fred2.

1. This problem asks you to do your own growth accounting exercise. Using data since 1948, make a table of annual growth rates of real GDP, the capital stock (private fixed assets from the Fixed Assets section of the BEA Web site, *www.bea.gov*, Table 6.1), and civilian employment. Assuming $a_K = 0.3$ and $a_N = 0.7$, find the productivity growth rate for each year.

   a. Graph the contributions to overall economic growth of capital growth, labor growth, and productivity growth for the period since 1948. Contrast the behavior of each of these variables in the post–1973 period to their behavior in the earlier period.

   b. Compare the post–1973 behavior of productivity growth with the graph of the relative price of energy, shown in Fig. 3.12. To what extent do you think the productivity slowdown can be blamed on higher energy prices?

2. Graph the U.S. capital–labor ratio since 1948 (use private fixed assets from the Fixed Assets section of the BEA Web site, *www.bea.gov*, Table 6.1 as the measure of capital, and civilian employment as the measure of labor). Do you see evidence of convergence to a steady state during the postwar period? Now graph real output per worker and real consumption per worker for the same period. According to the Solow model, what are the two basic explanations for the upward trends in these two variables? Can output per worker and consumption per worker continue to grow even if the capital–labor ratio stops rising?

3. According to the Solow model, if countries differed primarily in terms of their capital–labor ratios, with rich countries having high capital–labor ratios and poor countries having low capital–labor ratios, then countries that have a lower real GDP per capita income should grow faster than countries with a higher real GDP per capita. (This prediction of the Solow model assumes that countries have similar saving rates, population growth rates, and production functions.) You can test this idea using the Penn World Tables at *pwt.econ.upenn.edu*. Pick a group of ten countries and examine their initial levels of real GDP per capita in a year long ago, such as 1950. Then calculate the average growth rate of real GDP per capita since that initial year. Do your results suggest that countries that initially have lower real GDP per capita indeed grow faster than countries that initially have a higher real GDP per capita?

CHAPTER 7

The Asset Market, Money, and Prices

In Chapters 3 and 4 we discussed the labor market and the goods market, two of the three markets in our model of the macroeconomy. In this chapter we consider the third market, the asset market. By *asset market* we mean the entire set of markets in which people buy and sell real and financial assets, including, for example, gold, houses, stocks, and bonds.

A type of asset that has long been believed to have special macroeconomic significance is money. Money is the economist's term for assets that can be used in making payments, such as cash and checking accounts. One reason that money is important is that most prices are expressed in units of money, such as dollars, yen, and euros. Because prices are measured in money terms, understanding the role of money in the economy is basic to studying issues related to the price level, such as inflation and its causes. In addition, many economists believe that the amount of money in the economy affects real economic variables, such as output and employment. If it does, then it may be possible to use monetary policy to promote stable output growth and fight unemployment, as we discuss in Part 3.

Because money is such an important asset, it is the focus of our discussion of the asset market. In the first part of the chapter we explain what money is and why people choose to hold it. We show that a person's decision about how much money to hold (his or her money demand) is part of a broader decision about how to allocate wealth among the various assets that are available. We then bring together the demand for money and the supply of money (which is determined by the central bank) to analyze equilibrium in the asset market. This analysis demonstrates that the price level in an economy is closely related to the amount of money in the economy. Thus high rates of inflation—that is, rapid increases in prices—are likely when the money supply is growing rapidly.

7.1 What is Money?

In economics the meaning of the term *money* is different from its everyday meaning. People often say *money* when they mean *income* or *wealth*, as in: That job pays good money, or Her family has a lot of money. In economics, however, **money** refers specifically to assets that are widely used and accepted as payment. Historically, the forms of money have ranged from beads and shells to gold and silver—and even to

237

cigarettes (see "In Touch with Data and Research: Money in a Prisoner-of-War Camp"). In modern economies the most familiar forms of money are coins and paper money, or currency. Another common form of money is checkable deposits, or bank accounts on which checks can be written for making payments.

IN TOUCH WITH DATA AND RESEARCH

Money in a Prisoner-of-War Camp

Among the Allied soldiers liberated from German prisoner-of-war (POW) camps at the end of World War II was a young man named R. A. Radford. Radford had been trained in economics, and shortly after his return home he published an article entitled "The Economic Organisation of a POW Camp."* This article, a minor classic in the economics literature, is a fascinating account of the daily lives of soldiers in several POW camps. It focuses particularly on the primitive "economies" that grew up spontaneously in the camps.

The scope for economic behavior in a POW camp might seem severely limited, and to a degree that's so. There was little production of goods within the camps, although there was some trade in services, such as laundry or tailoring services and even portraiture. However, prisoners were allowed to move around freely within the compound, and they actively traded goods obtained from the Red Cross, the Germans, and other sources. Among the commodities exchanged were tinned milk, jam, butter, biscuits, chocolate, sugar, clothing, and toilet articles. In one particular camp, which at various times had up to fifty thousand prisoners of many nationalities, active trading centers were run entirely by the prisoners.

A key practical issue was how to organize the trading. At first, the camp economies used barter, but it proved to be slow and inefficient. Then the prisoners hit on the idea of using cigarettes as money. Soon prices of all goods were quoted in terms of cigarettes, and cigarettes were accepted as payment for any good or service. Even nonsmoking prisoners would happily accept cigarettes as payment, because they knew that they could easily trade the cigarettes for other things they wanted. The use of cigarette money greatly simplified the problem of making trades and helped the camp economy function much more smoothly.

Why were cigarettes, rather than some other commodity, used as money by the POWs? Cigarettes satisfied a number of criteria for a good money: A cigarette is a fairly standardized commodity whose value was easy for both buyers and sellers to ascertain. An individual cigarette is low enough in value that making "change" wasn't a problem. Cigarettes are portable, are easily passed from hand to hand, and don't spoil quickly.

A drawback was that, as a commodity money (a form of money with an alternative use), cigarette money had a resource cost: Cigarettes that were being used as money could not simultaneously be smoked. In the same way, the traditional use of gold and silver as money was costly in that it diverted these metals from alternative uses.

The use of cigarettes as money isn't restricted to POW camps. Just before the collapse of communism in Eastern Europe, cigarette money reportedly was used in Romania and other countries instead of the nearly worthless official money.

Economica, November 1945, pp. 189–201.

The Functions of Money

Since the earliest times almost all societies—from the most primitive to the most sophisticated and with many types of political and economic systems—have used money. Money has three useful functions in an economy: It is a medium of exchange, a unit of account, and a store of value.

Medium of Exchange.   In an economy with no money, trading takes the form of barter, or the direct exchange of certain goods for other goods. Even today some people belong to barter clubs, in which members swap goods and services among themselves. Generally, though, barter is an inefficient way to trade because finding someone who has the item you want and is willing to exchange that item for something you have is both difficult and time-consuming. In a barter system, if one of the authors of this book wanted a restaurant meal, he would first have to find a restaurateur willing to trade his blue-plate special for an economics lecture—which might not be easy to do.

Money makes searching for the perfect trading partner unnecessary. In an economy that utilizes money, the economics professor doesn't have to find a restaurant owner who is hungry for knowledge. Instead, he can first exchange his economics lecture to students for money and then use the money to buy a meal. In functioning as a **medium of exchange,** or a device for making transactions, money permits people to trade at less cost in time and effort. Having a medium of exchange also raises productivity by allowing people to specialize in economic activities at which they are most skilled. In an economy with money, specialized producers have no problem trading their goods or services for the things they need. In a barter economy, though, the difficulty of trading would leave people no choice but to produce most of their own food, clothing, and shelter. Thus in a barter economy the opportunity to specialize is greatly reduced.

Unit of Account.   As a **unit of account,** money is the basic unit for measuring economic value. In the United States, for example, virtually all prices, wages, asset values, and debts are expressed in dollars. Having a single, uniform measure of value is convenient. For example, pricing all goods in the United States in dollars—instead of some goods being priced in yen, some in gold, and some in Microsoft shares—simplifies comparison among different goods.

The medium-of-exchange and unit-of-account functions of money are closely linked. Because goods and services are most often exchanged for money (the medium-of-exchange function), expressing economic values in money terms (the unit-of-account function) is natural. Otherwise, we could just as well express economic values in terms of, say, bushels of wheat. However, the medium of exchange and the unit of account aren't always the same. In countries with high and erratic inflation, for example, fluctuating currency value makes money a poor unit of account because prices must be changed frequently. In such cases, economic values are commonly stated in terms of a more stable unit of account, such as dollars or ounces of gold, even though transactions may continue to be carried out in the local currency.

Store of Value.   As a **store of value,** money is a way of holding wealth. An extreme example is a miser who keeps his life's savings in cash under the mattress. But even someone who spends his cash wages fifteen minutes after receiving them is using money as a store of value for that short period.

In most cases, only money functions as a medium of exchange or a unit of account, but any asset—for example, stocks, bonds, or real estate—can be a store of value. As these other types of assets normally pay the holder a higher return than money does, why do people use money as a store of value? The answer is that money's usefulness as a medium of exchange makes it worthwhile to hold, even though its return is relatively low.

Measuring Money: The Monetary Aggregates. Money is defined as those assets that are widely used and accepted in payment. This definition suggests a hard-and-fast line between assets that should be counted as money and those that should not. Actually, the distinction between monetary assets and nonmonetary assets isn't so clear.

Consider, for example, money market mutual funds (MMMFs), which first became popular in the late 1970s. MMMFs are organizations that sell shares to the public and invest the proceeds in short-term government and corporate debt. MMMFs strive to earn a high return for their shareholders. At the same time, they typically allow their shareholders to write a small number of checks each month against their accounts, perhaps for a fee. Thus, although MMMF shares can be used to make payments, they are not as convenient as cash or regular checking accounts for this purpose. Should MMMF shares be counted as money? There is no definitive answer to this question.

Because assets differ in their "moneyness," no single measure of the amount of money in the economy—or the money stock, as it is often called—is likely to be completely satisfactory. For this reason, in most countries economists and policymakers use several different measures of the money stock. These official measures are known as **monetary aggregates.** The various monetary aggregates differ in how narrowly they define the concept of money. In the United States the two monetary aggregates are called M1 and M2. Summary definitions and data for these two aggregates are given in Table 7.1. Information about where to find data on the monetary aggregates is presented in "In Touch with Data and Research: The Monetary Aggregates."

The M1 Monetary Aggregate. The most narrowly defined official money measure, **M1,** consists primarily of currency and balances held in checking accounts. More precisely, M1 is made up of currency (including U.S. currency circulating outside the United States; see "In Touch with Data and Research: Where Have All

Table 7.1

U.S. Monetary Aggregates (June 2009)

M1	**1655.0**
Currency	852.4
Travelers' checks	5.2
Demand deposits	441.7
Other checkable deposits	355.6
M2	**8363.6**
Components of M1	1655.0
Savings deposits, including MMDAs	4477.7
Small-denomination time deposits	1272.0
MMMFs (noninstitutional)	958.9

Note: Numbers may not add to totals shown owing to rounding.
Source: Federal Reserve Statistical Release H.6, August 6, 2009.
Data are not seasonally adjusted.

IN TOUCH WITH DATA AND RESEARCH

The Monetary Aggregates

The official monetary aggregates—M1 and M2—are compiled and reported by the Board of Governors of the Federal Reserve System in Washington. Only data for M1 were reported until 1971, when the Fed introduced M2 and M3. Since then the definitions of the monetary aggregates have changed several times, reflecting the evolution of the financial system. In 2006, the Fed stopped reporting M3.

The Fed reports estimates of the aggregates both weekly and monthly, using data supplied by banks, the Treasury, money market mutual funds, foreign central banks, and other sources. Each Thursday at 4:30 p.m. Eastern time the Fed announces figures for M1 and M2 for the week ending the Monday of the previous week. Historical data are available in the *Federal Reserve Bulletin,* the Federal Reserve Bank of St. Louis FRED database at *research.stlouisfed.org/fred2,* the *Economic Report of the President,* and on the Federal Reserve System's Web site at *www.federalreserve.gov/releases/H6.* Monetary data are revised frequently, reflecting the receipt of new data by the Federal Reserve or changes in the definitions of monetary aggregates.

Publication of the monetary aggregates helps keep the public and Congress informed about how the Fed is changing the nation's money supply.

the Dollars Gone?", p. 242) and travelers' checks held by the public, demand deposits (non-interest-bearing checking accounts), and other checkable deposits. The category "other checkable deposits" mainly consists of interest-bearing checking accounts. M1 is perhaps the closest counterpart of the theoretical definition of money because all its components are actively used and widely accepted for making payments.

The M2 Monetary Aggregate.   Everything in M1 plus other assets that are somewhat less "moneylike" compose **M2.** The main additional assets in M2 include savings deposits, small-denomination (under $100,000) time deposits, noninstitutional holdings of money market mutual funds (MMMFs), and money market deposit accounts (MMDAs). Time deposits are interest-bearing deposits with a fixed term (early withdrawal usually involves a penalty). As mentioned, MMMFs invest their shareholders' funds in short-term securities, pay market-based interest rates, and allow holders to write checks. MMDAs are like MMMFs, except they are offered by banks or thrift institutions such as savings and loan associations. In Table 7.1 we followed the presentation in the *Federal Reserve Bulletin* and included MMDAs as part of savings deposits.

The Money Supply.   The **money supply** is the amount of money available in an economy.[1] In modern economies the money supply is determined by the central bank—in the United States, the Federal Reserve System.

A detailed explanation of how central banks control the money supply raises issues that would take us too far afield at this point, so we defer that discussion to

---

[1]The terms *money supply* and *money stock* are used interchangeably.

Chapter 14. To grasp the basic idea, however, let's consider the simple hypothetical situation in which the only form of money is currency. In this case, to increase the money supply the central bank needs only to increase the amount of currency in circulation. How can it do so?

IN TOUCH WITH DATA AND RESEARCH

Where Have All the Dollars Gone?

In June 2009 the stock of U.S. currency was $852 billion, or about $2800 for every man, woman, and child in the United States. This figure is surprisingly high. After all, how many people actually have $2800 of cash on hand at any given time, and how many families of four hold over $10,000 in cash? In fact, studies have found that the average person in the United States holds not much more than $100 in currency. So where is the remaining $2700 per person?

Businesses, especially retailers, hold currency for making transactions, but the amount of currency held by U.S. businesses appears to account for less than $100 of the "missing" $2700 per person. Currency also is extensively used in the underground economy, either to conduct illegal transactions (such as trade in illegal drugs) or to hide legal transactions from tax collectors. However, the Federal Reserve estimates that the amount of currency in the domestic underground economy amounts to less than $125 per person. Studies have found that most of the "missing" U.S. currency—amounting to 50% to 70% of currency outstanding—is held abroad.*

Why would people in other countries want to hold U.S. dollars? Even though the dollar may not serve as the medium of exchange or as a unit of account in a country, it can be a relatively attractive store of value, especially in countries that are economically or politically unstable. For example, in countries with high rates of inflation, the local currency is a particularly poor store of value because the real value (purchasing power) of the local currency decreases at the rate of inflation. In high-inflation countries the dollar, which has had a relatively stable purchasing power, may be much more attractive than local currency as a means of holding wealth. Political instability in a country might also induce residents to demand U.S. dollars because, if political upheaval forces people to flee the country, carrying dollars out may be the easiest way for them to take some of their wealth with them. About half the U.S. currency sent overseas between 1988 and 1995 went to Europe, much of it to Russia and other nations of Eastern Europe, which in recent years have experienced substantial economic and political instability (see the Application "Money Growth and Inflation in European Countries in Transition," p. 264).

Because currency is more than one-half of M1 in the United States and more than half of all U.S. currency is held abroad, more than one-fourth of U.S. M1 is in fact held by foreign interests. Therefore events abroad that change the foreign demand for U.S. dollars can cause substantial changes in measured U.S. monetary aggregates. Since 1947, many of the months with the fastest growth in U.S. currency holdings were months in which a foreign crisis occurred. For example, U.S. currency growth was

---

*Most of the data in this box (except the months of most rapid currency growth) are reported in United States Treasury Department, *The Use and Counterfeiting of United States Currency Abroad, Part 3*, September 2006, available at *www.federalreserve.gov/boarddocs/rptcongress/counterfeit2006.pdf*.

rapid in the months after lraq invaded Kuwait in 1990. And several of the months with the fastest growth occurred in late 2008 and early 2009 during the worldwide financial crisis, where many foreigners traded their own currency for the safety of U.S. dollars.** These large increases in U.S. currency outstanding were driven by foreign concerns about political, military, and financial instability rather than by domestic factors determining money demand in the U.S. economy.

Although foreign holdings of U.S. dollars reduce the reliability of measured monetary aggregates as indicators of conditions in the U.S. economy, the United States gets an important benefit from the foreign holdings of its currency. U.S. currency is a liability of the Federal Reserve System and thus represents a loan to the Federal Reserve System (and ultimately to the U.S. government, to which most Federal Reserve profits go). However, currency pays no interest, so this loan being provided by foreign holders of U.S. currency to the United States is interest-free! The interest savings associated with this interest-free loan to the U.S. government amount to several billion dollars each year.

**The month with the highest (seasonally adjusted) currency growth rate was December 1999, when businesses and individuals sharply increased their demand for cash in preparation for the century rollover, Y2K.

One way—which is close to what happens in practice—is for the central bank to use newly minted currency to buy financial assets, such as government bonds, from the public. In making this swap, the public increases its holdings of money, and the amount of money in circulation rises. When the central bank uses money to purchase government bonds from the public, thus raising the money supply, it is said to have conducted an *open-market purchase.*

To reduce the money supply, the central bank can make this trade in reverse, selling government bonds that it holds to the public in exchange for currency. After the central bank removes this currency from circulation, the money supply is lower. When the central bank sells government bonds to the public to reduce the money supply, the transaction is an *open-market sale.* Open-market purchases and sales together are called **open-market operations.**

In addition to buying government bonds from the public, the central bank can also increase the money supply by buying newly issued government bonds directly from the government itself. For example, if a country's treasury needs $1 billion to pay for some new fighter planes, it might give an IOU for $1 billion (government bonds) to the central bank in exchange for $1 billion in newly minted currency. The treasury then gives the $1 billion of currency to the manufacturer of the fighter planes. After the treasury has distributed this currency, the amount of money in circulation—the money supply—will be higher by $1 billion. Effectively, this second way of increasing the money supply amounts to the government financing its expenditures by printing money.[2] This practice is most common in poor countries

---

[2]In Chapter 2 we said that the portion of government outlays not covered by taxes had to be borrowed from the private sector. Is this still true when the government has the option of paying for its outlays by printing money? Yes; for national income accounting purposes, the Federal Reserve is treated as part of the private sector. So when the Treasury sells government bonds to the Federal Reserve in exchange for currency, it is still technically borrowing from the private sector.

or in countries wracked by war or natural disaster, in which government spending often greatly exceeds the amount that can be raised through taxes.[3]

For the rest of this chapter we assume that the economy has a money supply of M dollars, which is determined by the central bank. The term M may represent M1, M2, or some other measure of money. For the purpose of developing the theoretical model, which measure of money M refers to doesn't matter.

7.2 Portfolio Allocation and the Demand for Assets

Our next goal is to understand how people determine the amount of money they choose to hold. We begin by considering the broader question of how people allocate their wealth among the many different assets that are available, of which money is only one example.

A consumer, a business, a pension fund, a university, or any other holder of wealth must decide how to distribute that wealth among many types of assets. The set of assets that a holder of wealth chooses to own is called a *portfolio*. The decision about which assets and how much of each asset to hold is called the **portfolio allocation decision.**

The portfolio allocation decision can be complex. Many people make their living by giving financial advice to holders of wealth, and a major branch of economics, called financial economics, is devoted largely to the study of the portfolio allocation decision. But, fundamentally, only four characteristics of assets matter for the portfolio allocation decision: expected return, risk, liquidity, and time to maturity.

Expected Return

The rate of return to an asset is the rate of increase in its value per unit of time. For example, the return on a bank account is the interest rate on the account. The return on a share of stock is the dividend paid by the stock plus any increase in the stock's price. Clearly, a high return is a desirable feature for an asset to have: All else being equal, the higher the return a wealth holder's portfolio provides, the more consumption she can enjoy in the future for any given amount of saving done today.

Of course, the return on an asset is not always known in advance. Stock prices may go up or down, for example. Thus holders of wealth must base their portfolio allocation decisions on **expected returns,** or their best guesses about returns on assets. Everything else being equal, the higher an asset's expected return (after subtracting taxes and fees such as brokers' commissions), the more desirable the asset is and the more of it holders of wealth will want to own.[4]

---

[3]The financing of government spending through money creation is discussed further in Chapter 15.

[4]For the purpose of comparing expected returns among assets, returns may be expressed in either real or nominal terms. For any expected rate of inflation, if asset A's nominal return is 1% higher than asset B's nominal return, asset A's expected real return (its nominal return minus expected inflation) will also be 1% higher than asset B's expected real return.

Risk

The uncertainty about the return an asset will earn relates to the second important characteristic of assets—riskiness. An asset or a portfolio of assets has high **risk** if there is a significant chance that the actual return received will be very different from the expected return. An example of a risky asset is a share in a start-up Internet company that will be worthless if the company fails but will grow in value by a factor of ten if the company succeeds. Because most people don't like risk, they hold risky assets only if the expected return is higher than that on relatively safe assets, such as government bonds.

Liquidity

Besides risk and return a third characteristic, liquidity, affects the desirability of assets. The **liquidity** of an asset is the ease and quickness with which it can be exchanged for goods, services, or other assets. Because it is accepted directly in payment, money is a highly liquid asset. An example of an illiquid asset is your automobile: Time and effort are required to exchange a used car for other goods and services; you must find someone interested in buying the car and arrange legal transfer of ownership. Between liquid money and illiquid autos are many assets, such as stocks and bonds, of intermediate liquidity. A share of stock, for example, can't be used directly to pay for groceries as cash can, but stock can be transformed into cash with a short delay and at the cost of a broker's fee.

In addition to making transactions easier and cheaper, liquidity provides flexibility to the holder of wealth. A liquid asset can easily be disposed of if there is an emergency need for funds or if an unexpectedly good financial investment opportunity arises. Thus, everything else being equal, the more liquid an asset is, the more attractive it will be to holders of wealth.

Time to Maturity

Financial securities have a fourth and final key characteristic, which is their time to maturity. **Time to maturity** is the amount of time until a financial security matures and the investor is repaid his or her principal. Considering time to maturity is especially relevant for all types of bonds, as an investor can purchase bonds that will mature at any time—in one day, one week, one month, one year, or thirty years.

Let's consider a couple that wants to buy bonds and keep their money invested for two years. They could choose one of two plans: Plan A is simply to buy a two-year bond today; Plan B calls for buying a one-year bond today and another one-year bond when that one matures one year from today. Ignoring, for the moment, any differences in the risk between Plan A and Plan B, the investors would choose the plan that they expect to give them the highest return over the two years. For example, if today's interest rate on the two-year bond is 7% per year, today's interest rate on a one-year bond is 5% per year, and if they expect the interest rate on a one-year bond to be 6% per year one year from now, then their return from Plan A (buying the two-year bond) is 7% per year and the return they expect from Plan B is 5.5% per year, which is the average of the 5% per year return on the one-year bond purchased today and the expected 6% per year return expected on the bond to be bought one year from today. So the investors are likely to choose Plan A; that is, they are likely to buy the two-year bond today.

The idea that investors compare the returns on bonds with differing times to maturity to see which is expected to give them the highest return underlies the **expectations theory of the term structure** of interest rates. "Term structure" refers to the fact that the theory explains why bonds that are similar in all respects except their terms to maturity have different rates of return. In equilibrium, according to the expectations theory, Plans A and B, which involve holding bonds with different terms to maturity over the same two-year period, should yield the same expected return; that is, the interest rate on a two-year bond should equal the average interest rate expected on two successive one-year bonds, so that an investor does not prefer one investment over another. More generally, the expected rate of return on an N-year bond should equal the average of the expected rates of return on one-year bonds during the current year and the $N-1$ succeeding years.

Although the expectations theory of the term structure of interest rates is a useful starting point, it cannot explain why, on average, we observe that the interest rates on long-term bonds generally exceed the interest rates on short-term bonds. (See the graph of the yield curve on p. 115, which illustrates the term structure of interest rates.) When short-term interest rates are expected to be higher in the future than the current short-term rate, the expectations theory predicts that the long-term interest rate will exceed the short-term interest rate. However, when short-term interest rates are expected to be lower in the future than the current short-term interest rate, the expectations theory predicts that the long-term interest rate will be lower than the short-term interest rate. To see why long-term interest rates usually exceed short-term interest rates, we need to take account of the fact that longer-term bonds are riskier than shorter-term bonds because the prices of long-term bonds are more sensitive than the prices of short-term bonds are to changes in the interest rate. Because investors do not like risk, they must be compensated for holding longer-term bonds. The result is a **term premium:** an interest rate on long-term bonds that is somewhat higher than the expectations theory would suggest.

If we add the term premium to the expectations theory, we have a more complete theory of how interest rates vary with time to maturity. For example, suppose the interest rate on a one-year bond today is 5% per year, the interest rate on a one-year bond one year from now is expected to be 6% per year, and the term premium on a two-year bond is 0.75% per year. Then, in equilibrium, the interest rate on a two-year bond should equal the average interest rate on the one-year bonds, which equals $(5\% + 6\%)/2 = 5.5\%$, plus the term premium, 0.75%, or 6.25%.

Types of Assets and Their Characteristics

What types of assets do people hold, and how do the characteristics of those assets differ? Though there are many different assets, we will consider a few that are the most popular: money, bonds, stocks, houses, and consumer durable goods.

We have already seen in section 7.1 that there are different types of money. All types of money usually have a low expected rate of return compared with other assets. Money also usually does not have much risk, although there is always some risk that inflation will be higher than expected, so that the real return to holding money might turn out to be lower than expected. But money is very liquid compared with the other assets; indeed, its liquidity is generally the defining characteristic of what we call money. Because of its liquidity, money's time to maturity is generally very short. However, some assets included in M2, such as small time deposits, may have a longer time to maturity and are not very liquid.

Bonds are financial securities that are sometimes called fixed-income securities because they promise to pay bondholders specific amounts on specific dates. People often choose to own bonds issued by the U.S. government because these bonds have very little risk of default. Bonds issued by corporations are similar, but there is always some chance that a corporation will go bankrupt and fail to pay the interest or repay the principal it owes to its bondholders. Thus bonds offer a higher expected return than money, but the return is riskier. Many bonds, especially those sold by the U.S. government, are very liquid, as an investor can easily sell his or her bond quickly and with low transactions costs. However, some corporate bonds are not very liquid, especially in bad economic times, and it may be difficult to sell them without a high cost. Bonds are issued in a variety of times to maturity, generally ranging from 3 months to 30 years.

Stocks represent ownership in a company. Most stocks pay periodic dividends to the shareholders, but the dividend payments are not guaranteed. When the economy is weak and the company is not doing well, it may even stop paying dividends altogether for a time. Prices of stocks rise and fall every day, so the overall return to a shareholder consists of the dividends received plus any capital gain resulting from an increase in the value of the stock less any capital loss resulting from a decrease in the value of the stock. Because dividends and, especially, stock prices can change unpredictably, stocks are subject to a substantial amount of risk. Stocks in large companies are sold in very liquid markets, but when you buy or sell a stock there is a delay of several days for the transaction to clear and payment to be made. Most stocks do not have maturity dates, so the time to maturity is infinite.

Although most large companies are owned by shareholders who can readily buy and sell shares of stock in organized stock exchanges, such as the New York Stock Exchange, many small businesses are directly owned by one or a few people. These businesses, which are directly owned by their proprietors, are not incorporated and do not issue stock that can be traded on exchanges. Because there are no marketable shares of stock in these companies, it is difficult for the owners to quickly sell ownership in the companies, so this ownership is very illiquid. Indeed, because there are no marketable shares, it is difficult to measure accurately the value of the ownership stake in these companies. The return to the owners of the company takes the form of profits earned by the company plus the opportunity that they may someday sell the company.

For most homeowners, housing is their largest asset. The returns to owning a house come in two forms: (1) the benefits to the household in terms of shelter net of maintenance costs and property taxes, and (2) the change in the value of the house (or the land it sits on) over time. For a time in the 2000s, many people seemed to think that there was no risk to investing in housing, and the United States and many other countries went through a tremendous boom in which millions of homes were built and it was very easy for home purchasers to get mortgage loans. But the risk turned out to be much higher than investors thought, and an unexpected downturn in housing prices led to a financial crisis, as we discuss in "In Touch with Data and Research: The Housing Crisis That Began in 2007," p. 249. Compared with other assets, housing is very illiquid—it may take months or years for a household to sell its home, especially in a recession. However, the availability of home equity loans and home equity lines of credit permit households to quickly borrow money against a portion of the value of their house. There is, of course, no specified time to maturity on housing, as it is not a financial security.

Households also hold some of their assets in the form of consumer durable goods, such as automobiles and furniture. As in the case of housing, durable goods provide services (such as transportation) over a period of time but may also require maintenance expenditures and can depreciate over time. There is some risk to the value of consumer durables, and it may be difficult and costly to sell them, as the market for used consumer durables is not as well developed as the market for stocks and bonds. Thus, consumer durables are not very liquid, and, like housing, have no specified time to maturity.

Households must determine what mix of these various assets is ideal for them. Wealthier households generally purchase more financial assets (stocks and bonds) as a percentage of their total wealth than poorer households. Many households will also put aside funds for retirement by holding assets in pension funds, which hold stocks, bonds, and types of money (such as money-market mutual funds). Of course, their mix of different assets may change when market conditions change. For example, the housing crisis that began in 2007 and the financial crisis of 2008 dramatically reduced the value of housing and stock holdings, as Table 7.2 indicates. The table shows the amounts of each type of asset that households (and nonprofit organizations) held at the end of 2006 and at the end of the first quarter of 2009. Note that the amount of currency and checkable deposits is far less than the amounts listed in Table 7.1 under M1 because much currency is held overseas (see "In Touch with Data and Research: Where Have All the Dollars Gone?", p. 242) and because business firms have substantial holdings of currency and checkable deposits. The table also reports how much of each type of asset households held as a percentage of their total assets, so you can get a sense of how the relative amounts of each type of asset changed between 2006 and 2009.

Table 7.2

Household Assets, 2006 and 2009

	Amounts in trillions of dollars		Percentages of total assets	
	2006-IV	2009-I	2006-IV	2009-I
Real estate	24.3	19.9	31.6	30.5
Consumer durables	4.3	4.6	5.6	7.0
Currency and checkable deposits	0.2	0.2	0.3	0.4
Time, savings, and other deposits	6.5	7.6	8.5	11.7
Bonds	4.2	5.2	5.5	8.0
Stocks	13.9	8.4	18.1	12.9
Proprietors' investment in unincorporated businesses	8.7	7.3	11.3	11.1
Pension funds	12.7	9.9	16.5	15.2
Other assets	2.0	2.2	2.6	3.3
Total Assets	76.7	65.2	100.0	100.0

Note: Numbers may not add to totals owing to rounding.
Source: Federal Reserve Flow of Funds Accounts of the United States, Statistical Release Z.1, June 11, 2009.

IN TOUCH WITH DATA AND RESEARCH

The Housing Crisis That Began in 2007

U.S. households gained a tremendous amount of wealth in their houses throughout the late 1990s and early 2000s. The housing market was booming and the home-ownership rate rose to a record level of 68.6 percent of households by 2007. But as people became more and more convinced that housing was a "can't miss" investment and housing prices spiraled ever upwards, mortgage lenders and homeowners began to make some serious mistakes, which would lead to a major financial crisis.

As housing prices moved higher and higher in the early 2000s, many people found themselves unable to afford to buy a home, because the monthly mortgage payments would have been too high relative to their monthly incomes. Specifically, the lending standards of mortgage lenders required that borrowers have sufficient monthly income so that the monthly mortgage payment would not exceed a specified percentage of monthly income. But as housing prices increased rapidly, mortgage lenders began making loans to people who did not meet the lending standards. These people were known as *subprime borrowers*. The subprime mortgage market grew rapidly. To compensate the lenders for the additional risk and potential costs of lending to subprime borrowers, the interest rate on subprime mortgages was higher than the interest rate on conventional or prime mortgages. In many cases, subprime lenders even dispensed with the usual income verification of borrowers, thereby further subjecting themselves to the risk that the borrowers would not be able to repay. In addition, some loans had creative features that gave the appearance that the borrower could afford to make the monthly payments—at least for a while. For instance, most subprime loans were adjustable-rate loans with a low initial interest rate that would increase after two or three years in a process known as *mortgage reset*.

Why were lenders willing to offer these risky loans to subprime borrowers, and why were borrowers willing to take on these risky obligations? To a large degree, the answer is that they expected house prices to continue to rise rapidly for the foreseeable future. As long as house prices kept rising substantially, a borrower who might otherwise have trouble making mortgage payments in the future could either sell the house for a profit and pay off the mortgage or could borrow against the house's equity value, which would be higher as house prices increased further. So, both borrowers and lenders thought they were insulated from risk.

The problem with subprime mortgages is that the borrower and lender are insulated from risk only as long as house prices continue to rise substantially. In 2005, as mortgage interest rates across the country began to rise, the rate of increase of house prices began to slow. In 2006, defaults on subprime mortgages began to increase, as borrowers who had counted on rapidly rising house prices to bail them out found that their houses were not worth as much as they expected. In addition, as mortgage resets began to set in at higher interest rates, more and more borrowers could no longer make their monthly mortgage payments and began to default on their mortgages. And as defaults began to occur in increasing numbers, banks started to tighten their lending standards, so that by mid 2007, they were making few if any subprime mortgage loans. But that, in turn, reduced the demand for houses, thus causing the increase in housing prices to be even smaller. House prices even

(continued)

Figure 7.1

Increase in home prices from one year earlier, 1976–2009
The chart shows quarterly data on the percent increase in home prices from one year earlier, averaged across the United States, from the first quarter of 1976 to the first quarter of 2009. The appreciation in home prices averaged 5.4% per year over the entire period but exceeded 10% per year from early 2004 to early 2006. In 2007, the growth rate of home prices fell sharply, and in 2008, home prices began to decline, causing a crisis in mortgage markets.

Source: Federal Housing Finance Agency, *www.fhfa.gov.*

began to decline in some areas of the country in 2007 and by 2008 began to fall for the nation as a whole, as shown in Fig. 7.1.

Falling house prices caused a variety of problems, at both the micro level and macro level. Thousands of households that had bought houses with subprime mortgages lost their homes through foreclosure when they could not make their mortgage payments. Homeowners often found themselves owning homes whose value had fallen far below the amount they owed on their mortgage loans (a situation that came to be known as "underwater"), giving them the incentive to stop making mortgage payments and allow their homes to be repossessed. Financial institutions lost billions of dollars on such deals because they owned the rights to the mortgage payments, which would no longer occur. Since house prices had fallen, whoever came to own the house, usually a bank, would usually have to sell it for much less than the outstanding mortgage balance.

But what surprised many people about the problems in the mortgage market is that the impact was felt even more broadly. It turns out that most banks had sold bundles of their mortgages in the form of mortgage-backed securities (MBSs), and investors in MBSs suffered large losses. Once the losses began to materialize, investors all at once tried to bail out of such investments, driving their prices to very low levels. This, in turn, led to the financial crisis of 2008, when investors began to realize that many financial institutions had lost hundreds of billions of dollars through mortgage-related securities. Panic ensued, stock prices fell dramatically, especially for financial firms, and the government and Federal Reserve bailed out many financial firms, as we describe in more detail in the Application "The Financial Crisis of 2008," p. 551.

At the end of 2006, households had over $76 trillion in assets, with over $24 trillion worth of real estate and almost $13.9 trillion in stocks, as well as almost $13 trillion in pension fund assets. The steep declines in house prices and stock prices and the drop in proprietors' investment in unincorporated businesses reduced household wealth by more than $10 trillion. The value of real estate holdings declined by 18 percent, pension assets fell 22 percent, and the value of stock holdings fell almost 40 percent from the end of 2006 to early 2009. Over this period of time, households reallocated their portfolios, putting more of their wealth in the form of money (time and savings deposits) and bonds (especially government bonds with little default risk).

Asset Demands

Typically, there is a trade-off among the four characteristics that make an asset desirable: a high expected return, safety (low risk), liquidity, and time to maturity. For example, a safe and liquid asset with a short time to maturity, such as a checking account, is likely to have a low expected return. The essence of the portfolio allocation decision is determining which assets, taken together, achieve the wealth holder's preferred combination of expected return, safety, liquidity, and time to maturity. In addition to the risk of each asset separately, the investor should also consider **diversification,** the idea that spreading out his or her investment in different assets can reduce his or her overall risk, because when one asset has a low return, another may have a high return.

The amount of each particular asset that a holder of wealth desires to include in his or her portfolio is called his or her demand for that asset. Because all wealth must be held as some type of asset, the sum of a wealth holder's asset demands must equal his or her total wealth. For example, suppose that you have wealth of $10,000 and decide to hold $5000 in stock, $3000 in short-term bonds, $1000 in long-term bonds, and $1000 in cash. The sum of your four asset demands must equal your total wealth of $10,000.

7.3 The Demand for Money

The **demand for money** is the quantity of monetary assets, such as cash and checking accounts, that people choose to hold in their portfolios. Choosing how much money to demand is thus a part of the broader portfolio allocation decision. In general, the demand for money—like the demand for any other asset—will depend on the expected return, risk, liquidity, and time to maturity of money and other assets.

In practice, two features of money are particularly important. First, money is the most liquid asset. This liquidity is the primary benefit of holding money.[5] Second, money pays a low return (indeed, currency pays a zero nominal return). The low return earned by money, relative to other assets, is the major cost of holding money. People's demand for money is determined by how they trade off their desire for liquidity against the cost of a lower return.

---

[5]Money also has low risk, but many alternative assets (such as short-term government bonds) are not much riskier than money and pay a higher return.

In this section we look at how some key macroeconomic variables affect the demand for money. Although we primarily consider the aggregate, or total, demand for money, the same economic arguments apply to individual money demands. This relationship is to be expected, as the aggregate demand for money is the sum of all individual money demands.

The macroeconomic variables that have the greatest effects on money demand are the price level, real income, and interest rates. Higher prices or incomes increase people's need for liquidity and thus raise the demand for money. Interest rates affect money demand through the expected return channel: The higher the interest rate on money, the more money people will demand; however, the higher the interest rate paid on alternative assets to money, the more people will want to switch from money to those alternative assets.

The Price Level

The higher the general level of prices, the more dollars people need to conduct transactions and thus the more dollars people will want to hold. For example, seventy years ago the price level in the United States was about one-tenth of its level today; as your grandfather will tell you, in 1940 a good restaurant meal cost a dollar. Because less money was needed for transactions, the number of dollars your grandfather held in the form of currency or checking accounts—his nominal demand for money—was probably much smaller than the amount of money you hold today. The general conclusion is that a higher price level, by raising the need for liquidity, increases the nominal demand for money. In fact, because prices are ten times higher today than they were in 1940, an identical transaction takes ten times as many dollars today as it did back then. Thus, everything else being equal, the nominal demand for money is *proportional* to the price level.

Real Income

The more transactions that individuals or businesses conduct, the more liquidity they need and the greater is their demand for money. An important factor determining the number of transactions is real income. For example, a large, high-volume supermarket has to deal with a larger number of customers and suppliers and pay more employees than does a corner grocery. Similarly, a high-income individual makes more and larger purchases than a low-income individual. Because higher real income means more transactions and a greater need for liquidity, the amount of money demanded should increase when real income increases.

Unlike the response of money demand to changes in the price level, the increase in money demand need not be proportional to an increase in real income. Actually, a 1% increase in real income usually leads to less than a 1% increase in money demand. One reason that money demand grows more slowly than income is that higher-income individuals and firms typically use their money more efficiently. For example, a high-income individual may open a special cash management account in which money not needed for current transactions is automatically invested in nonmonetary assets paying a higher return. Because of minimum-balance requirements and fees, such an account might not be worthwhile for a lower-income individual.

Another reason that money demand grows more slowly than income is that a nation's financial sophistication tends to increase as national income grows. In poor countries people may hold much of their saving in the form of money, for lack of anything better; in richer countries people have many attractive alternatives to money. Money substitutes such as credit cards also become more common as a country becomes richer, again causing aggregate money demand to grow more slowly than income.

Interest Rates

The theory of portfolio allocation implies that, with risk and liquidity held constant, the demand for money depends on the expected returns of both money and alternative, nonmonetary assets. An increase in the expected return on money increases the demand for money, and an increase in the expected return on alternative assets causes holders of wealth to switch from money to higher-return alternatives, thus lowering the demand for money.

For example, suppose that, of your total wealth of $10,000, you have $8000 in government bonds earning 8% interest and $2000 in an interest-bearing checking account earning 3%. You are willing to hold the checking account at a lower return because of the liquidity it provides. But if the interest rate on bonds rises to 10%, and the checking account interest rate remains unchanged, you may decide to switch $1000 from the checking account into bonds. In making this switch, you reduce your holding of money (your money demand) from $2000 to $1000. Effectively, you have chosen to trade some liquidity for the higher return offered by bonds.

Similarly, if the interest rate paid on money rises, holders of wealth will choose to hold more money. In the example, if the checking account begins paying 5% instead of 3%, with bonds still at 8%, you may sell $1000 of your bonds, lowering your holdings of bonds to $7000 and increasing your checking account to $3000. The sacrifice in return associated with holding money is less than before, so you increase your checking account balance and enjoy the flexibility and other benefits of extra liquidity. Thus a higher interest rate on money makes the demand for money rise.

In principle, the interest rate on each of the many alternatives to money should affect money demand. However, as previously noted (see "In Touch with Data and Research: Interest Rates," p. 114), the many interest rates in the economy generally tend to move up and down together. For the purposes of macroeconomic analysis, therefore, assuming that there is just one nominal interest rate, i, which measures the nominal return on nonmonetary assets, is simpler and not too misleading. The nominal interest rate, i, minus the expected inflation rate, π^e, gives the expected real interest rate, r, that is relevant to saving and investment decisions, as discussed in Chapter 4.

Also, in reality, various interest rates are paid on money. For example, currency pays zero interest, but different types of checkable accounts pay varying rates. Again for simplicity, let's assume that there is just one nominal interest rate for money, i^m. The key conclusions are that an increase in the interest rate on nonmonetary assets, i, reduces the amount of money demanded and that an increase in the interest rate on money, i^m, raises the amount of money demanded.

The Money Demand Function

We express the effects of the price level, real income, and interest rates on money demand as

$$M^d = P \times L(Y, i), \tag{7.1}$$

where

M^d = the aggregate demand for money, in nominal terms;
P = the price level;
Y = real income or output;
i = the nominal interest rate earned by alternative, nonmonetary assets;
L = a function relating money demand to real income and the nominal interest rate.

Equation (7.1) holds that nominal money demand, M^d, is proportional to the price level, P. Hence, if the price level, P, doubles (and real income and interest rates don't change), nominal money demand, M^d, also will double, reflecting the fact that twice as much money is needed to conduct the same real transactions. Equation (7.1) also indicates that, for any price level, P, money demand depends (through the function L) on real income, Y, and the nominal interest rate on nonmonetary assets, i. An increase in real income, Y, raises the demand for liquidity and thus increases money demand. An increase in the nominal interest rate, i, makes nonmonetary assets more attractive, which reduces money demand.

We could have included the nominal interest rate on money, i^m, in Eq. (7.1) because an increase in the interest rate on money makes people more willing to hold money and thus increases money demand. Historically, however, the nominal interest rate on money has varied much less than the nominal interest rate on nonmonetary assets (for example, currency and a portion of checking accounts always have paid zero interest) and thus has been ignored by many statistical studies of Eq. (7.1). Thus for simplicity we do not explicitly include i^m in the equation.

An equivalent way of writing the demand for money expresses the nominal interest rate, i, in terms of the expected real interest rate and the expected rate of inflation. Recall from Eq. (2.13) that the expected real interest rate, r, equals the nominal interest rate, i, minus the expected rate of inflation, π^e. Therefore the nominal interest rate, i, equals $r + \pi^e$. Substituting $r + \pi^e$ for i in Eq. (7.1) yields

$$M^d = P \times L(Y, r + \pi^e). \tag{7.2}$$

Equation (7.2) shows that, for any expected rate of inflation, π^e, an increase in the real interest rate increases the nominal interest rate and reduces the demand for money. Similarly, for any real interest rate, an increase in the expected rate of inflation increases the nominal interest rate and reduces the demand for money.

Nominal money demand, M^d, measures the demand for money in terms of dollars (or yen or euros). But, sometimes, measuring money demand in real terms is more convenient. If we divide both sides of Eq. (7.2) by the price level, P, we get

$$\frac{M^d}{P} = L(Y, r + \pi^e). \tag{7.3}$$

The expression on the left side of Eq. (7.3), M^d/P, is called real money demand or, sometimes, the demand for **real balances.** Real money demand is the amount of money demanded in terms of the goods it can buy. Equation (7.3) states that real money demand, M^d/P, depends on real income (or output), Y, and on the nominal interest rate, which is the sum of the real interest rate, r, and expected inflation, π^e. The function L that relates real money demand to output and interest rates in Eq. (7.3) is called the **money demand function.**

Other Factors Affecting Money Demand

The money demand function in Eq. (7.3) captures the main macroeconomic determinants of money demand, but some other factors should be mentioned. Besides the nominal interest rate on money, which we have already discussed, additional factors influencing money demand include wealth, risk, liquidity of alternative assets, and payment technologies. Summary table 9 contains a comprehensive list of variables that affect the demand for money.

Wealth.   When wealth increases, part of the extra wealth may be held as money, increasing total money demand. However, with income and the level of transactions held constant, a holder of wealth has little incentive to keep extra wealth in money rather than in higher-return alternative assets. Thus the effect of an increase in wealth on money demand is likely to be small.

Risk.   Money usually pays a fixed nominal interest rate (zero in the case of cash), so holding money itself usually isn't risky. However, if the risk of alternative assets such as stocks and real estate increases greatly, people may demand safer assets, including money. Thus increased riskiness in the economy may increase money demand.[6]

SUMMARY 9

Macroeconomic Determinants of the Demand for Money

An increase in	Causes money demand to	Reason
Price level, P	Rise proportionally	A doubling of the price level doubles the number of dollars needed for transactions.
Real income, Y	Rise less than proportionally	Higher real income implies more transactions and thus a greater demand for liquidity.
Real interest rate, r	Fall	Higher real interest rate means a higher return on alternative assets and thus a switch away from money.
Expected inflation, π^e	Fall	Higher expected inflation means a lower real return on money and thus a switch away from money.
Nominal interest rate on money, i^m	Rise	Higher return on money makes people more willing to hold money.
Wealth	Rise	Part of an increase in wealth may be held in the form of money.
Risk	Rise, if risk of alternative asset increases	Higher risk of alternative asset makes money more attractive.
	Fall, if risk of money increases	Higher risk of money makes it less attractive.
Liquidity of alternative assets	Fall	Higher liquidity of alternative assets makes these assets more attractive.
Efficiency of payments technologies	Fall	People can operate with less money.

[6]For some evidence that this effect occurred in the early 1980s, see James M. McGibany and Farrokh Nourzad, "Interest Rate Volatility and the Demand for Money," *Quarterly Review of Economics and Business*, Autumn 1986, pp. 73–83.

However, money doesn't always carry a low risk. In a period of erratic inflation, even if the nominal return on money is fixed, the real return on money (the nominal return minus inflation) may become quite uncertain, making money risky. Money demand then will fall as people switch to inflation hedges (assets whose real returns are less likely to be affected by erratic inflation) such as gold, consumer durable goods, and real estate.

Liquidity of Alternative Assets. The more quickly and easily alternative assets can be converted into cash, the less need there is to hold money. In recent years the joint impact of deregulation, competition, and innovation in financial markets has made alternatives to money more liquid. For example, with a home equity line of credit, a family can now write checks that are backed by the value of its home. We have mentioned individual cash management accounts whose introduction allowed individuals to switch wealth easily between high-return assets, such as stocks, and more liquid forms. As alternative assets become more liquid, the demand for money declines.

Payment Technologies. Money demand also is affected by the technologies available for making and receiving payments. For example, the introduction of credit cards allowed people to make transactions without money—at least until the end of the month, when a check must be written to pay the credit card bill. Automatic teller machines (ATMs) probably have reduced the demand for cash because people know that they can obtain cash quickly whenever they need it. In the mid 2000s, check clearing became very efficient, thanks to the Check 21 law, which allowed for electronic clearing of images of checks. This process greatly reduces the costs of clearing checks and allows them to clear much more quickly than before. In the future more innovations in payment technologies undoubtedly will help people operate with less and less cash.[7] Some experts even predict that ultimately we will live in a "cashless society," in which almost all payments will be made through immediately accessible computerized accounting systems and that the demand for cash will be close to zero.

Elasticities of Money Demand. The theory of portfolio allocation helps economists identify factors that should affect the aggregate demand for money. However, for many purposes—such as forecasting and quantitative analyses of the economy—economists need to know not just which factors affect money demand but also how strong the various effects are. This information can be obtained only through statistical analysis of the data.

Over the past three decades, economists have performed hundreds of statistical studies of the money demand function. The results of these studies often are expressed in terms of elasticities, which measure the change in money demand resulting from changes in factors affecting the demand for money. Specifically, the **income elasticity of money demand** is the percentage change in money demand resulting from a 1% increase in real income. Thus, for example, if the income elasticity of money demand is 2/3, a 3% increase in real income will increase money

---

[7]In 2003, the number of electronic payments exceeded the number of check payments in the United States for the first time. The pace of change is accelerating, as just three years later, the number of electronic payments was twice the number of check payments. For more, see Geoffrey R. Gerdes, "Recent Payment Trends in the United States," *Federal Reserve Bulletin*, October 2008, pp. A75–A106.

demand by 2% (2/3 × 3% = 2%). Similarly, the **interest elasticity of money demand** is the percentage change in money demand resulting from a 1% increase in the interest rate.

When we work with the interest elasticity of money demand, some care is needed to avoid a potential pitfall. To illustrate, suppose that the interest rate increases from 5% per year to 6% per year. To describe this increase in the interest rate as a 1% increase in the interest rate is tempting (but incorrect). In fact, it is a 20% increase in the interest rate, because 6 is 20% larger than 5.[8] If the interest elasticity of money demand is −0.1, for example, an increase in the interest rate from 5% to 6% reduces money demand by 2% (−0.1 × 20% = −2%). Note that, if the interest elasticity of money demand is negative, as in this example, an increase in the interest rate reduces money demand.

What are the actual values of the income elasticity and interest elasticity of money demand? Although the many statistical studies of money demand provide a range of answers, some common results emerge. First, there is widespread agreement that the income elasticity of money demand is positive. For example, in his classic 1973 study of M1 money demand, which established the framework for many later studies, Stephen Goldfeld of Princeton University found this elasticity to be about 2/3.[9] A positive income elasticity of money demand implies that money demand rises when income rises, as predicted by our theory. Goldfeld's finding that the income elasticity of money demand is less than 1.0 is similar to that of many other empirical analyses, although some studies have found values for this elasticity as large as 1.0. An income elasticity of money demand smaller than 1.0 implies that money demand rises less than proportionally with income. Earlier in the chapter we discussed some reasons why, as an individual or nation has higher income, the demand for money might be expected to grow more slowly than income.

Second, for the interest elasticity of money demand, most studies find a small negative value. For example, Goldfeld found the interest elasticity of money demand to be about −0.1 or −0.2. A negative value for the interest elasticity of money demand implies that when interest rates on nonmonetary assets rise, people reduce their holdings of money, again as predicted by the theory.

Finally, Goldfeld's study and others have confirmed empirically that the nominal demand for money is proportional to the price level. Again, this result is consistent with the theory, as reflected in the money demand equation, Eq. (7.3).

Velocity and the Quantity Theory of Money

A concept related to money demand, which at times is used in discussions of monetary policy, is velocity. It measures how often the money stock "turns over" each period. Specifically, **velocity** is nominal GDP (the price level, P, times real output, Y) divided by the nominal money stock, M. If we let V represent velocity,

$$V = \frac{nominal\ GDP}{nominal\ money\ stock} = \frac{PY}{M}. \tag{7.4}$$

---

[8]The change from 5% to 6% can be described as "a one *percentage point* increase" or as "a twenty *percent* increase."

[9]"The Demand for Money Revisited," *Brookings Papers on Economic Activity,* 1973:4, pp. 577–638. Goldfeld reported elasticities of money demand that applied to the short run and the long run. The figures we present here are long-run elasticities.

Figure 7.2

Velocity of M1 and M2, 1959–2009

M1 velocity is nominal GDP divided by M1, and M2 velocity is nominal GDP divided by M2. M1 velocity moved steadily upward until about 1981, but in the early 1980s M1 velocity fell and it has behaved erratically since then. M2 velocity has no clear trend and is more stable than M1 velocity, but it has been unpredictable over some short periods.

Source: FRED database of the Federal Reserve Bank of St. Louis, *research.stlouisfed.org/ fred2*, series M1SL, M2SL, and GDP.

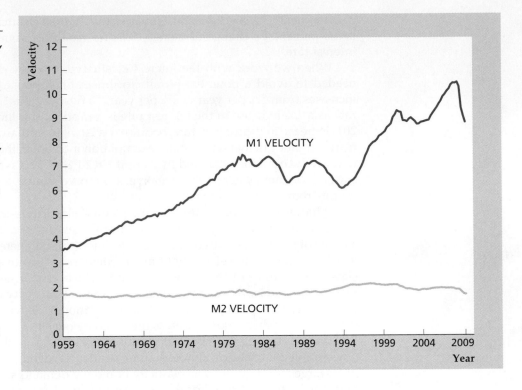

If velocity rises, each dollar of the money stock is being used in a greater dollar volume of transactions in each period, if we assume that the volume of transactions is proportional to GDP. Figure 7.2 shows the M1 and M2 velocities for the United States from 1959 through the second quarter of 2009.

The concept of velocity comes from one of the earliest theories of money demand, the quantity theory of money.[10] The **quantity theory of money** asserts that real money demand is proportional to real income, or

$$\frac{M^d}{P} = kY, \tag{7.5}$$

where M^d/P is real money demand, Y is real income, and k is a constant. In Eq. (7.5) the real money demand function, $L(Y, r + \pi^e)$, takes the simple form kY. This way of writing money demand is based on the strong assumption that velocity is a constant, $1/k$, and doesn't depend on income or interest rates.[11]

But is velocity actually constant? As Fig. 7.2 shows, M1 velocity clearly is not constant: M1 velocity rose steadily until about 1981, fell sharply in the early 1980s, and has behaved erratically since then. Financial innovations and foreign demand for dollars affected velocity at various times since the early 1980s. In the early 1980s, the introduction of interest-bearing checking accounts led to an increase in M1 demand at any level of GDP and thus a decline in velocity. Later in the decade, low interest

---

[10]The quantity theory of money was developed by several classical economists, notably Irving Fisher, in the late nineteenth and early twentieth centuries. A famous statement of the theory is contained in Fisher's book, *The Purchasing Power of Money* (New York: Macmillan, 1911).

[11]To derive velocity under the quantity theory, we must assume that nominal money demand, M^d, equals the actual money stock, M, an assumption that we justify later in the chapter. Under this assumption, you should verify that $V = 1/k$.

rates on nonmonetary assets raised the demand for M1 at any level of GDP and thus reduced M1 velocity. In the early 1990s, the breakup of the Soviet Union led to increased demand for U.S. dollars by foreigners, increasing M1 demand and reducing velocity. In the mid-1990s, banks developed accounts that were designed to reduce deposits held in transactions accounts (by transferring funds from checking accounts to savings accounts overnight), to reduce the reserves they were required to hold; this reduction in deposits had the effect of reducing M1 at any given level of GDP, thus increasing M1 velocity. More recently, M1 velocity fell sharply during the financial crisis of 2008, both because households increased their holdings of money and because GDP fell during the recession that began in December 2007.

M2 velocity, also shown in Fig. 7.2, is closer to being constant. It shows no upward or downward trend and doesn't exhibit the instability of M1 velocity. However, even M2 velocity has been somewhat unpredictable over short periods and most economists would be reluctant to treat M2 velocity as constant. Throughout the 1990s, people began investing their savings in a broader variety of financial assets than they had before, pulling funds out of bank accounts (which are included in M2) and investing in bonds and stocks (which are not in M2). As a result, demand for M2 at any level of GDP was reduced, raising M2 velocity. Further, when the housing market was booming from the late 1990s to the mid-2000s, funds from refinancing of mortgages were temporarily parked in M2 accounts, leading to increased M2 growth and lower velocity.

Figure 7.3 shows how M1 and M2 growth changed from 1960 to 2009. The graph shows how the instability in velocity is related to fluctuations in the growth rates of the monetary aggregates. Of course, these growth rates also reflect changes in the supply of money, not just demand, but you can see specific episodes, such as the increase in M1 demand in the early 1990s, caused by the surge in foreign demand for U.S. currency.

Figure 7.3

Growth rates of M1 and M2, 1960–2009
The growth rates of M1 and M2 plotted here show the percentage increase in both of the monetary aggregates from their levels one year earlier, using quarterly data. Growth of both M1 and M2 has fluctuated considerably because of financial innovations and foreign demand for currency.

Source: FRED database of the Federal Reserve Bank of St. Louis, *research.stlouisfed.org/ fred2*, series M1SL and M2SL.

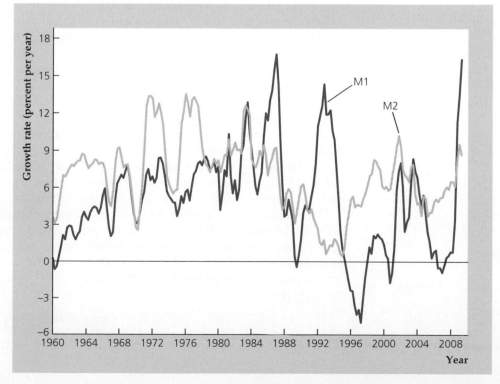

7.4 Asset Market Equilibrium

Recall that the asset market actually is a set of markets, in which real and financial assets are traded. The demand for any asset (say, government bonds) is the quantity of the asset that holders of wealth want in their portfolios. The demand for each asset depends on its expected return, risk, liquidity, and time to maturity relative to other assets. The supply of each asset is the quantity of that asset that is available. At any particular time the supplies of individual assets are typically fixed, although over time asset supplies change (the government may issue more bonds, firms may issue new shares, more gold may be mined, and so on).

The asset market is in equilibrium when the quantity of each asset that holders of wealth demand equals the (fixed) available supply of that asset. In this section we examine asset market equilibrium, focusing on the role of money. We then show how asset market equilibrium is linked to the price level.

Asset Market Equilibrium: An Aggregation Assumption

In analyzing the labor market in Chapter 3 and the goods market in Chapter 4, we relied on aggregation to keep things manageable. That is, instead of looking at the supply and demand for each of the many different types of labor and goods in the economy, we studied the supply and demand for both labor and goods in general. Aggregating in this way allowed us to analyze the behavior of the economy as a whole without getting lost in the details.

Because there are many different types of assets, aggregation is equally necessary for studying the asset market. Thus we adopt an aggregation assumption for the asset market that economists often make for macroeconomic analysis: We assume that all assets may be grouped into two categories, money and nonmonetary assets. Money includes assets that can be used in payment, such as currency and checking accounts. All money is assumed to have the same risk and liquidity and to pay the same nominal interest rate, i^m. The fixed nominal supply of money is M. Nonmonetary assets include all assets other than money, such as stocks, bonds, land, and so on. All nonmonetary assets are assumed to have the same risk and liquidity and to pay a nominal interest rate of $i = r + \pi^e$, where r is the expected real interest rate and π^e is the expected rate of inflation. The fixed nominal supply of nonmonetary assets is NM.

Although the assumption that assets can be aggregated into two types ignores many interesting differences among assets, it greatly simplifies our analysis and has proved to be very useful. One immediate benefit of making this assumption is that, if we allow for only two types of assets, *asset market equilibrium reduces to the condition that the quantity of money supplied equals the quantity of money demanded.*

To demonstrate this point, let's look at the portfolio allocation decision of an individual named Ed. Ed has a fixed amount of wealth that he allocates between money and nonmonetary assets. If m^d is the nominal amount of money and nm^d is the nominal amount of nonmonetary assets that Ed wants to hold, the sum of Ed's desired money holdings and his desired holdings of nonmonetary assets must be his total wealth, or

$$m^d + nm^d = \text{Ed's total nominal wealth.}$$

This equation has to be true for every holder of wealth in the economy.

Suppose that we sum this equation across all holders of wealth in the economy. Then the sum of all individual money demands, m^d, equals the aggregate demand for money, M^d. The sum of all individual demands for nonmonetary assets is the aggregate demand for nonmonetary assets, NM^d. Finally, adding nominal wealth for all holders of wealth gives the aggregate nominal wealth of the economy, or

$$M^d + NM^d = \text{aggregate nominal wealth.} \tag{7.6}$$

Equation (7.6) states that the total demand for money in the economy plus the total demand for nonmonetary assets must equal the economy's total nominal wealth.

Next, we relate the total supplies of money and nonmonetary assets to aggregate wealth. Because money and nonmonetary assets are the only assets in the economy, aggregate nominal wealth equals the supply of money, M, plus the supply of nonmonetary assets, NM, or

$$M + NM = \text{aggregate nominal wealth.} \tag{7.7}$$

Finally, we subtract Eq. (7.7) from Eq. (7.6) to obtain

$$(M^d - M) + (NM^d - NM) = 0. \tag{7.8}$$

The term $M^d - M$ in Eq. (7.8) is the *excess demand for money,* or the amount by which the total amount of money demanded exceeds the money supply. Similarly, the term $NM^d - NM$ in Eq. (7.8) is the *excess demand for nonmonetary assets.*

Now suppose that the demand for money, M^d, equals the money supply, M, so that the excess demand for money, $M^d - M$, is zero. Equation (7.8) shows that, if $M^d - M$ is zero, $NM^d - NM$ must also be zero; that is, if the amounts of money supplied and demanded are equal, the amounts of nonmonetary assets supplied and demanded also must be equal. By definition, if quantities supplied and demanded are equal for each type of asset, the asset market is in equilibrium.

If we make the simplifying assumption that assets can be lumped into monetary and nonmonetary categories, the asset market is in equilibrium if the quantity of money supplied equals the quantity of money demanded. This result is convenient, because it means that in studying asset market equilibrium we have to look at only the supply and demand for money and can ignore nonmonetary assets. As long as the amounts of money supplied and demanded are equal, the entire asset market will be in equilibrium.

The Asset Market Equilibrium Condition

Equilibrium in the asset market occurs when the quantity of money supplied equals the quantity of money demanded. This condition is valid whether money supply and demand are expressed in nominal terms or real terms. We work with this condition in real terms, or

$$\frac{M}{P} = L(Y, r + \pi^e). \tag{7.9}$$

The left side of Eq. (7.9) is the nominal supply of money, M, divided by the price level, P, which is the supply of money measured in real terms. The right side of the equation is the same as the real demand for money, M^d/P, as in Eq. (7.3). Equation (7.9), which states that the real quantity of money supplied equals the real quantity of money demanded, is called the asset market equilibrium condition.

The *asset market equilibrium condition* involves five variables: the nominal money supply, M; the price level, P; real income, Y; the real interest rate, r; and the expected rate of inflation, π^e. The nominal money supply, M, is determined by the central bank through its open-market operations. For now, we treat the expected rate of inflation, π^e, as fixed (we return to the determination of expected inflation later in the chapter). That leaves three variables in the asset market equilibrium condition whose values we haven't yet specified: output, Y; the real interest rate, r; and the price level, P.

In this part of the book we have made the assumption that the economy is at full employment or, equivalently, that all markets are in equilibrium. Both classical and Keynesian economists agree that the full-employment assumption is reasonable for analyzing the long-term behavior of the economy. If we continue to assume full employment,[12] we can use the analysis from previous chapters to describe how output and the real interest rate are determined. Recall from Chapter 3 that, if the labor market is in equilibrium—with employment at its full-employment level—output equals full-employment output, $\overline{Y}$. In Chapter 4 we showed that, for any level of output, the real interest rate in a closed economy must take the value that makes desired national saving and desired investment equal (the goods market equilibrium condition).

With the values of output and the real interest rate established by equilibrium in the labor and goods markets, the only variable left to be determined by the asset market equilibrium condition is the price level, P. To emphasize that the price level is the variable determined by asset market equilibrium, we multiply both sides of Eq. (7.9) by P and divide both sides by real money demand, $L(Y, r + \pi^e)$, to obtain

$$P = \frac{M}{L(Y, r + \pi^e)}. \tag{7.10}$$

According to Eq. (7.10), the economy's price level, P, equals the ratio of the nominal money supply, M, to the real demand for money, $L(Y, r + \pi^e)$. For given values of real output, Y, the real interest rate, r, and the expected rate of inflation, π^e, the real demand for money, $L(Y, r + \pi^e)$, is fixed. Thus Eq. (7.10) states that the price level is proportional to the nominal money supply. A doubling of the nominal money supply, M, for instance, would double the price level, P, with other factors held constant. The existence of a close link between the price level and the money supply in an economy is one of the oldest and most reliable conclusions about macroeconomic behavior, having been recognized in some form for hundreds if not thousands of years. We discuss the empirical support for this link in Section 7.5.

What forces lead the price level to its equilibrium value, Eq. (7.10)? A complete description of how the price level adjusts to its equilibrium value involves an analysis of the goods market as well as the asset market; we leave this task until Chapter 9, where we discuss the links among the three main markets of the economy in more detail. Briefly, in Chapter 9 we show that an increase in the money supply leads people to increase their nominal spending on goods and services; this increased nominal demand for output leads prices to rise. Prices continue to rise until people are content to hold the increased nominal quantity of money in their portfolios, satisfying the asset market equilibrium condition (rewritten as Eq. 7.10).

---

[12]We relax this assumption in Part 3 when we discuss short-run economic fluctuations.

7.5 Money Growth and Inflation

In Section 7.4 we established that, when the markets for labor, goods, and assets are all in equilibrium, the price level, P, is proportional to the nominal money supply, M. However, the price level itself generally is of less concern to policy-makers and the public than is the rate of inflation, or the percentage rate of increase of the price level. In this section we extend our analysis of the price level to show how inflation is determined. We conclude that the inflation rate, which is the growth rate of the price level, is closely related to the growth rate of the nominal money supply.

To obtain an equation for the rate of inflation, we set the growth rate of the left side of Eq. (7.10) equal to the growth rate of its right side to obtain

$$\frac{\Delta P}{P} = \frac{\Delta M}{M} - \frac{\Delta L(Y, r + \pi^e)}{L(Y, r + \pi^e)}, \tag{7.11}$$

where the symbol Δ indicates the change in a variable from one year to the next. The left side of Eq. (7.11) is the growth rate of the price level, $\Delta P/P$, which is the same as the inflation rate, π. The right side of Eq. (7.11) expresses the growth rate of the ratio on the right side of Eq. (7.10) as the growth rate of the numerator, M, minus the growth rate of the denominator, $L(Y, r + \pi^e)$. (In Appendix A, Section A.7, we provide some useful formulas for calculating growth rates.) Equation (7.11) shows that, if the asset market is in equilibrium, *the rate of inflation equals the growth rate of the nominal money supply minus the growth rate of real money demand.*

Equation (7.11) highlights the point that the rate of inflation is closely related to the rate of growth of the nominal money supply. However, to use Eq. (7.11) to predict the behavior of inflation we must also know how quickly real money demand is growing. The money demand function, Eq. (7.3), focused on two macroeconomic variables with significant effects on real money demand: income (or output), Y, and the nominal interest rate, $r + \pi^e$. We show later in this section that, in a long-run equilibrium with a constant growth rate of money, the nominal interest rate will be constant. Therefore here we look only at growth in income as a source of growth in real money demand.

Earlier we defined the income elasticity of money demand to be the percentage change in money demand resulting from a 1% increase in real income. If $\Delta Y/Y$ is the percentage change in real income from one year to the next and η_Y is the income elasticity of money demand, $\eta_Y \Delta Y/Y$ is the resulting increase in the real demand for money, with other factors affecting money demand held constant. Substituting π for $\Delta P/P$ and $\eta_Y \Delta Y/Y$ for the growth rate of real money demand in Eq. (7.11) yields

$$\pi = \frac{\Delta M}{M} - \eta_Y \frac{\Delta Y}{Y}. \tag{7.12}$$

Equation (7.12) is a useful simple expression for the rate of inflation. According to Eq. (7.12), the rate of inflation equals the growth rate of the nominal money supply minus an adjustment for the growth rate of real money demand arising from growth in real output. For example, suppose that nominal money supply growth is 10% per year, real income is growing by 3% per year, and the income elasticity of money demand is 2/3. Then Eq. (7.12) predicts that the inflation rate will be 10% − (2/3)(3%), or 8% per year.

APPLICATION

Money Growth and Inflation in European Countries in Transition

The fall of communism in Eastern Europe and the breakup of the Soviet Union led to economic, political, and social upheaval. All of these countries, to varying degrees, have introduced reforms intended to make their economies more market-oriented, and many (particularly the new countries formed from the breakup of the Soviet Union) have introduced new currencies. However, Russia and many of the Eastern European economies continued to face serious problems, including very high rates of inflation. The main reason for the high inflation rates is the rapid rates of money growth in these countries.

In general, both the growth of the nominal money supply and the growth of real money demand (resulting from real income growth, for example) affect the rate of inflation (see Eq. 7.12). In countries with high inflation, however, the growth of the nominal money supply usually is the much more important of these two factors. To illustrate, if the income elasticity of money demand in a country is 2/3, and real output were to grow at the stunning rate of 15% per year, then in Eq. (7.12) real money demand would grow at 10% per year ($2/3 \times 15\%$) in that country. If a second country also has an income elasticity of 2/3, but its income is falling at the painful rate of 15% per year, the rate of growth of real money demand is −10% per year. Thus even with these radically different income growth rates, the difference in the growth rates of real money demand is only 20 percentage points per year.

In contrast to the relatively modest differences among countries in the growth rates of real money demand, rates of growth of nominal money supplies may vary among countries by hundreds of percentage points per year. Thus large differences in inflation rates among countries almost always are the result of large differences in rates of money growth.

The link between the money growth rate and the inflation rate is illustrated in Fig. 7.4, which shows the average annual values of these rates during the period 1995–2001 for the European countries designated by the International Monetary Fund as "countries in transition." Most of these countries were in the process of moving from communism to free-market capitalism. The three countries that had inflation rates that averaged more than 80% per year during this period—Belarus, Turkey, and Bulgaria—also had money growth rates that averaged more than 80% per year. Whether we compare inflation rates among these three countries or compare the high inflation rates of these three countries with the relatively low inflation rates of the remaining sixteen countries, large differences in inflation rates clearly are associated with large differences in rates of money growth.

If rapid money growth causes inflation, why do countries allow their money supplies to grow so quickly? As we discussed earlier, governments sometimes find that printing money (borrowing from the central bank) is the only way that they can finance their expenditures. This situation is most likely to occur in poor countries or countries that undergo economic upheavals associated with war, natural disaster, or (as in the case of the European countries in transition) major political and economic change. Unfortunately, the almost inevitable result of financing government expenditures in this way is increased inflation.

Figure 7.4

The relationship between money growth and inflation
Nominal money growth and inflation during the period 1995–2001 are plotted for the European countries in transition for which complete data are available. There is a strong relationship between money growth rates and inflation rates, with countries having money growth rates in excess of 80% per year also having inflation rates in excess of 80% per year.

Source: Money growth rates and consumer price inflation from *International Financial Statistics,* February 2003, International Monetary Fund. Figure shows European countries in transition for which there are complete data.

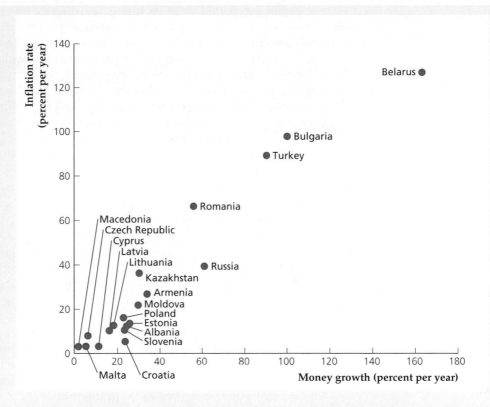

The Expected Inflation Rate and the Nominal Interest Rate

In our earlier discussion of asset market equilibrium, we made the assumption that the expected inflation rate is fixed. For a given real interest rate, r (which is determined by the goods market equilibrium condition), if the expected inflation rate, π^e, is fixed, so is the nominal interest rate, at $r + \pi^e$. We close the chapter with a brief look at the factors that determine the expected inflation rate and the nominal interest rate.

What should holders of wealth and others expect the inflation rate to be in the future? As we demonstrated, Eq. (7.12), which relates inflation to the growth rates of the nominal money supply and real income, is useful for predicting inflation. For expected values of money growth (based, for example, on plans announced by the central bank) and real income growth, as well as an estimate of the income elasticity of money demand, Eq. (7.12) can be used to calculate the expected inflation rate. Suppose that people in a particular country expect their nation's money supply to grow much more rapidly over the next two years because the government is committed to large military expenditures and can pay for these expenditures only by printing money. In this case, Eq. (7.12) shows that people should expect much higher inflation rates in the future.

The inflation prediction equation, Eq. (7.12), is particularly easy to apply when the growth rates of the nominal money supply and real income are constant over time. In this case, the expected growth rates of the nominal money supply and real income equal their current growth rates, and (from Eq. 7.12) the expected inflation rate equals the current inflation rate (assuming no change in the income elasticity of money demand). In practice, the current inflation rate often approximates the expected inflation rate, as long as people don't expect money or income growth to change too much in the near future.

The public's expected inflation rate is not directly observable, except perhaps through surveys and similar methods. However, an observable economic variable that is strongly affected by expected inflation is the nominal interest rate. At any real interest rate, r, which is determined by the goods market equilibrium condition that desired national saving equals desired investment, the nominal interest rate, $r + \pi^e$, changes one-for-one with changes in the expected inflation rate, π^e. Thus policy actions (such as rapid expansion of the money supply) that cause people to fear future increases in inflation should cause nominal interest rates to rise, all else being equal.

But, as already noted, if people don't expect large changes in the growth rates of the money supply or real income, expected inflation won't be much different from current inflation. In this case, nominal interest rates and current inflation rates should move together. If current inflation is high, for example, expected inflation also is likely to be high; but high expected inflation also causes nominal interest rates to be high, all else being equal.

The historical relationship between nominal interest rates and inflation is illustrated by Fig. 7.5, which shows monthly data on the nominal interest rate on one-year Treasury bills and the twelve-month inflation rate measured by the consumer price index in the United States from January 1960 to July 2009. The nominal interest rate and the inflation rate have tended to move together, rising during the 1960s and 1970s and then falling sharply after reaching a peak in the early 1980s. However, movements in the inflation rate aren't perfectly matched by movements in the nominal interest rate because the real interest rate hasn't been constant over this period. In particular, during the late 1970s and early 1980s, the rise in the nominal interest rate was much greater than the rise in the inflation rate, reflecting an increase in the real interest rate from a negative value in the mid 1970s to much higher, positive values in the 1980s. (See Fig. 2.3, p. 52, for a graph of the real interest rate.)

Figure 7.5

Inflation and the nominal interest rate in the United States, 1960–2009

The figure shows the nominal interest rate on one-year Treasury bills and the twelve-month rate of inflation as measured by the consumer price index. The nominal interest rate tends to move with inflation, although there are periods such as the early 1980s when the two variables diverge.

Source: FRED database of the Federal Reserve Bank of St. Louis, *research.stlouisfed.org /fred2*, series GS1 (interest rate) and CPIAUCNS (CPI).

APPLICATION

Measuring Inflation Expectations

Equilibrium in the asset market depends on people's expectations for the inflation rate. But how do people form expectations of inflation? They may do so by looking at surveys of economists who specialize in forecasting the economy.[13] If so, we can gather information about people's long-term inflation expectations from surveys that ask people what they think inflation will be in the long run, such as the Survey of Professional Forecasters or the University of Michigan Survey of Consumers. However, survey information may be unreliable if the people surveyed do not have a strong stake in understanding the determinants of the inflation rate. On the other hand, people who purchase bonds are more likely to care about inflation, because a change in the inflation rate affects the real return on their investments. So data from financial markets can reveal investors' expectations about the rate of inflation.[14]

The U.S. government borrows from the public by issuing nominal bonds and (since 1997) by issuing Treasury Inflation-Protected Securities (TIPS). Nominal bonds offer a certain nominal interest rate over the life of the bond, but the real rate of interest on nominal bonds depends on the rate of inflation during the life of the bond. The expected real interest rate on the nominal bond is (recall Eq. 2.13) $r = i - \pi^e$, where i is the nominal interest rate and π^e is the expected rate of inflation during the life of the bond. TIPS bonds offer a certain real interest rate over the life of the bond, regardless of the rate of inflation that occurs during the life of the bond. TIPS bonds insulate the real rate of return from fluctuations in the rate of inflation by adjusting both the interest payments and the principal repayments of the bonds.

Figure 7.6 shows the nominal interest rate on nominal bonds and the real interest rate on TIPS bonds. The real interest rate on ten-year TIPS bonds trended upward from 3.3% in early 1997 to 4.3% in early 2000. Beginning in 2000, the real interest rate generally trended down, falling to 1.6% in early 2005. From mid 2005 to mid 2007, the real interest rate increased somewhat. The real interest rate then fell during the recession that began in late 2007, except for a short-lived upward spike during the financial crisis in late 2008.

If nominal bonds and TIPS bonds were equally risky and equally liquid, then equilibrium in the asset market would imply that the expected real interest rate on nominal bonds, $i - \pi^e$, would equal the real interest rate on TIPS bonds, r_{TIPS}. Setting $i - \pi^e$ equal to r_{TIPS} implies that $\pi^e = i - r_{TIPS}$. Thus, the excess of the nominal interest rate over the TIPS rate, $i - r_{TIPS}$, which we will call the *interest rate differential*, provides a rough measure of expected inflation. However, because the risk to investors from unpredictable fluctuations in inflation is eliminated by the TIPS bond, some of the difference between the two rates is attributable to inflation risk rather than to expected inflation. That is, investors who buy nominal bonds know that they face greater risk from unpredictable changes in inflation than they would if they were to buy TIPS bonds, so the interest rate on nominal bonds is higher to compensate holders of nominal bonds for bearing that risk. On the other hand, the market for

[13]See Christopher D. Carroll, "Macroeconomic Expectations of Households and Professional Forecasters," *Quarterly Journal of Economics* 118 (February 2003), pp. 269–298.

[14]The following analysis is based on Ben S. Bernanke, "What Policymakers Can Learn from Asset Prices." Remarks before the Investment Analysts Society of Chicago, April 15, 2004.

(continued)

Figure 7.6

Interest rates on nominal and TIPS ten-year notes, 1997–2009
The chart shows quarterly values for the nominal interest rate on nominal ten-year U.S. government Treasury notes and the real interest rate on Treasury Inflation-Protected Securities (TIPS) ten-year notes for the period 1997:Q1 to 2009:Q2.

Sources: Nominal interest rate: Federal Reserve Board of Governors, available at *research. stlouisfed.org/fred2/series/GS10*; TIPS interest rates: constructed by authors from latest ten-year TIPS note yield, yield data available at *research.stlouisfed. org/fred2/series/TP10J07* to *TP10J19*.

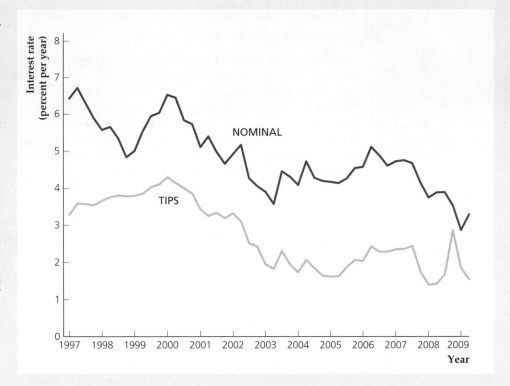

TIPS bonds is less liquid (that is, has fewer buyers and sellers), so the interest rate on TIPS bonds is higher than it would be if they were sold in a more liquid market. With these two conflicting effects, it is not clear whether the interest rate differential shown in Fig. 7.6 overstates or understates the expected inflation rate over the next ten years. However, these two effects are likely to be small, and they work in opposite directions, so their net effect is likely to be very small. Therefore, we will use the inflation rate differential as a measure of people's expected rate of inflation.

Figure 7.7 plots the inflation rate differential over time (the gap between the lines in Fig. 7.6). The graph suggests that people's expectations of inflation declined in 1997 and 1998, rose in 1999, fell slightly in 2000, remained roughly constant in 2001 and 2002, rose in 2003, were stable from 2004 to early 2008, and then declined sharply in the financial crisis that began in 2008.[15] This fluctuating behavior is in contrast to the smooth behavior of a survey measure of expected inflation, also shown in Fig. 7.7, from the Survey of Professional Forecasters. The survey measure of expected inflation fell from 3% in 1997 to 2.5% in 1998 and remained at about 2.5% throughout the period. It appears that professional forecasters did not change their views very much about expected inflation over the next ten years. However, market participants seem to have had much more volatile views on expected inflation, or else the degree of inflation risk and liquidity in the TIPS market fluctuated substantially in this period.

---

[15]Some observers explain the decline in the interest differential that occurred late in 2008 as the consequence of reduced liquidity of TIPS relative to conventional bonds issued by the Federal government. The perception that TIPS had become less liquid meant that investors required a higher expected rate of return on TIPS relative to the expected return on conventional bonds, thereby narrowing the differential between the interest rates on conventional bonds and on TIPS.

Figure 7.7

Alternative measures of expected inflation, 1997–2009

The chart shows quarterly values for two different measures of expected inflation: the interest rate differential, which equals the nominal interest rate on nominal ten-year U.S. government Treasury notes minus the real interest rate on Treasury Inflation-Protected Securities (TIPS) ten-year notes; and the ten-year expected inflation rate from the Survey of Professional Forecasters for the period 1997:Q1 to 2009:Q2.

Sources: Interest rate differential: authors' calculations from data for Fig. 7.6; Survey of Professional Forecasters: Federal Reserve Bank of Philadelphia, available at *www. philadelphiafed.org*.

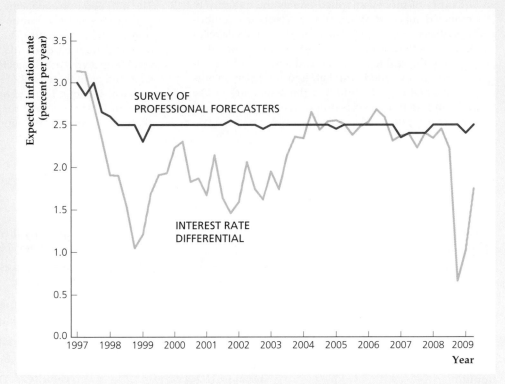

CHAPTER SUMMARY

1. Money is the set of assets that are widely used and accepted as payment, such as currency and checking accounts. Money functions as a medium of exchange, a unit of account, and a store of value.

2. The supply of money is set by the central bank—the Federal Reserve System in the United States. The central bank's official measures of money are called the monetary aggregates. M1 is made up primarily of currency and checking accounts and M2 includes a broader set of monetary assets.

3. A portfolio allocation decision is made by a holder of wealth when determining how much of each asset to hold. The characteristics of assets that most affect their desirability are expected return, risk, liquidity, and, for financial securities, time to maturity. The major assets that people hold are money, bonds, stocks, houses, and consumer durable goods.

4. Money demand is the total amount of money that people choose to hold in their portfolios. The principal macroeconomic variables that affect money demand are the price level, real income, and interest rates. Nominal money demand is proportional to the price level. Higher real income increases the number of transactions and thus raises real money demand. A higher interest rate on alternative, nonmonetary assets lowers real money demand by making the alternative assets more attractive relative to money. The money demand function measures the relationship between real money demand and these macroeconomic variables.

5. Velocity is the ratio of nominal GDP to the nominal money stock. The quantity theory of money is an early theory of money demand based on the assumption that velocity is constant, so that money demand is proportional to income. Historically, M2 velocity has been more stable than M1 velocity, although even M2 velocity isn't constant.

6. Under the simplifying assumption that assets can be grouped into two categories—money and nonmonetary assets—the asset market is in equilibrium if the

quantity of money supplied equals the quantity of money demanded. When all markets are in equilibrium (the economy is at full employment), the level of output is determined by equilibrium in the labor market, the real interest rate is determined by equilibrium in the goods market, and the price level is determined by equilibrium in the asset market. The equilibrium price level is proportional to the nominal money supply.

7. The inflation rate equals the growth rate of the nominal money supply minus the growth rate of real money demand. The growth rate of real money demand in turn depends primarily on the real income growth rate. Expected inflation depends on expected growth rates of the nominal money supply and real income. For a given real interest rate, the nominal interest rate responds one-for-one to changes in expected inflation.

KEY TERMS

demand for money, p. 251

diversification, p. 251

expectations theory of the term structure, p. 246

expected returns, p. 244

income elasticity of money demand, p. 256

interest elasticity of money demand, p. 257

liquidity, p. 245

M1, p. 240

M2, p. 241

medium of exchange, p. 239

monetary aggregates, p. 240

money, p. 237

money demand function, p. 254

money supply, p. 241

open-market operations, p. 243

portfolio allocation decision, p. 244

quantity theory of money, p. 258

real balances, p. 254

risk, p. 245

store of value, p. 239

term premium, p. 246

time to maturity, p. 245

unit of account, p. 239

velocity, p. 257

KEY EQUATIONS

$$\frac{M^d}{P} = L(Y, r + \pi^e) \qquad (7.3)$$

According to the money demand function, the real quantity of money demanded, M^d/P, depends on output and the nominal interest rate on alternative, nonmonetary assets. An increase in output, Y, raises the number of transactions people make and thus raises the demand for money. An increase in the nominal interest rate on nonmonetary assets, i (which equals the expected real interest rate, r, plus the expected rate of inflation, π^e) raises the attractiveness of alternative assets and thus reduces the demand for money.

$$V = \frac{\text{nominal GDP}}{\text{nominal money stock}} = \frac{PY}{M} \qquad (7.4)$$

Velocity, V, is nominal GDP, or P times Y, divided by the nominal money stock, M. Velocity is assumed to be constant by the quantity theory of money.

$$\frac{M}{P} = L(Y, r + \pi^e) \qquad (7.9)$$

The asset market equilibrium condition states that the real supply of money, M/P, and the real demand for money, $L(Y, r + \pi^e)$, are equal.

$$\pi = \frac{\Delta M}{M} - \eta_Y \frac{\Delta Y}{Y} \qquad (7.12)$$

The inflation rate, π, equals the growth rate of the nominal money supply, $\Delta M/M$, minus the growth rate of real money demand. In long-run equilibrium with a constant nominal interest rate, the growth rate of real money demand equals the income elasticity of money demand, η_Y, times the growth rate of real income or output, $\Delta Y/Y$.

REVIEW QUESTIONS

All review questions are available in at **www.myeconlab.com.**

1. Define *money*. How does the economist's use of this term differ from its everyday meaning?

2. What are the three functions of money? How does each function contribute to a more smoothly operating economy?

3. Who determines the nation's money supply? Explain how the money supply could be expanded or reduced in an economy in which all money is in the form of currency.

4. What are the four characteristics of assets that are most important to holders of wealth? How does money compare with other assets for each characteristic?

5. Describe what is meant by the expectations theory of the term structure of interest rates. Why isn't the expectations theory sufficient to describe the data on interest rates that we observe? What must be added to

the expectations theory to form a more accurate theory?

6. List and discuss the macroeconomic variables that affect the aggregate demand for money.

7. Define *velocity*. Discuss the role of velocity in the quantity theory of money.

8. Why is equilibrium in the asset market described by the condition that real money supply equal real money demand? What aggregation assumption is needed to allow ignoring the markets for other assets?

9. What is the relationship between the price level and the nominal money supply? What is the relationship between inflation and the growth rate of the nominal money supply?

10. Give an example of a factor that would increase the public's expected rate of inflation. All else being equal, how would this increase in the expected inflation rate affect interest rates?

NUMERICAL PROBLEMS

All numerical problems are available in at **www.myeconlab.com.**

1. Suppose the interest rate on a one-year bond today is 6% per year, the interest rate on a one-year bond one year from now is expected to be 4% per year, and the interest rate on a one-year bond two years from now is expected to be 3% per year. The term premium on a two-year bond is 0.5% per year and the term premium on a three-year bond is 1.0% per year. In equilibrium, what is the interest rate today on a two-year bond? On a three-year bond? What is the shape of the yield curve?

2. Money demand in an economy in which no interest is paid on money is

$$\frac{M^d}{P} = 500 + 0.2Y - 1000i.$$

a. Suppose that $P = 100$, $Y = 1000$, and $i = 0.10$. Find real money demand, nominal money demand, and velocity.

b. The price level doubles from $P = 100$ to $P = 200$. Find real money demand, nominal money demand, and velocity.

c. Starting from the values of the variables given in Part (*a*) and assuming that the money demand function as written holds, determine how velocity is affected by an increase in real income, by an increase in the nominal interest rate, and by an increase in the price level.

3. Mr. Midas has wealth of $100,000 that he invests entirely in money (a checking account) and government bonds. Mr. Midas instructs his broker to invest $50,000 in bonds, plus $5000 more in bonds for every percentage point that the interest rate on bonds exceeds the interest rate on his checking account.

a. Write an algebraic formula that gives Mr. Midas's demand for money as a function of bond and checking account interest rates.

b. Write an algebraic formula that gives Mr. Midas's demand for bonds. What is the sum of his demand for money and his demand for bonds?

c. Suppose that all holders of wealth in the economy are identical to Mr. Midas. Fixed asset supplies per person are $80,000 of bonds and $20,000 of checking accounts. Checking accounts pay no interest. What is the interest rate on bonds in asset market equilibrium?

4. Assume that the quantity theory of money holds and that velocity is constant at 5. Output is fixed at its full-employment value of 10,000, and the price level is 2.

   a. Determine the real demand for money and the nominal demand for money.

   b. In this same economy the government fixes the nominal money supply at 5000. With output fixed at its full-employment level and with the assumption that prices are flexible, what will be the new price level? What happens to the price level if the nominal money supply rises to 6000?

5. Consider an economy with a constant nominal money supply, a constant level of real output $Y = 100$, and a constant real interest rate $r = 0.10$. Suppose that the income elasticity of money demand is 0.5 and the interest elasticity of money demand is −0.1.

   a. By what percentage does the equilibrium price level differ from its initial value if output increases to $Y = 106$ (and r remains at 0.10)? (*Hint:* Use Eq. 7.11.)

   b. By what percentage does the equilibrium price level differ from its initial value if the real interest increases to $r = 0.11$ (and Y remains at 100)?

   c. Suppose that the real interest rate increases to $r = 0.11$. What would real output have to be for the equilibrium price level to remain at its initial value?

6. Suppose that the real money demand function is

   $$L(Y,r + \pi^e) = \frac{0.01Y}{r + \pi^e},$$

   where Y is real output, r is the real interest rate, and π^e is the expected rate of inflation. Real output is constant over time at $Y = 150$. The real interest rate is fixed in the goods market at $r = 0.05$ per year.

   a. Suppose that the nominal money supply is growing at the rate of 10% per year and that this growth rate is expected to persist forever. Currently, the nominal money supply is $M = 300$. What are the values of the real money supply and the current price level? (*Hint:* What is the value of the expected inflation rate that enters the money demand function?)

   b. Suppose that the nominal money supply is $M = 300$. The central bank announces that from now on the nominal money supply will grow at the rate of 5% per year. If everyone believes this announcement, and if all markets are in equilibrium, what are the values of the real money supply and the current price level? Explain the effects on the real money supply and the current price level of a slowdown in the rate of money growth.

7. The income elasticity of money demand is 2/3 and the interest elasticity of money demand is −0.1. Real income is expected to grow by 4.5% over the next year, and the real interest rate is expected to remain constant over the next year. The rate of inflation has been zero for several years.

   a. If the central bank wants zero inflation over the next year, what growth rate of the nominal money supply should it choose?

   b. By how much will velocity change over the next year if the central bank follows the policy that achieves zero inflation?

ANALYTICAL PROBLEMS

1. All else being equal, how would each of the following affect the demand for M1? The demand for M2? Explain.

   a. The maximum number of checks per month that can be written on money market mutual funds and money market deposit accounts is raised from three to thirty.

   b. Home equity lines of credit that allow homeowners to write checks against the value of their homes are introduced.

   c. The stock market crashes, and further sharp declines in the market are widely feared.

   d. Banks introduce overdraft protection, under which funds are automatically transferred from savings to checking as needed to cover checks.

   e. A crackdown reduces the illegal drug trade (which is carried out largely in currency).

2. Figure 7.2 shows that, before the 1980s, M1 velocity generally rose over time. Suggest some explanations for this upward trend.

3. The prisoner-of-war camp described by Radford ("In Touch with Data and Research: Money in a Prisoner-of-War Camp," p.238) periodically received large shipments of cigarettes from the Red Cross or other sources.

   a. How did cigarette shipments affect the price level (the prices of goods in terms of cigarettes) in the POW camp?

b. (More difficult) On some occasions the prisoners knew in advance when the cigarette shipments were to arrive. What happened to the demand for cigarette money and the price level in the camp in the days just before an anticipated shipment?

4. Assume that prices and wages adjust rapidly so that the markets for labor, goods, and assets are always in equilibrium. What are the effects of each of the following on output, the real interest rate, and the current price level?

a. A temporary increase in government purchases.
b. A reduction in expected inflation.
c. A temporary increase in labor supply.
d. An increase in the interest rate paid on money.

WORKING WITH MACROECONOMIC DATA

For data to use in these exercises, go to the Federal Reserve Bank of St. Louis FRED database at research.stlouisfed.org/fred2.

1. Graph the current yield curve (see the section, "Time to Maturity," p. 245 and the graph of the yield curve on p. 115), plotting the interest rate on bonds with different maturities against their time to maturity, using data from the Federal Reserve's H.15 release (*www.federalreserve.gov/releases/h15*). Use the Fed's "constant maturity" series of rates, which are designed for this purpose. Then look at the H.15 release from one year earlier and plot the yield curve for that date as well. What has happened to the term structure of interest rates over the past year? What economic events do you think have led to this change?

2. Graph the CPI inflation rate, M1 money growth, and M2 money growth for the United States, using annual data since 1959. (Find annual growth rates for December to December.) Also graph the three-year average rate of inflation and the three-year averages of M1 growth and M2 growth, starting with 1961. (The three-year average rate of inflation for, say, 1978 is the average of the inflation rates in 1976, 1977, and 1978. Similarly, the three-year average money growth rate for 1978 is the average of the money growth rates for 1976, 1977, and 1978.)

   Is the inflation rate more closely related to M1 growth or M2 growth? Is the relationship of inflation to money growth stronger in the short run (in annual data) or in the longer run (using three-year averages)? What has happened to the link between inflation and money growth during the past decade?

3. Graph the three-month Treasury bill interest rate, the ten-year government bond interest rate, and the CPI inflation rate on the same figure, using data since 1961. Make sure that the units are comparable.

a. In general, how are changes in interest rates related to changes in inflation? Why?
b. Is the three-month rate or the ten-year rate more sensitive to current changes in inflation? Give an economic explanation.

CHAPTER 8

Business Cycles

Since the Industrial Revolution, the economies of the United States and many other countries have grown tremendously. That growth has transformed economies and greatly improved living standards. Yet even in prosperous countries, economic expansion has been periodically interrupted by episodes of declining production and income and rising unemployment. Sometimes—fortunately, not very often—these episodes have been severe and prolonged. But whether brief or more extended, declines in economic activity have been followed almost invariably by a resumption of economic growth.

This repeated sequence of economic expansion giving way to temporary decline followed by recovery, is known as the *business cycle.* The business cycle is a central concern in macroeconomics because business cycle fluctuations—the ups and downs in overall economic activity—are felt throughout the economy. When the economy is growing strongly, prosperity is shared by most of the nation's industries and their workers and owners of capital. When the economy weakens, many sectors of the economy experience declining sales and production, and workers are laid off or forced to work only part-time. Because the effects of business cycles are so widespread, and because economic downturns can cause great hardship, economists have tried to find the causes of these episodes and to determine what, if anything, can be done to counteract them. The two basic questions of (1) what causes business cycles and (2) how policymakers should respond to cyclical fluctuations are the main concern of Part 3 of this book.

The answers to these two questions remain highly controversial. Much of this controversy involves the proponents of the classical and Keynesian approaches to macroeconomics, introduced in Chapter 1. In brief, classical economists view business cycles as generally representing the economy's best response to disturbances in production or spending. Thus classical economists do not see much, if any, need for government action to counteract these fluctuations. In contrast, Keynesian economists argue that, because wages and prices adjust slowly, disturbances in production or spending may drive the economy away from its most desirable level of output and employment for long periods of time. According to the Keynesian view, government should intervene to smooth business cycle fluctuations.

We explore the debate between classicals and Keynesians, and the implications of that debate for economic analysis and macroeconomic policy, in Chapters 9–11. In this chapter we provide essential background for that discussion by presenting the basic features of the business cycle. We begin with a definition and a brief history of the business cycle in the United States. We then turn to a more detailed discussion of business cycle characteristics, or "business cycle facts." We conclude the chapter with a brief preview of the alternative approaches to the analysis of business cycles.

8.1 What Is a Business Cycle?

Countries have experienced ups and downs in overall economic activity since they began to industrialize. Economists have measured and studied these fluctuations for more than a century. Marx and Engels referred to "commercial crises," an early term for business cycles, in their Communist Manifesto in 1848. In the United States, the National Bureau of Economic Research (NBER), a private nonprofit organization of economists founded in 1920, pioneered business cycle research. The NBER developed and continues to update the **business cycle chronology,** a detailed history of business cycles in the United States and other countries. The NBER has also sponsored many studies of the business cycle: One landmark study was the 1946 book *Measuring Business Cycles,* by Arthur Burns (who served as Federal Reserve chairman from 1970 until 1978) and Wesley Mitchell (a principal founder of the NBER). This work was among the first to document and analyze the empirical facts about business cycles. It begins with the following definition:

> Business cycles are a type of fluctuation found in the aggregate economic activity of nations that organize their work mainly in business enterprises. A cycle consists of expansions occurring at about the same time in many economic activities, followed by similarly general recessions, contractions, and revivals which merge into the expansion phase of the next cycle; this sequence of changes is recurrent but not periodic; in duration business cycles vary from more than one year to ten or twelve years.[1]

Five points in this definition should be clarified and emphasized.

1. *Aggregate economic activity.* Business cycles are defined broadly as fluctuations of "aggregate economic activity" rather than as fluctuations in a single, specific economic variable such as real GDP. Although real GDP may be the single variable that most closely measures aggregate economic activity, Burns and Mitchell also thought it important to look at other indicators of activity, such as employment and financial market variables.

2. *Expansions and contractions.* Figure 8.1—a diagram of a typical business cycle—helps explain what Burns and Mitchell meant by expansions and contractions. The dashed line shows the average, or normal, growth path of aggregate economic activity, as determined by the factors we considered in Chapter 6. The solid curve shows the rises and falls of actual economic activity. The period of time during which aggregate economic activity is falling is a **contraction** or **recession.** If the recession is particularly severe, it becomes a **depression.** After reaching the low point of the contraction, the **trough** (*T*), aggregate economic activity begins to increase. The period of time during which aggregate economic activity grows is an **expansion** or a **boom.** After reaching the high point of the expansion, the **peak** (*P*), aggregate economic activity begins to decline again. The

---

[1]Burns and Mitchell, *Measuring Business Cycles,* New York: National Bureau of Economic Research, 1946, p. 1.

Figure 8.1

A business cycle
The solid curve graphs the behavior of aggregate economic activity over a typical business cycle. The dashed line shows the economy's normal growth path. During a contraction aggregate economic activity falls until it reaches a trough, *T*. The trough is followed by an expansion during which economic activity increases until it reaches a peak, *P*. A complete cycle is measured from peak to peak or trough to trough.

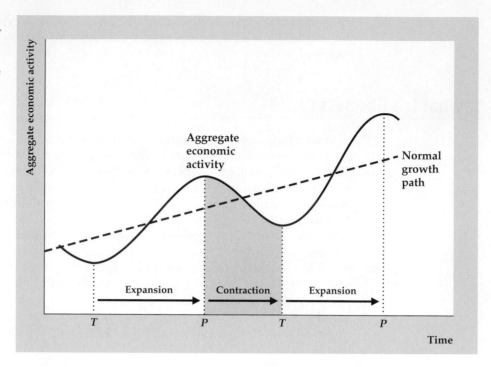

entire sequence of decline followed by recovery, measured from peak to peak or trough to trough, is a **business cycle.**

Figure 8.1 suggests that business cycles are purely temporary deviations from the economy's normal growth path. However, part of the output losses and gains that occur during a business cycle may become permanent.

Peaks and troughs in the business cycle are known collectively as **turning points.** One goal of business cycle research is to identify when turning points occur. Aggregate economic activity isn't measured directly by any single variable, so there's no simple formula that tells economists when a peak or trough has been reached.[2] In practice, a small group of economists who form the NBER's Business Cycle Dating Committee determine that date. The committee meets only when its members believe that a turning point may have occurred. By examining a variety of economic data, the committee determines whether a peak or trough has been reached and, if so, the month it happened. However, the committee's announcements usually come well after a peak or trough occurs, so their judgments are more useful for historical analysis of business cycles than as a guide to current policymaking.

3.   *Comovement.* Business cycles do not occur in just a few sectors or in just a few economic variables. Instead, expansions or contractions "occur at about the same time in many economic activities." Thus, although some industries are more sensitive to the business cycle than others, output and employment in most industries tend to

---

[2]A conventional definition used by the media—that a recession has occurred when there are two consecutive quarters of negative real GDP growth—isn't widely accepted by economists. The reason that economists tend not to like this definition is that real GDP is only one of many possible indicators of economic activity.

fall in recessions and rise in expansions. Many other economic variables, such as prices, productivity, investment, and government purchases, also have regular and predictable patterns of behavior over the course of the business cycle. The tendency of many economic variables to move together in a predictable way over the business cycle is called **comovement.**

4. *Recurrent but not periodic.* The business cycle isn't periodic, in that it does not occur at regular, predictable intervals and doesn't last for a fixed or predetermined length of time. ("In Touch with Data and Research: The Seasonal Cycle and the Business Cycle," p. 301, discusses the seasonal cycle—or economic fluctuations over the seasons of the year—which, unlike the business cycle, is periodic.) Although the business cycle isn't periodic, it is recurrent; that is, the standard pattern of contraction–trough–expansion–peak recurs again and again in industrial economies.

5. *Persistence.* The duration of a complete business cycle can vary greatly, from about a year to more than a decade, and predicting it is extremely difficult. However, once a recession begins, the economy tends to keep contracting for a period of time, perhaps for a year or more. Similarly, an expansion, once begun, usually lasts a while. This tendency for declines in economic activity to be followed by further declines, and for growth in economic activity to be followed by more growth, is called **persistence.** Because movements in economic activity have some persistence, economic forecasters are always on the lookout for turning points, which are likely to indicate a change in the direction of economic activity.

8.2 The American Business Cycle: The Historical Record

An overview of American business cycle history is provided by the NBER's monthly business cycle chronology,[3] as summarized in Table 8.1. It gives the dates of the troughs and peaks of the thirty-two complete business cycles that the U.S. economy has experienced since 1854. Also shown is the number of months that each contraction and expansion lasted.

The Pre–World War I Period

The period between the Civil War (1861–1865) and World War I (1917–1918) was one of rapid economic growth in the United States. Nevertheless, as Table 8.1 shows, recessions were a serious problem during that time. Indeed, the longest contraction on record is the 65-month-long decline between October 1873 and March 1879, a contraction that was worldwide in scope and is referred to by economic historians as the Depression of the 1870s. Overall, during the 1854–1914 period the economy suffered 338 months of contraction, or nearly as many as the 382 months of expansion. In contrast, from the end of World War II in 1945 through December 2007, the number of months of expansion (642) outnumbered months of contraction (104) by more than six to one.

---

[3]For a detailed discussion of the NBER chronologies, see Geoffrey H. Moore and Victor Zarnowitz, "The NBER's Business Cycle Chronologies," in Robert J. Gordon, ed., *The American Business Cycle: Continuity and Change,* Chicago: University of Chicago Press, 1986. The NBER chronology is available at the NBER's Web site, *www.nber.org.*

Table 8.1

NBER Business Cycle Turning Points and Durations of Post–1854 Business Cycles

Trough	Expansion (months from trough to peak)	Peak	Contraction (months from peak to next trough)
Dec. 1854	30	June 1857	18
Dec. 1858	22	Oct. 1860	8
June 1861	46 (Civil War)	Apr. 1865	32
Dec. 1867	18	June 1869	18
Dec. 1870	34	Oct. 1873	65
Mar. 1879	36	Mar. 1882	38
May 1885	22	Mar. 1887	13
Apr. 1888	27	July 1890	10
May 1891	20	Jan. 1893	17
June 1894	18	Dec. 1895	18
June 1897	24	June 1899	18
Dec. 1900	21	Sept. 1902	23
Aug. 1904	33	May 1907	13
June 1908	19	Jan. 1910	24
Jan. 1912	12	Jan. 1913	23
Dec. 1914	44 (WWI)	Aug. 1918	7
Mar. 1919	10	Jan. 1920	18
July 1921	22	May 1923	14
July 1924	27	Oct. 1926	13
Nov. 1927	21	Aug. 1929	43 (Depression)
Mar. 1933	50	May 1937	13 (Depression)
June 1938	80 (WWII)	Feb. 1945	8
Oct. 1945	37	Nov. 1948	11
Oct. 1949	45 (Korean War)	July 1953	10
May 1954	39	Aug. 1957	8
Apr. 1958	24	Apr. 1960	10
Feb. 1961	106 (Vietnam War)	Dec. 1969	11
Nov. 1970	36	Nov. 1973	16
Mar. 1975	58	Jan. 1980	6
July 1980	12	July 1981	16
Nov. 1982	92	July 1990	8
Mar. 1991	120	Mar. 2001	8
Nov. 2001	73	Dec. 2007	

Source: NBER Web site, *www.nber.org/cycles.html.*

The Great Depression and World War II

The worst economic contraction in the history of the United States was the Great Depression of the 1930s. After a prosperous decade in the 1920s, aggregate economic activity reached a peak in August 1929, two months before the stock market crash in October 1929. Between the 1929 peak and the 1933 trough, real GDP fell by nearly 30%. During the same period the unemployment rate rose from about 3% to nearly 25%, with many of those lucky enough to have jobs only able to work part-time. To appreciate how severe the Great Depression was, compare it with the two worst post–World War II recessions of 1973–1975 and 1981–1982. In contrast to the 30% real GDP decline and 25% unemployment rate of the Great Depression, in the 1973–1975 recession real GDP fell by 3.4% and the unemployment rate rose from about 4% to about 9%; in the 1981–1982 recession real GDP fell by 2.8% and the unemployment rate rose from about 7% to about 11%.

Although no sector escaped the Great Depression, some were particularly hard hit. In the financial sector, stock prices continued to collapse after the crash. Depositors withdrew their money from banks, and borrowers, unable to repay their bank loans, were forced to default; as a result, thousands of banks were forced to go out of business or merge with other banks. In agriculture, farmers were bankrupted by low crop prices, and a prolonged drought in the Midwest turned thousands of farm families into homeless migrants. Investment, both business and residential, fell to extremely low levels, and a "trade war"—in which countries competed in erecting barriers to imports—virtually halted international trade.

Although most people think of the Great Depression as a single episode, technically it consisted of two business cycles, as Table 8.1 shows. The contraction phase of the first cycle lasted forty-three months, from August 1929 until March 1933, and was the most precipitous economic decline in U.S. history. After Franklin Roosevelt took office as President in March 1933 and instituted a set of policies known collectively as the New Deal, a strong expansion began and continued for fifty months, from March 1933 to May 1937. By 1937 real GDP was almost back to its 1929 level, although at 14% the unemployment rate remained high. Unemployment remained high in 1937 despite the recovery of real GDP because the number of people of working age had grown since 1929 and because increases in productivity allowed employment to grow more slowly than output.

The second cycle of the Great Depression began in May 1937 with a contraction phase that lasted more than a year. Despite a new recovery that began in June 1938, the unemployment rate was still more than 17% in 1939.

The Great Depression ended dramatically with the advent of World War II. Even before the Japanese attack on Pearl Harbor brought the United States into the war in December 1941, the economy was gearing up for increased armaments production. After the shock of Pearl Harbor, the United States prepared for total war. With production supervised by government boards and driven by the insatiable demands of the military for more guns, planes, and ships, real GDP almost doubled between 1939 and 1944. Unemployment dropped sharply, averaging less than 2% of the labor force in 1943–1945 and bottoming out at 1.2% in 1944.

Post–World War II U.S. Business Cycles

As World War II was ending in 1945, economists and policymakers were concerned that the economy would relapse into depression. As an expression of this concern, Congress passed the Employment Act of 1946, which required the government to fight recessions and depressions with any measures at its disposal. But instead of falling into a new depression as feared, the U.S. economy began to grow strongly.

Only a few relatively brief and mild recessions interrupted the economic expansion of the early postwar period. None of the five contractions that occurred between 1945 and 1970 lasted more than a year, whereas eighteen of the twenty-two previous cyclical contractions in the NBER's monthly chronology had lasted a year or more. The largest drop in real GDP between 1945 and 1970 was 3.3% during the 1957–1958 recession, and throughout this period unemployment never exceeded 8.1% of the work force. Again, there was a correlation between economic expansion and war: The 1949–1953 expansion corresponded closely to the Korean War, and the latter part of the strong 1961–1969 expansion occurred during the military buildup to fight the Vietnam War.

Because no serious recession occurred between 1945 and 1970, some economists suggested that the business cycle had been "tamed," or even that it was "dead." This view was especially popular during the 106-month expansion of 1961–1969, which was widely attributed not only to high rates of military spending during the Vietnam War but also to the macroeconomic policies of Presidents Kennedy and Johnson. Some argued that policymakers should stop worrying about recessions and focus their attention on inflation, which had been gradually increasing over the 1960s.

Unfortunately, reports of the business cycle's death proved premature. Shortly after the Organization of Petroleum Exporting Countries (OPEC) succeeded in quadrupling oil prices in the fall of 1973, the U.S. economy and the economies of many other nations fell into a severe recession. In the 1973–1975 recession U.S. real GDP fell by 3.4% and the unemployment rate reached 9%—not a depression but a serious downturn, nonetheless. Also disturbing was the fact that inflation, which had fallen during most previous recessions, shot up to unprecedented double-digit levels. Inflation continued to be a problem for the rest of the 1970s, even as the economy recovered from the 1973–1975 recession.

More evidence that the business cycle wasn't dead came with the sharp 1981–1982 recession. This contraction lasted sixteen months, the same length as the 1973–1975 decline, and the unemployment rate reached 11%, a postwar high. Many economists claim that the Fed knowingly created this recession to reduce inflation, a claim we discuss in Chapter 11. Inflation did drop dramatically, from about 11% to less than 4% per year. The recovery from this recession was strong, however.

The "Long Boom"

The expansion that followed the 1981–1982 recession lasted almost eight years, until July 1990, when the economy again entered a recession. This contraction was relatively short (the trough came in March 1991, only eight months after the peak) and shallow (the unemployment rate peaked in mid 1992 at 7.7%—not particularly high for a recession). Moreover, after some initial sluggishness, the 1990–1991 recession was followed by another sustained expansion that lasted 120 months, making it the longest in U.S. history. Taking the expansions of the 1980s and 1990s together, you can see that the U.S. economy experienced a period of more than eighteen years during which only one relatively minor recession occurred. Some observers referred to this lengthy period of prosperity as the "long boom." The long boom ended with the business cycle peak in March 2001, after which the U.S. economy suffered a mild recession and sluggish growth. After six years of modest growth, the economy suffered a recession that began in December 2007 and worsened severely in the financial crisis of the fall of 2008. As the recession was still ongoing as of this writing, it had become the longest recession since the first phase of the Great Depression.

Have American Business Cycles Become Less Severe?

Until recently, macroeconomists believed that, over the long sweep of history, business cycles generally have become less severe. Obviously, no recession in the United States since World War II can begin to rival the severity of the Great Depression.

Even putting aside the Great Depression, economists generally believed that business downturns before 1929 were longer and deeper than those since 1945. According to the NBER business cycle chronology (Table 8.1), for example, the average contraction before 1929 lasted nearly twenty-one months and the average expansion lasted slightly more than twenty-five months. Since 1945, contractions have shortened to an average of eleven months, and expansions have lengthened to an average of more than fifty months, even excluding the lengthy expansion of the 1990s. Standard measures of economic fluctuations, such as real GDP growth and the unemployment rate, also show considerably less volatility since 1945, relative to data available for the pre–1929 era.

Since World War II a major goal of economic policy has been to reduce the size and frequency of recessions. If researchers found—contrary to the generally accepted view—that business cycles had *not* moderated in the postwar period, serious doubt would be cast on the ability of economic policymakers to achieve this goal. For this reason, although the question of whether the business cycle has moderated over time may seem to be a matter of interest only to economic historians, this issue is of great practical importance.

Thus Christina Romer, the Chair of President Obama's Council of Economic Advisers, sparked a heated controversy by writing a series of articles in the 1980s denying the claim that the business cycle has moderated over time.[4] Romer's main point concerned the dubious quality of the pre–1929 data. Unlike today, in earlier periods the government didn't collect comprehensive data on economic variables such as GDP. Instead, economic historians, using whatever fragmentary information they could find, have had to estimate historical measures of these variables.

Romer argued that methods used for estimating historical data typically overstated the size of earlier cyclical fluctuations. For example, widely accepted estimates of pre–1929 GNP[5] were based on estimates of just the goods-producing sectors of the economy, which are volatile, while ignoring less-volatile sectors such as wholesale and retail distribution, transportation, and services. As a result, the volatility of GNP was overstated. Measured properly, GNP varied substantially less over time than the official statistics showed. Romer's arguments sparked additional research, though none proved decisively whether volatility truly declined after 1929. Nonetheless, the debate served the useful purpose of forcing a careful reexamination of the historical data.

New research shows that economic volatility declined in the mid 1980s and has remained low since then. Because the quality of the data is not an issue for the period following World War II, the decline in volatility in the mid 1980s, relative to the preceding forty years, probably reflects a genuine change in economic volatility rather than a change in how economic data are produced.

---

[4]The articles included "Is the Stabilization of the Postwar Economy a Figment of the Data?" *American Economic Review,* June 1986, pp. 314–334; "The Prewar Business Cycle Reconsidered: New Estimates of Gross National Product, 1869–1908," *Journal of Political Economy,* February 1989, pp. 1–37; and "The Cyclical Behavior of Individual Production Series, 1889–1984," *Quarterly Journal of Economics,* February 1991, pp. 1–31.

[5]As discussed in Chapter 2, until 1991 the U.S. national income and product accounts focused on GNP rather than GDP. As a result, studies of business cycle behavior have often focused on GNP rather than GDP.

Figure 8.2

**GDP growth,
1960–2009**

The chart shows the annualized quarterly growth rate of seasonally adjusted GDP from the first quarter of 1960 to the second quarter of 2009. The growth rate is more volatile before 1984 than after 1984.

Source: Authors' calculations from data on real GDP from the Federal Reserve Bank of St. Louis FRED database, *research.stlouisfed.org/fred2/GDPC1.*

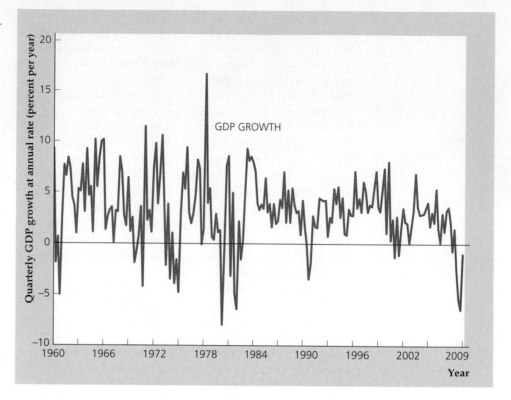

Other economic variables, including inflation, residential investment, output of durable goods, and output of structures, also appear to fluctuate less in the past twenty years than they did in the preceding forty years. Research by James Stock of Harvard University and Mark Watson of Princeton University[6] shows that the volatility, as measured by the standard deviation of a variable, declined by 20 to 40% for many of the twenty-one variables they examine, including a decline of 33% for real GDP, 27% for employment, and 50% for inflation. Because the decline in volatility of macroeconomic variables has been so widespread, economists have dubbed this episode "the Great Moderation."[7]

To see what we mean by the Great Moderation, let's begin by looking at real GDP growth since 1960. In Fig. 8.2, we have plotted the quarterly growth rate of real GDP (seasonally adjusted at an annual rate). You can see that from 1960 until about 1984, the growth rate changes significantly from quarter to quarter, but after 1984 it seems considerably more stable.

Another graphical device that will help us to see the Great Moderation is a plot of the standard deviation of quarterly real GDP growth. The standard deviation of a variable is a measure of its volatility. Because we think the volatility has changed over time, we are going to calculate the standard deviation over

---

[6]"Has the Business Cycle Changed and Why?" *NBER Macroeconomics Annual 2002* (Cambridge, MA: MIT Press, 2002), pp. 159–218.

[7]See Ben S. Bernanke, "The Great Moderation." Speech at the Eastern Economic Association meetings, February 20, 2004, available at *www.federalreserve.gov/boarddocs/speeches/2004/20040220/default.htm.*

Figure 8.3

Standard deviation of GDP growth, 1960–2009
The chart shows the standard deviation of the annualized quarterly growth rate of GDP, over seven-year periods, from 1960 to 2009. The seven-year standard deviation fell sharply in about 1984, but rose during the recession that began in 2007.

Source: Authors' calculations from data on real GDP from the Federal Reserve Bank of St. Louis FRED database, *research.stlouisfed.org/fred2/GDPC1.*

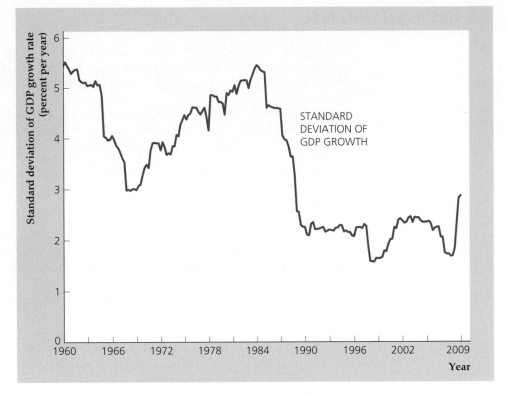

seven-year periods. The result is shown in Fig. 8.3. Note that each point shown on the graph represents the standard deviation of GDP growth for the preceding seven years. The graph shows a sharp decline in about 1984 in the seven-year standard deviation. The uptick in that standard deviation in 2009 might lead some to worry that the Great Moderation could be over; but we will need many more years of data to know for sure.

Somewhat surprisingly, the reduction in volatility seemed to come from a sudden, one-time drop rather than a gradual decline. The break seems to have come around 1984 for many economic variables, though for some variables the break occurred much later.

What accounts for this reduction in the volatility of the economy? Stock and Watson found that better monetary policy is responsible for about 20% to 30% of the reduction in output volatility, with reduced shocks to the economy's productivity accounting for about 15% and reduced shocks to food and commodity prices accounting for another 15%. The remainder is attributable to some unknown form of good luck in terms of smaller shocks to the economy.[8]

---

[8]Since the Stock and Watson paper was written, much additional research has been undertaken, with mixed results. For example, Shaghil Ahmed, Andrew Levin, and Beth Ann Wilson ["Recent Improvements in U.S. Macroeconomic Stability: Good Policy, Good Practices, or Good Luck?" *Review of Economics and Statistics*, vol. 86 (2004), pp. 824–832] suggest that good luck played the biggest role, while others find a larger role for monetary policy, including Peter M. Summers ["What Caused the Great Moderation? Some Cross-Country Evidence," Federal Reserve Bank of Kansas City, *Economic Review* (Third Quarter 2005), pp. 5–32].

8.3 Business Cycle Facts

Although no two business cycles are identical, all (or most) cycles have features in common. This point has been made strongly by a leading business cycle theorist, Nobel laureate Robert E. Lucas, Jr., of the University of Chicago:

> Though there is absolutely no theoretical reason to anticipate it, one is led by the facts to conclude that, with respect to the qualitative behavior of comovements among series [that is, economic variables], *business cycles are all alike.* To theoretically inclined economists, this conclusion should be attractive and challenging, for it suggests the possibility of a unified explanation of business cycles, grounded in the *general* laws governing market economies, rather than in political or institutional characteristics specific to particular countries or periods.[9]

Lucas's statement that business cycles are all alike (or more accurately, that they have many features in common) is based on examinations of comovements among economic variables over the business cycle. In this section, we study these comovements, which we call business cycle facts, for the post–World War II period in the United States. Knowing these business cycle facts is useful for interpreting economic data and evaluating the state of the economy. In addition, they provide guidance and discipline for developing economic theories of the business cycle. When we discuss alternative theories of the business cycle in Chapters 10 and 11, we evaluate the theories principally by determining how well they account for business cycle facts. To be successful, a theory of the business cycle must explain the cyclical behavior of not just a few variables, such as output and employment, but of a wide range of key economic variables.

The Cyclical Behavior of Economic Variables: Direction and Timing

Two characteristics of the cyclical behavior of macroeconomic variables are important to our discussion of the business cycle facts. The first is the *direction* in which a macroeconomic variable moves, relative to the direction of aggregate economic activity. An economic variable that moves in the same direction as aggregate economic activity (up in expansions, down in contractions) is **procyclical.** A variable that moves in the opposite direction to aggregate economic activity (up in contractions, down in expansions) is **countercyclical.** Variables that do not display a clear pattern over the business cycle are **acyclical.**

The second characteristic is the *timing* of the variable's turning points (peaks and troughs) relative to the turning points of the business cycle. An economic variable is a **leading variable** if it tends to move in advance of aggregate economic activity. In other words, the peaks and troughs in a leading variable occur before the corresponding peaks and troughs in the business cycle. A **coincident variable** is one whose peaks and troughs occur at about the same time as the corresponding business cycle peaks and troughs. Finally, a **lagging variable** is one whose peaks and troughs tend to occur later than the corresponding peaks and troughs in the business cycle.

---

[9]Robert E. Lucas, Jr., "Understanding Business Cycles," in K. Brunner and A. H. Meltzer, eds., *Carnegie-Rochester Conference Series on Public Policy*, vol. 5, Autumn 1977, p. 10.

The fact that some economic variables consistently lead the business cycle suggests that they might be used to forecast the future course of the economy. Some analysts have used downturns in the stock market to predict recessions, but such an indicator is not infallible. As Paul Samuelson noted: "Wall Street indexes predicted nine out of the last five recessions."[10]

In some cases, the cyclical timing of a variable is obvious from a graph of its behavior over the course of several business cycles; in other cases, elaborate statistical techniques are needed to determine timing. Conveniently, The Conference Board has analyzed the timing of dozens of economic variables. This information is published monthly in *Business Cycle Indicators*, along with the most recent data for these variables. For the most part, in this chapter we rely on The Conference Board's timing classifications.

Let's now examine the cyclical behavior of some key macroeconomic variables. We showed the historical behavior of several of these variables in Figs. 1.1–1.4. Those figures covered a long time period and were based on annual data. We can get a better view of short-run cyclical behavior by looking at quarterly or monthly data. The direction and timing of the variables considered are presented in Summary table 10 on page 290.

IN TOUCH WITH DATA AND RESEARCH

Coincident and Leading Indexes

In this chapter we discuss a large number of variables and describe how they behave as the economy goes through expansions and contractions. One difficulty faced by policymakers and economic analysts is how to sort through all of the different economic data and figure out where the economy stands overall; a more challenging problem is to forecast, in advance, when the economy will change course. To address these problems, economists have developed coincident and leading indexes. An index is a single number that combines data on a variety of economic variables. A *coincident index* is an index that is designed to have peaks and troughs that occur about the same time as the corresponding peaks and troughs in aggregate economic activity, and is useful for assessing whether the economy is currently in a recession or an expansion. A *leading index* is designed to have its peaks and troughs before the corresponding peaks and troughs in aggregate economic activity, and thus might be useful for forecasting turning points in the business cycle.

The first indexes were developed in the 1930s at the National Bureau of Economic Research (NBER) by Wesley Mitchell and Arthur Burns,* whose important early work on business cycles was mentioned earlier in this chapter. Today, these original indexes (with some modification and updating) are produced by The Conference Board, and other indexes have been developed by other economists. In this box, we discuss two recently developed coincident indexes and The Conference Board's **index of leading economic indicators**.

*Statistical Indicators of Cyclical Revivals (New York: National Bureau of Economic Research, 1938).

(continued)

[10]*Newsweek* column, September 19, 1966, as quoted in John Bartlett, *Bartlett's Familiar Quotations*, Boston: Little Brown, 2002.

The Chicago Fed National Activity Index (CFNAI) was developed in 2001 by economist Jonas Fisher of the Federal Reserve Bank of Chicago. This coincident index is based on 85 monthly economic variables in five categories: production and income, the labor market, consumption and housing, manufacturing and sales, and inventories and orders. The index is constructed so that it has an average value of 0 over time. Figure 8.4 shows the values of the CFNAI, averaged over the current and preceding two months, since March 1967. The graph includes recession bars, showing the dates of recessions as determined by the NBER. As the graph shows, the CFNAI turns significantly negative in recessions, falling much more in severe recessions (such as 1973–1975, 1981–1982, and the recession that began in December 2007) than in mild recession (such as 1990–1991 and 2001).**

Another recently developed coincident index is the Aruoba-Diebold-Scotti (ADS) Business Conditions Index, which doesn't use as many variables as the CFNAI, but uses variables that have different frequencies: some quarterly data (real GDP), some monthly data (payroll employment, industrial production, personal income less transfer payments, and manufacturing and trade sales), and some weekly data (initial jobless claims). Like the CFNAI, the ADS index is constructed so that it has an

Figure 8.4

Chicago Fed National Activity Index, 1967–2009

The chart shows monthly data on the Chicago Fed National Activity Index (CFNAI), averaged over the current and preceding two months. The peaks and troughs of the business cycle are shown by the vertical lines *P* and *T*. The shaded areas represent recessions. The index tracks recessions closely, falling more in severe recessions than in mild recessions.

Source: Federal Reserve Bank of Chicago Web site, *www.chicagofed.org/economic_research_and_data/cfnai.cfm.*

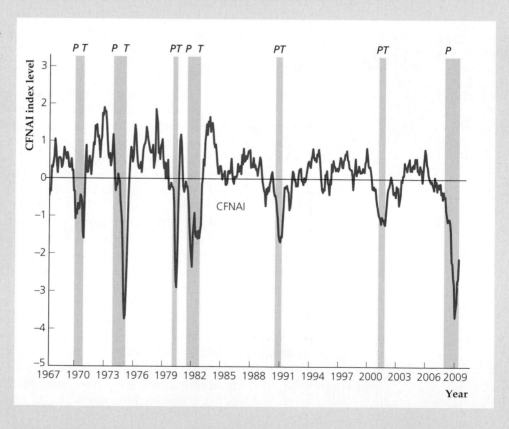

**For more details about the CFNAI, see the article by Charles L. Evans, Chin Te Liu, and Genevieve Pham-Kanter, "The 2001 Recession and the Chicago Fed National Activity Index: Identifying Business Cycle Turning Points," Federal Reserve Bank of Chicago *Economic Perspectives*, Third Quarter 2002, pp. 26–43; or read the discussion on the Chicago Fed's Web site at *www.chicagofed.org/economic_research_and_data/cfnai.cfm.*

average value of 0 over time. The developers of the model, Boragan Aruoba of the University of Maryland, Francis X. Diebold of the University of Pennsylvania, and Chiara Scotti of the Federal Reserve Board, sought an index that could be estimated to provide a measure of the state of the economy on a day-by-day basis. They implemented the index in partnership with the Federal Reserve Bank of Philadelphia, which updates the series once or twice each week. Figure 8.5 shows the values of the ADS index, averaged over the current and preceding two months.***

Comparing the two indexes, we can see that they are quite similar, despite using very different sets of data. Of course, it is not surprising that the two indexes are similar because they are both designed to measure the underlying state of aggregate economic activity. An advantage of the ADS index is that it is available very frequently (it gets updated once each week or more often). But the CFNAI has a longer history of reliability in real time, since it was developed in 2001, whereas the ADS index just began to be produced in real time in 2009.

Unlike the CFNAI and the ADS index, which were designed to measure the current state of the economy, the composite index of leading economic indicators was

Figure 8.5

ADS Business Conditions Index, 1967–2009

The chart shows monthly data on the ADS Business Conditions Index, averaged over the current and preceding two months. Like the CFNAI, the index tracks recessions closely, falling more in severe recessions than in mild recessions.

Source: Authors' calculations from data on Federal Reserve Bank of Philadelphia Web site, *www.philadelphiafed.org/research-and-data/real-time-center/business-conditions-index.*

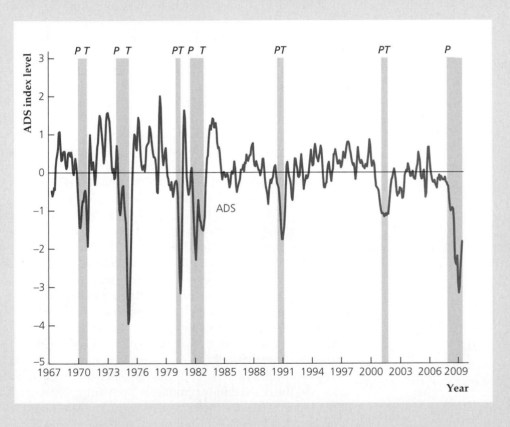

***For more on the ADS index, see S. Boragan Aruoba, Francis X. Diebold, and Chiara Scotti, "Real-Time Measurement of Business Conditions," *Journal of Business and Economic Statistics*, October 2009, pp. 417–427; the ADS index data are available at the Philadelphia Fed's Web site at *www.philadelphiafed.org/research-and-data/real-time-center/business-conditions-index.*

(continued)

designed to help anticipate or forecast turning points in aggregate economic activity. However, its record as a forecasting tool is mixed. When the index declines for two or three consecutive months, it warns that a recession is likely. However, its forecasting acumen in real time has not been very good because of the following problems:

1. Data on the components of the index are often revised when more complete data become available. Revisions change the value of the index and may even reverse a signal of a future recession.

2. The index is prone to giving false signals, predicting recessions that did not materialize.

3. The index does not provide any information on when a recession might arrive or how severe it might be.

4. Changes in the structure of the economy over time may cause some variables to become better predictors of the economy and others to become worse. For this reason, the index must be revised periodically, as the list of component indicators is changed.

Research by Francis X. Diebold and Glenn Rudebusch of the Federal Reserve Bank of San Francisco showed that the revisions were substantial.[†] The agency calculating the index (the Commerce Department or The Conference Board) often demonstrates the value of the index with a plot of the index over time, showing how it turns down just before every recession. But Diebold and Rudebusch showed that such a plot is illusory because the index plotted was not the one used at the time of each recession, but rather a revised index made many years after the fact. In real time, they concluded, the use of the index does not improve forecasts of industrial production.

For example, suppose you were examining the changes over time in the composite index of leading indicators, and used the rule of thumb that a decline in the index for three months in a row meant that a recession was likely in the next six months to one year. You would have noticed in December 1969 that the index had declined two months in a row; by January 1970 you would have seen the third monthly decline. In fact, the NBER declared that a recession had begun in December 1969, so the index did not give you any advance warning. Even worse, if you had been following the index in 1973 to 1974, you would have thought all was well until September 1974, when the index declined for the second month in a row, or October 1974, when the third monthly decline occurred. But the NBER declared that a recession had actually begun in November 1973, so the index was nearly a year late in calling the recession.

After missing a recession's onset so badly, the creators of the index naturally want to improve it. So, they may revise the index with different variables, give the variables different weights, or manipulate the statistics so that, if the new revised index had been available, it would have indicated that a recession were coming. For example, the revised index published in April 1979 would have given eight months of lead time before the recession that began in December 1969 and six months of lead time before the recession that began in November 1973. But of course, that index was not available to forecasters when it would have been useful—before the recessions began.

[†]"Forecasting Output with the Composite Leading Index: A Real-Time Analysis." *Journal of the American Statistical Association* (September 1991), pp. 603–610.

Because of the problems of the official composite index of leading indicators, James Stock and Mark Watson[‡] set out to create some new indexes that would improve the value of such indexes in forecasting. They created several experimental leading indexes, with the hope that such indexes would prove better at helping economists forecast turning points in the business cycle. However, it appears that the next two recessions were sufficiently different from earlier recessions that the experimental leading indexes did not suggest an appreciable probability of recession in either 1990 or 2001. In early 1990, the experimental recession index of Stock and Watson showed that the probability that a recession would occur in the next six months never exceeded 10%. Also, in late 2000 and early 2001, the index did not rise above 10%. So, although the Stock and Watson approach appeared promising in prospect, it did not deliver any improvement in forecasting recessions.

The inability of leading indicators to forecast recessions may simply mean that recessions are often unusual events, caused by large, unpredictable shocks such as disruptions in the world oil supply or a near-collapse of the financial system. If so, then the pursuit of the perfect index of leading indicators may prove to be frustrating.

[‡]"New Indexes of Coincident and Leading Economic Indicators," in Olivier J. Blanchard and Stanley Fischer, eds., *NBER Macroeconomics Annual, 1989* (Cambridge, MA: MIT Press, 1989), pp. 351–394.

Production

Because the level of production is a basic indicator of aggregate economic activity, peaks and troughs in production tend to occur at about the same time as peaks and troughs in aggregate economic activity. Thus production is a coincident and procyclical variable. Figure 8.6 shows the behavior of the industrial production index

Figure 8.6

Cyclical behavior of the index of industrial production, 1947-2009
The index of industrial production, a broad measure of production in manufacturing, mining, and utilities, is procyclical and coincident.

Source: Federal Reserve Bank of St. Louis FRED database at *research.stlouisfed.org/fred2/series/INDPRO*.

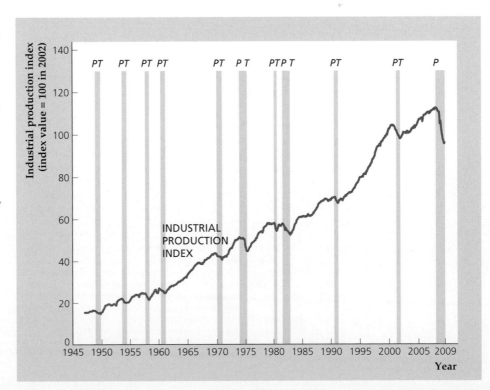

in the United States since 1947. This index is a broad measure of production in manufacturing, mining, and utilities. The vertical lines P and T in Figs. 8.4–8.14 indicate the dates of business cycle peaks and troughs, as determined by the NBER (see Table 8.1). The turning points in industrial production correspond closely to the turning points of the cycle.

Although almost all types of production rise in expansions and fall in recessions, the cyclical sensitivity of production in some sectors of the economy is greater than in others. Industries that produce relatively durable, or long-lasting, goods—houses, consumer durables (refrigerators, cars, washing machines), or capital goods (drill presses, computers, factories)—respond strongly to the business cycle, producing at high rates during expansions and at much lower rates during recessions. In contrast, industries that produce relatively nondurable or short-lived goods (foods, paper products) or services (education, insurance) are less sensitive to the business cycle.

SUMMARY 10

The Cyclical Behavior of Key Macroeconomic Variables (The Business Cycle Facts)

Variable	Direction	Timing
Production		
Industrial production	Procyclical	Coincident
Durable goods industries are more volatile than nondurable goods and services		
Expenditure		
Consumption	Procyclical	Coincident
Business fixed investment	Procyclical	Coincident
Residential investment	Procyclical	Leading
Inventory investment	Procyclical	Leading
Government purchases	Procyclical	__a
Investment is more volatile than consumption		
Labor Market Variables		
Employment	Procyclical	Coincident
Unemployment	Countercyclical	Unclassified[b]
Average labor productivity	Procyclical	Leading[a]
Real wage	Procyclical	__a
Money Supply and Inflation		
Money supply	Procyclical	Leading
Inflation	Procyclical	Lagging
Financial Variables		
Stock prices	Procyclical	Leading
Nominal interest rates	Procyclical	Lagging
Real interest rates	Acyclical	__a

[a]Timing is not designated by The Conference Board.
[b]Designated as "unclassified" by The Conference Board.
Source: Business Cycle Indicators, September 2008. Industrial production: series 47 (industrial production); consumption: series 57 (manufacturing and trade sales, constant dollars); business fixed investment: series 86 (gross private nonresidential fixed investment); residential investment: series 28 (new private housing units started); inventory investment: series 30 (change in business inventories, constant dollars); employment: series 41 (employees on nonagricultural payrolls); unemployment: series 43 (civilian unemployment rate); money supply: series 106 (money supply M2, constant dollars); inflation: series 120 (CPI for services, change over six-month span); stock prices: series 19 (index of stock prices, 500 common stocks); nominal interest rates: series 119 (Federal funds rate), series 114 (discount rate on new 91-day Treasury bills), series 109 (average prime rate charged by banks).

Expenditure

For components of expenditure, as for types of production, durability is the key to determining sensitivity to the business cycle. Figure 8.7 shows the cyclical behavior of consumption of nondurable goods, consumption of services, consumption expenditures on durable goods, and investment. Investment is made up primarily of spending on durable goods and is strongly procyclical. In contrast, consumption of nondurable goods and consumption of services are both much smoother. Consumption expenditures on durable goods are more strongly procyclical than consumption expenditures on nondurable goods or consumption of services, but not as procyclical as investment expenditures. With respect to timing, consumption and investment are generally coincident with the business cycle, although individual components of fixed investment vary in their cyclical timing.[11]

One component of spending that seems to follow its own rules is inventory investment, or changes in business inventories (not shown), which often displays large fluctuations that aren't associated with business cycle peaks and troughs. In general, however, inventory investment is procyclical and leading. Even though goods kept in inventory need not be durable, inventory investment is also very volatile. Although, on average, inventory investment is a small part (about 1%) of total spending, sharp declines in inventory investment represented a large part of the total decline in spending in some recessions, most notably those of 1973–1975, 1981–1982, and 2001.

Figure 8.7

Cyclical behavior of consumption and investment, 1959-2009
Both consumption and investment are procyclical. However, investment is more sensitive than consumption to the business cycle, reflecting the fact that durable goods are a larger part of investment spending than they are of consumption spending. Similarly, expenditures on consumer durables are more sensitive to the business cycle than is consumption of nondurable goods or services.

Source: Federal Reserve Bank of St. Louis FRED database at *research.stlouisfed.org/fred2* series*PCDGCC96* (durable goods), *PCNDGC96* (nondurable goods), *PCESVC96* (services), and *GPDIC1* (investment).

[11]Summary table 10 shows that residential investment leads the cycle.

Government purchases of goods and services generally are procyclical. Rapid military buildups, as during World War II, the Korean War, and the Vietnam War, are usually associated with economic expansions.

Employment and Unemployment

Business cycles are strongly felt in the labor market. In a recession, employment grows slowly or falls, many workers are laid off, and jobs become more difficult to find.

Figure 8.8 shows the number of civilians employed in the United States since 1955. Employment clearly is procyclical, as more people have jobs in booms than in recessions, and also is coincident with the cycle.

Figure 8.9 shows the civilian unemployment rate, which is the fraction of the civilian labor force (the number of people who are available for work and want to work) that is unemployed. The civilian unemployment rate is strongly counter-cyclical, rising sharply in contractions but falling more slowly in expansions. Although The Conference Board has studied the timing of unemployment, Summary table 10 shows that the timing of this variable is designated as "unclassified," owing to the absence of a clear pattern in the data. Figures 8.8 and 8.9 illustrate a worrisome change in the patterns of recent recessions: namely in both the 1990–1991 and 2001 recessions, employment growth stagnated and unemployment tended to rise for some time even after the recession's trough was reached. This pattern led observers to refer to the recovery period following these recessions as "jobless recoveries." Fortunately, both of these recoveries eventually gained strength and the economy showed employment growth and a decline in the rate of unemployment.

Figure 8.8

Cyclical behavior of civilian employment, 1955-2009

Civilian employment is procyclical and coincident with the business cycle.

Source: Federal Reserve Bank of St. Louis FRED database at *research.stlouisfed.org/fred2/series/ CE16OV.*

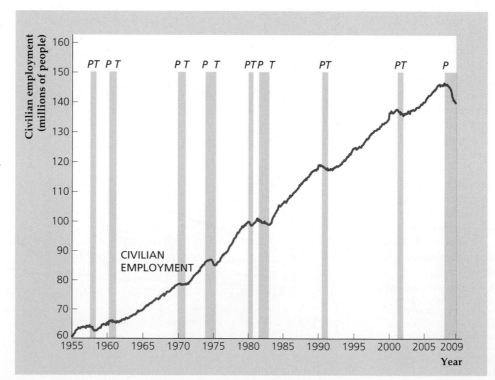

Figure 8.9

Cyclical behavior of the unemployment rate, 1959-2009

The unemployment rate is countercyclical and very sensitive to the business cycle. Its timing pattern relative to the cycle is unclassified, meaning that it has no definite tendency to lead, be coincident, or lag.

Source: Federal Reserve Bank of St. Louis FRED database at *research.stlouisfed.org/fred2/series/ UNRATE.*

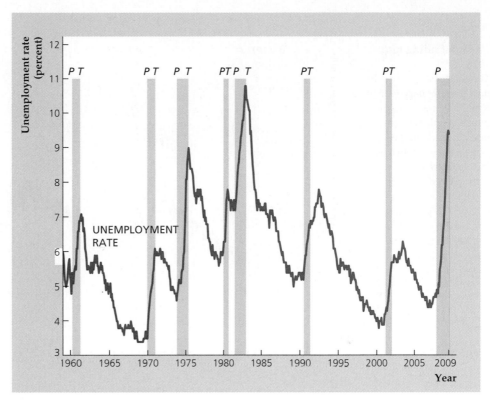

APPLICATION

The Job Finding Rate and the Job Loss Rate

In considering the cyclical movement of employment, we examined the total amount of employment in the economy. As we discussed in Chapter 3, in any given month, we can examine the probability that someone finds a job in that month or loses a job in that month. It turn out that those probabilities change over time, depending on whether the economy is in a recession or an expansion. For example, the probability that someone who is unemployed will find a job in the next month, which we call the **job finding rate**, declines during recessions and increases in expansions. As you might imagine, the probability that someone who is employed will lose his or her job in the next month, which we call the **job loss rate**, increases during recessions and decreases in expansions.[12]

Figure 8.10 shows the job finding rate over the course of the business cycle. Notice that the job finding rate generally rises during each economic expansion, and falls in recessions. The decline in recessions is a bit faster than the rise of the job finding rate in expansions. The job finding rate changes substantially over the business cycle. In the expansion of the 1980s, the job finding rate rose from a low of

---

[12]This discussion is based on the research by Shigeru Fujita and Garey Ramey, "The Cyclicality of Separation and Job Finding Rates," *International Economic Review* 50 (2009), pp. 415–430.

(continued)

Figure 8.10

The job finding rate, 1976–2009
The chart shows monthly data from January 1976 to June 2009 on the rate at which people who are unemployed find new jobs each month, that is, those who report being unemployed one month and employed the next month. The job finding rate rises in expansions and falls in recessions.

Source: Shigeru Fujita and Garey Ramey, "The Cyclicality of Separation and Job Finding Rates," *International Economic Review,* May 2009, pp. 415–430; data updated by Shigeru Fujita.

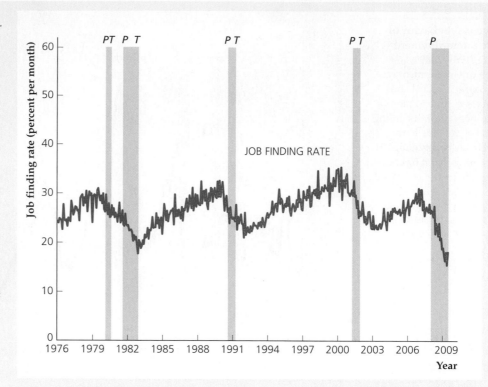

18% in November 1982 to a peak of 33% in late 1989, an increase of 15 percentage points. In the expansion of the 1990s, the job finding rate rose from 21% in late 1991 to 35% in April 2000, an increase of 14 percentage points. And in some recessions, such as the one in 2001, the decline in the job finding rate can be very sharp, and it sometimes continues to decline even after the recession ends, as occurred following the 1990–1991 recession and the 2001 recession. A particularly disturbing feature of the recession that began in December 2007 is the decline of the job finding rate to its lowest point since the data became available in 1976.

Figure 8.11 shows the job loss rate, which is the probability that a person employed in one month becomes unemployed the next month.[13] The first thing to notice is that the job loss rate is very low compared with the job finding rate (the scales on Figs. 8.10 and 8.11 are different, so be sure to look at the percentages shown on the vertical axes of both graphs). The job loss rate averaged 1.5% from 1976 to 2009. It appeared to be on a long steady decline over time in the 1980s and 1990s but did not decline much in the 2000s, and increased sharply in the recession that began in 2007. Even with the more recent upturn in the job loss rate, the probability remains less than 2% that an employed person will lose his or her job in any given month.

Over the course of the business cycle, the job loss rate generally declines in economic expansions and rises in recessions. Compared with the job finding rate, the changes in the job loss rate are very small. So, at first glance, you might think that

---

[13]People who lose jobs in a given month may become unemployed or may move out of the labor force in the following month. We use the term *job loss* to indicate only the transition from being employed in one month to being unemployed in the following month.

Figure 8.11

The job loss rate, 1976–2009

The chart shows monthly data from January 1976 to June 2009 on the rate at which people who are employed lose their jobs each month, that is, those who report being employed one month and unemployed the next month. The job loss rate declines in expansions and rises in recessions.

Source: Shigeru Fujita and Garey Ramey, "The Cyclicality of Separation and Job Finding Rates," *International Economic Review*, May 2009, pp. 415–430; data updated by Shigeru Fujita.

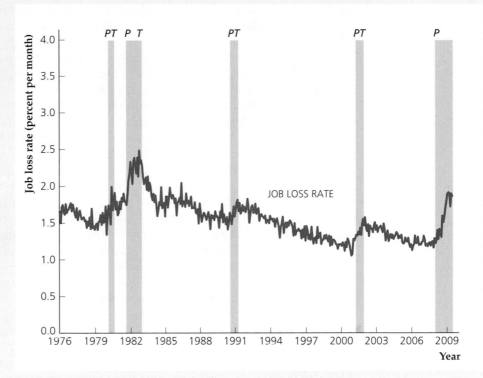

because the job finding rate falls substantially in recessions, while the job loss rate does not change very much, changes in the job finding rate are primarily responsible for changes in the overall unemployment rate for the economy.

To investigate this issue, we will use the data in Table 8.2 to examine job losses and jobs found in an economic expansion and in a recession. First consider changes in employment status during June 2007, which was near the end of the expansion that ended in December 2007. As shown in the first column of Table 8.2, in June 2007, the job loss rate was 1.2% and the number of employed workers was 147.0 million, so the number of people who were employed at the start of the month and who became unemployed during the month was 0.012×147.0 million $= 1.8$ million. Similarly, we can calculate the number of people who were unemployed at the start

Table 8.2

Jobs Lost and Gained In an Expansion and a Recession

	June 2007 (expansion)	October 2008 (recession)
Number of employed people	147.0 million	145.5 million
Job loss rate	1.2%	1.6%
Number of newly unemployed people	1.8 million	2.3 million
Number of unemployed people	7.3 million	9.5 million
Job finding rate	25.5%	20.7%
Number of newly employed people	1.9 million	2.0 million
Net change in number of unemployed	−0.1 million	0.3 million

(continued)

of the month and who became employed during the month. The job finding rate was 25.5% and the number of unemployed workers was 7.3 million, so the number of people who were unemployed at the start of the month and who became employed during the month was 0.255 × 7.3 million = 1.9 million. With 1.8 million workers losing jobs and 1.9 million workers finding jobs, the number of unemployed people fell by 0.1 million during June 2007.[14]

In a recession, the decline in the job finding rate combined with the rise in the job loss rate together cause the number of employed workers to decline and the number of unemployed workers to rise. For example, consider changes in employment during October 2008, in the middle of the financial crisis. As shown in the second column of Table 8.2, the job loss rate was 1.6% and the number of employed workers was 145.5 million, so the number of people who were employed at the start of the month and who became unemployed during the month was 0.016 × 145.5 million = 2.3 million. Similarly, we can calculate the number of people who were unemployed at the start of the month and who became employed during the month. The job finding rate was 20.7% and the number of unemployed workers was 9.5 million, so the number of people who were unemployed at the start of the month and who became employed during the month is 0.207 × 9.5 million = 2.0 million. With 2.3 million workers losing jobs and only 2.0 million workers finding jobs, the number of unemployed people increased by 0.3 million.

Notice in these calculations that the number of people who are employed is much larger than the number of people who are unemployed. Thus, even though the job finding rate falls by more than the job loss rate rises in recessions, the job loss rate is multiplied by a much larger number than is the job finding rate. For example, during October 2008, the ratio of employed to unemployed was 15 to 1. So, smaller changes in the job loss rate may lead to larger changes in the number of unemployed workers than larger changes in the job finding rate. Indeed, comparing October 2008 to June 2007, the number of newly unemployed people (those who suffered job losses in that month) increased by 0.5 million despite the small increase in the job loss rate, while the number of newly employed people (those who found jobs in that month) increased by only 0.1 million.[15]

In summary, economists have found interesting patterns to the changes in job losses and hiring over the course of the business cycle. The most surprising finding is that the job finding rate declines substantially more than the job loss rate rises during recessions. But since the job loss rate applies to many more people, job loss is the main force in increased unemployment rates during recessions, though the lower job finding rate also plays a role.

---

[14]For simplicity, we have ignored people who have moved into or out of the labor force in our calculations.

[15]Note that even though the job finding rate was lower in October 2008 than in June 2007, more unemployed people found jobs in October 2008 than in June 2007 because there were so many more unemployed people in October 2008 than in June 2007.

Average Labor Productivity and the Real Wage

Two other significant labor market variables are average labor productivity and the real wage. As discussed in Chapter 1, average labor productivity is output per unit of labor input. Figure 8.12 shows average labor productivity measured as total real

Figure 8.12

Cyclical behavior of average labor productivity and the real wage, 1959–2009
Average labor productivity, measured as real output per employee hour in the nonfarm business sector, is procyclical and leading. The economywide average real wage is mildly procyclical.

Source: Federal Reserve Bank of St. Louis FRED database at *research.stlouisfed.org/fred2* series *OPHNFB* (productivity) and *COMPRNFB* (real wage).

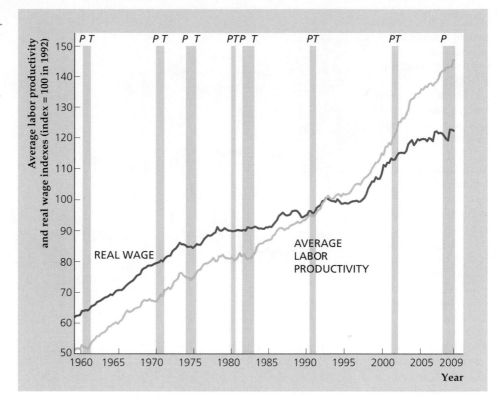

output in the U.S. economy (excluding farms) divided by the total number of hours worked to produce that output. Average labor productivity tends to be procyclical: In booms workers produce more output during each hour of work than they do in recessions.[16] Although The Conference Board doesn't designate the timing of this variable, studies show that average labor productivity tends to lead the business cycle.[17]

Recall from Chapter 3 that the real wage is the compensation received by workers per unit of time (such as an hour or a week) measured in real, or purchasing-power, terms. The real wage, as shown in Fig. 8.12, is an especially important variable in the study of business cycles because it is one of the main determinants of the amount of labor supplied by workers and demanded by firms. Most of the evidence points to the conclusion that real wages are mildly procyclical, but there is some controversy on this point.[18]

Money Growth and Inflation

Another variable whose cyclical behavior is somewhat controversial is the money supply. Figure 8.13 shows the behavior since 1959 of the growth in the M2 measure

---

[16]The Application in Chapter 3, "The Production Function of the U.S. Economy and U.S. Productivity Growth," p. 60, made the point that total factor productivity *A* also tends to be procyclical.

[17]See Robert J. Gordon, "The 'End of Expansion' Phenomenon in Short-Run Productivity Behavior," *Brookings Papers on Economic Activity,* 1979:2, pp. 447–461.

[18]Strong procyclicality for the real wage is claimed by Gary Solon, Robert Barsky, and Jonathan Parker, "Measuring the Cyclicality of Real Wages: How Important Is Composition Bias?" *Quarterly Journal of Economics,* February 1994, pp. 1–25. But their results are disputed by others, such as Paul J. Devereux, "The Cyclicality of Real Wages Within Employer-Employee Matches," *Industrial and Labor Relations Review,* July 2001, pp. 835–850.

Figure 8.13

Cyclical behavior of nominal money growth and inflation, 1959–2009

Nominal money growth, here measured as the six-month moving average of monthly growth rates in M2 (expressed in annual rates), is volatile. However, the figure shows that money growth often falls at or just before a cyclical peak. Statistical and historical studies suggest that, generally, money growth is procyclical and leading. Inflation, here measured as the six-month moving average of monthly growth rates of the CPI (expressed in annual rates), is procyclical and lags the business cycle.

Source: Federal Reserve Bank of St. Louis FRED database at *research.stlouisfed.org/fred2* series *M2SL* and *CPIAUCSL*.

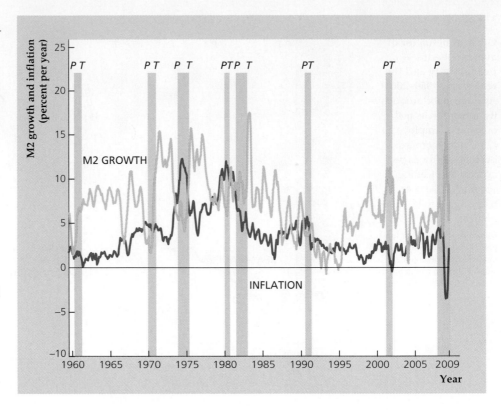

of the money supply.[19] Note that (nominal) money growth fluctuates a great deal and doesn't always display an obvious cyclical pattern. However, as Fig. 8.13 shows, money growth often falls sharply at or just before the onset of a recession. Moreover, many statistical and historical studies—including a classic work by Milton Friedman and Anna J. Schwartz[20] that used data back to 1867—demonstrate that money growth is procyclical and leads the cycle.

The cyclical behavior of inflation, also shown in Fig. 8.13, presents a somewhat clearer picture. Inflation is procyclical but with some lag. Inflation typically builds during an economic expansion, peaks slightly after the business cycle peak, and then falls until some time after the business cycle trough is reached. Atypically, inflation did *not* increase during the long boom of the 1990s.

Financial Variables

Financial variables are another class of economic variables that are sensitive to the cycle. For example, stock prices are generally procyclical (stock prices rise in good economic times) and leading (stock prices usually fall in advance of a recession).

Nominal interest rates are procyclical and lagging. The nominal interest rate shown in Fig. 8.14 is the rate on three-month Treasury bills. However, other interest rates, such as the prime rate (charged by banks to their best customers) and the

---

[19]See Table 7.1 for a definition of M2. To reduce the effect of high month-to-month volatility in money growth, Fig. 8.13 presents a six-month moving average of money growth rates; that is, the reported growth rate in each month is actually the average of the growth rate in the current month and in the previous five months.

[20]*A Monetary History of the United States, 1867–1960*, Princeton, N.J.: Princeton University Press for NBER, 1963. We discuss this study further in Chapter 10.

Figure 8.14

Cyclical behavior of the nominal interest rate, 1947–2009

The nominal interest rate, measured here as the interest rate on three-month Treasury bills, is procyclical and lagging.

Source: Federal Reserve Bank of St. Louis FRED database at *research.stlouisfed.org/fred2/series/ TB3MS.*

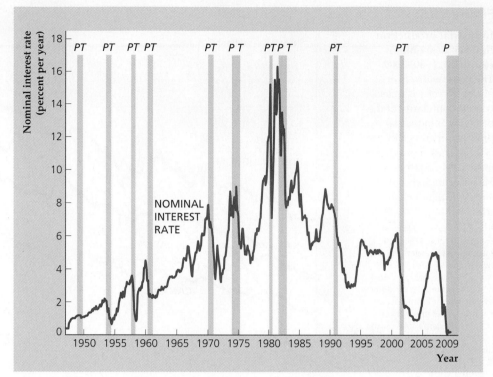

Federal funds rate (the interest rate on overnight loans made from one bank to another) also are procyclical and lagging. Note that nominal interest rates have the same general cyclical pattern as inflation; in Chapter 7 we discussed why nominal interest rates tend to move up and down with the inflation rate.

The real interest rate doesn't have an obvious cyclical pattern. For instance, the real interest rate actually was negative during the 1973–1975 recession but was very high during the 1981–1982 recession. (Annual values of the real interest rate are shown in Fig. 2.3.) The acyclicality of the real interest rate doesn't necessarily mean its movements are unimportant over the business cycle. Instead, the lack of a stable cyclical pattern may reflect the facts that individual business cycles have different causes and that these different sources of cycles have different effects on the real interest rate.

International Aspects of the Business Cycle

So far we have concentrated on business cycles in the United States. However, business cycles are by no means unique to the United States, having been regularly observed in all industrialized market economies. In most cases the cyclical behavior of key economic variables in these other economies is similar to that described for the United States.

The business cycle is an international phenomenon in another sense: Frequently, the major industrial economies undergo recessions and expansions at about the same time, suggesting that they share a common cycle. Figure 8.15 illustrates this common cycle by showing the index of industrial production since 1960 for each of six major industrial countries. Note in particular the effects of worldwide recessions in about 1975, 1982, 1991, 2001, and 2008. Figure 8.15 also shows that each economy experiences many small fluctuations not shared by the others.

Figure 8.15

Industrial production indexes in six major countries, 1960–2009
The worldwide effect of business cycles is reflected in the similarity of the behavior of industrial production in each of the six countries shown. But individual countries also have fluctuations not shared with other countries.

Source: International Financial Statistics, August 2009, from International Monetary Fund (with scales adjusted for clarity). *Note:* The scales for the industrial production indexes differ by country; for example, the figure does not imply that the United Kingdom's total industrial production is higher than that of Japan.

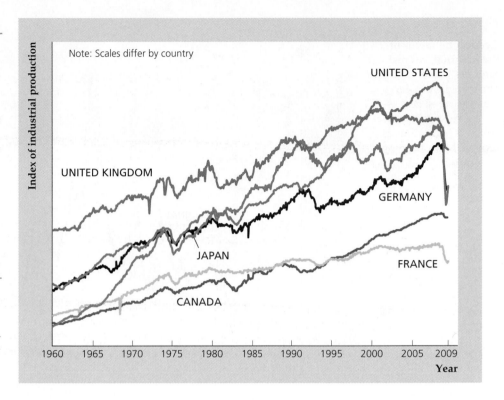

8.4 Business Cycle Analysis: A Preview

The business cycle facts presented in this chapter would be useful even if we took them no further. For example, being familiar with the typical cyclical patterns of key macroeconomic variables may help forecasters project the course of the economy, as we showed when discussing leading indicators. Knowing the facts about cycles also is important for businesspeople making investment and hiring decisions and for financial investors trying to choose portfolios that provide the desired combinations of risk and return. However, macroeconomists are interested not only in *what* happens during business cycles but also in *why* it happens. This desire to understand cycles isn't just idle intellectual curiosity. For example, as we demonstrate in Chapters 9–11, the advice that macroeconomists give to policymakers about how to respond to a recession depends on what they think is causing the recession. Thus, with the business cycle facts as background, in the rest of Part 3 we describe the primary alternative explanations of business cycle fluctuations, as well as policy recommendations based on these explanations.

In general, theories of the business cycle have two main components. The first is a description of the types of factors that have major effects on the economy—wars, new inventions, harvest failures, and changes in government policy are examples. Economists often refer to these (typically unpredictable) forces hitting the economy as *shocks*. The other component of a business cycle theory is a *model* of how the economy responds to the various shocks. Think of the economy as a car moving down a poorly maintained highway: The shocks can be thought of as the potholes and bumps in the road; the model describes how the components of the car (its tires and shock absorbers) act to smooth out or amplify the effects of the shocks on the passengers.

IN TOUCH WITH DATA AND RESEARCH

The Seasonal Cycle and the Business Cycle

Did you know that the United States has a large economic boom, followed by a deep recession, every year? The boom always occurs in the fourth quarter of the year (October through December). During this quarter output is 5% higher than in the third quarter (July–September) and about 8% higher than in the following first quarter (January–March). Fortunately, the first-quarter recession is always a short one, with output rising by almost 4% in the second quarter (April–June). This regular seasonal pattern, known as the seasonal cycle, actually accounts for more than 85% of the total fluctuation in the growth rate of real output!

Why don't large seasonal fluctuations appear in Figs. 8.4–8.14? Normally, macroeconomic data are seasonally adjusted, meaning that regularly recurring seasonal fluctuations are removed from the data. Seasonal adjustment allows users of economic data to ignore seasonal changes and focus on business cycle fluctuations and longer-term movements in the data. However, Robert Barsky of the University of Michigan and Jeffrey Miron of Boston University* argue that the practice of seasonally adjusting macroeconomic data may throw away information that could help economists better understand the business cycle. Using data that hadn't been seasonally adjusted, Barsky and Miron determined that the comovements of variables over the seasonal cycle are similar to their comovements over the business cycle. Specifically, they obtained the following results:

1. Of the types of expenditure, expenditures on durable goods vary most over the seasonal cycle and expenditures on services vary least.
2. Government spending is seasonally procyclical.
3. Employment is seasonally procyclical, and the unemployment rate is seasonally countercyclical.
4. Average labor productivity is seasonally procyclical, and the real wage hardly varies over the seasonal cycle.
5. The nominal money stock is seasonally procyclical.

Each observation appears to be true for both the business cycle and the seasonal cycle (although, as discussed, there is some controversy about the cyclical behavior of the real wage). However, the seasonal fluctuations of inventory investment, the price level, and the nominal interest rate are much smaller than their fluctuations over the business cycle.

The seasonal cycle illustrates three potential sources of aggregate economic fluctuations: (1) changes in consumer demand, as at Christmastime; (2) changes in productivity, as when construction workers become less productive because of winter weather in the first quarter; and (3) changes in labor supply, as when people take summer vacations in the third quarter. Each of these three sources of fluctuation may also contribute to the business cycle.

As we discuss in Chapter 10, classical economists believe that business cycles generally represent the economy's best response to changes in the economic environment, a response that macroeconomic policy need not try to eliminate. Although it doesn't necessarily confirm this view, the seasonal cycle shows that large economic fluctuations may be desirable responses to various factors (Christmas, the weather) and do not need to be offset by government policy.

*"The Seasonal Cycle and the Business Cycle," *Journal of Political Economy*, June 1989, pp. 503–534.

Figure 8.16

The aggregate demand–aggregate supply model
The aggregate demand (*AD*) curve slopes downward, reflecting the fact that the aggregate quantity of goods and services demanded, *Y*, falls when the price level, *P*, rises. The short-run aggregate supply (*SRAS*) curve is horizontal, reflecting the assumption that, in the short run, prices are fixed and firms simply produce whatever quantity is demanded. In the long run, firms produce their normal levels of output, so the long-run aggregate supply (*LRAS*) curve is vertical at the full-employment level of output, $\overline{Y}$. The economy's short-run equilibrium is at the point where the *AD* and *SRAS* curves intersect, and its long-run equilibrium is where the *AD* and *LRAS* curves intersect. In this example, the economy is in both short-run and long-run equilibrium at point *E*.

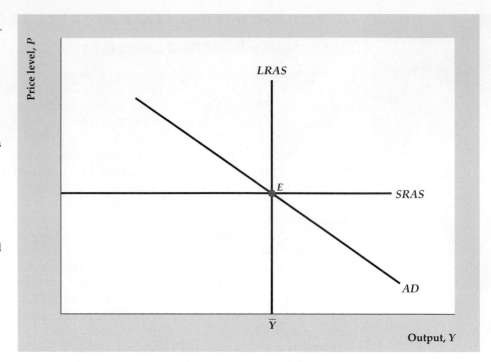

The two principal business cycle theories that we discuss in this book are the *classical* and the *Keynesian* theories. Fortunately, to present and discuss these two theories we don't have to develop two completely different models. Instead, both can be considered within a general framework called the *aggregate demand–aggregate supply*, or *AD–AS, model*. To introduce some of the key differences between the classical and Keynesian approaches to business cycle analysis, in the rest of this chapter we preview the *AD–AS* model and how it is used to analyze business cycles.

Aggregate Demand and Aggregate Supply: A Brief Introduction

We develop and apply the *AD–AS* model, and a key building block of the *AD–AS* model, the *IS–LM* model, in Chapters 9–11. Here, we simply introduce and briefly explain the basic components of the *AD–AS* model. The *AD–AS* model has three components, as illustrated in Fig. 8.16: (1) the aggregate demand curve, (2) the short-run aggregate supply curve, and (3) the long-run aggregate supply curve. Each curve represents a relationship between the aggregate price level, *P*, measured on the vertical axis in Fig. 8.16, and output, *Y*, measured along the horizontal axis.

The *aggregate demand (AD) curve* shows for any price level, *P*, the total quantity of goods and services, *Y, demanded* by households, firms, and governments. The *AD* curve slopes downward in Fig. 8.16, implying that, when the general price level is higher, people demand fewer goods and services. We give the precise explanation for this downward slope in Chapter 9. The intuitive explanation for the downward slope of the *AD* curve—that when prices are higher people can afford to buy fewer goods—is *not* correct. The problem with the intuitive explanation is that, although an increase in the general price level does reflect an increase in the prices of most goods, it also implies an increase in the incomes of the people who produce and sell those goods. Thus to say that a higher price level reduces the quantities of goods and services that people can afford to buy is not correct, because their incomes, as well as prices, have gone up.

The *AD* curve relates the amount of output demanded to the price level, if we hold other economic factors constant. However, for a specific price level, any change in the economy that increases the aggregate quantity of goods and services demanded will shift the *AD* curve to the right (and any change that decreases the quantity of goods and services demanded will shift the *AD* curve to the left). For example, a sharp rise in the stock market, by making consumers wealthier, would likely increase households' demand for goods and services, shifting the *AD* curve to the right. Similarly, the development of more efficient capital goods would increase firms' demand for new capital goods, again shifting the *AD* curve to the right. Government policies also can affect the *AD* curve. For example, a decline in government spending on military hardware reduces the aggregate quantity of goods and services demanded and shifts the *AD* curve to the left.

An aggregate supply curve indicates the amount of output producers are willing to *supply* at any particular price level. Two aggregate supply curves are shown in Fig. 8.16—one that holds in the short run and one that holds in the long run. The *short-run aggregate supply (SRAS) curve,* shown in Fig. 8.16, is a horizontal line. The horizontal *SRAS* curve captures the ideas that in the short run the price level is fixed and that firms are willing to supply any amount of output at that price. If the short run is a very short period of time, such as a day, this assumption is realistic. For instance, an ice cream store posts the price of ice cream in the morning and sells as much ice cream as is demanded at that price (up to its capacity to produce ice cream). During a single day, the owner typically won't raise the price of ice cream if the quantity demanded is unusually high; nor does the owner lower the price of ice cream if the quantity demanded is unusually low. The tendency of a producer to set a price for some time and then supply whatever is demanded at that price is represented by a horizontal *SRAS* curve.

However, suppose that the quantity of ice cream demanded remains high day after day, to the point that the owner is straining to produce enough ice cream to meet demand. In this case, the owner may raise her price to reduce the quantity of ice cream demanded to a more manageable level. The owner will keep raising the price of ice cream as long as the quantity demanded exceeds normal production capacity. In the long run, the price of ice cream will be whatever it has to be to equate the quantity demanded to the owner's normal level of output. Similarly, in the long run, all other firms in the economy will adjust their prices as necessary so as to be able to produce their normal level of output. As discussed in Chapter 3, the normal level of production for the economy as a whole is called the full-employment level of output, denoted $\overline{Y}$. In the long run, then, when prices fully adjust, the aggregate quantity of output supplied will simply equal the full-employment level of output, $\overline{Y}$. Thus the *long-run aggregate supply (LRAS) curve* is vertical, as shown in Fig. 8.16, at the point that output supplied, Y, equals $\overline{Y}$.

Figure 8.16 represents an economy that is simultaneously in short-run and long-run equilibrium. The short-run equilibrium is represented by the intersection of the *AD* and *SRAS* curves, shown as point *E*. The long-run equilibrium is represented by the intersection of the *AD* and *LRAS* curves, also shown as point *E*. However, when some change occurs in the economy, the short-run equilibrium can differ from the long-run equilibrium.

Aggregate Demand Shocks. Recall that a theory of business cycles has to include a description of the shocks hitting the economy. The *AD–AS* framework identifies shocks by their initial effects—on aggregate demand or aggregate supply. An *aggregate demand shock* is a change in the economy that shifts the *AD* curve. For example, a negative aggregate demand shock would occur if consumers became more pessimistic about the future and thus reduced their current consumption spending, shifting the *AD* curve to the left.

To analyze the effect of an aggregate demand shock, let's suppose that the economy initially is in both short-run and long-run equilibrium at point *E* in Fig. 8.17. We assume that, because consumers become more pessimistic, the aggregate demand curve shifts down and to the left from AD^1 to AD^2. In this case, the new short-run equilibrium (the intersection of AD^2 and *SRAS*) is at point *F*, where output has fallen to Y_2 and the price level remains unchanged at P_1. Thus the decline in household consumption demand causes a recession, with output falling below its normal level. However, the economy will not stay at point *F* forever, because firms won't be content to keep producing below their normal capacity. Eventually firms will respond to lower demand by adjusting their prices—in this case downward—until the economy reaches its new long-run equilibrium at point *H*, the intersection of AD^2 and *LRAS*. At point *H*, output is at its original level, $\overline{Y}$, but the price level has fallen to P_2.

Our analysis shows that an adverse aggregate demand shock, which shifts the *AD* curve down, will cause output to fall in the short run but not in the long run. How long does it take for the economy to reach the long run? This question is crucial to economic analysis and is one to which classical economists and Keynesian economists have very different answers. Their answers help explain why classicals and Keynesians have different views about the appropriate role of government policy in fighting recessions.

The classical answer is that prices adjust quite rapidly to imbalances in quantities supplied and demanded so that the economy gets to its long-run equilibrium quickly—in a few months or less. Thus a recession caused by a downward shift of the *AD* curve is likely to end rather quickly, as the price level falls and the economy reaches the original level of output $\overline{Y}$. In the strictest versions of the classical model, the economy is assumed to reach its long–run equilibrium essentially immediately, implying that the short-run aggregate supply curve is irrelevant and that the economy always operates on the long-run aggregate supply (*LRAS*) curve. Because the adjustment takes place quickly, classical economists argue that little is gained by the government actively trying to fight recessions. Note that this conclusion is consistent with the "invisible hand" argument described in Chapter 1, according to which the free market and unconstrained price adjustments are sufficient to achieve good economic results.

In contrast to the classical view, Keynesian economists argue that prices (and wages, which are the price of labor) do not necessarily adjust quickly in response to shocks. Hence the return of the economy to its long-run equilibrium may be slow, taking perhaps years rather than months. In other words, although Keynesians agree with classicals that the economy's level of output will eventually return from its recessionary level (represented by Y_2 in Fig. 8.17) to its full-employment level, $\overline{Y}$, they believe that this process may be slow. Because they lack confidence in the self-correcting powers of the economy, Keynesians tend to see an important role for the government in fighting recessions. For example, Keynes himself originally argued that government could fight recessions by increasing spending. In terms of Fig. 8. 17, an increase in government spending could in principle shift the *AD* curve up and to the right, from AD^2 back to AD^1, restoring the economy to full employment.

Figure 8.17

An adverse aggregate demand shock
An adverse aggregate demand shock reduces the aggregate quantity of goods and services demanded at a given price level; an example is that consumers become more pessimistic and thus reduce their spending. This shock is represented by a shift to the left of the aggregate demand curve from AD^1 to AD^2. In the short run, the economy moves to point F. At this short-run equilibrium, output has fallen to Y_2 and the price level is unchanged. Eventually, price adjustment causes the economy to move to the new long-run equilibrium at point H, where output returns to its full-employment level, $\overline{Y}$, and the price level falls to P_2. In the strict classical view, the economy moves almost immediately to point H, so the adverse aggregate demand shock essentially has no effect on output in both the short run and the long run. Keynesians argue that the adjustment process takes longer, so that the adverse aggregate demand shock may lead to a sustained decline in output.

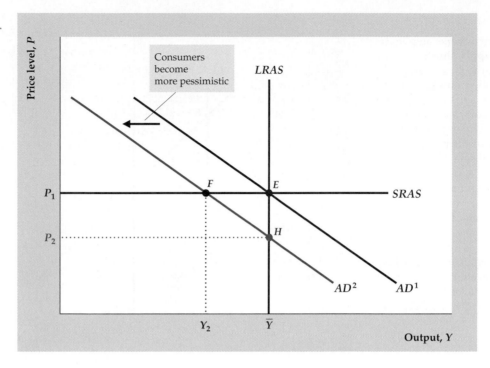

Aggregate Supply Shocks. Because classical economists believe that aggregate demand shocks don't cause sustained fluctuations in output, they generally view aggregate supply shocks as the major force behind changes in output and employment. An *aggregate supply shock* is a change in the economy that causes the long-run aggregate supply ($LRAS$) curve to shift. The position of the $LRAS$ curve depends only on the full-employment level of output, $\overline{Y}$, so aggregate supply shocks can also be thought of as factors—such as changes in productivity or labor supply, for example—that lead to changes in $\overline{Y}$.

Figure 8.18 illustrates the effects of an adverse supply shock—that is, a shock that reduces the full-employment level of output (an example would be a severe drought that greatly reduces crop yields). Suppose that the economy is initially in long-run equilibrium at point E in Fig. 8.18, where the initial long-run aggregate supply curve, $LRAS^1$, intersects the aggregate demand curve, AD. Now imagine that the adverse supply shock hits, reducing full-employment output from $\overline{Y}_1$ to $\overline{Y}_2$ and causing the long-run aggregate supply curve to shift to the left from $LRAS^1$ to $LRAS^2$. The new long-run equilibrium occurs at point F, where the level of output is lower than at point E. According to the classical view, the economy moves quickly from point E to point F and then remains at point F. The drop in output as the economy moves from point E to point F is a recession. Note that the new price level, P_2, is higher than the initial price level, P_1, so adverse supply shocks cause prices to rise during recessions. We return to this implication for the price level and discuss its relation to the business cycle facts in Chapter 10.

Although classical economists first emphasized supply shocks, Keynesian economists also recognize the importance of supply shocks in accounting for business cycle fluctuations in output. Keynesians agree that an adverse supply shock will reduce output and increase the price level in the long run. In Chapter 11, we discuss the Keynesian view of the process by which the economy moves from the short run to the long run in response to a supply shock.

Figure 8.18

An adverse aggregate supply shock
An adverse aggregate supply shock, such as a drought, reduces the full-employment level of output from $\overline{Y}_1$ to $\overline{Y}_2$. Equivalently, the shock shifts the long-run aggregate supply curve to the left, from $LRAS^1$ to $LRAS^2$. As a result of the adverse supply shock, the long-run equilibrium moves from point E to point F. In the new long-run equilibrium, output has fallen from $\overline{Y}_1$ to $\overline{Y}_2$ and the price level has increased from P_1 to P_2.

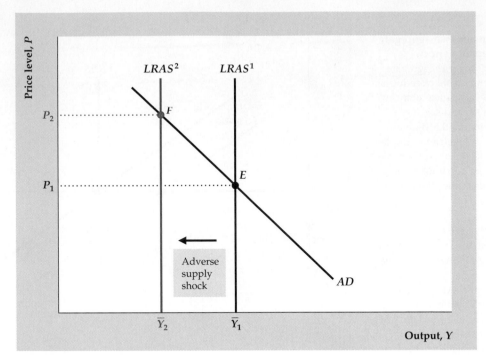

CHAPTER SUMMARY

1. A business cycle consists of a period of declining aggregate economic activity (a contraction or recession) followed by a period of rising economic activity (an expansion or a boom). The low point of the contraction is called the trough, and the high point of the expansion is called the peak. Business cycles have been observed in market economies since the beginning of industrialization.

2. The tendency of many economic variables to move together in regular and predictable ways over the course of the cycle is called comovement. We refer to the typical cyclical patterns of key macroeconomic variables as the "business cycle facts."

3. The fluctuations in aggregate economic activity that constitute business cycles are recurrent, having been observed again and again in industrialized market economies. However, they aren't periodic, in that they don't occur at regular or predictable intervals. Business cycle fluctuations also are persistent, which means that once a recession or expansion begins, it usually lasts for a while.

4. Many economists believe that the U.S. economy before 1929 had longer recessions and more cyclical

volatility than the post–World War II economy. However, data problems prevent precise measurements of how much more cyclical the pre–1929 economy was. The Great Depression that began in 1929 and didn't end until the onset of World War II was the most severe cyclical decline in U.S. history. Moderation of the business cycle after World War II led to premature pronouncements that the cycle was "dead." However, the U.S. economy suffered severe recessions in 1973–1975 and 1981–1982. Between 1982 and the end of the millennium the economy enjoyed a "long boom," with only one minor recession in 1990–1991.

5. The direction of a variable relative to the business cycle can be procyclical, countercyclical, or acyclical. A procyclical variable moves in the same direction as aggregate economic activity, rising in booms and falling in recessions. A countercyclical variable moves in the opposite direction to aggregate economic activity, falling in booms and rising in recessions. An acyclical variable has no clear cyclical pattern.

6. The timing of a variable relative to the business cycle may be coincident, leading, or lagging. A coincident variable's peaks and troughs occur at about the same

time as peaks and troughs in aggregate economic activity. Peaks and troughs in a leading variable come before, and peaks and troughs in a lagging variable come after, the corresponding peaks and troughs in aggregate economic activity.

7. The cyclical direction and timing of major macro-economic variables—the business cycle facts—are described in Summary table 10, p. 290. In brief, production, consumption, and investment are procyclical and coincident. Investment is much more volatile over the business cycle than consumption is. Employment is procyclical, but the unemployment rate is countercyclical. Average labor productivity and the real wage are procyclical, although according to most studies the real wage is only mildly so. Money and stock prices are procyclical and lead the cycle. Inflation and nominal interest rates are procyclical and lagging. The real interest rate is acyclical.

8. A theory of business cycles consists of (1) a description of shocks that affect the economy and (2) a model, such as the aggregate demand–aggregate supply (AD–AS) model, that describes how the economy responds to these shocks. In the AD–AS model, shocks to the aggregate demand (AD) curve cause output to change in the short run, but output returns to its full-employment level, $\bar{Y}$, in the long run. Shocks to the aggregate supply curve can affect output both in the long run and the short run.

9. Classical economists argue that the economy reaches its long-run equilibrium quickly, because prices adjust rapidly. This view implies that aggregate demand shocks have only very short-lived effects on real variables such as output; instead, classical economists emphasize aggregate supply shocks as the source of business cycles. Classicals also see little role for government policies to fight recessions. Keynesian economists, in contrast, believe that it takes a long time for the economy to reach long-run equilibrium. They conclude, therefore, that aggregate demand shocks can affect output for substantial periods of time. Furthermore, they believe that government policies may be useful in speeding the economy's return to full employment.

KEY TERMS

acyclical, p. 284
boom, p. 275
business cycle, p. 276
business cycle chronology, p. 275
coincident variable, p. 284
comovement, p. 277
contraction, p. 275

countercyclical, p. 284
depression, p. 275
expansion, p. 275
index of leading indicators, p. 285
job finding rate, p. 293
job loss rate, p. 293
lagging variable, p. 284

leading variable, p. 284
peak, p. 275
persistence, p. 277
procyclical, p. 284
recession, p. 275
trough, p. 275
turning points, p. 276

REVIEW QUESTIONS

All review questions are available in myeconlab at www.myeconlab.com.

1. Draw a diagram showing the phases and turning points of a business cycle. Using the diagram, illustrate the concepts of recurrence and persistence.

2. What is *comovement*? How is comovement related to the business cycle facts presented in this chapter?

3. What is the evidence for the view that the U.S. business cycle has become less severe over time? Why is the question of whether the cycle has moderated over time an important one?

4. What terms are used to describe the way a variable moves when economic activity is rising or falling? What terms are used to describe the timing of cyclical changes in economic variables?

5. If you knew that the economy was falling into a recession, what would you expect to happen to production during the next few quarters? To investment? To average labor productivity? To the real wage? To the unemployment rate?

6. How is the fact that some economic variables are known to lead the cycle used in macroeconomic forecasting?

7. What are the two components of a theory of business cycles?

8. How do Keynesians and classicals differ in their beliefs about how long it takes the economy to reach long-run equilibrium? What implications do these differences in beliefs have for Keynesian and classical views about the usefulness of antirecessionary policies? About the types of shocks that cause most recessions?

ANALYTICAL PROBLEMS

1. Figure 8.1 shows that business cycle peaks and troughs are identified with peaks and troughs in the level of aggregate economic activity, which is consistent with current NBER methodology. However, for business cycles before 1927, the NBER identified business cycle peaks and troughs with peaks and troughs in *detrended* aggregate economic activity (aggregate economic activity minus the "normal growth path" shown in Fig. 8.1). Show that this alternative methodology implies that peaks occur earlier and that troughs occur later than you would find when using the current methodology. Compared to the current methodology, does the alternative methodology increase or decrease the computed length of contractions and expansions? How might this change in measurement account for the differences in the average measured lengths of expansions and contractions since World War II compared to the period before World War I?[17]

2. Consumer expenditures on durable goods such as cars and furniture, as well as purchases of new houses, fall much more than expenditures on nondurable goods and services during most recessions. Why do you think that is?

3. Output, total hours worked, and average labor productivity all are procyclical.

   a. Which variable, output or total hours worked, increases by a larger percentage in expansions and falls by a larger percentage in recessions? (*Hint:* Average labor productivity = output ÷ total hours worked, so that the percentage change in average labor productivity equals the percentage change in output minus the percentage change in total hours worked.)

   b. How is the procyclical behavior of average labor productivity related to Okun's Law, discussed in Chapter 3?

4. During the period 1973–1975, the United States experienced a deep recession with a simultaneous sharp rise in the price level. Would you conclude that the recession was the result of a supply shock or a demand shock? Illustrate, using *AD–AS* analysis.

5. It is sometimes argued that economic growth that is "too rapid" will be associated with inflation. Use *AD–AS* analysis to show how this statement might be true. When this claim is made, what type of shock is implicitly assumed to be hitting the economy?

WORKING WITH MACROECONOMIC DATA

For data to use in these exercises, go to the Federal Reserve Bank of St. Louis FRED database at research.stlouisfed.org/fred2.

1. An economic variable is persistent if declines in the variable tend to be followed by more declines, and increases by more increases. This question asks you to study the persistence of the civilian unemployment rate.

   Using data since 1961, identify all quarters in which the unemployment rate changed by at least 0.2 percentage points from the previous quarter (either up or down). (Note: you may wish to use the data converter on the Web site for this textbook at *www.pearsonhighered.com/abel/* to help you calculate quarterly averages of the unemployment rate, which is a monthly variable.) How many of these changes by 0.2 percentage points or more were

followed in the subsequent quarter by (1) another change in the same direction, (2) a change in the opposite direction, or (3) no change? Based on your count, would you say that the unemployment rate is a persistent variable?

2. How does each of the following variables behave over the business cycle? Develop graphs to show your results and give economic explanations.

   a. Real imports

   b. Federal government receipts

   c. Housing starts

   d. Capacity utilization rate, manufacturing

   e. Average weekly hours, manufacturing

---

[17]For further discussion of these issues, see Christina D. Romer, "Remeasuring Business Cycles," *Journal of Economic History,* September 1994, pp. 573–609; and Randall E. Parker and Philip Rothman, "Further Evidence on the Stabilization of Postwar Economic Fluctuations," *Journal of Macroeconomics,* Spring 1996, pp. 289–298. Romer was the first to emphasize the potential importance of the change in business cycle dating methodology.

3. It has been argued that the stock market predicts recessions. Using quarterly data since 1961, plot the real value of the stock market index (the S&P 500 index in the last month of the quarter divided by the GDP deflator). [Note that data on the S&P 500 index may be found at *finance.yahoo.com*.] Draw in the business cycle peaks and troughs. Do you find the stock market to be a good economic forecaster?

4. Graph the levels of real GDP for the United States, Canada, and Germany (data can be found at *www.oecd.org* under Statistics and then under National Accounts). Are U.S. and Canadian business cycles closely related? U.S. and German business cycles?

5. In the FRED database, find a variable that is available in both a seasonally adjusted form and a not seasonally adjusted form. Plot both over time and describe how large the seasonal variation in the variable is.

9

The *IS–LM/AD–AS* Model: A General Framework for Macroeconomic Analysis

The main goal of Chapter 8 was to *describe* business cycles by presenting the business cycle facts. This and the following two chapters attempt to *explain* business cycles and how policymakers should respond to them. First, we must develop a macroeconomic model that we can use to analyze cyclical fluctuations and the effects of policy changes on the economy. By examining the labor market in Chapter 3, the goods market in Chapter 4, and the asset market in Chapter 7, we already have identified the three components of a complete macroeconomic model. Now we put these three components together into a single framework that allows us to analyze them simultaneously. This chapter, then, consolidates our previous analyses to provide the theoretical structure for the rest of the book.

The basic macroeconomic model developed in this chapter is known as the *IS–LM* model. (As we discuss later, this name originates in two of its basic equilibrium conditions: that investment, *I,* must equal saving, *S,* and that money demanded, *L,* must equal money supplied, *M.*) The *IS–LM* model was developed in 1937 by Nobel laureate Sir John Hicks,[1] who intended it as a graphical representation of the ideas presented by Keynes in his famous 1936 book, *The General Theory of Employment, Interest, and Money.* Reflecting Keynes's belief that wages and prices don't adjust quickly to clear markets (see Section 1.3), in his original *IS–LM* model Hicks assumed that the price level was fixed, at least temporarily. Since Hicks, several generations of economists have worked to refine the *IS–LM* model, and it has been widely applied in analyses of cyclical fluctuations and macroeconomic policy, and in forecasting.

Because of its origins, the *IS–LM* model is commonly identified with the Keynesian approach to business cycle analysis. Classical economists—who believe that wages and prices move rapidly to clear markets—would reject Hicks's *IS–LM* model because of his assumption that the price level is fixed. However, the conventional *IS–LM* model may be easily adapted to allow for rapidly adjusting wages

---

[1]Hicks outlined the *IS–LM* framework in an article entitled "Mr. Keynes and the Classics: A Suggested Interpretation," *Econometrica,* April 1937, pp. 137–159.

and prices. Thus the *IS–LM* framework, although originally developed by Keynesians, also may be used to present and discuss the classical approach to business cycle analysis. In addition, the *IS–LM* model is equivalent to the *AD–AS* model that we previewed in Section 8.4. We show how the *AD–AS* model is derived from the *IS–LM* model and illustrate how the *AD–AS* model can be used with either a classical or a Keynesian perspective.

Using the *IS–LM* model (and the equivalent *AD–AS* model) as a framework for both classical and Keynesian analyses has several practical benefits: First, it avoids the need to learn two different models. Second, utilizing a single framework emphasizes the large areas of agreement between the Keynesian and classical approaches while showing clearly how the two approaches differ. Moreover, because versions of the *IS–LM* model (and its concepts and terminology) are so often applied in analyses of the economy and macroeconomic policy, studying this framework will help you understand and participate more fully in current economic debates.

We use a graphical approach to develop the *IS–LM* model. Appendix 9.B presents the identical analysis in algebraic form. If you have difficulty understanding why the curves used in the graphical analysis have the slopes they do or why they shift, you may find the algebra in the appendix helpful.

To keep things as simple as possible, in this chapter we assume that the economy is closed. In Chapter 13 we show how to extend the analysis to allow for a foreign sector.

9.1 The *FE* Line: Equilibrium in the Labor Market

In previous chapters, we discussed the three main markets of the economy: the labor market, the goods market, and the asset market. We also identified some of the links among these markets, but now we want to be more precise about how they fit into a complete macroeconomic system.

Let's turn first to the labor market and recall from Chapter 3 the concepts of the full-employment level of employment and full-employment output. The *full-employment level of employment, $\overline{N}$,* is the equilibrium level of employment reached after wages and prices have fully adjusted. *Full-employment output, $\overline{Y}$,* is the amount of output produced when employment is at its full-employment level, for the current level of the capital stock and the production function. Algebraically, full-employment output, $\overline{Y}$, equals $AF(K,\overline{N})$, where K is the capital stock, A is productivity, and F is the production function (see Eq. 3.4).

Our ultimate goal is a diagram that has the real interest rate on the vertical axis and output on the horizontal axis. In such a diagram equilibrium in the labor market is represented by the **full-employment line,** or *FE,* in Fig. 9.1. The *FE* line is vertical at $Y = \overline{Y}$ because, when the labor market is in equilibrium, output equals its full-employment level, regardless of the interest rate.[2]

---

[2]The real interest rate affects investment and thus the amount of capital that firms will have in the future, but it doesn't affect the current capital stock, and hence does not affect current full-employment output.

Figure 9.1

The *FE* line
The full-employment (*FE*) line represents labor market equilibrium. When the labor market is in equilibrium, employment equals its full-employment level, $\overline{N}$, and output equals its full-employment level, $\overline{Y}$, regardless of the value of the real interest rate. Thus the *FE* line is vertical at $Y = \overline{Y}$.

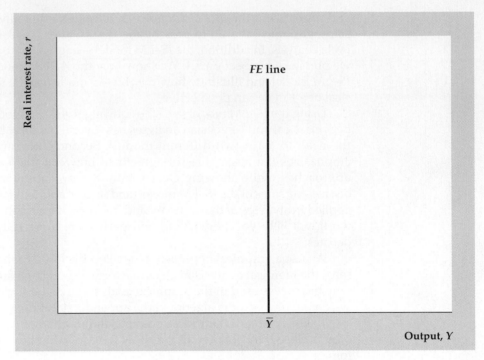

Factors That Shift the *FE* Line

The full-employment level of output is determined by the full-employment level of employment and the current levels of capital and productivity. Any change that affects the full-employment level of output, $\overline{Y}$, will cause the *FE* line to shift. Recall that full-employment output, $\overline{Y}$, increases—and thus the *FE* line shifts to the right—when the labor supply increases (which raises equilibrium employment $\overline{N}$), when the capital stock increases, or when there is a beneficial supply shock. Similarly, a drop in the labor supply or capital stock, or an adverse supply shock, lowers full-employment output, $\overline{Y}$, and shifts the *FE* line to the left. Summary table 11 lists the factors that shift the *FE* line.

SUMMARY 11

Factors That Shift the Full-Employment (*FE*) Line

A(n)	Shifts the *FE* line	Reason
Beneficial supply shock	Right	**1.** More output can be produced for the same amount of capital and labor.
		2. If the *MPN* rises, labor demand increases and raises employment. Full-employment output increases for both reasons.
Increase in labor supply	Right	Equilibrium employment rises, raising full-employment output.
Increase in the capital stock	Right	More output can be produced with the same amount of labor. In addition, increased capital may increase the *MPN*, which increases labor demand and equilibrium employment.

9.2 The *IS* Curve: Equilibrium in the Goods Market

The second of the three markets in our model is the goods market. Recall from Chapter 4 that the goods market is in equilibrium when desired investment and desired national saving are equal or, equivalently, when the aggregate quantity of goods supplied equals the aggregate quantity of goods demanded. Recall that adjustments in the real interest rate help bring about equilibrium in the goods market.

In a diagram with the real interest rate on the vertical axis and real output on the horizontal axis, equilibrium in the goods market is described by a curve called the *IS* curve. For any level of output (or income), Y, the **IS curve** shows the real interest rate, r, for which the goods market is in equilibrium. The *IS* curve is so named because at all points on the curve desired investment, I^d, equals desired national saving, S^d.

Figure 9.2 shows the derivation of the *IS* curve from the saving–investment diagram introduced in Chapter 4 (see Key Diagram 3, p. 142). Figure 9.2(a) shows the saving–investment diagram drawn for two randomly chosen levels of output, 4000 and 5000. Corresponding to each level is a saving curve, with the value of output indicated in parentheses next to it. Each saving curve slopes upward because an increase in the real interest rate causes households to increase their desired level of saving. An increase in current output (income) leads to more desired saving at any real interest rate, so the saving (S) curve for $Y = 5000$ lies to the right of the saving (S) curve for $Y = 4000$.

Also shown in Fig. 9.2(a) is an investment curve. Recall from Chapter 4 that the investment curve slopes downward. It slopes downward because an increase in the real interest rate increases the user cost of capital, which reduces the desired capital stock and hence desired investment. Desired investment isn't affected by current output, so the investment curve is the same whether $Y = 4000$ or $Y = 5000$.

Each level of output implies a different market-clearing real interest rate. When output is 4000, goods market equilibrium is at point D and the market-clearing real interest rate is 7%. When output is 5000, goods market equilibrium occurs at point F and the market-clearing real interest rate is 5%.

Figure 9.2(b) shows the *IS* curve for this economy, with output on the horizontal axis and the real interest rate on the vertical axis. For any level of output, the *IS* curve shows the real interest rate that clears the goods market. Thus $Y = 4000$ and $r = 7\%$ at point D on the *IS* curve. (Note that point D in Fig. 9.2b corresponds to point D in Fig. 9.2a.) Similarly, when output is 5000, the real interest rate that clears the goods market is 5%. This combination of output and the real interest rate occurs at point F on the *IS* curve in Fig. 9.2(b), which corresponds to point F in Fig. 9.2(a). In general, because a rise in output increases desired national saving, thereby reducing the real interest rate that clears the goods market, the *IS* curve slopes downward.

The slope of the *IS* curve may also be interpreted in terms of the alternative (but equivalent) version of the goods market equilibrium condition, which states that in equilibrium the aggregate quantity of goods demanded must equal the aggregate quantity of goods supplied. To illustrate, let's suppose that the economy is initially at point F in Fig. 9.2(b). The aggregate quantities of goods supplied and

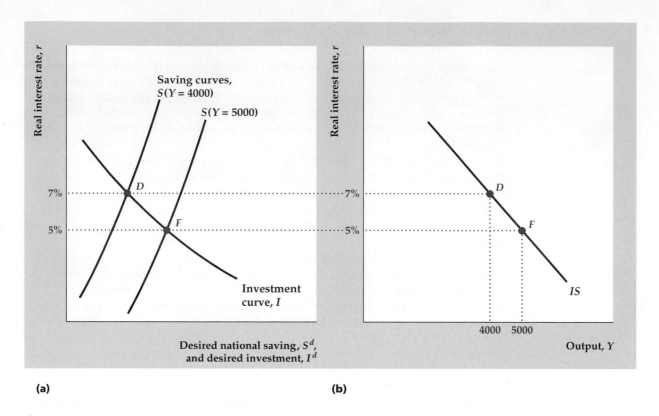

(a)   **(b)**

Figure 9.2

Deriving the IS curve

(a) The graph shows the goods market equilibrium for two different levels of output: 4000 and 5000 (the output correspond-ing to each saving curve is indicated in parentheses next to the curve). Higher levels of output (income) increase desired national saving and shift the saving curve to the right. When output is 4000, the real interest rate that clears the goods market is 7% (point D). When output is 5000, the market-clearing real interest rate is 5% (point F).

(b) For each level of output the IS curve shows the corresponding real interest rate that clears the goods market. Thus each point on the IS curve corresponds to an equilibrium point in the goods market. As in (a), when output is 4000, the real interest rate that clears the goods market is 7% (point D); when output is 5000, the market-clearing real interest rate is 5% (point F). Because higher output raises saving and leads to a lower market-clearing real interest rate, the IS curve slopes downward.

demanded are equal at point F because F lies on the IS curve, which means that the goods market is in equilibrium at that point.[3]

Now suppose that for some reason the real interest rate r rises from 5% to 7%. Recall from Chapter 4 that an increase in the real interest rate reduces both desired consumption, C^d (because people desire to save more when the real interest rate rises), and desired investment, I^d, thereby reducing the aggregate quantity of goods demanded. If output, Y, remained at its initial level of 5000, the increase in the real interest rate would imply that more goods were being supplied than demanded. For the goods market to reach equilibrium at the higher real interest rate, the quan-tity of goods supplied has to fall. At point D in Fig. 9.2(b), output has fallen enough

---

[3]We have just shown that desired national saving equals desired investment at point F, or $S^d = I^d$. Substituting the definition of desired national saving, $Y - C^d - G$, for S^d in the condition that desired national saving equals desired investment shows also that $Y = C^d + I^d + G$ at F.

SUMMARY 12

Factors That Shift the *IS* Curve

An increase in	Shifts the *IS* curve	Reason
Expected future output	Up and to the right	Desired saving falls (desired consumption rises), raising the real interest rate that clears the goods market.
Wealth	Up and to the right	Desired saving falls (desired consumption rises), raising the real interest rate that clears the goods market.
Government purchases, *G*	Up and to the right	Desired saving falls (demand for goods rises), raising the real interest rate that clears the goods market.
Taxes, *T*	No change or down and to the left	No change, if consumers take into account an offsetting future tax cut and do not change consumption (Ricardian equivalence); down and to the left, if consumers don't take into account a future tax cut and reduce desired consumption, increasing desired national saving and lowering the real interest rate that clears the goods market.
Expected future marginal product of capital, MPK^f	Up and to the right	Desired investment increases, raising the real interest rate that clears the goods market.
Effective tax rate on capital	Down and to the left	Desired investment falls, lowering the real interest rate that clears the goods market.

(from 5000 to 4000) that the quantities of goods supplied and demanded are equal, and the goods market has returned to equilibrium.[4] Again, higher real interest rates are associated with less output in goods market equilibrium, so the *IS* curve slopes downward.

Factors That Shift the *IS* Curve

For any level of output, the *IS* curve shows the real interest rate needed to clear the goods market. With output held constant, any economic disturbance or policy change that changes the value of the goods-market-clearing real interest rate will cause the *IS* curve to shift. More specifically, for constant output, *any change in the economy that reduces desired national saving relative to desired investment will increase the real interest rate that clears the goods market and thus shift the* IS *curve up and to the right*. Similarly, for constant output, changes that increase desired saving relative to desired investment, thereby reducing the market-clearing real interest rate, shift the *IS* curve down and to the left. Factors that shift the *IS* curve are described in Summary table 12.

---

[4]Although a drop in output, *Y*, obviously reduces the quantity of goods supplied, it also reduces the quantity of goods demanded. The reason is that a drop in output is also a drop in income, which reduces desired consumption. However, although a drop in output of one dollar reduces the supply of output by one dollar, a drop in income of one dollar reduces desired consumption, C^d, by less than one dollar (that is, the marginal propensity to consume, defined in Chapter 4, is less than 1). Thus a drop in output, *Y*, reduces goods supplied more than goods demanded and therefore reduces the excess supply of goods.

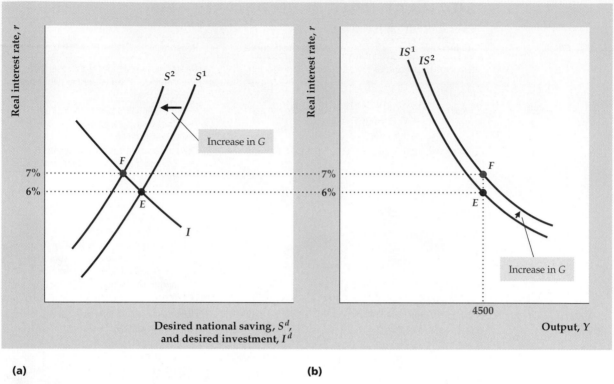

(a)   **(b)**

Figure 9.3

Effect on the *IS* curve of a temporary increase in government purchases

(a) The saving–investment diagram shows the effects of a temporary increase in government purchases, *G*, with output, *Y*, constant at 4500. The increase in *G* reduces desired national saving and shifts the saving curve to the left, from S^1 to S^2. The goods market equilibrium point moves from point *E* to point *F*, and the real interest rate rises from 6% to 7%.

(b) The increase in *G* raises the real interest rate that clears the goods market for any level of output. Thus the *IS* curve shifts up and to the right from IS^1 to IS^2. In this example, with output held constant at 4500, an increase in government purchases raises the real interest rate that clears the goods market from 6% (point *E*) to 7% (point *F*).

We can use a change in current government purchases to illustrate *IS* curve shifts in general. The effects of a temporary increase in government purchases on the *IS* curve are shown in Fig. 9.3. Figure 9.3(a) shows the saving–investment diagram, with an initial saving curve, S^1, and an initial investment curve, *I*. The S^1 curve represents saving when output (income) is fixed at *Y* = 4500. Figure 9.3(b) shows the initial *IS* curve, IS^1. The initial goods market equilibrium when output, *Y*, equals 4500 is represented by point *E* in both (a) and (b). At *E*, the initial market-clearing real interest rate is 6%.

Now suppose that the government increases its current purchases of goods, *G*. Desired investment at any level of the real interest rate isn't affected by the increase in government purchases, so the investment curve doesn't shift. However, as discussed in Chapter 4, a temporary increase in government purchases reduces desired national saving, $Y - C^d - G$ (see Summary table 5, p. 118), so the saving curve shifts to the left from S^1 to S^2 in Fig. 9.3(a). As a result of the reduction in desired national saving, the real interest rate that clears the goods market when output equals 4500 increases from 6% to 7% (point *F* in Fig. 9.3a).

The effect on the *IS* curve is shown in Fig. 9.3(b). With output constant at 4500, the real interest rate that clears the goods market increases from 6% to 7%, as shown by the shift from point *E* to point *F*. The new *IS* curve, IS^2, passes through *F* and lies above and to the right of the initial *IS* curve, IS^1. Thus a temporary increase in government purchases shifts the *IS* curve up and to the right.

So far our discussion of *IS* curve shifts has focused on the goods market equilibrium condition that desired national saving must equal desired investment. However, factors that shift the *IS* curve may also be described in terms of the alternative (but equivalent) goods market equilibrium condition—that the aggregate quantities of goods demanded and supplied are equal. In particular, for a given level of output, *any change that increases the aggregate demand for goods shifts the* IS *curve up and to the right*.

This rule works because, for the initial level of output, an increase in the aggregate demand for goods causes the quantity of goods demanded to exceed the quantity supplied. Goods market equilibrium can be restored at the same level of output by an increase in the real interest rate, which reduces desired consumption, C^d, and desired investment, I^d. For any level of output, an increase in aggregate demand for goods raises the real interest rate that clears the goods market, so we conclude that an increase in the aggregate demand for goods shifts the *IS* curve up and to the right.

To illustrate this alternative way of thinking about shifts in the *IS* curve, we again use the example of a temporary increase in government purchases. Note that an increase in government purchases, *G*, directly raises the demand for goods, $C^d + I^d + G$, leading to an excess demand for goods at the initial level of output. The excess demand for goods can be eliminated and goods market equilibrium at the initial level of output restored by an increase in the real interest rate, which reduces C^d and I^d. Because a higher real interest rate is required for goods market equilibrium when government purchases increase, an increase in *G* causes the *IS* curve to shift up and to the right.

9.3 The *LM* Curve: Asset Market Equilibrium

The third and final market in our macroeconomic model is the asset market, presented in Chapter 7. The asset market is in equilibrium when the quantities of assets demanded by holders of wealth for their portfolios equal the supplies of those assets in the economy. In reality, there are many different assets, both real (houses, consumer durables, office buildings) and financial (checking accounts, government bonds). Recall, however, that we aggregated all assets into two categories—money and nonmonetary assets. We assumed that the nominal supply of money is *M* and that money pays a fixed nominal interest rate, i^m. Similarly, we assumed that the nominal supply of nonmonetary assets is *NM* and that these assets pay a nominal interest rate, *i*, and (given expected inflation, π^e) an expected real interest rate, *r*.

With this aggregation assumption, we showed that the asset market equilibrium condition reduces to the requirement that the quantities of money supplied and demanded be equal. In this section we show that asset market equilibrium can be represented by the *LM* curve. However, to discuss how the asset market comes into equilibrium—a task that we didn't complete in Chapter 7—we first introduce an important relationship used every day by traders in financial markets: the relationship between the *price* of a nonmonetary asset and the *interest rate* on that asset.

The Interest Rate and the Price of a Nonmonetary Asset

The price of a nonmonetary asset, such as a government bond, is what a buyer has to pay for it. Its price is closely related to the interest rate that it pays (sometimes called its *yield*). To illustrate this relationship with an example, let's consider a bond that matures in one year. At maturity, we assume, the bondholder will redeem it and receive $10,000; the bond doesn't pay any interest before it matures.[5] Suppose that this bond can now be purchased for $9615. At this price, over the coming year the bond will increase in value by $385 ($10,000 − $9615), or approximately 4% of its current price of $9615. Therefore the nominal interest rate on the bond, or its yield, is 4% per year.

Now suppose that for some reason the current price of a $10,000 bond that matures in one year drops to $9524. The increase in the bond's value over the next year will be $476 ($10,000 − $9524), or approximately 5% of the purchase price of $9524. Therefore, when the current price of the bond falls to $9524, the nominal interest rate on the bond increases to 5% per year. More generally, for the promised schedule of repayments of a bond or other nonmonetary asset, the higher the price of the asset, the lower the nominal interest rate that the asset pays. Thus a media report that, in yesterday's trading, the bond market "strengthened" (bond prices rose), is equivalent to saying that nominal interest rates fell.

We have just indicated why the price of a nonmonetary asset and its nominal interest rate are negatively related. For a given expected rate of inflation, π^e, movements in the nominal interest rate are matched by equal movements in the real interest rate, so the price of a nonmonetary asset and its *real* interest rate are also inversely related. This relationship is a key to deriving the *LM* curve and explaining how the asset market comes into equilibrium.

The Equality of Money Demanded and Money Supplied

To derive the *LM* curve, which represents asset market equilibrium, we recall that the asset market is in equilibrium only if the quantity of money demanded equals the currently available money supply. We depict the equality of money supplied and demanded using the *money supply–money demand diagram,* shown in Fig. 9.4(a). The real interest rate is on the vertical axis and money, measured in real terms, is on the horizontal axis.[6] The *MS* line shows the economy's real money supply, M/P. The nominal money supply, M, is set by the central bank. Thus, for a given price level, P, the real money supply, M/P, is a fixed number and the *MS* line is vertical. For example, if $M = 2000$ and $P = 2$, the *MS* line is vertical at $M/P = 1000$.

[5]A bond that doesn't pay any interest before maturity is called a *discount bond* or a *zero-coupon bond.*
[6]Asset market equilibrium may be expressed as either nominal money supplied equals nominal money demanded, or as real money supplied equals real money demanded. As in Chapter 7, we work with the condition expressed in real terms.

(a)

(b)

Figure 9.4

Deriving the *LM* curve

(a) The curves show real money demand and real money supply. Real money supply is fixed at 1000. When output is 4000, the real money demand curve is *MD* ($Y = 4000$); the real interest rate that clears the asset market is 3% (point *A*). When output is 5000, more money is demanded at the same real interest rate, so the real money demand curve shifts to the right to *MD* ($Y − 5000$). In this case the real interest rate that clears the asset market is 5% (point *C*).
(b) The graph shows the corresponding *LM* curve. For each level of output, the *LM* curve shows the real interest rate that clears the asset market. Thus when output is 4000, the *LM* curve shows that the real interest rate that clears the asset market is 3% (point *A*). When output is 5000, the *LM* curve shows a market-clearing real interest rate of 5% (point *C*). Because higher output raises money demand, and thus raises the real interest rate that clears the asset market, the *LM* curve slopes upward.

Real money demand at two different levels of income, Y, is shown by the two *MD* curves in Fig. 9.4(a). Recall from Chapter 7 that a higher real interest rate, r, increases the relative attractiveness of nonmonetary assets and causes holders of wealth to demand less money. Thus the money demand curves slope downward. The money demand curve, *MD*, for $Y = 4000$ shows the real demand for money when output is 4000; similarly, the *MD* curve for $Y = 5000$ shows the real demand for money when output is 5000. Because an increase in income increases the amount of money demanded at any real interest rate, the money demand curve for $Y = 5000$ is farther to the right than the money demand curve for $Y = 4000$.

Graphically, asset market equilibrium occurs at the intersection of the money supply and money demand curves, where the real quantities of money supplied and demanded are equal. For example, when output is 4000, so that the money demand curve is *MD* ($Y = 4000$), the money demand and money supply curves intersect at point *A* in Fig. 9.4(a). The real interest rate at *A* is 3%. Thus when output is 4000, the real interest rate that clears the asset market (equalizes the quantities of money supplied and demanded) is 3%. At a real interest rate of 3% and an output of 4000, the real quantity of money demanded by holders of wealth is 1000, which equals the real money supply made available by the central bank.

What happens to the asset market equilibrium if output rises from 4000 to 5000? People need to conduct more transactions, so their real money demand increases at any real interest rate. As a result, the money demand curve shifts to the right, to MD ($Y = 5000$). If the real interest rate remained at 3%, the real quantity of money demanded would exceed the real money supply. At point B in Fig. 9.4(a) the real quantity of money demanded is 1200, which is greater than the real money supply of 1000. To restore equality of money demanded and supplied and thus bring the asset market back into equilibrium, the real interest rate must rise to 5%. When the real interest rate is 5%, the real quantity of money demanded declines to 1000, which equals the fixed real money supply (point C in Fig. 9.4a).

How does an increase in the real interest rate eliminate the excess demand for money, and what causes this increase in the real interest rate? Recall that the prices of nonmonetary assets and the interest rates they pay are negatively related. At the initial real interest rate of 3%, the increase in output from 4000 to 5000 causes people to demand more money (the MD curve shifts to the right in Fig. 9.4a). To satisfy their desire to hold more money, people will try to sell some of their nonmonetary assets for money. But when people rush to sell a portion of their nonmonetary assets, the prices of these assets will fall, which will cause the real interest rates on these assets to rise. Thus it is the public's attempt to increase its holdings of money by selling nonmonetary assets that causes the real interest rate to rise.

Because the real supply of money in the economy is fixed, the public as a whole cannot increase the amount of money it holds. As long as people attempt to do so by selling nonmonetary assets, the real interest rate will continue to rise. But the increase in the real interest rate paid by nonmonetary assets makes those assets more attractive relative to money, reducing the real quantity of money demanded (here the movement is *along* the MD curve for $Y = 5000$, from point B to point C in Fig. 9.4a). The real interest rate will rise until the real quantity of money demanded again equals the fixed supply of money and restores asset market equilibrium. The new asset market equilibrium is at C, where the real interest rate has risen from 3% to 5%.

The preceding example shows that when output rises, increasing real money demand, a higher real interest rate is needed to maintain equilibrium in the asset market. In general, the relationship between output and the real interest rate that clears the asset market is expressed graphically by the LM curve. For any level of output, the **LM curve** shows the real interest rate for which the asset market is in equilibrium, with equal quantities of money supplied and demanded. The term LM comes from the asset market equilibrium condition that the real quantity of money demanded, as determined by the real money demand function, L, must equal the real money supply, M/P.

The LM curve corresponding to our numerical example is shown in Fig. 9.4(b), with the real interest rate, r, on the vertical axis and output, Y, on the horizontal axis. Points A and C lie on the LM curve. At A, which corresponds to point A in the money supply–money demand diagram of Fig. 9.4(a), output, Y, is 4000 and the real interest rate, r, is 3%. Because A lies on the LM curve, when output is 4000 the real interest rate that clears the asset market is 3%. Similarly, because C lies on the LM curve, when output is 5000 the real interest rate that equalizes money supplied and demanded is 5%; this output–real interest rate combination corresponds to the asset market equilibrium at point *C* in Fig. 9.4(a).

Figure 9.4(b) illustrates the general point that the *LM* curve always slopes upward from left to right. It does so because increases in output, by raising money demand, also raise the real interest rate on nonmonetary assets needed to clear the asset market.

Factors That Shift the *LM* Curve

In deriving the *LM* curve we varied output but held constant other factors, such as the price level, that affect the real interest rate that clears the asset market. Changes in any of these other factors will cause the *LM* curve to shift. In particular, for constant output, *any change that reduces real money supply relative to real money demand will increase the real interest rate that clears the asset market and cause the* LM *curve to shift up and to the left*. Similarly, for constant output, anything that raises real money supply relative to real money demand will reduce the real interest rate that clears the asset market and shift the *LM* curve down and to the right. Here we discuss in general terms how changes in real money supply or demand affect the *LM* curve. Summary table 13 describes the factors that shift the *LM* curve.

Changes in the Real Money Supply.   An increase in the real money supply M/P will reduce the real interest rate that clears the asset market and shift the *LM* curve down and to the right. Figure 9.5 illustrates this point and extends our previous numerical example.

Figure 9.5(a) contains the money supply–money demand diagram. Initially, suppose that the real money supply M/P is 1000 and output is 4000, so the money

SUMMARY 13

Factors That Shift the *LM* Curve

An increase in	Shifts the *LM* curve	Reason
Nominal money supply, *M*	Down and to the right	Real money supply increases, lowering the real interest rate that clears the asset market (equates money supplied and money demanded).
Price level, *P*	Up and to the left	Real money supply falls, raising the real interest rate that clears the asset market.
Expected inflation, π^e	Down and to the right	Demand for money falls, lowering the real interest rate that clears the asset market.
Nominal interest rate on money, i^m	Up and to the left	Demand for money increases, raising the real interest rate that clears the asset market.

In addition, for constant output, any factor that increases real money demand raises the real interest rate that clears the asset market and shifts the *LM* curve up and to the left. Other factors that increase real money demand (see Summary table 9, p. 255) include

- ◼ an increase in wealth;
- ◼ an increase in the risk of alternative assets relative to the risk of holding money;
- ◼ a decline in the liquidity of alternative assets; and
- ◼ a decline in the efficiency of payment technologies.

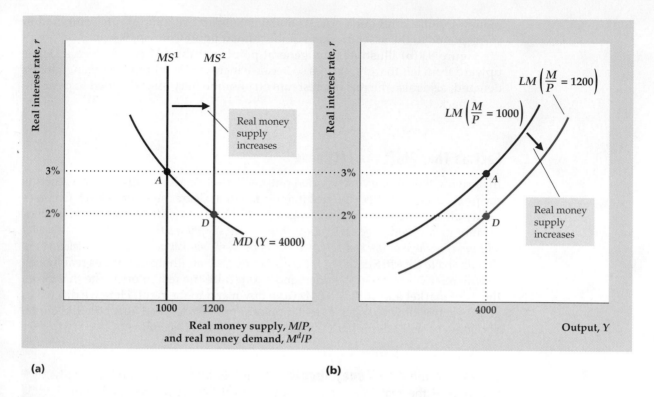

Figure 9.5

An increase in the real money supply shifts the *LM* curve down and to the right
(a) An increase in the real supply of money shifts the money supply curve to the right, from MS^1 to MS^2. For a constant level of output, the real interest rate that clears the asset market falls. If output is fixed at 4000, for example, the money demand curve is MD $(Y = 4000)$ and the real interest rate that clears the asset market falls from 3% (point A) to 2% (point D).
(b) The graph shows the effect of the increase in real money supply on the *LM* curve. For any level of output, the increase in the real money supply causes the real interest rate that clears the asset market to fall. So, for example, when output is 4000, the increase in the real money supply causes the real interest rate that clears the asset market to fall from 3% (point A) to 2% (point D). Thus the *LM* curve shifts down and to the right, from LM $(M/P = 1000)$ to LM $(M/P = 1200)$.

demand curve is MD $(Y = 4000)$. Then equilibrium in the asset market occurs at point A with a market-clearing real interest rate of 3%. The *LM* curve corresponding to the real money supply of 1000 is shown as LM $(M/P = 1000)$ in Fig. 9.5(b). At point A on this *LM* curve, as at point A in the money supply–money demand diagram in Fig. 9.5(a), output is 4000 and the real interest rate is 3%. Because A lies on the initial *LM* curve, when output is 4000 and the money supply is 1000, the real interest rate that clears the asset market is 3%.

Now suppose that, with output constant at 4000, the real money supply rises from 1000 to 1200. This increase in the real money supply causes the vertical money supply curve to shift to the right, from MS^1 to MS^2 in Fig. 9.5(a). The asset market equilibrium point is now point D, where, with output remaining at 4000, the market-clearing real interest rate has fallen to 2%.

Why has the real interest rate that clears the asset market fallen? At the initial real interest rate of 3%, there is an excess supply of money—that is, holders of wealth have more money in their portfolios than they want to hold and, consequently, they have a smaller share of their wealth than they would like in nonmonetary assets. To eliminate this imbalance in their portfolios, holders of wealth will want to use some of their money to buy nonmonetary assets. However, when holders of wealth as a group try to purchase nonmonetary assets, the price of nonmonetary assets is bid up and hence the real interest rate paid on these assets declines. As the real interest rate falls, nonmonetary assets become less attractive relative to money. The real interest rate continues to fall until it reaches 2% at point *D* in Fig. 9.5(a), where the excess supply of money and the excess demand for nonmonetary assets are eliminated and the asset market is back in equilibrium.

The effect of the increase in the real money supply on the *LM* curve is illustrated in Fig. 9.5(b). With output constant at 4000, the increase in the real money supply lowers the real interest rate that clears the asset market, from 3% to 2%. Thus point *D*, where *Y* = 4000 and *r* = 2%, is now a point of asset market equilibrium, and point *A* no longer is. More generally, for any level of output, an increase in the real money supply lowers the real interest rate that clears the asset market. Therefore the entire *LM* curve shifts down and to the right. The new *LM* curve, for *M/P* = 1200, passes through the new equilibrium point *D* and lies below the old *LM* curve, for *M/P* = 1000.

Thus, with fixed output, an increase in the real money supply lowers the real interest rate that clears the asset market and causes the *LM* curve to shift down and to the right. A similar analysis would show that a drop in the real money supply causes the *LM* curve to shift up and to the left.

What might cause the real money supply to increase? In general, because the real money supply equals *M/P*, it will increase whenever the nominal money supply, *M*, which is controlled by the central bank, grows more quickly than the price level, *P*.

Changes in Real Money Demand.   A change in any variable that affects real money demand, other than output or the real interest rate, will also shift the *LM* curve. More specifically, with output constant, an increase in real money demand raises the real interest rate that clears the asset market and thus shifts the *LM* curve up and to the left. Analogously, with output constant, a drop in real money demand shifts the *LM* curve down and to the right.

Figure 9.6 shows a graphical analysis of an increase in money demand similar to that for a change in money supply shown in Fig. 9.5. As before, the money supply–money demand diagram is shown on the left, Fig. 9.6(a). Output is constant at 4000, and the real money supply again is 1000. The initial money demand curve is MD^1. The initial asset market equilibrium point is at *A*, where the money demand curve, MD^1, and the money supply curve, *MS*, intersect. At initial equilibrium, point *A*, the real interest rate that clears the asset market is 3%.

Now suppose that, for a fixed level of output, a change occurs in the economy that increases real money demand. For example, if banks decided to increase the interest rate paid on money, i^m, the public would want to hold more money at the same levels of output and the real interest rate. Graphically, the increase in money demand shifts the money demand curve to the right, from MD^1 to MD^2 in Fig. 9.6(a). At the initial real interest rate of 3%, the real quantity of money demanded is 1300, which exceeds the available supply of 1000; so 3% is no longer the value of the real interest rate that clears the asset market.

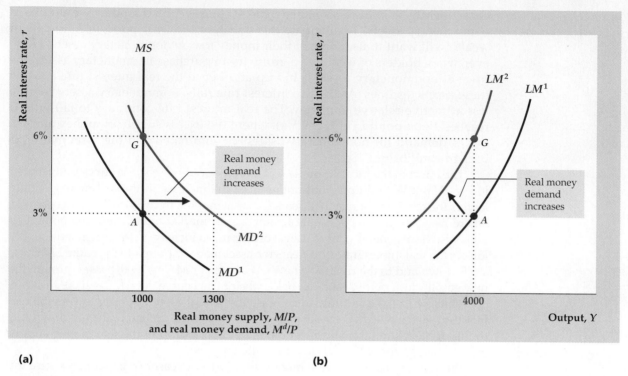

(a)   **(b)**

Figure 9.6

An increase in real money demand shifts the *LM* curve up and to the left
(a) With output constant at 4000 and the real money supply at 1000, an increase in the interest rate paid on money raises real money demand. The money demand curve shifts to the right, from MD^1 to MD^2, and the real interest rate that clears the asset market rises from 3% (point *A*) to 6% (point *G*).
(b) The graph shows the effect of the increase in real money demand on the *LM* curve. When output is 4000, the increase in real money demand raises the real interest rate that clears the asset market from 3% (point *A*) to 6% (point *G*). More generally, for any level of output, the increase in real money demand raises the real interest rate that clears the asset market. Thus the *LM* curve shifts up and to the left, from LM^1 to LM^2.

How will the real interest rate that clears the asset market change after the increase in money demand? If holders of wealth want to hold more money, they will exchange nonmonetary assets for money. Increased sales of nonmonetary assets will drive down their price and thus raise the real interest rate that they pay. The real interest rate will rise, reducing the attractiveness of holding money, until the public is satisfied to hold the available real money supply (1000). The real interest rate rises from its initial value of 3% at *A* to 6% at *G*.

Figure 9.6(b) shows the effect of the increase in money demand on the *LM* curve. The initial *LM* curve, LM^1, passes through point *A*, showing that when output is 4000, the real interest rate that clears the asset market is 3%. (Point *A* in Fig. 9.6b corresponds to point *A* in Fig. 9.6a.) Following the increase in money demand, with output fixed at 4000, the market-clearing real interest rate rises to 6%. Thus the new *LM* curve must pass through point *G* (corresponding to point *G* in Fig. 9.6a), where $Y = 4000$ and $r = 6\%$. The new *LM* curve, LM^2, is higher than LM^1 because the real interest rate that clears the asset market is now higher for any level of output.

9.4 General Equilibrium in the Complete *IS–LM* Model

The next step is to put the labor market, the goods market, and the asset market together and examine the equilibrium of the economy as a whole. A situation in which all markets in an economy are simultaneously in equilibrium is called a **general equilibrium.** Figure 9.7 shows the complete *IS–LM* model, illustrating how the general equilibrium of the economy is determined. Shown are:

- the full-employment, or *FE,* line, along which the labor market is in equilibrium;
- the *IS* curve, along which the goods market is in equilibrium; and
- the *LM* curve, along which the asset market is in equilibrium.

The three curves intersect at point *E,* indicating that all three markets are in equilibrium at that point. Therefore *E* represents a general equilibrium and, because it is the only point that lies on all three curves, the only general equilibrium for this economy.

Although point *E* obviously is a general equilibrium point, not so clear is which forces, if any, act to bring the economy to that point. To put it another way, although the *IS* curve and *FE* line must intersect somewhere, we haven't explained why the *LM* curve must pass through that same point. In Section 9.5 we discuss the economic forces that lead the economy to general equilibrium. There we show that (1) the general equilibrium of the economy always occurs at the intersection of the *IS* curve and the *FE* line; and (2) adjustments of the price level cause the *LM* curve to shift until it passes through the general equilibrium point defined by the intersection of the *IS* curve and the *FE* line. Before discussing the details of this adjustment process, however, let's consider an example that illustrates the use of the complete *IS–LM* model.

Figure 9.7

General equilibrium in the *IS–LM* model
The economy is in general equilibrium when quantities supplied equal quantities demanded in every market. The general equilibrium point, *E,* lies on the *IS* curve, the *LM* curve, and the *FE* line. Thus at *E,* and only at *E,* the goods market, the asset market, and the labor market are simultaneously in equilibrium.

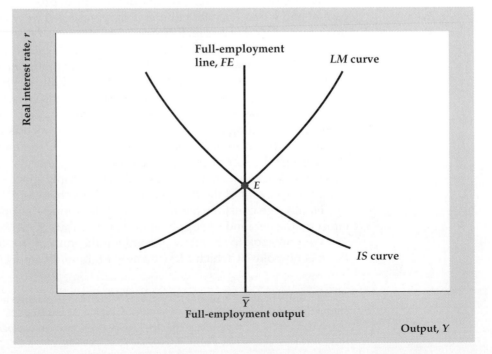

Applying the *IS–LM* Framework: A Temporary Adverse Supply Shock

An economic shock relevant to business cycle analysis is an adverse supply shock. Specifically, suppose that (because of bad weather or a temporary increase in oil prices) the productivity parameter, A, in the production function drops temporarily.[7] We can use the *IS–LM* model to analyze the effects of this shock on the general equilibrium of the economy and the general equilibrium values of economic variables such as the real wage, employment, output, the real interest rate, the price level, consumption, and investment.

Suppose that the economy is initially in general equilibrium at point E in Fig. 9.8(a), where the initial FE line, FE^1, IS curve, and LM curve, LM^1, for this economy intersect. To determine the effects of a temporary supply shock on the general equilibrium of this economy, we must consider how the temporary drop in productivity A affects the positions of the FE line and the IS and LM curves.

The FE line describes equilibrium in the labor market. Hence to find the effect of the supply shock on the FE line we must first look at how the shock affects labor supply and labor demand. In Chapter 3 we demonstrated that an adverse supply shock reduces the marginal product of labor and thus shifts the labor demand curve down (see Fig. 3.11). Because the supply shock is temporary, we assume that it doesn't affect workers' wealth or expected future wages and so doesn't affect labor supply. As a result of the decline in labor demand, the equilibrium values of the real wage and employment, $\overline{N}$, fall.

The FE line shifts only to the degree that full-employment output, $\overline{Y}$, changes. Does $\overline{Y}$ change? Yes. Recall from Chapter 3 that an adverse supply shock reduces full-employment output, $\overline{Y}$, which equals $AF(K,\overline{N})$, for two reasons: (1) as we just mentioned, the supply shock reduces the equilibrium level of employment, $\overline{N}$, which lowers the amount of output that can be produced; and (2) the drop in productivity A directly reduces the amount of output produced by any combination of capital and labor. The reduction in $\overline{Y}$ is represented by a shift to the left of the FE line, from FE^1 to FE^2 in Fig. 9.8(b).

Now consider the effects of the temporary adverse supply shock on the IS curve. Recall that we derived the IS curve by changing the level of current output in the saving–investment diagram (Fig. 9.2) and finding for each level of current output the real interest rate for which desired saving equals desired investment. A *temporary* adverse supply shock reduces current output but doesn't change any other factor affecting desired saving or investment (such as wealth, expected future income, or the future marginal product of capital). Therefore a temporary supply shock is just the sort of change in current output that we used to trace out the IS curve. We conclude that a temporary adverse supply shock is a movement *along* the IS curve, *not a shift* of the IS curve, leaving it unchanged.[8]

Finally, we consider the LM curve. A temporary supply shock has no direct effect on the demand or supply of money and thus doesn't shift the LM curve.

We now look for the new general equilibrium of the economy. In Fig. 9.8(b), there is no point at which FE^2 (the new FE line), IS, and LM^1 all intersect. As we

---

[7]Recall that the production function, Eq. (3.1), is $Y = AF(K, N)$, so a drop in A reduces the amount of output that can be produced for any quantities of capital, K, and labor, N.

[8]Analytical Problem 2 at the end of the chapter examines the effect of a permanent adverse supply shock and identifies factors that shift the IS curve in that case.

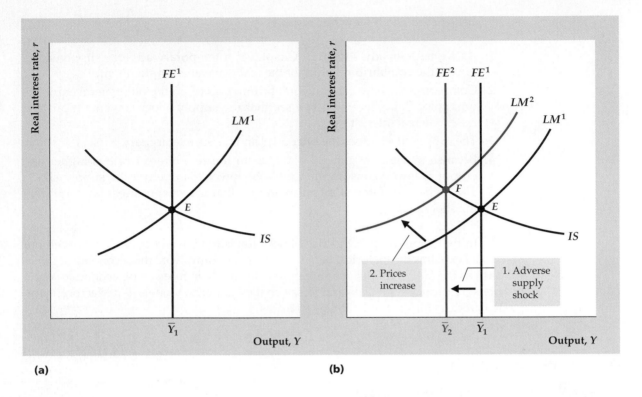

(a)   **(b)**

Figure 9.8

Effects of a temporary adverse supply shock
(a) Initially, the economy is in general equilibrium at point E, with output at its full-employment level, $\overline{Y}_1$.
(b) A temporary adverse supply shock reduces full-employment output from $\overline{Y}_1$ to $\overline{Y}_2$ and shifts the FE line to the left from FE^1 to FE^2. The new general equilibrium is represented by point F, where FE^2 intersects the unchanged IS curve. The price level increases and shifts the LM curve up and to the left, from LM^1 to LM^2, until it passes through F. At the new general equilibrium point, F, output is lower, the real interest rate is higher, and the price level is higher than at the original general equilibrium point, E.

mentioned—and demonstrate in Section 9.5—when the FE line, the IS curve, and the LM curve don't intersect at a common point, the LM curve shifts until it passes through the intersection of the FE line and IS curve. This shift in the LM curve is caused by changes in the price level, P, which change the real money supply, M/P, and thus affect the equilibrium of the asset market. As Fig. 9.8(b) shows, to restore general equilibrium at point F, the LM curve must shift up and to the left, from LM^1 to LM^2. For it to do so, the real money supply M/P must fall (see Summary table 13, p. 321) and thus the price level, P, must rise. We infer (although we haven't yet given an economic explanation) that an adverse supply shock will cause the price level to rise.

What is the effect of a temporary supply shock on the inflation rate, as distinct from the price level? As the inflation rate is the growth rate of the price level, during the period in which prices are rising to their new, higher level, a burst of inflation will occur. However, after the price level stabilizes at its higher value (and is no longer rising), inflation will subside. Thus a temporary supply shock should cause a temporary, rather than a permanent, increase in the rate of inflation.

Let's pause and review our results.

1. As we had already shown in Chapter 3, a temporary adverse supply shock lowers the equilibrium values of the real wage and employment.
2. Comparing the new general equilibrium, point *F,* to the old general equilibrium, point *E,* in Fig. 9.8(b), we see that the supply shock lowers output and raises the real interest rate.
3. The supply shock raises the price level and causes a temporary burst of inflation.
4. Because in the new general equilibrium the real interest rate is higher and output is lower, consumption must be lower than before the supply shock. The higher real interest rate also implies that investment must be lower after the shock.

In the Application "Oil Price Shocks Revisited," we check out how well our model explains the historical behavior of the economy. Note that economic models, such as the *IS–LM* model, also are used extensively in forecasting economic conditions ("In Touch with Data and Research: Econometric Models and Macroeconomic Forecasts for Economic Policy Analysis").

APPLICATION

Oil Price Shocks Revisited

In Chapter 3 we pointed out that an increase in the price of oil is an example of an adverse supply shock, and we looked at the effects of the 1973–1974 and 1979–1980 oil price shocks on the U.S. economy (see the Application "Output, Employment, and the Real Wage During Oil Price Shocks," p. 85). The theory's predictions—that adverse supply shocks reduce output, employment, and the real wage—were confirmed for those two episodes. Our analysis using the complete *IS–LM* model is consistent with that earlier discussion. However, it adds the predictions that, following an oil price shock, consumption and investment decline, inflation increases, and the real interest rate rises.

Figure 8.7 shows that consumption fell slightly and that investment fell sharply immediately after these oil price shocks. From the beginning of the recession in the fourth quarter of 1973 until the fourth quarter of 1974, real consumption fell by 1.8% and real investment fell by 11.1%. Following the onset of the recession in the first quarter of 1980, real consumption fell by 2.3% and real investment fell by 9.0% in just one quarter. Inflation also behaved as predicted by our analysis, surging temporarily in 1973–1974 and again in 1979–1980 (see Fig. 8.13).

Our analysis also predicted that an oil price shock will cause the real interest rate to rise. However, this result depends somewhat on the assumption we made that people expected the oil price shock to be temporary. In Analytical Problem 2 at the end of the chapter, you will find that, if the adverse supply shock is expected to be permanent, the rise in the real interest rate will be less than when the adverse supply shock is expected to be temporary (and the real interest rate may not rise). However, we don't really know what people's expectations were about the duration of the two major oil price shocks. Therefore we can't state with confidence what the effect of such a shock on the real interest rate should have been. Actually, the real interest rate rose during the 1979–1980 shock but not during the 1973–1974 shock (see Fig. 2.3). On the basis of these data only, our model suggests that people expected the 1973–1974 oil shock to be permanent and the 1979–1980 shock to be temporary. Interestingly, those expectations were essentially correct: Figure 3.12 shows that the oil price increase of 1979–1980 was reversed rather quickly but that the price increase of 1973–1974 was not.

IN TOUCH WITH DATA AND RESEARCH

Econometric Models and Macroeconomic Forecasts for Monetary Policy Analysis

The *IS–LM* model developed in this chapter is a relatively simple example of a macroeconomic model. Much more complicated models of the economy (many, though not all of them, based on the *IS–LM* framework) are used in applied macroeconomic research and analysis.

A common use of macroeconomic models is to help economists forecast the course of the economy. In general, using a macroeconomic model to obtain quantitative economic forecasts involves three steps. First, numerical values for the parameters of the model (such as the income elasticity of money demand) must be obtained. In *econometric* models, these values are estimated through statistical analyses of the data. Second, projections must be made of the likely behavior of relevant *exogenous* variables, or variables whose values are not determined within the model. Examples of exogenous variables include policy variables (such as government spending and the money supply), oil prices, and changes in productivity. Third, based on the expected path of the exogenous variables and the model parameters, the model can be solved (usually on a computer) to give forecasts of variables determined within the model (such as output, employment, and interest rates). Variables determined within the model are *endogenous* variables.

Although a relatively simple model like the *IS–LM* model developed in this chapter could be used to create real forecasts, the results probably would not be very good. Because real-world economies are complex, macroeconomic models actually used in forecasting tend to be much more detailed than the *IS–LM* model presented here. For example, the Federal Reserve Board has long had such a model in place for analyzing the economy and for developing forecasts for use in monetary policy.

In 1996, the Federal Reserve Board produced a new model for policy analysis and forecasting, known as the FRB/US model, and has been continually upgrading the model since then. FRB/US was based on a previous model known as the MPS model, which was developed closely from the theoretical *IS–LM* model but with hundreds of equations representing different industries and sectors of the economy. The new FRB/US model differed from the old MPS model in a number of ways: It featured a much better ability to handle people's expectations about the future values of inflation and other variables, improved modeling of people's and firms' reactions to economic shocks, and used newer statistical techniques to estimate the model.

(continued)

The staff economists at the Federal Reserve Board now use the model as a workhorse for policy analysis. They apply results from the model to analyze alternative monetary policy scenarios—for example, what would happen to the economy over the next two years if the Fed raised the Federal funds interest rate to 5%, compared with a scenario in which the rate were set at a lower level, such as 2%. This analysis gives policymakers an idea of how policy affects the economy and what are the likely outcomes of policy choices.

The model contains three main sectors of the economy, just as the *IS–LM* model does: households, firms, and financial markets. Households supply labor, as we discussed in Section 3.3, and decide how much to consume and save, as we saw in Section 4.1 and Appendix 4.A. Firms maximize their profits, choosing appropriate levels of investment, as we discussed in Section 4.2, and demand labor, as we saw in Section 3.2. Firms' and households' demand and supply of financial assets determine equilibrium in the financial markets, as we discussed in Chapter 7. The model is solved with general equilibrium concepts, as we showed in Sections 3.4 for labor markets, 4.3 for goods markets, and 7.4 for asset markets. Overall economic growth is governed by the principles discussed in Chapter 6. Other assumptions of the model are based on new Keynesian theory, as we will discuss in Chapter 11.

Although the model is quite detailed, no macro model is able to provide accurate forecasts without some human judgment. So, to produce the forecasts that the Fed uses internally in its Greenbook publication, the FRB/US model forecasts are analyzed by the staff at the Federal Reserve Board and are often modified somewhat before being presented to monetary policymakers. The judgment of the staff economists who are experts in various sectors of the economy is an important input into the Greenbook forecasts. Evidently, this method of producing forecasts works well, as the Greenbook forecasts have been found to be superior to private sector forecasts.*

---

*See Christina Romer and David Romer, "Federal Reserve Information and the Behavior of Interest Rates," *American Economic Review* (June 2000), pp. 429–457, and Christopher Sims, "The Role of Models and Probabilities in the Monetary Policy Process," *Brookings Papers on Economic Activity* (2:2002), pp. 1–62.

9.5 Price Adjustment and the Attainment of General Equilibrium

We now explain the economic forces that lead prices to change and shift the *LM* curve until it passes through the intersection of the *IS* curve and the *FE* line. In discussing the role of price adjustments in bringing the economy back to general equilibrium, we also show the basic difference between the two main approaches to business cycle analysis, classical and Keynesian.

To illustrate the adjustment process, let's use the complete *IS–LM* model to consider what happens to the economy if the nominal money supply increases. This analysis allows us to discuss monetary policy (the control of the money supply) and to introduce some ongoing controversies about the effects of monetary policy on the economy.

The Effects of a Monetary Expansion

Suppose that the central bank decides to raise the nominal money supply, M, by 10%. For now we hold the price level, P, constant so that the real money supply, M/P, also increases by 10%. What effects will this monetary expansion have on the economy? Figure 9.9 helps us answer this question with the complete *IS–LM* model.

The three parts of Fig. 9.9 show the sequence of events involved in the analysis. For simplicity, suppose that the economy initially is in general equilibrium so that in Fig. 9.9(a) the *IS* curve, the *FE* line, and the initial *LM* curve, LM^1, all pass through the general equilibrium point, E. At E output equals its full-employment value of 1000, and the real interest rate is 5%. Both the *IS* and *LM* curves pass through E, so we know that 5% is the market-clearing real interest rate in both the goods and asset markets. For the moment the price level, P, is fixed at its initial level of 100.

The 10% increase in the real supply of money, M/P, doesn't shift the *IS* curve or the *FE* line because, with output and the real interest rate held constant, a change in M/P doesn't affect desired national saving, desired investment, labor demand, labor supply, or productivity. However, Fig. 9.5 showed that an increase in the real money supply does shift the *LM* curve down and to the right, which we show here as a shift of the *LM* curve from LM^1 to LM^2, in Fig. 9.9(b). The *LM* curve shifts down and to the right because, at any level of output, an increase in the money supply lowers the real interest rate needed to clear the asset market.

Note that, after the *LM* curve has shifted down to LM^2, there is no point in Fig. 9.9(b) at which all three curves intersect. In other words, the goods market, the labor market, and the asset market no longer are simultaneously in equilibrium.

Figure 9.9

Effects of a monetary expansion
(a) The economy is in general equilibrium at point E. Output equals the full-employment level of 1000, the real interest rate is 5%, and the price level is 100.
(b) With the price level fixed, a 10% increase in the nominal money supply, M, raises the real money supply, M/P, and shifts the *LM* curve down and to the right from LM^1 to LM^2. At point F, the intersection of the *IS* curve and the new *LM* curve, LM^2, the real interest rate has fallen to 3%, which raises the aggregate demand for goods. If firms produce extra output to meet the increase in aggregate demand, output rises to 1200 (higher than full-employment output of 1000).
(c) Because aggregate demand exceeds full-employment output at point F, firms raise prices. A 10% rise in P, from 100 to 110, restores the real money supply to its original level and shifts the *LM* curve back to its original position at LM^1. This returns the economy to point E, where output again is at its full-employment level of 1000, but the price level has risen 10% from 100 to 110.

(a)

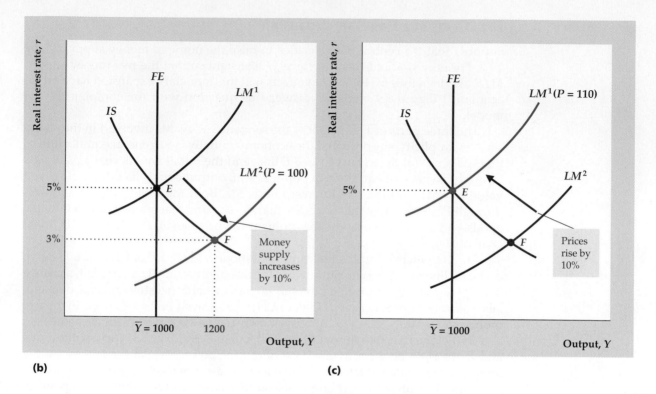

(b)   **(c)**

We now must make some assumptions about how the economy behaves when it isn't in general equilibrium.

Of the three markets in the *IS–LM* model, the asset market (represented by the *LM* curve) undoubtedly adjusts the most quickly, because financial markets can respond within minutes to changes in economic conditions. The labor market (the *FE* line) is probably the slowest to adjust, because the process of matching workers and jobs takes time and wages may be renegotiated only periodically. The adjustment speed of the goods market (*IS* curve) probably is somewhere in the middle. We assume that, when the economy isn't in general equilibrium, the asset market and the goods market are in equilibrium so that *output and the real interest rate are given by the intersection of the* IS *and* LM *curves.* Note that, when the economy isn't in general equilibrium, the *IS–LM* intersection doesn't lie on the *FE* line, so the labor market isn't in equilibrium.

Immediately after the increase in the nominal money supply, therefore, the economy is out of general equilibrium with the level of output and the real interest rate represented by point *F* in Fig. 9.9(b), where the new *LM* curve, LM^2, intersects the *IS* curve. At *F*, output (1200) is higher and the real interest rate (3%) is lower than at the original general equilibrium, point *E*. We refer to *F*, the point at which the economy comes to rest before any adjustment occurs in the price level, as the *short-run equilibrium* point. (Although we refer to *F* as a short-run equilibrium point, keep in mind that only the asset and goods markets are in equilibrium there—the labor market isn't.)

In economic terms, why does the increase in the money supply shift the economy to point *F*? The sequence of events can be described as follows: After the increase in the money supply, holders of wealth are holding more money in their portfolios than they desire at the initial values of output and the real interest rate. To bring their portfolios back into balance, they will try to use their excess money to buy non-monetary assets. However, as holders of wealth bid for nonmonetary assets, they put upward pressure on the prices of those assets, which reduces their interest rate. Thus, after an increase in the money supply, wealth-holders' attempts to achieve their desired mix of money and nonmonetary assets cause the interest rate to fall.

The drop in the real interest rate isn't the end of the story, however. Because the lower real interest rate increases the demand by households for consumption, C^d, and the demand by firms for investment, I^d, the aggregate demand for goods rises. Here we make a fundamental assumption, to which we return shortly: When demanders increase their spending on goods, firms are willing (at least temporarily) to produce enough to meet the extra demand for their output. After the decline in the real interest rate raises the aggregate demand for goods, therefore, we assume that firms respond by increasing production, leading to higher output at the short-run equilibrium point, *F*.

To summarize, with the price level constant, an increase in the nominal money supply takes the economy to the short-run equilibrium point, *F*, in Fig. 9.9(b), at which the real interest rate is lower and output is higher than at the initial general equilibrium point, *E*. We made two assumptions: (1) when the economy isn't in general equilibrium, the economy's short-run equilibrium occurs at the intersection of the *IS* and *LM* curves; and (2) when the aggregate demand for goods rises, firms are willing (at least temporarily) to produce enough extra output to meet the expanded demand.

The Adjustment of the Price Level.   So far we have simply taken the price level, *P*, as fixed. In reality, prices respond to conditions of supply and demand in the economy. The price level, *P*, refers to the price of output (goods), so to think about how prices are likely to adjust in this example, let's reconsider the effects of the increase in the money supply on the goods market.

In Fig. 9.9(b), the short-run equilibrium point, *F*, lies on the *IS* curve, implying that the goods market is in equilibrium at that point with equal aggregate quantities of goods supplied and demanded. Recall our assumption that firms are willing to meet any increases in aggregate demand by producing more. In that sense, then, the aggregate quantity of goods supplied equals the aggregate quantity of goods demanded. However, in another sense the goods market is *not* in equilibrium at point *F*. The problem is that, to meet the aggregate demand for goods at *F*, firms have to produce more output than their full-employment level of output, $\overline{Y}$. Full-employment output, $\overline{Y}$, is the level of output that maximizes firms' profits because that level of output corresponds to the profit-maximizing level of employment (Chapter 3). Therefore, in meeting the higher level of aggregate demand, firms are producing more output than they would like. In the sense that, at point *F*, the production of goods by firms is *not* the level of output that maximizes their profits, the goods market isn't truly in equilibrium.

At point *F* the aggregate demand for goods exceeds firms' desired supply of output, $\overline{Y}$, so we can expect firms to begin raising their prices, causing the price level, *P*, to rise. With the nominal money supply, *M*, set by the central bank, an increase in the price level, *P*, lowers the real money supply, *M/P*, which in turn causes the *LM* curve to shift up and to the left. Indeed, as long as the aggregate quantity of goods demanded exceeds what firms want to supply, prices will keep rising. Thus the *LM* curve will keep shifting up and to the left until the aggregate quantity of goods demanded equals full-employment output. Aggregate demand equals full-employment output only when the LM curve has returned to its initial position, LM^1 in Fig. 9.9(c), where it passes through the original general equilibrium point, E. At E all three markets of the economy again are in equilibrium, with output at its full-employment level.

Compare Fig. 9.9(c) to the initial situation in Fig. 9.9(a) and note that after the adjustment of the price level the 10% increase in the nominal money supply has had no effect on output or the real interest rate. Employment also is unchanged from its initial value, as the economy has returned to its original level of output. However, as a result of the 10% increase in the nominal money supply, the price level is 10% higher (so that $P = 110$). How do we know that the price level changes by exactly 10%? To return the LM curve to its original position, the increase in the price level had to return the real money supply, M/P, to its original value. Because the nominal money supply, M, was raised by 10%, to return M/P to its original value, the price level, P, had to rise by 10% as well. Thus the change in the nominal money supply causes the price level to change proportionally. This result is the same result obtained in Chapter 7 (see Eq. 7.10), where we assumed that all markets are in equilibrium.

Note that, because in general equilibrium the price level has risen by 10% but real economic variables are unaffected, all nominal economic variables must also rise by 10%. In particular, for the real wage to have the same value after prices have risen by 10% as it did before, the nominal wage must rise by 10%. Thus the return of the economy to general equilibrium requires adjustment of the nominal wage (the price of labor) as well as the price of goods.

Trend Money Growth and Inflation.   In Fig 9.9 we analyzed the effects of a one-time 10% increase in the nominal money supply, followed by a one-time 10% adjustment in the price level. In reality, in most countries the money supply and the price level grow continuously. Our framework easily handles this situation. Suppose that in some country both the nominal money supply, M, and the price level, P, are growing steadily at 7% per year, which implies that the real money supply, M/P, is constant. The LM curve depends on the real money supply, M/P, so in this situation the LM curve won't shift, even though the nominal money supply and prices are rising.

Now suppose that for one year the money supply of this country is increased an additional 3%—for a total of 10%—while prices rise 7%. Then the real money supply, M/P, grows by 3% (10% minus 7%), and the LM curve shifts down and to the right. Similarly, if for one year the nominal money supply increased by only 4%, with inflation still at 7% per year, the LM curve would shift up and to the left, reflecting the 3% drop ($-3\% = 4\% - 7\%$) in the real money supply.

This example illustrates that changes in M or P *relative to the expected or trend rate of growth of money and inflation* (7% in this example) shift the LM curve. Thus, when we analyze the effects of "an increase in the money supply," we have in mind an increase in the money supply relative to the expected, or trend, rate of money growth (for example, a rise from 7% to 10% growth for one year); by a "decrease in the money supply," we mean a drop relative to a trend rate (such as a decline from 7% to 4% growth in money). Similarly, if we say something like "the price level falls to restore general equilibrium," we don't necessarily mean that the price level literally falls but only that it rises by less than its trend or expected rate of growth would suggest.

Classical Versus Keynesian Versions of the *IS–LM* Model

Our diagrammatic analysis of the effects of a change in the money supply highlights two questions that are central to the debate between the classical and Keynesian approaches to macroeconomics: (1) How rapidly does the economy reach general equilibrium? and (2) What are the effects of monetary policy on the economy? We previewed the first of these questions in Section 8.4, using the *AD–AS* model. Now we examine both questions, using the *IS–LM* model.

Price Adjustment and the Self-Correcting Economy.   In our analysis of the effects of a monetary expansion, we showed that *the economy is brought into general equilibrium by adjustment of the price level.* In graphical terms, if the intersection of the *IS* and *LM* curves lies to the right of the *FE* line—so that the aggregate quantity of goods demanded exceeds full-employment output, as in Fig. 9.9(b)—the price level will rise. The increase in *P* shifts the *LM* curve up and to the left, reducing the quantity of goods demanded, until all three curves intersect at the general equilibrium point, as in Fig. 9.9(c). Similarly, if the *IS–LM* intersection lies to the left of the full-employment line—so that desired spending on goods is below firms' profit-maximizing level of output—firms will cut prices. A decrease in the price level raises the real money supply and shifts the *LM* curve down and to the right, until all three curves again intersect, returning the economy to general equilibrium.

There is little disagreement about the idea that, after some sort of economic disturbance, price level adjustments will eventually restore the economy to general equilibrium. However, as discussed in Section 8.4, the *speed* at which this process takes place is a controversial issue in macroeconomics. Under the classical assumption that prices are flexible, the adjustment process is rapid. When prices are flexible, the economy is effectively self-correcting, automatically returning to full employment after a shock moves it away from general equilibrium.[9] Indeed, if firms respond to increased demand by raising prices rather than by temporarily producing more (as we earlier assumed), the adjustment process would be almost immediate.

According to the opposing Keynesian view, however, sluggish adjustment of prices (and of wages, the price of labor) might prevent general equilibrium from being attained for a much longer period, perhaps even several years. While the economy is not in general equilibrium, Keynesians argue, output is determined by the level of aggregate demand, represented by the intersection of the *IS* and *LM* curves; the economy is not on the *FE* line, and the labor market is not in equilibrium. This assumption of sluggish price adjustment, and the consequent disequilibrium in the labor market, distinguishes the Keynesian version of the *IS–LM* model from the classical version.

Monetary Neutrality.   Closely related to the issue of how fast the economy reaches general equilibrium is the question of how a change in the nominal money supply affects the economy. We showed that, after the economy reaches its general equilibrium, an increase in the nominal money supply has no effect on real variables such as output, employment, or the real interest rate but raises the price level. Economists say that there is **monetary neutrality,** or simply that

---

[9]The proposition that a free-market economy with flexible prices is automatically self-correcting is consistent with Adam Smith's invisible-hand idea, discussed in Chapter 1.

money is neutral, if a change in the nominal money supply changes the price level proportionally but has no effect on real variables. Our analysis shows that, after the complete adjustment of prices, money is neutral in the *IS–LM* model.

The practical relevance of monetary neutrality is much debated by classicals and Keynesians. The basic issue again is the speed of price adjustment. In the classical view a monetary expansion is rapidly transmitted into prices and has, at most, a transitory effect on real variables; that is, the economy moves quickly from the situation shown in Fig. 9.9(a) to the situation shown in Fig. 9.9(c), spending little time in the position shown in Fig. 9.9(b). Keynesians agree that money is neutral after prices fully adjust but believe that, because of slow price adjustment, the economy may spend a long time in disequilibrium. During this period the increased money supply causes output and employment to rise and the real interest rate to fall (compare Fig. 9.9b with Fig. 9.9a).

In brief, Keynesians believe in monetary neutrality in the long run (after prices adjust) but not in the short run. Classicals are more accepting of the view that money is neutral even in the relatively short run. We return to the issue of monetary neutrality when we develop the classical and Keynesian models of the business cycle in more detail in Chapters 10 and 11.

9.6 Aggregate Demand and Aggregate Supply

The *IS–LM* model introduced in this chapter is a complete model representing the general equilibrium of the economy. In this section we use the *IS–LM* model to develop the aggregate demand–aggregate supply (*AD–AS*) model, which we previewed in Chapter 8. The *AD–AS* model appears to be different from the *IS–LM* model, but in fact the two models are equivalent. They are based on the same assumptions about economic behavior and price adjustment, and they give the same answers when used to analyze the effects of various shocks on the economy. Why then do we bother to present both models? The reason is that, depending on the issue being addressed, one way of representing the economy may be more convenient than the other. The *IS–LM* model relates the real interest rate to output, and the *AD–AS* model relates the price level to output. Thus the *IS–LM* model is more useful for examining the effect of various shocks on the real interest rate and on variables, such as saving and investment, that depend on the real interest rate. In Chapter 13, for example, when we discuss international borrowing and lending in open economies, the behavior of the real interest rate is crucial; therefore, in that chapter we emphasize the *IS–LM* approach. However, for issues related to the price level, or inflation, use of the *AD–AS* model is more convenient. For example, we rely on the *AD–AS* framework in Chapter 12 when we describe the relationship between inflation and unemployment. Keep in mind, though, that the choice of the *IS–LM* framework or the *AD–AS* framework is a matter of convenience; the two models express the same basic macroeconomic theory.

The Aggregate Demand Curve

The **aggregate demand curve** shows the relation between the aggregate quantity of goods demanded, $C^d + I^d + G$, and the price level, P. The aggregate demand curve slopes downward, as does the demand curve for a single product (apples, for example). Despite the superficial similarity between the *AD* curve and the demand curve for a specific good, however, there is an important difference between these two types of curves. The demand curve for apples relates the demand for apples to the price of apples *relative to the prices of other goods.* In contrast, the *AD* curve relates the aggregate quantity of output demanded to the *general price level.* If the prices of all goods increase by 10%, the price level, P, also increases by 10%, even though all relative prices of goods remain unchanged. Nevertheless, the increase in the price level reduces the aggregate quantity of goods demanded.

The reason that an increase in the price level, P, reduces the aggregate quantity of output demanded is illustrated in Fig. 9.10. Recall that, for a *given price level,* the aggregate quantity of output that households, firms, and the government choose to demand is where the *IS* curve and the *LM* curve intersect. Suppose that the nominal money supply is M and that the initial price level is P_1. Then the real money supply is M/P_1, and the initial *LM* curve is LM^1 in Fig. 9.10(a). The *IS* and LM^1 curves intersect at point E, where the amount of output that households, firms, and the government want to buy is Y_1. Thus we conclude that, when the price level is P_1, the aggregate amount of output demanded is Y_1.

Now suppose that the price level increases to P_2. With a nominal money supply of M, this increase in the price level reduces the real money supply from M/P_1 to M/P_2. Recall (Summary table 13, p. 321) that a decrease in the real money supply shifts the *LM* curve up and to the left, to LM^2. The *IS* and LM^2 curves intersect at point F, where the aggregate quantity of output demanded is Y_2. Thus the increase in the price level from P_1 to P_2 reduces the aggregate quantity of output demanded from Y_1 to Y_2.

This negative relation between the price level and the aggregate quantity of output demanded is shown as the downward-sloping *AD* curve in Fig. 9.10(b). Points E and F in Fig. 9.10(b) correspond to points E and F in Fig. 9.10(a), respectively. The *AD* curve slopes downward because an increase in the price level reduces the real money supply, which shifts the *LM* curve up and to the left; the reduction in the real money supply increases the real interest rate, which reduces the demand for goods by households and firms.

Factors That Shift the AD Curve.   The *AD* curve relates the aggregate quantity of output demanded to the price level. For a constant price level, any factor that changes the aggregate demand for output will cause the *AD* curve to shift, with increases in aggregate demand shifting the *AD* curve up and to the right and decreases in aggregate demand shifting it down and to the left. Aggregate demand is determined by the intersection of the *IS* and *LM* curves, so we can also say that, holding the price level constant, any factor that causes the intersection of the *IS* curve and the *LM* curve to shift to the right raises aggregate demand and shifts the *AD* curve up and to the right. Similarly, for a constant price level, any factor that causes the intersection of the *IS* and *LM* curves to shift to the left shifts the *AD* curve down and to the left.

An example of a factor that shifts the *AD* curve up and to the right, which we have considered before, is a temporary increase in government purchases. The effect of the increase in government purchases on the *AD* curve is illustrated in Fig. 9.11. The initial *IS* curve, IS^1, intersects the *LM* curve at point E in Fig. 9.11(a) so that the initial aggregate quantity of output demanded is Y_1. As we have shown, a temporary increase in government purchases shifts the *IS* curve up and to the right to IS^2. With the price level held constant at its initial value of P_1, the intersection of the *IS* and *LM* curves moves to point F so that the aggregate quantity of output demanded increases from Y_1 to Y_2.

Figure 9.10

Derivation of the aggregate demand curve

For a given price level, the aggregate quantity of output demanded is determined where the *IS* and *LM* curves intersect. If the price level, *P*, is P_1 and the initial *LM* curve is LM^1, the initial aggregate quantity of output demanded is Y_1, corresponding to point *E* in both (a) and (b). To derive the aggregate demand curve, we examine what happens to the quantity of output demanded when the price level changes. **(a)** An increase in the price level from P_1 to P_2 reduces the real money supply and shifts the *LM* curve up and to the left, from LM^1 to LM^2. Therefore the aggregate quantity of output demanded, represented by the intersection of the *IS* and *LM* curves, falls from Y_1 to Y_2. **(b)** The increase in the price level from P_1 to P_2 reduces the aggregate quantity of output demanded from Y_1 to Y_2, so the aggregate demand curve slopes downward.

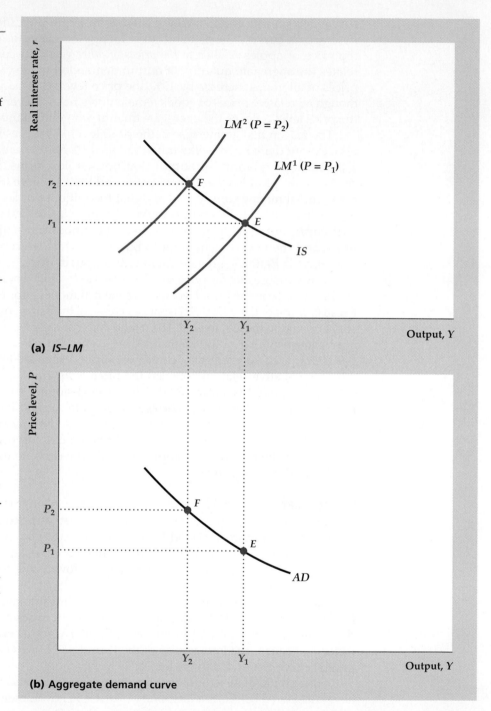

(a) *IS–LM*

(b) Aggregate demand curve

The shift of the *AD* curve resulting from the increase in government purchases is shown in Fig. 9.11(b). The increase in the aggregate quantity of output demanded at price level P_1 is shown by the movement from point *E* to point *F*. Because the increase in government purchases raises the aggregate quantity of output demanded at any price level, the entire *AD* curve shifts up and to the right, from AD^1 to AD^2. Other factors that shift the *AD* curve are listed in Summary table 14, p. 340, and an algebraic derivation of the *AD* curve is presented in Appendix 9.B.

Figure 9.11

The effect of an increase in government purchases on the aggregate demand curve

(a) An increase in government purchases shifts the *IS* curve up and to the right, from IS^1 to IS^2. At price level P_1, the aggregate quantity of output demanded increases from Y_1 to Y_2, as shown by the shift of the *IS–LM* intersection from point *E* to point *F*. **(b)** Because the aggregate quantity of output demanded rises at any price level, the *AD* curve shifts up and to the right. Points *F* and *F* in (b) correspond to points *E* and *F* in (a), respectively.

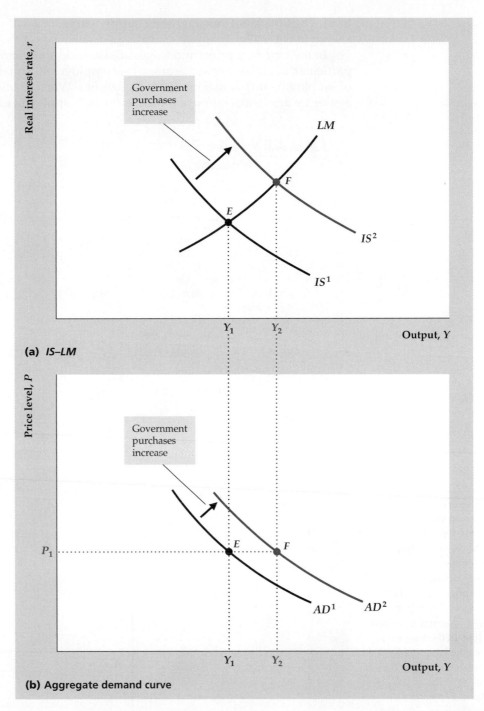

(a) *IS–LM*

(b) Aggregate demand curve

The Aggregate Supply Curve

The **aggregate supply curve** shows the relationship between the price level and the aggregate amount of output that firms supply. Recall from the preview in Chapter 8 and our discussion of the *IS–LM* model that firms are assumed to behave differently in the short run than in the long run. The assumption is that prices remain fixed in the short run and that firms supply the quantity of output demanded at this fixed price level. Thus the **short-run aggregate supply curve,** or *SRAS*, is a horizontal line, as shown in Fig. 9.12.

In the long run, prices and wages adjust to clear all markets in the economy. In particular, the labor market clears so that employment equals $\overline{N}$, which is the level of employment that maximizes firms' profits. When employment equals $\overline{N}$, the aggregate amount of output supplied is the full-employment level, $\overline{Y}$, which equals

SUMMARY 14

Factors That Shift the *AD* Curve

For a constant price level, any factor that shifts the intersection of the *IS* and *LM* curves to the right increases aggregate output demanded and shifts the *AD* curve up and to the right.

Factors that shift the *IS* curve up and to the right, and thus shift the *AD* curve up and to the right (see Summary table 12, p. 315) include

- an increase in expected future output;
- an increase in wealth;
- an increase in government purchases, *G;*
- a reduction in taxes, *T* (assuming no Ricardian equivalence so that consumers respond by raising desired consumption);
- an increase in the expected future *MPK;* and
- a reduction in the effective tax rate on capital.

Factors that shift the *LM* curve down and to the right, and thus shift the *AD* curve up and to the right (see Summary table 13, p. 321) include

- an increase in the nominal money supply, *M;*
- a rise in expected inflation, π^e;
- a decrease in the nominal interest rate on money, i^m; and
- any other change that reduces the real demand for money.

Figure 9.12

The short-run and long-run aggregate supply curves
In the short run, firms supply the amount of output demanded at the fixed price, so the short-run aggregate supply (*SRAS*) curve is a horizontal line. In the long run, when the labor market clears, firms supply the full-employment level of output, $\overline{Y}$, regardless of the price level. Thus the long-run aggregate supply (*LRAS*) curve is a vertical line at $Y = \overline{Y}$.

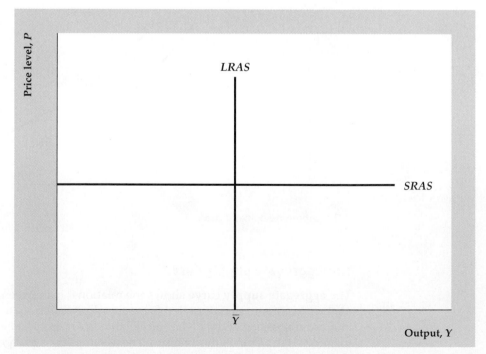

$AF(K,\overline{N})$, regardless of the price level. In the long run, firms supply $\overline{Y}$ at any price level, so the **long-run aggregate supply curve,** or *LRAS*, is a vertical line at $Y = \overline{Y}$, as shown in Fig. 9.12.

Factors That Shift the Aggregate Supply Curves.   Any factor that increases the full-employment level of output, $\overline{Y}$, shifts the long-run aggregate supply (*LRAS*) curve to the right, and any factor that reduces $\overline{Y}$ shifts the *LRAS* curve to the left. Thus any change that shifts the *FE* line to the right in the *IS–LM* diagram also shifts the *LRAS* curve to the right. For instance, an increase in the labor force raises the full-employment levels of employment and output, shifting the *LRAS* curve to the right.

The short-run aggregate supply curve shifts whenever firms change their prices in the short run. Any factor, such as an increase in costs, that leads firms to increase prices in the short run will shift the *SRAS* curve up, and any factor that leads firms to decrease prices in the short run will shift the *SRAS* curve down.

Equilibrium in the *AD–AS* Model

When we previewed the *AD–AS* model in Section 8.4, we introduced the distinction between short-run equilibrium (equilibrium when prices are fixed) and long-run equilibrium (equilibrium when prices have fully adjusted). Short-run equilibrium is represented by the intersection of the *AD* and *SRAS* curves, as at point *E* in Fig. 9.13. Long-run equilibrium is represented by the intersection of the *AD* and *LRAS* curves, which is also at point *E* in Fig. 9.13. Thus point *E* represents both the short-run and long-run equilibria of the economy. When the economy is in

Figure 9.13

Equilibrium in the *AD–AS* model
Short-run equilibrium is represented by the intersection of the *AD* and *SRAS* curves at point *E*. At short-run equilibrium, prices are fixed and firms meet demand at those prices. Long-run equilibrium, which occurs after prices have fully adjusted, is represented by the intersection of the *AD* and *LRAS* curves, also at point *E*. Long-run equilibrium is the same as general equilibrium, because in long-run equilibrium all markets clear.

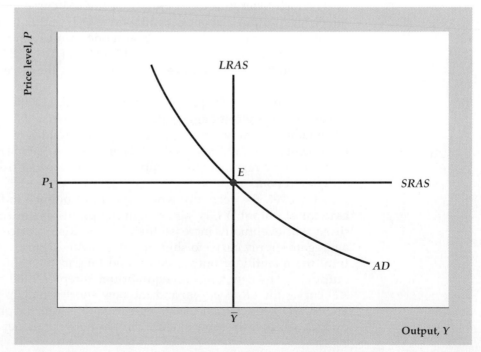

long-run equilibrium, output equals its full-employment level, $\overline{Y}$. Long-run equilibrium is the same as general equilibrium, because in long-run equilibrium all markets clear.

When the economy reaches general, or long-run, equilibrium, all three curves—AD, $SRAS$, and $LRAS$—intersect at a common point, as in Fig. 9.13. This condition isn't a coincidence. As with the IS curve, the LM curve, and the FE line, strong economic forces lead the economy to arrive eventually at a common point of intersection of the three curves. Indeed, the forces leading the AD, $SRAS$, and $LRAS$ curves to intersect at a common point are the same as the forces leading the IS curve, the LM curve, and FE line to intersect at a common point. To illustrate, we use the AD–AS framework to examine the effects on the economy of an increase in the money supply, which we previously analyzed with the IS–LM model.

Monetary Neutrality in the *AD–AS* Model

Suppose that the economy is initially in equilibrium at point E in Fig. 9.14, where the level of output is $\overline{Y}$ and the price level is P_1, and that the money supply then increases by 10%. In the IS–LM model an increase in the money supply shifts the LM curve down and to the right, raising the aggregate quantity of output demanded at any particular price level. Thus an increase in the money supply also shifts the AD curve up and to the right, from AD^1 to AD^2.

Moreover, *when the money supply rises by 10%, points on the new* AD *curve are those for which the price level is 10% higher at each level of output demanded.* To see why, compare points E and H. Because H lies on AD^2 and E lies on AD^1, the nominal money supply, M, is 10% higher at H than at E. However, the aggregate quantity of output demanded is the same ($\overline{Y}$) at H and E. The aggregate quantity of output demanded can be the same at H and E only if the real money supply, M/P, which determines the position of the LM curve and hence the aggregate quantity of output demanded, is the same at H and E. With the nominal money supply 10% higher at H, for the real money supply to be the same at the two points the price level at H must be 10% higher than at E. Therefore P_2 is 10% higher than P_1. Indeed, for every level of output, the price level is 10% higher on AD^2 than on AD^1.

In the short run, the price level remains fixed, and the increase in the nominal money supply shifts the aggregate demand curve from AD^1 to AD^2. Thus the short-run equilibrium moves from point E to point F (which corresponds to movement from point E to point F in the IS–LM diagram in Fig. 9.9b). Thus in the short run the increase in the nominal money supply increases output from $\overline{Y}$ to Y_2, causing an economic boom.

However, the economy won't remain at point F indefinitely. Because the amount of output, Y_2, is higher than the profit-maximizing level of output, $\overline{Y}$, firms will eventually increase their prices. Rising prices cause the short-run aggregate supply curve to shift up from $SRAS^1$. Firms will increase their prices until the quantity of output demanded falls to the profit-maximizing level of output, $\overline{Y}$. The new long-run equilibrium is represented by point H, where the AD curve, the $LRAS$ curve, and the new short-run aggregate supply curve, or $SRAS^2$, all intersect. In the new long-run equilibrium, the price level has increased by 10%, which is the same amount that the nominal money supply has increased.

Figure 9.14

Monetary neutrality in the *AD–AS* framework
If we start from general equilibrium at point E, a 10% increase in the nominal money supply shifts the *AD* curve up and to the right from AD^1 to AD^2. The points on the new *AD* curve are those for which the price level is 10% higher at each level of output demanded, because a 10% increase in the price level is needed to keep the real money supply, and thus the aggregate quantity of output demanded, unchanged. In the new short-run equilibrium at point F, the price level is unchanged, and output is higher than its full-employment level. In the new long-run equilibrium at point H, output is unchanged at $\overline{Y}$, and the price level P_2 is 10% higher than the initial price level P_1. Thus money is neutral in the long run.

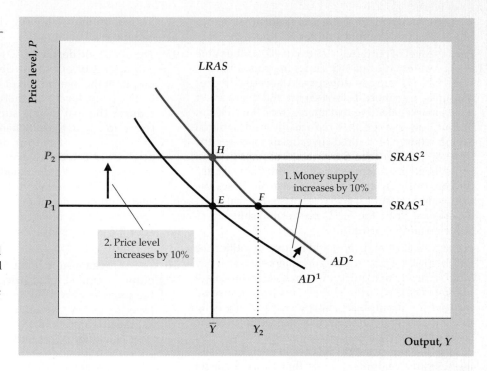

Output is the same in the new long-run equilibrium at point H as at point E. Thus we conclude that money is neutral in the long run, as we did when using the *IS–LM* model.

Our analysis highlights the distinction between the short-run and long-run effects of an increase in the money supply, but it leaves open the crucial question of how long it takes the economy to reach long-run equilibrium. As we have emphasized in both Chapter 8 and this chapter, classical and Keynesian economists have very different answers to this question. Classical economists argue that the economy reaches its long-run equilibrium quickly. Indeed, in its strictest form, the classical view is that the economy reaches long-run equilibrium almost immediately, so that the long-run aggregate supply (*LRAS*) curve is the only aggregate supply curve that matters [the short-run aggregate supply (*SRAS*) curve is irrelevant]. However, Keynesians argue that the economy may take years to reach long-run equilibrium and that in the meantime output will differ from its full-employment level. We elaborate on these points of view in Chapter 10, which is devoted to the classical model, and in Chapter 11, which is devoted to the Keynesian model.

CHAPTER SUMMARY

1. The *IS–LM* model represents the three main markets of the economy—the labor market, the goods market, and the asset market—simultaneously, in a diagram that has the real interest rate on the vertical axis and output on the horizontal axis. Although the *IS–LM* model was originally developed by Keynesians, it may be used to illustrate both classical and Keynesian analyses of the economy.

2. In the *IS–LM* model, equilibrium in the labor market is represented graphically by the full-employment, or *FE*, line, which is vertical at full-employment output. Factors that raise full-employment output

shift the *FE* line to the right, and factors that reduce full-employment output shift the *FE* line to the left.

3. For any level of output, the *IS* curve shows the value of the real interest rate that clears the goods market. The *IS* curve slopes downward because higher output leads to more desired saving and thus a lower goods-market-clearing real interest rate. For constant output, any change that reduces desired national saving relative to desired investment increases the real interest rate that clears the goods market and shifts the *IS* curve up and to the right. Equivalently, for constant output, any change that increases the aggregate demand for goods increases the real interest rate that clears the goods market and shifts the *IS* curve up and to the right.

4. For any level of output, the *LM* curve identifies the real interest rate that equates the quantities of money supplied and demanded and thus clears the asset market. The *LM* curve slopes upward because an increase in output raises money demand, implying that a higher real interest rate is needed to clear the asset market. With output fixed, any change that reduces the money supply relative to money demand increases the real interest rate that clears the asset market and causes the *LM* curve to shift up and to the left.

5. General equilibrium in the macroeconomy occurs when all markets are in equilibrium. Graphically, the general equilibrium point is where the *IS* curve, the *FE* line, and the *LM* curve intersect. Price level adjustments push the economy toward general equilibrium. Specifically, changes in the price level, *P*, change the real money supply, *M*/*P*, which causes the *LM* curve to shift until it passes through the point at which the *FE* line and the *IS* curve intersect.

6. A temporary adverse supply shock causes the general equilibrium levels of the real wage, employment, output, consumption, and investment to fall, and the general equilibrium levels of the real interest rate and price level to increase.

7. A change in the money supply is neutral if it leads to a proportional change in the price level but doesn't affect real variables. In the *IS*–*LM* model, money is neutral after prices have adjusted and the economy has returned to general equilibrium.

8. The aggregate demand–aggregate supply (*AD*–*AS*) model is based on the *IS*–*LM* model and in fact is equivalent to it. However, the two models allow us to focus on the behavior of different macroeconomic variables: The *IS*–*LM* model is most useful for studying the relationship between the real interest rate and the level of output, whereas the *AD*–*AS* model focuses on the relationship between the price level and the level of output.

9. The aggregate demand (*AD*) curve relates the aggregate quantity of output demanded—the level of output at the intersection of the *IS* and *LM* curves—to the price level. An increase in the price level reduces the real money supply and shifts the *LM* curve up and to the left, thereby reducing the aggregate quantity of output demanded. Because an increase in the price level reduces the aggregate quantity of goods demanded, the aggregate demand curve slopes downward. Factors that increase the aggregate quantity of output demanded at a given price level, such as increases in government purchases or the money supply, shift the *AD* curve up and to the right.

10. The aggregate supply curve relates the quantity of output supplied to the price level. In the short run, the price level is fixed and firms supply whatever level of output is demanded, so the short-run aggregate supply (*SRAS*) curve is horizontal. In the long run, after prices and wages have fully adjusted and all markets are in equilibrium, firms produce the profit-maximizing level of output. Hence, in the long run, aggregate output, Y, equals its full-employment level, $\overline{Y}$. In the long run, firms supply $\overline{Y}$ regardless of the price level, so the long-run aggregate supply (*LRAS*) curve is a vertical line at $Y = \overline{Y}$.

11. Classical macroeconomists argue that prices and wages adjust rapidly in response to changes in supply or demand. This argument implies that, following shocks or changes in policy, the economy quickly reaches its general equilibrium, represented by the *IS*–*LM*–*FE* intersection or, equivalently, by the intersection of the *AD* and *LRAS* curves. In contrast, Keynesian macroeconomists argue that prices and wages adjust slowly enough that the economy can remain away from its general equilibrium (long-run equilibrium) for a prolonged period of time. Keynesians agree with classicals, however, that eventually prices and wages fully adjust so that the economy reaches its general equilibrium.

12. Classicals and Keynesians agree that money is neutral in the long run, after the economy has reached its general equilibrium. Because classicals believe that long-run equilibrium is reached quickly, they dismiss the short-run equilibrium in which money is not neutral as essentially irrelevant. Keynesians, who believe that it may take several years for the economy to reach general equilibrium, ascribe much more importance to the short-run period in which money is not neutral.

KEY DIAGRAM 6

The *IS–LM* model
The *IS–LM* model shows general equilibrium in the goods, asset, and labor markets. It can be used to analyze the effects of economic shocks on output, the real interest rate, the price level, and other macroeconomic variables.

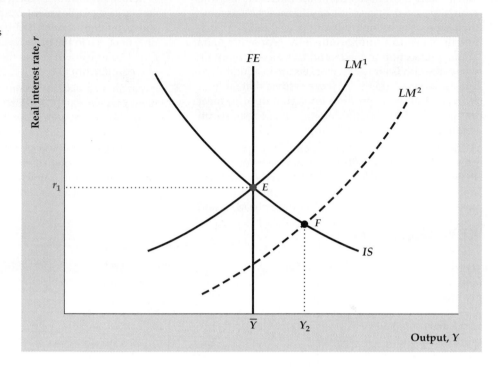

Diagram Elements

■ The real interest rate, r, is on the vertical axis, and output, Y, is on the horizontal axis.

■ The full-employment line, *FE*, is vertical at full-employment output. Full-employment output, $\overline{Y}$, is the level of output that firms supply when wages and prices have fully adjusted, so employment is at its full-employment level, $\overline{N}$. Full-employment output is determined by the equation $\overline{Y} = AF(K, \overline{N})$.

■ For any level of output, Y, the *IS* curve gives the real interest rate, r, that clears the goods market—or, in other words, the rate that equalizes desired national saving, S^d, and desired investment, I^d. Because higher output raises desired saving and lowers the real interest rate that clears the goods market, the *IS* curve slopes downward. Equivalently, the *IS* curve gives combinations of output, Y, and the real interest rate, r, that equalize the aggregate quantities of goods supplied and demanded, $Y = C^d + I^d + G$.

■ For given values of the price level and output, the *LM* curve gives the real interest rate that clears the asset market, making the real money supply, M/P, and the real quantity of money demanded, $L(Y, r + \pi^e)$, equal. Because an increase in income raises real money demand, which raises the real interest rate that clears the asset market, the *LM* curve slopes upward.

Factors That Shift the Curves

■ Any factor that raises full-employment output shifts the *FE* line to the right. See Summary table 11, p. 312.

■ For constant output, any change that reduces desired national saving relative to desired investment increases the real interest rate that clears the goods market and shifts the *IS* curve up and to the right. Equivalently, any change that increases the aggregate demand for goods at a specific level of income raises the real interest rate that clears the goods market and shifts the *IS* curve up and to the right. See Summary table 12, p. 315.

■ For constant output, any change that reduces real money supply relative to real money demand increases the real interest rate that clears the asset market and shifts the *LM* curve up and to the left. See Summary table 13, p. 321.

Analysis

■ If we assume that the *LM* curve is LM^1, the economy is in general equilibrium at point E, which lies on all three curves. At E the labor market (*FE* line), the goods market (*IS* curve), and the asset market (*LM* curve) are all in equilibrium. At E output equals full-employment output, $\overline{Y}$; and the real interest rate, r_1, clears both the goods and asset markets.

- If we assume that the *LM* curve is LM^2, the *FE* line and *IS* and *LM* curves don't all intersect, and the economy is out of general equilibrium. We assume that, when the economy is out of general equilibrium, the short-run equilibrium of the economy occurs at the intersection of the *IS* and *LM* curves (point *F*), where the goods and asset markets are in equilibrium but the labor market isn't. If we assume that (at least temporarily) firms produce enough output to meet the increased aggregate demand at *F*, in short-run equilibrium the economy's output is Y_2.

- At the short-run equilibrium point, *F*, output, Y_2, is greater than firms' profit-maximizing level of output, $\overline{Y}$. Because aggregate demand at *F* exceeds what firms want to produce, they raise prices. An increase in the price level, *P*, lowers the real money supply, *M/P*, and shifts the *LM* curve up and to the left, to LM^1, and general equilibrium is reached at *E*. At *E* output again equals full-employment output, $\overline{Y}$. Similarly, if the short-run equilibrium had been to the left of the *FE* line, declines in the price level, *P*, would have shifted the *LM* curve down and to the right and restored general equilibrium at *E*.

- According to classical economists, the price adjustment process quickly restores the economy to general equilibrium at point *E*, so the economy spends little or no time at point *F*, away from full employment. Keynesians argue that prices and wages are slow to adjust, so the economy may remain at the short-run equilibrium point, *F*, with output different from $\overline{Y}$, for an extended period of time.

KEY DIAGRAM 7

The aggregate demand–aggregate supply model
The *AD–AS* model shows the determination of the price level and output. In the short run, before prices adjust, equilibrium occurs at the intersection of the *AD* and *SRAS* curves. In the long run, equilibrium occurs at the intersection of the *AD* and *LRAS* curves.

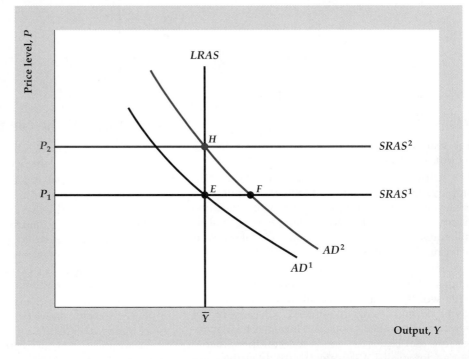

Diagram Elements

- The price level, *P*, is on the vertical axis, and the level of output, *Y*, is on the horizontal axis.

- The aggregate demand (*AD*) curve shows the aggregate quantity of output demanded at each price level. The aggregate amount of output demanded is determined by the intersection of the *IS* and *LM* curves (see Fig. 9.10, p. 338). An increase in the price level, *P*, reduces the real money supply, shifting the *LM* curve up and to the left, and reduces the aggregate quantity of output demanded. Thus the *AD* curve slopes downward.

- The aggregate supply curves show the relationship between the price level and the aggregate quantity of output supplied in the short run and in the long run. In the short run, the price level is fixed, and firms supply whatever level of output is demanded. Thus the short-run aggregate supply (*SRAS*) curve is horizontal. In the long run, firms produce the amount of output that maximizes their profits, which is the full-employment level of output, $\overline{Y}$. Because aggregate output in the long run equals $\overline{Y}$ regardless of the price level, *P*, the long-run aggregate supply (*LRAS*) curve is a vertical line at $Y = \overline{Y}$.

Factors That Shift the Curves

▇ The aggregate quantity of output demanded is determined by the intersection of the *IS* and the *LM* curves. At a constant price level, any factor that shifts the *IS–LM* intersection to the right increases the aggregate quantity of goods demanded and thus also shifts the *AD* curve up and to the right. Factors that shift the *AD* curve are listed in Summary table 14, p. 340.

▇ Any factor, such as an increase in the costs of production, that leads firms to increase prices in the short-run will shift the short-run aggregate supply (*SRAS*) curve up. Any factor that increases the full-employment level of output, $\overline{Y}$, shifts the long-run aggregate supply (*LRAS*) curve to the right. Factors that increase $\overline{Y}$ are listed in Summary table 11, p. 312.

Analysis

▇ The economy's short-run equilibrium is represented by the intersection of the *AD* and *SRAS* curves, as at

point *E*. The long-run equilibrium of the economy is represented by the intersection of the *AD* curve and *LRAS* curve, also at point *E*. In the long run, output equals its full-employment level, $\overline{Y}$.

▇ The short-run equilibrium can temporarily differ from the long-run equilibrium as a result of shocks or policy changes that affect the economy. For instance, an increase in the nominal money supply shifts the aggregate demand curve up and to the right from AD^1 to AD^2. The new short-run equilibrium is represented by point *F*, where output is higher than its full-employment level, $\overline{Y}$. At point *F*, firms produce an amount of output that is greater than the profit-maximizing level, and they begin to increase prices. In the new long-run equilibrium at point *H*, output is at its full-employment level and the price level is higher than its initial value, P_1. Because the new price level is P_2, the short-run aggregate supply curve shifts up to $SRAS^2$, which is a horizontal line at $P = P_2$.

KEY TERMS

aggregate demand curve, p. 336
aggregate supply curve, p. 339
full-employment line, p. 311
general equilibrium, p. 325

IS curve, p. 313
LM curve, p. 320
long-run aggregate supply curve, p. 341

monetary neutrality, p. 335
short-run aggregate supply curve, p. 340

REVIEW QUESTIONS

All review questions are available in **myeconlab** at www.myeconlab.com.

1. What determines the position of the *FE* line? Give two examples of changes in the economy that would shift the *FE* line to the right.

2. What relationship does the *IS* curve capture? Derive the *IS* curve graphically and show why it slopes as it does. Give two examples of changes in the economy that would cause the *IS* curve to shift down and to the left.

3. What relationship does the *LM* curve capture? Derive the *LM* curve graphically and show why it slopes as it does. Give two examples of changes in the economy that would cause the *LM* curve to shift down and to the right.

4. For constant output, if the real money supply exceeds the real quantity of money demanded, what will happen to the real interest rate that clears the asset market? In describing the adjustment of the real interest rate, use the relationship that exists between the price of a nonmonetary asset and the interest rate that it pays.

5. Define *general equilibrium* and show the general equilibrium point in the *IS–LM* diagram. If the economy isn't in general equilibrium, what determines output and the real interest rate? What economic forces act to bring the economy back to general equilibrium?

6. Define *monetary neutrality*. Show that, after prices adjust completely, money is neutral in the *IS–LM* model. What are the classical and Keynesian views about whether money is neutral in the short run? In the long run?

7. What two variables are related by the aggregate demand (*AD*) curve? Why does the *AD* curve slope downward? Give two examples of changes in the economy that shift the *AD* curve up and to the right and explain why the shifts occur.

8. Describe the short-run aggregate supply (*SRAS*) curve and the long-run aggregate supply (*LRAS*) curve. Why is one of these curves horizontal and the other vertical?

9. Use the *AD–AS* framework to analyze whether money is neutral in the short run and whether it is neutral in the long run.

NUMERICAL PROBLEMS

All numerical problems are available in X myeconlab at www.myeconlab.com.

1. Desired consumption and investment are

$$C^d = 4000 - 4000r + 0.20Y;$$

$$I^d = 2400 - 4000r.$$

As usual, Y is output and r is the real interest rate. Government purchases, G, are 2000.

a. Find an equation relating desired national saving, S^d, to r and Y.

b. What value of the real interest rate clears the goods market when $Y = 10,000$? Use both forms of the goods market equilibrium condition. What value of the real interest rate clears the goods market when $Y = 10,200$? Graph the IS curve.

c. Government purchases rise to 2400. How does this increase change the equation for national saving in Part (a)? What value of the real interest rate clears the goods market when $Y = 10,000$? Use both forms of the goods market equilibrium condition. How is the IS curve affected by the increase in G?

2. In a particular economy the real money demand function is

$$\frac{M^d}{P} = 3000 + 0.1Y - 10,000i.$$

Assume that $M = 6000$, $P = 2.0$, and $\pi^e = 0.02$.

a. What is the real interest rate, r, that clears the asset market when $Y = 8000$? When $Y = 9000$? Graph the LM curve.

b. Repeat Part (a) for $M = 6600$. How does the LM curve in this case compare with the LM curve in Part (a)?

c. Use $M = 6000$ again and repeat Part (a) for $\pi^e = 0.03$. Compare the LM curve in this case with the one in Part (a).

3. An economy has full-employment output of 1000. Desired consumption and desired investment are

$$C^d = 200 + 0.8(Y - T) - 500r;$$

$$I^d = 200 - 500r.$$

Government purchases are 196, and taxes are

$$T = 20 + 0.25Y.$$

Money demand is

$$\frac{M^d}{P} = 0.5Y - 250(r + \pi^e),$$

where the expected rate of inflation, π^e, is 0.10. The nominal supply of money $M = 9890$.

a. What are the general equilibrium values of the real interest rate, price level, consumption, and investment?

b. Suppose that government purchases are increased to $G = 216$. What are the new general equilibrium values of the real interest rate, the price level, consumption, and investment?

4. The production function in an economy is

$$Y = A(5N - 0.0025N^2),$$

where A is productivity. With this production function, the marginal product of labor is

$$MPN = 5A - 0.005AN.$$

Suppose that $A = 2$. The labor supply curve is

$$NS = 55 + 10(1 - t)w,$$

where NS is the amount of labor supplied, w is the real wage, and t is the tax rate on wage income, which is 0.5.

Desired consumption and investment are

$$C^d = 300 + 0.8(Y - T) - 200r;$$

$$I^d = 258.5 - 250r.$$

Taxes and government purchases are

$$T = 20 + 0.5Y;$$

$$G = 50.$$

Money demand is

$$\frac{M^d}{P} = 0.5Y - 250(r + \pi^e).$$

The expected rate of inflation, π^e, is 0.02, and the nominal money supply M is 9150.

a. What are the general equilibrium levels of the real wage, employment, and output?

b. For any level of output, Y, find an equation that gives the real interest rate, r, that clears the goods market; this equation describes the IS curve. (*Hint*: Write the goods market equilibrium condition and solve for r in terms of Y and other variables.) What are the general equilibrium values of the real interest rate, consumption, and investment?

c. For any level of output, Y, find an equation that gives the real interest rate that clears the asset market; this equation describes the LM curve.

[*Hint:* As in Part (*b*), write the appropriate equilibrium condition and solve for *r* in terms of *Y* and other variables.] What is the general equilibrium value of the price level?

d. Suppose that government purchases increase to *G* = 72.5. Now what are the general equilibrium values of the real wage, employment, output, the real interest rate, consumption, investment, and price level?

5. Consider the following economy:

Desired consumption	$C^d = 1275 + 0.5(Y - T) - 200r.$
Desired investment	$I^d = 900 - 200r.$
Real money demand	$L = 0.5Y - 200i.$
Full-employment output $\overline{Y}$	$= 4600.$
Expected inflation	$\pi^e = 0.$

a. Suppose that *T* = *G* = 450 and that *M* = 9000. Find an equation describing the *IS* curve. (*Hint:* Set desired national saving and desired investment equal, and solve for the relationship between *r* and *Y*.) Find an equation describing the *LM* curve. (*Hint:* Set real money supply and real money demand equal, and again solve for the relationship between *r* and *Y*, given *P*.) Finally, find an equation for the aggregate demand curve. (*Hint:* Use the *IS* and *LM* equations to find a relationship between *Y*

and *P*.) What are the general equilibrium values of output, consumption, investment, the real interest rate, and price level?

b. Suppose that *T* = *G* = 450 and that *M* = 4500. What is the equation for the aggregate demand curve now? What are the general equilibrium values of output, consumption, investment, the real interest rate, and price level? Assume that full-employment output $\overline{Y}$ is fixed.

c. Repeat Part (*b*) for *T* = *G* = 330 and *M* = 9000.

6. (Appendix 9.B) This question asks you to use the formulas in Appendix 9.B to find the general equilibrium values of variables for the economy described in Numerical Problem 4. Assume that *G* = 50.

a. Use the data from Numerical Problem 4 to find the numerical values of the parameters $A, f_1, f_2, n_0, n_w, c_0, c_Y, c_r, t_0, t, i_0, i_r, \ell_0, \ell_Y,$ and ℓ_r defined in Appendix 9.B.

b. Substitute the values of these behavioral parameters into the relevant equations in Appendix 9.B to compute the general equilibrium values of the real wage, employment, output, the real interest rate, and the price level.

c. Assume that government purchases, *G*, increase to 72.5, and repeat Part (*b*).

ANALYTICAL PROBLEMS

1. Use the *IS–LM* model to determine the effects of each of the following on the general equilibrium values of the real wage, employment, output, real interest rate, consumption, investment, and price level.

a. A reduction in the effective tax rate on capital increases desired investment.

b. The expected rate of inflation rises.

c. An influx of working-age immigrants increases labor supply (ignore any other possible effects of increased population).

d. Increased usage of automatic teller machines reduces the demand for money.

2. Use the *IS–LM* model to analyze the general equilibrium effects of a permanent increase in the price of oil (a permanent adverse supply shock) on current output, employment, the real wage, national saving, consumption, investment, the real interest rate, and the price level. Assume that, besides reducing the current productivity of capital and labor, the permanent supply shock lowers both the expected future *MPK* and households' expected future incomes. (Assume

that the rightward shift in labor supply is smaller than the leftward shift in labor demand.) Show that, if the real interest rate rises at all, it will rise less than in the case of a temporary supply shock that has an equal effect on current output.

3. Suppose that the price level is fixed in the short run so that the economy doesn't reach general equilibrium immediately after a change in the economy. For each of the following changes, what are the short-run effects on the real interest rate and output? Assume that, when the economy is in disequilibrium, only the labor market is out of equilibrium; assume also that for a short period firms are willing to produce enough output to meet the aggregate demand for output.

a. A decrease in the expected rate of inflation.

b. An increase in consumer optimism that increases desired consumption at each level of income and the real interest rate.

c. A temporary increase in government purchases.

d. An increase in lump-sum taxes, with no change in government purchases (consider both the case in which Ricardian equivalence holds and the case in which it doesn't).

e. A scientific breakthrough that increases the expected future *MPK*.

4. (Appendix 9.B) In some macroeconomic models, desired investment depends on both the current level of output and the real interest rate. One possible reason that desired investment may depend on output is that, when current production and sales are high, firms may expect continued strong demand for their products in the future, which leads them to want to expand capacity.

Algebraically, we can allow for a link between desired investment and current output by replacing Eq. (9.B.10) with

$$I^d = i_0 - i_r r + i_Y Y,$$

where i_Y is a positive number. Use this alternative equation for desired investment to derive the algebraic expressions for the general equilibrium values of employment, the real wage, output, the real interest rate, and the price level.

5. (Appendix 9.B) Recall from Chapter 7 that an increase in i^m, the nominal interest rate on money, increases the demand for money. To capture that effect, let's replace Eq. (9.B.17) with

$$\frac{M^d}{P} = \ell_0 + \ell_Y Y - \ell_r(r + \pi^e - i^m).$$

How does this modification change the solutions for the general equilibrium values of the variables discussed in Appendix 9.B, including employment, the real wage, output, the real interest rate, and the price level?

APPENDIX 9.A

Worked-Out Numerical Exercise for Solving the *IS–LM/AD–AS* Model

To help you work through the algebra needed for numerical problems in this chapter, here is a worked-out numerical exercise as an example for solving the *IS–LM* model:

Consider an economy that is described by the following equations:

$$C^d = 300 + 0.75(Y - T) - 300r$$
$$T = 100 + 0.2Y$$
$$I^d = 200 - 200r$$
$$L = 0.5Y - 500i$$

$$\overline{Y} = 2500; G = 600; M = 133{,}200; \pi^e = 0.05; P_{sr} = 120.$$

In the short run, the price level is fixed at P_{sr}. Find the short-run and long-run equilibrium values of Y, P, r, C, I, and i.

To solve this problem, we will follow these steps:

Step 1: Find the equation for the *IS* curve by using the goods market equilibrium condition, $Y = C^d + I^d + G$. Substitute the equation for T into the equation for C^d from above. Then substitute the resulting equation and the equation for I^d from above, along with the value of G, into $Y = C^d + I^d + G$ to obtain: $Y = \{300 + 0.75[Y - (100 + 0.2Y)] - 300r\} + [200 - 200r] + 600$. Rearrange this equation as an equation for r in terms of Y: $Y = [300 + 0.75Y - 75 - 0.15Y - 300r] + [200 - 200r] + 600$, so $0.4Y = [300 - 75 + 200 + 600] - (300 + 200)r$, so $500r = 1025 - 0.4Y$. Therefore, $r = 1025/500 - (0.4/500)Y$, so $r = 2.05 - 0.0008Y$. This is the *IS* curve.

Step 2: Find the equation for the *LM* curve by using the asset market equilibrium condition.

a. First, find the equation for the *LM* curve with an unspecified value of the price level. The asset market equilibrium condition equates real money supply to real money demand. Real money demand is given by $L = 0.5Y - 500i = 0.5Y - 500(r + \pi^e) = 0.5Y - 500(r + 0.05)$, and real money supply is $M/P = 133{,}200/P$. In asset market equilibrium, $133{,}200/P = 0.5Y - 500(r + 0.05)$, so $500r = 0.5Y - 25 - 133{,}200/P$. Therefore, $r = (0.5/500)Y - (25/500) - (133{,}200/500)/P = 0.001Y - 0.05 - 266.4/P$. This is the equation of the *LM* curve for an unspecified value of P.

b. Then find the equation for the *LM* curve when $P = P_{sr}$. Set $P = P_{sr} = 120$ in the *LM* curve to obtain $r = 0.001Y - 0.05 - 266.4/120$, so $r = 0.001Y - 0.05 - 2.22$. Therefore, $r = 0.001Y - 2.27$. This is the equation of the *LM* curve when $P = P_{sr}$.

Step 3: Find the short-run equilibrium.

a. Find the intersection of the *IS* and *LM* curves to find the short-run equilibrium values of Y and r. We have written the equations of the *IS* and *LM* curves so that the left side of each equation is simply r. Setting the right side of the *IS* curve equal to the right side of the *LM* curve yields $2.05 - 0.0008Y = 0.001Y - 2.27$, so $4.32 = 0.0018Y$. Therefore, $Y = 4.32/0.0018 = 2400$. Now use the value of Y in either the *IS* or the *LM* curve. In the IS curve, $r = 2.05 - 0.0008Y = 2.05 - (0.0008 \times 2400) = 2.05 - 1.92 = 0.13$. In the LM curve, $r = 0.001Y - 2.27 = (0.001 \times 2400) - 2.27 = 2.40 - 2.27 = 0.13$.

b. Plug these equilibrium values of Y and r into other equations to find equilibrium values for T, C, I, and i.

$T = 100 + 0.2Y = 100 + (0.2 \times 2400)$, so $T = 580$.
$C = 300 + 0.75(Y - T) - 300r = 300 + [0.75(2400 - 580)] - (300 \times 0.13)$
$\quad = 300 + 1365 - 39 = 1626$.
$I = 200 - 200r = 200 - (200 \times 0.13) = 200 - 26 = 174$.

(Note that $C + I + G = 1626 + 174 + 600 = 2400$, which equals Y.)

$i = r + \pi^e = 0.13 + 0.05 = 0.18$.

Step 4: Find the long-run equilibrium.

a. Use the fact that in long-run equilibrium, $Y = \bar{Y}$. Plug the equilibrium level of output into the IS equation to find the equilibrium real interest rate. Use $\bar{Y} = 2500$ and the IS equation, $r = 2.05 - 0.0008Y$, to obtain $r = 2.05 - (0.0008 \times 2500) = 2.05 - 2.00 = 0.05$.

b. Plug the equilibrium values of Y and r into other equations to find equilibrium values for T, C, I, and i.

$T = 100 + 0.2Y = 100 + (0.2 \times 2500)$, so $T = 600$.
$C = 300 + 0.75(Y - T) - 300r = 300 + [0.75(2500 - 600)] - (300 \times 0.05)$
$\quad = 300 + 1425 - 15 = 1710$.
$I = 200 - 200r = 200 - (200 \times 0.05) = 200 - 10 = 190$.

(Note that $C + I + G = 1710 + 190 + 600 = 2500$, which equals Y.)

$i = r + \pi^e = 0.05 + 0.05 = 0.10$.

c. Plug the equilibrium values of Y and i into the money demand equation to obtain the value of real money demand L. Then find the value of P that equates real money supply, M/P, with real money demand, L. The money demand curve is $L = 0.5Y - 500i = (0.5 \times 2500) - (500 \times 0.10) = 1250 - 50 = 1200$. Setting real money supply equal to real money demand gives $133{,}200/P = 1200$, so $P = 133{,}200/1200 = 111$.

Step 5: Find the equation for the AD curve by using the IS and LM curves. Use the form of the LM curve for an unspecified value of P.

The IS and LM curves are both written so that r appears alone on the left side, so the right sides of both can be equated to obtain:

$2.05 - 0.0008Y = 0.001Y - 0.05 - 266.4/P$, so $0.0018Y = 2.10 + 266.4/P$.

Dividing this equation through by 0.0018 yields $Y = 2.10/0.0018 + (266.4/0.0018)/P$, so $Y = 1166\frac{2}{3} + 148{,}000/P$. This is the AD curve.

Step 6: Illustrate the use of the AD curve and short-run and long-run aggregate supply curves. In the short run, the $SRAS$ curve is $P = P_{sr} = 120$, which means it is a horizontal line. The short-run equilibrium occurs at the intersection of the AD and $SRAS$ curves. Plug $P = 120$ into the AD curve to obtain $Y = 1166\frac{2}{3} + 148{,}000/120 = 1166\frac{2}{3} + 1233\frac{1}{3}$. Therefore $Y = 2400$, the same result we found in Step 3.

In the long run, output equals its full-employment level, so the $LRAS$ curve is $Y = \bar{Y} = 2500$, which means it is a vertical line. The long-run equilibrium occurs at the intersection of the AD and $LRAS$ curves. Plug $Y = \bar{Y} = 2500$, into the AD curve to obtain $2500 = Y = 1166\frac{2}{3} + 148{,}000/P$, so $1333\frac{1}{3} = 148{,}000/P$, which implies $P = 148{,}000/1333\frac{1}{3} = 111$, the same result we found in Step 4.

APPENDIX **9.B**

Algebraic Versions of the *IS–LM* and *AD–AS* Models

In this appendix we present algebraic versions of the *IS–LM* and *AD–AS* models. For each of the three markets—labor, goods, and assets—we first present equations that describe demand and supply in that market, then find the market equilibrium. After considering each market separately, we solve for the general equilibrium of the complete *IS–LM* model. We use the *IS–LM* model to derive the aggregate demand (*AD*) curve and then introduce the short-run and long-run aggregate supply curves to derive the short-run and long-run equilibria.

The Labor Market

The demand for labor is based on the marginal product of labor, as determined by the production function. Recall from Chapter 3 (Eq. 3.1) that the production function can be written as $Y = AF(K, N)$, where Y is output, K is the capital stock, N is labor input, and A is productivity. Holding the capital stock K fixed, we can write the production function with output Y as a function only of labor input N and productivity A. A useful specific production function is

$$Y = A\left(f_1 N - \frac{1}{2} f_2 N^2\right), \tag{9.B.1}$$

where f_1 and f_2 are positive numbers.

The marginal product of labor, *MPN*, is the slope of the production function. The slope of the production function in Eq. (9.B.1) at any level of employment N equals[10] $A(f_1 - f_2 N)$, so the marginal product of labor is

$$MPN = A(f_1 - f_2 N). \tag{9.B.2}$$

Firms hire labor to the point at which the marginal product of labor equals the real wage. Thus the relation between the real wage, w, and the amount of labor demanded, *ND*, is

$$w = A(f_1 - f_2 ND). \tag{9.B.3}$$

The supply of labor is an increasing function of the current, after-tax real wage. If t is the tax rate on wage income (we assume that $0 \le t < 1$) so that $(1 - t)w$ is the after-tax real wage, a simple form of the labor supply curve is

$$NS = n_0 + n_w(1 - t)w, \tag{9.B.4}$$

---

[10]Students who know calculus can derive the slope of the production function by taking the derivative of Eq. (9.B.1) with respect to N.

where NS is the amount of labor supplied, and n_w is a positive number. Factors other than the after-tax real wage that affect labor supply, such as wealth or the working-age population, are captured by the constant term n_0 in Eq. (9.B.4).

Equilibrium in the Labor Market

In equilibrium, the amounts of labor demanded, ND, and supplied, NS, are equal; their common value is the full-employment level of employment, $\overline{N}$. If we substitute $\overline{N}$ for NS and ND in Eqs. (9.B.3) and (9.B.4), we have two linear equations in the two variables $\overline{N}$ and w. Solving these equations for w and $\overline{N}$ yields[11]

$$w = A\left[\frac{f_1 - f_2 n_0}{1 + (1 - t)A f_2 n_w}\right] \tag{9.B.5}$$

and

$$\overline{N} = \frac{n_0 + (1 - t)A f_1 n_w}{1 + (1 - t)A f_2 n_w}. \tag{9.B.6}$$

Using the full-employment level of employment, $\overline{N}$, in Eq. (9.B.6), we obtain the full-employment level of output, $\overline{Y}$, by substituting $\overline{N}$ into the production function (9.B.1):

$$\overline{Y} = A\left[f_1\overline{N} - \frac{1}{2}f_2\overline{N}^2\right], \qquad FE \text{ line} \tag{9.B.7}$$

The value of full-employment output in Eq. (9.B.7) is the horizontal intercept of the *FE* line.

We use these equations to analyze the effects on the labor market of changes in productivity and labor supply. First consider an increase in productivity A. Equation (9.B.5) shows that an increase in A leads to an increase in the equilibrium real wage (an increase in A raises the ratio $A/[1 + (1 - t)A f_2 n_w]$). Although not directly evident from Eq. (9.B.6), an increase in A also increases $\overline{N}$.[12] To see why, note first that an increase in A doesn't affect the labor supply curve, Eq. (9.B.4). Second, an increase in A raises the real wage. Hence the implication is that an increase in A raises the equilibrium amount of labor supplied and thus also the full-employment level of employment, $\overline{N}$. Because an increase in A raises $\overline{N}$, it must also raise full-employment output, $\overline{Y}$ (see Eq. 9.B.7), and shift the *FE* line to the right.

Now consider an increase in the amount of labor supplied at each level of the after-tax real wage, represented algebraically as an increase in n_0 in Eq. (9.B.4). Equations (9.B.5) and (9.B.6) show that an increase in n_0 reduces the equilibrium real wage and increases employment, $\overline{N}$. Because an increase in labor supply raises $\overline{N}$, it also raises full-employment output, $\overline{Y}$, and shifts the *FE* line to the right.

---

[11]We assume that the constants f_1, f_2, and n_0 are such that $f_1 - f_2 n_0 > 0$. This assumption is needed to guarantee that the marginal product of labor and the equilibrium real wage are positive.

[12]Students who know calculus can compute the derivative of $\overline{N}$ with respect to A in Eq. (9.B.6) and will find that the sign of this derivative is positive if and only if $f_1 - f_2 n_0 > 0$. As we have assumed that $f_1 - f_2 n_0 > 0$ (see preceding footnote), an increase in A does indeed increase $\overline{N}$.

The Goods Market

To find equilibrium in the goods market, we start with equations describing desired consumption and desired investment. Desired consumption is

$$C^d = c_0 + c_Y(Y - T) - c_r r, \tag{9.B.8}$$

where $Y - T$ is disposable income (income Y minus taxes T), r is the real interest rate, and c_0, c_Y, and c_r are positive numbers. The number c_Y in Eq. (9.B.8) is the marginal propensity to consume, as defined in Chapter 4; because people consume only part of an increase in disposable income, saving the rest, a reasonable assumption is that $0 < c_Y < 1$. According to Eq. (9.B.8), an increase in disposable income causes desired consumption to increase, and an increase in the real interest rate causes desired consumption to fall (and desired saving to rise). Other factors that affect desired consumption, such as wealth or expected future income, are included in the constant term c_0.[13]

Taxes in Eq. (9.B.8) are

$$T = t_0 + tY, \tag{9.B.9}$$

where t is the tax rate on income (the same tax rate that is levied on wages) and t_0 is a lump-sum tax. As mentioned earlier, $0 \leqslant t < 1$, so an increase in income, Y, increases total taxes, T, and also increases disposable income, $Y - T$.

Desired investment is

$$I^d = i_0 - i_r r, \tag{9.B.10}$$

where i_0 and i_r are positive numbers. Equation (9.B.10) indicates that desired investment falls when the real interest rate rises. Other factors affecting desired investment, such as the expected future marginal product of capital, are included in the constant term i_0.

Equilibrium in the Goods Market

The goods market equilibrium condition in a closed economy is given by Eq. (4.7), which we repeat here:

$$Y = C^d + I^d + G. \tag{9.B.11}$$

Equation (9.B.11) is equivalent to the goods market equilibrium condition, $S^d = I^d$, which could be used equally well here.

If we substitute the equations for desired consumption (Eq. 9.B.8, with taxes T as given by Eq. 9.B.9) and desired investment (Eq. 9.B.10) into the goods market equilibrium condition (Eq. 9.B.11), we get

$$Y = c_0 + c_Y(Y - t_0 - tY) - c_r r + i_0 - i_r r + G. \tag{9.B.12}$$

---

[13]Because an increase in taxes, T, reduces desired consumption in Eq. (9.B.8), this formulation of desired consumption appears, at first glance, to be inconsistent with the Ricardian equivalence proposition discussed in Chapter 4. However, essential to the idea of Ricardian equivalence is that consumers expect an increase in current taxes, T, to be accompanied by lower taxes in the future. This decrease in expected future taxes would increase desired consumption, which would be captured in Eq. (9.B.8) as an increase in c_0. According to the Ricardian equivalence proposition, after an increase in T with no change in current or planned government purchases, an increase in c_0 would exactly offset the reduction in $c_Y(Y - T)$ so that desired consumption would be unchanged.

Collecting the terms that multiply Y on the left side yields

$$[1 - (1 - t)c_Y]Y = c_0 + i_0 + G - c_Y t_0 - (c_r + i_r)r. \tag{9.B.13}$$

Equation (9.B.13) relates output, Y, to the real interest rate, r, that clears the goods market. This relationship between Y and r defines the IS curve. Because the IS curve is graphed with r on the vertical axis and Y on the horizontal axis, we rewrite Eq. (9.B.13) with r on the left side and Y on the right side. Solving Eq. (9.B.13) for r gives

$$r = \alpha_{IS} - \beta_{IS}Y, \quad IS \text{ curve.} \tag{9.B.14}$$

In Eq. (9.B.14), α_{IS} and β_{IS} are positive numbers defined as

$$\alpha_{IS} = \frac{c_0 + i_0 + G - c_Y t_0}{c_r + i_r} \tag{9.B.15}$$

and

$$\beta_{IS} = \frac{1 - (1 - t)c_Y}{c_r + i_r}. \tag{9.B.16}$$

Equation (9.B.14) yields the graph of the IS curve. In Eq. (9.B.14), the coefficient of Y, or $-\beta_{IS}$, is the slope of the IS curve; because this slope is negative, the IS curve slopes downward. Changes in the constant term α_{IS} in Eq. (9.B.14), which is defined in Eq. (9.B.15), shift the IS curve. Anything that increases α_{IS}—such as (1) an increase in consumer optimism that increases desired consumption by increasing c_0; (2) an increase in the expected future marginal product of capital, MPK^f, that raises desired investment by raising i_0; or (3) an increase in government purchases, G—shifts the IS curve up and to the right. Similarly, anything that decreases α_{IS} shifts the IS curve down and to the left.

The Asset Market

In general, the real demand for money depends on real income, Y, and the nominal interest rate on nonmonetary assets, i, which in turn equals the expected real interest rate, r, plus the expected rate of inflation, π^e. We assume that the money demand function takes the form

$$\frac{M^d}{P} = \ell_0 + \ell_Y Y - \ell_r(r + \pi^e), \tag{9.B.17}$$

where M^d is the nominal demand for money, P is the price level, and ℓ_Y and ℓ_r are positive numbers. The constant term ℓ_0 includes factors other than output and the interest rate that affect money demand, such as the liquidity of alternative assets. The real supply of money equals the nominal supply of money, M, which is determined by the central bank, divided by the price level, P.

Equilibrium in the Asset Market

As we showed in Chapter 7, if we assume that there are only two types of assets (money and nonmonetary assets), the asset market is in equilibrium when the real quantity of money demanded equals the real money supply, M/P. Using the money demand function in Eq. (9.B.17), we write the asset market equilibrium condition as

$$\frac{M}{P} = \ell_0 + \ell_Y Y - \ell_r(r + \pi^e). \qquad \text{(9.B.18)}$$

For fixed levels of the nominal money supply, M, price level, P, and expected rate of inflation, π^e, Eq. (9.B.18) relates output, Y, and the real interest rate, r, that clears the asset market. Thus Eq. (9.B.18) defines the *LM* curve. To get Eq. (9.B.18) into a form that is easier to interpret graphically, we rewrite the equation with r alone on the left side:

$$r = \alpha_{LM} - \left(\frac{1}{\ell_r}\right)\left(\frac{M}{P}\right) + \beta_{LM}Y, \quad \textit{LM curve} \qquad \text{(9.B.19)}$$

where

$$\alpha_{LM} = \left(\frac{\ell_0}{\ell_r}\right) - \pi^e \qquad \text{(9.B.20)}$$

and

$$\beta_{LM} = \left(\frac{\ell_Y}{\ell_r}\right). \qquad \text{(9.B.21)}$$

The graph of Eq. (9.B.19) is the *LM* curve. In Eq. (9.B.19), the coefficient of Y, or β_{LM}, is the slope of the *LM* curve; because this coefficient is positive, the *LM* curve slopes upward. Variables that change the intercept of the equation in Eq. (9.B.19), $\alpha_{LM} - (1/\ell_r)$ (M/P), shift the *LM* curve. An increase in the real money supply, M/P, reduces this intercept and thus shifts the *LM* curve down and to the right. An increase in the expected rate of inflation π^e reduces α_{LM} and shifts the *LM* curve down and to the right. An increase in real money demand arising from (for example) reduced liquidity of alternative assets raises ℓ_0, which raises α_{LM} and shifts the *LM* curve up and to the left.

General Equilibrium in the *IS–LM* Model

From the supply and demand relationships and equilibrium conditions in each market, we can calculate the general equilibrium values for the most important macroeconomic variables. We have already solved for the general equilibrium levels of the real wage, employment, and output in the labor market: The real wage is given by Eq. (9.B.5); employment equals its full-employment level, $\overline{N}$, given by Eq. (9.B.6); and, in general equilibrium, output equals its full-employment level, $\overline{Y}$, as given by Eq. (9.B.7).

Turning to the goods market, we obtain the general equilibrium real interest rate by substituting $\overline{Y}$ for Y in Eq. (9.B.14):

$$r = \alpha_{IS} - \beta_{IS}\overline{Y}. \qquad \text{(9.B.22)}$$

Having output, Y, and the real interest rate, r (determined by Eq. 9.B.22), we use Eqs. (9.B.9), (9.B.8), and (9.B.10) to find the general equilibrium values of taxes, T, consumption, C, and investment, I, respectively.

The final important macroeconomic variable whose equilibrium value needs to be determined is the price level, P. To find the equilibrium price level, we work with the asset market equilibrium condition, Eq. (9.B.18). In Eq. (9.B.18), we substitute full-employment output, $\overline{Y}$, for Y and use Eq. (9.B.22) to substitute the equilibrium value of the real interest rate for r. Solving Eq. (9.B.18) for the price level gives

$$P = \frac{M}{\ell_0 + \ell_Y \overline{Y} - \ell_r(\alpha_{IS} - \beta_{IS}\overline{Y} + \pi^e)}. \tag{9.B.23}$$

Equation (9.B.23) confirms that the equilibrium price level, P, is proportional to the nominal money supply, M.

We can use these equations to analyze the effects of an adverse productivity shock on the general equilibrium, as in the text. We have already shown that an increase in the productivity parameter, A, increases the equilibrium real wage, the full-employment level of employment, and the full-employment level of output. Thus an adverse productivity shock (a reduction in A) reduces the general equilibrium levels of the real wage, employment, and output. Equation (9.B.22) indicates that an adverse productivity shock, because it reduces $\overline{Y}$, must increase the equilibrium real interest rate. Lower output and a higher real interest rate imply that both consumption and investment must decline (Eqs. 9.B.8 and 9.B.10). Finally, the decrease in $\overline{Y}$ resulting from an adverse productivity shock reduces the denominator of the right side of Eq. (9.B.23), so the price level, P, must rise. All these results are the same as those found by graphical analysis.

The *AD–AS* Model

Building on the algebraic version of the *IS–LM* model just derived, we now derive an algebraic version of the *AD–AS* model presented in this chapter. We present algebraic versions of the aggregate demand (*AD*) curve, the short-run aggregate supply (*SRAS*) curve, and the long-run aggregate supply (*LRAS*) curve and then solve for short-run and long-run equilibria.

The Aggregate Demand Curve

Aggregate output demanded at any price level, P, is the amount of output corresponding to the intersection of the *IS* and *LM* curves. We find the value of Y at the intersection of the *IS* and *LM* curves by setting the right sides of Eqs. (9.B.14) and (9.B.19) equal and solving for Y:

$$Y = \frac{\alpha_{IS} - \alpha_{LM} + (1/\ell_r)(M/P)}{\beta_{IS} + \beta_{LM}}. \tag{9.B.24}$$

Equation (9.B.24) is the aggregate demand curve. For constant nominal money supply, M, Eq. (9.B.24) shows that the aggregate quantity of goods demanded, Y, is a decreasing function of the price level, P, so that the *AD* curve slopes downward. Note that the numerator of the right side of Eq. (9.B.24) is the intercept of the *IS* curve minus the intercept of the *LM* curve. Thus, for a constant price level, any change that shifts the *IS* curve up and to the right (such as an increase in the government purchases) or shifts the *LM* curve down and to the right (such as an increase in the nominal money supply) increases aggregate output demanded and shifts the *AD* curve up and to the right.

The Aggregate Supply Curve

In the short run, firms supply the output demanded at the fixed price level, which we denote P_{sr}. Thus the short-run aggregate supply (*SRAS*) curve is a horizontal line:

$$P = P_{sr}, \quad SRAS. \tag{9.B.25}$$

The long-run aggregate supply curve is a vertical line at the full-employment level of output, $\overline{Y}$, or

$$Y = \overline{Y}, \quad LRAS. \tag{9.B.26}$$

Short-Run and Long-Run Equilibrium

The short-run equilibrium of the economy is represented by the intersection of the aggregate demand (*AD*) curve and the short-run aggregate supply (*SRAS*) curve. We find the quantity of output in short-run equilibrium simply by substituting the equation of the *SRAS* curve (Eq. 9.B.25) into the equation of the *AD* curve (Eq. 9.B.24) to obtain

$$Y = \frac{\alpha_{IS} - \alpha_{LM} + (1/\ell_r)(M/P_{sr})}{\beta_{IS} + \beta_{LM}}. \tag{9.B.27}$$

The long-run equilibrium of the economy, which is reached when the labor, goods, and asset markets are all in equilibrium, is represented by the intersection of the aggregate demand curve and the long-run aggregate supply curve. Thus $Y = \overline{Y}$ in long-run equilibrium, from the *LRAS* curve in Eq. (9.B.26). We find the price level in long-run equilibrium by setting the right sides of the equation of the *AD* curve (Eq. 9.B.24) and the equation of the *LRAS* curve (Eq. 9.B.26) equal and solving for P to obtain

$$P = \frac{M}{\ell_r[\alpha_{LM} - \alpha_{IS} + (\beta_{IS} + \beta_{LM})\overline{Y}]}. \tag{9.B.28}$$

The long-run equilibrium price level in Eq. (9.B.28) is the same as that at the *IS–LM–FE* intersection in Eq. (9.B.23). You can verify that the price level is the same in both equations by substituting the definitions of α_{LM} and β_{LM} from Eqs. (9.B.20) and (9.B.21), respectively, into Eq. (9.B.28).

CHAPTER 10

Classical Business Cycle Analysis: Market-Clearing Macroeconomics

Economists generally agree about the basic business cycle facts outlined in Chapter 8. They know that economic growth isn't necessarily smooth and that occasionally there are periods of recession in which output declines and unemployment rises. They know that recessions typically are followed by periods of recovery in which the economy grows more strongly than normal. And they also know a great deal about how other macroeconomic variables—such as productivity, interest rates, and inflation—behave during recessions.

Recall that recessions and booms in the economy raise two basic questions: (1) What are the underlying economic causes of these business cycles? and (2) What, if anything, should government policymakers do about them? Unfortunately, economists agree less about the answers to these two questions than about the basic business cycle facts.

The main disagreements about the causes and cures of recessions are between two broad groups of macroeconomists, the classicals and the Keynesians. As discussed first in Chapter 1 and again in Chapters 8 and 9, classicals and Keynesians—although agreeing on many points—differ primarily in their views on how rapidly prices and wages adjust to restore general equilibrium after an economic shock. Classical macroeconomists assume that prices and wages adjust quickly to equate quantities supplied and demanded in each market; as a result, they argue, a market economy is largely "self-correcting," with a strong tendency to return to general equilibrium on its own when it is disturbed by an economic shock or a change in public policy. Keynesians usually agree that prices and wages *eventually* change as needed to clear markets; however, they believe that *in the short run* price and wage adjustment is likely to be incomplete. That is, in the short run, quantities supplied and demanded need not be equal and the economy may remain out of general equilibrium. Although this difference in views may seem purely theoretical, it has a practical implication: Because Keynesians are skeptical about the economy's ability to reach equilibrium rapidly on its own, they are much more inclined than are classicals to recommend that government act to raise output and employment during recessions and to moderate economic growth during booms.

In this chapter and Chapter 11 we develop and compare the classical and Keynesian theories of the business cycle and the policy recommendations of the two groups, beginning with the classical perspective in this chapter. Conveniently, both the classical and Keynesian analyses can be expressed in terms of a common analytical framework, the *IS–LM/AD–AS* model. In this chapter we use the classical (or market-clearing) version of the *IS–LM/AD–AS* model, composed of the *IS–LM/AD–AS* model and the assumption that prices and wages adjust rapidly. The assumption that prices and wages adjust rapidly implies that the economy always is in or near general equilibrium and therefore that variables such as output and employment always are close to their general equilibrium levels.

In comparing the principal competing theories of the business cycle, we are particularly interested in how well the various theories explain the business cycle facts. The classical theory is consistent with many of the most important facts about the cycle. However, one business cycle fact that challenges the classical theory is the observation that changes in the money stock lead the cycle. Recall the implication of the classical assumption that wages and prices adjust quickly to clear markets, so that the economy reaches long-run equilibrium quickly. Money is neutral, which means that changes in the money supply do not affect output and other real variables. However, most economists interpret the fact that money leads the cycle as evidence that money is not neutral in all situations. If money isn't neutral, we must either modify the basic classical model to account for monetary nonneutrality or abandon the classical model in favor of alternative theories (such as the Keynesian approach) that are consistent with nonneutrality. In Section 10.3 we extend the classical model to allow for nonneutrality of money. We then examine the implications of this extended classical approach for macroeconomic policy.

10.1 Business Cycles in the Classical Model

We have identified two basic questions of business cycle analysis: What causes business cycles? and What can (or should) be done about them? Let's examine the classical answers to these questions, beginning with what causes business cycles.

The Real Business Cycle Theory

Recall from Section 8.4 that a complete theory of the business cycle must have two components. The first is a description of the types of shocks or disturbances believed to affect the economy the most. Examples of economic disturbances emphasized by various theories of the business cycle include supply shocks, changes in monetary or fiscal policy, and changes in consumer spending. The second component is a model that describes how key macroeconomic variables, such as output, employment, and prices, respond to economic shocks. Classical economists prefer to build their models from microeconomic foundations, describing how people maximize their utility and how firms maximize profits. Thus their preferred models are quite complex and we cannot represent them easily in this textbook. However, the main results of their detailed models are similar to those from the market-clearing version of the *IS–LM* model, so in this textbook we will use that model to represent the views of classical macroeconomists. In addition, the issue of which shocks are crucial in driving cyclical fluctuations remains.

An influential group of classical macroeconomists, led by Nobel laureates Edward Prescott of Arizona State University and the Federal Reserve Bank of

Minneapolis and Finn Kydland of the University of California at Santa Barbara, developed a theory that takes a strong stand on the sources of shocks that cause cyclical fluctuations. This theory, the **real business cycle theory** (or RBC theory), argues that real shocks to the economy are the primary cause of business cycles.[1] **Real shocks** are disturbances to the "real side" of the economy, such as shocks that affect the production function, the size of the labor force, the real quantity of government purchases, and the spending and saving decisions of consumers. Economists contrast real shocks with **nominal shocks,** or shocks to money supply or money demand. In terms of the *IS–LM* model, real shocks directly affect the *IS* curve or the *FE* line, whereas nominal shocks directly affect only the *LM* curve.

Although many types of real shocks could contribute to the business cycle, RBC economists give the largest role to production function shocks—what we've called supply shocks and what the RBC economists usually refer to as **productivity shocks.** Productivity shocks include the development of new products or production methods, the introduction of new management techniques, changes in the quality of capital or labor, changes in the availability of raw materials or energy, unusually good or unusually bad weather, changes in government regulations affecting production, and any other factor affecting productivity. According to RBC economists, most economic booms result from beneficial productivity shocks, and most recessions are caused by adverse productivity shocks.

The Recessionary Impact of an Adverse Productivity Shock.   Does the RBC economists' idea that adverse productivity shocks lead to recessions (and, similarly, that beneficial productivity shocks lead to booms) make sense? We examined the theoretical effects on the economy of a temporary adverse productivity shock in Chapters 3, 8, and 9.[2] In Chapter 3 we showed that an adverse productivity shock (or supply shock), such as an increase in the price of oil, reduces the marginal product of labor (*MPN*) and the demand for labor at any real wage. As a result, the equilibrium values of the real wage and employment both fall (see Fig. 3.11). The equilibrium level of output (the full-employment level of output $\overline{Y}$) also falls, both because equilibrium employment declines and because the adverse productivity shock reduces the amount of output that can be produced by any amount of capital and labor.

We later used the complete *IS–LM* model (Fig. 9.8) to explore the general equilibrium effects of a temporary adverse productivity shock. We confirmed our earlier conclusion that an adverse productivity shock lowers the general equilibrium levels of the real wage, employment, and output. In addition, we showed that an adverse productivity shock raises the real interest rate, depresses consumption and investment, and raises the price level.

Broadly, then, our earlier analyses of the effects of an adverse productivity shock support the RBC economists' claim that such shocks are recessionary, in that they lead to declines in output. Similar analyses show that a beneficial productivity shock leads to a rise in output (a boom). Note that, in the RBC approach, output declines in

---

[1]For a more detailed introduction to real business cycles, see Charles Plosser, "Understanding Real Business Cycles," *Journal of Economic Perspectives,* Summer 1989, pp. 51–78, and Robert G. King and Sergio Rebelo, "Resuscitating Real Business Cycles," in J. Taylor and M. Woodford, eds., *Handbook of Macroeconomics,* Elsevier, 1999.

[2]RBC economists analyze permanent as well as temporary productivity shocks; we focus on temporary shocks because it is the slightly easier case.

recessions and rises in booms because the general equilibrium (or full-employment) level of output has changed and because rapid price adjustment ensures that actual output always equals full-employment output. As classical economists, RBC economists would reject the Keynesian view (discussed in Chapter 11) that recessions and booms are periods of disequilibrium, during which actual output is below or above its general equilibrium level for a protracted period of time.

Real Business Cycle Theory and the Business Cycle Facts.   Although the RBC theory—which combines the classical, or market-clearing, version of the *IS–LM* model with the assumption that productivity shocks are the dominant form of economic disturbance—is relatively simple, it is consistent with many of the basic business cycle facts. First, under the assumption that the economy is being continuously buffeted by productivity shocks, the RBC approach predicts recurrent fluctuations in aggregate output, which actually occur. Second, the RBC theory correctly predicts that employment will move procyclically—that is, in the same direction as output. Third, the RBC theory predicts that real wages will be higher during booms than during recessions (procyclical real wages), as also occurs.

A fourth business cycle fact explained by the RBC theory is that average labor productivity is procyclical; that is, output per worker is higher during booms than during recessions. This fact is consistent with the RBC economists' assumption that booms are periods of beneficial productivity shocks, which tend to raise labor productivity, whereas recessions are the results of adverse productivity shocks, which tend to reduce labor productivity. The RBC economists point out that without productivity shocks—allowing the production function to remain stable over time—average labor productivity wouldn't be procyclical. With no productivity shocks, the expansion of employment that occurs during booms would tend to reduce average labor productivity because of the principle of diminishing marginal productivity of labor. Similarly, without productivity shocks, recessions would be periods of relatively higher labor productivity, instead of lower productivity as observed. Thus RBC economists regard the procyclical nature of average labor productivity as strong evidence supporting their approach.

A business cycle fact that does not seem to be consistent with the simple RBC theory is that inflation tends to slow during or immediately after a recession. The theory predicts that an adverse productivity shock will both cause a recession and increase the general price level. Thus, according to the RBC approach, periods of recession should also be periods of inflation, contrary to the business cycle fact.

Some RBC economists have responded by taking issue with the conventional view that inflation is procyclical. For example, in a study of the period 1954–1989, RBC proponents Kydland and Prescott[3] showed that the finding of procyclical inflation is somewhat sensitive to the statistical methods used to calculate the trends in inflation and output. Using a different method of calculating these trends, Kydland and Prescott found evidence that, when aggregate output has been above its long-run trend, the price level has tended to be below its long-run trend, a result more nearly consistent with the RBC prediction about the cyclical behavior of prices. Kydland and Prescott suggested that standard views about the procyclicality of prices and inflation are based mostly on the experience of the economy between the two world wars (1918–1941), when the economy had a different structure and was

---

[3]"Business Cycles: Real Facts and a Monetary Myth," *Quarterly Review,* Federal Reserve Bank of Minneapolis, Spring 1990, pp. 3–18.

subject to different types of shocks than the more recent economy. For example, many economists believe that the Great Depression—the most important macroeconomic event between the two world wars—resulted from a sequence of large, adverse aggregate demand shocks. As we illustrated in Fig. 8.17, an adverse aggregate demand shock shifts the *AD* curve down and to the left, leading first to a decline in output and then to a decline in prices; this pattern is consistent with the conventional business cycle fact that inflation is procyclical and lagging. Kydland and Prescott argue, however, that since World War II large adverse supply shocks have caused the price level to rise while output fell. Most notably, inflation surged during the recessions that followed the oil price shocks of 1973–1974 and 1979–1980. The issue of the cyclical behavior of prices remains controversial, however.

APPLICATION

Calibrating the Business Cycle

If we put aside the debate about price level behavior, the RBC theory can account for some of the business cycle facts, including the procyclical behavior of employment, productivity, and real wages. However, real business cycle economists argue that an adequate theory of the business cycle should be *quantitative* as well as *qualitative*. In other words, in addition to predicting generally how key macroeconomic variables move throughout the business cycle, the theory should predict numerically the size of economic fluctuations and the strength of relationships among the variables.

To examine the quantitative implications of their theories, RBC economists developed a method called *calibration*. The idea is to work out a detailed numerical example of a more general theory. The results are then compared to macroeconomic data to see whether model and reality broadly agree.

The first step in calibration is to write down a model of the economy—such as the classical version of the *IS–LM* model—except that specific functions replace general functions. For example, instead of representing the production function in general terms as

$$Y = AF(K, N),$$

the person doing the calibration uses a specific algebraic form for the production function, such as[4]

$$Y = AK^a N^{1-a},$$

where *a* is a number between 0 and 1. Similarly, specific functions are used to describe the behavior of consumers and workers.

Next, the specific functions chosen are made even more specific by expressing them in numerical terms. For example, for *a* = 0.3, the production function becomes

$$Y = AK^{0.3} N^{0.7}.$$

In the same way, specific numbers are assigned to the functions describing the behavior of consumers and workers. Where do these numbers come from? Generally, they are *not* estimated from macroeconomic data but are based on other sources.

---

[4]This production function is the Cobb–Douglas production function (Chapter 3). As we noted, although it is relatively simple, it fits U.S. data quite well.

Figure 10.1

Actual versus simulated volatilities of key macroeconomic variables

The figure compares the actual volatilities of key macroeconomic variables observed in post–World War II U.S. data with the volatilities of the same variables predicted by computer simulations of Edward Prescott's calibrated RBC model. Prescott set the size of the random productivity shocks in his simulations so that the simulated volatility of GNP would match the actually observed volatility of GNP exactly. For these random productivity shocks, the simulated volatilities of the other five macroeconomic variables (with the possible exception of consumption) match the observed volatilities fairly well.

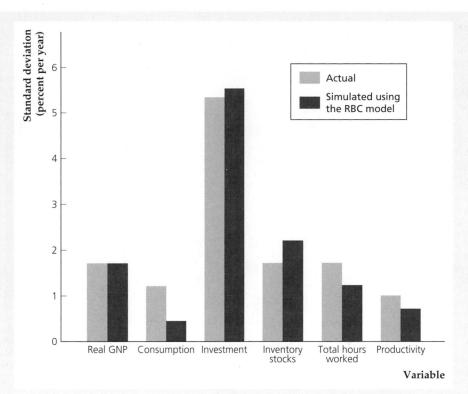

For example, the numbers assigned to the functions in the model may come from previous studies of the production function or of the saving behavior of individuals and families.

The third step, which must be carried out on a computer, is to find out how the numerically specified model behaves when it is hit by random shocks, such as productivity shocks. The shocks are created on the computer with a random number generator, with the size and persistence of the shocks (unlike the numbers assigned to the specific functions) being chosen to fit the actual macroeconomic data. For these shocks, the computer tracks the behavior of the model over many periods and reports the implied behavior of key macroeconomic variables such as output, employment, consumption, and investment. The results from these simulations are then compared to the behavior of the actual economy to determine how well the model fits reality.

Edward Prescott[5] performed an early and influential calibration exercise. He used a model similar to the RBC model we present here, the main difference being that our version of the RBC model is essentially a two-period model (the present and the future), and Prescott's model allowed for many periods. The results of his computer simulations are shown in Figs. 10.1 and 10.2.

[5]"Theory Ahead of Business Cycle Measurement," *Carnegie-Rochester Conference Series on Public Policy,* Volume 25, Autumn 1986, pp. 11–39. Reprinted in *Quarterly Review,* Federal Reserve Bank of Minneapolis, Fall 1986, pp. 9–22.

(continued)

Figure 10.2

Actual versus simulated correlations of key macroeconomic variables with GNP
How closely a variable moves with GNP over the business cycle is measured by its correlation with GNP, with higher correlations implying a closer relationship. The figure compares the correlations of key variables with GNP that were actually observed in the post–World War II U.S. economy with the correlations predicted by computer simulations of Prescott's calibrated RBC model. Except for productivity, whose predicted correlation with GNP is too high, the simulations predicted correlations of macroeconomic variables with GNP that closely resemble the actual correlations of these variables with GNP.

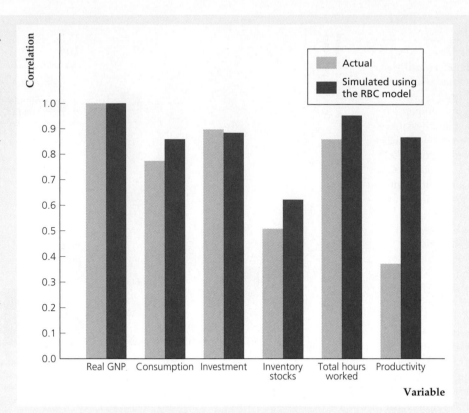

Figure 10.1 compares the actually observed volatilities of six macroeconomic variables, as calculated from post–World War II U.S. data, with the volatilities predicted by Prescott's calibrated RBC model.[6] Prescott set the size of the random productivity shocks in his simulations so that the volatility of GNP in his model would match the actual volatility in U.S. GNP.[7] That choice explains why the actual and simulated volatilities of GNP are equal in Fig. 10.1. But he did nothing to guarantee that the simulation would match the actual volatilities of the other five variables. Note, however, that the simulated and actual volatilities for the other variables in most cases are quite close.

Figure 10.2 compares the actual economy with Prescott's calibrated model in another respect: how closely important macroeconomic variables move with GNP over the business cycle. The statistical measure of how closely variables move together is called *correlation*. If a variable's correlation with GNP is positive, the variable tends to move in the same direction as GNP over the business cycle (that is, the variable is procyclical). A correlation with GNP of 1.0 indicates that the variable's movements track the movements of GNP perfectly (thus the correlation of GNP with itself is 1.0), and a correlation with GNP of 0 indicates no relationship to

---

[6]The measure of volatility used is called the *standard deviation*. The higher the standard deviation, the more volatile the variable being measured.

[7]At the time of Prescott's study, the national income and product accounts of the United States focused on GNP rather than GDP, so Prescott also focused on GNP.

GNP. Correlations with GNP between 0 and 1.0 reflect relationships with GNP of intermediate strength. Figure 10.2 shows that Prescott's model generally accounts well for the strength of the relationships between some of the variables and GNP, although the correlation of productivity and GNP predicted by Prescott's model is noticeably larger than the actual correlation.

The degree to which relatively simple calibrated RBC models can match the actual data is impressive. In addition, the results of calibration exercises help guide further development of the model. For example, the version of the RBC model discussed here has been modified to improve the match between the actual and predicted correlations of productivity with GNP.

Are Productivity Shocks the Only Source of Recessions? Although RBC economists agree in principle that many types of real shocks buffet the economy, in practice much of their work rests on the assumption that productivity shocks are the dominant, or even the only, source of recessions. Many economists, including both classicals and Keynesians, have criticized this assumption as being unrealistic. For example, some economists challenged the RBC economists to identify the specific productivity shocks that they believe caused each of the recessions since World War II. The critics argue that, except for the oil price shocks of 1973, 1979, and 1990, and the tech revolution of the late 1990s, historical examples of economywide productivity shocks are virtually nonexistent.

An interesting RBC response to that argument is that, in principle, economy-wide fluctuations could also be caused by the cumulative effects of a series of small productivity shocks. To illustrate the point that small shocks can cause large fluctuations, Fig. 10.3 shows the results of a computer simulation of productivity shocks and the associated behavior of output for a simplified RBC model. In this simple RBC model, the change in output from one month to the next has two parts: (1) a fixed part that arises from normal technical progress or from a normal increase in population and employment; and (2) an unpredictable part that reflects a random shock to productivity during the current month.[8] The random, computer-generated productivity shocks are shown at the bottom of Fig. 10.3, and the implied behavior of output is displayed above them. Although none of the individual shocks is large, the cumulative effect of the shocks causes large fluctuations in output that look something like business cycles. Hence business cycles may be the result of productivity shocks, even though identifying specific, large shocks is difficult.

Does the Solow Residual Measure Technology Shocks? Because productivity shocks are the primary source of business cycle fluctuations in RBC models, RBC economists have attempted to measure the size of these shocks. The most common measure of productivity shocks is known as the **Solow residual,** which

---

[8]Specifically, the model is $Y_t = Y_{t-1} + 0.01 + e_t$, where Y_t is output in month t, Y_{t-1} is output in the previous month, and e_t is the random productivity shock in month t. The productivity shocks are randomly chosen numbers between -1.0 and 1.0. A similar example is given in Numerical Problem 6 at the end of this chapter.

Figure 10.3

Small shocks and large cycles

A computer simulation of a simple RBC model is used to find the relationship between computer-generated random productivity shocks (shown at the bottom of the figure) and aggregate output (shown in the middle of the figure). Even though all of the productivity shocks are small, the simulation produces large cyclical fluctuations in aggregate output. Thus large productivity shocks aren't necessary to generate large cyclical fluctuations.

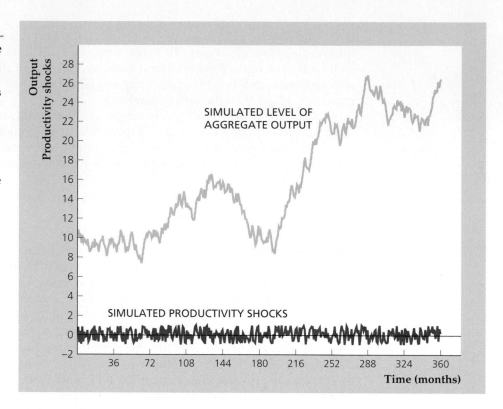

is an empirical measure of total factor productivity, A. The Solow residual is named after the originator of modern growth theory, Robert Solow,[9] who used this measure in the 1950s.

Recall from Chapter 3 that, to measure total factor productivity A, we need data on output, Y, and the inputs of capital, K, and labor, N. In addition, we need to use a specific algebraic form for the production function. Then we have,

$$\text{Solow residual} = \frac{Y}{K^a N^{1-a}} = A. \qquad (10.1)$$

The Solow residual is called a "residual" because it is the part of output that cannot be directly explained by measured capital and labor inputs.

When the Solow residual is computed from actual U.S. data, using Eq. (10.1), it turns out to be strongly procyclical, rising in economic expansions and falling in recessions. This procyclical behavior is consistent with the premise of RBC theory that cyclical fluctuations in aggregate output are driven largely by productivity shocks.

However, some economists have questioned whether the Solow residual should be interpreted solely as a measure of technology, as early RBC proponents tended to do. If changes in the Solow residual reflect only changes in the technologies available to an economy, its value should be unrelated to factors such as government purchases or monetary policy that don't directly affect scientific and technological progress (at least in the short run). However, statistical studies reveal

---

[9]"Technical Change and the Aggregate Production Function," *Review of Economics and Statistics*, 1957, pp. 312–320. In Chapter 6 we described Solow's contributions to growth theory.

that the Solow residual is in fact correlated with factors such as government expenditures, suggesting that movements in the Solow residual may also reflect the impacts of other factors.[10]

To understand why measured productivity can vary, even if the actual technology used in production doesn't change, we need to recognize that capital and labor sometimes are used more intensively than at other times and that more intensive use of inputs leads to higher output. For instance, a printing press used full-time contributes more to production than an otherwise identical printing press used half-time. Similarly, workers working rapidly (for example, restaurant workers during a busy lunch hour) will produce more output and revenue than the same number of workers working more slowly (the same restaurant workers during the afternoon lull). To capture the idea that capital and labor resources can be used more or less intensively at different times, we define the *utilization rate of capital*, u_K, and the *utilization rate of labor*, u_N. The utilization rate of a factor measures the intensity at which it is being used. For example, the utilization rate of capital for the printing press run full-time would be twice as high as for the printing press used half-time; similarly, the utilization rate of labor is higher in the restaurant during lunch hour. The actual usage of the capital stock in production, which we call *capital services*, equals the utilization rate of capital times the stock of capital, or $u_K K$. Capital services are a more accurate measure of the contribution of the capital stock to output than is the level of capital itself, because the definition of capital services adjusts for the intensity at which capital is used. Similarly, we define *labor services* to be the utilization rate of labor times the number of workers (or hours) employed by the firm, or $u_N N$. Thus the labor services received by an employer are higher when the same number of workers are working rapidly than when they are working slowly (that is, the utilization of labor is higher).

Recognizing that capital services and labor services go into the production of output, we rewrite the production function as

$$Y = AF(u_K K, u_N N) = A(u_K K)^a (u_N N)^{1-a}, \qquad (10.2)$$

where we have replaced the capital stock, K, with capital services, $u_K K$, and labor, N, with labor services, $u_N N$. Now we can use the production function in Eq. (10.2) to substitute for Y in Eq. (10.1) to obtain an expression for the Solow residual that incorporates utilization rates for capital and labor:

$$\text{Solow residual} = \frac{A(u_K K)^a (u_N N)^{1-a}}{K^a N^{1-a}} = A u_K{}^a u_N{}^{1-a}. \qquad (10.3)$$

Equation (10.3) shows that the Solow residual, as conventionally measured, includes not only parameter A (which reflects technology and perhaps other factors affecting productivity) but also utilization rates of capital and labor, u_K and u_N. Thus, even if technology were unchanging, the calculated Solow residual would be procyclical if the utilization rates of capital and labor were procyclical.

There is evidence that utilization is procyclical (so that capital and labor are worked harder in boom periods than in economic slumps). For example, Craig

---

[10]Changes in technology might well be correlated with changes in government spending on research and development (R&D). However, the Solow residual is also highly correlated with non-R&D government spending and with lags too short to be accounted for by the effects of spending on the rate of invention.

Burnside of Duke University, Martin Eichenbaum of Northwestern University, and Sergio Rebelo[11] of Northwestern University studied the cyclical behavior of capital utilization by using data on the amount of electricity used by producers. Their rationale for using data on electricity is that additional electricity is needed to increase capital utilization, whether the increased utilization is achieved by operating capital for an increased number of hours per day or by increasing the speed at which the capital is operated. This study revealed that electricity used per unit of capital rises in economic upturns, leading the authors to conclude that capital utilization is strongly procyclical. In addition, this study showed that a measure of technology, analogous to the term A in Eq. (10.2), is much less procyclical than is the Solow residual.

Measuring the cyclical behavior of labor utilization is more difficult, but various studies have found evidence that the utilization rate of labor is also procyclical. For example, Jon Fay and James Medoff[12] of Harvard University sent questionnaires to large manufacturing enterprises, asking about employment and production during the most recent downturn experienced at each plant. Fay and Medoff found that during a downturn the average plant surveyed cut production by 31% and cut its total use of blue-collar hours to 23% below the normal level. Plant managers estimated that total hours could have been reduced by an additional 6% of the normal level without further reducing output. Of this 6% of normal hours, about half (3% of normal hours) were typically assigned to various types of useful work, including equipment maintenance and overhaul, painting, cleaning, reworking output, and training. The remaining 3% of normal hours were assigned to "make-work" and other unproductive activities. These numbers suggest that firms utilize labor less intensively during recessions.

The tendency to use workers less intensively in recessions than in expansions has been referred to as labor hoarding. **Labor hoarding** occurs when, because of the costs of firing and hiring workers, firms retain some workers in a recession that they would otherwise lay off. Firms keep these workers on the payroll to avoid the costs of laying off workers and then rehiring them or hiring and training new workers when the economy revives. Hoarded labor either works less hard during the recession (there is less to do) or is put to work doing tasks, such as maintaining equipment, that aren't measured as part of the firm's output. When the economy revives, the hoarded labor goes back to working in the normal way. In much the same way, it may not pay the restaurant owner to send her workers home between the lunch and dinner rush hours, with the result that restaurant workers are less productive during the slow afternoon period. This lower rate of productivity during recessions (or during the afternoon slow period, in the restaurant) doesn't reflect changes in the available technology, but only changes in the rate at which firms utilize capital and labor. Hence you should be cautious about interpreting cyclical changes in the Solow residual (equivalently, total factor productivity, A) as solely reflecting changes in technology.

Although changes in technology or the utilization rates of capital and labor might cause aggregate cyclical fluctuations, history suggests that shocks other than

[11]"Capital Utilization and Returns to Scale," in B. Bernanke and J. Rotemberg, eds., *NBER Macroeconomics Annual*, 1995.

[12]"Labor and Output Over the Business Cycle," *American Economic Review*, September 1985, pp. 638–655.

productivity shocks also affect the economy; wars and the corresponding military buildups are but one obvious example. Thus many classical economists favor a broader definition of classical business cycle theory that allows for both productivity and other types of shocks to have an impact on the economy. Because the models they use allow for shocks other than "real" productivity shocks, the models are not called RBC models but rather dynamic, stochastic, general equilibrium (DSGE) models, as they model behavior over time (dynamic), allow for shocks to the economy (stochastic), and are based on general equilibrium concepts.

The macroeconomic effects of shocks other than productivity shocks can be analyzed with the classical *IS–LM* model. Let's use it to examine the effects of a fiscal policy shock.

Fiscal Policy Shocks in the Classical Model

Another type of shock that can be a source of business cycles in the classical model is a change in fiscal policy, such as an increase or decrease in real government purchases of goods and services.[13] Examples of shocks to government purchases include military buildups and the initiation of large road-building or other public works programs. Because government purchases are procyclical—and in particular, because national output tends to be above normal during wars and at other times when military spending is high—we need to explore how shocks to government purchases affect aggregate output and employment.

Let's consider what happens when the government purchases more goods, as it would, for example, when the country is at war. (Think of the increase in government purchases as temporary. Analytical Problem 2 at the end of the chapter asks you to work out what happens if the increase in government purchases is permanent.)

Figure 10.4 illustrates the effects of an increase in government purchases in the classical *IS–LM* model. Before the fiscal policy change, the economy's general equilibrium is represented by point *E* in both (a) and (b). To follow what happens after purchases rise, we start with the labor market in Fig. 10.4(a). The change in fiscal policy doesn't affect the production function or the marginal product of labor (the *MPN* curve), so the labor demand curve doesn't shift.

However, classical economists argue that an increase in government purchases will affect labor supply by reducing workers' wealth. People are made less wealthy because, if the government increases the amount of the nation's output that it takes for military purposes, less output will be left for private consumption and investment. This negative impact of increased government purchases on private wealth is most obvious if the government pays for its increased military spending by raising current taxes.[14] However, even if the government doesn't raise current taxes to pay for the extra military spending and borrows the funds it needs,

---

[13]Another important example of a change in fiscal policy is a change in the structure of the tax code. Classical economists argue that the greatest effects of tax changes are those that affect people's incentives to work, save, and invest, and thus affect full-employment output. However, because most classical economists accept the Ricardian equivalence proposition, they wouldn't expect lump-sum changes in taxes without accompanying changes in government purchases to have much effect on the economy.

[14]For simplicity, we assume that the tax increase is a lump sum. A tax increase that isn't a lump sum—for example, one that changes the effective tax rate on capital—has complicating effects.

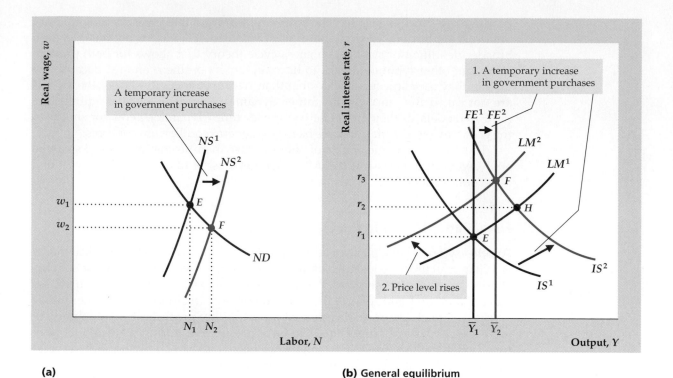

(a)

(b) General equilibrium

Figure 10.4

Effects of a temporary increase in government purchases

Initial equilibrium is at point E in both (a) and (b).

(a) A temporary increase in government purchases raises workers' current or future taxes. Because workers feel poorer, they supply more labor and the labor supply curve shifts to the right, from NS^1 to NS^2. The shift in the labor supply curve reduces the real wage and increases employment, as indicated by point F.

(b) The increase in employment raises full-employment output and shifts the FE line to the right, from FE^1 to FE^2. The increase in government purchases also reduces desired national saving and shifts the IS curve up and to the right, from IS^1 to IS^2. Because the intersection of IS^2 and LM^1 is to the right of FE^2, the aggregate quantity of output demanded is higher than the full-employment level of output, $\overline{Y}_2$, so the price level rises. The rise in the price level reduces the real money supply and shifts the LM curve up and to the left, from LM^1 to LM^2, until the new general equilibrium is reached at point F. The effect of the increase in government purchases is to increase output, the real interest rate, and the price level.

taxes will still have to be raised in the future to pay the principal and interest on this extra government borrowing. So, whether or not taxes are currently raised, under the classical assumption that output is always at its full-employment level, an increase in government military spending effectively makes people poorer.

In Chapter 3 we showed that a decrease in wealth increases labor supply because someone who is poorer can afford less leisure. Thus, according to the classical analysis, an increase in government purchases—which makes people financially worse off—should lead to an increase in aggregate labor supply.[15] The

---

[15]In theory, the effect on labor supply of an increase in government purchases should be the strongest for spending, such as military spending, that extracts resources without providing any direct benefits to the private sector. Government purchases that effectively replace private consumption expenditures—for example, purchases of medical services, roads, or playgrounds—should in principle have a smaller negative impact on people's economic well-being and thus a smaller positive effect on labor supply.

increase in government purchases causes the labor supply curve to shift to the right, from NS^1 to NS^2 in Fig. 10.4(a). Following the shift of the labor supply curve, the equilibrium in the labor market shifts from point E to point F, with employment increasing and the real wage decreasing.[16]

The effects of the increase in government purchases in the classical IS–LM framework are shown in Fig. 10.4(b). First, note that, because equilibrium employment increases, full-employment output, $\overline{Y}$, also increases. Thus the FE line shifts to the right, from FE^1 to FE^2.

In addition to shifting the FE line to the right, the fiscal policy change shifts the IS curve. Recall that, at any level of output, a temporary increase in government purchases reduces desired national saving and raises the real interest rate that clears the goods market. Thus the IS curve shifts up and to the right, from IS^1 to IS^2. (See also Summary table 12, p. 315.) The LM curve isn't directly affected by the change in fiscal policy.

The new IS curve, IS^2, the initial LM curve, LM^1, and the new FE line, FE^2, have no common point of intersection. For general equilibrium to be restored, prices must adjust, shifting the LM curve until it passes through the intersection of IS^2 and FE^2 (point F). Will prices rise or fall? The answer to this question is ambiguous because the fiscal policy change has increased both the aggregate demand for goods (by reducing desired saving and shifting the IS curve up and to the right) and the full-employment level of output (by increasing labor supply and shifting the FE line to the right). If we assume that the effect on labor supply and full-employment output of the increase in government purchases isn't too large (probably a reasonable assumption), after the fiscal policy change the aggregate quantity of goods demanded is likely to exceed full-employment output. In Fig. 10.4(b) the aggregate quantity of goods demanded (point H at the intersection of IS^2 and LM^1) exceeds full-employment output, $\overline{Y}_2$. Thus the price level must rise, shifting the LM curve up and to the left and causing the economy to return to general equilibrium at F. At F both output and the real interest rate are higher than at the initial equilibrium point, E.

Therefore the increase in government purchases increases output, employment, the real interest rate, and the price level. Because the increase in employment is the result of an increase in labor supply rather than an increase in labor demand, real wages fall when government purchases rise. Because of diminishing marginal productivity of labor, the increase in employment also implies a decline in average labor productivity when government purchases rise.

That fiscal shocks play some role in business cycles seems reasonable, which is itself justification for including them in the model. However, including fiscal shocks along with productivity shocks in the RBC model has the additional advantage of improving the match between model and data. We previously noted that government purchases are procyclical, which is consistent with the preceding analysis. Another advantage of adding fiscal shocks to a model that also contains productivity shocks is that it improves the model's ability to explain the behavior of labor productivity.

Refer back to Fig. 10.2 to recall a weakness of the RBC model with only productivity shocks: It predicts that average labor productivity and GNP are highly

---

[16]Note that this labor supply effect was omitted from our discussion of the impact of increased government purchases in Chapter 4, as illustrated in Fig. 4.9.

correlated. In fact, RBC theory predicts a correlation that is more than twice the actual correlation. However, as we have just shown, a classical business cycle model with shocks to government purchases predicts a negative correlation between labor productivity and GNP because a positive shock to government purchases raises output but lowers average productivity. A classical business cycle model that includes *both* shocks to productivity and shocks to government purchases can match the empirically observed correlation of productivity and GNP well, without reducing the fit of the model in other respects.[17] Thus adding fiscal shocks to the real business cycle model seems to improve its ability to explain the actual behavior of the economy.

Should Fiscal Policy Be Used to Dampen the Cycle?   Our analysis shows that changes in government purchases can have real effects on the economy. Changes in the tax laws can also have real effects on the economy in the classical model, although these effects are more complicated and depend mainly on the nature of the tax, the type of income or revenue that is taxed, and so on. Potentially, then, changes in fiscal policy could be used to offset cyclical fluctuations and stabilize output and employment; for example, the government could increase its purchases during recessions. This observation leads to the second of the two questions posed in the introduction to the chapter: Should policymakers use fiscal policy to smooth business cycle fluctuations?

Recall that classical economists generally oppose active attempts to dampen cyclical fluctuations because of Adam Smith's invisible-hand argument that free markets produce efficient outcomes without government intervention. The classical view holds that prices and wages adjust fairly rapidly to bring the economy into general equilibrium, allowing little scope for the government to improve the macroeconomy's response to economic disturbances. Therefore, although in principle fiscal policy could be used to fight recessions and reduce output fluctuations, classical economists advise against using this approach. Instead, classicals argue that not interfering in the economy's adjustment to disturbances is better.

This skepticism about the value of active antirecessionary policies does not mean that classical economists don't regard recessions as a serious problem. If an adverse productivity shock causes a recession, for example, real wages, employment, and output all fall, which means that many people experience economic hardship. But would offsetting the recession by, for example, increasing government purchases help? In the classical analysis, a rise in government purchases increases output by raising the amount of labor supplied, and the amount of labor supplied is increased by making workers poorer (as a result of higher current or future taxes). Thus, under the classical assumption that the economy is always in general equilibrium, increasing government purchases for the sole purpose of increasing output and employment makes people worse off rather than better off. Classical economists conclude that government purchases should be increased only if the benefits of the expanded government program—in terms of improved military security or public services, for example—exceed the costs to taxpayers.

---

[17]See Lawrence Christiano and Martin Eichenbaum, "Current Real-Business-Cycle Theories and Aggregate Labor-Market Fluctuations," *American Economic Review,* June 1992, pp. 430–450. The analysis of this paper is technically complex but it gives a flavor of research in classical business cycle analysis.

Classicals apply this criterion for useful government spending—that the benefits should exceed the costs—whether or not the economy is currently in recession.

So far we have assumed that, because fiscal policy affects the equilibrium levels of employment and output, the government is capable of using fiscal policy to achieve the levels of employment and output it chooses. In fact, the legislative process can lead to lengthy delays, or *lags,* between the time that a fiscal policy change is proposed and the time that it is enacted. Additional lags occur in implementing the new policies and in the response of the economy to the policy changes. Because of these lags, fiscal policy changes contemplated today should be based on where the economy will be several quarters in the future; unfortunately, forecasting the future of the economy is an inexact art at best. Beyond the problems of forecasting, policymakers also face uncertainties about how and by how much to modify their policies to get the desired output and employment effects. Classical economists cite these practical difficulties as another reason for not using fiscal policy to fight recessions.

Unemployment in the Classical Model

A major weakness of the classical model is that it doesn't explain why unemployment rises during business downturns. Indeed, in the simple classical, or supply–and–demand, model of the labor market, unemployment is literally zero: Anyone who wants to work at the market-clearing wage can find a job. Of course, in reality unemployment is never zero. Furthermore, the sharp increases in unemployment that occur during recessions are a principal reason that policymakers and the public are so concerned about economic downturns.

Classical economists are perfectly aware of this issue, and they have developed more sophisticated versions of the classical business cycle model to account for unemployment. The main modification they make to the simple supply–and–demand model of the labor market is to drop the model's implicit assumption that all workers and jobs are the same. Rather than all being the same, workers in the real world have different abilities, skills, and interests, among other things; jobs entail different skill requirements, work environments, locations, and other characteristics. Because workers and jobs both vary in so many ways, matching workers to jobs isn't instantaneous and free, but time-consuming and costly. The fact that someone who has lost a job or has just entered the labor force must spend time and effort to find a new job helps explain why there always are some unemployed people.

Some classical economists suggest that differences among workers and among jobs explain not only why the unemployment rate is always greater than zero, but also why unemployment rises so sharply in recessions. They argue that productivity shocks and other macroeconomic disturbances that cause recessions also often increase the degree of mismatch between workers and firms.[18] Thus a major adverse productivity shock might affect the various industries and regions within the country differently, with jobs being destroyed in some sectors but new opportunities emerging in others. An oil price shock, for example, would eliminate jobs

---

[18]This idea was proposed in David Lilien, "Sectoral Shifts and Cyclical Unemployment," *Journal of Political Economy,* August 1982, pp. 777–793.

in energy-intensive industries but create new opportunities in industries that supply energy or are light energy users.

Following such a shock, workers in industries and regions where labor demand has fallen will be induced to search elsewhere for jobs, which raises the frictional component of unemployment. Some of these workers will find that their skills don't match the requirements of industries with growing labor demand; these workers may become chronically unemployed, raising structural unemployment.[19] With many unemployed workers looking for jobs, and because creating new jobs takes a while, the time necessary to find a new job is likely to increase. For all these reasons, an adverse productivity shock may raise unemployment as well as reduce output and employment. Note that this predicted rise in frictional and structural unemployment during recessions is the same as an increase in the natural rate of unemployment (the sum of frictional and structural unemployment rates).

What is the evidence of worker–job mismatch and unemployment? The process of job creation and job destruction in U.S. manufacturing has been studied in some detail by Steven Davis of the University of Chicago and John Haltiwanger[20] of the University of Maryland. Using data for 160,000 manufacturing plants, the authors showed that, during the 1973–1986 period, about 11% of all existing manufacturing jobs disappeared, on average, each year, reflecting plant closings and cutbacks. During a typical year, about 81% of these lost jobs were replaced by newly created jobs elsewhere in the manufacturing sector (so that, overall, employment in manufacturing shrank over the period). Thus Davis and Haltiwanger confirmed that a great deal of "churning" of jobs and workers occurs in the economy. They also showed that much of this churning reflected closing of old plants and opening of new ones *within the same industries*, rather than a general decline in some industries and growth in others. Thus reallocation of workers within industries seems to be as important as movement of workers between industries as a source of unemployment.

Figure 10.5 shows the rates of job creation and destruction in U.S. nonfarm private businesses for the years 1977–2005.[21] You can see that in recession years, such as 1981–1982, 1990–1991, and 2001, many more jobs were destroyed than created—although a significant number of new jobs were created even in recession years, reflecting shifts of workers among firms and industries.

It seems clear that increased mismatches between workers and jobs can't account for *all* the increase in unemployment that occurs during recessions. Much of that increase is in the form of temporary layoffs; rather than search for new jobs, many workers who are temporarily laid off simply wait until they are called back by their old firm. Moreover, if recessions were times of increased mismatch in the labor market, more postings of vacancies and help-wanted ads during recessions would

[19]See Chapter 3 for definitions and discussion of frictional and structural unemployment.

[20]"Gross Job Creation, Gross Job Destruction, and Employment Reallocation," *Quarterly Journal of Economics,* August 1992, pp. 819–864.

[21]The data shown in Fig. 10.5 are published by the Census Bureau, based on the methods developed by Davis and Haltiwanger in the paper cited in footnote 20. Job creation and destruction data are based on data collected from business firms; job creation is net new jobs from expanding establishments and job destruction is the net loss of jobs from contracting establishments. By comparison, the data in Figs. 8.10 and 8.11 on the job finding rate and the job loss rate are based on data on individuals and show the probability that a given worker found or lost a job in a given month. Thus, there may be substantial differences between job creation and job finding, as well as between job destruction and job loss.

Figure 10.5

Rates of job creation and job destruction in U.S. private, nonfarm businesses, 1977-2005
The graph shows the rates of job creation and job destruction in the U.S. nonfarm private business sector between 1977 and 2005. Job creation is the number of new jobs created during the year in expanding firms as a percentage of existing jobs. Job destruction is the number of jobs lost during the year as a result of closing or downsizing plants, as a percentage of existing jobs.

Source: Data from U.S. Census Bureau, Business Dynamic Statistics, *www.ces.census.gov/index.php/bds/bds_home.*

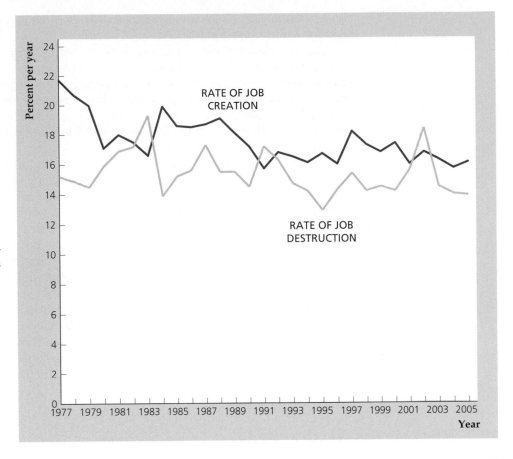

be expected; in fact, both vacancies and new job openings fall in recessions.[22] Despite these objections, however, economists generally agree that the dynamic reallocation of workers from shrinking to growing sectors is an important source of unemployment.

Modifying the classical model to allow for unemployment doesn't change the classical view that fiscal policy should not be actively used to combat recessions. Classical economists point out that raising the aggregate demand for goods (by increasing government purchases, for example) doesn't directly address the problem of unemployment arising from the mismatch that exists at the microeconomic level between workers and jobs. A better approach, in the classical view, is to eliminate barriers to labor market adjustment, such as high legal minimum wages that price low-skilled workers out of the labor market or burdensome regulations that raise businesses' costs of employing additional workers.

Household Production

In recent years, researchers have found that the RBC model can better match the U.S. data on business cycles if the model explicitly accounts for household production, which is output produced at home instead of in a market. Household

---

[22]See Katharine Abraham and Lawrence Katz in "Cyclical Unemployment: Sectoral Shifts or Aggregate Disturbances?" *Journal of Political Economy,* June 1986, pp. 507–522.

production includes such goods and services as cooking, child care, sewing, and food grown in a home garden.

The U.S. national income accounts described in Chapter 2 count mainly the output of businesses, not households. But people clearly switch between the two. For example, when times are good and a person is employed, she may hire someone else to mow her lawn. Because those lawn-mowing services are paid for in a market, they count in GDP. But if times are bad, someone losing her job may mow the lawn herself; such services are not counted in GDP but nonetheless represent output.

When household production is incorporated into an RBC model, the match between the model and the data improves, as shown by Jeremy Greenwood of the University of Pennsylvania, Richard Rogerson of Arizona State University, and Randall Wright of the University of Wisconsin.[23] A household-production model has a higher standard deviation of (market) output than a standard RBC model and more closely matches the U.S. data.

Models with household production may also be used to improve our understanding of foreign economies, especially those not as well developed as the United States. In less-developed countries, a greater proportion of output is produced at home, such as home-sewn clothes and food grown in a home garden. In their study of development, Stephen L. Parente of the University of Illinois, Richard Rogerson, and Randall Wright[24] show that once household production is accounted for, income differences across countries are not as big as the GDP data suggest. So, modeling household production is vital in understanding differences in the well-being of people in different countries.

10.2 Money in the Classical Model

So far we have focused on real shocks to the economy, such as productivity shocks and changes in government purchases. However, many macroeconomists believe that nominal shocks—shocks to money supply and money demand—also affect the business cycle. In the rest of the chapter we discuss the role of money and monetary policy in the classical approach to the business cycle.

Monetary Policy and the Economy

Monetary policy refers to the central bank's decisions about how much money to supply to the economy (Chapter 7). Recall that the central bank (the Federal Reserve in the United States) can control the money supply through open market operations, in which it sells government bonds to the public in exchange for money (to reduce the money supply) or uses newly created money to buy bonds from the public (to increase the money supply).

In Chapter 9 we examined the effects of changes in the money supply, using the *IS–LM* model (Fig. 9.9) and the *AD–AS* model (Fig. 9.14). With both models we

---

[23]"Putting Home Economics into Macroeconomics," *Quarterly Review,* Federal Reserve Bank of Minneapolis, Summer 1993, pp. 2–11.

[24]"Household Production and Development," *Economic Review,* Federal Reserve Bank of Cleveland, Third Quarter 1999, pp. 21–35.

found that, after prices fully adjust, changes in the money supply are neutral: A change in the nominal money supply, M, causes the price level, P, to change proportionally, but a change in the money supply has no effect on real variables, such as output, employment, or the real interest rate. Our analysis left open the possibility that a change in the money supply would affect real variables, such as output, in the short run before prices had a chance to adjust. However, because classical economists believe that the price adjustment process is rapid, they view the period of time during which the price level is fixed—and money is not neutral—to be too short to matter. That is, for practical purposes, they view money as neutral for any relevant time horizon.

Monetary Nonneutrality and Reverse Causation

The prediction that money is neutral is a striking result of the classical model, but it seems inconsistent with the business cycle fact that money is a leading, procyclical variable. If an expansion of the money supply has no effect, why are expansions of the money supply typically followed by increased rates of economic activity? And, similarly, why are reductions in the money supply often followed by recessions?

Some classical economists have responded to these questions by pointing out that, although increases in the money supply tend to *precede* expansions in output, this fact doesn't necessarily prove that economic expansions are caused by those increases. After all, just because people put storm windows on their houses before winter begins doesn't mean that winter is caused by putting on storm windows. Rather, people put storm windows on their houses because they know that winter is coming.

Many classical economists, including RBC economists in particular, argue that the link between money growth and economic expansion is like the link between putting on storm windows and the onset of winter, a relationship they call reverse causation. Specifically, **reverse causation** means that expected future increases in output cause increases in the current money supply and that expected future decreases in output cause decreases in the current money supply, rather than the other way around. Reverse causation explains how money could be a procyclical and leading variable even if the classical model is correct and changes in the money supply are neutral and have no real effects.[25]

Reverse causation might arise in one of several ways. One possibility (which you are asked to explore in more detail in Analytical Problem 4 at the end of the chapter) is based on the idea that money demand depends on both expected future output and current output. Suppose that a firm's managers expect business to pick up considerably in the next few quarters. To prepare for this expected increase in output, the firm may need to increase its current transactions (for example, to purchase raw materials, hire workers, and so on) and thus it will demand more money now. If many firms do so, the aggregate demand for money may rise in advance of the actual increase in output.

---

[25]Robert King and Charles Plosser, "Money, Credit, and Prices in a Real Business Cycle," *American Economic Review*, June 1984, pp. 363–380, explain reverse causation and present supporting evidence for the idea.

Now suppose that the Fed observes this increase in the demand for money. If the Fed does nothing, leaving the money supply unchanged, the increase in money demand will cause the equilibrium value of the price level to fall. As one of the Fed's objectives is stable prices, it won't like this outcome; to keep prices stable, instead of doing nothing, the Fed should provide enough extra money to the economy to meet the higher money demand. But if the Fed does so, the money supply will rise in advance of the increase in output, consistent with the business cycle fact—even though money is neutral.

Undoubtedly, reverse causation explains at least some of the tendency of money to lead output. However, this explanation doesn't rule out the possibility that changes in the money supply also sometimes cause changes in output so that money is nonneutral. That is, a combination of reverse causation and monetary nonneutrality could account for the procyclical behavior of money.

The Nonneutrality of Money: Additional Evidence

Because of reverse causation, the leading and procyclical behavior of money can't by itself establish that money is nonneutral. To settle the issue of whether money is neutral, we need additional evidence. One useful source is a historical analysis of monetary policy. The classic study is Milton Friedman and Anna J. Schwartz's, *A Monetary History of the United States, 1867–1960*.[26] Using a variety of sources, including Federal Reserve policy statements and the journals and correspondence of monetary policymakers, Friedman and Schwartz carefully described and analyzed the causes of money supply fluctuations and the interrelation of money and other economic variables. They concluded (p. 676):

Throughout the near-century examined in detail we have found that:

1. Changes in the behavior of the money stock have been closely associated with changes in economic activity, [nominal] income, and prices.
2. The interrelation between monetary and economic change has been highly stable.
3. Monetary changes have often had an independent origin; they have not been simply a reflection of changes in economic activity.

The first two conclusions restate the basic business cycle fact that money is procyclical. The third conclusion states that reverse causation can't explain the entire relationship between money and real income or output. Friedman and Schwartz focused on historical episodes in which changes in the supply of money were not (they argued) responses to macroeconomic conditions but instead resulted from other factors such as gold discoveries (which affected money supplies under the gold standard), changes in monetary institutions, or changes in the leadership of the Federal Reserve. In the majority of these cases "independent" changes in money growth were followed by changes in the same direction in real output. This evidence suggests that money isn't neutral.

More recently, Christina Romer and David Romer[27] of the University of California at Berkeley reviewed and updated the Friedman-Schwartz analysis. Although they disputed some of Friedman and Schwartz's interpretations, they

---

[26]Princeton, N.J.: Princeton University Press for NBER, 1963.

[27]"Does Monetary Policy Matter? A New Test in the Spirit of Friedman and Schwartz," in Olivier Blanchard and Stanley Fischer, eds., NBER *Macroeconomics Annual*, Cambridge, Mass.: M.I.T. Press, 1989.

generally agreed with the conclusion that money isn't neutral. In particular, they argued that since 1960 half a dozen additional episodes of monetary nonneutrality have occurred. Probably the most famous one occurred in 1979, when Federal Reserve Chairman Paul Volcker announced that money supply procedures would change and that the money growth rate would be reduced to fight inflation. A minor recession in 1980 and a severe downturn in 1981–1982 followed Volcker's change in monetary policy. An economic boom followed relaxation of the Fed's anti-inflationary monetary policy in 1982.

Because of the Friedman-Schwartz evidence and episodes such as the 1979–1982 Volcker policy (and a similar experience in Great Britain at the same time), most economists now believe that money is not neutral. If we accept that evidence, contrary to the prediction of the classical model, we are left with two choices: Either we must adopt a different framework for macroeconomic analysis, or we must modify the classical model. In Section 10.3 we take the second approach and consider how monetary nonneutrality can be explained in a classical model.

10.3 The Misperceptions Theory and the Nonneutrality of Money

According to the classical model, prices do not remain fixed for any substantial period of time, so the horizontal short-run aggregate supply curve developed in Chapter 9 is irrelevant. The only relevant aggregate supply curve is the long-run aggregate supply curve, which is vertical. As we showed in Fig. 9.14, changes in the money supply cause the *AD* curve to shift; because the aggregate supply curve is vertical, however, the effect of the *AD* shift is simply to change prices without changing the level of output. Thus money is neutral in the classical model.

For money to be nonneutral, the relevant aggregate supply curve must not be vertical. In this section, we extend the classical model to incorporate the assumption that producers have imperfect information about the general price level and thus sometimes misinterpret changes in the general price level as changes in the relative prices of the goods that they produce. We demonstrate that the assumption that producers may misperceive the aggregate price level—the *misperceptions theory*—implies a short-run aggregate supply curve that isn't vertical. Unlike the short-run aggregate supply curve developed in Chapter 9, however, the short-run aggregate supply curve based on the misperceptions theory doesn't require the assumption that prices are slow to adjust. Even though prices may adjust instantaneously, the short-run aggregate supply curve slopes upward, so money is nonneutral in the short run.

The misperceptions theory was originally proposed by Nobel laureate Milton Friedman and then was rigorously formulated by another Nobel laureate, Robert E. Lucas, Jr., of the University of Chicago.[28] According to the **misperceptions theory,** *the aggregate quantity of output supplied rises above the full-employment level, $\overline{Y}$, when the aggregate price level, P, is higher than expected.* Thus for any expected price level, the aggregate supply curve relating the price level and the aggregate quantity of output supplied slopes upward.

---

[28]See Friedman, "The Role of Monetary Policy," *American Economic Review,* March 1968, pp. 1–17. Lucas's formalization of Friedman's theory was first presented in Lucas's article, "Expectations and the Neutrality of Money," *Journal of Economic Theory,* April 1972, pp. 103–124.

If you took a course in the principles of economics, you learned that supply curves generally slope upward, with higher prices leading to increased production. However, just as the demand curves for individual goods differ from the aggregate demand curve, the supply curves for individual goods differ from the aggregate supply curve. An ordinary supply curve relates the supply of some good to the price of that good *relative to other prices.* In contrast, the aggregate supply curve relates the aggregate amount of output produced to the *general price level.* Changes in the general price level can occur while the relative prices of individual goods remain unchanged.

To understand the misperceptions theory and why it implies an upward-sloping aggregate supply curve, let's think about an individual producer of a particular good, say bread. For simplicity, consider a bakery owned and operated by one person, a baker. The baker devotes all his labor to making bread and earns all his income from selling bread. Thus the price of bread is effectively the baker's nominal wage, and the price of bread relative to the general price level is the baker's real wage. When the relative price of bread increases, the baker responds to this increase in his current real wage by working more and producing more bread. Similarly, when the price of bread falls relative to the other prices in the economy, the baker's current real wage falls and he decreases the amount of bread he produces.

But how does an individual baker know whether the relative price of bread has changed? To calculate the relative price of bread, the baker needs to know both the nominal price of bread and the general price level. The baker knows the nominal price of bread because he sells bread every day and observes the price directly. However, the baker probably is not as well informed about the general price level, because he observes the prices of the many goods and services he might want to buy less frequently than he observes the price of bread. Thus, in calculating the relative price of bread, the baker can't use the actual current price level. The best he can do is to use his previously formed expectation of the current price level to estimate the actual price level.

Suppose that before he observes the current market price of bread, the baker expected an overall inflation rate of 5%. How will he react if he then observes that the price of bread increases by 5%? The baker reasons as follows: I expected the overall rate of inflation to be 5%, and now I know that the price of bread has increased by 5%. This 5% increase in the price of bread is consistent with what I had expected. My best estimate is that all prices increased by 5%, and thus I think that the relative price of bread is unchanged. There is no reason to change my output.

The baker's logic applies equally to suppliers of output in the aggregate. Suppose that all suppliers expected the nominal price level to increase by 5% and that in fact all prices do increase by 5%. Then each supplier will estimate that its relative price hasn't changed and won't change its output. Hence, if expected inflation is 5%, an actual increase in prices of 5% won't affect aggregate output.

For a change in the nominal price of bread to affect the quantity of bread produced, the increase in the nominal price of bread must differ from the *expected* increase in the general price level. For example, suppose that the baker expected the general price level to increase by 5% but then observes that the price of bread rises by 8%. The baker then estimates that the relative price of bread has increased so that the real wage he or she earns from baking is higher. In response to the perceived increase in the relative price, he or she increases the production of bread.

Again, the same logic applies to the economy in the aggregate. Suppose that everyone expects the general price level to increase by 5%, but instead it actually increases by 8%, with the prices of all goods increasing by 8%. Now all producers will estimate that the relative prices of the goods they make have increased, and hence the production of all goods will increase. Thus a greater than expected increase of the price level will tend to raise output. Similarly, if the price level actually increases by only 2% when all producers expected a 5% increase, producers will think that the relative prices of their own goods have declined; in response, all suppliers reduce their output.

Thus, according to the misperceptions theory, the amount of output that producers choose to supply depends on the actual general price level compared to the expected general price level. When the price level exceeds what was expected, producers are fooled into thinking that the relative prices of their own goods have risen, and they increase their output. Similarly, when the price level is lower than expected, producers believe that the relative prices of their goods have fallen, and they reduce their output. This relation between output and prices is captured by the equation

$$Y = \overline{Y} + b(P - P^e), \tag{10.4}$$

where b is a positive number that describes how strongly output responds when the actual price level exceeds the expected price level. Equation (10.4) summarizes the misperceptions theory by showing that output, Y, exceeds full-employment output, $\overline{Y}$, when the price level, P, exceeds the expected price level, P^e.

To obtain an aggregate supply curve from the misperceptions theory, we graph Eq. (10.4) in Fig. 10.6. Given full-employment output, $\overline{Y}$, and the expected price level, P^e, the aggregate supply curve slopes upward, illustrating the relation between the amount of output supplied, Y, and the actual price level, P. Because an increase in the price level of ΔP increases the amount of the output supplied by $\Delta Y = b\Delta P$, the slope of the aggregate supply curve is $\Delta P/\Delta Y = 1/b$. Thus the aggregate supply curve is steep if b is small and is relatively flat if b is large.

Point E helps us locate the aggregate supply curve. At E the price level, P, equals the expected price level, P^e, so that (from Eq. 10.4) the amount of output supplied equals full-employment output, $\overline{Y}$. When the actual price level is higher than expected ($P > P^e$), the aggregate supply curve shows that the amount of output supplied is greater than $\overline{Y}$; when the price level is lower than expected ($P < P^e$), output is less than $\overline{Y}$.

The aggregate supply curve in Fig. 10.6 is called the short-run aggregate supply (*SRAS*) curve because it applies only to the short period of time that P^e remains unchanged. When P^e rises, the *SRAS* curve shifts up because a higher value of P is needed to satisfy Eq. (10.4) for given values of Y and $\overline{Y}$. When P^e falls, the *SRAS* curve shifts down. In the long run, people learn what is actually happening to prices, and the expected price level adjusts to the actual price level ($P = P^e$). When the actual price level equals the expected price level, no misperceptions remain and producers supply the full-employment level of output. In terms of Eq. (10.4), in the long run P equals P^e, and output, Y, equals full-employment output, $\overline{Y}$. In the long run, then, the supply of output doesn't depend on the price level. Thus, as in Chapters 8 and 9, the long-run aggregate supply (*LRAS*) curve is vertical at the point where output equals $\overline{Y}$.

Figure 10.6

The aggregate supply curve in the misperceptions theory
The misperceptions theory holds that, for a given value of the expected price level, P^e, an increase in the actual price level, P, fools producers into increasing output. This relationship between output and the price level is shown by the short-run aggregate supply (SRAS) curve. Along the SRAS curve, output equals $\overline{Y}$ when prices equal their expected level ($P = P^e$, at point E), output exceeds $\overline{Y}$ when the price level is higher than expected ($P > P^e$), and output is less than $\overline{Y}$ when the price level is lower than expected ($P < P^e$). In the long run, the expected price level equals the actual price level so that output equals $\overline{Y}$. Thus the long-run aggregate supply (LRAS) curve is vertical at $Y = \overline{Y}$.

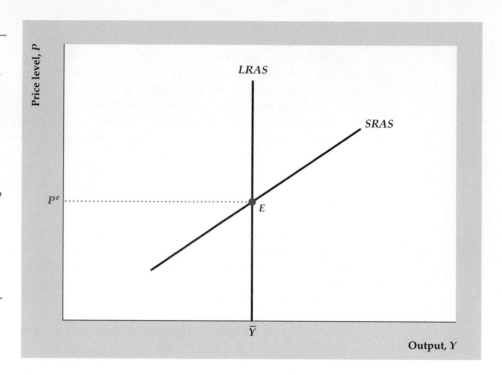

Monetary Policy and the Misperceptions Theory

Let's now reexamine the neutrality of money in the extended version of the classical model based on the misperceptions theory. This framework highlights an important distinction between anticipated and unanticipated changes in the money supply: Unanticipated changes in the nominal money supply have real effects, but anticipated changes are neutral and have no real effects.

Unanticipated Changes in the Money Supply. Suppose that the economy is initially in general equilibrium at point E in Fig. 10.7, where AD^1 intersects $SRAS^1$. Here, output equals the full-employment level, $\overline{Y}$, and the price level and the expected price level both equal P_1. Suppose that everyone expects the money supply and the price level to remain constant but that the Fed unexpectedly and without publicity increases the money supply by 10%. A 10% increase in the money supply shifts the AD curve up and to the right, from AD^1 to AD^2, such that for a given Y, the price level on AD^2 is 10% higher than the price level on AD^1. With the expected price level equal to P_1, the SRAS curve remains unchanged, still passing through point E.

The increase in aggregate demand bids up the price level to the new equilibrium level, P_2, where AD^2 intersects $SRAS^1$ (point F). In the new short-run equilibrium at F, the actual price level exceeds the expected price level and output exceeds $\overline{Y}$. Because the increase in the money supply leads to a rise in output, money isn't neutral in this analysis.

The reason money isn't neutral is that producers are fooled. Each producer misperceives the higher nominal price of her output as an increase in its relative price, rather than as an increase in the general price level. Although output increases in the short run, producers aren't better off. They end up producing more than they would have if they had known the true relative prices.

Figure 10.7

An unanticipated increase in the money supply

If we start from the initial equilibrium at point E, an unanticipated 10% increase in the money supply shifts the AD curve up and to the right, from AD^1 to AD^2, such that for a given Y, the price level on AD^2 is 10% higher than the price level on AD^1. The short-run equilibrium is located at point F, the intersection of AD^2 and the short-run aggregate supply curve $SRAS^1$, where prices and output are both higher than at point E. Thus an unanticipated change in the money supply isn't neutral in the short run. In the long run, people learn the true price level and the equilibrium shifts to point H, the intersection of AD^2 and the long-run aggregate supply curve $LRAS$. In the long-run equilibrium at H, the price level has risen by 10% but output returns to its full-employment level, $\overline{Y}$, so that money is neutral in the long run. As expectations of the price level rise from P_1 to P_3, the $SRAS$ curve also shifts up until it passes through H.

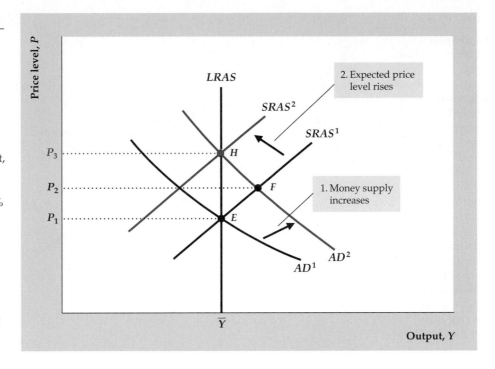

The economy can't stay long at the equilibrium represented by point F because at F the actual price level, P_2, is higher than the expected price level, P_1. Over time, people obtain information about the true level of prices and adjust their expectations accordingly. The only equilibrium that can be sustained in the long run is one in which people do not permanently underestimate or overestimate the price level so that the expected price level and the actual price level are equal. Graphically, when people learn the true price level, the relevant aggregate supply curve is the long-run aggregate supply ($LRAS$) curve, along which P always equals P^e. In Fig. 10.7 the long-run equilibrium is point H, the intersection of AD^2 and $LRAS$. At H output equals its full-employment level, $\overline{Y}$, and the price level, P_3, is 10% higher than the initial price level, P_1. Because everyone now expects the price level to be P_3, a new $SRAS$ curve with $P^e = P_3$, $SRAS^2$, passes through H.

Thus, according to the misperceptions theory, an unanticipated increase in the money supply raises output and isn't neutral *in the short run*. However, an unanticipated increase in the money supply is neutral in the long run, after people have learned the true price level.

Anticipated Changes in the Money Supply.   In the extended classical model based on the misperceptions theory, the effects of an anticipated money supply increase are different from the effects of a surprise money supply increase. Figure 10.8 illustrates the effects of an anticipated money supply increase. Again, the initial general equilibrium point is at E, where output equals its full-employment level and the actual and expected price levels both equal P_1, just as in Fig. 10.7. Suppose that the Federal Reserve announces that it is going to increase the money supply by 10% and that the public believes this announcement.

As we have shown, a 10% increase in the money supply shifts the AD curve, from AD^1 to AD^2, where for each output level Y, the price level P on AD^2 is 10% higher than on AD^1. However, in this case the $SRAS$ curve also shifts up. The reason is that the

Figure 10.8

An anticipated increase in the money supply

The economy is in initial equilibrium at point *E* when the Fed publicly announces a 10% increase in the money supply. When the money supply increases, the *AD* curve shifts up by 10%, from AD^1 to AD^2. In addition, because the increase in the money supply is anticipated by the public, the expected price level increases by 10%, from P_1 to P_3. Thus the short-run aggregate supply curve shifts up from $SRAS^1$ to $SRAS^2$. The new short-run equilibrium, which is the same as the long-run equilibrium, is at point *H*. At *H* output is unchanged at $\overline{Y}$ and the price level is 10% higher than in the initial equilibrium at *E*. Thus an anticipated increase in the money supply is neutral in the short run as well as in the long run.

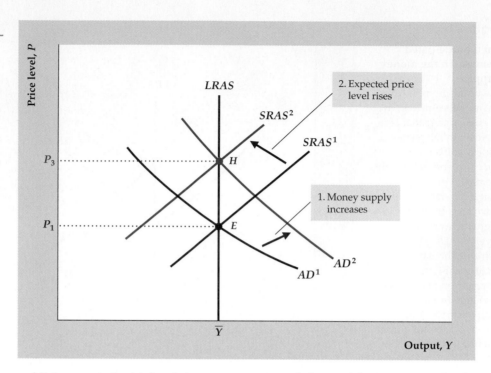

public's expected price level rises as soon as people learn of the increase in the money supply. Suppose that people expect—correctly—that the price level will also rise by 10% so that P^e rises by 10%, from P_1 to P_3. Then the new *SRAS* curve, $SRAS^2$, passes through point *H* in Fig. 10.8, where *Y* equals $\overline{Y}$ and both the actual and expected price levels equal P_3. The new equilibrium also is at *H*, where AD^2 and $SRAS^2$ intersect. At the new equilibrium, output equals its full-employment level, and prices are 10% higher than they were initially. The anticipated increase in the money supply hasn't affected output but has raised prices proportionally. Similarly, an anticipated drop in the money supply would lower prices but not affect output or other real variables. Thus *anticipated changes in the money supply are neutral in the short run as well as in the long run.* The reason is that, if producers know that increases in the nominal prices of their products are the result of an increase in the money supply and do not reflect a change in relative prices, they won't be fooled into increasing production when prices rise.

Rational Expectations and the Role of Monetary Policy

In the extended classical model based on the misperceptions theory, *unanticipated* changes in the money supply affect output, but *anticipated* changes in the money supply are neutral. Thus, if the Federal Reserve wanted to use monetary policy to affect output, it seemingly should use only unanticipated changes in the money supply. So, for example, when the economy is in recession, the Fed would try to use surprise increases in the money supply to raise output; when the economy is booming, the Fed would try to use surprise decreases in the money supply to slow the economy.

A serious problem for this strategy is the presence of private economic forecasters and "Fed watchers" in financial markets. These people spend a good deal of time and effort trying to forecast macroeconomic variables such as the money supply and the price level, and their forecasts are well publicized. If the Fed began a pattern of raising the money supply in recessions and reducing it in booms, forecasters and Fed watchers would quickly understand and report this fact. As a result, the Fed's manipulations of the money supply would no longer be unanticipated, and the changes in the money supply would have no effect other than possibly causing instability in the price level. More generally, according to the misperceptions theory, to achieve any systematic change in the behavior of output, the Fed must conduct monetary policy in a way that systematically fools the public. But there are strong incentives in the financial markets and elsewhere for people to try to figure out what the Fed is doing. Thus most economists believe that attempts by the Fed to surprise the public in a systematic way cannot be successful.

The idea that the Federal Reserve cannot systematically surprise the public is part of a larger hypothesis that the public has rational expectations. The hypothesis of **rational expectations** states that the public's forecasts of various economic variables, including the money supply, the price level, and GDP, are based on reasoned and intelligent examination of available economic data.[29] (The evidence for rational expectations is discussed in "In Touch with Data and Research: Are Price Forecasts Rational?", p. 388.) If the public has rational expectations, it will eventually understand the Federal Reserve's general pattern of behavior. If expectations are rational, purely random changes in the money supply may be unanticipated and thus nonneutral. However, because the Fed won't be able to surprise the public systematically, it can't use monetary policy to stabilize output. Thus, even if smoothing business cycles were desirable, according to the combination of the misperceptions theory and rational expectations, the Fed can't systematically use monetary policy to do so.

Propagating the Effects of Unanticipated Changes in the Money Supply.

The misperceptions theory implies that unanticipated changes in the money supply are nonneutral because individual producers are temporarily fooled about the price level. However, money supply data are available weekly and price level data are reported monthly, suggesting that any misperceptions about monetary policy or the price level—and thus any real effects of money supply changes—should be quickly eliminated.

To explain how changes in the money supply can have real effects that last more than a few weeks, classical economists stress the role of propagation mechanisms. A **propagation mechanism** is an aspect of the economy that allows short-lived shocks to have relatively long-term effects on the economy.

An important example of a propagation mechanism is the behavior of inventories. Consider a manufacturing firm that has both a normal level of monthly sales and a normal amount of finished goods in inventory that it tries to maintain. Suppose that an unanticipated rise in the money supply increases aggregate demand and raises prices above their expected level. Because increasing production sharply in a short period of time is costly, the firm will respond to the increase in demand partly by producing more goods and partly by selling some finished goods from inventory, thus depleting its inventory stocks below their normal level.

Next month suppose that everyone learns the true price level and that the firm's rate of sales returns to its normal level. Despite the fact that the monetary shock has passed, the firm may continue to produce for a while at a higher than normal rate. The reason for the continued high level of production is that besides meeting its normal demand, the firm wants to replenish its inventory stock. The need to rebuild inventories illustrates a propagation mechanism that allows a short-lived shock (a monetary shock, in this case) to have a longer-term effect on the economy.

---

[29]The idea of rational expectations was first discussed by John F. Muth in his classic 1961 paper, "Rational Expectations and the Theory of Price Movements," *Econometrica*, July 1961, pp. 315–335. However, this idea wasn't widely used in macroeconomics until the new classical "revolution" of the early 1970s.

IN TOUCH WITH DATA AND RESEARCH

Are Price Forecasts Rational?

Most classical economists assume that people have rational expectations about economic variables; that is, people make intelligent use of available information in forecasting variables that affect their economic decisions. The rational expectations assumption has important implications. For example, as we have demonstrated, if monetary nonneutrality is the result of temporary misperceptions of the price level and people have rational expectations about prices, monetary policy is not able to affect the real economy systematically.

The rational expectations assumption is attractive to economists—including many Keynesian as well as classical economists—because it fits well economists' presumption that people intelligently pursue their economic self-interests. If people's expectations aren't rational, the economic plans that individuals make won't generally be as good as they could be. But the theoretical attractiveness of rational expectations obviously isn't enough; economists would like to know whether people really do have rational expectations about important economic variables.

The rational expectations idea can be tested with data from surveys, in which people are asked their opinions about the future of the economy. To illustrate how such a test would be conducted, suppose that we have data from a survey in which people were asked to make a prediction of the price level one year in the future. Imagine that this survey is repeated each year for several years. Now suppose that, for each individual in the survey, we define

P_t^e = the individual's forecast, made in year $t-1$, of the price level in year t.

Suppose also that we let P_t represent the price level that actually occurs in year t. Then the individual's forecast error for year t is the difference between the actual price level and the individual's forecast:

$P_t - P_t^e$ = the individual's forecast error in year t.

If people have rational expectations, these forecast errors should be unpredictable random numbers. However, if forecast errors are consistently positive or negative—meaning that people systematically tend to underpredict or overpredict the price level—expectations are not rational. If forecast errors have a systematic pattern—for example, if people tend to overpredict the price level when prices have been rising in the recent past—again, expectations are not rational.

Early statistical studies of price level forecasts made by consumers, journalists, professional economists, and others tended to reject the rational expectations theory. These studies, which were conducted in the late 1970s and early 1980s, followed the period in which inflation reached unprecedented levels, in part because of the major increases in oil prices and expansionary monetary policy in 1973–1974 and in 1979. It is perhaps not surprising that people found forecasting price changes to be unusually difficult during such a volatile period.

More recent studies of price level forecasts have been more favorable to the rational expectations theory. Michael Keane and David Runkle* of the Federal

---

*"Are Economic Forecasts Rational?" *Quarterly Review,* Federal Reserve Bank of Minneapolis, Spring 1989, pp. 26–33.

Reserve Bank of Minneapolis studied the price level forecasts of a panel of professional forecasters that has been surveyed by the American Statistical Association and the National Bureau of Economic Research since 1968. They found no evidence to refute the hypothesis that the professional forecasters had rational expectations. In another article, Dean Croushore[†] of the University of Richmond analyzed a variety of forecasts made not only by economists and forecasters but also by members of the general public, as reported in surveys of consumers. Croushore found that the forecasts of each of these groups were broadly consistent with rational expectations, although there appeared to be some tendency for expectations to lag behind reality in periods when inflation rose or fell sharply.

[†]"Inflation Forecasts: How Good Are They?" *Business Review,* Federal Reserve Bank of Philadelphia, May/June 1996, pp. 15–25.

CHAPTER SUMMARY

1. Classical business cycle analysis uses the classical *IS–LM* model along with the assumption that wages and prices adjust quickly to bring the economy into general equilibrium.

2. The real business cycle (RBC) theory is a version of the classical theory that emphasizes productivity shocks (shocks to the production function) as the source of business cycle fluctuations. In the classical *IS–LM* model, a temporary decline in productivity reduces the real wage, employment, and output, while raising the real interest rate and the price level. The RBC theory can account for the observed procyclical behavior of employment, real wages, and labor productivity. However, the prediction of the RBC theory that prices are countercyclical is viewed by some as a failing.

3. The Solow residual is an empirical measure of total factor productivity, *A*, in the production function. It increases as a result of technical progress that increases the amount of output that can be produced with the same amounts of labor and capital services (inputs). The Solow residual also changes as a result of changes in the utilization rates of capital and labor. It is procyclical at least partly because the utilization rates of capital and labor are procyclical. The procyclical behavior of the utilization rate of labor may reflect labor hoarding, which occurs when firms continue to employ workers during recessions but use them less intensively or on tasks, such as maintenance, that don't contribute directly to measured output.

4. Classical business cycle analysis allows for other shocks to the economy besides changes in productivity, including changes in fiscal policy. According to

the classical *IS–LM* model, an increase in government purchases raises employment, output, the real interest rate, and the price level. Including both fiscal and productivity shocks in the classical model improves its ability to fit the data. Although fiscal policy can affect employment and output, classical economists argue that it should not be used to smooth the business cycle because the invisible hand leads the economy to an efficient outcome without government interference. Instead, decisions about government purchases should be based on comparisons of costs and benefits.

5. In the basic classical model (which includes RBC theory), money is neutral, which means that changes in the nominal money supply change the price level proportionally but do not affect real variables such as output, employment, and the real interest rate.

6. The basic classical model can account for the procyclical and leading behavior of money if there is reverse causation—that is, if anticipated changes in output lead to changes in the money supply in the same direction. For example, if firms increase their money demand in anticipation of future output increases, and if the Fed (to keep the price level stable) supplies enough extra money to meet the increase in money demand, increases in the money stock precede increases in output. This result holds even though changes in the money stock don't *cause* subsequent changes in output.

7. Examination of historical monetary policy actions suggests that money isn't neutral. Friedman and Schwartz identified occasions when the money supply changed for independent reasons, such as gold discoveries or changes in monetary institutions,

and changes in output followed these changes in the money supply in the same direction. More recent experiences, such as the severe economic slowdown that followed Federal Reserve Chairman Volcker's decision to reduce money growth in 1979, also provide evidence for the view that money isn't neutral.

8. The misperceptions theory is based on the idea that producers have imprecise information about the current price level. According to the misperceptions theory, the amount of output supplied equals the full-employment level of output, $\overline{Y}$, only if the actual price level equals the expected price level. When the price level is higher than expected, suppliers are fooled into thinking that the relative prices of the goods they supply have risen, so they supply a quantity of output that exceeds $\overline{Y}$. Similarly, when the price level is lower than expected, the quantity of output supplied is less than $\overline{Y}$.

9. The short-run aggregate supply (SRAS) curve based on the misperceptions theory slopes upward in describing the relationship between output and the actual price level, with the expected price level held constant. In the long run, the price level equals the expected price level so that the supply of output equals

$\overline{Y}$; thus the long-run aggregate supply (LRAS) curve is a vertical line at the point where output equals $\overline{Y}$.

10. With the upward-sloping SRAS curve based on the misperceptions theory, an *unanticipated* increase in the money supply increases output (and is thus nonneutral) in the short run. However, because the long-run aggregate supply curve is vertical, an unanticipated increase in the money supply doesn't affect output (and so is neutral) in the long run. An *anticipated* increase in the money supply causes price expectations to adjust immediately and leads to no misperceptions about the price level; thus an anticipated increase in the money supply is neutral in both the short and long runs.

11. According to the extended classical model based on the misperceptions theory, only surprise changes in the money supply can affect output. If the public has rational expectations about macroeconomic variables, including the money supply, the Fed cannot systematically surprise the public because the public will understand and anticipate the Fed's pattern of behavior. Thus classical economists argue that the Fed cannot systematically use changes in the money supply to affect output.

KEY DIAGRAM 8

The misperceptions version of the AD–AS model

The misperceptions version of the AD–AS model shows how the aggregate demand for output and the aggregate supply of output interact to determine the price level and output in a classical model in which producers misperceive the aggregate price level.

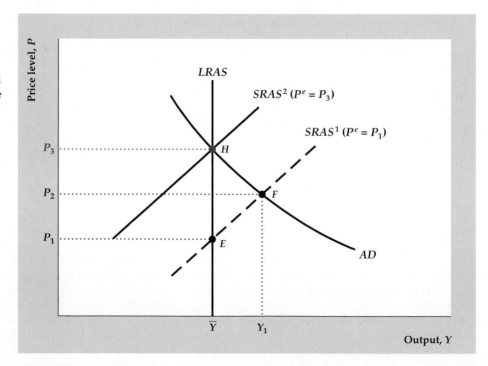

Diagram Elements

■ The price level, P, is on the vertical axis, and the level of output, Y, is on the horizontal axis.

■ The aggregate demand (AD) curve shows the aggregate quantity of output demanded at each price level.

It is identical to the AD curve in Key Diagram 7, p. 346. The aggregate amount of output demanded is determined by the intersection of the IS and LM curves (see Fig. 9.10). An increase in the price level, P, reduces the real money supply, shifting the *LM* curve up and to the left and reducing the aggregate quantity of output demanded. Thus the *AD* curve slopes downward.

■ The misperceptions theory is based on the assumption that producers have imperfect information about the general price level and hence don't know precisely the relative prices of their products. When producers misperceive the price level, an increase in the general price level above the expected price level fools suppliers into thinking that the relative prices of their goods have increased, so all suppliers increase output. The short-run aggregate supply (*SRAS*) curve shows the aggregate quantity of output supplied at each price level, with the expected price level held constant. Because an increase in the price level fools producers into supplying more output, the short-run aggregate supply curve slopes upward, as shown by $SRAS^1$.

■ The short-run aggregate supply curve, $SRAS^1$, is drawn so that the expected price level, P^e, equals P_1. When the actual price level equals the expected price level, producers aren't fooled and so supply the full-employment level of output, $\overline{Y}$. Therefore at point *E*, where the actual price level equals the expected price level (both equal P_1), the short-run aggregate supply curve, $SRAS^1$, shows that producers supply $\overline{Y}$.

■ In the long run, producers learn about the price level and adjust their expectations until the actual price level equals the expected price level. Producers then supply the full-employment level of output, $\overline{Y}$, regardless of the price level. Thus, the long-run aggregate supply (*LRAS*) curve is vertical at $Y = \overline{Y}$, just as in the basic *AD–AS* model in Key Diagram 7, p. 346.

Factors That Shift the Curves

■ The aggregate quantity of output demanded is determined by the intersection of the *IS* curve and the *LM* curve. At a constant price level, any factor that shifts the *IS–LM* intersection to the right increases the aggregate quantity of goods demanded and thus also shifts the *AD* curve up and to the right. Factors that shift the *AD* curve are listed in Summary table 14, p. 340.

■ Any factor that increases full-employment output, $\overline{Y}$, shifts both the short-run and the long-run aggregate supply curves to the right. Factors that increase full-employment output are listed in Summary table 11, p. 312. An increase in government purchases, because it induces workers to supply more labor, also shifts the short-run and long-run aggregate supply curves to the right in the classical model.

■ An increase in the expected price level shifts the short-run aggregate supply curve up.

Analysis

■ The short-run equilibrium is at the intersection of the *AD* curve and the *SRAS* curve. For example, if the expected price level is P_1, the *SRAS* curve is $SRAS^1$, and the short-run equilibrium is at point *F*. At *F* output, Y_1, is higher than the full-employment level, $\overline{Y}$, and the price level, P_2, is higher than the expected price level, P_1. As producers obtain information about the price level, the expected price level is revised upward, which shifts the *SRAS* curve up. The long-run equilibrium is at point *H*, where the long-run aggregate supply (*LRAS*) curve intersects the *AD* curve. In the long run (1) output equals $\overline{Y}$, and (2) the price level equals the expected price level (both equal P_3). In the long run, when the expected price level has risen to P_3, the short-run aggregate supply curve, $SRAS^2$, passes through *H*.

KEY TERMS

KEY EQUATION

$$Y = \overline{Y} + b(P - P^e) \qquad (10.4)$$

The short-run aggregate supply curve based on the misperceptions theory indicates that the aggregate amount of output supplied, Y, equals full-employment output, $\overline{Y}$, when the price level, P, equals the expected price level, P^e. When the price level is higher than expected ($P > P^e$), output exceeds $\overline{Y}$; when the price level is lower than expected ($P < P^e$), output is less than $\overline{Y}$.

REVIEW QUESTIONS

All review questions are available in ⓧ myeconlab at www.myeconlab.com.

1. What main feature of the classical *IS–LM* model distinguishes it from the Keynesian *IS–LM* model? Why is the distinction of practical importance?

2. What are the two main components of any theory of the business cycle? Describe these two components for the real business cycle theory.

3. Define *real shock* and *nominal shock*. What type of real shock do real business cycle economists consider the most important source of cyclical fluctuations?

4. What major business cycle facts does the RBC theory explain successfully? Does it explain any business cycle facts less well?

5. What is the Solow residual and how does it behave over the business cycle? What factors cause the Solow residual to change?

6. What effects does an increase in government purchases have on the labor market, according to the classical theory? What effects does it have on output, the real interest rate, and the price level? According to classical economists, should fiscal policy be used to smooth out the business cycle? Why or why not?

7. In the context of the relationship between the money supply and real economic activity, what is meant by *reverse causation*? Explain how reverse causation could occur. What business cycle fact is it intended to explain?

8. According to the misperceptions theory, what effect does an increase in the price level have on the amount of output supplied by producers? Explain. Does it matter whether the increase in the price level was expected?

9. What conclusion does the basic classical model (with no misperceptions of the price level) allow about the neutrality or nonneutrality of money? In what ways is this conclusion modified by the extended classical model based on the misperceptions theory?

10. Define *rational expectations*. According to the classical model, what implications do rational expectations have for the ability of the central bank to use monetary policy to smooth business cycles?

NUMERICAL PROBLEMS

All numerical problems are available in ⓧ myeconlab at www.myeconlab.com.

1. In a certain economy the production function is

$$Y = A(100N - 0.5N^2),$$

where Y is output, A is productivity, and N is total hours worked. The marginal product of labor associated with this production function is

$$MPN = A(100 - N).$$

Initially, $A = 1.0$, but a beneficial productivity shock raises A to 1.1.

a. The supply of labor is

$$NS = 45 + 0.1w,$$

where w is the real wage. Find the equilibrium levels of output, hours worked, and the real wage before and after the productivity shock. Recall (Chapter 3) that the *MPN* curve is the same as the labor demand curve, with the real wage replacing the *MPN*.

b. Repeat Part (*a*) if the labor supply is

$$NS = 10 + 0.8w.$$

c. Some studies show that the real wage is only slightly procyclical. Assume for the sake of argument that this finding is correct. Would a calibrated RBC model fit the facts better if the labor supply is relatively insensitive to the real wage, or if it is relatively sensitive? Justify your answer diagrammatically and relate it to your answers to Parts (*a*) and (*b*).

2. An economy is described as follows.

Desired consumption	$C^d = 600 + 0.5(Y - T) - 50r.$
Desired investment	$I^d = 450 - 50r.$
Real money demand	$L = 0.5Y - 100i.$
Full-employment output	$\bar{Y} = 2210.$
Expected inflation	$\pi^e = 0.05.$

In this economy the government always has a balanced budget, so $T = G$, where T is total taxes collected.

a. Suppose that $M = 4320$ and $G = 150$. Use the classical *IS–LM* model to find the equilibrium values of output, the real interest rate, the price level, consumption, and investment. (*Hint:* In the classical model, output always equals its full-employment level.)

b. The money supply rises to 4752. Repeat Part (*a*). Is money neutral?

c. With the money supply back at 4320, government purchases and taxes rise to 190. Repeat Part (*a*).

Assume for simplicity that $\overline{Y}$ is fixed (unaffected by G). Is fiscal policy neutral in this case? Explain.

3. Consider the following economy.

Desired consumption	$C^d = 250 + 0.5(Y - T) - 500r.$
Desired investment	$I^d = 250 - 500r.$
Real money demand	$L = 0.5Y - 500i.$
Full-employment output	$\overline{Y} = 1000.$
Expected inflation	$\pi^e = 0.$

a. Suppose that $T = G = 200$ and that $M = 7650$. Find an equation describing the IS curve. Find an equation describing the LM curve. Finally, find an equation for the aggregate demand curve. What are the equilibrium values of output, consumption, investment, the real interest rate, and the price level? Assume that there are no misperceptions about the price level.

b. Suppose that $T = G = 200$ and that $M = 9000$. What is the equation for the aggregate demand curve now? What are the equilibrium values of output, consumption, investment, the real interest rate, and the price level? Assume that full-employment output, $\overline{Y}$, is fixed.

c. Repeat Part (b) for $T = G = 300$ and $M = 7650$.

4. An economy has the following AD and AS curves.

AD curve	$Y = 300 + 30(M/P).$
AS curve	$Y = \overline{Y} + 10(P - P^e).$

Here, $\overline{Y} = 500$ and $M = 400$.

a. Suppose that $P^e = 60$. What are the equilibrium values of the price level, P, and output, Y? (*Hint:* The solutions for P in this Part and in Part (b) are multiples of 10.)

b. An unanticipated increase raises the money supply to $M = 700$. Because the increase is unanticipated, P^e remains at 60. What are the equilibrium values of the price level, P, and output, Y?

c. The Fed announces that the money supply will be increased to $M = 700$, which the public believes. Now what are the equilibrium values of the price level, P, the expected price level, P^e, and output, Y?

5. Output in an economy is given by the production function $Y = AK^{0.3}N^{0.7}$, where Y is output, A measures productivity, the capital stock, K, is fixed at 30, and employment N is fixed at 100. Output equals 100 in the year 2009 and equals 105 in 2010.

a. Find the Solow residual in the years 2009 and 2010, and its growth rate between those two years.

b. What is the relationship between the growth in the Solow residual between 2009 and 2010 and the growth in productivity (as measured by the parameter A) in

the same years? Assume that the rates of utilization of capital and labor remain unchanged.

c. Repeat Part (b) under the assumption that utilization of labor increases by 3% between 2009 and 2010. You will have to modify the production function along the lines of Eq. (10.2).

d. Repeat Part (b) under the assumption that the utilization rates of both labor and capital increase by 3% between 2009 and 2010.

6. Try the following experiment: Flip a coin fifty times, keeping track of the results. Think of each "heads" as a small positive shock that increases output by one unit; similarly, think of each "tails" as a small negative shock that reduces output by one unit. Let the initial value of output, Y, be 50, and graph the level of output over time as it is hit by the "positive" and "negative" shocks (coin flips). For example, if your first four flips are three heads and a tail, output takes the values 51, 52, 53, 52. After fifty flips, have your small shocks produced any large cycles in output?

7. In a particular economy the labor force (the sum of employed and unemployed workers) is fixed at 100 million. In this economy, each month 1% of the workers who were employed at the beginning of the month lose their jobs, and 19% of the workers who were unemployed at the beginning of the month find new jobs.

a. The January unemployment rate is 5%. For the rates of job loss and job finding given, what will the unemployment rate be in February? In March?

b. In April an adverse productivity shock raises the job loss rate to 3% of those employed. The job loss rate returns to 1% in May, while the job finding rate remains unchanged at 19% throughout. Find the unemployment rate for April, May, June, and July.

8. (Appendix 10.B) Consider the following economy.

IS curve	$r = 2.47 - 0.0004Y.$
Real money demand	$L = 0.5Y - 500(r + \pi^e).$
Short-run aggregate supply	$Y = \overline{Y} + 100(P - P^e).$

Here, r is the real interest rate, Y is output, and P is the price level. Assume that expected inflation, π^e, is 0, nominal money supply, M, is 88,950, and full-employment output, $\overline{Y}$, is 6000.

a. Use the notation of Appendixes 9.B and 10.B. What are the values of the parameters $\alpha_{IS}, \beta_{IS}, \alpha_{LM}, \beta_{LM}, l_r$, and b? (*Hint:* Solve for asset market equilibrium to obtain the coefficients of the LM equation.)

b. What is the equation of the aggregate demand curve?

c. Suppose that the expected price level, P^e, is 29.15. What are the short-run equilibrium values of the price level, P, and output, Y?

d. What are the long-run equilibrium values of the price level, P, and output, Y?

ANALYTICAL PROBLEMS

1. The discovery of a new technology increases the expected future marginal product of capital.

   a. Use the classical *IS–LM* model to determine the effect of the increase in the expected future *MPK* on current output, the real interest rate, employment, real wages, consumption, investment, and the price level. Assume that expected future real wages and future incomes are unaffected by the new technology. Assume also that current productivity is unaffected.

   b. Find the effects of the increase in the expected future *MPK* on current output and prices from the *AD–AS* diagram based on the misperceptions theory. What accounts for the difference with Part (*a*)?

2. Use the classical *IS–LM* model to analyze the effects of a permanent increase in government purchases of 100 per year (in real terms). The increase in purchases is financed by a permanent increase in lump-sum taxes of 100 per year.

   a. Begin by finding the effects of the fiscal change on the labor market. How does the effect of the permanent increase in government purchases of 100 compare with the effect of a temporary increase in purchases of 100?

   b. Because the tax increase is permanent, assume that at any constant levels of output and the real interest rate, consumers respond by reducing their consumption each period by the full amount of the tax increase. Under this assumption, how does the permanent increase in government purchases affect desired national saving and the *IS* curve?

   c. Use the classical *IS–LM* model to find the effects of the permanent increase in government purchases and taxes on output, the real interest rate, and the price level in the current period. What happens if consumers reduce their current consumption by less than 100 at any level of output and the real interest rate?

3. Consider a business cycle theory that combines the classical *IS–LM* model with the assumption that temporary changes in government purchases are the main source of cyclical fluctuations. How well would this theory explain the observed cyclical behavior of each of the following variables? Give reasons for your answers.

   a. Employment
   b. The real wage
   c. Average labor productivity
   d. Investment
   e. The price level

4. This problem asks you to work out in more detail the example of reverse causation described in the text. Suppose that firms that expect to increase production in the future have to increase their current transactions (for example, they may need to purchase more raw materials). For this reason, current real money demand rises when expected future output rises.

   a. Under the assumption that real money demand depends on expected future output, use the classical *IS–LM* model to find the effects of an increase in expected future output on the current price level. For simplicity, assume that any effects of the increase in expected future output on the labor market or on desired saving and investment are small and can be ignored.

   b. Suppose that the Fed wants to stabilize the current price level. How will the Fed respond to the increase in expected future output? Explain why the Fed's response is an example of reverse causation.

5. Starting from a situation with no government spending and no taxes, the government introduces a foreign aid program (in which domestically produced goods are shipped abroad) and pays for it with a temporary 10% tax on current wages. Future wages are untaxed.

   What effects will the temporary wage tax have on labor supply? Use the classical *IS–LM* model to find the effects of the fiscal change on output, employment, the (before-tax) real wage, the real interest rate, and the price level.

WORKING WITH MACROECONOMIC DATA

For data to use in these exercises, go to the Federal Reserve Bank of St. Louis FRED database at research.stlouisfed.org/fred2.

1. According to the real business cycle theory, productivity shocks are an important source of business cycles. Using the Cobb–Douglas production function (for example, Eq. 3.2, p. 60) and annual data since 1961, calculate and graph U.S. total factor productivity. Use real GDP for *Y*, the capital stock from the source listed in Table 3.1 for *K*, and civilian employment for *N*. Look for periods marked by sharp changes up or down in productivity. How well do

these changes match up with the dates of business cycle peaks and troughs? (See Chapter 8.)

2. This question asks you to study whether unanticipated declines in the money stock tend to raise interest rates and lead to recessions, as implied by the misperceptions theory.

    a. Using quarterly data from 1960 to the present, define unanticipated money growth in each quarter to be the rate of M2 growth (expressed as an annual rate) from the preceding quarter to the current quarter, minus average M2 growth over the preceding four quarters. (Average M2 growth over the preceding four quarters is a simple approximation of expected money growth.) Graph unanticipated money growth along with the nominal three-month Treasury bill interest rate. On a separate figure, graph unanticipated money growth against the real three-month Treasury bill interest rate (the nominal rate minus the inflation rate). Are unanticipated changes in M2 associated with changes in interest rates in the theoretically predicted direction?

    b. In a separate figure, graph unanticipated money growth and the unemployment rate. Are increases in the unemployment rate generally preceded by periods in which unanticipated money growth is negative?

    What happens to unanticipated money growth following increases in the unemployment rate? Why do you think it happens? Why should the response of this measure of unanticipated money growth to increases in unemployment make you worry about whether this measure captures the unanticipated component of money growth?

3. Are people's inflation forecasts rational? To investigate this question, go to the Web site of the Federal Reserve Bank of Philadelphia at www.philadelphiafed.org. Find the Web pages for Research and Data and look for data from the Survey of Professional Forecasters on forecasts of CPI inflation. Then, go to FRED and get actual data on the CPI. Make a plot showing the forecast of inflation at a given date on the horizontal axis against the actual inflation rate on the vertical axis. If forecasts are rational, what pattern should you see in the data? What pattern do you observe in your plot? Does the evidence support the idea that people's inflation forecasts are rational?

APPENDIX 10.A

Worked-Out Numerical Exercise for Solving the Classical *AD–AS* Model with Misperceptions

Consider an economy that is described by the following equations:

$$AD \text{ curve: } Y = 1166\tfrac{2}{3} + 148{,}000/P.$$
$$SRAS \text{ curve: } Y = \overline{Y} + 10(P - P^e).$$
$$\overline{Y} = 2500; P^e = 130.$$

The *AD* curve is identical to the *AD* curve derived in Appendix 9.A, Step 5. So, we could have started with the functions for consumption, taxes, investment, and money demand, as well as the money supply from Appendix 9.A, and derived this *AD* curve.

The short-run equilibrium is found by the intersection of the *AD* curve and the *SRAS* curve: $1166\tfrac{2}{3} + 148{,}000/P = Y = \overline{Y} + 10(P - P^e)$. Substituting 2500 for $\overline{Y}$ and 130 for P^e yields $1166\tfrac{2}{3} + 148{,}000/P = 2500 + 10(P - 130)$, which implies $1166\tfrac{2}{3} + 148{,}000/P = 1200 + 10P$. Therefore $10P + 33\tfrac{1}{3} - 148{,}000/P = 0$.

Now multiply both sides of this equation by P and divide both sides by 10 to obtain the quadratic equation $P^2 + 3\tfrac{1}{3}P - 14{,}800 = 0$.

This quadratic equation has two solutions (known as roots): $P = 120$ and $P = -123\tfrac{1}{3}$. [*Hint:* You can find these roots either by using the formula for the roots of a quadratic equation* or by factoring the quadratic equation to obtain $(P - 120)(P + 123\tfrac{1}{3}) = 0$.] The positive root, $P = 120$, is the price level in short-run equilibrium. The level of output in short-run equilibrium can be found by plugging $P = 120$ into either the *AD* curve or the *SRAS* curve. In the *AD* curve, $Y = 1166\tfrac{2}{3} + 148{,}000/P = 1166\tfrac{2}{3} + 148{,}000/120 = 1166\tfrac{2}{3} + 1233\tfrac{1}{3}$, so $Y = 2400$. In the *SRAS* curve, $Y = \overline{Y} + 10(P - P^e) = 2500 + 10(120 - 130) = 2500 - 100$, so $Y = 2400$.

In the long run, there are no misperceptions, so the long-run equilibrium is the same as we found in Appendix 9.A, where $Y = 2500$ and $P = 111$.

---

*The roots of a general quadratic equation $AX^2 + BX + C = 0$ are given by $X = (-B \pm \sqrt{B^2 - 4AC})/2A$.

An Algebraic Version of the Classical *AD–AS* Model with Misperceptions

Building on the algebraic version of the *AD–AS* model developed in Appendix 9.B, in this appendix we derive an algebraic version of the classical *AD–AS* model with misperceptions. We present algebraic versions of the aggregate demand (*AD*) curve and the aggregate supply (*AS*) curve and then solve for the general equilibrium.

The Aggregate Demand Curve

Because misperceptions by producers don't affect the demand for goods, the aggregate demand curve is the same as in Appendix 9.B. Recall from Eq. (9.B.24) that the equation of the aggregate demand (*AD*) curve is

$$Y = \frac{\alpha_{IS} - \alpha_{LM} + (1/\ell_r)(M/P)}{\beta_{IS} + \beta_{LM}}, \tag{10.B.1}$$

where the coefficients of the *IS* curve, α_{IS} and β_{IS}, are given by Eqs. (9.B.15) and (9.B.16), respectively, the coefficients of the *LM* curve, α_{LM} and β_{LM}, are given by Eqs. (9.B.20) and (9.B.21), respectively, and ℓ_r is the coefficient of the nominal interest rate in the money demand equation, Eq. (9.B.17).

The Aggregate Supply Curve

The short-run aggregate supply curve based on the misperceptions theory is represented by Eq. (10.4), which, for convenience, we repeat here:

$$Y = \overline{Y} + b(P - P^e), \tag{10.B.2}$$

where b is a positive number.

General Equilibrium

For a given expected price level, P^e, the short-run equilibrium value of the price level is determined by the intersection of the aggregate demand curve (Eq. 10.B.1) and the short-run aggregate supply curve (Eq. 10.B.2). Setting the right sides of Eqs. (10.B.1) and (10.B.2) equal and multiplying both sides of the resulting equation by $P(\beta_{IS} + \beta_{LM})$ and rearranging yields a quadratic equation for the price level P:

$$a_2 P^2 + a_1 P - a_0 = 0, \tag{10.B.3}$$

where

$$a_2 = (\beta_{IS} + \beta_{LM})b;$$
$$a_1 = (\beta_{IS} + \beta_{LM})(\overline{Y} - bP^e) - \alpha_{IS} + \alpha_{LM};$$
$$a_0 = \frac{M}{\ell_r}.$$

The coefficients a_2 and a_0 are positive, and the coefficient a_1 could be positive, negative, or zero. Because both a_2 and a_0 are positive, the solution of Eq. (10.B.3) yields one positive value of P and one negative value of P. The price level can't be negative, so the short-run equilibrium price level is the positive solution of this equation. Using the standard quadratic formula, we find the positive solution of equation (10.B.3) to be

$$P = \frac{-a_1 + \sqrt{a_1^2 + 4a_2a_0}}{2a_2} \qquad\qquad \textbf{(10.B.4)}$$

We obtain the short-run equilibrium level of output by substituting the value of the price level from Eq. (10.B.4) into either the aggregate demand curve Eq. (10.B.1) or the aggregate supply curve Eq. (10.B.2).

Note that an increase in the nominal money supply, M, increases the constant a_0 and thus, according to Eq. (10.B.4), it increases the equilibrium price level. Because an increase in M doesn't affect the aggregate supply curve but does increase the equilibrium price level, Eq. (10.B.2) shows that it increases output.

We focused on short-run equilibrium in this appendix. In the long run, the actual price level equals the expected price level so that, according to Eq. (10.B.2), output equals its full-employment level, $\overline{Y}$. In the long run, the economy reaches the general equilibrium described in Appendix 9.B.

CHAPTER 11

Keynesianism: The Macroeconomics of Wage and Price Rigidity

In Chapter 10 we presented the classical, or market-clearing, approach to business cycle analysis. In the classical approach wages and prices are assumed to adjust quickly so that markets are almost always in equilibrium. Classical economists argue that business cycles represent the economy's best response to disturbances, such as productivity shocks, so there is little justification for government attempts to smooth the cycle.

In contrast to the classicals, Keynesians are less optimistic about the ability of free-market economies to respond quickly and efficiently to shocks. One of the central ideas of Keynesianism is that wages and prices are "rigid" or "sticky" and do *not* adjust quickly to market-clearing levels. Wage and price rigidity implies that the economy can be away from its general equilibrium for significant periods of time. Thus a deep recession is not an optimal response of the free market to outside shocks; rather, it is a disequilibrium situation in which high unemployment reflects an excess of labor supplied over labor demanded. Keynesians believe that the government should act to eliminate—or at least minimize—these periods of low output and high unemployment.

As wage and price rigidity is the basis for Keynesian theory and policy recommendations, understanding the potential causes of rigidity is important. A telling criticism that the classicals aimed at the Keynesians in the early 1970s was that the Keynesians simply assumed that wages and prices are rigid, without giving a good economic explanation of why these rigidities occur. After all, argued the classicals, wages and prices are not simply "given" to the economy but are the results of decisions made by millions of individuals and firms. If excessively high wages are causing unemployment, why don't unemployed workers offer to work for lower wages until firms are willing to hire them? If prices aren't at the levels at which quantities supplied equal quantities demanded, why don't firms just change their prices? In effect, the classicals challenged the Keynesians to show how wage and price rigidity could be consistent with the idea—basic to almost all of economics—that individuals and firms are economically rational; that is, they do the best they can for themselves when making economic decisions.

Keynesian researchers accepted this challenge and have made progress in explaining wage and price rigidity in terms consistent with economic rationality. In the first part of this chapter we discuss some leading Keynesian explanations for wage and price rigidity. We then show how slow adjustment of wages and prices can be incorporated into the *IS–LM* model, converting it from a classical model to a Keynesian model. Using this model, we discuss the Keynesian answers to the two central questions about business cycles—namely, What causes business cycles? and What should policymakers do about them?

11.1 Real-Wage Rigidity

Because Keynesian analysis and policy prescriptions depend so greatly on the assumption that wages and prices do not move rapidly to clear markets, we begin by discussing in some detail the possible economic reasons for slow or incomplete adjustment. In this section we focus on the rigidity of real wages, and in Section 11.2 we look at the slow adjustment of prices.

The main reason that Keynesians bring wage rigidity into their analysis is their dissatisfaction with the classical explanation of unemployment. Recall that classicals believe that most unemployment, including the increases in unemployment that occur during recessions, arises from mismatches between workers and jobs (frictional or structural unemployment). Keynesians don't dispute that mismatch is a major source of unemployment, but they are skeptical that it explains all unemployment.

Keynesians are particularly unwilling to accept the classical idea that recessions are periods of increased mismatch between workers and jobs. If higher unemployment during downturns reflected increased mismatch, Keynesians argue, recessions should be periods of particularly active search by workers for jobs and by firms for new employees. However, surveys suggest that unemployed workers spend relatively little time searching for work (many are simply waiting, hoping to be recalled to their old jobs), and help-wanted advertising and vacancy postings by firms fall rather than rise during recessions. Rather than times of increased worker–job mismatch, Keynesians believe that recessions are periods of generally low demand for both output and workers throughout the economy.

To explain the existence of unemployment without relying solely on worker–job mismatch, Keynesians argue for rejecting the classical assumption that real wages adjust relatively quickly to equate the quantities of labor supplied and demanded. In particular, if the real wage is above the level that clears the labor market, unemployment (an excess of labor supplied over labor demanded) will result. From the Keynesian perspective, the idea that the real wage moves "too little" to keep the quantity of labor demanded equal to the quantity of labor supplied is called **real-wage rigidity**.

Some Reasons for Real-Wage Rigidity

For a rigid real wage to be the source of unemployment, the real wage that firms are paying must be higher than the market-clearing real wage, at which quantities of labor supplied and demanded are equal. But if the real wage is higher than necessary to attract workers, why don't firms save labor costs by simply reducing the wage that they pay, as suggested by the classical analysis?

Various explanations have been offered for why real wages might be rigid, even in the face of an excess supply of labor. One possibility is that there are legal and institutional factors that keep wages high, such as the minimum-wage law and union contracts. However, most U.S. workers are neither union members nor minimum-wage earners, so these barriers to wage cutting can't be the main reason for real-wage rigidity. Furthermore, the minimum wage in the United States is specified in nominal terms so that workers who are paid the minimum wage would have rigid nominal wages rather than rigid real wages. (Union contracts may help explain real-wage rigidity in Western European and other countries in which a high proportion of workers are unionized, and in which nominal wages are typically adjusted for inflation so as to maintain the real wage at its negotiated level.)

Another explanation for why a firm might pay a higher real wage than it "has" to is that this policy might reduce the firm's **turnover costs**, or the costs associated with hiring and training new workers. By paying a high wage, the firm can keep more of its current workers, which saves the firm the cost of hiring and training replacements. Similarly, by developing a reputation for paying well, the firm can assure itself of more and better applicants for any position that it may have to fill.

A third reason that firms might pay real wages above market-clearing levels is that workers who are paid well may have greater incentives to work hard and effectively. If highly paid workers are more productive, the firm may profit from paying its employees well, even though it could attract all the workers it needs at a lower real wage. The idea that a worker's productivity depends on the real wage received, and that therefore firms may pay wages above the market-clearing level, is the essence of the **efficiency wage model**. Because this model of wage determination has played a key role in recent Keynesian analyses and because it has several interesting aspects, we focus on it for the remainder of this section.

The Efficiency Wage Model

If better-paid workers are more productive, firms may gain by paying wages higher than the minimum necessary to attract workers. But why might a worker's productivity depend on the real wage received? The answer has both "carrot" and "stick" aspects.

The *carrot,* or positive incentive, is based on the idea that workers who feel well treated will work harder and more efficiently. George Akerlof,[1] a Nobel laureate at the University of California at Berkeley, argued that workers who believe that their employer is treating them fairly—say, by paying higher wages than required to retain them and by not cutting wages in slack times—will in turn want to treat the employer fairly by doing a good job. Akerlof called this motivation the *gift exchange motive* because it's similar to the one that leads people to exchange gifts.

The *stick,* or threat, aspect of why a firm would pay a higher wage than necessary has been analyzed in an economic model called the "shirking" model of wage determination.[2] According to the *shirking model,* if a worker is paid only the minimum amount needed to attract her to a particular job, she won't be too concerned about the possibility of being fired if she doesn't perform well. After all, if the job pays the minimum amount necessary to induce her to take the job, she isn't much happier with the job than without the job. In this case the worker will be more

---

[1]See George Akerlof, "Labor Contracts as Partial Gift Exchange," *Quarterly Journal of Economics,* November 1982, pp. 543–569.

[2]See Carl Shapiro and Joseph E. Stiglitz, "Equilibrium Unemployment as a Worker Discipline Device," *American Economic Review,* June 1984, pp. 433–444.

Figure 11.1

Determination of the efficiency wage

The effort curve shows the relation between worker effort, E, and the real wage workers receive, w. A higher real wage leads to more effort, but above a certain point higher wages are unable to spur effort much, so the effort curve is S-shaped. For any point on the curve, the amount of effort per dollar of real wage is the slope of the line from the origin to that point. At point A, effort per dollar of real wage is E_A/w_A. The highest level of effort per dollar of real wage is at point B, where the line from the origin is tangent to the curve. The real wage rate at B is the efficiency wage, w^*, and the corresponding level of effort is E^*.

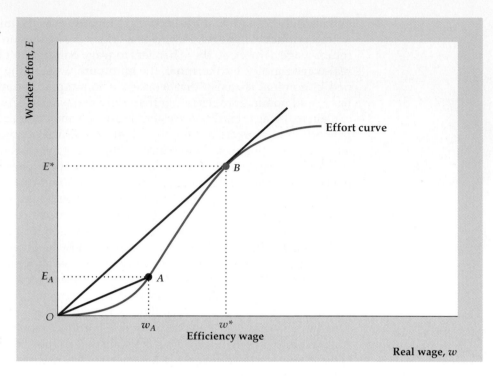

inclined to take it easy at work and shirk her duties, and the employer will have to bear the cost either of the shirking or of paying supervisors to make sure that the work gets done. In contrast, a worker receiving a higher wage will place a greater value on keeping her job (it's not that easy to find another job as good) and will work hard to avoid being fired for shirking.

The gift exchange idea and the shirking model both imply that workers' effort on the job depends on the real wages they receive. Graphically, the relationship between the real wage and the level of effort is shown by the **effort curve** in Fig. 11.1. The real wage, w, is measured along the horizontal axis, and the level of effort, E, is measured along the vertical axis. The effort curve passes through points O, A, and B. When real wages are higher, workers choose to work harder, for either carrot or stick reasons; therefore the effort curve slopes upward. We assume that the effort curve is S-shaped. At the lowest levels of the real wage, workers make hardly any effort, and effort rises only slowly as the real wage increases. At higher levels of the real wage, effort rises sharply, as shown by the steeply rising portion of the curve. The curve flattens at very high levels of the real wage because there is some maximum level of effort that workers really can't exceed no matter how motivated they are.

Wage Determination in the Efficiency Wage Model

The effort curve shows that effort depends on the real wage, but what determines the real wage? To make as much profit as possible, *firms will choose the level of the real wage that gets the most effort from workers for each dollar of real wages paid.* The amount of effort per dollar of real wages equals the amount of effort, E, divided by the real wage, w. The ratio of E to w can be found graphically from Fig. 11.1. Consider, for example, point A on the effort curve, at which the real wage w_A induces workers to supply effort E_A. The slope of the line from the origin to A equals the height of the curve at point A, E_A, divided by the horizontal distance, w_A. Thus the slope of the line from the origin to A equals the amount of effort per dollar of real wages at A.

The real wage that achieves the highest effort per dollar of wages is at point B. The slope of the line from the origin to B, which is the amount of effort per dollar of real wage at B, is greater than the slope of the line from the origin to any other point on the curve. In general, to locate the real wage that maximizes effort per dollar of real wage, we draw a line from the origin tangent to the effort curve; the real wage at the tangency point maximizes effort per dollar of real wage. We call the real wage that maximizes effort or efficiency per dollar of real wages the **efficiency wage**. In Fig. 11.1 the efficiency wage is w^*, and the corresponding level of effort is E^*.

The efficiency wage theory helps explain real-wage rigidity. Because the employer chooses the real wage that maximizes effort received per dollar paid, as long as the effort curve doesn't change, the employer won't change the real wage. Therefore the theory implies that the real wage is permanently rigid and equals the efficiency wage.

Employment and Unemployment in the Efficiency Wage Model

According to the efficiency wage theory, the real wage is rigid at the level that maximizes effort per dollar of wages paid. We now consider how the levels of employment and unemployment in the labor market are determined.

The workings of the labor market when there is an efficiency wage are shown in Fig. 11.2. The efficiency wage, w^*, is indicated by a horizontal line. Because the efficiency wage is determined solely by the effort curve, for the purpose of analyzing the labor market we can take w^* to be fixed. Similarly, we can take the level of effort, E^*, induced by the efficiency wage, w^*, as fixed at this stage of the analysis.

The upward-sloping curve is the standard labor supply curve, NS. As in the classical model, this curve shows the number of hours of work that people would like to supply at each level of the real wage.[3]

The downward-sloping curve is the demand curve for labor in the efficiency wage model. Recall from Chapter 3 that the amount of labor demanded by a firm depends on the marginal product of labor, or MPN. Specifically, the labor demand curve is identical to the MPN curve, which in turn relates the marginal product of labor, MPN, to the quantity of labor input, N, being used. The MPN curve—and hence the labor demand curve—slopes down because of the diminishing marginal productivity of labor.

In the classical model, the marginal product of labor depends only on the production function and the capital stock. A complication of the efficiency wage model is that the amount of output produced by an extra worker (or hour of work) also depends on the worker's effort. Fortunately, as we noted, the efficiency wage, w^*, and the effort level induced by that wage, E^*, are fixed at this stage of the analysis. Thus the labor demand curve in Fig. 11.2, ND^*, reflects the marginal product of labor *when worker effort is held fixed at E^**. As in the classical case, an increase in productivity or in the capital stock shifts the labor demand curve, ND^*, to the right. In addition, any change in the effort curve that led to an increase in the optimal level of effort E^* would raise the MPN, and the labor demand curve, ND^*, again would shift to the right.

---

[3]For simplicity, we assume that the number of hours of labor that people want to supply doesn't depend on the effort they must exert while on the job.

Figure 11.2

Excess supply of labor in the efficiency wage model
When the efficiency wage, w^*, is paid, the firm's demand for labor is $\overline{N}$, represented by point A. However, the amount of labor that workers want to supply at a real wage of w^* is NS_1. The excess supply of labor equals distance AB. We assume that the efficiency wage, w^*, is higher than the market-clearing wage, w_E, that would prevail if the supply of labor equaled the demand for labor at point E.

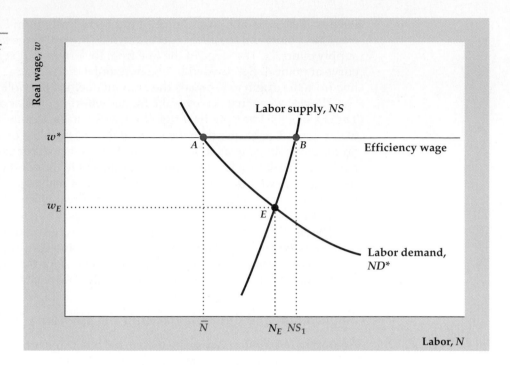

Now we can put the elements of Fig. 11.2 together to show how employment is determined. Point A on the labor demand curve, ND^*, indicates that, when the real wage is fixed at w^*, firms want to employ $\overline{N}$ hours of labor. Point B on the labor supply curve indicates that, when the real wage is fixed at w^*, workers want to supply NS_1 hours of labor, which is greater than the amount demanded by firms. At the efficiency wage, the quantity of labor supplied is greater than the quantity demanded,[4] so the level of employment is determined by the labor demand of firms and hence equals $\overline{N}$. The demand-determined level of employment is labeled $\overline{N}$ because it represents the full-employment level of employment for this model; that is, $\overline{N}$ is the level of employment reached after full adjustment of wages and prices. (Note that the value of $\overline{N}$ in the efficiency wage model differs from the full-employment level of employment in the classical model of the labor market, which would correspond to N_E in Fig. 11.2.) Because the efficiency wage is rigid at w^*, in the absence of shocks the level of employment in this economy remains at $\overline{N}$ indefinitely.

Perhaps the most interesting aspect of Fig. 11.2 is that it provides a new explanation of unemployment. It shows that, even when wages have adjusted as much as they are going to and the economy is technically at "full employment," an excess supply of labor, $NS_1 - \overline{N}$, remains.[5]

Why don't the unemployed bid down the real wage and thus gain employment, as they would in the classical model of the labor market? Unlike the classical case, in a labor market with an efficiency wage the real wage can't be bid down by

---

[4]The result that there is an excess supply of labor requires the assumption that the efficiency wage, w^*, is higher than the real wage that would clear the labor market, shown as w_E in Fig. 11.2. We always assume that the efficiency wage is higher than the market-clearing wage; if it weren't, firms would have to pay the market-clearing wage to attract workers.

[5]Because the unemployment represented by the excess supply of labor persists even when the economy is at full employment, it is considered part of structural unemployment.

people offering to work at lower wages because employers won't hire them. Employers know that people working at lower wages will not put out as much effort per dollar of real wages as workers receiving the higher efficiency wage. Thus the excess supply of labor shown in Fig. 11.2 will persist indefinitely. The efficiency wage model thus implies that unemployment will exist even if there is no mismatch between jobs and workers.

The efficiency wage model is an interesting theory of real wages and unemployment. But does it explain actual behavior? "In Touch with Data and Research: Henry Ford's Efficiency Wage," p. 406, interprets a famous episode in labor history in terms of efficiency wage theory. In addition to this anecdotal evidence, studies of wages and employment in various firms and industries provide some support for the efficiency wage model. For example, Peter Cappelli of the University of Pennsylvania and Keith Chauvin of the University of Kansas[6] found that, consistent with one aspect of the theory, plants that paid higher wages to workers experienced less shirking, measured by the number of workers fired for disciplinary reasons. Also, research by Michelle Alexopoulos and Jon Cohen of the University of Toronto[7] showed that when wages became compressed in Sweden in the 1970s, workers' effort declined dramatically.

A criticism of the efficiency wage model presented here is that it predicts that the real wage is literally fixed (for no change in the effort curve). Of course, this result is too extreme because the real wage does change over time (and over the business cycle, as demonstrated in Chapter 8). However, the basic model can be extended to allow for changes in the effort curve that bring changes in the efficiency wage over time. For example, a reasonable assumption would be that workers are more concerned about losing their jobs during recessions, when finding a new job is more difficult, than during booms. Under this assumption, the real wage necessary to obtain any specific level of effort will be lower during recessions; hence the efficiency wage paid in recessions also may be lower. This extension may help the efficiency wage model match the business cycle fact that real wages are lower in recessions than in booms (procyclical real wages).

Efficiency Wages and the *FE* Line

In the Keynesian version of the *IS–LM* model, as in the classical version, the *FE* line is vertical, at a level of output that equals the full-employment level of output, $\overline{Y}$. If we assume that employers pay efficiency wages, full-employment output, $\overline{Y}$, in turn is the output produced when employment is at the full-employment level of employment, $\overline{N}$, as shown in Fig. 11.2, and the level of worker effort is E^*.

As in the classical model, anything that changes full-employment output, $\overline{Y}$, shifts the *FE* line. The classical model emphasizes two factors that shift the *FE* line: changes in the supply of labor and changes in productivity. In the efficiency wage model, however, labor supply doesn't affect employment, so *changes in labor supply don't affect the* FE *line in the Keynesian model* with efficiency wages. A change in

---

[6]"An Interplant Test of the Efficiency Wage Hypothesis," *Quarterly Journal of Economics*, August 1991, pp. 769–787.

[7]"Centralized Wage Bargaining and Structural Change in Sweden," *European Review of Economic History*, December 2003, pp. 331–366.

IN TOUCH WITH DATA AND RESEARCH

Henry Ford's Efficiency Wage

During 1908–1914 Henry Ford instituted at Ford Motor Company a radically new way of producing automobiles.* Prior to Ford's innovations, automobile components weren't produced to uniform specifications. Instead, cars had to be assembled one by one by skilled craftsmen, who could make the parts fit even if sizes or shapes were off by fractions of an inch. Ford introduced a system of assembly-line production in which a standardized product, the Model T automobile, was produced from precisely made, interchangeable components. The production process also was broken into numerous small, simple steps, replacing the skilled craftsmen who had built cars from start to finish with unskilled workers who performed only a few operations over and over.

The high speed at which Ford ran the assembly line and the repetitiveness of the work were hard on the workers. As one laborer said, "If I keep putting on Nut No. 86 for about 86 more days, I will be Nut No. 86 in the Pontiac bughouse."[†] As a result, worker turnover was high, with the typical worker lasting only a few months on the job. Absenteeism also was high—about 10% on any given day—and morale was low. Worker slowdowns and even sabotage occurred.

In January 1914 Ford announced that the company would begin paying $5 a day to workers who met certain criteria, one being that the worker had been with the company at least six months. Five dollars a day was more than double the normal wage for production workers at the time. Although the motivation for Ford's announcement has been debated, its effect was stunning: Thousands of workers lined up outside the plant, hoping for jobs. Within the plant the number of people quitting dropped by 87%, absenteeism dropped by 75%, and productivity rose by 30% or more. The productivity increases helped increase Ford's profits, despite the higher wage bill and a cut in the price of a Model T.

Many results of Ford's $5 day can be predicted by the efficiency wage model, including improved efficiency and higher profits. As other automakers adopted Ford's technological innovations, they also adopted his wage policies. By 1928, before unions were important in the industry, auto industry wages were almost 40% higher than those in the rest of manufacturing.

---

*The source for this box is Daniel M. G. Raff and Lawrence H. Summers, "Did Henry Ford Pay Efficiency Wages?" *Journal of Labor Economics,* October 1987, pp. S57–S86.

[†]This quote is originally from Stephen Meyer, *The Five-Dollar Day: Labor Management and Social Control in the Ford Motor Company, 1908–1921,* Albany: State University of New York Press, 1981.

productivity, however, does affect the *FE* line in the Keynesian model, as in the classical model. A drop in productivity reduces full-employment output, $\overline{Y}$, and shifts the *FE* line to the left, for two reasons. First, by reducing the marginal product of labor at any given level of employment, a drop in productivity reduces the demand for labor at any fixed real wage. With the real wage fixed at w^*, the full-employment level of employment, $\overline{N}$, falls. Second, a drop in productivity reduces the amount of output that can be produced with any particular amount of capital, labor, and effort.

11.2 Price Stickiness

The rigidity created by efficiency wages is a real rigidity in that the real wage, rather than the nominal wage, remains fixed. Keynesian theories also emphasize *nominal* rigidities that occur when a price or wage is fixed in nominal, or dollar, terms and doesn't readily change in response to changes in supply or demand. Keynesians often refer to rigidity of nominal prices—a tendency of prices to adjust only slowly to changes in the economy—as **price stickiness**.

We explained in Section 11.1 that Keynesians introduced real-wage rigidity because of their dissatisfaction with the classical explanation of unemployment. Similarly, the assumption of price stickiness addresses what Keynesians believe is another significant weakness of the basic classical model: the classical prediction that money is neutral.

Recall that, in the basic classical model without misperceptions, the assumption that wages and prices adjust quickly implies that money is neutral. If money is neutral, an increase or decrease in the money supply changes the price level by the same proportion but has no effect on real variables, such as output, employment, or the real interest rate. However, recall also that empirical studies—including analyses of historical episodes—have led most economists to conclude that money probably is not neutral in the real world.

One approach to accounting for monetary nonneutrality (pursued in Chapter 10) is to extend the classical model by assuming that workers and firms have imperfect information about the current price level (the misperceptions theory). However, Keynesians favor an alternative explanation of monetary nonneutrality: Prices are sticky; that is, they don't adjust quickly. If prices are sticky, the price level can't adjust immediately to offset changes in the money supply, and money isn't neutral. Thus, for Keynesians, the importance of price stickiness is that it helps explain monetary nonneutrality.

Although we focus on nominal-price rigidity in this section, a long Keynesian tradition emphasizes nominal wage rigidity instead of nominal-price rigidity. We discuss an alternative version of the Keynesian model that rests on the assumption of nominal-wage rigidity in Appendix 11.A. This alternative model has similar implications to the Keynesian model with price rigidity—in particular, that money is not neutral.

Sources of Price Stickiness: Monopolistic Competition and Menu Costs

To say that price stickiness gives rise to monetary nonneutrality doesn't completely explain nonneutrality because it raises another question: Why are prices sticky? The Keynesian explanation for the existence of price rigidity relies on two main ideas: (1) most firms actively set the prices of their products rather than taking the prices of their output as given by the market; and (2) when firms change prices, they incur a cost, known as a menu cost.

Monopolistic Competition. Talking about price stickiness in a highly competitive, organized market—such as the market for corn or the stock exchange—wouldn't make much sense. In these markets, prices adjust rapidly to reflect changes in supply or demand. Principal reasons for price flexibility in these competitive, highly organized markets include standardization of the product being traded (one bushel of corn of a certain grade, or one share of Microsoft stock, is much like any other) and the large number of actual or potential market participants. These two factors make it worthwhile to organize a centralized market (such as the New York Stock Exchange) in which prices can react swiftly to changes in supply and demand. These same two factors also promote keen competition among buyers and sellers, which greatly reduces the ability of any individual to affect prices.

Most participants in the corn market or stock market think of themselves as price takers. A *price taker* is a market participant who takes the market price as given. For example, a small farmer correctly perceives that the market price of corn is beyond his control. In contrast, a *price setter* has some power to set prices.

Markets having fewer participants and less standardized products than the corn or stock markets may exhibit price-setting rather than price-taking behavior. For example, consider the market for movies in a medium-sized city. This market may be fairly competitive, with many different movie theaters, each trying to attract customers from other theaters, home video stores, and so on. Although the market for movies is competitive, it isn't competitive to the same degree as the corn market. If a farmer tried to raise the price of a bushel of his corn by 5¢ above the market price, he would sell no corn; but a movie theater that raised its ticket prices by 5¢ above its competitors' prices wouldn't lose all its customers. Because the movie theater's product isn't completely standardized (it is showing a different movie than other theaters, its location is better for some people, it has different candy bars in the concession stand, a larger screen, or more comfortable seats, and so on), the theater has some price-setting discretion. It is a price setter, not a price taker.

Generally, a situation in which all buyers and sellers are price takers (such as the market for corn) is called **perfect competition.** In contrast, a situation in which there is some competition, but in which a smaller number of sellers and imperfect standardization of the product allow individual producers to act as price setters, is called **monopolistic competition.**

Perfect competition is the model underlying the classical view of price determination, and, as we have said, price rigidity or stickiness is extremely unlikely in a perfectly competitive market. Keynesians agree that price rigidity wouldn't occur in a perfectly competitive market but point out that a relatively small part of the economy is perfectly competitive. Keynesians argue that price rigidity is possible, even likely, in a monopolistically competitive market.

To illustrate the issues, let's return to the example of the competing movie theaters. If the market for movie tickets were perfectly competitive, how would tickets be priced? Presumably, there would be some central meeting place where buyers and sellers of tickets would congregate. Market organizers would call out "bids" (prices at which they are willing to buy) and "asks" (prices at which they are willing to sell). Prices would fluctuate continuously as new information hit the market, causing supplies and demands to change. For example, a "two thumbs up" review by leading movie critics would instantly drive up the price of tickets to that movie, but news of a prospective shortage of baby-sitters would cause all movie ticket prices to fall.

Obviously, though, this scheme isn't how movie tickets are priced. Actual pricing by most theaters has the following three characteristics, which are also common to most price-setting markets:

1. Rather than accept the price of movies as completely determined by the market, a movie theater *sets* the price of tickets (or a schedule of prices), in *nominal* terms, and maintains the nominal price for some period of time.

2. At least within some range, the theater *meets the demand* that is forthcoming at the fixed nominal price. By "meets the demand" we mean that the theater will sell as many tickets as people want to buy at its fixed price, to the point that all its seats are filled.

3. The theater readjusts its price from time to time, generally when its costs or the level of demand changes significantly.

Can this type of pricing behavior maximize profits? Keynesian theory suggests that it can, if costs are associated with changing nominal prices, and if the market is monopolistically competitive.

Menu Costs and Price Setting. The classic example of a cost of changing prices is the cost that a restaurant faces when it has to reprint its menu to show changes in the prices of its offerings. Hence the cost of changing prices is called a **menu cost.** More general examples of menu costs (which can apply to any kind of firm) include costs of remarking merchandise, reprinting price lists and catalogues, and informing potential customers. Clearly, if firms incur costs when changing prices, they will change prices less often than they would otherwise, which creates a certain amount of price rigidity.

A potential problem with the menu cost explanation for price rigidity is that these costs seem to be rather small. How, then, can they be responsible for an amount of nominal rigidity that could have macroeconomic significance?

Here is the first point at which the monopolistic competition assumption is important. For a firm in a perfectly competitive market, getting the price "a little bit wrong" has serious consequences: The farmer who prices his corn 5¢ a bushel above the market price sells no corn. Therefore the existence of a menu cost wouldn't prevent the farmer from pricing his product at precisely the correct level. However, the demand for the output of a monopolistically competitive firm responds much less sharply to changes in its price; the movie theater doesn't lose many of its customers if its ticket price is 5¢ higher than its competitors'. Thus, as long as the monopolistic competitor's price is in the right general range, the loss of profits from not getting the price exactly right isn't too great. If the loss in profits is less than the cost of changing prices—the menu costs—the firm won't change its price.

Over time, the production function and the demand curve the firm faces will undergo a variety of shocks so that eventually the profit-maximizing price for a firm may be significantly different from the preset price. When the profits lost by having the "wrong" price clearly exceed the cost of changing the price, the firm will change its nominal price. Thus movie theaters periodically raise their ticket and popcorn prices to reflect general inflation and other changes in market conditions.

Empirical Evidence on Price Stickiness. Several studies have examined the degree of rigidity or stickiness in actual prices.

To investigate whether firms perceive their own prices as being sticky or not, Alan Blinder[8] of Princeton University, assisted by a team of Princeton graduate students during 1990–1992, interviewed the managers of 200 randomly selected firms about their pricing behavior. Table 11.1 summarizes the evidence on price stickiness

---

[8]"On Sticky Prices: Academic Theories Meet the Real World," in N. G. Mankiw, ed., *Monetary Policy,* University of Chicago Press, 1994.

Table 11.1

Frequency of Price Adjustment Among Interviewed Firms

Frequency of price change (number of times per year)	Percentage of firms
Less than once	10.2%
Once	39.3
1.01 to 2	15.6
2.01 to 4	12.9
4.01 to 12	7.5
12.01 to 52	4.3
More than 52	10.2

Source: Alan S. Blinder, "On Sticky Prices: Academic Theories Meet the Real World," in N. G. Mankiw, ed., *Monetary Policy*, University of Chicago Press, 1994, Table 4.1.

by showing the percentage of firms in the study that reported changing their prices at various frequencies. For example, the first line of Table 11.1 tells us that 10.2% of these firms reported changing their prices less than once per year. Almost half (49.5%) of managers interviewed said that their firms changed prices once a year or less. Only 22% of the firms changed prices more than four times per year.

Besides probing into pricing behavior, Blinder and his students also asked firm managers *why* they tend to change prices infrequently. Direct costs of changing prices (menu costs) did appear to play a role for many firms. Nevertheless, many managers stressed as a reason for price stickiness their concern that, if they changed their own prices, their competitors would not necessarily follow suit. Managers were particularly reluctant to be the first in their market to raise prices, fearing that they would lose customers to their rivals. For this reason, many firms reported delaying price changes until it was evident throughout the industry that changes in costs or demand made price adjustment necessary.

In another study of price stickiness Anil Kashyap,[9] of the University of Chicago, examined the prices of twelve individual items listed in the catalogues of L. L. Bean, Orvis, and Recreational Equipment, Inc., over a thirty-five-year period. Changing the prices listed in a new catalogue is virtually costless, yet Kashyap found that the nominal prices of many goods remained fixed in successive issues of the catalogue. When nominal prices were changed, Kashyap found both large and small changes. He interpreted the combination of small price changes and long periods of unchanged prices as evidence against menu costs. If menu costs are the reason that prices aren't changed frequently, prices should be changed only when they are relatively far out of line, and the price changes should be large; small changes seem to contradict this implication of menu costs. Even if menu costs aren't the underlying cause of pricing behavior, however, Kashyap's study confirms Binder's findings of substantial nominal-price rigidity in the economy.

However, recent evidence based on a larger data set suggests that price stickiness may not be as pervasive as earlier studies indicated. In their 2004 paper, Mark Bils of the University of Rochester and Peter Klenow of Stanford University[10]

[9]"Sticky Prices: New Evidence from Retail Catalogs," *Quarterly Journal of Economics*, February 1995, pp. 245–274.
[10]"Some Evidence on the Importance of Sticky Prices," *Journal of Political Economy*, October 2004, pp. 947–985.

found that the average time between price changes among 350 categories of goods (whose prices were recorded by the Bureau of Labor Statistics for use in calculating the Consumer Price Index) was just 4.3 months, suggesting that prices are changed much more frequently than reported by Blinder and by Kashyap. Prices of some goods and services, such as men's haircuts, taxicab fares, and newspapers, change very rarely and are clearly sticky. But prices of other goods and services, including food and gasoline, change very frequently.

The results by Bils and Klenow thus suggest that some prices are not too sticky, and these findings could cast doubt on the price stickiness view. But one reason that economists continue to use the assumption of price stickiness in their models is that many of the price changes are caused by shifts in demand or supply in a particular industry. For example, day-to-day news about the supply of oil causes gasoline prices to change. But the assumption about price stickiness is going to be relevant in our macroeconomic model for how prices respond to changes in monetary policy and how prices change to restore general equilibrium, not how they respond to supply and demand shocks in their own industry. Recent research by Jean Boivin of HEC-Montreal, Marc Giannoni of Columbia University and Ilian Mihov of INSEAD[11] shows that in response to monetary policy, prices of many goods are very sticky, whereas those same prices respond quickly in response to shocks to supply and demand that affect the relative price of the good compared with other goods. Thus, in our macroeconomic model, the assumption of sticky prices is a useful one, even in the face of the Bils and Klenow evidence.

Meeting the Demand at the Fixed Nominal Price. When prices are sticky, firms react to changes in demand by changing the amount of production rather than by changing prices. According to Keynesians, why are firms willing to meet demand at a fixed nominal price? To answer this question, we again rely on the assumption of monopolistic competition. We've stated that a monopolistically competitive firm can raise its price some without risk of losing all its customers. The profit-maximizing strategy for a monopolistically competitive firm is to charge a price higher than its **marginal cost,** or the cost of producing an additional unit of output. The excess of the price over the marginal cost is the **markup.** For example, if a firm charges a price 15% above its marginal cost, the firm has a markup of 15%. More generally, if the firm charges a constant markup of η over marginal cost, the following markup rule describes its price:

$$P = (1 + \eta)MC, \tag{11.1}$$

where P is the nominal price charged by the firm and MC is the nominal marginal cost.[12]

[11]"Sticky Prices and Monetary Policy: Evidence from Disaggregated U.S. Data." *American Economic Review,* March 2009, pp. 350–384.

[12]Technical note: For a monopolistically competitive firm that faces a demand curve with a constant price elasticity and a fixed wage, the constant-markup rule in Eq. (11.1) will maximize profit. Also, in this case the labor demand curve is proportional to (rather than equal to) the marginal product of labor curve. Specifically, to maximize profits the firm equates the MPN to $(1 + \eta)w^*$, where w^* is the efficiency wage, rather than equating the MPN to w^* itself. This qualification doesn't affect any conclusions presented in this chapter.

When the firm sets its price according to Eq. (11.1), it has an idea of how many units it will sell. Now suppose that, to the firm's surprise, customers demand several more units than the firm expected to sell at that price. Will it be profitable for the firm to meet the demand at this price?

The answer is "yes." Because the price the firm receives for each extra unit exceeds its cost of producing that extra unit (its marginal cost), the firm's profits increase when it sells additional units at the fixed price. Thus, as long as the marginal cost remains below the fixed price of its product, the firm gladly supplies more units at this fixed price. Furthermore, if the firm is paying an efficiency wage, it can easily hire more workers to produce the units needed to meet the demand, because there is an excess supply of labor.

The macroeconomic importance of firms' meeting demand at the fixed nominal price is that *the economy can produce an amount of output that is not on the full-employment line.* Recall that the *FE* line shows the amount of output that firms would produce after complete adjustment of all wages and prices. However, with nominal-price stickiness the prices of goods do not adjust rapidly to their general equilibrium values. During the period in which prices haven't yet completely adjusted, the amount of output produced need not be on the *FE* line. Instead, as long as marginal cost is below the fixed price, monopolistically competitive firms will produce the level of output demanded.

Effective Labor Demand.   When a firm meets the demand for its output at a specific price, it may produce a different amount of output and employ a different amount of labor than it had planned. How much labor will a firm actually employ when it meets the demand? The answer is given by the effective labor demand curve, $ND^e(Y)$, shown in Fig. 11.3. For any amount of output, Y, the **effective labor demand curve**

Figure 11.3

The effective labor demand curve
When a firm meets the demand for its output, it employs just the amount of labor needed to produce the quantity of output demanded. Because more labor is required to produce more output, firms must employ more labor when the demand for output is higher. This relationship between the amount of output demanded and the amount of labor employed is the effective labor demand curve. The effective labor demand curve is the same as the production function relating output and labor, except that labor is plotted on the vertical axis and output is plotted on the horizontal axis.

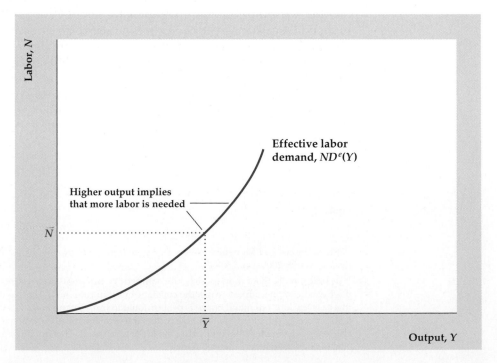

indicates how much labor is needed to produce that output, with productivity, the capital stock, and effort held constant.

We already have a concept that expresses the relationship between the amount of labor used and the amount of output produced: the production function. Indeed, the effective labor demand curve in Fig. 11.3 is simply a graph of the production function relating output and labor input, except that output, Y, is measured on the horizontal axis and labor, N, is measured on the vertical axis. (This reversal of the axes is convenient later.) The effective labor demand curve slopes upward from left to right because a firm needs more labor to produce more output.

We use the effective labor demand curve to determine the level of employment in the Keynesian model in Section 11.3. When the economy is not on the FE line and the price level is fixed, the effective labor demand curve gives the level of employment. Then, after complete adjustment of wages and prices, the economy returns to the FE line and the level of employment is given by the labor demand curve, ND^* (Fig. 11.2). After wages and prices have completely adjusted, with output at its full-employment level, $\overline{Y}$, the effective labor demand curve indicates that employment equals $\overline{N}$, as shown in Fig. 11.3.

11.3 Monetary and Fiscal Policy in the Keynesian Model

Let's now consider the complete Keynesian model. Like the classical model, the Keynesian model can be expressed in terms of the IS–LM diagram or, alternatively, in terms of the AD–AS diagram. Rather than describe the Keynesian model in the abstract, we put it to work analyzing the effects of monetary and fiscal policy.

Monetary Policy

The main reason for introducing nominal-price stickiness into the Keynesian model was to explain monetary nonneutrality. We examine the link between price stickiness and monetary nonneutrality first in the Keynesian IS–LM framework and then in the Keynesian version of the AD–AS model.

Monetary Policy in the Keynesian *IS*–*LM* Model.   The Keynesian version of the IS–LM model is quite similar to the IS–LM model discussed in Chapters 9 and 10. In particular, the IS curve and the LM curve are the same as in our earlier analyses. The FE line in the Keynesian model also is similar to the FE line used earlier. The Keynesian FE line is vertical at the full-employment level of output, $\overline{Y}$, which in turn depends on the full-employment level of employment determined in the labor market. However, the Keynesian and classical FE lines differ in two respects. First, in the Keynesian model the full-employment level of employment is determined at the intersection of the labor demand curve and the efficiency wage line, not at the point where the quantities of labor demanded and supplied are equal, as in the classical model. Second, because labor supply doesn't affect employment in the efficiency wage model, changes in labor supply don't affect the Keynesian FE line, although changes in labor supply do affect the classical FE line.

Because of price stickiness, in the Keynesian model the economy doesn't have to be in general equilibrium in the short run. However, in the long run when prices adjust, the economy reaches its general equilibrium at the intersection of the IS curve, the LM curve, and the FE line, as in the classical model.

According to Keynesians, what happens to the economy in the short run, if sticky prices prevent it from reaching general equilibrium? Keynesians assume that the asset market clears quickly and that the level of output is determined by aggregate demand. Thus, according to Keynesians, *the economy always lies at the intersection of the IS and LM curves.* However, because monopolistically competitive firms are willing to meet the demand for goods at fixed levels of prices, output can differ from full-employment output and the economy may not be on the *FE* line in the short run. When the economy is off the *FE* line, firms use just enough labor to produce the output needed to meet demand. Under the assumption that the efficiency wage is higher than the market-clearing real wage, there are always unemployed workers who want to work, and firms are able to change employment as needed to meet the demand for output without changing the wage.

Figure 11.4 analyzes the effect of an increase in the nominal money supply in the Keynesian *IS–LM* model. We assume that the economy starts at its general equilibrium point, *E*. Recall that an increase in the money supply shifts the *LM* curve down and to the right, from LM^1 to LM^2 (Fig. 11.4a). Because an increase in the money supply doesn't directly affect the goods or labor markets, the *IS* curve and the *FE* line are unaffected. So far this analysis is like that of the classical model.

Unlike the classical model, however, the Keynesian model is based on the assumption that prices are temporarily fixed (because of menu costs) so that the general equilibrium at *E* isn't restored immediately. Instead, the short-run equilibrium of the economy—that is, the resting point of the economy at the fixed price level—lies at the intersection of *IS* and LM^2 (point *F*), where output rises to Y_2 and the real interest rate falls to r_2.

Because the *IS–LM* intersection at point *F* is to the right of the *FE* line, aggregate output demanded, Y_2, is greater than the full-employment level of output, $\overline{Y}$. Monopolistically competitive firms facing menu costs don't raise their prices in the short run, as competitive firms do. Instead they increase production to Y_2 to satisfy the higher level of demand. To increase production, firms raise employment—for example, by hiring additional workers or by having employees work overtime. The level of employment is given by the effective labor demand curve in Fig. 11.4(b). Because the level of output increases from $\overline{Y}$ to Y_2 in the short run, the level of employment increases from $\overline{N}$ to N_2.

We refer to a monetary policy that shifts the *LM* curve down and to the right—and thus increases output and employment—as an expansionary monetary policy, or "easy" money. Analogously, a contractionary monetary policy, or "tight" money, is a decrease in the money supply that shifts the *LM* curve up and to the left, decreasing output and employment.

Why does easy money increase output in the Keynesian model? In the Keynesian model, prices are fixed in the short run, so an increase in the nominal money supply, M, also is an increase in the real money supply, M/P. Recall that, for holders of wealth to be willing to hold more real money, and a correspondingly smaller amount of nonmonetary assets, the real interest rate must fall.[13] Finally, the lower real interest rate increases both consumption spending (because saving falls) and investment spending. With more demand for their output, firms increase production and employment, taking the economy to point *F* in Fig. 11.4.

---

[13]As discussed in Chapter 9, the real interest rate is driven down by wealth-holders' attempts to exchange money for nonmonetary assets. The purchase of nonmonetary assets drives up their prices, which is the same as decreasing the real interest rate that they pay.

Figure 11.4

An increase in the money supply

(a) If we start from an initial general equilibrium at point E, an increase in the money supply shifts the LM curve down and to the right, from LM^1 to LM^2; the IS curve and the FE line remain unchanged. Because prices are fixed and firms meet the demand for output in the short run, the economy moves to point F, which is to the right of the FE line. Output rises to Y_2 and the real interest rate falls.

(b) Because firms produce more output, employment rises to N_2, as shown by the effective labor demand curve. In the long run, the price level rises in the same proportion as the money supply, the real money supply returns to its initial level, and the LM curve returns to its initial position, LM^1, in (a). The economy returns to E in both (a) and (b), and money is neutral in the long run.

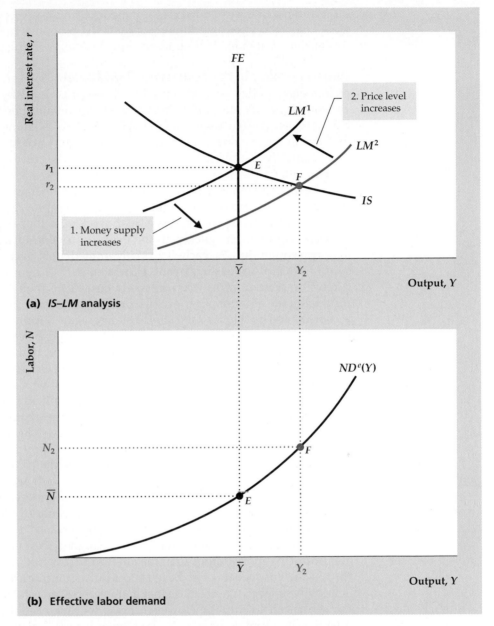

(a) *IS–LM* analysis

(b) Effective labor demand

The rigidity of the price level isn't permanent. Eventually, firms will review and readjust their prices, allowing the economy to reach its long-run equilibrium. In the case of monetary expansion, firms find that demand for their products in the short run is greater than they had planned (aggregate output demanded, Y_2, is greater than full-employment output, $\overline{Y}$), so eventually they raise their prices. The rise in the price level returns the real money supply to its initial level, which shifts the LM curve back to LM^1 and restores the general equilibrium at point E in Fig. 11.4(a). This adjustment process is exactly the same as in the classical model, but it proceeds more slowly.

Thus, the Keynesian model predicts that *money is not neutral in the short run but is neutral in the long run*. In this respect the predictions of the Keynesian model are the same as those of the extended classical model with misperceptions. In the Keynesian model, short-run price stickiness prevents the economy from reaching its general equilibrium, but in the long run prices are flexible, ensuring general equilibrium.

Monetary Policy in the Keynesian *AD–AS* Model.   We can also analyze the effect of monetary policy on real output and the price level by using the Keynesian version of the *AD–AS* model. In fact, we have already performed this analysis in Fig. 9.14, where we used the *AD–AS* model to examine the effects of a 10% increase in the nominal money supply. Although we didn't identify that analysis as specifically Keynesian or classical, it can be readily given a Keynesian interpretation.

The distinguishing feature that determines whether an analysis is Keynesian or classical is the speed of price adjustment. As we emphasized in Chapter 10, classical economists argue that prices adjust quickly so that the economy reaches its long-run equilibrium quickly. In the extreme version of the classical model, the long-run equilibrium is reached virtually immediately, and the short-run aggregate supply (*SRAS*) curve is irrelevant. However, in the Keynesian model, monopolistically competitive firms that face menu costs keep their prices fixed for a while, producing the amount of output demanded at the fixed price level. This behavior is represented by a horizontal short-run aggregate supply curve such as $SRAS^1$ in Fig. 9.14. If we assume that firms maintain fixed prices and simply meet the demand for output for a substantial period of time, so that the departure from long-run equilibrium lasts for months or perhaps even years, the analysis illustrated in Fig. 9.14 reflects the Keynesian approach.

Let's briefly review that analysis from an explicitly Keynesian perspective. Figure 9.14 depicts the effects of a 10% increase in the nominal money supply on an economy that is initially in both short-run and long-run equilibrium (at point *E*). The increase in the nominal money supply causes the *AD* curve to shift up from AD^1 to AD^2. In fact, as we explained in Chapter 9, the 10% increase in the nominal money supply shifts the *AD* curve up by 10% at each level of output. The initial effect of this shift in the *AD* curve is to move the economy to a short-run equilibrium at point *F*, where output is higher than its full-employment level, $\overline{Y}$. Because of menu costs, firms don't immediately react to increased demand by raising prices, but instead increase production to meet the higher demand. Thus, at point *F*, firms are producing more output than the amount that would maximize their profits in the absence of menu costs. Because output is temporarily higher than its full-employment level, we conclude that in the Keynesian model money isn't neutral in the short run. Eventually, however, firms will increase their prices to bring the quantity of output demanded back to the profit-maximizing level of output. In the long-run equilibrium, represented by point *H* in Fig. 9.14, output equals the full-employment level, $\overline{Y}$, and the price level, P_2, is 10% higher than the initial price level, P_1. In long-run equilibrium the expansion of the money supply affects only nominal quantities, such as the price level, not real quantities, such as output or employment, so we conclude that in the Keynesian model (as in the classical model) money is neutral in the long run.

Fiscal Policy

The Keynesian model was initially developed during the Great Depression as economists struggled to explain the worldwide economic collapse and find policies to help the economy return to normal. The early Keynesians stressed that fiscal policy—the government's decisions about government purchases and taxes—can significantly affect output and employment levels. Let's look at the Keynesians' conclusion that both increased government purchases and lower taxes can be used to raise output and employment.

The Effect of Increased Government Purchases. The Keynesian analysis of how increased government purchases affect the economy is shown in Fig. 11.5. Again, we assume that the economy starts from full employment (later we discuss what happens if the economy starts from a recession). Point E represents the initial equilibrium in both (a) and (b). As before, a temporary increase in government purchases increases the demand for goods and reduces desired national saving at any level of the real interest rate, so that the IS curve shifts up and to the right, from IS^1 to IS^2 (see Summary table 12, p. 315). In the short run, before prices can adjust, the economy moves to point F in Fig. 11.5(a), where the new IS curve, IS^2, and LM^1 intersect. At F both output and the real interest rate have increased. Because firms meet the higher demand at the fixed price level, employment also rises, as shown by the movement from point E to point F along the effective labor demand curve in Fig. 11.5(b). A fiscal policy change, such as this one, that shifts the IS curve up and to the right and raises output and employment is an expansionary change. Similarly, a fiscal policy change (such as a reduction in government purchases) that shifts the IS curve down and to the left and reduces output and employment is a contractionary change.

In discussing the effects of increased government purchases or other types of spending, Keynesians often use the multiplier concept. The **multiplier** associated with any particular type of spending is the short-run change in total output resulting from a one-unit change in that type of spending. So, for example, if the increase in government purchases analyzed in Fig. 11.5 is ΔG and the resulting short-run increase in output between points E and F in Fig. 11.5 is ΔY, the multiplier associated with government purchases is $\Delta Y / \Delta G$. Keynesians usually argue that the fiscal policy multiplier is greater than 1, so that if government purchases rise by \$1 billion, output will rise by more than \$1 billion. We derive an algebraic expression for the government purchases multiplier in Appendix 11.C.

Recall that the classical version of the IS–LM model also predicts that a temporary increase in government purchases increases output, but in a different way. The classical analysis focuses on the fact that increased government purchases require higher current or future taxes to pay for the extra spending. Higher taxes make workers (who are taxpayers) effectively poorer, which induces them to supply more labor. This increase in labor supply shifts the FE line to the right and causes output to rise in the classical model. In contrast, the FE line in the Keynesian model doesn't depend on labor supply (because of efficiency wages) and thus is unaffected by the increase in government purchases. Instead, the increase in government purchases affects output by raising aggregate demand (that is, by shifting the IS–LM intersection to the right). Output increases above its full-employment level in the short run as firms satisfy extra demand at the initial price level.

The effect of increased government purchases on output in the Keynesian model lasts only as long as needed for the price level to adjust. (However, many Keynesians believe that price adjustment is sufficiently slow that this effect could be felt for several years.) In the long run, when firms adjust their prices, the LM curve moves up and to the left, from LM^1 to LM^2 in Fig. 11.5(a), and the economy

Figure 11.5

An increase in government purchases
(a) If we start from the general equilibrium at point E, an increase in government purchases reduces desired national saving and shifts the IS curve up and to the right, from IS^1 to IS^2. The short-run equilibrium is at point F, with output increasing to Y_2 and the real interest rate rising to r_2.
(b) As firms increase production to meet the demand, employment increases from $\overline{N}$ to N_2, as shown by the effective labor demand curve. However, the economy doesn't remain at point F. Because aggregate output demanded exceeds $\overline{Y}$ in the short run, the price level increases, reducing the real money supply and shifting the LM curve up and to the left, from LM^1 to LM^2. In the long run, with equilibrium at point H, output returns to $\overline{Y}$ and employment returns to $\overline{N}$, but the real interest rate rises further to r_3.

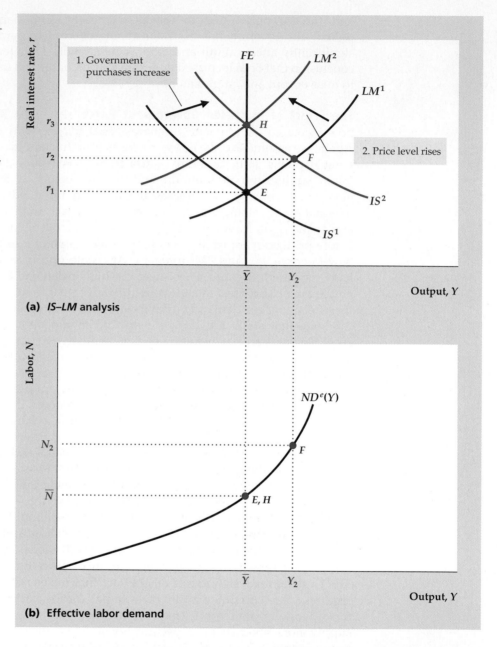

(a) *IS–LM* analysis

(b) Effective labor demand

reaches general equilibrium at point H, with output again at $\overline{Y}$. Thus an increase in government purchases doesn't raise output in the long run.

The effects of more government purchases also appear in the Keynesian AD–AS framework (Fig. 11.6). Increased government purchases shift the IS curve up and to the right and raise the aggregate demand for output at any given price level. Thus, as a result of expansionary fiscal policy, the aggregate demand curve shifts to the right, from AD^1 to AD^2. The increase in aggregate demand raises output above $\overline{Y}$, as shown by the shift from the initial equilibrium at point E to the short-run equilibrium at point F. At F the aggregate demand for output is greater than full-employment output, so firms eventually raise their prices. In the long run

Figure 11.6

An increase in government purchases in the Keynesian *AD–AS* framework

An increase in government purchases raises aggregate demand for output at any price level (see Fig. 11.5). Thus the aggregate demand curve shifts to the right, from AD^1 to AD^2. In the short run the increase in aggregate demand increases output to Y_2 (point F) but doesn't affect the price level, because prices are sticky in the short run. Because aggregate output demanded, Y_2, exceeds $\overline{Y}$ at F, firms eventually raise their prices. The long-run equilibrium is at H, where AD^2 intersects the $LRAS$ curve. At H, output has returned to $\overline{Y}$ and the price level has risen from P_1 to P_2. The higher price level raises the short-run aggregate supply curve, from $SRAS^1$ to $SRAS^2$.

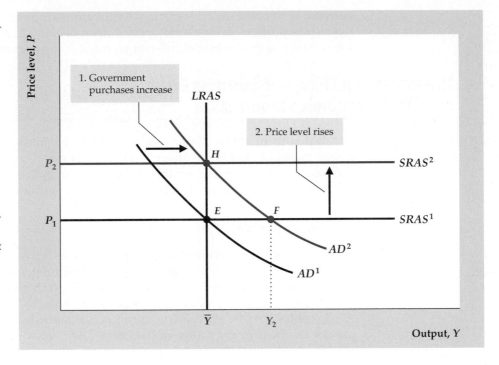

the economy reaches the full-employment general equilibrium at point H, with output again at $\overline{Y}$ and with a higher price level. These results are identical to those we obtained using the Keynesian *IS–LM* framework.

The Effect of Lower Taxes.   Keynesians generally believe that, like an increase in government purchases, a lump-sum reduction in current taxes is expansionary. In other words, they expect that a tax cut will shift the *IS* curve up and to the right, raising output and employment in the short run. Similarly, they expect a tax increase to be contractionary, shifting the *IS* curve down and to the left.

Why does a tax cut affect the *IS* curve, according to Keynesians? The argument is that if consumers receive a tax cut, they will spend part of it on increased consumption. For any output, Y, and level of government purchases, G, an increase in desired consumption arising from a tax cut will lower desired national saving, $Y-C^d-G$. A drop in desired saving raises the real interest rate that clears the goods market and shifts the *IS* curve up.[14]

If a tax cut raises desired consumption and shifts the *IS* curve up, as Keynesians claim, the effects on the economy are similar to the effects of increased government purchases (Figs. 11.5 and 11.6). In the short run, a tax cut raises aggregate demand and thus output and employment at the initial price level. In the long run, after complete price adjustment, the economy returns to full employment with a higher real interest rate than in the initial general equilibrium. The only difference

---

[14]In arguing that a tax cut raises desired consumption and lowers desired national saving, Keynesian economists reject the Ricardian equivalence proposition (Chapter 4), which states that a lump-sum tax cut should *not* affect consumption or national saving. We discuss Ricardian equivalence further in Chapter 15.

between the tax cut and the increase in government purchases is that, instead of raising the portion of full-employment output devoted to government purchases, a tax cut raises the portion of full-employment output devoted to consumption.

11.4 The Keynesian Theory of Business Cycles and Macroeconomic Stabilization

Recall that there are two basic questions about business cycles that a macroeconomic theory should try to answer: (1) What causes recurrent fluctuations in the economy? and (2) What, if anything, should policymakers try to do about cycles? We are now ready to give the Keynesian answers to these two questions.

Keynesian Business Cycle Theory

An explanation of the business cycle requires not only a macroeconomic model but also some assumptions about the types of shocks hitting the economy. For example, RBC economists believe that productivity shocks, which directly shift the *FE* line, are the most important type of macroeconomic shock.

In contrast to RBC economists, most Keynesians believe that aggregate demand shocks are the primary source of business cycle fluctuations. **Aggregate demand shocks** are shocks to the economy that shift *either* the *IS* curve or the *LM* curve and thus affect the aggregate demand for output. Examples of aggregate demand shocks affecting the *IS* curve are changes in fiscal policy, changes in desired investment arising from changes in the expected future marginal product of capital,[15] and changes in consumer confidence about the future that affect desired saving. Examples of aggregate demand shocks affecting the *LM* curve are changes in the demand for money or changes in the money supply. The Keynesian version of the *IS–LM* model, combined with the view that most shocks are aggregate demand shocks, constitutes the Keynesian theory of business cycles.

Figure 11.7 uses the Keynesian model to illustrate a recession caused by an aggregate demand shock. Suppose that consumers become pessimistic about the long-term future of the economy and thus reduce their current desired consumption; equivalently, they raise their current desired saving. For any level of income, an increase in desired saving lowers the real interest rate that clears the goods market and thus shifts the *IS* curve down, from IS^1 to IS^2. The economy goes into recession at point *F,* and, as prices don't adjust immediately to restore full employment, it remains in recession for some period of time with output below its full-employment level. Because firms face below-normal levels of demand, they also cut employment.

Note that a decline in investment spending (reflecting, for example, pessimism of business investors) or reduced government purchases would have similar recessionary effects as the decline in consumer spending analyzed in Fig. 11.7. Alternatively, a shift up and to the left of the *LM* curve (because of either increased money demand or reduced money supply) also could cause a recession in the Keynesian

---

[15]A change in the expected future *MPK* might also be thought of as a technological shock because it involves a change in the future production function. However, because a change in the future *MPK* shifts the *IS* curve but doesn't affect the current *FE* line, Keynesians classify it as an aggregate demand shock.

Figure 11.7

A recession arising from an aggregate demand shock
The figure illustrates how an adverse aggregate demand shock can cause a recession in the Keynesian model. The economy starts at general equilibrium at point E. A decline in consumer confidence about the future of the economy reduces desired consumption and raises desired saving so that the IS curve shifts down, from IS^1 to IS^2. The economy falls into recession at point F, with output below its full-employment level, $\bar{Y}$.

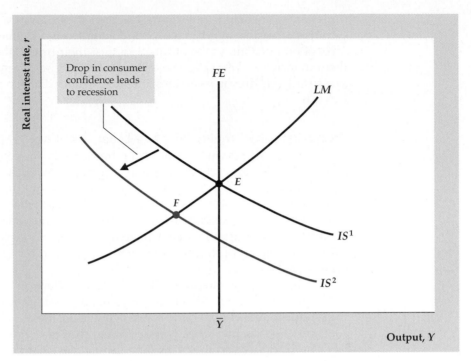

framework; in this case, high real interest rates caused by the "shortage" of money would cause the declines in consumer spending and investment. Thus Keynesians attribute recessions to "not enough demand" for goods, in contrast to classical economists who attribute recessions to "not enough supply."

Like the real business cycle theory, the Keynesian theory of cycles can account for several of the business cycle facts: (1) in response to occasional aggregate demand shocks, the theory predicts recurrent fluctuations in output; (2) the theory correctly implies that employment will fluctuate in the same direction as output; and (3) because it predicts that shocks to the money supply will be nonneutral, the theory is consistent with the business cycle fact that money is procyclical and leading.

A business cycle fact that we previously emphasized (Chapter 8) is that spending on investment goods and other durable goods is strongly procyclical and volatile. This cyclical behavior of durable goods spending can be explained by the Keynesian theory if shocks to durable goods demand are themselves a main source of cycles. The demand for durable goods would be a source of cyclical fluctuations if, for example, investors frequently reassessed their expectations of the future MPK. Keynes himself thought that waves of investor optimism and pessimism, which he called "animal spirits," were a significant source of cyclical fluctuations. A rise in the demand for investment goods or consumer durables (at fixed levels of output and the real interest rate) is expansionary because it shifts the IS curve up and to the right. Investment will also be procyclical in the Keynesian model whenever cycles are caused by fluctuations in the LM curve; for example, an increase in the money supply that shifts the LM curve down and to the right both increases output and (by reducing the real interest rate) increases investment.

Another important business cycle fact that is consistent with the Keynesian theory is the observation that inflation tends to slow during or just after recessions (inflation is procyclical and lagging). In the Keynesian view, as Fig. 11.7 illustrates, during a recession, aggregate output demanded is less than the full-employment level of output. Thus, when firms do adjust their prices, they will be likely to cut them to increase their sales. According to the Keynesian model, because demand pressure is low during recessions, inflation will tend to subside when the economy is weak.

Procyclical Labor Productivity and Labor Hoarding.   Although the Keynesian model is consistent with many of the business cycle facts, one fact—that labor productivity is procyclical—presents problems for this approach. Recall that procyclical labor productivity is consistent with the real business cycle assumption that cycles are caused by productivity shocks—that recessions are times when productivity is unusually low and booms are times when productivity is unusually high. Unlike the RBC economists, however, Keynesians assume that demand shocks rather than supply (productivity) shocks cause most cyclical fluctuations.

Because supply shocks are shifts of the production function, the Keynesian assumption that supply shocks usually are unimportant is the same as saying that the production function is fairly stable over the business cycle. But if the production function is stable, increases in employment during booms should *reduce* average labor productivity because of the diminishing marginal productivity of labor. Thus the Keynesian model predicts that average labor productivity is countercyclical, contrary to the business cycle fact.

To explain the procyclical behavior of average labor productivity, Keynesians have modified their models to include labor hoarding. As discussed in Section 10.1, labor hoarding occurs if firms retain, or "hoard," labor in a recession rather than laying off or firing workers. The reason that firms might hoard labor during a recession is to avoid the costs of letting workers go and then having to rehire them or hire and train new workers when the recession ends. Thus hoarded labor may be used less intensively (for example, store clerks may wait on fewer customers in a day) or be assigned to activities such as painting, cleaning, maintaining equipment, and training. If labor is utilized less intensively during a recession, or workers spend time on activities such as maintenance that don't directly contribute to measured output, labor productivity may fall during a recession even though the production function is stable. Thus labor hoarding provides a way of explaining the procyclical behavior of average labor productivity without assuming that recessions and expansions are caused by productivity shocks.

Macroeconomic Stabilization

From the Keynesian explanation of why business cycles occur, we turn to the Keynesian view on how policymakers should respond to recessions and booms. Briefly, Keynesians—unlike classical economists—generally favor policy actions to "stabilize" the economy by eliminating large fluctuations in output and employment. Keynesian support of more active policy measures follows from the theory's characterization of business cycle expansions and contractions as periods in which the economy is temporarily away from its general equilibrium (or not at the *IS–LM–FE* intersection). According to Keynesians, recessions are particularly undesirable because in a recession, employment may be far below the amount of labor that

Figure 11.8

Stabilization policy in the Keynesian model
From point E the economy is driven into a recession at point F by a drop in consumer confidence and spending, which shifts the IS curve down, from IS^1 to IS^2. If the government took no action, in the long run price adjustment would shift the LM curve from LM^1 to LM^2 and restore general equilibrium at point H (Scenario 1).

Alternatively, the government could try to offset the recession through stabilization policy. For example, the Fed could increase the money supply, which would shift the LM curve directly from LM^1 to LM^2, speeding the recovery in output (Scenario 2).

Another possibility is a fiscal expansion, such as an increase in government purchases, which would shift the IS curve from IS^2 back to IS^1, again restoring full employment at E (Scenario 3).

Compared to a strategy of doing nothing, expansionary monetary or fiscal policy helps the economy recover more quickly but leads to a higher price level in the long run.

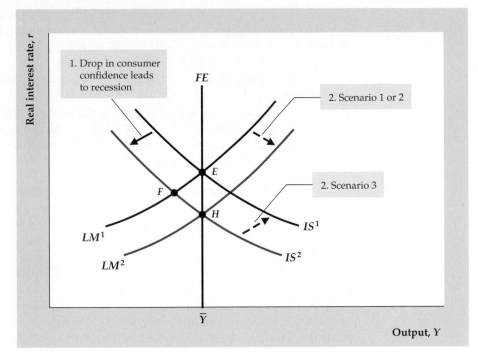

workers want to supply, which leads to hardships for the unemployed and to output that is "too low." Keynesians therefore argue that average economic well-being would be increased if governments tried to reduce cyclical fluctuations, especially recessions.

The Keynesian analysis of monetary and fiscal policies suggests that these policies could be used to smooth the business cycle. To understand how, consider Fig. 11.8. Suppose that the economy, initially in general equilibrium at point E, has been driven into recession at point F. Various types of shocks could have caused this recession. In Fig. 11.7, for example, we considered a drop in consumer confidence about the future of the economy. A drop in confidence would reduce current desired consumption and increase current desired saving, thereby shifting the IS curve down from IS^1 to IS^2. This sort of change in consumer attitudes may have contributed to the 1990–1991 recession.

How might policymakers respond to this recession? We consider three possible scenarios: (1) no change in monetary or fiscal policy; (2) an increase in the money supply; and (3) an increase in government purchases.

■ *Scenario 1: No change in macroeconomic policy.* One policy option is to do nothing. With no government intervention, the economy eventually will correct itself. At point F in Fig. 11.8, aggregate output demanded is below the full-employment level of output $\overline{Y}$. Therefore, over time, prices will begin to fall, increasing the real money supply and shifting the LM curve down and to the right. In the long run, price declines shift the LM curve from LM^1 to LM^2, restoring the economy to general equilibrium at point H. However, a disadvantage of this strategy is that, during the (possibly lengthy) price adjustment process, output and employment remain below their full-employment levels.

■ *Scenario 2: An increase in the money supply.* Instead of waiting for the economy to reach general equilibrium through price adjustment, the Fed could increase the money supply, which also would shift the *LM* curve from LM^1 to LM^2 in Fig. 11.8. If prices adjust slowly, this expansionary policy would move the economy to general equilibrium at point *H* more quickly than would doing nothing.

■ *Scenario 3: An increase in government purchases.* An alternative policy of raising government purchases will shift the *IS* curve up and to the right, from IS^2 to IS^1. This policy also takes the economy to full employment, although at point *E* in Fig. 11.8 rather than at point *H*.

In all three scenarios, the economy eventually returns to full employment. However, the use of monetary or fiscal policy to achieve full employment leads to two important differences from the scenario in which no policy action is taken. First, if the government uses monetary or fiscal expansion to end the recession, the economy returns directly to full employment; if policy isn't changed, the economy remains in recession in the short run, returning to full employment only when prices have fully adjusted. Second, if there is no policy change (Scenario 1), in the long run the price level falls relative to the nominal money supply. Indeed, the drop in the price level relative to the money supply increases the real money supply, shifts the *LM* curve down and to the right, and restores full employment at point *H*. In contrast, when monetary or fiscal policy is used to restore full employment (Scenarios 2 and 3), the downward adjustment of the price level doesn't occur because expansionary policy directly returns aggregate demand to the full-employment level. Thus, according to the Keynesian analysis, using expansionary monetary or fiscal policy has the advantage of bringing the economy back to full employment more quickly but the disadvantage of leading to a higher price level than if no policy action is undertaken.

Usually, either monetary or fiscal policy can be used to bring the economy back to full employment. Does it matter which policy is used? Yes, there is at least one basic difference between the outcomes of the two policies: Monetary and fiscal policies affect the composition of spending (the amount of output that is devoted to consumption, the amount to investment, and so on) differently. In Fig. 11.8, although total output is the same at the alternative general equilibrium points *E* and *H*, at *E* (reached by an increase in government purchases) government purchases are higher than at *H* (reached by an increase in the money supply). Because government purchases are higher at *E*, the remaining components of spending—in a closed economy, consumption and investment—must be lower at *E* than at *H*. Relative to a monetary expansion, an increase in government purchases crowds out consumption and investment by raising the real interest rate, which is higher at *E* than at *H*. In addition, increased government purchases imply higher current or future tax burdens, which also reduces consumption relative to what it would be with monetary expansion.

Difficulties of Macroeconomic Stabilization. The use of monetary and fiscal policies to smooth or moderate the business cycle is called **macroeconomic stabilization.** Using macroeconomic policies to try to smooth the cycle is also sometimes called **aggregate demand management** because monetary and fiscal policies shift the aggregate demand curve. Macroeconomic stabilization was a popular concept in the heyday of Keynesian economics in the 1960s, and it still influences policy discussions. Unfortunately, even putting aside the debates between classicals and Keynesians about whether smoothing the business cycle is desirable, actual macroeconomic stabilization has been much less successful than the simple Keynesian theory suggests.

As discussed earlier in connection with fiscal policy (Section 10.1), attempts to stabilize the economy run into some technical problems. First, because the ability to measure and analyze the economy is imperfect, gauging how far the economy is from full employment at any particular time is difficult. Second, the amount that output will increase in response to a monetary or fiscal expansion isn't known exactly. These uncertainties make assessing how much of a monetary or fiscal change is needed to restore full employment difficult. Finally, even knowing the size of the policy change needed still wouldn't provide enough information. Because macroeconomic policies take time to implement and more time to affect the economy, their optimal use requires knowledge of where the economy will be six months or a year from now. But such knowledge is, at best, very imprecise.

Because of these problems, aggregate demand management has been likened to trying to hit a moving target in a heavy fog. These problems haven't persuaded most Keynesians to abandon stabilization policy; however, many Keynesians agree that policymakers should concentrate on fighting major recessions and not try to fine-tune the economy by smoothing every bump and wiggle in output and employment.

Supply Shocks in the Keynesian Model

Until the 1970s, the Keynesian business cycle theory focused almost exclusively on aggregate demand shocks as the source of business cycle fluctuations. Because aggregate demand shocks lead to procyclical movements in inflation, however, the Keynesian theory failed to account for the stagflation—high inflation together with a recession—that hit the U.S. economy following the 1973–1975 oil price shock.

This experience led to much criticism of the traditional theory by both economists and policymakers, so Keynesians recast the theory to allow for both supply and demand shocks. Although Keynesians wouldn't go so far as to agree with RBC economists that supply (productivity) shocks are a factor in most recessions, they now concede that there have been occasional episodes—the oil price shocks of the 1970s being the leading examples—in which supply shocks have played a primary role in an economic downturn. (See "In Touch with Data and Research: DSGE Models and the Classical–Keynesian Debate," p. 427, for further discussion of agreement and disagreement between Keynesians and classicals.)

Figure 11.9 shows a Keynesian analysis of the effects of a sharp temporary increase in the price of oil (a similar analysis would apply to other supply shocks, such as a drought). As we showed in Chapter 3, if firms respond to an increase in the price of oil by using less energy, the amount of output that can be produced with the same amount of capital and labor falls. Thus the increase in the price of oil is an adverse supply shock, which reduces the full-employment level of output and shifts the FE line to the left, from FE^1 to FE^2. After complete wage and price adjustment, which occurs virtually immediately in the basic classical model but only in the long run in the Keynesian model, output falls to its new full-employment level, $\overline{Y}_2$. Thus, in the long run (after full wage and price adjustment), the Keynesian analysis and the classical analysis of a supply shock are the same.

Figure 11.9

An oil price shock in the Keynesian model

An increase in the price of oil is an adverse supply shock that reduces full-employment output from $\overline{Y}_1$ to $\overline{Y}_2$ and thus shifts the FE line to the left. In addition, the increase in the price of oil increases prices in sectors that depend heavily on oil, whereas prices in other sectors remain fixed in the short run. Thus the average price level rises, which reduces the real money supply, M/P, and shifts the LM curve up and to the left, from LM^1 to LM^2. In the short run, the economy moves to point F, with output falling below the new, lower value of full-employment output and the real interest rate increasing. Because the aggregate quantity of goods demanded at F is less than the full-employment level of output, $\overline{Y}_2$, in the long run the price level falls, partially offsetting the initial increase in prices. The drop in the price level causes the LM curve to shift down and to the right, from LM^2 to LM^3, moving the economy to full-employment equilibrium at point H.

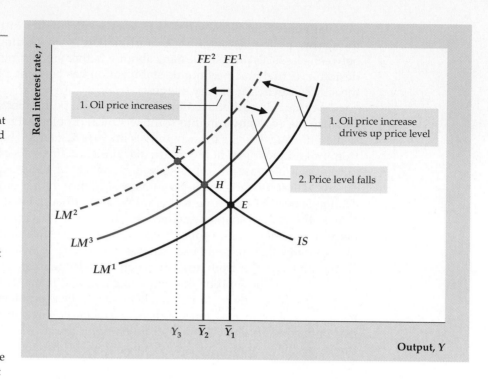

However, the Keynesian analysis of the short-run effects of an oil price shock is slightly different from the classical analysis. To understand the short-term effects of the oil price shock in the Keynesian model, first think about the effects of the increase in the oil price on the general price level. Recall that firms facing menu costs will not change their prices if the "right" prices are only a little different from the preset prices. However, if the right prices are substantially different from the preset prices, so that firms would lose considerable profits by maintaining the preset prices, they will change their prices. In the case of a large increase in the price of oil, firms whose costs are strongly affected by the price of oil—including gas stations, suppliers of home heating oil, and airlines, for example—find that the right prices for their products are substantially higher than the preset prices. These oil-dependent firms increase their prices quickly, whereas firms in other sectors maintain their preset prices in the short run. Thus there is price stickiness in the sense that not all prices adjust to their equilibrium values, and yet the average price level rises in the short run.

Because a sharp increase in the price of oil raises the price level, P, in the short run, it also reduces the real money supply, M/P. A decline in the real money supply shifts the LM curve up and to the left, from LM^1 to LM^2 in Fig. 11.9. As drawn, the intersection of the LM curve and the IS curve is located to the left of the new FE line, although this outcome isn't logically necessary. The short-run equilibrium is at point F, where LM^2 intersects the IS curve. Because F is to the left of the FE line, the economy is in a recession at F, with output (at Y_3) below the new value of full-employment output, $\overline{Y}_2$. In the short run, the economy experiences stagflation, with both a drop in output and a burst of inflation. Note that, according to this analysis, the short-run decline in output has two components: (1) the drop in full-employment output from $\overline{Y}_1$ to $\overline{Y}_2$; and (2) the drop in output below the new

IN TOUCH WITH DATA AND RESEARCH

DSGE Models and the Classical–Keynesian Debate

In Chapters 10 and 11, we have compared and contrasted the classical and Keynesian approaches to analyzing the business cycle and to determining stabilization policy. For many years, classical and Keynesian economists pursued research on business cycles and stabilization policy using very different types of models, and they argued about the data using very different empirical methods. As a result, communication between the two groups was difficult.

However, in the past decade, some classical economists have been incorporating Keynesian ideas into their models, and some Keynesian economists have been incorporating classical ideas into their models. Many young economists coming from top Ph.D. programs have been well trained in dynamic, stochastic, general equilibrium (DSGE) models, which we discussed briefly in Chapter 10. Roughly speaking, those models use techniques that were developed by classical RBC economists in the 1980s and 1990s, so many Keynesian economists have adopted classical methods of analysis. But many of the models, even those used by classical economists, incorporate Keynesian features, especially sticky prices (but not usually efficiency wages) and imperfect competition among firms. As a result, classical and Keynesian economists are now speaking the same language and can communicate with each other more clearly, and research on macroeconomic ideas is advancing more easily.

One fundamental area of difference between classical and Keynesian economists had always been the degree to which a model incorporated microeconomic foundations. Many classical economists, especially after ideas about rational expectations came to the forefront in the early 1980s, believed that good models could be developed only by modeling microeconomic foundations, which means showing how households choose labor supply and consumption spending to maximize their own welfare, how firms chose labor demand and investment spending to maximize their own profits, and so on. Keynesian economists, however, often believed that the attempt to find microeconomic foundations was unlikely to be fruitful, and instead they focused on large-scale macroeconomic models that were based on demand curves and supply curves of aggregates rather than worrying about individual decision making. The result was that classical economists thought Keynesian models were both wrong and worthless, and Keynesians thought the same of classical models. After decades of fighting over the right type of modeling to perform (some of which continues), some researchers found ways to reconcile the two approaches.* The basic idea was to show under what circumstances the Keynesian-type model with a few equations describing behavior was consistent with a classical model containing detailed microeconomic foundations. This research helped to reconcile the classical and Keynesian approaches, even though it did not convince everyone on both sides.

However, despite the gains that have been made in the past decade, classicals and Keynesians still differ in some fundamental ways. Keynesians tend to believe that prices and wages are slow to adjust, while classicals think they adjust faster. Keynesians tend to have more faith that government policy actions can improve people's welfare, while classical economists often think just the opposite—that many government policies make people worse off, especially when it comes to attempts to stabilize the business cycle. But at least the two sides now are speaking to each other.

---

*See, for example, Michael Woodford, *Interest and Prices: Foundations of a Theory of Monetary Policy* (Princeton, N.J.: Princeton University Press, 2003).

full-employment level arising from the shift up and to the left of the *LM* curve (the difference between $\overline{Y}_2$ and Y_3).

Supply shocks of the type analyzed in Fig. 11.9 pose tremendous difficulties for Keynesian stabilization policies. First, monetary or fiscal policy can do little about the portion of the decline in output resulting from the shift of the *FE* line; attempts to expand the economy beyond the new full-employment output level, $\overline{Y}_2$, will increase output only temporarily and worsen inflation. In contrast, the portion of the output decline arising from the shift up and to the left of the *LM* curve (the difference between $\overline{Y}_2$ and Y_3) represents an output level below the full-employment level and could, in principle, be eliminated by expansionary monetary or fiscal policies that raise output to $\overline{Y}_2$. However, by using expansionary policies at point *F*, rather than doing nothing, the government risks worsening the already-high rate of inflation. Hence, in the face of a shock that induces stagflation like the one shown in Fig. 11.9, macroeconomic policy can neither avoid a sharp decline in output nor restore output even to its new, lower full-employment level without potentially worsening inflation.

CHAPTER SUMMARY

1. Keynesians are skeptical that a mismatch between workers and jobs can explain all unemployment. They argue that some unemployment is caused by real wages that are rigid and above the level at which the quantities of labor demanded and supplied are equal.

2. One explanation for real-wage rigidity is based on the efficiency wage model, which assumes that workers work harder in response to an increase in the real wage. Firms can attain the highest level of profit by paying the real wage, known as the efficiency wage, that elicits the most worker effort per dollar of wages. If the effort curve relating effort provided by workers to the real wage doesn't change, the efficiency wage, and hence the real wage actually paid, is rigid.

3. At the efficiency wage, firms demand the level of employment, $\overline{N}$, at which the marginal product of labor equals the efficiency wage. If the efficiency wage is above the market-clearing real wage, employment is determined by labor demand. The difference between the quantity of labor supplied and the quantity of labor demanded at the efficiency wage represents unemployment.

4. Full-employment output, $\overline{Y}$, is the output that can be produced when employment is at its full-employment level, $\overline{N}$, and worker effort is at the level induced by the efficiency wage. The *FE* line in the Keynesian *IS–LM* model is vertical where output equals its full-employment level. In the Keynesian model, full-employment output and the *FE* line are affected by productivity shocks but not by changes in labor supply because changes in labor supply don't affect employment in the efficiency wage model.

5. Keynesians attribute the nonneutrality of money to price stickiness, which means that some firms may not change their prices in the short run even though the demand for or supply of their product has changed. Price stickiness is contrary to the assumption of the basic classical model that prices and wages are completely flexible.

6. Price stickiness can arise from the profit-maximizing behavior of monopolistically competitive firms that face menu costs, or costs of changing prices. Such firms are price setters rather than price takers, and once they set their prices they meet customer demand at that fixed price. These firms readjust prices only occasionally, generally when costs or demand have changed significantly.

7. In the Keynesian model with sticky prices, output is determined in the short run at the intersection of the *IS* and *LM* curves. The economy can be off the *FE* line in the short run because firms are willing to meet demand at predetermined prices. The level of employment in the short run is given by the effective labor demand curve, which shows the amount of labor needed to produce any given amount of output. In the long run, after prices and wages have completely adjusted, the *LM* curve moves to restore general equilibrium with full employment.

8. The short-run and long-run equilibria in the Keynesian model can also be analyzed with the *AD–AS* model. The short-run equilibrium is represented by the intersection of the downward-sloping aggregate demand (*AD*) curve and the horizontal short-run aggregate supply (*SRAS*) curve. In short-run equilibrium, monopolistically competitive firms produce

whatever level of output is demanded at the fixed price level. Eventually, however, the price level adjusts and the economy reaches its long-run equilibrium, represented by the intersection of the AD curve and the vertical long-run aggregate supply ($LRAS$) curve. In long-run equilibrium, output equals its full-employment level, $\overline{Y}$.

9. In the Keynesian model, an increase in the money supply shifts the LM curve down and to the right, raising output and lowering the real interest rate in the short run. Thus money isn't neutral in the short run. In the long run, however, money is neutral; monetary expansion raises the price level proportionally but has no real effects.

10. In the Keynesian model, an increase in government purchases or a cut in taxes shifts the IS curve up and to the right, raising output and the real interest rate in the short run. In the long run, output returns to the full-employment level but the real interest rate increases. Fiscal policy isn't neutral in the long run because it affects the composition of output among consumption, investment, and government purchases.

11. Keynesians attribute most business cycles to aggregate demand shocks. These shocks hit the IS curve (changes in government purchases, desired consumption, or desired investment) or the LM curve (changes in money supply or money demand). Keynesian business cycle theory, which has traditionally emphasized the importance of aggregate demand shocks, can account for the procyclical behavior of employment, money, inflation, and investment. To explain the procyclical behavior of average labor productivity, the Keynesian theory must include the additional assumption that firms hoard labor—that is, they employ more workers than necessary during recessions.

12. Macroeconomic stabilization, also called aggregate demand management, is the use of monetary or fiscal policy to try to eliminate recessions and keep the economy at full employment. The Keynesian theory suggests that macroeconomic stabilization is both desirable and possible. However, practical problems include the difficulty of measuring and forecasting the state of the economy and determining how much monetary and fiscal stimulus is needed at any particular time. Keynesian antirecessionary policies also lead to a higher price level than would occur in the absence of policy changes.

13. Following the oil price shocks of the 1970s, the Keynesian theory was modified to allow for supply shocks. Supply shocks lead to stagflation (a combination of inflation and recession) and pose great difficulties for stabilization policy.

KEY TERMS

aggregate demand management, p. 424
aggregate demand shocks, p. 420
effective labor demand curve, p. 412
efficiency wage, p. 403
efficiency wage model, p. 401

effort curve, p. 402
macroeconomic stabilization, p. 424
marginal cost, p. 411
markup, p. 411
menu cost, p. 409
monopolistic competition, p. 408

multiplier, p. 417
perfect competition, p. 408
price stickiness, p. 407
real-wage rigidity, p. 400
turnover costs, p. 401

REVIEW QUESTIONS

All review questions are available in myeconlab at www.myeconlab.com.

1. Define *efficiency wage*. What assumption about worker behavior underlies the efficiency wage theory? Why does it predict that the real wage will remain rigid even if there is an excess supply of labor?

2. How is full-employment output, $\overline{Y}$, determined in the Keynesian model with efficiency wages? In this model, how is full-employment output affected by changes in productivity (supply shocks)? How is it affected by changes in labor supply?

3. What is price stickiness? Why do Keynesians believe that allowing for price stickiness in macroeconomic analysis is important?

4. Define *menu cost*. Why might small menu costs lead to price stickiness in monopolistically competitive markets but not in perfectly competitive markets? Why can a monopolistically competitive firm profitably meet

demand at its fixed price when actual demand is greater than the firm anticipated?

5. What does the Keynesian model predict about monetary neutrality (both in the short run and in the long run)? Compare the Keynesian predictions about neutrality with those of the basic classical model and the extended classical model with misperceptions.

6. In the Keynesian model, how do increased government purchases affect output and the real interest rate in the short run? In the long run? How do increased government purchases affect the composition of output in the long run?

7. Describe three alternative responses available to policymakers when the economy is in recession. What are the advantages and disadvantages of each strategy? Be sure

to discuss the effects on employment, the price level, and the composition of output. What are some of the practical difficulties in using macroeconomic stabilization policies to fight recessions?

8. Use the Keynesian model to explain the procyclical behavior of employment, money, inflation, and investment.

9. What does the Keynesian model predict about the cyclical behavior of average labor productivity? How does the idea of labor hoarding help bring the prediction of the model into conformity with the business cycle facts?

10. According to the Keynesian analysis, in what two ways does an adverse supply shock reduce output? What problems do supply shocks create for Keynesian stabilization policies?

NUMERICAL PROBLEMS

All numerical problems are available in **myeconlab** at www.myeconlab.com.

1. A firm identifies the following relationship between the real wage it pays and the effort exerted by its workers:

Real Wage	Effort
8	7
10	10
12	15
14	17
16	19
18	20

The marginal product of labor for this firm is

$$MPN = \frac{E(100 - N)}{15},$$

where E is the effort level and N is the number of workers employed. If the firm can pay only one of the six wage levels shown, which should it choose? How many workers will it employ?

There are 200 workers in the town where the firm is located, all willing to work at a real wage of 8. Does this fact change your answer to the first part of this question? If so, how?

2. An economy is described by the following equations:

Desired consumption	$C^d = 130 + 0.5(Y - T) - 500r.$
Desired investment	$I^d = 100 - 500r.$
Government purchases	$G = 100.$
Taxes	$T = 100.$
Real money demand	$L = 0.5Y - 1000r.$
Money supply	$M = 1320.$
Full-employment output	$\overline{Y} = 500.$

Assume that expected inflation is zero so that money demand depends directly on the real interest rate.

a. Write the equations for the IS and LM curves. (These equations express the relationship between r and Y when the goods and asset markets, respectively, are in equilibrium.)

b. Calculate the full-employment values of output, the real interest rate, the price level, consumption, and investment.

c. Suppose that, because of investor optimism about the future marginal product of capital, the investment function becomes

$$I^d = 200 - 500r.$$

Assuming that the economy was initially at full employment, what are the new values of output, the real interest rate, the price level, consumption, and investment in the short run? In the long run? Show your results graphically.

3. Consider the following Keynesian closed economy:

Consumption	$C = 388 + 0.4(Y - T) - 600r.$
Investment	$I = 352 - 400r.$
Government purchases	$G = 280.$
Taxes	$T = 300.$
Full-employment output	$\overline{Y} = 1400.$
Nominal money supply	$M = 12,600.$
Real money demand	$L = 1750 + 0.75Y$
	$\quad - 8750(r + \pi^e).$
Expected inflation	$\pi^e = 0.02.$

a. What is the equation of the IS curve?

b. Suppose that the price level is fixed at $P_{sr} = 7$ in the short run. What is the equation of the LM curve in the short run, while the price level remains fixed?

c. What are the short-run equilibrium values of output, the real interest rate, consumption, and investment?

d. What are the long-run equilibrium values of output, the real interest rate, consumption, investment, and the price level?

e. What is the value of velocity in long-run equilibrium?

f. Suppose that the government wants to increase its purchases to $G = 350$ and to achieve a long-run equilibrium with investment, I, equal to 320, and the price level, P, equal to 6. What level of taxes, T, and money supply, M, will achieve this long-run equilibrium? The following questions will guide you to the answer. (1) What value of the real interest rate leads to $I = 320$? (2) What is the value of consumption in long-run equilibrium when $I = 320$ and $G = 350$? (3) What value of taxes, T, will lead to the level of consumption, C, in part (2), thereby achieving $I = 320$ and $G = 350$ in long-run equilibrium? (4) What value of the nominal money supply, M, will lead to a price level of 6 in long-run equilibrium with $I = 320$ and $G = 350$? (Note: continue to assume that $\pi^e = 0.02$.)

4. An economy is described by the following equations:

Desired consumption	$C^d = 300 + 0.5(Y - T) - 300r.$
Desired investment	$I^d = 100 - 100r.$
Government purchases	$G = 100.$
Taxes	$T = 100.$
Real money demand	$L = 0.5Y - 200r.$
Money supply	$M = 6300.$
Full-employment output	$\bar{Y} = 700.$

a. Write the equation for the aggregate demand curve. (*Hint:* Find the equations describing the goods market and asset market equilibria. Use these two equations to eliminate the real interest rate. For any given price level, the equation of the aggregate demand curve gives the level of output that satisfies both goods market and asset market equilibria.)

b. Suppose that $P = 15$. What are the short-run equilibrium values of output, the real interest rate, consumption, and investment?

c. What are the long-run equilibrium values of output, the real interest rate, consumption, investment, and the price level?

5. (Appendix 11.A) Consider an economy in which all workers are covered by contracts that specify the nominal wage and give the employer the right to choose the amount of employment. The production function is

$$Y = 20\sqrt{N},$$

and the corresponding marginal product of labor is

$$MPN = \frac{10}{\sqrt{N}}.$$

Suppose that the nominal wage is $W = 20$.

a. Derive an equation that relates the real wage to the amount of labor demanded by firms (the labor demand curve).

b. For the nominal wage of 20, what is the relationship between the price level and the amount of labor demanded by firms?

c. What is the relationship between the price level and the amount of output supplied by firms? Graph this relationship.

Now suppose that the IS and LM curves of the economy (the goods market and asset market equilibrium conditions) are described by the following equations:

IS curve	$Y = 120 - 500r.$
LM curve	$M/P = 0.5Y - 500r.$

d. The money supply M is 300. Use the IS and LM equations to derive a relationship between output, Y, and the price level, P. This relationship is the equation for the aggregate demand curve. Graph it on the same axis as the relationship between the price level and the amount of output supplied by firms (the aggregate supply curve) from Part (c).

e. What are the equilibrium values of the price level, output, employment, real wage, and real interest rate?

f. Suppose that the money supply, M, is 135. What are the equilibrium values of the price level, output, employment, real wage, and real interest rate?

6. (Appendix 11.C) Consider the following economy.

Desired consumption	$C^d = 325 + 0.5(Y - T)$ $- 500r.$
Desired investment	$I^d = 200 - 500r.$
Government purchases	$G = 150.$
Taxes	$T = 150.$
Real money demand	$L = 0.5Y - 1000r.$
Money supply	$M = 6000.$
Full-employment output	$\bar{Y} = 1000.$

a. Calculate the full-employment values of the real interest rate, the price level, consumption, and investment.

b. What are the values of α_{IS}, β_{IS}, α_{LM}, β_{LM}, and ℓ_r for this economy? (You'll have to refer back to Appendix 9.B for definitions of these coefficients.)

c. Suppose that the price level is fixed at $P_{sr} = 15$. What are the short-run equilibrium values of output and the real interest rate?

d. With the price level still fixed at $P_{sr} = 15$, suppose that government purchases increase from $G = 150$ to $G = 250$. What are the new values of α_{IS} and the short-run equilibrium level of output?

e. Use Eq. (11.C.5) to compute the government purchases multiplier. Use your answer to compute the short-run change in Y resulting from an increase in government purchases from $G = 150$ to $G = 250$. How does your answer here compare to your answer in Part (d)?

ANALYTICAL PROBLEMS

1. According to the Keynesian *IS–LM* model, what is the effect of each of the following on output, the real interest rate, employment, and the price level? Distinguish between the short run and the long run.

   a. Increased tax incentives for investment (the tax breaks for investment are offset by lump-sum tax increases that keep total current tax collections unchanged).

   b. Increased tax incentives for saving [as in Part (a), lump-sum tax increases offset the effect on total current tax collections].

   c. A wave of investor pessimism about the future profitability of capital investments.

   d. An increase in consumer confidence, as consumers expect that their incomes will be higher in the future.

2. According to the Keynesian *IS–LM* model, what is the effect of each of the following on output, the real interest rate, employment, and the price level? Distinguish between the short run and the long run.

   a. Financial deregulation allows banks to pay a higher interest rate on checking accounts.

   b. The introduction of sophisticated credit cards greatly reduces the amount of money that people need for transactions.

   c. A severe water shortage causes sharp declines in agricultural output and increases in food prices.

   d. A temporary beneficial supply shock affects most of the economy, but no individual firm is affected sufficiently to change its prices in the short run.

3. Suppose that the Fed has a policy of increasing the money supply when it observes that the economy is in recession. However, suppose that about six months are needed for an increase in the money supply to affect aggregate demand, which is about the same amount of time needed for firms to review and reset their prices. What effects will the Fed's policy have on output and price stability? Does your answer change if (a) the Fed has some ability to forecast recessions or (b) price adjustment takes longer than six months?

4. Classical economists argue that using fiscal policy to fight a recession doesn't make workers better off. Suppose, however, that the Keynesian model is correct. Relative to a policy of doing nothing, does an increase in government purchases that brings the economy to full employment make workers better off? In answering the question, discuss the effects of the fiscal expansion on the real wage, employment, consumption, and current and future taxes. How does your answer depend on (a) the direct benefits of the government spending program and (b) the speed with which prices adjust in the absence of fiscal stimulus?

5. Some labor economists argue that it is useful to think of the labor market as being divided into two sectors: a primary sector, where "good" (high-paying, long-term) jobs are located, and a secondary sector, which has "bad" (low-paying, short-term) jobs. Suppose that the primary sector has a high marginal product of labor and that (because effort is costly for firms to monitor) firms pay an efficiency wage. The secondary sector has a low marginal product of labor and no efficiency wage; instead, the real wage in the secondary sector adjusts so that the quantities of labor demanded and supplied are equal in that sector. Workers are alike, and all would prefer to work in the primary sector. However, workers who can't find jobs in the primary sector work in the secondary sector.

   What are the effects of each of the following on the real wage, employment, and output in both sectors?

   a. Expansionary monetary policy increases the demand for primary sector output.

   b. Immigration increases the labor force.

   c. The effort curve changes so that a higher real wage is needed to elicit the greatest effort per dollar in the primary sector. Effort exerted at the higher real wage is the same as before the change in the effort curve.

   d. There is a temporary productivity improvement in the primary sector.

   e. There is a temporary productivity improvement in the secondary sector.

WORKING WITH MACROECONOMIC DATA

For data to use in these exercises, go to the Federal Reserve Bank of St. Louis FRED database at research.stlouisfed.org/fred2.

1. Keynesian theory predicts that expansionary fiscal policy—either higher spending or lower taxes—will raise the real interest rate.

    Using data since 1960, graph the Federal government budget deficit, the state-local government budget deficit (both relative to GDP), and the real interest rate (three-month Treasury bill rate minus the CPI inflation rate over the preceding twelve-month period). Do you see a link between deficits and real interest rates? In what period does the relationship seem clearest? Do your answers change when the ten-year government bond interest rate is used instead of the three-month rate?

2. Because of price stickiness, the Keynesian model predicts that an increase in the growth rate of money will lead to higher inflation only after some lag, when firms begin to adjust their prices. Using data since 1960, graph the inflation rate and the rate of growth of M2. Prior to 1980, is it true that increases in money growth only affected inflation with a lag? What has happened since 1980?

    Keynesians argue that financial innovations, such as the introduction of money market deposit accounts at banks, led to a large increase in the demand for M2 in the early 1980s. If this claim is true, how does it help explain the relationship between money growth and inflation that you observe after 1980?

3. Working with Macroeconomic Data Exercise 1, Chapter 10, asked you to look at the cyclical behavior of total factor productivity. If you have not completed that problem, do it now and compare productivity changes with changes in the producer price index for fuels and related products and power. How would Keynesian interpretations differ from those offered by classical macroeconomics?

APPENDIX 11.A

Labor Contracts and Nominal-Wage Rigidity

In the Keynesian theory, the nonneutrality of money is a consequence of nominal rigidity. In this chapter we emphasized nominal-*price* rigidity. An alternative nominal rigidity that could account for the nonneutrality of money, which many Keynesians emphasize, is nominal-*wage* rigidity. Nominal-wage rigidity could reflect long-term labor contracts between firms and unions in which wages are set in nominal terms (the case we study here). In terms of the *AD–AS* framework the difference between nominal-price rigidity and nominal-wage rigidity is that nominal-price rigidity implies a horizontal short-run aggregate supply curve, whereas nominal-wage rigidity implies a short-run aggregate supply curve that slopes upward. However, this difference doesn't really affect the results obtained from the Keynesian model. In particular, in the Keynesian model with nominal-wage rigidity, money remains nonneutral in the short run and neutral in the long run.

The Short-Run Aggregate Supply Curve with Labor Contracts

In the United States most labor contracts specify employment conditions and nominal wages for a period of three years. Although labor contracts specify the nominal wage rate, they usually don't specify the total amount of employment. Instead, employers unilaterally decide how many hours will be worked and whether workers will be laid off. These factors imply that the short-run aggregate supply curve slopes upward.

We can see why the short-run aggregate supply curve slopes upward when labor contracts prespecify the nominal wage by considering what happens when the price level increases. With the nominal wage, W, already determined by the contract, an increase in the price level, P, reduces the real wage, w, or W/P. In response to the drop in the real wage, firms demand more labor. Because firms unilaterally choose the level of employment, the increase in the amount of labor demanded leads to an increase in employment and therefore an increase in output. Thus an increase in the price level leads to an increase in the amount of output supplied, as shown by the *SRAS* curves in Fig. 11.A.1.

Nonneutrality of Money

Money is nonneutral in the short run in the model with long-term labor contracts, as illustrated in Fig. 11.A.1. The initial general equilibrium is at point E, where the initial aggregate demand curve, AD^1, intersects the short-run aggregate supply curve, $SRAS^1$. A 10% increase in the money supply shifts the AD curve up to AD^2. (For any level of output the price level is 10% higher on AD^2 than on AD^1.) In the

Figure 11.A.1

Monetary nonneutrality with long-term contracts

With labor contracts that fix the nominal wage in the short run, an increase in the price level lowers the real wage and induces firms to employ more labor and produce more output. Thus the short-run aggregate supply curve $SRAS^1$ slopes upward. When nominal wages are rigid, money isn't neutral. From the initial equilibrium point, E, a 10% increase in the money supply shifts the AD curve up, from AD^1 to AD^2. In the short run, both output and the price level increase, as shown by point F. Over time, contracts are renegotiated and nominal wages rise to match the increase in prices. As wages rise, the short-run aggregate supply curve shifts up, from $SRAS^1$ to $SRAS^2$, so that general equilibrium is restored at H. At H both the price level, P, and the nominal wage, W, have risen by 10%, so the real wage is the same as it was initially, and firms supply the full-employment level of output, $\overline{Y}$.

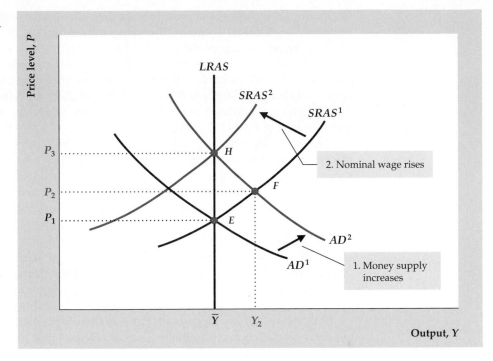

short run, the increase in the money supply raises the price level to P_2 and output to Y_2 at point F. Output at F is higher than its full-employment level because the rise in prices lowers the real wage, which leads firms to employ more labor and produce more output.

At the short-run equilibrium point, F, however, workers will be dissatisfied because their real wages are lower than they had expected. Over time, as contracts are renewed or renegotiated, nominal wages will rise to offset the increase in prices. At any price level, a rise in the nominal wage also raises the real wage, inducing firms to employ less labor and produce less output. Thus rising nominal wages cause the short-run aggregate supply curve to shift up and to the left, from $SRAS^1$ to $SRAS^2$. Eventually, general equilibrium is restored at point H.

In the long run at point H, the price level rises to P_3, which is 10% higher than its initial value, P_1. At H the nominal wage, W, has also increased by 10% so that the real wage, W/P, has returned to its initial value. With the real wage back at its original value, firms employ the same amount of labor and produce the same amount of output ($\overline{Y}$) as they did at the initial equilibrium point, E. Thus, as in the Keynesian model based on efficiency wages and price stickiness, in the Keynesian model with nominal-wage rigidity, money is neutral in the long run but not in the short run.

Although nominal-wage rigidity arising from labor contracts can explain short-run monetary nonneutrality, some economists object to this explanation. One objection is that less than one-sixth of the labor force in the United States is unionized and covered by long-term labor contracts. However, many nonunion workers receive wages similar to those set in union contracts. For example, although most nonunion workers don't have formal wage contracts, they may have "implicit contracts" with their employers, or informal unwritten arrangements for comparable wages.

A second objection is that many labor contracts contain cost-of-living adjustments (COLAs), which tie the nominal wage to the overall price level, as measured, for example, by the consumer price index. Contracts with *complete* indexation increase the nominal wage by the same percentage as the increase in the price level. If wages are completely indexed to the price level, the short-run aggregate supply curve is vertical and money is neutral. To show why, let's suppose that the price level increases by 6%. If labor contracts are completely indexed, nominal wages also increase by 6% and the real wage, W/P, remains unchanged. Because the real wage doesn't change, firms choose the same levels of employment and output independent of the price level.

However, in most U.S. labor contracts, wages aren't completely indexed to prices. In recent years, fewer than one-fourth of the workers covered by major private industry bargaining agreements have had any COLA provisions. Furthermore, most contracts with COLA provisions have partial rather than complete indexation. For example, under a contract that calls for 50% indexation, the nominal wage will increase by 50% of the overall rate of increase in prices. Thus, if the price level increases by 6%, the nominal wage increases by 3%. As a result, the real wage falls by 3% (a 3% increase in the nominal wage, W, minus a 6% increase in the price level, P). The reduction in the real wage induces firms to increase employment and production. Thus with partial indexation the short-run aggregate supply curve again slopes upward, and money isn't neutral in the short run.

A third and final objection is that this theory predicts that real wages will be countercyclical, contrary to the business cycle fact that real wages are procyclical. For example, at point F in Fig. 11.A.1, output is higher than the full-employment level, but the real wage is lower than at full employment (indeed, the low real wage induces firms to produce the extra output). Thus the theory holds that real wages will fall in booms—that is, the real wage is countercyclical—which is inconsistent with the evidence.

However, perhaps both supply shocks and aggregate demand shocks affect real wages. For the real business cycle theory we showed that, if productivity shocks cause cyclical fluctuations, the real wage should be procyclical, perhaps strongly so. A combination of supply shocks (which cause the real wage to move procyclically) and aggregate demand shocks (which, as in Fig. 11.A.1, cause the real wage to move countercyclically) might average out to a real wage that is at least mildly procyclical. Some evidence for this view was provided in a study by Scott Sumner of Bentley College and Stephen Silver[18] of Virginia Military Institute, which shows that the real wage has been procyclical during periods dominated by supply shocks but has been countercyclical during periods in which aggregate demand shocks were more important.

---

[18]"Real Wages, Employment and the Phillips Curve," *Journal of Political Economy*, June 1989, pp. 706–720.

APPENDIX **11.B**

Worked-Out Numerical Exercise for Calculating the Multiplier in a Keynesian Model

This is a worked-out numerical exercise, as an example for solving the model from Appendix 9.A, applied to a question about the government spending multiplier. In that problem, the economy is given by the following equations:

$$C^d = 300 + 0.75(Y - T) - 300r$$
$$T = 100 + 0.2Y$$
$$I^d = 200 - 200r$$
$$L = 0.5Y - 500i$$
$$\overline{Y} = 2500; G = 600; M = 133,200; \pi^e = 0.05; P_{sr} = 120.$$

In Appendix 9.A, we found the short-run and long-run equilibrium values of Y, P, r, T, C, I, and i. Now we want to calculate the government spending multiplier in the short run if government spending rises from 600 to 690. (Of course, in the long run, the multiplier is zero, because output will be at its full-employment level, and increases in government spending do not affect the full-employment level of output in the Keynesian model.) To do this, we use the short-run equilibrium results from Appendix 9.A and then repeat our procedure with the higher level of government spending to see how output is affected. From that, we can calculate the multiplier, which is the change in output divided by the change in government spending.

In Appendix 9.A, we found that in the short run, $Y = 2400$. With an increase in government spending, in the short run, the IS curve will change, but the LM curve will be the same as before, $r = 0.001Y - 2.27$.

First, we find the equation for the IS curve by using the goods market equilibrium condition. The goods market equilibrium condition is $Y = C^d + I^d + G$. Substitute the equation for T into the equation for C^d from above. Then substitute the resulting equation and the equation for I^d from above, along with the value of G, into $Y = C^d + I^d + G$ to obtain: $Y = \{300 + 0.75[Y - (100 + 0.2Y)] - 300r\} + [200 - 200r] + 690$. Rearrange this equation as an equation for r in terms of Y: $Y = \{300 + 0.75Y - [(0.75 \times 100) + (0.75 \times 0.2Y)] - 300r\} + [200 - 200r] + 690$, so $Y = [300 + 0.75Y - 75 - 0.15Y - 300r] + [200 - 200r] + 690$, so $0.4Y = [300 - 75 + 200 + 690] - (300 + 200)r$, so $500r = 1115 - 0.4Y$. Therefore, $r = (1115/500) - (0.4/500)Y$, so $r = 2.23 - 0.0008Y$. This is the IS curve.

Next, we find the intersection of the IS and LM curves to calculate the short-run equilibrium values of Y and r. We have written the equations of the IS and LM curves so that the left side of each equation is simply r. Setting the right side of the IS equation equal to the right side of the LM equation yields $2.23 - 0.0008Y = 0.001Y - 2.27$, so $4.5 = 0.0018Y$. Therefore, $Y = 4.5/0.0018 = 2500$.

The multiplier is the change in output divided by the change in government spending, which is $(2500 - 2400)/(690 - 600) = {}^{10}\!/_9 = 1\tfrac{1}{9}$. In this example, output rises by 100 when government spending rises by 90.

Equation (11.C.5) in Appendix 11.C shows that the multiplier equals

$$\Delta Y/\Delta G = 1/[(c_r + i_r)(\beta_{IS} + \beta_{LM})].$$

Filling in the data, we find that $\Delta Y/\Delta G = 1/[(c_r + i_r)(\beta_{IS} + \beta_{LM})] = 1/[(300 + 200)(0.0008 + 0.001)] = 1/(500 \times 0.0018) = {}^{1}\!/_{0.9} = 1\tfrac{1}{9}$, exactly as we found above.

APPENDIX 11.C

The Multiplier in the Keynesian Model

In Chapter 11 we defined the multiplier associated with any particular type of spending as the short-run change in total output resulting from a one-unit change in that type of spending. Here we use the analysis in Appendix 9.B to derive the multiplier associated with government purchases G. We proceed in three steps: First, we calculate the effect on α_{IS} (the intercept of the IS curve in Eq. 9.B.14) of an increase in G. Then, we calculate the effect on the short-run equilibrium value of Y, shown by Eq. (9.B.27), of an increase in α_{IS}. Finally, we combine these two effects to calculate the effect on output, Y, of an increase in G.

To calculate the effect on α_{IS} of an increase in G, we repeat the definition of α_{IS}, Eq. (9.B.15):

$$\alpha_{IS} = \frac{c_0 + i_0 + G - c_Y t_0}{c_r + i_r}, \tag{11.C.1}$$

where c_0, i_0, c_Y, c_r, i_r, and t_0 are parameters that determine desired consumption and desired investment (see Appendix 9.B). If G increases by ΔG, then α_{IS} increases by $\Delta G / (c_r + i_r)$, so

$$\Delta \alpha_{IS} = \frac{\Delta G}{c_r + i_r}. \tag{11.C.2}$$

Next, recall from Eq. (9.B.27) that, in the short run when $P = P_{sr}$ the level of output is

$$Y = \frac{\alpha_{IS} - \alpha_{LM} + (1/\ell_r)(M/P_{sr})}{\beta_{IS} + \beta_{LM}}. \tag{11.C.3}$$

Observe from Eq. (11.C.3) that, if α_{IS} increases by $\Delta \alpha_{IS}$, output, Y, increases by $\Delta \alpha_{IS}/(\beta_{IS} + \beta_{LM})$, or

$$\Delta Y = \frac{\Delta \alpha_{IS}}{\beta_{IS} + \beta_{LM}}. \tag{11.C.4}$$

Finally, if we substitute the right side of Eq. (11.C.2) for $\Delta \alpha_{IS}$ on the right side of Eq. (11.C.4) and then divide both sides of the resulting equation by ΔG, we obtain

$$\frac{\Delta Y}{\Delta G} = \frac{1}{(c_r + i_r)(\beta_{IS} + \beta_{LM})}. \tag{11.C.5}$$

The right side of Eq. (11.C.5) is the increase in short-run equilibrium output, Y, that occurs for each one-unit increase in government purchases, G. In other words, it is the government purchases multiplier. Similar calculations show that changes in desired consumption or desired investment (as reflected in the terms c_0 and i_0) have the same multiplier as government purchases.

Because c_r, i_r, β_{IS}, and β_{LM} all are positive, the multiplier is positive. However, depending on the specific values of those parameters, the multiplier may be greater or less than 1. A case in which the multiplier is likely to be large occurs when the LM curve is horizontal (that is, when the slope of the LM curve, β_{LM}, is 0). If the LM curve is horizontal, shifts in the IS curve induced by changes in spending have relatively large effects on output. Recall that Eq. (9.B.16) gives the slope of the IS curve, β_{IS}, as $[1 - (1 - t)c_Y]/(c_r + i_r)$. Making this substitution and setting the slope of the LM curve, β_{LM}, at 0 yield a simple form of the multiplier:

$$\frac{\Delta Y}{\Delta G} = \frac{1}{1 - (1 - t)c_Y}. \tag{11.C.6}$$

For example, suppose that the marginal propensity to consume, c_Y, is 0.8 and that the tax rate, t, is 0.25. Then the multiplier defined in Eq. (11.C.6) is $1/[(1 - (0.75)(0.8)] = 1/0.4$, or 2.5. If the LM curve is very steep, by contrast—that is, β_{LM} is large—then the multiplier could be quite small, as you can see from Eq. (11.C.5).

12

Unemployment and Inflation

In the past several chapters we focused on the concepts of the business cycle, macroeconomic stabilization, and classical and Keynesian approaches to business cycle analysis. Although these concepts are central to today's macroeconomics, actual policy discussions rarely involve such abstract terms. Policy debates tend to focus on highly publicized economic statistics such as inflation and unemployment. To make a stronger connection between business cycle theories and policy debates, we now take a closer look at unemployment and inflation, first together and then separately.

Unemployment and inflation—sometimes referred to as the "twin evils" of macroeconomics—are among the most difficult and politically sensitive economic issues that policymakers face. High rates of unemployment and inflation generate intense public concern because their effects are direct and visible: Almost everyone is affected by rising prices, and few workers can be confident that they will never lose their jobs.

Moreover, there is a long-standing idea in macroeconomics that unemployment and inflation are somehow related. In the first part of this chapter we discuss in some detail the concept of the Phillips curve—an empirical relationship between inflation and unemployment. According to the Phillips curve, inflation tends to be low when unemployment is high and high when unemployment is low. The Phillips curve relationship raises some important questions about how the economy works and how macroeconomic policies should be used.

We then look at unemployment and inflation separately. We examine the costs that each imposes on society and consider the options that policymakers have for dealing with these problems.

This chapter begins Part 4 of the book, the purpose of which is to explore macroeconomic policymaking in detail. Following the discussion of inflation and unemployment in this chapter, in Chapter 13 we address the issue of how economic openness—as reflected in the trading and financial links among countries—affects macroeconomic policy. In Chapter 14 we take a closer look at institutions and debates related to the making of monetary policy and in Chapter 15 we provide a similar overview of fiscal policy.

12.1 Unemployment and Inflation: Is There a Trade-Off?

Newspaper editorials and public discussions about economic policy often refer to the "trade-off" between inflation and unemployment. The idea is that, to reduce inflation, the economy must tolerate high unemployment, or alternatively that, to reduce unemployment, more inflation must be accepted. This section examines the idea of an inflation–unemployment trade-off and its implications for macroeconomic policy.

The origin of the idea of a trade-off between inflation and unemployment was a 1958 article by economist A. W. Phillips.[1] Phillips examined ninety-seven years of British data on unemployment and nominal wage growth and found that, historically, unemployment tended to be low in years when nominal wages grew rapidly and high in years when nominal wages grew slowly. Economists who built on Phillips's work shifted its focus slightly by looking at the link between unemployment and inflation—that is, the growth rate of prices—rather than the link between unemployment and the growth rate of wages. During the late 1950s and the 1960s, many statistical studies examined inflation and unemployment data for numerous countries and time periods, in many cases finding a negative relationship between the two variables. This negative empirical relationship between unemployment and inflation is known as the **Phillips curve.**

A striking example of a Phillips curve, shown in Fig. 12.1, occurred in the United States during the 1960s. The U.S. economy expanded throughout most of the 1960s, with unemployment falling and inflation rising steadily. In Fig. 12.1, the inflation rate is measured on the vertical axis, and the unemployment rate is measured on the horizontal axis. Note that years, such as 1961, that had high unemployment also had low inflation, and that years, such as 1969, that had high inflation also had low unemployment. The data produce an almost perfect downward-sloping relation between inflation and unemployment—that is, a Phillips curve. The experience of the United States in the 1960s, which came after Phillips's article had been published and widely disseminated, was viewed by many as a confirmation of his basic finding.

The policy implications of these findings were much debated. Initially, the Phillips curve seemed to offer policymakers a "menu" of combinations of inflation and unemployment from which they could choose. Indeed, during the 1960s some economists argued that, by accepting a modest amount of inflation, macroeconomic policymakers could keep the unemployment rate low indefinitely. This belief seemed to be borne out during the 1960s, when rising inflation was accompanied by falling unemployment.

In the following decades, however, this relationship between inflation and unemployment failed to hold: Figure 12.2 shows inflation and unemployment for the period 1970–2008. During those years, unlike the 1960s, there seemed to be no reliable relationship between unemployment and inflation. From the perspective of the Phillips curve the most puzzling period was the mid 1970s, during which the country experienced high inflation and high unemployment simultaneously (stagflation). In 1975, for example, unemployment reached 8.5% of the labor force and the annual inflation rate was 9.1%. High unemployment, together with high inflation, is inconsistent with the Phillips curve.

The original empirical results of Phillips and others who extended his work, together with the unexpected experience of the U.S. economy after 1970, raise at least three important questions:

■   Why was the original Phillips curve relationship between inflation and unemployment frequently observed historically, as in the cases of Great Britain in the century before 1958 and the United States in the 1960s?

---

[1]"The Relation Between Unemployment and the Rate of Change of Money Wage Rates in the United Kingdom, 1861–1957," *Economica*, November 1958, pp. 283–299.

Figure 12.1

The Phillips curve and the U.S. economy during the 1960s

During the 1960s, U.S. rates of inflation and unemployment seemed to lie along a Phillips curve. Inflation rose and unemployment fell fairly steadily during this decade, and policymakers apparently had decided to live with higher inflation so as to reduce unemployment.

Source: Federal Reserve Bank of St. Louis FRED database at *research.stlouisfed.org/fred2*, series CPIAUCSL and UNRATE.

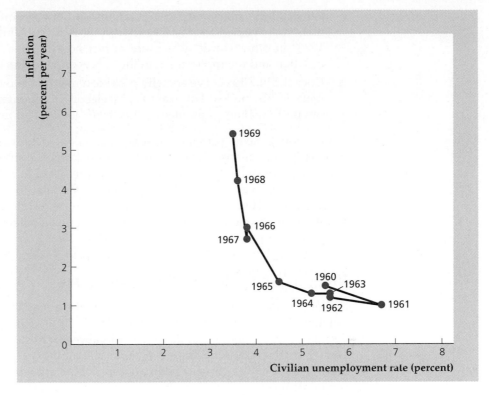

Figure 12.2

Inflation and unemployment in the United States, 1970–2008

The figure shows the combinations of inflation and unemployment experienced in the United States each year from 1970 to 2008. Unlike during the 1960s (see Fig. 12.1), after 1970 a clear negative relationship between inflation and unemployment in the United States didn't seem to exist.

Source: Federal Reserve Bank of St. Louis FRED database at *research.stlouisfed.org/fred2*, series CPIAUCSL and UNRATE.

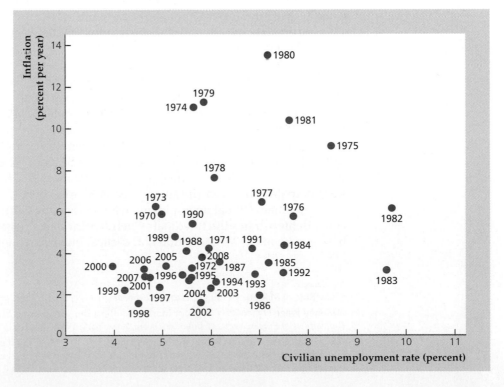

■ Why did the simple negative relationship between inflation and unemployment that seemed to exist during the 1960s in the United States vanish after 1970? In other words, was there in fact no systematic relationship between inflation and unemployment in the U.S. economy after 1970?

■ Does the Phillips curve actually provide a menu of choices from which policymakers can choose? For example, by electing to maintain a high inflation rate can policymakers guarantee a *permanently* low rate of unemployment?

Economic theory provides reasonable answers to these questions; in particular, it explains the collapse of the Phillips curve after 1970. Interestingly, the key economic analysis of the Phillips curve—which predicted that this relationship would not be stable—was done during the 1960s, *before* the Phillips curve had actually broken down. Thus we have at least one example of economic theorists predicting an important development in the economy that policymakers and the public didn't anticipate.

The Expectations-Augmented Phillips Curve

Although the Phillips curve seemed to describe adequately the unemployment–inflation relationship in the United States in the 1960s, during the second half of the decade some economists, notably Nobel Laureates Milton Friedman[2] of the University of Chicago and Edmund Phelps[3] of Columbia University, questioned the logic of the Phillips curve. Friedman and Phelps argued—purely on the basis of economic theory—that there should not be a stable negative relationship between inflation and unemployment. Instead, a negative relationship should exist between *unanticipated* inflation (the difference between the actual and expected inflation rates) and *cyclical* unemployment (the difference between the actual and natural unemployment rates).[4] Although these distinctions appear to be merely technical, they are crucial in understanding the relationship between the actual rates of inflation and unemployment.

Before discussing the significance of their analyses, we need to explain how Friedman and Phelps arrived at their conclusions. To do so we use the extended classical model, which includes the misperceptions theory. (Analytical Problem 3 at the end of the chapter asks you to perform a similar analysis using the Keynesian model.) We proceed in two steps, first considering an economy at full employment with steady, fully anticipated inflation. In this economy, both unanticipated inflation and cyclical unemployment are zero. Second, we consider what happens when aggregate demand growth increases unexpectedly. In this case both positive unanticipated inflation (inflation greater than expected) and negative cyclical unemployment (actual unemployment lower than the natural rate) occur. This outcome demonstrates the Friedman–Phelps point that a negative relationship exists between unanticipated inflation and cyclical unemployment.

---

[2]"The Role of Monetary Policy," *American Economic Review,* March 1968, pp. 1–17.
[3]"Money Wage Dynamics and Labor Market Equilibrium," in Edmund Phelps, ed., *Microeconomic Foundations of Employment and Inflation Theory,* New York: W. W. Norton, 1970, pp. 124–166.
[4]In Chapter 3 we defined cyclical unemployment. Recall that the natural rate of unemployment is the unemployment rate that exists when output is at its full-employment level. The natural rate exceeds zero because of frictional and structural unemployment, also defined in Chapter 3.

Figure 12.3

Ongoing inflation in the extended classical model

If the money supply grows by 10% every year, the AD curve shifts up by 10% every year, from AD^1 in year 1 to AD^2 in year 2, and so on. If the money supply has been growing by 10% per year for some time and the rate of inflation has been 10% for some time, the expected rate of inflation also is 10%. Thus the expected price level also grows by 10% each year, from 100 in year 1 to 110 in year 2, and so on. The 10% annual increase in the expected price level shifts the $SRAS$ curve up by 10% each year, for example, from $SRAS^1$ in year 1 to $SRAS^2$ in year 2. The economy remains in full-employment equilibrium at the intersection of the AD curve and the $SRAS$ curve in each year (point E in year 1 and point F in year 2), with output at $\overline{Y}$, unemployment at the natural rate of unemployment, $\overline{u}$, and inflation and expected inflation both at 10% per year.

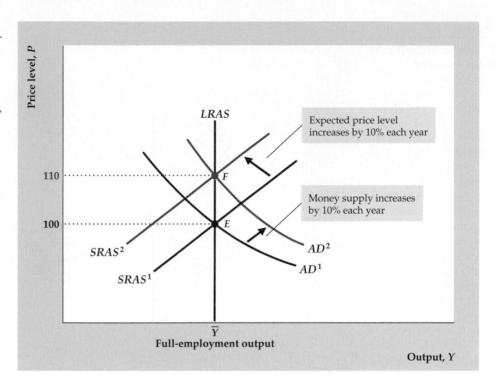

We develop the first step of this analysis by using the extended classical model to analyze an economy with steady inflation (see Fig. 12.3). We assume that this economy is in full-employment equilibrium in which the money supply has been growing at 10% per year for many years and is expected to continue to grow at this rate indefinitely. With the money supply growing by 10% per year, the aggregate demand curve shifts up by 10% each year, from AD^1 in year 1 to AD^2 in year 2, and so on. For simplicity we assume that full-employment output, $\overline{Y}$, is constant, but relaxing that assumption wouldn't affect our basic conclusions.

In Fig. 12.3 the short-run aggregate supply ($SRAS$) curve shifts up by 10% each year. Why? With the growth in money supply fully anticipated, there are no misperceptions. Instead, people expect the price level to rise by 10% per year (a 10% inflation rate), which in turn causes the $SRAS$ curve to shift up by 10% per year. With no misperceptions, the economy remains at full employment with output at $\overline{Y}$. For example, when the expected price level is 100 in year 1, the short-run aggregate supply curve is $SRAS^1$. At point E the price level is 100 (the same as the expected price level) and output is $\overline{Y}$. In year 2 the expected price level is 110, and the short-run aggregate supply curve is $SRAS^2$. In year 2 equilibrium occurs at point F, again with output of $\overline{Y}$ and equal expected and actual price levels. Each year, both the AD curve and the $SRAS$ curve shift up by 10%, increasing the actual price level and expected price level by 10% and maintaining output at its full-employment level.

What happens to unemployment in this economy? Because output is continuously at its full-employment level, $\overline{Y}$, unemployment remains at the natural rate, $\overline{u}$. With unemployment at its natural rate, cyclical unemployment is zero. Hence this economy has zero unanticipated inflation *and* zero cyclical unemployment.

Against this backdrop of 10% monetary growth and 10% inflation, suppose now that in year 2 the money supply grows by 15% rather than by the expected

Figure 12.4

Unanticipated inflation in the extended classical model
If the money supply has been growing by 10% per year for a long time and is expected to continue growing by 10%, the expected price level increases by 10% each year. The 10% increase in the expected price level shifts the SRAS curve up from $SRAS^1$ in year 1 to $SRAS^2$ in year 2. Then, if the money supply actually increases by 15% in year 2 rather than by the expected 10%, the AD curve is $AD^{2,new}$ rather than $AD^{2,old}$. As a result of higher-than-expected money growth, output increases above $\overline{Y}$ in year 2 and the price level increases to 113, at point G. Because the price level rises by 13% rather than the expected 10%, unanticipated inflation is 3% in year 2. This unanticipated inflation is associated with output higher than $\overline{Y}$ and unemployment below the natural rate, $\overline{u}$ (negative cyclical unemployment).

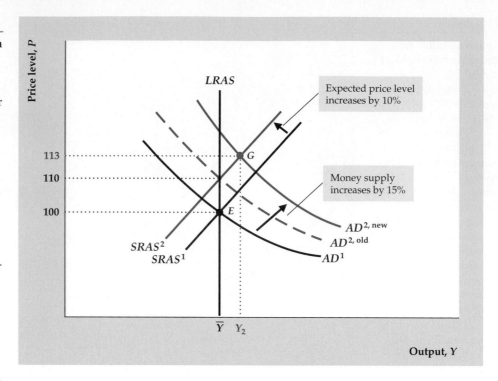

10% (Fig. 12.4). In this case, instead of being 10% higher than AD^1 (as shown by $AD^{2,old}$), the aggregate demand curve in year 2 will be 15% higher than AD^1 (as shown by $AD^{2,new}$). If this increase in the rate of monetary growth is *unanticipated* at the beginning of year 2, the expected price level in year 2 remains at 110, and the short-run aggregate supply curve is $SRAS^2$, as before. The short-run equilibrium in year 2 is at point G, the intersection of the $AD^{2,new}$ and $SRAS^2$ curves. At G the price level is 113, so the actual rate of inflation in year 2 is 13%. Because the expected rate of inflation was 10%, the 13% inflation rate implies unanticipated inflation of 3% in year 2. Furthermore, because output is above its full-employment level, $\overline{Y}$, at G, the actual unemployment rate is below the natural rate and cyclical unemployment is negative.

Why is output above its full-employment level in year 2? Note that, in year 2, the 13% rate of inflation is less than the 15% rate of money growth but greater than the 10% expected rate of inflation. Because the price level grows by less than does the nominal money supply in year 2, the real money supply, M/P, increases, lowering the real interest rate and raising the aggregate quantity of goods demanded above $\overline{Y}$. At the same time, because the price level grows by more than expected, the aggregate quantity of goods supplied also is greater than $\overline{Y}$, as producers are fooled into thinking that the relative prices of their products have increased.

Producers can't be fooled about price behavior indefinitely, however. In the long run, producers learn the true price level, the economy returns to full employment, and the inflation rate again equals the expected inflation rate, as in Fig. 12.3. In the meantime, however, as long as actual output is higher than full-employment output, $\overline{Y}$, and actual unemployment is below the natural rate, $\overline{u}$, the actual price level must be higher than the expected price level. Indeed, according to the misperceptions theory, output can be higher than $\overline{Y}$ only when prices are higher than expected (and therefore when inflation is also higher than expected).

Thus, in this economy, when the public correctly predicts aggregate demand growth and inflation, unanticipated inflation is zero, actual unemployment equals the natural rate, and cyclical unemployment is zero (Fig. 12.3). However, if aggregate demand growth unexpectedly speeds up, the economy faces a period of positive unanticipated inflation and negative cyclical unemployment (Fig. 12.4). Similarly, an unexpected slowdown in aggregate demand growth could occur, causing the AD curve to rise more slowly than expected; for a time unanticipated inflation would be negative (actual inflation less than expected) and cyclical unemployment would be positive (actual unemployment greater than the natural rate).

The relationship between unanticipated inflation and cyclical unemployment implied by this analysis is

$$\pi - \pi^e = -h(u - \overline{u}),$$

where

$\pi - \pi^e =$ unanticipated inflation (the difference between actual inflation, π, and expected inflation, π^e);

$u - \overline{u} =$ cyclical unemployment (the difference between the actual unemployment rate, u, and the natural unemployment rate, $\overline{u}$);

$h =$ a positive number that measures the slope of the relationship between unanticipated inflation and cyclical unemployment.

The preceding equation expresses mathematically the idea that unanticipated inflation will be positive when cyclical unemployment is negative, negative when cyclical unemployment is positive, and zero when cyclical unemployment is zero.[5] If we add π^e to both sides of the equation, it becomes

$$\pi = \pi^e - h(u - \overline{u}), \tag{12.1}$$

Equation (12.1) describes the expectations-augmented Phillips curve. According to the **expectations-augmented Phillips curve,** actual inflation, π, exceeds expected inflation, π^e, if the actual unemployment rate, u, is less than the natural rate, $\overline{u}$; actual inflation is less than expected inflation if the unemployment rate exceeds the natural rate.

The Shifting Phillips Curve

Let's return to the original Phillips curve, which links the levels of inflation and unemployment in the economy. The insight gained from the Friedman–Phelps analysis is that the relationship illustrated by the Phillips curve depends on the expected rate of inflation and the natural rate of unemployment. If either factor changes, the Phillips curve will shift.

Changes in the Expected Rate of Inflation.
Figure 12.5 shows how a change in the expected inflation rate affects the relationship between inflation and

---

[5]The equation also implies that the relationship between unanticipated inflation and cyclical unemployment is linear, but this formulation is for convenience only. The relationship of the two variables might as easily be a curve as a line.

Figure 12.5

The shifting Phillips curve: an increase in expected inflation

The Friedman–Phelps theory implies that there is a different Phillips curve for every expected inflation rate. For example, PC^1 is the Phillips curve when the expected rate of inflation is 3%. To verify this claim, note from Eq. (12.1) that, when the actual unemployment rate equals the natural rate, $\bar{u}$ (6% here), the actual inflation rate equals the expected inflation rate. At point A, the unemployment rate equals the natural rate and the inflation rate equals 3% on PC^1, so the expected inflation rate is 3% on PC^1. Similarly, at point B on PC^2, where the unemployment rate equals its natural rate, the inflation rate is 12%, so the expected inflation rate is 12% along PC^2. Thus an increase in the expected inflation rate from 3% to 12% shifts the Phillips curve up and to the right, from PC^1 to PC^2.

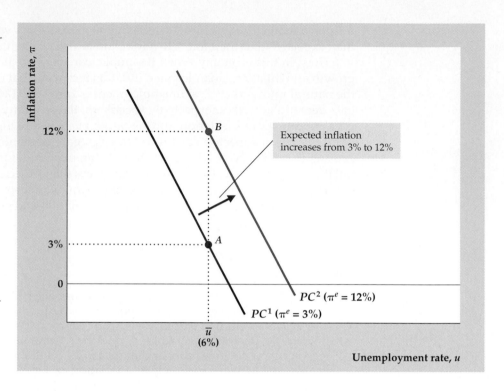

unemployment, according to the Friedman–Phelps theory. The curve PC^1 is the Phillips curve for an expected rate of inflation of 3%. What identifies the expected rate of inflation as 3% along PC^1? Equation (12.1) indicates that, when the actual unemployment rate equals the natural rate (6% in this example), the actual inflation rate equals the expected inflation rate. Thus, to determine the expected inflation rate on a Phillips curve, we find the inflation rate at the point where the actual unemployment rate equals the natural rate. For instance, at point A on curve PC^1, the unemployment rate equals the natural rate, and the actual and expected rates of inflation both equal 3%. As long as the expected inflation rate remains at 3% (and the natural unemployment rate remains at 6%), the Phillips curve PC^1 will describe the relationship between inflation and unemployment.

Now suppose that the expected rate of inflation increases from 3% to 12%. Figure 12.5 shows that this 9 percentage point increase in the expected rate of inflation shifts the Phillips curve up by 9 percentage points at each level of the unemployment rate, from PC^1 to PC^2. When the actual unemployment rate equals the natural rate on PC^2 (at point B), the inflation rate is 12%, confirming that the expected inflation rate is 12% along PC^2. Comparing PC^2 and PC^1 reveals that an increase in the expected inflation rate shifts the Phillips curve relationship between inflation and unemployment up and to the right.

Changes in the Natural Rate of Unemployment.   The Phillips curve relationship between inflation and unemployment also is shifted by changes in the natural unemployment rate, as illustrated by Fig. 12.6. The Phillips curve PC^1 shows a natural unemployment rate at 6% and an expected inflation rate at 3% (PC^1 in Fig. 12.6 is the same as PC^1 in Fig. 12.5). Now suppose that the natural unemployment rate increases to 7% but that the expected inflation rate remains

Figure 12.6

The shifting Phillips curve: an increase in the natural unemployment rate
According to the Friedman–Phelps theory, an increase in the natural unemployment rate shifts the Phillips curve up and to the right. At point A on PC^1, the actual inflation rate and the expected inflation rate are equal at 3%, so the natural unemployment rate equals the actual unemployment rate at A, or 6%. Thus PC^1 is the Phillips curve when the natural unemployment rate is 6% and the expected inflation rate is 3%, as in Fig. 12.5. If the natural unemployment rate increases to 7%, with expected inflation unchanged, the Phillips curve shifts to PC^3. At point C on PC^3, both expected and actual inflation equal 3%, so the natural unemployment rate equals the actual unemployment rate at C, or 7%.

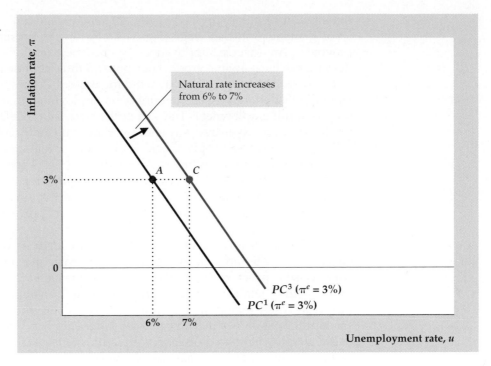

unchanged at 3%. As Fig. 12.6 shows, the increase in the natural unemployment rate causes the Phillips curve to shift, from PC^1 to PC^3.

To confirm that the natural unemployment rate corresponding to Phillips curve PC^3 in Fig. 12.6 is 7%, look at point C on PC^3: At C, where the actual and expected inflation rates are equal, the unemployment rate is 7%. Thus the natural unemployment rate associated with Phillips curve PC^3 is 7%. This example illustrates that—like an increase in expected inflation—an increase in the natural unemployment rate causes the Phillips curve relationship between inflation and unemployment to shift up and to the right.

Supply Shocks and the Phillips Curve. The Friedman–Phelps theory holds that changes in either expected inflation or the natural unemployment rate will shift the Phillips curve. One type of economic disturbance that is likely to affect both factors is a supply shock. Recall that an adverse supply shock causes a burst of inflation, which may lead people to expect higher inflation.[6] An adverse supply shock also tends to increase the natural unemployment rate, although the reasons for this effect are different in the classical and Keynesian models.

Recall that, from the classical perspective, an adverse supply shock raises the natural rate of unemployment by increasing the degree of mismatch between workers and jobs. For example, an oil price shock eliminates jobs in heavy-energy-using industries but increases employment in energy-providing industries.

In the Keynesian model, recall that much of the unemployment that exists even when the economy is at the full-employment level is blamed on rigid real wages. In particular, if the efficiency wage is above the market-clearing real wage,

---

[6]The inflationary impact of a supply shock will be reinforced if, in an attempt to moderate the rise in unemployment caused by the shock, the central bank increases the money supply.

the amount of labor supplied at the efficiency wage will exceed the amount of labor demanded at that wage (Fig. 11.2), leading to persistent structural unemployment. An adverse supply shock has no effect on the supply of labor,[7] but it does reduce the marginal product of labor and thus labor demand. With a rigid efficiency wage, the drop in labor demand increases the excess of labor supplied over labor demanded, raising the amount of unemployment that exists when the economy is at full employment. Thus, as in the classical model, the Keynesian model predicts that an adverse supply shock will raise the natural unemployment rate.

Because adverse supply shocks raise both expected inflation and the natural unemployment rate, according to the Friedman–Phelps analysis they should cause the Phillips curve to shift up and to the right. Similarly, beneficial supply shocks should shift the Phillips curve down and to the left. Overall, the Phillips curve should be particularly unstable during periods of supply shocks.

The Shifting Phillips Curve in Practice.   Our analysis of the shifting Phillips curve (Figs. 12.5 and 12.6) helps answer the basic questions about the Phillips curve raised earlier in the chapter. The first question was: Why did the original Phillips curve relationship between inflation and unemployment apply to many historical cases, including the United States during the 1960s? The Friedman–Phelps analysis shows that a negative relationship between the levels of inflation and unemployment holds *as long as expected inflation and the natural unemployment rate are approximately constant.* As shown in Fig. 12.9 later in this chapter, the natural unemployment rate changes relatively slowly, and during the 1960s it changed very little. Expected inflation probably was also nearly constant in the United States in the 1960s, because at that time people were used to low and stable inflation and inflation remained low for most of the decade. Thus, not surprisingly, the U.S. inflation and unemployment data for the 1960s seem to lie along a single Phillips curve (Fig. 12.1).

The second question was: Why did the Phillips curve relationship, so apparent in the United States in the 1960s, seem to disappear after 1970 (Fig. 12.2)? The answer suggested by the Friedman–Phelps analysis is that, in the period after 1970, the expected inflation rate and the natural unemployment rate varied considerably more than they had in the 1960s, causing the Phillips curve relationship to shift erratically.

Contributing to the shifts of the Phillips curve after 1970 were the two large supply shocks associated with sharp increases in the price of oil that hit the U.S. economy in 1973–1974 and 1979–1980. Recall that adverse supply shocks are likely to increase both expected inflation and the natural rate of unemployment, shifting the Phillips curve up and to the right.

Beyond the direct effects of supply shocks, other forces may have increased the variability of expected inflation and the natural unemployment rate after 1970. As we discuss later in the chapter, the natural unemployment rate first rose, then fell during this period as a result of changes in the composition of the labor force and other changes in the economy.

Expected inflation probably varied more after 1970 because actual inflation varied more (see Fig. 2.1 for the U.S. inflation rate for 1960–2008). After being relatively low

---

[7]This statement is strictly true only for a temporary adverse supply shock. A permanent adverse supply shock, if it reduces expected future wages, would increase labor supply and thus cause an even larger rise in the natural rate of unemployment.

for a long time, inflation—driven by monetary and fiscal policies that had probably been over-expansionary for several years—emerged as a problem at the end of the 1960s.[8] The 1970s were a period of high and erratic inflation, the result of the oil price shocks and macroeconomic policies that again were probably too expansionary, especially in the latter part of the decade. In contrast, following the tough anti-inflationary policies of the Federal Reserve during 1979–1982, inflation returned to a relatively low level during the 1980s. To the extent that expected inflation followed the path of actual inflation—high and erratic in the 1970s, low in the 1980s—our analysis suggests that the Phillips curve relationship between inflation and unemployment wouldn't have been stable over the period.

Does the unstable Phillips curve during 1970–2008 imply that there was no systematic relationship between inflation and unemployment during that period? The answer is "no." According to the Friedman–Phelps analysis, a negative relationship between *unanticipated* inflation and *cyclical* unemployment should appear in the data, even if expected inflation and the natural unemployment rate are changing. Measures of unanticipated inflation and cyclical unemployment for each year during the period 1970–2008 are shown in Fig. 12.7. These measures are approximate because we can't directly observe either expected inflation (needed to calculate unanticipated inflation) or the natural unemployment rate (needed to find cyclical unemployment). We used the forecast of CPI inflation from the Federal Reserve Bank of Philadelphia's Livingston Survey to represent expected inflation for each year, and we used estimates of the natural unemployment rate presented later in the chapter in Fig. 12.9.

Figure 12.7 suggests that, despite the instability of the traditional Phillips curve relationship between inflation and unemployment, a negative relationship between *unanticipated* inflation and *cyclical* unemployment did exist during the period 1970–2008, as predicted by the Friedman–Phelps analysis (compare Fig. 12.7 to Fig. 12.2). In particular, note that inflation was much lower than expected and that cyclical unemployment was high during 1982 and 1983, both years that followed Fed Chairman Paul Volcker's attempt to reduce inflation through tight monetary policy.

Macroeconomic Policy and the Phillips Curve

We have addressed two of the questions about the Phillips curve raised earlier in the chapter—the questions of why the Phillips curve was observed in historical data and why it seemed to shift after 1970. We still must answer the third question: Can the Phillips curve be thought of as a "menu" of inflation–unemployment combinations from which policymakers can choose? For example, can policymakers reduce the unemployment rate by increasing the rate of inflation (moving up and to the left along the Phillips curve)?

According to the expectations-augmented Phillips curve, unemployment will fall below the natural rate only when inflation is unanticipated. So the question becomes: Can macroeconomic policy be used systematically to create unanticipated inflation?

Classical and Keynesian economists disagree on the answer to this question. Classicals argue that wages and prices adjust quickly in response to new eco-

---

[8]Two sources of fiscal expansion during the 1960s were military expenditures associated with the Vietnam War and increased social spending for the Great Society programs.

Figure 12.7

The expectations-augmented Phillips curve in the United States, 1970–2008

The expectations-augmented Phillips curve is a negative relationship between unanticipated inflation and cyclical unemployment. Shown is this relationship for the years 1970–2008 in the United States. Unanticipated inflation equals actual minus expected inflation, where expected inflation in any year is the forecast of CPI inflation from the Livingston Survey. Cyclical unemployment for each year is actual unemployment minus an estimate of the natural unemployment rate for that year (see Fig. 12.9). Note that years in which unanticipated inflation is high usually are years in which cyclical unemployment is low.

Source: Federal Reserve Bank of St. Louis FRED database at *research.stlouisfed.org/fred2,* series CPIAUCSL (inflation) and UNRATE (unemployment rate); expected inflation: Federal Reserve Bank of Philadelphia Livingston Survey at *www.philadelphiafed.org*; natural rate of unemployment: Congressional Budget Office, *www.cbo.gov/ftpdocs/100xx/ doc10014/Mar09Web_ Tbl_ potential.xls.*

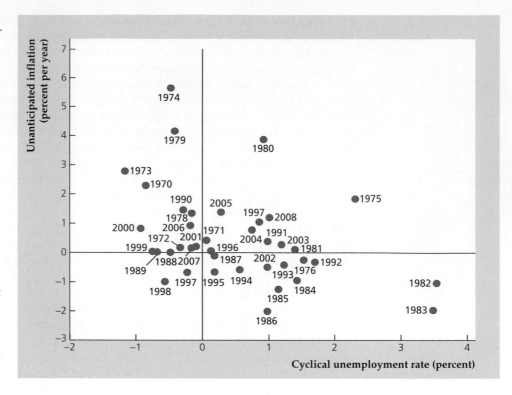

nomic information, including information about changes in government policies. Furthermore, classicals believe that people have rational expectations, meaning that they make intelligent forecasts of future policy changes. Because prices and price-level expectations respond quickly to new information, the government can't keep actual inflation above expected inflation—as would be needed to drive unemployment below the natural rate—except perhaps for a very short time. According to classicals, policies (such as more rapid monetary expansion) that increase the growth rate of aggregate demand act primarily to raise actual *and* expected inflation and so do not lead to a sustained reduction in unemployment. Because any systematic attempt to affect the unemployment rate will be thwarted by the rapid adjustment of inflation expectations, classicals conclude that the Phillips curve does *not* represent a usable trade-off for policymakers. ("In Touch with Data and Research: The Lucas Critique," p. 453, explores a general lesson for policymakers of the shifting Phillips curve.)

In contrast, Keynesians contend that policymakers do have some ability—in the short run, at least—to create unanticipated inflation and thus to bring unemployment below the natural rate.[9] Although many Keynesians accept the notion that people have rational expectations, they argue that the expected rate of inflation that should be included in the expectations-augmented Phillips curve is the forecast of inflation made at the time that the oldest sticky prices in the economy were set.

---

[9]As we discussed in Chapter 11, Keynesian economists also believe that macroeconomic policy can be used to return the unemployment rate to its natural level, if the economy starts out in a recession or a boom.

IN TOUCH WITH DATA AND RESEARCH

The Lucas Critique

Suppose that you observed, in a particular season, that the New York Giants of the National Football League punted 100% of the time when faced with fourth down in their own territory. Could you safely conclude, based on this empirical evidence, that the Giants would punt on fourth down in their own territory next season? In most cases, you probably could safely make this prediction, even if you didn't know anything about football. But what if, during the offseason, the rules were changed to allow six attempts to make a first down? Would you still expect the Giants to follow historical precedent and punt on fourth down? Certainly no one familiar with football would expect them to follow their old strategy, which would be foolish under the new rules. The simple lesson from this example is that, when the rules of the game change, people's behaviors also change.[*]

In an influential article,[†] Robert E. Lucas, Jr., of the University of Chicago, applied this lesson to macroeconomic policymaking. Frequently, in attempting to forecast the effects of a new set of policies, economists and policymakers assume that historical relationships between macroeconomic variables will continue to hold after the new policies are in place. Lucas objected to this assumption, asserting what has become known as the *Lucas critique*. According to the Lucas critique, because new policies change the economic "rules" and thus affect economic behavior, no one can safely assume that historical relationships between variables will hold when policies change.

A good example of the Lucas critique in action is the shifting Phillips curve. Historically, there seemed to be a stable relationship between inflation and unemployment, which led some policymakers to believe that they could permanently reduce unemployment by increasing inflation. However, as we have discussed, when policymakers allowed inflation to rise, the public's inflation expectations also rose. As a result, the Phillips curve shifted and the historical relationship between inflation and unemployment broke down.

The main message of the Lucas critique for economists is that, to predict the effects of policy changes on the economy, they must understand how economic behavior will change under the new policies. Understanding the impact of policy changes on behavior—particularly the introduction of policies that haven't been tried before—requires the use of economic theory as well as empirical analysis.

---

[*]The example is from Thomas Sargent, *Rational Expectations and Inflation*, New York: Harper & Row, 1986, pp. 1–2.

[†]"Econometric Policy Evaluation: A Critique," in K. Brunner and A. H. Meltzer, eds., *Carnegie-Rochester Conference Series on Public Policy*, vol. 1, 1976.

Because of price stickiness, when policymakers cause aggregate demand to rise above the expected level, time is needed for prices to fully reflect this new information. In the meantime, some prices reflect older information, and the rate of inflation is higher than the expected inflation rate based on this older information. In response to increased inflation, therefore, unemployment may remain below the natural rate for a while.

Figure 12.8

The long-run Phillips curve

People won't permanently overestimate or underestimate the rate of inflation, so in the long run the expected and actual inflation rates are equal and the actual unemployment rate equals the natural unemployment rate. Because actual unemployment equals the natural rate in the long run, regardless of the inflation rate, the long-run Phillips curve is vertical.

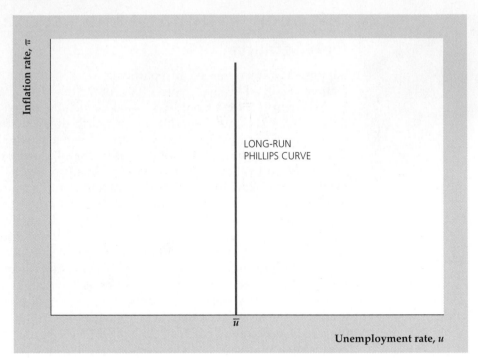

The Long-Run Phillips Curve

Although classicals and Keynesians disagree about whether the Phillips curve relationship can be exploited to reduce unemployment temporarily, they agree that policymakers can't keep the unemployment rate *permanently* below the natural rate by maintaining a high rate of inflation. Expectations about inflation eventually will adjust so that the expected and actual inflation rates are equal, or $\pi^e = \pi$. The expectations-augmented Phillips curve (Eq. 12.1) implies that, when $\pi^e = \pi$, the actual unemployment rate, u, equals the natural unemployment rate, $\bar{u}$. Thus the actual unemployment rate equals the natural rate in the long run regardless of the inflation rate maintained.

The long-run relationship of unemployment and inflation is shown by the **long-run Phillips curve.** In the long run, because unemployment equals the natural rate regardless of the inflation rate, the long-run Phillips curve is a vertical line at $u = \bar{u}$, as shown in Fig. 12.8.

The vertical long-run Phillips curve is related to the long-run neutrality of money, discussed in Chapters 10 and 11. Classicals and Keynesians agree that changes in the money supply will have no long-run effects on real variables, including unemployment. The vertical long-run Phillips curve carries the notion of monetary neutrality one step further by indicating that changes in the *growth rate* of money, which lead to changes in the inflation rate, also have no real effects in the long run.

12.2 The Problem of Unemployment

In the rest of the chapter we look more closely at unemployment and inflation, beginning with unemployment in this section. We start by discussing the costs of unemployment, then consider the factors that determine the long-run unemployment level, and conclude by exploring some ways in which macroeconomic policy can address unemployment.

The Costs of Unemployment

There are two principal costs of unemployment. The first is the loss of output that occurs because fewer people are productively employed. This cost is borne disproportionately by unemployed workers themselves, in terms of the income they lose because they are out of work. However, because the unemployed may stop paying taxes and instead receive unemployment insurance benefits or other government payments, society (in this case, the taxpayer) also bears some of the output cost of unemployment.

How big is the output cost of unemployment? One estimate is provided by Okun's law (see Eq. 3.5), which states that each percentage point of *cyclical* unemployment is associated with a loss equal to 2% of full-employment output. Thus, if full-employment output is $14,000 billion, Okun's law indicates that each percentage point of unemployment sustained for one year reduces output by $280 billion.

The loss of output predicted by Okun's law reflects not only the direct impact of increased unemployment, but also other labor market changes that occur during recessions, such as shorter workweeks, reduced labor force participation, and lower productivity (Numerical Problem 10 in Chapter 3 illustrates these effects). Thus the output cost of unemployment estimated by Okun's law probably is too high. Nevertheless, an output loss that was only one-fourth of that predicted by Okun's law would still be a significant cost, particularly if it were borne largely by the relatively poor and disadvantaged members of society.

The other substantial cost of unemployment is the personal or psychological cost faced by unemployed workers and their families. This cost is especially important for workers suffering long spells of unemployment and for the chronically unemployed. Workers without steady employment for long periods lose job skills and self-esteem, and suffer from stress.

The costs of unemployment are real and serious, but two offsetting factors should be noted. First, to the extent that unemployed workers engage in economically productive activities such as searching for a job or acquiring new skills, the loss of output arising from current unemployment may be compensated for by increased output in the future. In particular, frictional unemployment—the result of workers and firms seeking appropriate matches—raises future productivity and output and thus may impose little net economic cost, or even lead to an economic gain.

A second offsetting factor is that unemployed people have more leisure time—to spend with family and friends, work around the house, and so on. However, the benefits of extra leisure time decrease as the amount of leisure increases, and most unemployed workers wouldn't feel that increased leisure was adequate compensation for their lost income.

The Long-Term Behavior of the Unemployment Rate

Classical and Keynesian economists agree that, although the actual unemployment rate may deviate from the natural unemployment rate in the short run, in the long run the actual rate equals the natural rate. Thus understanding the behavior

Figure 12.9

Actual and natural unemployment rates in the United States, 1960–2008

The figure shows the actual unemployment rate and an estimate of the natural rate of unemployment in the United States for the period 1960–2008. The difference between the actual and natural unemployment rates is the cyclical unemployment rate. Note that the natural rate of unemployment rose from the 1960s until the late 1970s and declined from 1980 to 2001.

Sources: Actual unemployment rate, Federal Reserve Bank of St. Louis FRED database at *research.stlouisfed.org/fred2*, series UNRATE; natural rate of unemployment: Congressional Budget Office, *www.cbo. gov/ftpdocs/100xx/doc10014/ Mar09Web_Tbl_potential.xls.*

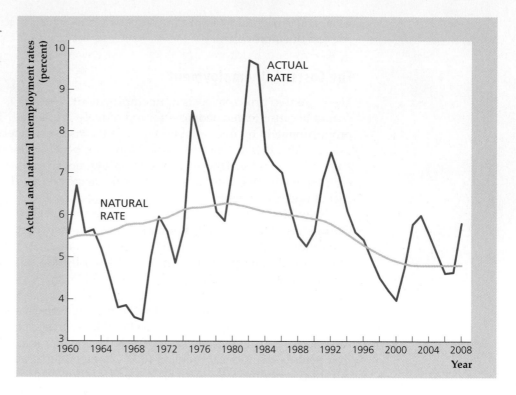

of unemployment in all but the short run requires identifying the determinants of the natural rate of unemployment. In Chapter 3 we discussed the reasons for the natural unemployment rate always being greater than zero; here we focus more narrowly on the reasons for changes in the natural rate in the United States.

The Changing Natural Rate.   The natural unemployment rate corresponds to full-employment output. Unfortunately, because we can't be sure when the economy is at full employment, we can't directly observe the natural rate and so must estimate it. Inevitably, therefore, there is some uncertainty about the value of the natural rate at any particular time. Figure 12.9 shows estimated values of the natural unemployment rate, published by the Congressional Budget Office, along with the actual unemployment rate, for the period 1960–2008. Most current estimates, including those in Fig. 12.9, suggest a natural unemployment rate of about 5% to 5.5% of the labor force, similar to or below what it was in the 1960s. In contrast, in much of the 1970s and 1980s the natural rate was about 6% of the labor force.

Giving a fully satisfactory explanation of the rise and fall in the natural rate of unemployment is difficult, but part of the story seems to have been the result of demographic changes. The proportion of workers from differing demographic groups (based on age, gender, or race) changes gradually over time. Because some groups have higher unemployment rates than others, the natural rate of unemployment changes over time. For example, in the 1960s, as women entered the labor force in greater numbers, the natural rate of unemployment rose because women's average unemployment rate was higher than men's.[10] Teenagers have particularly high unemployment rates both because they move in and out of the labor force frequently while in school and because many teenagers work at low-skill jobs that do not provide long-term employment.

From World War II through about 1980, teenagers and women made up an increasingly large portion of the labor force in the United States. This shift in the composition of the labor force toward groups that have traditionally experienced higher unemployment rates may have raised the overall unemployment rate during that period, particularly in the 1960s and 1970s. In contrast, since about 1980, demographic factors have tended to reduce the natural rate of unemployment. Most striking is the decline in recent decades in the share of young people in the labor force—a trend that reflects the aging of the population as a whole. Indeed, only about 16% of the U.S. labor force was aged sixteen to twenty-four in 1998, compared to about 25% of the labor force in 1980. A study by Robert Shimer[11] of the University of Chicago concluded that the declining share of unemployment-prone younger workers can account for the bulk of the decline in the natural rate of unemployment in the United States since 1980.

Some economists have been skeptical of estimates of the U.S. natural unemployment rate in the range of 5% to 5.5%, noting that, at the end of the 1990s, the U.S. unemployment rate remained close to 4% for a substantial period without generating inflation. They conclude that the natural rate must be 4.5% or even lower. This disagreement illustrates the difficulty of obtaining precise estimates of the natural rate—an important problem for policymakers as well as for economists in general. If the U.S. natural rate at the end of the millennium was as low as, say 4.5%, what explains this favorable development? One possibility is that the labor market has become more efficient at matching workers and jobs, thereby reducing frictional and structural unemployment. For example, temporary help agencies have become far more prominent in the United States in recent years. These agencies specialize in helping firms fill their temporary vacancies with qualified workers. In many cases, these temporary jobs become permanent. If temporary help agencies, Internet employment services, and other innovations have improved the matching of workers and jobs, these developments might explain further declines in the natural rate of unemployment.[12]

Another possibility is that increased productivity of workers caused the natural rate of unemployment to decline, especially in the second half of the 1990s. In long-run equilibrium, the real wage paid to workers will equal their marginal productivity. But there may be a lag between the time when productivity rises and the time when real wages increase. For example, if real wages and productivity have been growing at 2% per year for some time, and then productivity begins to grow at 4% per year, workers accustomed to 2% real-wage growth may be slow to raise their wage aspirations. With productivity growing faster than the real wage, firms

---

[10]However, since the early 1980s, the average unemployment rates for men and women have been about the same, so changes in the proportion of women in the labor force would no longer change the natural rate of unemployment.

[11]Robert Shimer, "Why Is the U.S. Unemployment Rate So Much Lower?" in B. Bernanke and J. Rotemberg, eds., NBER *Macroeconomics Annual*, 1998.

[12]Lawrence Katz of Harvard University and Alan Krueger of Princeton University argue that temporary help agencies may deserve credit for part of the falling natural rate. See their article "The High-Pressure U.S. Labor Market of the 1990s," *Brookings Papers on Economic Activity*, 1999:1, pp. 1–88.

will hire more workers and the natural rate of unemployment will decline temporarily.[13]

Measuring the Natural Rate of Unemployment.
Because of the prominent role played by the natural rate of unemployment in economic theory, policymakers would like to use measures of the natural rate when they formulate economic policy. In simple terms, if policymakers observe that the unemployment rate is above the natural rate, then the intersection of the *AD* and *SRAS* curves must be to the left of the *LRAS* curve. Thus a policymaker might consider using expansionary monetary policy (which we discuss in Chapter 14) or expansionary fiscal policy (which we discuss in Chapter 15) to shift the *AD* curve to the right, to bring the economy to its full-employment equilibrium. To use the unemployment rate as an indicator for setting policy, however, the policymaker needs a good measure of the natural rate of unemployment.

Although Fig. 12.9 shows a measure of the natural rate of unemployment created by the Congressional Budget Office (CBO), economists widely disagree about how to measure the natural rate. In addition, even the CBO has often revised its measures of the natural rate of unemployment over time.[14] Economists Douglas Staiger of Dartmouth University, James Stock of Harvard University, and Mark Watson of Princeton University[15] performed a detailed econometric analysis of the precision with which the natural rate can be measured. They concluded that the number could not be measured at all precisely, despite trying many alternative methods of doing so. Their best estimate for the natural rate of unemployment in 1994, for example, is that it equaled $5\frac{3}{4}\%$, but that there was so much uncertainty about the number that they were 95% confident that it was between 4.8% and 6.6%. That interval is far too large to be of any use to policymakers.

In the face of this evidence, researchers in the late 1990s pondered what policymakers should do. Given uncertainty about the natural rate of unemployment, policymakers may want to be less aggressive with policy changes than they would be if they knew the value of the natural rate more precisely.[16] Some researchers have even blamed the rise of inflation in the 1970s on the Federal Reserve's failure to estimate the natural rate of unemployment properly.[17] Policymakers face the problem, though, that measures of full-employment output may be even more imprecise. So, although economic theory relies on the concepts of full-employment output and the natural rate of unemployment, policymaking is difficult because economists cannot measure these concepts in a precise manner.

---

[13]Laurence Ball of Johns Hopkins University and N. Gregory Mankiw of Harvard University find support for this hypothesis in explaining the declining natural rate of unemployment in the 1990s in their article, "The NAIRU in Theory and Practice," *Journal of Economic Perspectives,* Fall 2002, pp. 115–136.

[14]To appreciate how dramatically the CBO has revised its numbers, see the article by Sharon Kozicki, "How Do Data Revisions Affect the Evaluation and Conduct of Monetary Policy?" Federal Reserve Bank of Kansas City, *Economic Review,* First Quarter 2004, pp. 5–38.

[15]"The NAIRU, Unemployment and Monetary Policy," *Journal of Economic Perspectives*, Winter 1997, pp. 33–49.

[16]For example, see Volker Wieland, "Monetary Policy and Uncertainty about the Natural Unemployment Rate: Brainard-Style Conservatism versus Experimental Activism," *Advances in Macroeconomics,* vol. 6, no. 1, 2006.

[17]See Athanasios Orphanides and John Williams, "The Decline of Activist Stabilization Policy: Natural Rate Misperceptions, Learning, and Expectations," *Journal of Economic Dynamics and Control,* November 2005, pp. 1927–1950.

12.3 The Problem of Inflation

In August 1971 President Richard M. Nixon instituted a set of wage and price controls in an attempt to reduce U.S. inflation. These strong measures were taken even though the inflation rate was only 5% at the time. During the late 1970s, when the U.S. inflation rate approached "double-digits," surveys of voters found that they thought inflation was "public enemy number one"; one victim of the public's fear of inflation was President Jimmy Carter, who lost his reelection bid to Ronald Reagan in 1980 in part because of his perceived inability to control inflation. In this section we look at inflation, beginning with a discussion of inflation costs and then turning to the question of what can be done to control inflation.

The Costs of Inflation

The costs of inflation depend primarily on whether consumers, investors, workers, and firms are able to predict the inflation before it occurs. To illustrate this point, we discuss two extreme cases: an inflation that everyone is able to predict and an inflation that comes as a complete surprise.

Perfectly Anticipated Inflation.   Let's first consider the case of an inflation that is perfectly anticipated by the public. Imagine, for example, that everyone knew that the inflation rate would be 4% per year. To keep things simple, assume no change in relative prices so that the prices of all individual goods and services also are rising at the rate of 4% per year.

Why then does a fully anticipated inflation impose any costs? The prices you pay for groceries, movie tickets, and other goods would increase by 4% per year but so would your nominal wage or the nominal value of the goods or services you produce. Because your nominal income is rising along with prices, your purchasing power isn't hurt by the perfectly anticipated inflation.[18]

What about the money that you hold in your savings account? Although inflation reduces the purchasing power of money, perfectly anticipated inflation wouldn't hurt the value of your savings account. The reason is that the nominal interest rate would adjust to offset the drop in the purchasing power of money. For instance, with a zero inflation rate and a nominal interest rate on savings deposits of 3%, the real interest rate also is 3% per year. If inflation rises to a perfectly anticipated rate of 4% per year, an increase in the nominal interest rate to 7% per year will leave the real interest rate unchanged at 3%. Because both savers and banks care only about the real interest rate, when inflation rises to 4% banks should be willing to offer 7% nominal interest, and savers should be willing to accept that nominal return. Thus neither banks nor savers are hurt by an anticipated increase in inflation.[19]

---

[18]It may be true that, psychologically, people think of increases in their wages arising from ongoing inflation as being earned and thus "fair," but that increases in the prices they pay because of inflation are "unfair." This is a confusion, although one that may have real political consequences if it causes the public to demand strong action on inflation.

[19]This argument ignores the fact that interest is taxed on a nominal basis. If the after-tax real interest rate is to be kept constant, the nominal interest rate will have to rise by somewhat more than the increase in inflation. See Section 4.1 on the after-tax real interest rate.

The suggestion that perfectly anticipated inflation imposes no economic costs isn't quite correct: Inflation erodes the value of currency, which leads people to keep less currency on hand—for example, by going to the bank or the automatic teller machine to make withdrawals every week instead of twice a month. Similarly, inflation may induce firms to reduce their cash holdings by introducing computerized cash management systems or adding staff to the accounting department. The costs in time and effort incurred by people and firms who are trying to minimize their holdings of cash are called **shoe leather costs.** For modest inflation rates, shoe leather costs are small but not completely trivial. For example, the shoe leather costs of a 10% perfectly anticipated inflation have been estimated to be about 0.3% of GDP, which is a little more than $40 billion per year in the United States.[20]

A second cost of perfectly anticipated inflation arises from menu costs, or the costs of changing nominal prices. When there is inflation and prices are continually rising, sellers of goods and services must use resources to change nominal prices. For instance, mail-order firms have to print and mail catalogues frequently to report the increases in prices. Although some firms face substantial menu costs, for the economy as a whole these costs probably are small. Furthermore, technological progress, such as the introduction of electronic scanners in supermarkets, reduces the cost of changing prices.

Unanticipated Inflation.   Much of the public's aversion to inflation is aversion to unanticipated inflation—inflation that is different from the rate expected. For example, if everyone expects the inflation rate to be 4% per year, but it actually is 6% per year, unanticipated inflation is 2% per year.

What is the effect of 6% inflation if (1) you expected 4% inflation and (2) your savings account pays 7% interest? When inflation is 6% per year instead of 4% per year, the actual real interest rate on your savings account is only 1% per year (the nominal interest rate of 7% minus the inflation rate of 6%) instead of the 3% per year that you expected. By earning a lower actual real interest rate, you lose as a result of the unanticipated inflation. However, your loss is the bank's gain because the bank pays a lower real interest rate than it expected. Note that the roles would have been reversed if the actual inflation rate had been lower than expected; in that case the real interest rate that you earn, and that the bank has to pay, would be higher than anticipated.

Similarly, suppose that your nominal salary is set in advance. If inflation is higher than expected, the real value of your salary is less than you expected, and your loss is your employer's gain. If inflation is lower than expected, however, you benefit and your employer loses.

These examples show that a primary effect of unanticipated inflation is to transfer wealth from one person or firm to another. People who lend or save at fixed interest rates (creditors) and those with incomes set in nominal terms are hurt by unanticipated inflation, whereas people who borrow at fixed interest rates (debtors) or who must make fixed nominal payments are helped by unanticipated inflation.

For the economy as a whole, a transfer of wealth from one group to another isn't a net loss of resources and hence doesn't represent a true cost. However, from the viewpoints of individual people and firms in the economy, the *risk* of gaining or

---

[20]See Stanley Fischer, "Towards an Understanding of the Costs of Inflation: II," in K. Brunner and A. Meltzer, eds., *Carnegie-Rochester Conference Series on Public Policy,* vol. 15, Autumn 1981.

losing wealth as a result of unanticipated inflation is unwelcome. Because most people don't like risk, the possibility of significant gains or losses arising from unexpected inflation makes people feel worse off and hence is a cost of unanticipated inflation. Furthermore, any resources that people use in forecasting inflation and trying to protect themselves against the risks of unanticipated inflation represent an additional cost. However, some of these costs of unanticipated inflation can be eliminated by contracts that are indexed to the price level, as we discuss in "In Touch with Data and Research: Indexed Contracts."

IN TOUCH WITH DATA AND RESEARCH

Indexed Contracts

In principle, much of the risk of gains and losses associated with unanticipated inflation can be eliminated by using contracts in which payments are indexed to inflation. If a bank wanted to offer a guaranteed 3% real interest rate on savings accounts, for instance, it could index the nominal interest rate to the rate of inflation by offering to pay a nominal interest rate equal to 3% plus whatever the rate of inflation turns out to be. Then if the actual inflation rate is 6%, the bank would end up paying a nominal interest rate of 9%—giving the depositor the promised 3% real interest rate. Similarly, other financial contracts, such as loans, mortgages, and bonds, can be indexed to protect the real rate of return against unanticipated inflation. Wage payments set by labor contracts can also be indexed to protect workers and employers against unanticipated inflation (we discussed the macroeconomic effects of wage indexation in Appendix 11.A).

How widespread is indexing? Most financial contracts in the United States are not indexed to the rate of inflation, although payments on some long-term financial contracts (adjustable-rate mortgages, for example) are indexed to nominal interest rates such as the prime rate charged by banks or the Treasury bill interest rate. Because nominal interest rates move roughly in step with inflation, these long-term financial contracts are to some extent indexed to inflation. Many labor contracts in the United States are indexed to the rate of inflation through provisions called cost-of-living adjustments, or COLAs. They provide for some increase in nominal wages if inflation is higher than expected, but usually a 1% increase in unanticipated inflation results in somewhat less than a 1% adjustment of wages. In January 1997 the U.S. Treasury began to sell bonds indexed to the rate of inflation.

In countries that have experienced high and unpredictable inflation rates, indexed contracts are common. A case in point is Israel, which had a CPI inflation rate of 445% per year in 1984. At that time, more than 80% of liquid financial assets in Israel were indexed: For example, long-term government bonds were indexed to the CPI, and banks offered short-term deposits whose purchasing power was tied to that of the U.S. dollar. However, the fraction of financial assets that were indexed decreased after the Israeli hyperinflation ended in the second half of 1985, and continued to decrease as Israeli inflation fell to single digits.*

*See Stanley Fischer, "Israeli Inflation and Indexation," in J. Williamson, ed., *Inflation and Indexation: Argentina, Brazil, and Israel,* Institute for International Economics, 1985, reprinted in Stanley Fischer, *Indexing, Inflation, and Economic Policy,* Cambridge, Mass.: M.I.T. Press, 1986; and Zalman F. Shiffer, "Adjusting to High Inflation: The Israeli Experience," Federal Reserve Bank of St. Louis *Review,* May 1986, pp. 18–29.

Another cost of unanticipated inflation relates to the fact that prices serve as signals in a market economy. For example, if wheat becomes more expensive than corn, that is a signal to consumers to switch from wheat to corn and to farmers to produce more wheat and less corn. However, the prices that act as signals in the economy are *relative* prices, such as the price of wheat relative to the price of corn. Knowing that wheat is so many dollars per bushel doesn't help the consumer and farmer make good economic decisions unless they also know the price of corn. When inflation is unanticipated, particularly if it is erratic, people may confuse changes in prices arising from changes in the general price level with changes in prices arising from shifts in the supply or demand for individual goods. Because the signals provided by prices may be distorted by unanticipated inflation, the market economy works less efficiently. In addition, when there is a great deal of uncertainty about the true inflation rate, people must spend time and effort learning about different prices, by comparison shopping, for example.

The Costs of Hyperinflation. **Hyperinflation** occurs when the inflation rate is extremely high for a sustained period of time.[21] For example, during a twelve-month period beginning in August 1945, the average rate of inflation in Hungary was 19,800% *per month*.[22] In the more recent hyperinflation in Bolivia, the annual rate of inflation was 1281% in 1984, and soared to 11,750% in 1985, before dropping to 276% in 1986.[23] The costs of inflation during these hyperinflations were much greater than the costs associated with moderate inflation. For example, when prices are increasing at such mind-boggling rates, the incentives to minimize holdings of currency are powerful and the resulting shoe leather costs are enormous. In severe hyperinflations, workers are paid much more frequently—perhaps even more than once a day—and they rush out to spend their money (or to convert their money into some other form, such as a foreign currency) before prices rise even further. The time and energy devoted to getting rid of currency as fast as possible wastes resources and disrupts production.

One early casualty of hyperinflations is the government's ability to collect taxes. In a hyperinflation, taxpayers have an incentive to delay paying their taxes as long as possible. Because tax bills usually are set in nominal terms, the longer the taxpayer delays, the less the real value of that obligation is. The real value of taxes collected by the government falls sharply during hyperinflations, with destructive effects on the government's finances and its ability to provide public services.

Finally, the disruptive effect of inflation on market efficiency that we discussed earlier becomes most severe in the case of a hyperinflation. If prices change so often that they cease to be reliable indicators of the supply and demand for different goods and services, the invisible hand of the free market can't allocate resources efficiently.

---

[21]Philip Cagan, in his classic study of hyperinflation ("The Monetary Dynamics of Hyperinflation," in Milton Friedman, ed., *Studies in the Quantity Theory of Money*, Chicago: University of Chicago Press, 1956), defined a hyperinflation as beginning in the month in which the rate of inflation first exceeds 50% *per month*.

[22]*Ibid.*, Table 1.

[23]See Table 7.3, Juan-Antonio Morales, "Inflation Stabilization in Bolivia," in Michael Bruno, Guido Di Tella, Rudiger Dornbusch, and Stanley Fischer, eds., *Inflation Stabilization: The Experience of Israel, Argentina, Brazil, Bolivia, and Mexico*, Cambridge, Mass.: M.I.T. Press, 1988.